Handbook of
Metamemory and Memory

Handbook of
Metamemory and Memory

EDITED BY
JOHN DUNLOSKY
ROBERT A. BJORK

Psychology Press
Taylor & Francis Group

New York   Hove

Psychology Press
Taylor & Francis Group
270 Madison Avenue
New York, NY 10016

Psychology Press
Taylor & Francis Group
27 Church Road
Hove, East Sussex BN3 2FA

© 2008 by Taylor & Francis Group, LLC

Printed in the United States of America on acid-free paper
10 9 8 7 6 5 4 3 2 1

International Standard Book Number-13: 978-0-8058-6214-0 (Hardcover)

Library of Congress Cataloging-in-Publication Data

Handbook of metamemory and memory / [edited by] John Dunlosky, Robert A. Bjork.
    p. cm.
  Includes bibliographical references and index.
  ISBN 978-0-8058-6214-0 (hardback : alk. paper)
  1. Metacognition. 2. Memory. I. Dunlosky, John. II. Bjork, Robert A.

BF311.H3343 2008
153.1'2--dc22
                     2008011715

Visit the Taylor & Francis Web site at
http://www.taylorandfrancis.com

and the Psychology Press Web site at
http://www.psypress.com

Dedicated

This volume is dedicated to Thomas O. Nelson
— Friend, Colleague, Mentor, and Scientist.

Contents

Contemporary Issues Involving the Metamemory-Memory Framework

Preface

Take a moment to think of activities that involve memory in some way: taking a test, driving a car, reading a book, making breakfast, and even developing this list of activities. Now, name a daily activity that does not in some way involve memory. This list will be much shorter, and most people have difficulties even coming up with one activity, except for an occasional "breathing" or "blinking." It is this ubiquitous nature of memory — the foundation of almost every human behavior — that has made it central to scholarly and personal inquiry since antiquity. Now consider metamemory, which involves people's knowledge, monitoring, and control of their memories. A quintessential aspect of metamemory is people's ability to self-reflect on their memories, and in contrast to memories that all species rely on, self-reflection may be uniquely human. Thus, memory essentially underlies most human behaviors, and metamemory essentially defines us as human.

In the present handbook, we examine the interplay between metamemory and memory. It is their interplay that increases the flexibility of human memory by releasing us from stimulus control. For each chapter, the authors' charge was to discuss cutting-edge theory and research that would in some manner showcase the symbiotic relationship between metamemory and memory, and in our introductory chapter, "The Integrated Nature of Metamemory and Memory," we discuss how individual chapters satisfied this charge. Together, these chapters support a central thesis of this volume, which is that a complete understanding of either metamemory or memory will not be possible without investigating their mutual influence. We were especially pleased with how responsive all the contributors of this volume were to their charge, and it was gratifying working with all of them on this project. Our sincere hope is that these chapters will encourage others to join the growing number of researchers who are dedicated to developing a deeper understanding of metamemory and memory.

The inspiration for this volume was the life and research of Thomas O. Nelson, who at some time influenced all the contributors of this volume through his research, collaboration, mentorship, and friendship. He was a pioneer in the fields of both metamemory and memory, and his work consistently highlighted their integrated nature. As Harry Bahrick (this volume) reflects on Tom's contributions to the field, "His early work examined relations among traditional methods, but he soon concluded that an individual's knowledge and control of their own memory functions are crucial to understanding memory performance" (p. 1). Tom's unexpected death in 2005 shocked the entire community. To celebrate and honor his memory, many of his colleagues and friends met to discuss how Tom had influenced their work and their lives, and this symposium provided the foundations for the present handbook.

Open this volume to any chapter — and almost to any page — and the fingerprints of his life's work will be evident. For those of you who were not fortunate enough to work with or to even have met him, we are positive this volume will provide a fitting introduction to Tom's research and influence on the field as well as a general introduction into the integrated nature of metamemory and memory.

John Dunlosky
Robert A. Bjork

Acknowledgments

We would like to thank Kent State University for funding the symposium at Psychonomics, Metamemory and Memory: Papers in Honor of Thomas O. Nelson. We extend much gratitude to Lori Handelman, who worked diligently with us to develop this handbook for Lawrence Erlbaum, and to Steve Rutter for thoughtful advice on how to shape the chapters and for his assistance as it was passed on to Taylor & Francis. Anthony Messina of Lawrence Erlbaum assisted with many details as well. Special thanks go to Paul Dukes, who provided much support and guidance as we fine-tuned the handbook for Taylor & Francis. Finally, sincerest thanks go to Katherine Rawson for support and encouragement to the first editor as he came to terms with the untimely death of his mentor and as he helped to complete this handbook.

Participants in the Symposium on Memory and Metamemory in Honor of Thomas O. Nelson, Psychonomics, 2005. Back (L to R): Louis Narens, Lisa Son, Colin MacLeod, Janet Metcalfe, Harry Bahrick, Jim Van Overschelde, Bobbie Spellman, William Batchelder, Marie Carroll, Ken Malmberg, Ruth Maki, and Charles Weaver; Front (L to R): Giuliana Mazzoni, Aaron Benjamin, Richard Shiffrin, Robert Bjork, John Dunlosky, Bennett Schwartz, and Asher Koriat.

Contributors

Elisabeth Bacon
University Hospital
Strasbourg, France

Harry P. Bahrick
Ohio Wesleyan University
Delaware, Ohio

Ece Batchelder
University of California, Irvine
Irvine, California

William H. Batchelder
University of California, Irvine
Irvine, California

Aaron S. Benjamin
University of Illinois
Champaign, Illinois

Robert A. Bjork
University of California at Los Angeles
Los Angeles, California

Herbert Bless
University of Mannheim
Mannheim, Germany

Aaron Bloomfield
University of Virginia
Charlottesville, Virginia

Linda Bol
OId Dominion University
Norfolk, Virginia

Marie Carroll
Australian National University
Canberra, Australia

Michael Diaz
University of Illinois
Champaign, Illinois

John Dunlosky
Kent State University
Kent, Ohio

Douglas J. Hacker
University of Utah
Salt Lake City, Utah

Matt C. Keener
University of Utah
Salt Lake City, Utah

William L. Kelemen
California State University, Long Beach
Long Beach, California

Asher Koriat
University of Haifa
Haifa, Israel

Nate Kornell
University of California at Los Angeles
Los Angeles, California

Kevin S. Krug
Louisiana State University, Shreveport
Shreveport, Louisiana

R. Jacob Leonesio
University of Washington
Seattle, Washington

Kathrin Lockl
University of Bamberg
Bamberg, Germany

Colin M. MacLeod
University of Waterloo
Waterloo, Ontario, Canada

Ruth H. Maki
Texas Tech University
Lubbock, Texas

Kenneth J. Malmberg
University of South Florida
Tampa, Florida

Guiliana Mazzoni
University of Hull
Hull, United Kingdom

Janet Metcalfe
Columbia University
New York, New York

Louis Narens
University of California, Irvine
Irvine, California

Ravit Nussinson
University of Haifa
Haifa, Israel

Timothy J. Perfect
University of Plymouth
Plymouth, United Kingdom

Petra Scheck
University of Maryland
College Park, Maryland

Wolfgang Schneider
University of Würzburg
Würzburg, Germany

Bennett L. Schwartz
Florida International University
Miami, Florida

Nira Shaked
University of Haifa
Haifa, Israel

Arthur P. Shimamura
University of California, Berkeley
Berkeley, California

Lisa K. Son
Barnard College
New York, New York

Barbara A. Spellman
University of Virginia
Charlottesville, Virginia

Louisa J. Stark
University of Plymouth
Plymouth, United Kingdom

J. Trent Terrell
Baylor University
Waco, Texas

James P. Van Overschelde
University of Maryland
College Park, Maryland

Charles A. Weaver III
Baylor University
Waco, Texas

Thomas O. Nelson:
His Life and Comments on Implications of His Functional View of Metacognitive Memory Monitoring

Harry P. Bahrick

Introduction

This book celebrates the life and the career of Thomas O. Nelson, who died unexpectedly following open-heart surgery on January 14, 2005. Tom was born July 30, 1942, in Newark, New Jersey. He earned his bachelor's degree at Trenton State College (1965); at the University of Illinois, Tom earned his master's degree in educational psychology (1966) and his doctorate (1970) with Charles Osgood as a mentor. Subsequently, he completed a postdoctoral fellowship at Stanford University with Gordon Bower as his sponsor. Tom accepted a position at the University of Washington in 1971 and was promoted through the ranks to professor; while at Washington, he also held a part-time appointment at the University of California, Irvine. In 1995, he moved to the University of Maryland.

At the time of his death, Tom was professor of psychology and head of the Cognitive Area at the University of Maryland. He was also the editor of the *Journal of Experimental Psychology: Learning, Memory, and Cognition* and the principal investigator of a research grant from the National Institute of Education Sciences. These activities illustrate the wide range of Tom's contributions to psychology as a teacher, editor, and research scientist.

Throughout his career, Tom's research was focused on memory and methodology, and he was a pioneer in the field of metacognition. His contribution to metamemory was huge. He believed that the scientific study of cognitive processes is limited by the available methods, and that methodological innovations are needed to expand research to previously unexplored aspects of cognition. His early work examined relations among traditional methods, but he soon concluded that an individual's knowledge and control of their own memory functions are crucial to understanding memory performance; accordingly, he devoted his later research to methods of investigating metacognition and metamemory.

He will be remembered best for the seminal 1990 publication (Nelson & Narens, 1990) that provided a conceptual framework to guide subsequent research on metacognition. The article outlined the interaction of monitoring and control processes during encoding and retrieval of information, and it gave coherence to and energized the then-fragmented research on metacognition. In a broader sense, the article gave impetus to the evolution of memory research from a focus on subjects

1

who respond mechanically to experimental controls to a focus on individuals who consciously and continuously monitor and control their cognitive activities in accord with the perceived demands of a situation. The paradigmatic shift to a focus on cognitive processes had been initiated much earlier, but the Nelson and Narens article and the ensuing programmatic research in metacognition provided the concepts and tools essential for an objective study of how individuals guide their learning and memory processes.

Two examples suffice here to illustrate the range and impact of Tom's research program. First, his highly influential research with Dunlosky (e.g., Nelson & Dunlosky, 1991) showed that individuals make far more accurate predictions of their future recall of memory content if their predictions are delayed after the content has been studied rather than assessed immediately. This important discovery continues to stimulate scholarship aimed at clarifying metacognitive processes. The second example is Tom's articles on measurement (Gonzalez & Nelson, 1996; Nelson, 1984), which demonstrate the limitations of available statistics when assessing metacognitive indicants and their relations to measures of learning and memory. The articles showed why the Goodman-Kruskal gamma coefficient should be the measure of choice, and as a consequence, the gamma coefficient became a standard measure in research on metacognition.

As a teacher and mentor, Tom attracted outstanding scholars to the field, and he was responsible for the postdoctoral training of others. Among these are John Dunlosky, Ken Malmberg, Colin McLeod, Martin Meeter, Tom Schreiber, and Jim Van Overschelde. His students describe him as demanding, exacting, loyal, and supportive. Tom's courses on methodology and on the philosophy of science were famous for their excellence and rigor, and his publication on the relation of consciousness to metacognition in the *American Psychologist* (Nelson, 1996) attracted wide interest among psychologists as well as philosophers and served as the inspiration for the subsequent content of this chapter.

Tom's high standards as an editor and his devotion to the field were widely recognized. Prior to his appointment as editor of the *Journal of Experimental Psychology: Learning, Memory, and Cognition,* he served as associate editor of *Memory and Cognition.* Among the honors and awards Tom received were a National Institutes of Mental Health KO5 career development grant (1993) to support his international metacognitive research coordinating activities and a coveted Alexander von Humboldt senior science research award in Germany (1994).

Two of Tom's outstanding personal characteristics were his courage and his disciplined, tenacious thoroughness. He was an outstanding mountaineer who scaled summits all over the world, participating in a Mount Everest expedition during which he collected memory data that he later presented in a riveting talk accompanied by a dramatic slide show. He was a competitive athlete who remained involved in basketball, skiing, sailing, and biking. Whenever a domain caught his interest, he pursued it relentlessly until he became an expert. Examples of this include the psychological literature, billiards, and his knowledge of the best restaurants and bars in any city he planned to visit.

Tom was a devoted and generous father to his two children and a very talented man who will be missed and remembered by his family, friends, students, and colleagues. His work will be known and respected by many future generations of psychologists.

His former wife, Liz Witter, and his children, Jake and Ashley Nelson of Potomac, Maryland, survive him.

Introspection in the History of Psychology and in Current Metacognitive Research

This discussion focuses on a historical aspect of metacognitive research that was a foundation of Tom Nelson's functional view of metacognitive monitoring. It is important to examine what we do in the light of our history to avoid repeating past mistakes. Tom Nelson was keenly aware of the need to do so, and he addressed this topic in his previously mentioned paper on consciousness and metacognition (Nelson, 1996).

Introspective analysis of conscious content was the primary task of psychology in the beginning of our science. We abandoned this approach during the behaviorist era, only to reclaim consciousness as a legitimate area of study under the cognitive paradigm. I believe that both paradigmatic changes occurred for solid reasons, and my basic theme is that it is important to keep these reasons in mind when we conduct research in metacognition.

We abandoned the analysis of consciousness into elements because the introspective methods used by structuralists often failed to yield verifiable results. Trained introspectionists in various laboratories reported conflicting findings, and their research yielded irresolvable stalemates, such as the controversy over imageless thought (Boring, 1950, p. 403; Heidbreder, 1933, p. 145). What survives from the early, introspective approach to psychology are primarily the methods and findings of psychophysics that focused not on introspective reports of sensory intensity or quality per se, but on the relations of these reports to specified stimulus characteristics.

The methodological shift to behaviorism was designed to escape the impasse attributed to introspective methods by changing the subject matter of psychology from conscious content to publicly observed behavior. Behaviorism yielded a plethora of valuable findings, but the exclusion of introspective reports made it impossible to investigate cognitive processes involved in memory, perception, thought, decision making, problem solving, and other domains.

The shift to the cognitive paradigm was motivated by the desire to regain access to these critically important phenomena. This was accomplished by inferring cognitive processes from their behavioral consequences or by metacognitive research that focused on the relations between conscious judgments and objective indicants reflecting the predictive validity of these judgments. Sperling's (1960) research illustrates this inferential procedure. He inferred the existence of an iconic memory from the superior recall of a tachistoscopically presented matrix of letters when subjects were instructed to recall any specific portion of the matrix versus the entire content of the matrix. Hart's (1965) study illustrates the metacognitive approach. He asked subjects to report their feeling of knowing (FOK) for memory targets they could not recall, and he subsequently tested how well the introspective reports of these feelings predicted whether they would recognize such targets on a forced-choice recognition test. His data showed that subjects' predictions of their recognition performance were more accurate than chance but far from perfect.

Nelson's (1996) article contrasts the current metacognitive approach with the earlier use of introspective reports. He pointed out that the goal of the earlier approach was to analyze participants' conscious content on the basis of their introspective reports, and that these reports were viewed as valid and reliable conduits to the mind. In contrast, the goal of metacognitive research is to examine introspective reports as a source of data that can be related to behavioral observations and thereby yield inferences about the nature of cognitive processes. I believe that this approach follows in the tradition of psychophysics in that reports of conscious phenomena are related to objective data, and the observed relations yield inferences about the reliability and predictive validity of the reported conscious judgments. In psychophysics, introspective reports of changes of intensity or quality of sensory experience are related to observed characteristics of stimuli, and the results yield conclusions about the sensitivity of sensory experiences.

Nelson emphasized that the metacognitive approach makes no assumptions about the reliability or predictive validity of introspections. As in psychophysics, the validity of metacognitive judgments is inferred from their relations to objective data. Thus, introspective reports or judgments are viewed as imperfect indicants of cognitive phenomena. Metacognitive investigations are open to the possibility that introspective reports may reflect illusions or intuitions that lack a consistent relationship to objective data. For example, Maki (1998) and others have shown that most metacognitive judgments of text comprehension share only a small amount of variance with objective indicants of comprehension. Some introspective reports, on the other hand, may be relatively valid predictors of subsequent behavioral data, as illustrated in the investigations of Nelson and Dunlosky (1991). These investigators found that delayed judgments of learning predicted future recall with high accuracy. Identifying and differentiating conditions that affect the validity of metacognitive judgments has yielded important inferences and contributed to the development of cognitive theory.

The Need to Link Metacognitive Reports to Distinctive Behavioral Anchors

My thesis here is that the success of metacognitive research in generating inferences about the nature of cognitions depends crucially on the availability of specific behavioral indicants that differentiate and validate various types of metacognitive reports. Thus, introspective reports of the feeling of knowing are validated by exploring their relations to performance on subsequent recognition tests, and ease of learning judgments can be validated and understood by relating them to subsequent acquisition data.

Absent such differential validation, metacognitive reports have no distinctive objective meaning, and if it turns out that two or more types of metacognitive reports relate similarly to objective indicants of performance, then we cannot infer from the data that the reports represent functionally different cognitions. We must keep in mind that the words we use to label or categorize metacognitive reports are imperfect indicants of the underlying cognitive experiences, and that the distinctive names we give to various metacognitive judgments may reflect in part the demand characteristics of the experiment.

Not withstanding this caveat, investigators have neglected to observe systematically this critical requirement for validating metacognitive inferences. Nelson (1996) cited Wilson (1994), who concluded, "It is striking how many studies that use verbal protocols make this error by failing to include an independent means of assessing the validity of the reports" (p. 250).

A domain of metacognitive research that seems to me to illustrate this problem involves the tip-of-the-tongue (TOT) phenomenon. I believe that the TOT literature fails to establish unambiguous, objective criteria that distinguish TOTs from confident judgments of the FOK. We therefore do not know to what extent reports of TOTs and FOKs reflect distinct cognitive phenomena.

The TOT phenomenon has spawned substantial research literature, but a parsimonious interpretation of that literature requires research designed to clarify the degree of overlap of the behavioral anchors of TOT reports and of confident reports of FOK.

Bennett Schwartz (2002, p. 14) pointed out that the literature for TOTs evolved largely independent of and in a different context from the work on FOKs, and he suggested this historical explanation for the dearth of investigations designed to achieve conceptual parsimony in that domain. However, the independent historical development of concepts does not justify maintaining their independence and should not deter the pursuit of establishing parsimonious categories of metacognitive monitoring.

To be sure, investigators of TOTs have identified objective criteria (e.g., the partial recall of a target name or the ability to recall certain target characteristics), and participants are usually instructed to report a TOT state only if they experience a feeling of imminent recall. In his excellent book on TOT states, Bennett Schwartz (2002, p. 5) noted that operational definitions of TOTs have varied considerably, and his preferred definition is "a strong feeling of knowing that a target word currently unrecallable, is known, and will be recalled." Further, reports of TOT states are usually validated by the probability of subsequent target recall, while confident judgments of FOK are validated by subsequent recognition of unrecalled targets. However, TOT states are also likely to yield the recognition of unrecalled targets, and confident judgments of FOK may involve feelings of imminent recall, may involve partial recall of a target name, and may lead to subsequent recall. My point is that we need to determine the degree of overlap and the degree of independence of reports of TOTs and confident FOKs on various behavioral criteria and, depending on results, decide whether reports of TOTs can be maintained as functionally distinct from reports of confident FOKs.

Investigators have reported that FOKs and TOTs involve differential degrees of involvement of the prefrontal cortex (Widner, Smith, & Graziano, 1996). However, the critical data for validating independent metamemory judgment categories are the functional relations of these categories to memory performance, not data regarding differential engagement of cortical structures or differential frequency of such reports as a function of experimenter instructions. The wording of instructions may affect differential cortical involvement as well as the decision of subjects to report

TOTs versus confident FOKs without affecting the crucial relation of these metacognitive judgments to memory performance.

The degree of functional overlap between the memorial consequences of TOTs and confident FOKs is best determined by comparing subsequent recovery of temporarily inaccessible targets designated as TOTs to recovery of the same types of targets designated as confident FOKs. If it turns out that recovery probabilities at various retention intervals and for various types of targets are comparable, and if this remains true when additional criteria for TOTs, such as partial recall or a feeling of imminent recall, are imposed, then the TOT phenomenon should be redefined as a confident FOK. Redefining TOTs as confident FOKs on the basis of such data would not only serve parsimony but also would substitute a scalable dimension of metacognitive expectation for what is usually reported as an arbitrary dichotomy. Individuals may differ in the degree of perceived imminence of recall they require to report a TOT state, and such differences diminish the overall relation of metacognitive judgments to objective data.

Metacognitive research has been remarkably successful in allowing scholars to recover the scientific study of cognitive processes that play a key role in monitoring and guiding learning, memory, and decision making. We succeeded where earlier psychologists failed by focusing not on the conscious phenomena per se but on the linkages between reports of these phenomena and their behavioral consequences. To avoid repeating past mistakes, we must therefore continue to focus on these relationships and take care that the language we use to label and classify metacognitive reports remains unambiguously linked to behavioral data.

Acknowledgments

Preparation of this manuscript was supported by National Institute of Aging grant 5 RO1 AGO19803-04. I wish to thank Lynda Hall and Ann Daunic for many helpful suggestions.

References

Boring, E. G. (1950). *A history of experimental psychology.* New York: Appleton-Century-Crofts.

Gonzalez, R., & Nelson, T. O. (1996). Measuring ordinal association in situations that contain tied scores. *Psychological Bulletin, 119,* 159–165.

Hart, J. T. (1965). Memory and the feeling-of-knowing experience. *Journal of Educational Psychology, 56,* 208–216.

Heidbreder, E. (1933). *Seven psychologies.* New York: Appleton-Century-Crofts.

Maki, R. (1998). Test prediction over text material. In D. J. Hacker, J. Dunlosky, & A. C. Graesser (Eds.), *Metacognition in educational theory and practice* (pp. 117–145). Mahwah, NJ: Erlbaum.

Nelson, T. O. (1984). A comparison of current measures of the accuracy of feeling-of-knowing predictions. *Psychological Bulletin, 95,* 109–133.

Nelson, T. O. (1996). Consciousness and metacognition. *American Psychologist, 51,* 102–116.

Nelson, T. O., & Dunlosky, J. (1991). The delayed-JOL effect: When delaying your judgments of learning can improve the accuracy of your metacognitive monitoring. *Psychological Science, 2*, 267–270.

Nelson, T.O., & Narens, L. (1990). Metamemory: A theoretical framework and some new findings. In G. H. Bower (Ed.), *The psychology of learning and motivation* (Vol. 26, pp. 125–173). San Diego, CA: Academic Press.

Schwartz, B. L. (2002). *Tip-of-the-tongue states.* Mahwah, NJ: Erlbaum.

Sperling, G. (1960). The information available in brief visual presentations. *Psychological Monographs, 74,* Whole Number 11.

Widner, R. L., Smith, S. M., & Graziano, W. G. (1996). The effects of demand characteristics on the reporting of tip-of-the-tongue and feeling-of-knowing states. *American Journal of Psychology, 109,* 525–538.

Wilson, T. D. (1994). The proper protocol: Validity and completeness of verbal reports. *Psychological Science, 5,* 249–254.

Primers on Metamemory and Memory

The Integrated Nature of Metamemory and Memory

John Dunlosky and Robert A. Bjork

Introduction

Memory has been of interest to scholars and laypeople alike for over 2,000 years. In a rather gruesome example from antiquity, Cicero tells the story of Simonides (557–468 BC), who discovered the method of loci, which is a powerful mental mnemonic for enhancing one's memory. Simonides was at a banquet of a nobleman, Scopas. To honor him, Simonides sang a poem, but to Scopas's chagrin, the poem also honored two young men, Castor and Pollux. Being upset, Scopas told Simonides that he was to receive only half his wage. Simonides was later called from the banquet, and legend has it that the banquet room collapsed, and all those inside were crushed. To help bereaved families identify the victims, Simonides reportedly was able to name everyone according to the place where they sat at the table, which gave him the idea that order brings strength to our memories and that to employ this ability people "should choose localities, then form mental images of things they wanted to store in their memory, and place these in the localities" (Cicero, 2001).

This example highlights an early discovery that has had important applied implications for improving the functioning of memory (see, e.g., Yates, 1997). Memory theory was soon to follow. Aristotle (385–322 BC) claimed that memory arises from three processes: Events are associated (1) through their relative similarity or (2) relative dissimilarity and (3) when they co-occur together in space and time. Although Aristotle did not have sophisticated methodologies to develop or test his theory, these processes are strikingly reminiscent of modern theories of memory based on distinctiveness (e.g., Hunt & Worthen, 2006).

Metamemory versus Memory

Metamemory refers to people's knowledge of, monitoring of, and control of their own learning and memory processes. In the present chapter, we use the term *metamemory* or *metamemorial processes* to refer to any of these components of metamemory. The history of metamemory as a topic of experimental inquiry is very brief, relative to the history of memory research and theorizing. The first empirical work traces to Joseph Hart's research on feeling-of-knowing (FOK) judgments, reported in 1965, and the term metamemory was not even coined until 1970, when John Flavell introduced it.

The short experimental history of metamemory research notwithstanding, metamemory per se was evident as early as Simonides' tale and Aristotle's theory of memory. Using a mnemonic like the method of loci itself is a metacognitive act because individuals are using the mnemonic to control — and in this case, to improve — their memories, and Aristotle's distinction between having passive memories for a past event, versus attempting to recollect the past, has metacognitive implications as well. As Robinson (1989) explained in his treatise on *Aristotle's Psychology*:

> With recollection ... the process is initiated by the actor and entails a knowing, striving, *conscious* [italics original] being. It is the active nature of this search that distinguishes recollection from memory, and it is for this reason that Aristotle considers recollection to involve an inferential process. (pp. 71, 73)

For Aristotle, recollection involved an investigation of the mind — or self-observation and reflection — that relied on inferential processes, and although many animals evidently have memories, according to Aristotle, "None, we venture to say, except man, shares in the faculty of recollection" (Robinson, 1989, p. 71). Whether nonhuman animals have metamemories is perhaps one of the most debated topics in the field today and is relevant to the evolution of metamemory (Terrace & Metcalfe, 2005). As argued by Metcalfe (this volume), current evidence suggests that Aristotle was largely correct, although some nonhuman primates and other animals may possess preliminary forms of memory monitoring.

Metamemory and the Cognitive Renaissance

Even before metamemory was considered a subfield of cognition, early and groundbreaking work in cognitive psychology during the cognitive renaissance of the late 1950s and early 1960s included processes that are quintessentially metamemorial. Miller, Galanter, and Pribram (1960), for example, in their classic book, *Plans and the Structure of Behavior*, postulated a test-operate-test-exit (TOTE) unit, which was to supplant behaviorists' stimulus–response reflex arc as the fundamental unit of analysis of controlled behavior (see Figure 1). In brief, while controlling behavior, individuals presumably develop plans to achieve a certain goal and then test their current progress against that goal. If this test reveals a discrepancy between the current state and goal, the individual continues to operate (or work toward) achieving the sought-after goal. If no discrepancy remains, then the individual would terminate that particular goal-oriented behavior. This TOTE mechanism has been foundational to many theories and frameworks of metamemory, which assume that monitoring (analogous to "the tests" in TOTE) is used to control (analogous to "operate") memory in service of a learning goal (for a review, see Son & Kornell, this volume).

As a second example, consider Atkinson and Shiffrin's (1968) landmark article on memory. They proposed that external stimuli, if attended to, are transferred from a sensory store to a short-term memory. At that point, an individual could rely on a number of *control processes* to maintain the information in the short-term store or to transform the information. If one were trying to associate two words in a pair (e.g., dog–spoon), for example, one could elect to repeat the words over and over to

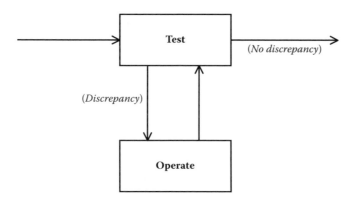

Figure 1 The test-operate-test-exit mechanism. (Adapted from G. A. Miller, E. Galanter, & K. H. Pribram, *Plans and the Structure of Behavior*, Holt, New York, 1960.)

oneself (a form of maintenance rehearsal) or one could develop an image of a dog swimming in a large spoon (a form of elaborative rehearsal). In either case, one is taking an active part in learning by manipulating the contents of one's short-term store. Thus, metamemory processes take center stage even in one of the first modern — and computational — theories of memory. It is important to emphasize, however, that although metamemory processes were implicated in these and other early theories of memory and cognition, most research on memory in the late 1960s and 1970s focused almost exclusively on memory qua memory, such as exploring the structure of the short-term store or the longevity of long-term memories.

The histories of thought and research on both memory and metamemory are quite extensive and go well beyond the scope of this introductory chapter (for further details on these histories, see Bower, 2000; Dunlosky & Metcalfe, in press). In the remainder of this chapter, we first discuss the rise of metamemory research and then argue that in many (if not all) situations, memory and metamemory are inextricably linked, to the point that understanding one may be a necessary, if not sufficient, condition for understanding the other. Our goal is to demonstrate and highlight how current research integrates memory and metamemory theories and phenomena.

Metamemory: Finding Its Identity

Consider the following classic quotation from Tulving and Madigan (1970):

> Why not start looking for ways of experimentally studying and incorporating into theories and models of memory one of the truly unique characteristics of human memory: its knowledge of its own knowledge. ... We cannot help but feel that if there is ever going to be a genuine breakthrough in the psychological study of memory ... it will, among other things, relate the knowledge stored in the individual's memory to his knowledge of that knowledge. (p. 477)

Why would Tulving and Madigan (1970) have to make this call for metamemory research, especially given the presence of metacognitive processes in early theories of memory? One answer to this question was provided by Nelson and Narens (1994) in their chapter, "Why Investigate Metacognition?" They argued that much of the early research on memory (1) overemphasized the human organism as nonreflective and, accordingly, (2) used methods to describe human memory that would short-circuit reflective control of learning and memory. Nelson and Narens (1994) discussed numerous examples to support these claims, one of which —having to do with Craik and Lockhart's (1972) levels-of-processing framework — seems particularly relevant and instructive. In Craik and Lockhart's framework, stored memory representations are essentially by-products of perception and comprehension. After watching the movie, *The Maltese Falcon*, for example, you may remember much of the plot but little of what the actors were wearing because you specifically attended to and comprehended the former and did not even perceive the latter. Note that the *intent* to remember in this account did not play a causal role in memory. That is, you would later remember the plot not because you had intended to do so but because you perceived and comprehended it.

For the levels-of-processing framework, it is quite evident that reflection about memory is not *directly* relevant to learning per se. Of course, intent to remember may indirectly influence memory because intent may increase the likelihood that we perceive and comprehend an event, yet intent itself is not proximally causal. In fact, to evaluate predictions from this framework (which claims that deeper, or more semantically oriented, levels of processing yield longer-lasting memories), researchers often employ incidental learning procedures to short-circuit any control processes that individuals might naturally use when attempting to learn new information. That is, experimental subjects were often not even informed that they would later be given a test of their memory and instead were given instructions to orient themselves to a particular level of processing.

In the history and development of memory theory, there is no doubt that the levels-of-processing framework has had a profound and important influence (see, e.g., Roediger & Gallo, 2001), and we would never argue that research within this and other traditions like it should not continue. Instead, we use the levels-of-processing example to illustrate that early memory research often deliberately downplayed metamemorial processes. The potential importance of self-reflection and control in learning was ignored; in fact, there was often an effort to minimize, via experimental controls and constraints, people's ability to rely on metamemorial processes. As noted by Nelson and Narens (1994), attempts to short-circuit people's control of learning is quite ironic given that doing so implicitly acknowledges that they will attempt to self-direct their learning to achieve task goals. That is, if people were not self-reflective and self-directed as they studied for an upcoming test, then why attempt to undermine such self-regulation?

The Influence of John Flavell

During the 1970s, other scientists, such as Ann Brown, Joseph Hart, Ellen Markman, and Henry Wellman, joined Tulving and Madigan in recognizing the importance of understanding the nature and influence of self-reflective processes — and people's knowledge about their memory and cognitive processes. Perhaps most influential among such early advocates was John Flavell. In his classic book, *The Developmental Psychology of Jean Piaget*, Flavell (1963) noted that Piaget and his colleagues argued that children's capability of having thoughts about thoughts were perhaps the crowning achievement of cognitive development (for further discussion, see Hacker, 1998). Flavell (1979) also, in a highly provocative *American Psychologist* article, "Metacognition and Cognitive Monitoring: A New Area of Cognitive-Developmental Inquiry," argued persuasively for the importance of understanding the role of metacognition in development, and he defined basic concepts and posed questions that ultimately helped define and promote the field. As but one example, Flavell (1979) asked, "How much good does cognitive monitoring actually do us in various type of cognitive enterprises?" (p. 910). Son and Kornell's review (this volume) of the field on study time allocation illustrates that definitive answers to this question have been elusive, although it appears that, at least under some conditions, memory monitoring can enhance the effectiveness of learning.

The Influence of Nelson and Narens's (1990) Unifying Framework

Certainly, by the late 1980s and early 1990s, metamemory research — and, more broadly, metacognitive research — had obtained an identity in the field. Even so, research on metamemory was often conducted in isolation, not only from research on memory, but also from other research on metamemory. There were pockets of interesting work, with some researchers, for example, focusing on how people judged their learning during study and other researchers focusing on how people judged their retrieval. Thus, metamemory was developing as a discipline in its own right, but metamemory research was itself fragmented.

In 1990, Nelson and Narens offered a framework for metamemory research that unified the field by illustrating how various metamemory judgments and control processes were interrelated. Their framework, which highlighted the temporal order during learning and retrieval of various judgments and control processes, is shown in Figure 2, and definitions of each of these metamemorial components are provided in Table 1. The framework allowed researchers to place their particular programs of research on a given judgment or control process within a larger perspective, and equally important, it stimulated questions — such as "Are specific judgments (e.g., judgment of learning, JOL) used in the control of learning?" and "Are the bases of the various metamemory judgments essentially the same?" — that led to additional research in the field. Basically, Nelson and Narens's framework unified the field by illustrating how research in one area of metamemory may be related to research in other areas.

Nelson and Narens (1990) also offered a straightforward model of metamemory, which itself implied that metamemory and memory were by their very nature integrated. This model contains a metalevel representation and an object-level representation (Figure 3), which loosely corresponds to metamemory and memory, respectively. This model is discussed extensively by Van Overschelde (this volume), who notes that "in this model, information flows hierarchically, with the metalevel acquiring information from (i.e., monitoring) the object level, and the metalevel

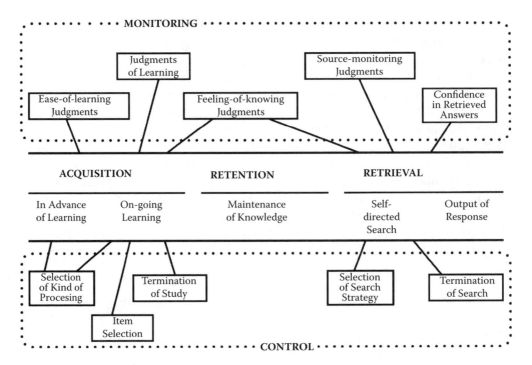

Figure 2 The Nelson and Narens (1990) framework. (Adapted by J. Dunlosky, M. Serra, and J. M. C. Baker, in F. Durso, R. S. Nickerson, S. T. Dumais, S. Lewandowsky, & T. J. Perfect, *Handbook of Applied Cognition,* 2nd ed., Wiley, New York, 2007.)

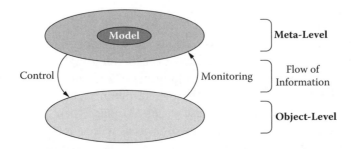

Figure 3 A framework relating metacognition (meta-level) and cognition (object-level) that gives rise to monitoring and control processes. (Adapted from Nelson and Narens, in G. H. Bower, *The Psychology of Learning and Motivation*, vol. 26 (pp. 125–173), Academic Press, New York, 1990.)

sending information to, and thereby changing (i.e., controlling), the object level" (p. 47). Van Overschelde also discusses a component of their model that had largely been neglected in research on metamemory. In particular, he expands on the idea that the metalevel itself contains a dynamic model of the underlying object level — which he calls the *meta-model* — that may play an essential role in people's decisions about how to control their learning and retrieval.

TABLE 1 Definitions of Metamemory Judgments and Control Processes

Term	Definition
Metamemory Judgments	
Ease-of-learning (EOL) judgments	Judgments of how easy to-be-studied items will be to learn
Judgments of learning (JOL)	Judgments of the likelihood of remembering recently studied items on an upcoming test
Feeling-of-knowing (FOK) judgments	Judgments of the likelihood of recognizing currently unrecallable answers on an upcoming test
Source-monitoring judgments	Judgments made during a criterion test pertaining to the source of a particular memory
Confidence in retrieved answers	Judgments of the likelihood that a response on a test is correct; often referred to as retrospective confidence (RC) judgments
Control Processes	
Selection of kind of processing	Selection of strategies to employ when attempting to commit an item to memory
Item selection	Decision about whether to study an item on an upcoming trial
Termination of study	Decision to stop studying an item currently being studied
Selection of search strategy	Selecting a particular strategy to produce a correct response during a test
Termination of search	Decisions to terminate searching for a response

Source: Adapted from J. Dunlosky, M. Serra, and J. M. C. Baker, in F. Durso, R. S. Nickerson, S. T. Dumais, S. Lewandowsky, & T. J. Perfect, *Handbook of Applied Cognition,* 2nd ed., Wiley, New York, 2007.

With respect to our main theme, Nelson and Narens's (1990) model in Figure 3 is notable in highlighting the symbiotic nature of metamemorial and memory processes: Metamemory itself involves monitoring an underlying memory system, but then metamemory processes in turn can act on the memory system. Put differently (and in rather general terms), memory influences metamemory, and metamemory influences memory (cf. Koriat, Ma'ayan, & Nussinson, 2006). Accordingly, they act together to decide the fate of learning, retrieval, and long-term retention.

The Integrated Nature of Metamemory and Memory

Given that self-reflective processes were often neglected in early research on memory, it may not be too surprising why Tulving and Madigan (1970) called for investigation of people's knowledge about their knowledge, or even why Nelson and Narens (1994) felt it necessary to ask (and then answer) the question, Why investigate metacognition? Such calls for research on metacognition are no longer necessary given that interest in metamemory — and more generally, in metacognition — has been growing steadily over the past several decades. Publications abound; specialized edited volumes have been appearing (e.g., Hacker, Dunlosky, & Graesser, 1998; Perfect & Schwartz, 2002;

Terrace & Metcalfe, 2005), and associations, such as the International Association for Metacognition (dept.kent.edu/psychology/iam.org) and the special interest
group on Metacognition for the European Association for Research on Learning and
Instruction, have been formed to support communication and collaboration among
researchers. With such a focus on metamemory and metacognition, our aim here
is partly to make sure the pendulum does not swing too far in the other direction,
so that future researchers of metamemory will not need to raise the question, Why
investigate memory in understanding metamemory?

In this *Handbook of Metamemory and Memory*, the charge to the contributors
was to provide an overview of their particular area of research and to discuss recent
evidence relevant to current directions for the field. The handbook chapters are biased
somewhat toward emphasizing metamemory processes, in part because other excellent and comprehensive volumes have recently been dedicated to learning and memory (e.g., Naveh-Benjamin, Moscovitch, & Roediger, 2001; Tulving & Craik, 2000).
In many instances, however, a by-product of this emphasis on cutting-edge research
on metamemory has been a demonstration of the many ways that memory processes
rely on, and are integrated with, metamemorial processes.

Is Metamemory a Necessary Component of All Memory?

Our basic argument is that attempting to study one construct (metamemory or
memory) in isolation will likely fall short of completely understanding either because
metamemory and memory are inextricably linked. This particular claim, however, is
admittedly too strong because the mutual reliance between the constructs is likely
asymmetrical. More specifically, understanding some forms of memory may not
require a concurrent understanding of metamemory, whereas most metamemory
research will likely benefit from knowledge about memory theory and phenomena.
In the following sections, we briefly illustrate these ideas.

Even Aristotle realized that memory itself is present in nonhuman animals that do
not have recollective — that is, reflective — capabilities. And although some recent
research suggests, at least to some researchers, that even rats have the ability to monitor memory, Metcalfe (this volume) argues that the methods used in this research fall
short of providing a convincing demonstration of rats' monitoring abilities. Thus, at
least in some nonhuman species, metamemory is evidently not a necessary support
for memory.

The first empirical research on human memory, published in 1885 by Hermann
Ebbinghaus, relied on a method to investigate memory that allegedly sidestepped
conscious awareness and perhaps the recruitment of metamemorial processes. In
particular, Ebbinghaus developed nonsense syllables, consonant-vowel-consonant
trigrams that do not form a word (e.g., VAL or DAX). He studied a given list of syllables during initial trials, and then, sometime later, he restudied that list. Among
Ebbinghaus's multiple contributions to research on human memory was the development of a very sensitive empirical measure of retention, a *savings score*, defined as the
percentage of the trials that were required to learn a given list to criteria that were
saved on relearning. Thus, if relearning required the same number of trials as did

original learning, there were no savings and, hence, complete forgetting of the list. As noted by MacLeod (this volume), Ebbinghaus's method "did not rely on conscious recollection at all: Savings can and does occur even when the subject has no recollection of the targeted item from the originally learned material" (p. 245). Thus, the savings score represents memory qua memory — no metamemory added.

In the decades following Ebbinghaus's pioneering research, the focus of research tended to be on explicit-memory tasks, that is, on tasks in which research participants were explicitly instructed to remember the past. In the 1980s, however, researchers turned their attention to implicit-memory tasks (e.g., Lewandowsky, Dunn, & Kirsner, 1989; Richardson-Klavehn & Bjork, 1988). As in Ebbinghaus realizing savings on relearning a list, even when he was unaware that the list was one he had learned earlier, implicit tests of memory do not require that people are aware that they are remembering a past event or being influenced by a past event. By definition, then, implicit memory is, at least in some cases, memory without metamemory.

Our conclusion may seem trivial to aficionados of memory because the answer to our question, Is metamemory a necessary component of all memory? most certainly is, No. The three related points we discuss next are much less trivial, and each echoes the subtle influences of metamemory on memory.

The first point is that even tests of implicit memory are often contaminated by people's explicit attempts to control their learning or explicitly recollect the past. Consider, for example, the nonsense syllables Ebbinghaus invented in an effort to study memory uncontaminated by earlier learning. Ebbinghaus (1885/1964) generated roughly 2,300 different, supposedly meaningless, syllables (e.g., VAL, MEV), but as Hothersall (1995) explained, Ebbinghaus was fluent in German, English, and French, making it virtually certain that many of his nonsense syllables were meaningful to him semantically. For VAL, for example, one can imagine him interpreting this alleged nonsense syllable as *valise*, the French word for "a small suitcase." In fact, researchers have subsequently generated meaningfulness norms for allegedly non-meaningful nonsense syllables (e.g., Taylor, 1970). These observations suggest that even Ebbinghaus's savings score may have been tainted by strategic behavior.

The second point returns to more contemporary tests of implicit memory. MacLeod (this volume) explains that almost all tests of implicit memory are susceptible to intrusions of conscious memory. Thus, if we want to use implicit memory tasks to understand memory that is stripped of metamemory, we will need to devise techniques to minimize reflective processes while people perform them (for nine techniques to do so, see MacLeod, this volume). An intriguing observation is that adults usually attempt to be strategic — that is, choose to engage in various metamemorial processes — even during tasks that have been designed to isolate memory from metamemory. Thus, metamemorial processes may not be entirely ubiquitous in the use of our memories, but memory and metamemory processes are closely aligned, and people almost automatically turn to self-reflection, monitoring, and explicit control to achieve memory goals.

The third point is that, implicit memory aside, it is apparent that many forms of learning and retrieval *do* explicitly elicit metamemorial processes. Thus, even though metamemory may not be a necessary component of all memory, metamemorial processes arguably cannot be overlooked in any comprehensive theory of memory or in most specialized theories that focus on particular memory phenomena. As we discuss next, the chapters is this volume serve to emphasize that conclusion.

Contributions of a Metamemory Perspective to the Understanding of Memory Phenomena

Multiple chapters in the current volume showcase this potential contribution of metamemory for understanding phenomena that can be identified, mistakenly, as entirely "memory" phenomena. The following are examples:

Batchelder and Batchelder (this volume) explore source monitoring, which involves remembering the source of a particular memory. One may recall that someone said that "you probably shouldn't eat grapefruit while taking your cholesterol medication," but remembering *who* gave you this tidbit of information (your doctor, perhaps, or maybe your mother) is a different type of memory — namely, source memory. Importantly, optimizing source memory can enhance the quality of decision making. If, for example, you incorrectly remember your mother, rather than your doctor, warning you against eating your beloved grapefruit, then you may unwisely decide to have some for breakfast.

People, of course, often have faulty source memories. When they do, according to Batchelder and Batchelder (this volume), "They utilize metacognitive inferences derived from monitoring their own experimentally induced memory processes coupled with extra experimental experiences and beliefs" (p. 211). Their chapter provides an extensive exploration of these metacognitive inferences in source memory and how they can be actualized within multinomial models.

In a similar vein, Malmberg (this volume) demonstrates how metacognitive monitoring influences retrieval processes, which in turn affects performance on an associative memory task (cf. Reder & Schunn, 1996). Imagine studying a paired associate, such as turtle–board, and later being cued with "turtle" and asked to recall the correct response (in this case, "board"). This cued-recall task involves both retrieval processes and a global-matching process. The latter process serves to compute a familiarity response to the probe word (turtle); individuals presumably monitor this familiarity, which then drives the retrieval process itself. According to Malmberg (this volume), memory researchers have given relatively little attention to these familiarity processes in cued-recall tasks, partly because "familiarity alone is insufficient for successfully performing a recall task" (p. 266). He also provides new evidence that people's monitoring of cue familiarity influences the duration of search during retrieval. Perhaps more intriguing, although such familiarity is used to control retrieval, it appears to be abandoned as a guide when familiarity itself is not attributed to memory strength.

Other examples of how metamemory informs theories of memory are provided by Perfect and Stark (this volume) and Mazzoni (this volume), who explore forms of false memory. Perfect and Stark, in "Tales from the Crypt ... omnesia," provides an impressive review of the extant literature on cryptomnesia, which refers to unconscious plagiarism — that is, inadvertently stating an idea is one's own idea when in fact it is not. One issue Perfect and Stark raises is whether cryptomnesia that is produced in the laboratory is actually an error in output monitoring. If so, lab-based cryptomnesia may be more indicative of a monitoring deficit than a true underlying memory deficiency, and Perfect and Stark review evidence relevant to this intriguing possibility.

Mazzoni (this volume) explores how people come to believe that an entire event occurred to them when in fact it did not. She describes how people can be made to believe that a seemingly implausible event — for example, witnessing a demonic possession — actually occurred earlier in their lives. A variety of metamemorial processes may be involved in the development of such false memories, such as evaluations of event plausibility and whether memories are available that are believed to be related to that event. Thus, people may come to believe that they had even witnessed demonic possession given that it seems plausible to them and they believe that their childhood memories are relevant to such an unlikely event.

In summary, by considering the possible metamemorial processes that could contribute to memory errors and performance, the chapters by Batchelder and Batchelder, Malmberg, Perfect and Stark, and Mazzoni highlight the contribution of metamemory theory to advances in understanding memory.

Is Memory a Necessary Component of All Metamemory?

As we elaborate later in this chapter, the answer to this question is decidedly No, yet given the nature of metamemory, research in memory has also led to new insights into metamemory. In this section, we describe how both memory theories and memory phenomena have provided foundations for advances in metamemory research.

Joseph Hart's (1965) groundbreaking research on FOK judgments provides an instructive illustration. Hart asked this question: When people say they know an answer that they cannot recall, do they really know the answer? Put differently, do these feelings of knowing have any accuracy? Before Hart, William James eloquently described these tip-of-the tongue experiences in a manner that made them seem real and valid, but Hart asked, *are* they real — that is, do they really reflect the nature of one's underlying memory system? To reveal whether people's FOK judgments were accurate, Hart capitalized on the established memory phenomenon that people can often recognize sought-after targets that they cannot recall:

> To answer the question about the accuracy of FOK experiences it is necessary to find a research paradigm within which the experiences can be produced and their accuracy evaluated. Use was made of one of the best-established facts of verbal learning — recognition exceeds recall. People can almost always recognize more answers than they can produce. (pp. 208–209)

This simple memory phenomenon — that memories can be recognized even when they were not recalled — inspired Hart to develop the now-famous recall-judge-recognize (RJR) method, which is the genesis of many of the methods used today to explore the accuracy of metamemory judgments. In general, the RJR method involves asking people to *recall* the answer to questions, such as, "Who sang the hit song, 'Back on the Chain Gang?'" For questions they cannot answer, they then make an FOK *judgment* by predicting the likelihood that they will *recognize* the correct answer. Given that some unrecalled answers would be recognized while others would not, Hart reasoned that participants should be able, if FOK judgments reflect genuine memories, to predict which answers they would and would not be able to correctly recognize on a later test. Using this method, Hart (1965) demonstrated that people's FOK judgments were accurate, which was quite surprising because, How can we know that a memory exists when we don't have access to it? In the present volume, Leonesio offers one answer to this question. To do so, he relies on the distinction, in current memory theorizing, between familiarity with an event and recollection of an event (e.g., Yonelinas, 2002). Based on the accuracy for FOK judgments for dream memories, Leonesio concludes that having recollection for some details of an event is critical to achieving above-chance FOK accuracy. In this case, memory theory and phenomena led to insight into the accuracy of metamemory judgments.

More generally, virtually all theories about the accuracy of metamemory judgments are at least partly inspired by memory theory or phenomena. Notable examples in the field include Reder's use of the source of activation confusion (SAC) model of declarative memory to explore FOK decisions (e.g., Reder & Schunn, 1996); Metcalfe's (1993) use of the composite holographic associative model of memory to understand Korsakoff patients' deficits in FOK accuracy; Dougherty's (2001) use of a multiple-trace memory model to account for the accuracy of retrospective confidence judgments; and Sikström and Jönsson's (2005) application of a stochastic drift model of memory strength to explain the delayed JOL effect.

Memory Versus Metamemory: The Delayed Judgment-of-Learning Controversy

In the present volume, several other chapters also focus on the delayed JOL effect, which sparked controversy about the contribution of memory versus metamemory to the accuracy of JOLs. To comprehend the nature of the controversy, it is necessary to understand how the accuracy of JOLs (which are predictions of the likelihood of correctly remembering a recently studied item on an upcoming test) is estimated. Typically, experimental subjects study paired associates (e.g., turtle–board) and predict the likelihood of correctly recalling the target when later shown the cue (i.e., turtle– ?). The relative accuracy of JOLs is often computed by correlating each individual's JOLs to his or her own later recall performance, with higher correlations indicating better relative accuracy. The most commonly used correlation to estimate judgment accuracy has been the gamma coefficient, mainly because Nelson (1984) argued persuasively that this particular coefficient is the best available. Benjamin and Diaz (this volume) closely scrutinize gamma and other measures of relative accuracy. They provide a detailed argument and supporting analyses that a measure based on the application of signal-detection theory (d_a) can provide superior estimates of relative accuracy. In particular, they conclude that using d_a (or a transform of gamma) may be especially important when one desires to evaluate the differential effectiveness of a manipulation on relative accuracy.

Returning to the delayed JOL effect itself, the timing of the JOLs in relation to initial study matters: When JOLs are prompted by the stimulus of a pair (e.g., turtle– ?) and are made immediately after studying items, relative accuracy is quite poor, in the range of +.30. By contrast, when JOLs are delayed until after all items have been studied (e.g., a delay of a minute or more), relative accuracy is close to perfect (Nelson & Dunlosky, 1991). The first theories for the delayed JOL effect, which are considered in detail by Narens, Nelson, and Scheck (this volume) and by Spellman, Blumenthal, and Bjork (this volume), provide prime examples of how memory theory and phenomena are foundational to understanding metamemory. The monitoring-dual-memories (MDM) hypothesis was inspired by Atkinson and Shiffrin's (1968) model of memory. According to MDM, delayed JOL accuracy is excellent because memory monitoring is based on retrieval of information about a to-be-judged response from long-term memory (which would be predictive of eventual test performance), whereas immediate JOL accuracy suffers because noise about the to-be-judged item from short-term memory disrupts monitoring information stored in long-term memory. By contrast, the self-fulfilling prophecy (SFP) hypothesis was inspired by the memory phenomenon that success on a delayed retrieval test influences subsequent test performance. According to this hypothesis, delayed JOLs are accurate because people attempt to retrieve the correct answer when making the judgment at a delay, and it is this retrieval attempt that ensures high levels of accuracy (Spellman & Bjork, 1992).

Narens et al. (this volume) and Spellman et al. (this volume) offer new tools to evaluate these hypotheses. Narens et al. decompose the relative accuracy of JOLs into subcomponents that reflect the contribution of (1) monitoring processes relevant to the MDM hypothesis and (2) memory processes relevant to the SFP hypothesis. Based on this decomposition, the data modeled in their article were better explained by the SFP than the MDM hypothesis — the latter of which appeared to contribute minimally to relative accuracy under the conditions investigated. Even so, Narens et al. explain that experimental circumstances that yield the delayed JOL effect can be devised that could be explained best by the MDM hypothesis (as in Weaver, Terrell, Krug, & Kelemen, this volume) and others that could be explained best by the SFP hypothesis (as in their data set). Importantly, their analysis also demonstrates that changes in standard measures of relative accuracy (whether it be gamma or d_a) cannot be used to evaluate theories of the delayed JOL effect without further decomposition.

Spellman et al. (this volume) also consider the delayed JOL effect, and like Narens et al. (this volume), they use a new technique to explore the contribution of memory to the effect. In particular, Monte Carlo simulations were used to provide estimates of whether, and how much, changes in memory (due to making delayed JOLs) boost the relative accuracy of those JOLs. They discuss the underlying assumptions of the simulations and describe how the simulation can be used to explore the delayed JOL effect in particular and relative judgment accuracy in general. Their simulation, which supports the SFP hypothesis, is available on the Web and is user friendly. Thus, both Narens et al. and Spellman et al. offer new tools for the field that researchers can readily use to answer questions about the potential influence of memory on metamemory.

In a creative application of a memory phenomenon to explore metamemory, Weaver et al. (this volume) used flashbulb memories to explore explanations for the delayed JOL effect. Not only are they the first to demonstrate the delayed JOL effect involving "flashbulb memories," but their data also cannot readily be explained by the SFP hypothesis. Another intriguing issue raised in this chapter, and also pursued by Maki (this volume), is the degree to which a person has privileged access to his or her own memories. Put differently, when you predict your own performance on a memory task, do you really access your own personal memory, or is your prediction instead based on other factors (e.g., normative item difficulty) that anyone could potentially access? As concluded by Maki, "People do seem to have privileged access after they have answered a question … [People] showed less evidence for privileged access when they made predictions about future performance over text. Rather than accessing information about their own learning from text, participants may have used common intrinsic factors related to the difficulty of the texts" (p. 188). Thus, in both chapters, the evidence suggests that people do demonstrate at least some privileged access when they are evaluating the quality of their memories, but it is equally clear that privileged access is limited.

The Cues That Support Metamemorial Judgments

Such limited privileged access can be readily accommodated by the metamemory framework from Koriat, Nussinson, Bless, and Shaked (this volume), who propose that people's metamemorial judgments are based on two classes of cues: information-based cues or experienced-based cues. Information-based cues, such as the time spent studying or normative test difficulty, can influence a person's judgments of memory. Given that other people also have access to these information-based cues, they may be responsible for the fact that one person can accurately judge another person's learning. By contrast, experienced-based cues "involve a two-stage process (Koriat, 2000), first a process that gives rise to a sheer subjective feeling and second a process that uses that feeling as a basis for memory predictions" (Koriat et al., this volume, p. 118). These experience-based cues apparently reflect privileged access. The take-home message is that metamemory is often closely tied to an individual's memory, so the two are closely linked, but metamemory judgments can also rely on information-based cues that do not recruit memories about the to-be-judged items. Thus, although memory is a necessary component of some forms of metamemory, certain metamemory judgments are not based on memory per se.

Contemporary Issues

A variety of contemporary issues covered in this volume also illustrate the integrated nature of memory and metamemory. Research on neuroscience explores the neurological substrates of both constructs and how one may function in the service of the other. For instance, Schwartz and Bacon (this volume) discuss pharmacological approaches for exploring the relations between metamemory and memory. Their review highlights how various drugs, such as benzodiazepines, can dissociate metamemory from memory. Their review of neuroimaging, neuropsychology, and pharmacological literatures converges on what has become the received view: Metacognitive monitoring relies on the prefrontal cortex (PFC) (see also Pannu & Kaszniak, 2005).

Shimamura (this volume) explores further the relations among the PFC, metamemory, and memory. According to Shimamura, a major role of metamemorial processes is to control information processing by suppressing, or inhibiting, unwanted information, which in turn improves the efficiency and success of information processing. More specifically, according to his dynamic filtering theory, the "PFC, with its extensive projections to and from many cortical regions, regulates posterior cortical circuits by way of a filtering or gating mechanism. By this view, object-level processors are distributed in posterior cortical regions and are controlled by metalevel processors in PFC regions. The PFC implements metacognitive control by dynamic filtering, that is, by the selection of appropriate signals and suppression of inappropriate signals" (pp. 374–375). Shimamura argues further that the PFC is segregated, and hence it should not be viewed as *the* central executive but more like a board of executives that act to control memory and cognition. Most relevant to our thesis here, both Shimamura (this volume) and Schwartz and Bacon (this volume) conjecture that, although the neural substrates underlying metamemory and memory are distinct, it is the coordinated interaction between these neural substrates that leads to efficient information processing.

The final set of chapters explores the developmental trajectory of metamemory in childhood as well as the relevance of metamemory to learning and student scholarship. These chapters herald the integrated nature of metamemory and memory because they focus directly on questions such as, When do children demonstrate the metamemorial ability to accurately evaluate their memories, and how can students use metamemorial processes to improve their learning of classroom materials? Concerning the first question, Schneider and Lockl (this volume) begin by describing the history of research on metacognition, focusing especially on issues relevant to child development. Their analysis of this history is impressive in that they lucidly illustrate the relationship between a metamemorial approach and a theory-of-mind approach to investigating memory development. After a thorough review of the literature on metamemory and child development, Schneider and Lockl conclude that "although monitoring accuracy tends to improve over the school years, even preschoolers show remarkable monitoring in learning situations they are familiar with. In contrast, the available evidence on the development of self-regulation skills shows that there are clear increases from middle childhood to adolescence" (p. 405).

Given that even preschoolers may have remarkable monitoring abilities, one might conjecture that students of all ages could readily use these abilities to improve their in-class performance. Although some students certainly rely on their monitoring of progress to guide their learning, the chapters by Carroll (this volume) and Hacker, Bol, and Keener (this volume) indicate that many challenges remain. Carroll describes a variety of situations in which even college students' judgments about their learning show poor relative accuracy. For instance, students' judgments do not appear to reflect the major benefits that overlearning can have on retention. Perhaps more important, however, Carroll emphasizes that such faulty judgment appears more prevalent when factors (e.g., overlearning vs. criterion learning) are manipulated between subjects than when manipulated within each subject. In the latter case, when students can experience and compare learning across levels of a factor, they are more likely to accurately judge the relative differences in memory across those factors.

Achieving high levels of relative accuracy is desirable, of course, but students' judgments of their learning often need to also show excellent absolute accuracy.

Unfortunately, Hacker et al. (this volume) document that laboratory-based research has repeatedly shown that students are typically quite overconfident in their learning. Such overconfidence can have detrimental effects on performance because a student who believes he or she has learned all the concepts in a chapter (when he or she really only knows 50%) will stop studying well before they are ready for an exam. Hacker et al.'s review of research conducted in classrooms yields even more sobering news: Poor students are overconfident in how well they have learned course materials, and various interventions involving feedback and practice do not improve their calibration. In such cases, the disconnect between metamemory and memory is serious and will contribute to poor performance, which is unfortunate given mandates to leave no child behind. Certainly, a major research agenda is to develop techniques that help students accurately evaluate their progress so that they can effectively and reliably obtain their learning goals.

Closing Remarks

The integrated nature of metamemory and memory is evident in the histories of both subfields of cognition and is showcased in the chapters in this volume. The main argument in this introductory chapter is that although one may investigate either construct alone, such isolationism runs a dire risk of providing an incomplete understanding of either. The chapters in this volume constitute not only a handbook of research on metamemory and memory, but also a demonstration of the importance of a dualistic, rather than isolationistic, approach to investigating metamemory and memory.

Acknowledgment

Many thanks to Katherine Rawson for comments on this chapter.

References

Atkinson, R. C., & Shiffrin, R. M. (1968). Human memory: A proposed system and its control processes. In K. Spence & J. Spence (Eds.), *The psychology of learning and motivation* (Vol. 2, pp. 90–197). New York: Academy Press.

Bower, G. (2000). A brief history of memory research. In E. Tulving & F. I. M. Craik (Eds.), *The Oxford handbook of memory* (pp. 3–32). New York: Oxford Press.

Cicero, M. T. (2001). *On the ideal orator (de oratore)* (J. M. May & J. Wisse, Trans.). New York: Oxford University Press.

Craik, F.I.M., & Lockhart, R. S. (1972). Levels of processing: A framework for memory research. *Journal of Verbal Learning and Verbal Behavior, 11,* 671–684.

Dougherty, M. R. P. (2001). Integration of the ecological and error models of overconfidence using a multiple-trace memory model. *Journal of Experimental Psychology: General, 130,* 579–599.

Dunlosky, J., & Metcalfe, J. (2008). *Metacognition: A textbook for cognitive, educational, life-span and applied psychology.* Thousand Oaks, CA: SAGE.

Dunlosky, J., Serra, M. J., & Baker, J. M. C. (2007). Metamemory applied. In F. Durso, R. S. Nickerson, S. T. Dumais, S. Lewandowsky, & T. J. Perfect (Eds.), *Handbook of applied cognition* (2nd ed.).

Ebbinghaus, H. (1964). *Memory: A contribution to experimental psychology*. New York: Dover. (Original work published 1885)

Flavell, J. H. (1963). *The developmental psychology of Jean Piaget*. New York: Van Nostrand.

Flavell, J. H. (1979). Metacognition and cognitive monitoring: A new area of cognitive-developmental inquiry. *American Psychologist, 34*, 906–911.

Hacker, D. J. (1998). Definitions and empirical foundations. In D. J. Hacker, J. Dunlosky, & A. Graesser (Eds.), *Metacognition in educational theory and practice* (pp. 1–24). Hillsdale, NJ: Erlbaum.

Hacker, D. J., Dunlosky, J., & Graesser, A. (Eds.) (1998). *Metacognition in educational theory and practice*. Hillsdale, NJ: Erlbaum.

Hart, J. T. (1965). Memory and the feeling-of-knowing experience. *Journal of Educational Psychology, 56*, 208–216.

Hothersall, D. (1995). *History of psychology* (3rd ed.). New York: McGraw Hill.

Hunt. R. R., & Worthen, J. B. (Eds.). (2006). Distinctiveness and memory. New York: Oxford University Press.

Koriat, A. (2000). The feeling of knowing: Some metatheoretical implications for consciousness and control. *Consciousness and Cognition, 9*, 149–171.

Koriat, A., Ma'ayan, H., & Nussinson, R. (2006). The intricate relationships between monitoring and control in metacognition: Lessons for the cause-and-effect relation between subjective experience and behavior. *Journal of Experimental Psychology: General, 135*, 36–69.

Lewandowsky, S., Dunn, J. C., & Kirsner, K. (Eds.). (1989). *Implicit memory: Theoretical issues*. Hillsdale, NJ: LEA.

Metcalfe, J. (1993). Novelty monitoring, metacognition, and control in a composite holographic associative recall model: Implications for Korsakoff amnesia. *Psychological Review, 100*, 3–22.

Miller, G. A., Galanter, E., & Pribram, K. H. (1960). *Plans and the structure of behavior*. New York: Holt.

Naveh-Benjamin, M., Moscovitch, M., & Roediger, H. L., III (Eds.). (2001). *Perspective on human memory and cognitive aging: Essays in honor of Fergus Craik*. New York: Psychology Press.

Nelson, T. O. (1984). A comparison of current measures of the accuracy of feeling-of-knowing predictions. *Psychological Bulletin, 95*, 109–133.

Nelson, T. O., & Dunlosky, J. (1991). When people's judgments of learning (JOLs) are extremely accurate at predicting subsequent recall: The "delayed-JOL effect." *Psychological Science, 2*, 267–270.

Nelson, T. O., & Narens, L. (1990). Metamemory: a theoretical framework and new findings. In G. H. Bower (Ed.), *The psychology of learning and motivation* (Vol. 26, pp. 125–173). New York: Academic Press.

Nelson, T. O., & Narens, L. (1994). Why investigate metacognition? In J. Metcalfe, & A. J. Shimamura (Eds.), *Metacognition: Knowing about knowing* (pp. 1–26). Cambridge, MA: MIT Press.

Pannu, J. K., & Kaszniak, A. W. (2005). Metamemory experiments in neurological populations: A review. *Neuropsychological Review, 15*, 105–130.

Perfect, T. J., & Schwartz, B. L. (Eds.). (2002). *Applied metacognition*. New York: Cambridge University Press.

Reder, L. M., & Schunn, C. D. (1996). Metacognition does not imply awareness: Strategy choice is governed by implicit learning and memory. In L. M. Reder (Ed.), *Implicit memory and metacognition* (pp. 79–122). Hillsdale, NJ: LEA.

Richardson-Klavehn, A., & Bjork, R. A. (1988). Measures of memory. *Annual Review of Psychology, 39*, 475–543.

Robinson, D. N. (1989). *Aristotle's psychology.* New York: Columbia University Press.

Roediger, H. L., III, & Gallo, D. (2001). Levels of processing: Some unanswered questions. In M. Naveh-Benjamin, M. Moscovitch, & H. L. Roediger, III (Eds.), *Perspectives on human memory and cognitive aging. Essays in honor of Fergus Craik* (pp. 28–47). New York: Psychology Press.

Sikström, S., & Jönsson, F. (2005). A model for stochastic drift in memory strength to account for judgments of learning. *Psychological Review, 112*, 932–950.

Spellman, B. A., & Bjork, R. A. (1992). When predictions create reality: Judgments of learning may alter what they are intended to assess. *Psychological Science, 3*, 315–316.

Taylor, K. (1970). An information-theory measurement of CVC trigram meaningfulness. *Psychonomic Science, 21*, 101–103.

Terrace, H. S., & Metcalfe, J. (2005). (Eds.) The missing link in cognition: Origins of self-reflective consciousness. *New York: Oxford University Press.*

Tulving, E., & Craik, F. I. M. (2000). *The Oxford handbook of memory.* New York: Oxford Press.

Tulving, E., & Madigan, S. A. (1970). Memory and verbal learning. In P. H. Mussen & M. R. Rosenzweig (Eds.), *Annual review of psychology* (pp. 437–484). Palo Alto, CA: Annual Reviews.

Yates, F. A. (1997). *The art of memory.* London: Pimlico.

Yonelinas, A. P. (2002). The nature of recollection and familiarity: A review of 30 years of research. *Journal of Memory and Language, 46*, 441–517.

Evolution of Metacognition

Janet Metcalfe

Introduction

The importance of metacognition, in the evolution of human consciousness, has been emphasized by thinkers going back hundreds of years. While it is clear that people have metacognition, even when it is strictly defined as it is here, whether any other animals share this capability is the topic of this chapter. The empirical data on non-human metacognition are reviewed. It is concluded that three monkeys have now shown evidence of metacognition. Even in these primates, however, the capabilities are limited. Despite claims that rats have metacognition, the data can be explained in terms of mere conditioning contingencies. No other species has been shown to have metacognition. Thus, metacognition appears to be a very recently evolved capability. It is one that may confer on humans an ability to escape from being stimulus bound and allow self-control of their learning and actions.

Even before psychology was recognized as a separate discipline, scholars were fascinated by what we now call metacognition because self-reflective knowledge (i.e., metacognition) was thought to embody a particular kind of consciousness unique to human beings. According to a number of thinkers, this kind of consciousness bears a special connection to our "self" or our knowledge of ourselves, as in the maxim, "know thyself." The notion that there is a looker, embedded within our cognitive fabric, that is somehow able to look at our other cognitive processes, has such compelling force as being a special entity to have provoked early philosophers from St. Augustine (see Harrison, 2006) to Descartes (1637/1999) to suppose that there is a disembodied soul. The modern analogue, while disavowing a nonphysical soul, is to claim that this self-reflective capability is nevertheless a special mental capability and a phenomenological experience that is specific to humans. This view has been articulately espoused by moderns from Armstrong (1968) to Rosenthal (2002) and holds considerable appeal. The idea is that whereas other species may have evolved adaptive characteristics such as the ability to fly, or, like the raptors, to see tiny movements many miles away, or, like the monarch butterfly, to eat foods that are poisonous to other animals, the human species has evolved — as its unique adaptive strength — a particular form of consciousness. The most elementary component of this form of consciousness is metacognition.

Is Metacognition a Special Kind of Consciousness?

Descartes, in what we now consider to be elaborate metacognitive musings, reached the conclusion that the fact of these musings — that he was able to think about his thinking — gave indisputable proof of his own existence. What Descartes was doing, when he was isolated in his poêle (a small cabin with a woodstove) thinking about the basis of all knowledge, was deeply metacognitive. He was considering whether his physical body might be different, and he acknowledged that it might. He was thinking about whether his perceptions might be faulty — which all modern psychologists and an entire tradition focused on illusions and distortions and biases of perception (see, e.g., Hochberg, 2003) resonate to. He was deliberating over whether his memories of his own personal experience might be wrong. The vulnerability of memory is, of course, now well established (Loftus, 2004). Despite all these possibilities of cognitive and perceptual distortions, which we now know extend even to the metacognitions themselves (see Bjork, 1994; Jacoby, Bjork, & Kelley, 1994; Metcalfe, 1998), what Descartes was unable to deny (cf., Russell, 1945/1972) was that there was somebody doing all of this reflection: him. This observation, that such metacognitive musings implicated a self who is the muser, had deep significance for Descartes and for subsequent thinkers.

Descartes reached a conclusion that most modern neuroscientists (e.g., Damasio, 1994), even those who ascribe to the importance of metacognition as entailing a special state of consciousness, might shy away from, namely, that the existence of such self-reflection implies that there must be a nonphysical soul. Descartes, of course, was a dualist and used his meditations to that end. However, one need not take a dualist stance to acknowledge the special status of metacognition in determining a particular kind of consciousness that may be available to humans and perhaps to other animals. The possible extension of this kind of consciousness to nonhumans was explicitly denied by Descartes, who believed that it, and hence the possibility of a soul, existed only in humans. The primary evidence weighing in on Descartes' conclusion was that animals did not have language. And, to this day, although there have been many studies attempting to demonstrate that at least some nonhuman primates have language, none have done so definitively (Terrace, 2005; Terrace & Metcalfe, 2005).

To the nondualist, who might nevertheless acknowledge self-reflective consciousness as a unique cognitive capability, it seems plausible that this special kind of consciousness may have arisen during the course of evolution, and it may have had a particular adaptive value for the animals who have it, namely, us. It may allow them to do things (e.g., to reflect on their actions and their outcomes and change those actions as indicated by the reflection to obtain better results) that other animals cannot do. This ability to gain reflective control over their own behaviors may well have allowed our ancestors to survive under circumstances fatal to other animals. The advantages of being able to foresee and evaluate events in one's mind's eye beforehand rather than having one's actions driven solely by the afferent stimuli seems self-evident. Being able to reflect on past occurrences also has its own adaptive value, freeing such an animal from the constraints of the stimulus and allowing more rational, adaptive future responding. Such consciousness may also have a benefit, to those who had it, in terms of sexual selection — its presence being particularly attractive to potential mates. Being able to take another's point of view — a sophisticated kind of metacognition known as *theory of mind* (Frith & Happe, 1999; Heyes, 1998; Leslie, 1987; Perner, 1991; Povinelli, 2000) — is indisputably appealing. People like feeling understood. It could also allow the person who has this ability to deceive more effectively, a trait that although despicable might provide certain evolutionary advantages for the person who has it (see Byrne & Whiten, 1992; de Waal, 1992; Whiten & Byrne, 1988, for anecdotes about the deceptive behavior of nonhuman primates and the consequences for mating success). One can entertain the idea that such a special kind of consciousness could evolve without necessarily accepting the postulate of Descartes that its existence is proof positive against materialism.

Comte's Paradox

The introspection that there is inside of us some special-status looker who can observe its own internal cognitions resurfaced, in the last century, as Comte's paradox. A *paradox* is defined as an apparently true statement that leads to a contradiction or to a situation that defies intuition. For Comte, how the mind or consciousness could both function and observe itself function seemed paradoxical. The fact that metacognition was, until very recently, perceived as a paradox is based on the deeply felt idea that consciousness is unitary and indivisible rather than piecemeal and fragmentary. The paradox depends on the statement being truly self-referential, in the strictest sense. But, as many perceptual psychologists have demonstrated (see Hochberg, 2003), perception is, itself, piecemeal and fragmentary, even though there is an illusion of a continuous whole. Perhaps the most dramatic example of this comes from recent change blindness (Simons & Chabris, 1999) studies, in which a person can be, for example, watching a videotape of a game of catch among several players and appear to have a whole and continuous perception of the entire field, with all of the players in this field. But this apparent wholeness and continuity is belied by the fact that a full-size person in a gorilla costume walks through the scene, stopping to beat his chest in the middle of the screen, and people, watching the ball throwing, do not see it. When told about the gorilla and shown the video again, they see it clearly, of course. Despite this gross omission — an enormous blind spot — they had no notion that there were any holes in their consciousness. It is simply that the notion of the unity of consciousness, and its apparent wholeness, is illusory. Our illusion of perceptual continuity (see Hochberg, 2003) is constructed from what we see and hear, from what we expect, and in a fragmentary way, from what we infer, with all of these components and a number of different modalities contributing in parallel.

Across modalities, it is straightforward to follow more than one line of consciousness, of course (so, cross-modal monitoring would not be paradoxical). One can drive and listen to the radio at the same time, being aware of both. But, even within a single modality, it has now been shown that the "spotlight of attention" (Treisman, 1986), which was originally thought to be a single indivisible spotlight (as would be consistent with the idea that Comte's paradox might really be paradoxical) can be divided into two different and spatially discontinuous locations (Müller, Malinowski, Gruber,

& Hillyard, 2003) at the same time. Thus, as many elegant experimental studies of perception have shown, the assumption of a unitary consciousness does not hold.

Furthermore, even if consciousness were unitary in each moment of psychological time, the possibility remains that "function" and the reflection do not in fact co-occur in the same psychological moment. We might be able to observe our own mental function by taking a snapshot of it in one moment and looking at that snapshot (or its ghost in working memory) in the next — alternating back and forth. Many studies of working memory illustrate this capability.

Finally, there is no contradiction of logic that people might be conscious of more than one thing at a time, simultaneously entertaining the cognition or memory and one's assessment of it in parallel. For Comte's paradox to be a paradox and self-referential, the object reflected and the reflector must really be one and the same entity. From a neuroscience perspective, though, the brain is constantly monitoring and feeding back information at all levels. For example, Oschner and Gross (2006) elaborated how the prefrontal cortex and the cingulate control system work in concert with subcortical (especially amygdala) emotional-generative systems to allow the modulation of emotional responses. Attentional regulation directs and controls other cognitive processes, and different aspects interact in a complex manner, as has been illustrated by a meta-analysis conducted by Wager and Smith (2003). To suppose that this could not be so — that doing and monitoring, or functioning and observing the functioning, could not co-occur — might well be considered quaint by modern neuroscience criteria. Thus, for Comte's paradox to be a puzzle, one must affirm as unassailable certain assumptions about consciousness and about brain function — assumptions that modern research refutes.

Even so, the postulation of a "paradox" was taken seriously enough by early experimental researchers in metacognition to provoke an explicit theoretical solution. Nelson and Narens (1990), in response to this supposed conundrum, proposed that to allow that the mind could both function cognitively and observe its own cognitive functions there must exist *two* levels (of consciousness), a base, or object, level and a metalevel. This solution, of course, says that consciousness is not unitary, just as much modern neuroscience would affirm. This framework has been widely accepted.

Does Metacognition Imply an Infinite Regress?

The idea that there is a looker of sorts, functioning at the metalevel in Nelson and Narens's framework, also withstands the "turtles all the way down," or infinite regress, criticism. The criticism is based on the idea that if one has to have observation of cognition, then there must be a conscious observer inside the person's head. That observer needs to be able to see what is going on at the basic cognitive level, and so it needs to be a full-blown internal person, or homunculus, complete with a fully elaborated perceptual-cognitive apparatus. But, then one needs to propose that there is a homunculus inside the head of the homunculus to be conscious of what it is seeing, and so on ad infinitum. This dissolves into absurdity. The "turtles" criticism depends on the postulate that observation, or monitoring, entails an elaborate observer, essentially a full-blown person. But monitoring, computationally at least, can be extremely simple. A simple thermostat monitors the room temperature and can trigger an action (turn off the heat) without anything like a full-blown cognitive-perceptual apparatus. A model of metacognitive monitoring sufficient to produce the kind of metacognitive data people give in feeling-of-knowing experiments may involve only simple computation; see the work of Metcalfe (1993), who within the Composite Holographic Associative Recall Model or CHARM framework, was able to model nearly all of the known data on the feeling-of-knowing phenomenon by postulating only a simple computation of a correlation between an input vector and a trace vector. This entails only one computation, and it is one that is well documented as existing in the nervous system. Certainly, then, the possibility of metacognition — if it entails only such straightforward computations — is not threatened by the criticism of turtles all the way down.

It is interesting to note that it was not until our modern familiarity with ideas like semimodular brain function, parallel distributed cognitive processing capabilities, and a systems approach to the mind-brain that researchers were able to free themselves of the idea that a self-reflective capability was a deeply perplexing paradox. We now find the puzzlement puzzling and agree with Humphrey (1987) in saying, "The problem of self-observation producing an infinite regress is, I think, phony. No one would say that a person cannot use his own eyes to observe his own feet. No one would say, moreover, that he cannot use his own eyes, with the aid of a mirror, to observe his own eyes. Then why should anyone say a person cannot, at least in principle, use his own brain to observe his own brain?" (p. 11).

Although we no longer view humans' metacognitive capability either as a paradox or as bearing some kind of mystical meaning, we do not rule out the possibility that this particular capability may be unique to humans, or that it bestows on them some cognitive, and adaptive, capabilities that may be missing in other creatures. Despite being demystified, it may still be special. But, to determine whether it is indeed specific to humans and to investigate empirically this question, we need first to define what is meant by *metacognitive* monitoring and control.

Definition of Metacognition

There are monitoring and control at all levels of the human and the animal mind-brain system. Indeed, the entire brain can be thought of as a giant feedback system, with virtually every pathway having both feedforward and feedback connections and multiple connections among different brain regions serving to allow the outcomes of one kind of processing to modulate other processes. So, if monitoring and feedback were all that was meant by metacognition, it would be pervasive, and there would be no question at all that most other animals also use such feedback. But, it is not simple feedback from one level interacting with processing at another that, alone, characterizes metacognition.

Furthermore, it is not simply the ability to make a discrimination or a judgment. Even very simple animals are able to make discriminating judgments about events in the world. Indeed, even nonanimals can make some of these. A plant apparently "judges" the lightness in its environment and moves, very slowly, toward the light.

Among animals, judgments about things in the world can be much more complex. A pigeon can make line-length discriminations. A rat can make at least eight alternative discriminations and reliably take the correct arm of a radial maze. Many animals can make duration discriminations. And, animals can show differential responses, including severe anxiety, when discriminations become very difficult. Pavlov (1927) made a circle a conditioned response to feeding, and an oval was made a food-negative response. Whenever a circle appeared, the dog would get food. When an oval appeared, it would not be fed. The poor dogs that, after this training, were exposed to stimuli halfway between the ovals and the circles showed symptoms of severe anxiety. Tolman (1932) also showed that animals given choices of stimuli between two discriminable categories can be "caught at the choice point" and be tugged simultaneously in two directions. The anxiety of Pavlov's dogs suggests that such conflict may well have visceral (and noticeable) consequences. But even such dramatic responding to very difficult discriminations do not qualify as metacognition since they are merely responses to the afferent stimuli and do not concern judgments about internal representations.

Furthermore, the responses animals make can be quite complex without making them qualify as metacognition. Circus trainers are able to get animals — through well-understood conditioning techniques — to exhibit behaviors that are both complex, that are not seen in the animals in their normal untrained repertoire, and may involve multiple steps. This training typically starts with a simple response (perhaps as insignificant as getting the animal to turn in a certain direction or move a certain way) and through many trials builds on those initial small responses until an elaborate sequence of moves — like getting an elephant to stand on one foot on a bucket — can be produced. Thus, through this kind of shaping, animals can be trained to make fine-grained nonbinary discriminations about what they see and hear in the world, and they can perform multiple-step and complex responses. None of this requires metacognition.

Metacognition, then, is not merely a judgment among options, however refined, and regardless of the number of discriminanda. It is not merely the production of a complex multistep response, to get a reward. And, it is not the combination of a multistep response to a difficult discriminative judgment. Instead, it is a very special kind of judgment or commentary that involves a level of processing that we, here, call *representational* or *cognitive* (and that Nelson & Narens, 1990, 1994, called the object level) and a higher-level monitoring that we call *metacognitive*. A simple case of a cognition or a representation is a word or a symbol. A word is not the object in the world itself, but rather it refers to the object and is about the object. A memory is also a representation. It is not present in the world, but rather it is internal. If a memory is represented internally, and a person makes a judgment about that memory, then that judgment is a metacognitive judgment. Note, however, that judgments in some recognition tasks, in which the probes are given in the testing environment, do not qualify as being metacognitive since the person can make the judgment based on the probe that is present in the afferent environment and not the memory to which the probe refers. The probe, present in the stimuli environment, is not properly considered to be a mental representation even if its ongoing processing has been influenced by something that happened in the past. (Note that this critique applies to virtually all implicit memory tasks. They are not metacognitive by the present criterion.) If a person just makes a judgment about something that he or she sees or hears, or even about his or her current fluency of processing, it is not metacognitive since it is not a judgment about a mental representation. Metacognition must be a judgment about an internal representation. Metacognition differs from mere judgment insofar as it is not stimulus bound or directly related to something in the animal's afferent environment. Rather, it is about a mental representation. While denying metacognition, so defined, is supernatural, we might still maintain that it could be a truly extraordinary capability and explore its implications and evolution.

Usually, metacognition requires language (as Descartes intuited). The individual is asked whether he or she will know the answer to a question. To be unequivocal that the cognition queried is representational, a question can be posed about something that is not present in the immediate environment, like a memory. The participant then gives a rating on some scale about the answer or about whether he or she will be able to retrieve the answer later, for example. The question and the answer to the question are indisputably mental representations, or concepts at a cognitive level, so the rating is true metacognition. Although language is typically used in these assessments, if a researcher were clever enough to be able to administer metacognitive tests that were about nonverbal internal representations using responses such as betting rather than, say, verbally based rating scales, then it should be possible to determine whether animals have metacognition. And, indeed, there have been several recent attempts to do just that.

Do Other Primates Have Metacognition?

The attempt to determine whether any nonhumans have metacognition is important for a number of reasons, not the least of which is the question of whether we can use an animal model to gain understanding of human thought. While nobody would dispute that animal models of human responding hold huge promise in some domains, such as pain, fear, and stress reactions, there may be distinct limits. If no animals other than humans have metacognition, then certain states of consciousness simply cannot be studied with any subject other than a human one. But, perhaps animals have metacognition.

Call and Carpenter (2001) were among the first researchers to systematically attempt to investigate whether any nonhumans have metacognition. They asked whether there was any evidence that great apes knew what they themselves knew. The paradigm that they used was clever. They showed chimps or orangutans a choice food morsel hidden in one of two tubes. The apes reached immediately into the appropriate tube for the food. Then, the researcher placed a barrier between his hand, hiding the food in one of two tubes, and the line of sight of the ape. The apes, in this condition, did not know where the food was hidden. The question they asked was, Do the apes seek information when they know they do not know where the food is hidden? If they seek information, by looking into the tubes, before reaching, Call argued that this gives evidence that they know that they do not know, and that knowing that one does or does not know is metacognition. The looking behavior of the great apes was much greater in the situation in which the hiding was hidden than when it was exposed. Young children of two years of age performed in much the same way as did the apes. But dogs, in contrast, did not seek information first (see Call, as cited in Terrace & Metcalfe, 2005).

Is this metacognition? The basic tenet in this research is that information seeking indicates metacognition. This is an interesting perspective on the question, but one that deserves intensive scrutiny. Does moving one's eyes before reaching for an apple imply that one is using metacognition? If one found, for example, that squirrels or chipmunks or birds looked around — scanning the skies with their eyes or listening carefully with their ears for predators — before venturing out on an open field, would one thereby grant them metacognition? If an animal were running on a rough pathway or swinging through the jungle through the trees, would looking first before stepping or leaping, to see whether there was a hole at the next step or whether the branch was thick or thin that they were going to grasp, be an indication of metacognition? Probably not.

Other researchers have investigated the possibility of metacognition in animals other than humans as well. Smith, Shields, and Washburn (2003) reviewed a series of experiments, mostly from their own labs, investigating the possibility of metacognition with apes, monkeys, and dolphins. They likened metacognition to uncertainty judgments or, for those not willing to say that nonhumans are really "judging," to indications of uncertainty. So, if the animal gave evidence that it was not sure of the answer or of the course of action to follow, then this was taken by Smith and colleagues to be evidence for metacognition. It is interesting that Smith appears to have picked up on a different aspect of Descartes' thinking — the ability to doubt — rather than the more standard self-reflective component.

Smith and colleagues (see Shields, Smith, & Washburn, 1997) conducted many classification tasks with animals in which the animals were trained to make one response to a particular category and a different response to a second category on the same dimension. Then, they would expose the animal to a situation in which the two categories blended smoothly into one another. An example would be a dot density discrimination task in which the animals were trained to make Response A to dense displays and Response B to less-dense displays. They were then given displays of intermediate density. They allowed the animals to give an escape response to get some reward reliably and found that in these intermediate or what they called "don't know" situations, the animal would often choose to hit the escape button. These "uncertainty" responses held along a number of dimensions, such as loudness, length of sound, pitch discrimination, density, and so on. They also held for a number of species: apes, monkeys, and dolphins.

Furthermore, Shields, Smith, Guttmannova, and Washburn (2005) have shown that the uncertainty functions in these animals have much the same form as did analogous functions when humans were the participants. Undoubtedly, humans and nonhuman animals respond in a similar way on these materials. The question remains, though, regarding whether these results indicate metacognition either in the nonhumans or in the humans?

On several grounds, I suggest that the answer is no. First, it is not obvious that the escape button really does mean to the animal that the animal does not know (even if it does have that meaning to the human). Maybe it just means that there is a third category — intermediate-length lines or moderate density — for which it can get the best possible rewards by hitting the button that the experimenter thinks is the escape or uncertainty button. But, to the animal this button is just a third category label. There is no question that even animals less intelligent than dolphins can make at least eight item discriminations, witness the eight-arm radial maze used universally in studies with rats. So, showing that a nonhuman animal can make a three-part rather than just a binary discrimination is not evidence for metacognition.

Second, the stimuli about which the animals are responding are present in the environment that the animal can see, hear, smell, or touch when they start to make their responses in these studies. They are not memories. Thus, even if the responses they are making are judgments (but see above), because they are not about internal representations, they are not metacognitive judgments. The elementary qualification that metacognition be a judgment about a representation is not met.

It is interesting that Smith et al. (2003) noted in their review article that it had been recommended by early researchers that the judgments animals make be done retrospectively — allowing them to give the primary response *then* make their confidence judgment, as is usually done with humans. This procedure would increase the chance that the judgment was about a representation rather than about the stimulus itself. But, they noted that, "The catch is that animals have so far not been able to report their confidence this way" (p. 8). Because these studies do not meet this fundamental criterion of being about a representation, it seems prudent to be skeptical about whether any of these studies indicated metacognition in nonhumans.

Hampton (2001, 2005), however, devised a task that, while not involving long-term memory, did involve an elementary form of memory. In an experiment with two rhesus monkeys, Hampton (2001) used a task called a delayed-match-to-sample task, in which the stimulus was no longer present in the environment when the monkeys had to make a decision about whether to take a test. Thus, Hampton's paradigm goes a long way toward countering criticisms of Smith's procedures. The stimulus being judged was not present, so there was at least the possibility that the judgment was about an internal representation rather than about a stimulus that was present at the time of judgment. Furthermore, Hampton rotated through four stimuli each day, randomly choosing one of the four as the target on each trial. The monkey had to remember which stimulus was correct on each trial, and all four of the alternatives had been equally reinforced in this role. Thus, it was not merely a discrimination conditioning task (as could have been the case in the studies Smith reviewed), but instead Hampton's task was a difficult memory task.

At each session, Hampton presented the monkeys one of four images that it had to touch on the computer touch screen three times. This multiple touching was designed to improve the chances that the monkey saw the to-be-remembered item. Then, a delay was intervened, during which, on two thirds of the trials, the animal was given a choice of whether it wanted to take the test or decline to take the test. If it wanted to take the test, it touched one icon; to decline, it touched another icon. If the monkey chose to take the test, it was given a four-alternative forced-choice test, with all four of the stimuli that had been used in that session as the alternatives, a few moments later. If it touched the item that it had seen on the present trial, it got a peanut. If it touched one of the three incorrect items, it got nothing. If the monkey declined to take the test, it got a primate pellet (which it liked more than nothing but not as much as peanuts). On the remaining one third of the trials, the monkey was forced to take the test, without an intervening choice.

The data on the first experiment showed that accuracy was better, for both monkeys, when they had chosen to take the test than when they had been forced to take the test. In an additional experiment, a time delay was manipulated. Although both monkeys chose to take the test more often at short intervals, and both monkeys numerically showed better performance at all time intervals when they chose, the data for only one monkey showed this difference in performance to be significant.

Did this study show that monkeys have metacognition? First, since only one of the two monkeys showed a significant effect on all criteria, we might, at best, have evidence that one monkey has shown metacognition. Experimental psychologists testing humans, though, prefer larger sample sizes and more consistency before reaching important conclusions and would prefer a criterion of something like 1/20 that their results are not just an accident. Still, the second monkey did show effects in the right direction. Second, the delays in the match-to-sample task were rather short (at the longest only 240 seconds) relative to those used in some metacognitive studies with humans. Thus, it may be controversial that these working memory representations should really be considered memories rather than something more akin to afterimages. Still, the stimulus itself was *not* present at the time the judgment was made, and this is a great improvement in methodology. Third, the task was not a simple discrimination learning task but involved an ongoing and changing memory (albeit with a brief delay), so the experiment avoids this criticism. Finally, the alternatives were not present when the judgment was made, so the judgment could not be made by simply assessing the fluency of each alternative. (When the test questions are present, even pigeons can do such tasks.) The fact that the alternatives were not present when the judgment was made allows this experiment to avoid another criticism. These data, then, suggest — although perhaps not as strongly as one would like — that monkeys may have some metacognitive capabilities. It was the first to do so.

Son and Kornell (2005) also provided some data indicating that rhesus monkeys have at least a glimmering of metacognition. They trained two monkeys (Lashley and Ebbinghaus) to do a line-length discrimination task. After the monkeys had seen the lines and made their choice of which was the longer (or shorter) line, they were then trained to select, on a touch screen, whether they wanted "to bet" on their answer. Note that neither the stimulus nor their choice on the test was present on the screen (although there was no extended time interval between the response and the judgments; note that this paradigm fits what early researchers had suggested and Shields et al., 2005, had thought could not be done). If the monkeys chose the "high-risk" icon on the touch screen and their response had been correct, they received several token rewards that, when enough tokens had been accumulated, resulted in a food reward. If they chose the "low-risk" icon, only one token reward was given, but it was given whether the answer had been correct or not. Son and Kornell reasoned that if the monkeys knew if they had made the correct response, that is, they had high confidence in their response, they should choose the high-risk icon. If they either were not sure or knew they had made the wrong response, they should choose the low-risk icon. This is just what they did. The data showed that both monkeys were more likely to choose the high-risk button when they had been right rather than wrong. The animals were also able to make these confidence judgments appropriately about a dot density discrimination task. However, it might be possible to criticize these results on the grounds that the monkeys had simply learned to make a two-part response, through some shaping procedure, to a conditioned discrimination. The high-confidence response might not have been analogous to a human confidence judgment about the choice but instead might have been a shaped single response. Such shaped responses, involving multiple steps, are common in animal training. For example, a circus trainer might achieve the final result of getting an elephant to stand on a bucket by such shaped multiple steps. The training might first involve getting the elephant to get close to the bucket and only then to raise its foot, then touch the bucket, and finally put its foot on the bucket and stand on it. However, such shaping would not be expected to transfer to a novel situation, as did the judgment in Son and Kornell's experiment.

Even more impressive, then, was the fact that these retrospective confidence judgments were observed to be appropriate immediately on a previously learned bona fide memory task, suggesting that they really were something like confidence judgments rather than part of a single shaping sequence. Kornell, Son, and Terrace (2007) showed transfer of the high-risk/low-risk response on the first trial to a memory task that the monkeys had independently been trained to perform. The monkeys saw a series of six pictures and then had to do a recognition task in which they chose the correct picture from an array of one target and eight distracters. After doing the immediate recognition task (and having the screen clear, so that the test alternatives and their response were no longer in view), the monkeys were given the high-risk/low-risk icon choice. They immediately chose appropriately. The correlation between choosing high risk on trials in which they had given the correct response and low risk on trials in which they had not was significantly greater than zero for both monkeys. The three panels of Figure 1 show Ebbinghaus first doing the memory task correctly, then being exposed to the confidence icons, and then expressing his high confidence in his correct choice.

While the time lags in Hampton's (2001) and Kornell et al.'s (2007) tasks were both small, so the depth of the representation that was judged was not very impressive, they nevertheless were experiments in which the stimuli were not present in the environment when the judgment was made. In addition, in neither task were the test alternatives present when the judgment was being made. Furthermore, they were about memories; they were not conditioned discriminations. The rewarded stimulus changed on every trial in both experiments. These factors provide some reassurance that the animals may actually have been making some kind of assessments about their own knowledge, in the former case whether they knew the answer or not, and in the latter whether they had given the correct response or not. These experiments are the most rigorous that have given positive results suggesting that any nonhuman animal is capable of metacognition of any sort (even though the limitations on the metacognition are, of course, extreme). It appears that three monkeys alive today have metacognitive abilities. It remains to be seen if this is a more general cognitive capability.

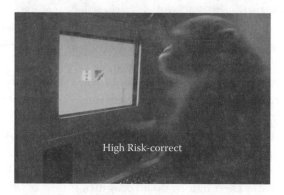

Figure 1   Panel A shows Ebbinghaus correctly choosing the to-be-remembered item in a recognition task. Panel B shows him thinking when the confidence icons appear. Panel C shows him choosing the high-risk (high-confidence) icon.

Do Any Nonprimates Have Metacognition?

We can, in good conscience, grant some limited metacognitive abilities to these three monkeys. Are any animals, other than primates, capable of metacognition? Of course, the answer must be that we do not know. Most animals have not been tested. However, Inman and Shettleworth (1999) and Sutton and Shettleworth (2007) have tested pigeons and have concluded that they do not show evidence for metacognition. The task that the former used was somewhat similar to that used by Hampton (2001).

It was a three-alternative (rather than a four-alternative) delayed-match-to-sample task. When the delay was increased, much as had been the case with the monkeys, the chance that the pigeons chose the escape (or uncertain) option increased. However, in striking contrast to the results found with the monkeys, who were able to do this task with above-chance accuracy when the test stimuli were not present, the pigeons were unable to perform the task unless the test alternatives were present when they made their choice. This is telling. If metacognition entails a judgment about a memory or an internal representation and the delay was needed to ensure that the judgment was about a representation, then this was the correct way to test for metacognition. The pigeons were unable to do it, and this is just what the researchers concluded.

Furthermore, Sutton and Shettleworth (2007) tried to elicit retrospective confidence judgments, similar to those studied by Kornell et al. (2007), from pigeons. Again, the birds were at chance unless the test stimuli were present. The conclusion, to date, is that although they have been tested, the results on pigeons indicate no metacognition.

Recently, Foote and Crystal (2007) have claimed, to much fanfare, that rats have metacognition. This conclusion, while well publicized in the popular media, is far from universally accepted. Staddon, Jozefowiez, and Cerutti (2007), for example, have written a detailed rebuttal, based on risk assessment.

Foote and Crystal (2007) trained 8 rats to do a duration discrimination task in which a tone was heard for either a long time or a short time. The rats were given considerable training in this discrimination task, being reinforced for choosing the correct button to get a reward for "saying" long — by choosing one button — or saying short by choosing the other button. In the next phase, the rats were allowed to poke their noses into one hole if they "wanted to take the test" and into another hole if they did not want to take the test. If they chose to take the test, they were then given the button-pressing test, and if they chose the "long" button when the tone was long, they got six rat pellets. If they chose the "short" button when the tone was short, they got six rat pellets. If, however, they chose the wrong button, they got nothing. A second hole for nose poking was introduced, and if they poked their noses into that hole — the "don't take the test" hole — they got three rat pellets, regardless.

Rather than having only long and short durations, at the critical series of tests, the researchers included critical stimuli that were in between. Their logic was that if the trained up rats took the don't-take-the-test nose poke, selectively, when the stimuli were of intermediate length, then they would be indicating that they did not know. If they were more accurate when they decided to take the test than when they were forced to take the test, this, they thought, would be an indication of metacognition.

Data were presented for 3 rats that were more likely to choose the don't-take-the-test nose poke when the stimuli were intermediate stimuli than when they were either distinctively long or distinctively short. When those trials on which the animals were forced to take the test and those on which they chose to take the test were compared, they performed better with their own choice on the difficult intermediate stimuli. These results were interpreted as indicating that the rats were metacognitive.

It was a clever experiment and seems similar, on the surface, to that of Hampton, which did provide some evidence of metacognition. There are some critical differences, however. Most important is that the task was not a memory task but rather a conditioned discrimination task. It is not clear that mental representation or memory proper was involved in this task at all. The animals may simply have learned a three-part discrimination. Second, there was no indication that the don't-take-the-test button meant that to the rats who chose it. Instead, it may have been nothing more than a shaped multistep response. There was no transfer test, such as Kornell et al. (2007) had used, to show that the meaning of the decline-the-test button had any relevance to another task in which the animal might also opt to decline the test.

How would a nonmetacognitive animal do this task to give the results obtained? Well, certainly, one problem, and the first thing a skeptic might note is that only 3 of the 8 animals did it. So, the first possibility is that it was simply accidental.

Second, the fact that there were two linked responses — the nose poke and the button press — can easily be explained by ordinary shaping behavior. The elephant rewarded for putting its foot on the bucket first has to put its other foot beside it. The initial nose poke may be no more than part of the complex rewarded pattern of motion that was reinforced over many trials. Finally, it is well known (from Pavlov on) that animals are responsive to intermediate categories in a conditioned discrimination task. Thus, the animals may well have been sensitive to the degree of discrepancy a test stimulus exhibited from the long and short stimuli on which they were trained.

What about the contingencies under the conditions in the experiment? The reward, in the case of a clear long or short tone, was six pellets as long as the animal got it right, which it nearly always did. If not, the animal did not get pellets. But, the animal did not get the discrimination right when the stimuli were in the intermediate range. Indeed, the expected reward for tones exactly in the middle of the to-be-discriminated distribution was three. This was true if the rats decided to take the test, in which case they had a 50–50 chance of being right and getting six pellets or wrong and getting no pellets, yielding an expected gain of three pellets. It was also true if they decided not to take the test, in which case they got a sure three pellets. A nonmetacognitive rat might have learned that if the to-be-discriminated stimulus was in the middle of the range, it did not matter what it did: The expected gain was three pellets regardless. So, it is not surprising to see that when the stimulus duration was extreme — either very long or very short — the rats reliably did the thing they had been trained to do: poke their nose into the correct hole and choose the correct button. When the stimulus duration was in the middle — since it did not matter what the rat did, the expected gain is the same three pellets regardless — the rat is more likely to show random behavior. That is exactly what the data show. No metacognition need be involved.

One more thing: Why, on these intermediate stimuli, would the nonmetacognitive rat be more likely to be right when it has poked its nose into the hole that the experimenters think meant that it wanted to take the test? The answer is simple. The stimuli in question had a correct answer, according to the experimenter's measurements: They were either slightly longer or slightly shorter in duration. They were not, in fact, exactly in the middle, where the odds were exactly the same for the different response combinations. When the rat perceived that a given stimulus was long (or short), it could get six pellets rather than three. The difference in performance in the intermediate range of stimuli only indicated that the rats had some discrimination of stimulus duration, even in this range, and that the responses allowed them to use their own discrimination of the fine gradients when they were available. As Staddon et al. (2007) noted, this variability alone is enough to account for this seemingly convincing result. Rats, then, have not (yet) been shown to have metacognition.

Conclusion

Metacognition in humans provides them with the cognitive capability to assess their learning, their knowledge, and what would otherwise be their automatic responses to the stimuli in the world that drive behavior. How they do this has been the subject of intensive research (Blake, 1973; Butterfield, Nelson, & Peck, 1988; Costermans, Lories, & Ansay, 1992; Dunlosky, Rawson, & Middleton, 2005; Hertzog & Dixon, 1994; Koriat, 1993; Schneider, Visé, Lockl, & Nelson, 2000; Sikström & Jönsson, 2005). Not only do they have the capability to reflect on their mental representations, but also they take these reflections and put them to use in controlling how they will study (Finn, in press; Metcalfe & Finn, 2008); what they will choose to attempt to retrieve (Reder, 1987; Reder & Ritter, 1992); how they solve problems (Simon, 1979; Simon & Reed, 1976); and how they will behave with respect to other people (Call & Tomasello, 1999; Wimmer & Perner, 1983). All of these refined capabilities — both at the metacognitive and control levels — are highly elaborated in humans. And, although they are sometimes susceptible to biases and errors (Bjork, 1994; Metcalfe, 1986), they nevertheless provide a buffer between what might correctly be called "mindless" responding. Being reflections, which allow control of mental representations, these particular capabilities form the basis of what is usually referred to as *mind* (Donald, 1991; Suddendorf & Whiten, 2001). They are our escape from stimulus control and into self-control.

Was Descartes right in attributing this kind of consciousness only to humans? Insofar as he was describing a highly elaborated self-reflective capability, the answer has to be yes. However, that does not mean that Darwin (1859) was wrong. This capability, while highly developed in people, shows antecedents in nonhuman species, most particularly in primates. To date, no studies with any animals other than primates have provided convincing evidence for this particular capability, although one has to be impressed by the remarkable nonmetacognitive learning capabilities of nonprimates, such as rats. Panskepp and Burgdorf (2003), for example, claimed that rats laugh. There are a number of claims about the superior theory of mind capabilities of dogs. Perhaps most strikingly, the representational and time travel capabilities, as well as the deceptive capabilities, and episodic memory-like abilities of birds documented by Clayton (see, e.g., Dally, Emery, & Clayton, 2006) all seem astonishing. Perhaps, with further research, we will find traces of self-reflective consciousness — however elementary — in animals other than the three monkeys who have so far given evidence of some preliminary metacognitive capabilities.

References

Armstrong, D. (1968). *A materialist theory of the mind*. London: Routledge and Kegan Paul.

Bjork, R. A. (1994). Memory and metamemory considerations in the training of human beings. In J. Metcalfe & A. P. Shimamura (Eds.), *Metacognition: Knowing about knowing* (pp. 185–206). Cambridge, MA: MIT Press.

Blake, M. (1973). Prediction of recognition when recall fails: Exploring the feeling-of-knowing phenomenon. *Journal of Verbal Learning and Verbal Behavior, 12,* 311–319.

Butterfield, E. C., Nelson, T. O., & Peck, V. (1988). Developmental aspects of the feeling of knowing. *Developmental Psychology, 24,* 654–663.

Byrne, R. W., & Whiten, A. (1992). Cognitive evolution in primates: Evidence from tactical deception. *Man, 27,* 609–627.

Call, J. (2005). The self and other: A missing link in comparative social cognition. In H. S. Terrace & J. Metcalfe (Eds.), *The missing link in cognition: Origins of self-reflective consciousness* (pp. 321–342). New York: Oxford University Press.

Call, J., & Carpenter, M. (2001). Do apes and children know what they have seen? *Animal Cognition, 4,* 207–220.

Call, J., & Tomasello, T. (1999). A nonverbal false belief task: The performance of children and great apes. *Child Development, 70,* 381–395.

Costermans, J., Lories, G., & Ansay, C. (1992). Confidence level and feeling of knowing in question answering: The weight of inferential processes. *Journal of Experimental Psychology: Learning, Memory, and Cognition, 18,* 142–150.

Dally, J. M., Emery, N. J., & Clayton, N. S. (2006). Food-caching Western Scrub-Jays keep track of who was watching when. *Science, 312,* 1662–1665.

Damasio, A. (1994) *Descartes' error: Emotion, reason, and the human brain.* New York: Putnam.

Darwin, C. (1859). *On the origin of species by means of natural selection.* London: Murray.

Descartes, R. (1999). *Discourse on method.* London: Penguin Books. (Original work published 1637.)

de Waal, F. B. M. (1992). Intentional deception in primates. *Evolutionary Anthropology, 1,* 86–92.

Donald, M. (1991). *Origins of the modern mind.* Cambridge, MA: Harvard University Press.

Dunlosky, J., Rawson, K. A., & Middleton, E. L. (2005). What constrains the accuracy of metacomprehension judgments? Testing the transfer-appropriate-monitoring and accessibility hypotheses. *Journal of Memory and Language, 52,* 551–565.

Finn, B. (in press). Framing effects on metacognitive monitoring and control, *Memory & Cognition.*

Foote, A. L., & Crystal, J. D. (2007). Metacognition in the rat. *Current Biology, 17,* 551–555.

Frith, U., & Happe, F. (1999). Theory of mind and self-consciousness: What is it like to be Autistic? *Mind & Language, 14,* 1–22.

Hampton, R. R. (2001). Rhesus monkeys know when they remember. *Proceedings of the National Academy of Sciences, 98,* 5359–5362.

Hampton, R. R. (2005). Can rhesus monkeys discriminate between remembering and forgetting? In H. S. Terrace & J. Metcalfe (Eds.), *The missing link in cognition: Origins of self-reflective consciousness* (pp. 272–295). New York: Oxford University Press.

Harrison, S. (2006). *Augustine's way into the will: The theological and philosophical significance of* De libero arbitrio. Oxford: Oxford University Press.

Hertzog, C., & Dixon, R. A. (1994). Metacognitive development in adulthood and old age. In J. Metcalfe & A. P. Shimamura (Eds.), *Metacognition: Knowing about knowing* (pp. 227–252). Cambridge, MA: MIT Press.

Heyes, C. M. (1998). Theory of mind in nonhuman primates. *Behavioral and Brain Sciences, 21,* 101–114.

Hochberg, J. (2003). Acts of perceptual inquiry: Problems for any stimulus-based simplicity theory. *Acta Psychologica, 114,* 215–228.

Humphrey, N. K. (1987). *The uses of consciousness.* New York: American Museum of Natural History.

Inman, A., & Shettleworth, S. J. (1999). Detecting metamemory in nonverbal subjects. *Journal of Experimental Psychology: Animal Behavior Processes, 25,* 389–395.

Jacoby, L. L., Bjork, R. A., & Kelley, C. M. (1994). Illusions of comprehension, competence, and remembering. In D. Druckman & R. A. Bjork (Eds.), *Learning, remembering, believing: Enhancing human performance* (pp. 57–80). Washington, DC: National Academy Press.

Koriat, A. (1993). How do we know that we know? The accessibility model of the feeling of knowing. *Psychological Review, 100,* 609–639.

Kornell, N., Son, L. K., & Terrace, H. S. (2007). Transfer of metacognitive skills and hint seeking in monkeys. *Psychological Science, 18,* 64–71.

Leslie, A. M. (1987). Pretense and representation: Origins of "theory of mind." *Psychological Review, 94,* 412–426.

Loftus, E. F. (2004) Memories of things unseen. *Current Directions in Psychological Science, 13,* 145–147.

Metcalfe, J. (1986). Premonitions of insight predict impending error. *Journal of Experimental Psychology: Learning, Memory, and Cognition, 12,* 623–634.

Metcalfe, J. (1993). Novelty monitoring, metacognition, and a control in a composite holographic associative recall model: Implications for Korsakoff amnesia. *Psychological Review, 100,* 3–22.

Metcalfe, J. (1998). Cognitive optimism: Self deception or memory-based processing heuristics? *Personality and Social Psychological Review, 2,* 100–110.

Metcalfe, J., & Finn, B. (2008). Judgments of learning are causally related to study choice. *Psychonomic Bulletin & Review, 15,* 174–179.

Müller, M. M., Malinowski, P., Gruber, T., & Hillyard, S. A. (2003). Sustained division of the attentional spotlight. *Nature, 42,* 309–312.

Nelson, T. O., & Narens, L. (1990). Metamemory: A theoretical framework and new findings. In G. H. Bower (Ed.), *The psychology of learning and motivation* (Vol. 26, pp. 125–173). New York: Academic Press.

Nelson, T. O., & Narens, L. (1994). Why investigate metacognition? In J. Metcalfe & A. P. Shimamura (Eds.), *Metacognition: Knowing about knowing* (pp. 1–25). Cambridge, MA: MIT Press.

Oschner, K. N., &. Gross, J. J. (2006). The cognitive control of emotion. *Trends in Cognitive Sciences, 9,* 242–250.

Panskepp, J., & Burgdorf, J. (2003). "Laughing" rats and the evolutionary antecedents of human joy? *Physiology and Behavior, 79,* 533–547.

Pavlov, I. P. (1927). *Conditioned reflexes: an investigation of the physiological activity of the cerebral cortex* (G. V. Anrep, Trans.). London: Oxford University Press.

Perner, J. (1991). *Understanding the representational mind.* Cambridge, MA: MIT Press.

Povinelli, D. J. (2000). *Folk physics for apes.* New York: Oxford University Press.

Reder, L. M. (1987). Strategy selection in question answering. *Cognitive Psychology, 19,* 90–138.

Reder, L. M., & Ritter, F. E. (1992). What determines initial feeling of knowing? Familiarity with question terms, not with the answer. *Journal of Experimental Psychology: Learning, Memory, and Cognition, 18,* 435–451.

Rosenthal, D. (2002). Consciousness and higher-order thought, *Macmillan Encyclopedia of Cognitive Science* (pp. 717–726). New York: Macmillan.

Russell, B. (1945/1972). *A history of Western philosophy.* New York: Simon & Schuster.

Schneider, W., Visé, M., Lockl, K., & Nelson, T. O. (2000) Developmental trends in children's memory monitoring: Evidence from a judgment of learning task. *Cognitive Development, 15,* 115–134.

Shields, W. E., Smith, J. D., & Washburn, D. A. (1997). Uncertain responses by humans and rhesus monkeys (*Macaca mulatta*) in a psychophysical same-different task. *Journal of Experimental Psychology: General, 126,* 147–164.

Shields, W. E., Smith, J. D., Guttmannova, K., & Washburn, D. A. (2005). Confidence judgments by humans and rhesus monkeys. *Journal of General Psychology, 132,* 165–186.

Sikström, S., & Jönsson, F. (2005). A model for stochastic drift in memory strength to account for judgments of learning. *Psychological Review, 112,* 932–950.

Simon, H. A. (1979). Information processing models of cognition. *Annual Review of Psychology, 30,* 363–396.

Simon, H. A., & Reed, S. K. (1976). Modeling strategy shifts in a problem-solving task. *Cognitive Psychology, 8,* 86–97.

Simons, D. J., & Chabris, C. F. (1999). Gorillas in our midst: Sustained inattentional blindness for dynamic events. *Perception, 28,* 1059–1074.

Smith, J. D., Shields, W. E., & Washburn, D. A. (2003). The comparative psychology of uncertainty monitoring and metacognition. *Behavioral and Brain Sciences, 26,* 317–339.

Son, L. K., & Kornell, N. (2005). Meta-confidence judgments in rhesus macaques: Explicit versus implicit mechanisms. In H. S. Terrace & J. Metcalfe (Eds.), *The missing link in cognition: Origins of self-reflective consciousness* (pp. 296–320). New York: Oxford University Press.

Terrace, H. S. (2005). Metacognition and the evolution of language. In H. S. Terrace & J. Metcalfe (Eds.), *The missing link in cognition: Origins of self-reflective consciousness* (pp. 84–115). New York: Oxford University Press.

Terrace, H. S., & Metcalfe, J. (2005). Introduction. In H. S. Terrace & J. Metcalfe (Eds.), *The missing link in cognition: Origins of self-reflective consciousness* (pp. i–viii). New York: Oxford University Press.

Treisman, A. (1986). Features and objects in visual processing. *Scientific American, 255*(5), 114–125.

Staddon, J. E. R., Jozefowiez, J., & Cerutti, D. (2007) Metacognition: A problem not a process: "Metacognition" in animals can be explained by familiar learning principles. *PsyCrit,* April 13, 2007, http://psycrit.com/index.php/Metacognition_in_the_Rat.

Suddendorf, T., & Whiten, A. (2001). Mental evolution and development: Evidence for secondary representation in children, great apes, and other animals. *Psychological Bulletin, 127,* 629–650.

Sutton, J. E., & Shettleworth, S. J. (2007). *Pigeons still don't have metamemory.* Paper presented at the annual meeting of the Comparative Cognition Society.

Tolman, E. C. (1932). *Purposive behavior in animals and men.* New York: Century.

Wager, T. D., & Smith, E. E. (2003). Neuroimaging studies of working memory: A meta-analysis, *Cognitive, Affective, and Behavioral Neuroscience, 3,* 255–274.

Whiten, A., & Byrne, R. W. (1988). Tactical deception in primates. *Behavioral and Brain Sciences, 11,* 233–273.

Wimmer, H., & Perner, J. (1983). Beliefs about beliefs: Representation and constraining function of wrong beliefs in young children's understanding of deception. *Cognition, 13,* 103–128.

Metacognition:
Knowing About Knowing

James P. Van Overschelde

Introduction

Metacognition involves the scientific study of the mind's ability to monitor and control itself or, in other words, the study of our ability to know about our knowing. Philosophical discussions on this topic go back at least to Aristotle's *On the Soul* (~350 BCE/2006) and probably as early as the Upanishads of Vedantic Hinduism (~1800 BCE, as cited in Aurobindo, 1998), but scientific research on this topic is considered by many to have started with Hart (1965). In the more than 40 years since this inaugural research, thousands of journal articles, book chapters, and books have been published on this topic.[1]

This chapter begins with a review of Nelson and Narens's "classic" metacognitive model (Nelson, 1996; Nelson & Narens, 1990, 1994). To this model, I add components that I believe were originally implied by Nelson and Narens. Following this, I propose a new way of conceptualizing and theorizing about metacognition. Finally, using this expanded metacognitive model as a framework, I present a large selection of research on metacognition.

Nelson and Narens's Metacognitive Model

Nelson and Narens (1990, 1994; Nelson, 1996) outlined a metacognitive model that consists of three critical features. The first critical feature is the division of cognitive processes or functions into multiple interrelated levels. Figure 1 illustrates the simplest case in which there exists a single "metalevel" and a single "object level." The object level consists of cognitions, which are often associated with external objects (e.g., that thing I see is a dog), and the metalevel consists of cognitions about object-level cognitions (Nelson, 1996; e.g., why do I keep thinking about that dog?). The second critical feature concerns the manner in which information flows between these two levels. In this model, information flows hierarchically, with the metalevel acquiring information from (i.e., monitoring) the object level and the metalevel sending information to, and thereby changing (i.e., controlling), the object level. The third critical feature of the metacognitive model is that the metalevel contains (1) a dynamic model of the current state of the object level (Nelson & Narens, 1990, 1994); (2) a metalevel goal, or

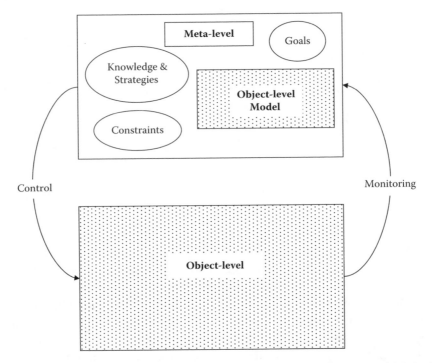

Figure 1   A basic representation of Nelson and Narens' metacognitive model (Nelson & Narens, 1990, 1994) with a single metalevel and a single object level. The metalevel contains a model of the object level, goals, knowledge of how the metalevel can control the object level, and a list of constraints on these control actions.

goal state, for the object level; and (3) knowledge and strategies for how the metalevel can change or control the object level to attain the metalevel's goal (Nelson, 1996).

Taking together these three features, the metacognitive model consists of upper-level metacognitive processes that monitor, dynamically model, and control lower-level cognitive processes in an attempt to attain a goal. These three goal-driven processes (i.e., monitoring, controlling, and modeling) are examined in more detail next.

Monitoring

Nelson and Narens (1990) originally described *monitoring* as a passive process equivalent to someone eavesdropping on a telephone conversation. In this analogy, the cognitive information simply flows from the object level to the metalevel, thereby informing the metalevel about the current state of the object level. However, Nelson's subsequent work (e.g., Nelson, 1996) described monitoring as a more active process, one that is often operating in the service of the metalevel and therefore influenced by current metagoals.

No claim was made by Nelson and Narens (1990, 1994) regarding what object-level information could be monitored by the metalevel or how much object-level information could be monitored simultaneously. Given known attentional capacity limits (e.g., Engle & Kane, 2004), it seems highly unlikely that the metalevel would be capable of monitoring all, or even most, of the object-level information. More likely is the idea that object-level information is preferentially selected by the metalevel: Some information is perceived as relevant to the current metagoal and some is not. For example, if the active metagoal is to generate a highly accurate metacognitive judgment, then the speed with which information comes to mind in the object level may be interpreted as insignificant (and therefore ignored) compared with the sheer quantity and the perceived quality (e.g., high integrality) of that information. Furthermore, the fact that the different metacognitive judgments have repeatedly been found to be weakly correlated implies that, at least to some degree, different information is being used as the basis of the different judgments (e.g., Leonesio & Nelson, 1990; Schwartz, 1994). In other words, the different judgments have different goals, and possibly different inputs, and therefore monitor different information as the basis for the judgment.

Although metacognitive *judgments* are often lumped under the monitoring moniker, in this chapter I treat monitoring as consisting only of the metalevel processes responsible for gathering and interpreting information about the object level and nothing more. In this way, monitoring is analogous to sensory perception, but in this case it is a *metaperception* process by which raw data about cognitions are evaluated, organized, and interpreted into meaningful percepts and incorporated into a dynamic mental model of the cognitive environment (cf. Whittlesea, 1997).

Control

Nelson and Narens (1990) likened the control function with that of speaking into a telephone. In this analogy, control information (generically called *control actions*) flows from the metalevel to the object level and thereby modifies the object level. By this definition, all information flowing from the metalevel to the objective will be called a *control action*. To accomplish these tasks, the metalevel must maintain a list of possible control actions, including (1) initiating a process, (2) changing the state of the current process, (3) changing from one process to another, or (4) terminating a process. It must also maintain a list of specific control actions and their possible consequences.

Because the metalevel contains a model of the object level (details of which are described in the next section), control actions are based on the metalevel's current model of the object level and not on the actual current state of the object level. Therefore, the accuracy of the control actions depends critically on the accuracy of the metalevel model as well as on the accuracy of the knowledge about how the metalevel can control the object level (i.e., metacognitive knowledge). Put differently, if the wrong information or variables are monitored or if the variables are interpreted incorrectly, then the control actions are likely to be ineffective (e.g., Benjamin, Bjork, & Schwartz, 1998).

Although control is often assumed to follow monitoring (for a review, see Dunlosky, Hertzog, Kennedy, & Thiede, 2005), Koriat and his colleagues (Koriat, Ma'ayan, & Nussinson, 2006) demonstrated that control and monitoring should be more accurately considered as ongoing and mutually informing processes. Still others have argued that control must precede monitoring in a negative-feedback loop so that the metalevel can minimize differences between the current state and the goal state while taking into consideration all perceived constraints and known possible courses of action (e.g., Dunlosky & Hertzog, 1998; Joslyn, 2001).

Research on the control aspect of metacognition includes topics like the allocation of study time, the selection of items for additional study, and the selection of different kinds of cognitive and learning strategies (e.g., memory search, problem solving, rote rehearsal).

Goal-Driven Modeling

As mentioned, Nelson and Narens (1990, 1994; Nelson 1996) explicitly stated that the metalevel contains the first three items in the following list, and they implied the metalevel contains the last two items on this list.

1. A dynamic model of the current state of the object level based on input from the monitoring process
2. A representation of a goal or a goal state
3. A list of known, possible control actions by which the metalevel can change/control the object level, details about when to use each control action, and the potential consequences
4. A list of perceived constraints on potential control actions (e.g., time limits, beliefs, expectations)
5. A judgment or decision-making process that evaluates the metamodel and makes a decision about which course of action to take or which response to make (if any) in an attempt to attain the goal.

I use the term *metamodel* to represent the information described in items 1 through 4, and these four components are examined in more detail next. For each component, I summarize a large selection of existing research on the topic. Following these, the metacognitive judgment and decision-making (JDM) process and the heuristics and biases that influence the JDM process are examined.

Modeling the Object Level

In *The Nature of Explanation*, Craik (1943) argued on logical grounds that it is important for an organism to model its environment. He said:

> If the organism carries a "small-scale model" of external reality and of its own possible actions within its head, it is able to try out various alternatives, conclude which is the best of them, react to future situations before they arise, utilize the knowledge of past events in dealing with the present and future, and in every way to react in a much fuller, safer, and more competent manner to the emergencies which face it. (p. 61)

A decade later, Ashby (1956) proposed the "law of requisite variety" in his groundbreaking work in cybernetics and system theory. This law states that a controller (also called a regulator) can only effectively regulate a system if the controller can represent (i.e., model) a sufficiently large number of distinct possible states (i.e., variety) of the controlled system. In other words, for effective control to occur, the variety in the controller must be equal to or greater than the variety in the system being controlled. For example, for a controller to make a decision between two possible control actions, the controller must be capable of representing at least two alternative states of the system and one distinction between the states. Conant and Ashby (1970) provided a theoretical proof regarding the regulation of complex systems in which they concluded that it was necessary for any effective and efficient regulator of a complex system to "have a model of that system" and that "there can no longer be [a] question about *whether* [italics added] the brain models its environment: it must" (p. 97).

As a result of this prior research, in particular that of Conant and Ashby (1970), Nelson and Narens (1990) concluded that it was necessary for the metalevel, as a regulator or controller of the object level, to contain a dynamic, goal-driven model of the object level. Since then, researchers have argued, mainly on theoretical grounds, that the accuracy of the control actions should depend critically on the accuracy of the monitoring (for a review, see Dunlosky, Herzog, et al., 2005). However, scant research has been done to investigate this issue directly.

Clearly, it is important to understand the factors affecting the construction of an accurate metamodel. A partial list of potential factors includes the completeness of the monitored information and the accuracy of its interpretation, the relationships and dynamics between the variables being monitored and the variables being controlled, the accuracy with which the monitored information is incorporated into the metamodel, the accuracy of the representation of the goal state, the accuracy of the list of possible control actions (or judgments) and their consequences, the accuracy of the list of perceived constraints, and the quality of the decision process that evaluates all of the available information.

We now review research on how different goals, metacognitive and metastrategic knowledge, and intrinsic and extrinsic constraints affect the accuracy of metacognitive judgments and control actions.

Goals

According to the Nelson and Narens model, any active goal should affect the metamodel, or the way in which the meta-model is constructed, and the influence of a range of different goals on metacognitive judgments and control decisions has been examined. Goals that are examined in more detail here include speed, accuracy, informativeness, high or low performance, minimizing effort or cost, and maximizing payoff or gains.

Mastery People who hold the goal of mastery (or a goal that is more generally referred to as a high-performance goal) focus on obtaining a highly developed skill in or knowledge of something. One of the most widely studied effects that the goal of mastery can have on learning concerns how learners allocate their time during study as a function of item or task difficulty. In general, the findings indicate that learners allocate more study time to items that are objectively or subjectively most difficult, but only when study time is unconstrained (for reviews, see Son & Metcalfe, 2000; Thiede & Dunlosky, 1999). When study time is constrained and the goal of mastery becomes more difficult to attain, then learners shift to the easier items (e.g., Kornell & Metcalfe, 2006; Thiede & Dunlosky, 1999). In fact, research has shown in this situation that learning is most effective (comes closer to mastery) if learners adopt a strategy of studying the easiest items first and gradually transitioning to more difficult items as learning progresses. This strategy has been labeled the *region of proximal learning* (e.g., Kornell & Metcalfe, 2006).

Researchers have also found that it is generally better to give learners control over the allocation of study time when the goal is mastery because they perform at a higher level than when the allocation of study time is done randomly (Mazzoni & Cornoldi, 1993, Experiment 3). Unfortunately, even when learners hold the goal of mastery and are given control over their allocation of study time, they are unlikely actually to attain this goal (Nelson & Leonesio, 1988).

Finally, the accuracy of the metacognitive judgments is also affected by this goal. For example, Nelson and Leonesio (1988, Experiment 2) had participants learn a list of word–trigram pairs during two rounds of study–test trials. Half of the participants were given speeded instructions, and half were given mastery instructions; all participants gave ease-of-learning (EOL) judgments before study trials. When the goal was speed, then the correlation between the amount of time spent studying an item and its EOL judgment was negative, and when the goal was accuracy, then the correlation was less negative. In other words, more time was spent studying items given low EOLs (i.e., difficult items), and this relationship was stronger for speeded instructions than for accuracy instructions. In addition, the accuracy of metacognitive judgments increased when individuals were given instructions to learn the list quickly than when given instructions to master the list.

Low Performance   When learners hold a low-performance goal, they shift from studying more difficult items to easier items (Dunlosky & Thiede, 2004; Thiede & Dunlosky, 1999). In addition, learners allocate more study time to easier items when they implicitly are given a low-performance goal as when they are encouraged to minimize the study time allocated to each item (e.g., Mazzoni & Cornoldi, 1993) or when the total amount of study time is limited and therefore mastery cannot be the goal (e.g., Kornell & Metcalfe, 2006).

Maximize Extrinsic Gains   People sometimes adopt a goal of maximizing extrinsic gains or payoffs, including doing better than others, getting a reward, or attempting to improve the image others have of them. However, doing so can affect their metacognitive control strategies. For example, when a goal is externally oriented, people prefer tasks for which they are more likely to do well or succeed, and they are more likely to give up when faced with difficulty (e.g., Wolters, 2003).

Minimize Effort or Cost   People sometimes adopt a goal of minimizing the amount of effort they expend on a task (also called work avoidance). People with this goal prefer tasks that can be completed easily and quickly or tasks that do not require much effort (e.g., Thorkildsen & Nicholls, 1998).

One can also adopt a goal of minimizing the cost associated with a task. Goldsmith, Koriat, and Pansky, 2005 (Experiment 2) found that both the quantity and quality (detail vs. gist) of information provided by participants, who were responding to questions about eyewitness transcripts, were influenced when the costs associated with being wrong were high. When the cost for being wrong was high, then participants provided more generic than detailed answers, presumably because they were attempting to minimize the potential costs. If, however, participants were required to give detailed answers, then they wanted to feel a higher level of confidence in their answer before responding. The effect has been replicated many times (e.g., Kelley & Sahakyan, 2003; Koriat, Goldsmith, Schneider, & Nakash-Dura, 2001). Together, these studies indicated that people can control their responses (including not responding) to reduce the cost associated with a task.

Balancing Accuracy and Informativeness   Similar to the goal of minimizing costs, extensive research showed that learners can strategically regulate the amount and quality (details vs. gist) of information they report after searching memory, and they seem to do so to accommodate the competing pragmatic goals of accuracy and informativeness (e.g., Goldsmith et al., 2005). For example, Goldsmith et al. (2005) had participants study eyewitness transcripts, and their memory was tested immediately, at 1 day after, or 7 days later. As expected, memory performance decreased as the testing delay increased, and the rate of decline was less for gist information than for detailed information. From a metacognitive standpoint, they found that participants switched from reporting detailed information to reporting gist information as the delay increased. Goldsmith et al. concluded that participants set a criterion for reporting accuracy and selectively report only retrieved information that is perceived to exceed that criterion, presumably because being wrong is a negative outcome (cost).

Knowledge

The amount of knowledge that a learner possesses about how his or her mind works and how it can be controlled is known to affect metacognitive judgments and control decisions. *Metacognitive knowledge* is explicit, factual knowledge about how the mind works, and *metastrategic knowledge* is implicit, procedural knowledge about how one can use the mind to accomplish goals (e.g., Kuhn, 2000).

Metacognitive knowledge is known to increase with age and with training (e.g., Schneider & Bjorklund, 1998; Weinert, 1986). A prime example of this development is the understanding that forgetting occurs. When 4-year-olds were shown 10 pictures and asked how many they would be able to recall, most said 10, thereby indicating that their knowledge about the functioning of their memory was inaccurate (Flavell, Friedrichs, & Hoyt, 1970). By 5 years of age, 30% of the children still believed that no forgetting occurs, and around 6 years of age almost all children knew that they forget (Kreutzer, Leonard, & Flavell, 1975). In addition, almost all 10- to 11-year-olds know that a recognition test is usually easier than a recall test, and that gist recall of stories is better than verbatim recall, but only half of all 5- to 6-year-olds do (Speer & Flavell, 1979). I assume that the growth of metacognitive knowledge is due, in part, to the cognitive demands of our educational system and to the frequent feedback children receive about the accuracy of their performance. A few meta-analyses indicated that the relationship between changes in metacognitive knowledge and general memory performance is positive and fairly strong (e.g., Schneider & Bjorklund, 1998).

Some basic metastrategic knowledge is present by the age of two. For example, two-year-olds will monitor their speech and spontaneously correct errors in word selection, pronunciation, and grammar (Clark, 1978). Two-year-olds also monitor what others say, inferring what others know and what others are capable of cognitively. With this knowledge, they can adjust their speech accordingly (Clark, 1978). Four-year-olds are capable of making relatively accurate feeling-of-knowing (FOK) judgments when presented with photographs of children, who they know to varying degrees and for which they have failed to recall the children's names (Cultice, Somerville, & Wellman, 1983). Finally, very young (4 years old) learners allocate about equal amounts of time to easy and difficult items, but older (12–13 years) learners allocate more study time to the difficult items (e.g., Kobasigawa & Dufresne, 1992, as cited in Metcalfe & Kornell, 2003). This is not to say that metastrategic knowledge is fully developed at an early age; it is not. Monitoring improves during elementary school (Zabrucky & Ratner, 1986) and is not even close to perfect in adults (e.g., Nelson & Dunlosky, 1992).

Much of the theorizing about adult metacognitive knowledge focuses on the kinds of information (cues) used when making metacognitive judgment, or control decisions, and a wide range of factors have been examined. For example, dozens of different kinds of information are known to influence the accuracy of judgments of learning (JOLs) (e.g., Koriat, 1997; Schwartz, 1994) and FOKs (e.g., Schwartz, 1994). One goal of research in the last decade has been to determine what kinds of information learners use versus what kinds of information they should use if they want to make accurate metacognitive judgments and control decisions. With regard to JOLs, Koriat (1997) outlined three general classes of information that may affect metacognitive processes: (1) information intrinsic to the studied items themselves (e.g., concreteness, degree of association between words in a pair, word frequency); (2) information associated with the conditions or cognitive processes occurring during learning (e.g., degree of learning, delay until testing, levels of processing); and (3) information associated with cognitive processes that are interpreted as indicating something about the state of one's memory (e.g., fluency of processing, quantity of available information). Knowledge about all three kinds of information can influence the accuracy of metacognitive processes. For example, JOL accuracy can improve when learners make JOLs after receiving a test of the to-be-judged items (e.g., Shaughnessy & Zechmeister, 1992) or simply with repeated study trials (Lovelace, 1984). For older adults, simply practicing making metacognitive judgments can result in improvements in self-paced associative learning, presumably because they more effectively allocate their study time (Dunlosky, Kubat-Silman, & Hertzog, 2003). However, a growing body of research has also found that the absolute accuracy of JOLs often changes from overconfident to underconfident with repeated study–test practice (Koriat, Ma'ayan,

Sheffer, & Bjork, 2006; Scheck & Nelson, 2005; Serra & Dunlosky, 2005). Together, these results give a mixed picture. Sometimes the knowledge gained by making metacognitive judgments improves their accuracy, and sometimes it does not. More research is needed to determine why these different patterns are observed.

Much of the theorizing about adult metastrategic knowledge focuses on how learners make decisions about which mnemonic or problem-solving strategy to use in a particular situation. For example, Reder (1988) examined peoples' ability to rapidly assess their knowledge when making metacognitive control decisions. She found that learners can quickly estimate whether they know an answer, and they do so before they can recall the actual answer. Furthermore, Reder and Ritter (1992) found that learners can decide rapidly which cognitive strategy to use (e.g., recall vs. calculate answer) in these situations. Pressley, Levin, and Ghatala (1984) observed that adult learners knew that an associative elaboration study technique was more effective than a rote rehearsal technique, but only when they received a practice test. On the other hand, 11- to 13-year-old children did not know about the differences between the two study techniques, and they did not benefit from practice testing unless they were given feedback about their test performance.

Intrinsic and Extrinsic Constraints

There are a number of constraints that can be incorporated into the metamodel. These constraints can be internally generated, as may happen when one holds expectations or constraining beliefs about one's cognitions, or externally generated, as when an experimenter limits the amount of time one has to study a list of word pairs.

Intrinsic Constraints   Beliefs and expectations are forms of internally generated constraints. For example, if one believes that Strategy X will not work in the current situation, then Strategy X is unlikely to be used. The belief imposes a constraint on current processing[2] (cf. Koriat, Bjork, Sheffer, & Bar, 2004).

If your goal is to make an accurate judgment about a word pair (e.g., pudding–cup) for which you are currently being shown only the cue word (e.g., pudding–), and you expect a recognition test, then your judgment is likely to be different from when you expect a recall test (e.g., Thiede, 1996), presumably because your expectations about the test's characteristics influence the construction of your metamodel, and your metamodel is assumed to be the basis of your metacognitive judgment or control decision. In fact, the relative accuracy of JOLs is greater when the learner expects a recall test than when expecting a recognition test (Thiede & Dunlosky, 1994). Furthermore, the metamodel that learners develop about test difficulty is often rigidly held, and they are generally unwilling to change it even when faced with evidence counter to their expectations. For example, Thiede (1996, Experiment 3) manipulated test difficulty (easy vs. difficult) and kind of test (recall vs. recognition) and found that participants consistently rated the objectively less-difficult recall tests as more difficult than the objectively more difficult recognition test, even after extensive experience.

Expectations about characteristics of a future test can also affect metacognitive judgments and control decisions. For example, learners who expect a recall test will spend more time studying than students expecting a recognition test (d'Ydewalle, Swerts, & DeCorte, 1983; Mazzoni & Cornoldi, 1993; Thiede, 1996; for a review, see Lundeberg & Fox, 1991). Again, this finding implies that people generally expect a recall test to be more difficult than a recognition test, and they adjust their allocation of study time according to this belief or expectation. Metacognitive judgments of item difficulty are affected by expectations of the relative difficulty of test formats (e.g., Thiede & Dunlosky, 1994).

Expectations about mnemonic changes can also affect metacognitive judgments and control decisions. As noted, people expect forgetting to occur, and for a prospective metacognitive judgment to be accurate, it must take into consideration the object-level changes that are most likely to occur during the delay between the time of the judgment and the time of the test. For example, when making JOLs, learners must take into consideration the forgetting that will occur during the delay between the JOL and the test (D_{jt}). Unfortunately, the mnemonic changes during D_{jt} are not linear, and these changes are usually highly dependent on the length of the delay between study and JOL (D_{sj}; see Figure 2). Therefore, people must possess accurate metacognitive knowledge about the variability of forgetting that occurs as a function of both D_{sj} and D_{jt} for the JOLs to be accurate. Koriat and colleagues (e.g., Koriat & Bjork, 2005) have shown that learners are incredibly insensitive to D_{jt}.[3] In fact, in Experiment 1 (Koriat et al., 2004), D_{jt} was manipulated between subjects and varied from approximately 10 minutes to 1 week. They found no significant differences in JOL ratings as a function of D_{jt} even though there were large and highly significant differences in actual recall performance. When D_{jt} values ranged from 10 minutes to 1 year and were manipulated between subjects, learners still gave similar JOL ratings across the different delays (Koriat et al., 2004, Experiment 4C). By contrast, Rawson

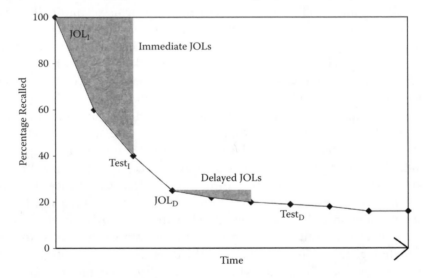

Figure 2 Hypothetical forgetting curve and the amounts of forgetting that occur between the immediate judgments of learning (JOL_I) and the test of those items ($Test_I$), represented by the large shaded area, and between the delayed JOLs (JOL_D) and the test of those items ($Test_D$), represented by the small shaded area.

and colleagues (Rawson, Dunlosky, & McDonald, 2002) found that learners were sensitive to D_{jt} when estimating performance on future tests of story comprehension but not when estimating their level of text comprehension.

Research indicates that the differences in JOL accuracy between immediate and delayed JOLs may be attributable, in part, to learners' insensitivity to the changes in the rate of forgetting (Van Overschelde & Nelson, 2006; cf. Carroll, Nelson, & Kirwan, 1997). For example, Van Overschelde and Nelson (2006) compared the accuracy of immediate and delayed JOLs only for items that were recallable at the time of the JOL, thereby allowing a direct comparison of the learner's estimations of forgetting during a subsequent 10-minute retention interval (D_{jt}). We found that learners expected moderate forgetting to occur when none was likely to occur (delayed JOLs), and they expected little forgetting to occur when much forgetting was likely to occur (immediate JOLs).

Other beliefs and expectations that have been found to influence metacognitive judgments and control decisions include beliefs about one's abilities (e.g., Perfect, 2004); beliefs about how the amount of time spent studying affects memory (e.g., Nelson & Leonesio, 1988); beliefs about the influence of external constraints (e.g., Carroll et al., 1997); and beliefs about how cognitive processes affect memory (e.g., Koriat, 1997).

Extrinsic Constraints   When deciding which control actions to take, it is important to consider extrinsic constraints on those potential courses of action. For example, if one holds the goal of getting the highest grade possible on a test but is afforded only a limited amount of time to study for it, then allocating study time to only a few items on a list of to-be-studied items would likely be counterproductive. Metcalfe and her colleagues have demonstrated that the constraints placed on the learner can dramatically influence how they allocate study time. As noted, when study time is limited, learners show preference for easier items than more difficult items, and they are generally correct in doing so (e.g., Metcalfe, 2002). However, when study time is unlimited, then learners tend to study the most difficult items longer (for a review, see Son & Metcalfe, 2000). These findings indicate that learners can use information about extrinsic constraints when making metacognitive judgments and control decisions.

Metacognitive Judgment and Decision Making

As described, the construction of the metamodel is based on information about (1) the current state of the object level, (2) the current meta level goal, (3) knowledge about possible courses of control actions and their consequences, and (4) perceived intrinsic and extrinsic constraints. A judgment or decision about which metacognitive control action to take, which is based on this metamodel, is then made. These four aspects of the metamodel are essentially identical to those of the problem-space or state-space hypothesis proposed by Newell and Simon (1972; see also Newell, 1980). As such, it may be fruitful to consider metacognitive control decisions as attempts to navigate through a metacognitive state-space that is represented here by the metamodel. We have a current state (e.g., unlearned items) and a goal state (e.g., mastery of the list), and we have to figure out how to get from here to there.

Characterizing metacognitive judgments as judgments about the metamodel allows us to think about them as either (1) predictions under varying degrees of uncertainty or (2) estimations of probability or frequency. Examples of the former include JOLs, EOLs, and FOKs. These are all judgments under uncertainty — prospective judgments. In fact, in a traditional JOL experiment, immediate JOLs, which are followed by much forgetting, are judgments under greater uncertainly than delayed JOLs, which are followed by almost no forgetting (Van Overschelde & Nelson, 2006). This difference in uncertainty may help explain why the relative accuracy of delayed JOLs is substantially greater than for immediate JOLs.

Examples of estimations of probability or frequency include old–new recognition and retrospective confidence judgments. In old–new recognition, participants have to judge the probability that the item currently being perceived was presented or learned earlier, and in retrospective confidence, participants have to judge the probability that their answer is correct.

Characterizing metacognition as essentially the navigation of a metamodel or as judgments about the current metamodel has several advantages. It provides a comprehensive framework for examining and classifying the many factors that can influence the construction of the metamodel and the navigation of a learner through the metacognitive state-space and concomitantly the accuracy of the metacognitive judgments and control decisions. By making these factors explicit, it then seems more likely that we will find effective techniques for improving the accuracy of metacognitive judgments and control decisions, which could have profound pedagogical ramifications. Furthermore, it permits us to draw on the extant JDM literature about heuristics and biases. Heuristics are called "rules of thumb," and they are generally less cognitively demanding than algorithms (precise rules), but unlike algorithms they are not guaranteed to give the correct answer, or even the same answer, every time. In fact, there are numerous heuristics and biases (errors or deviations from a norm) that have been identified and researched in the JDM literature (see Gilovich, Griffin, & Kahneman, 2002, for a recent summary), far more than have been examined in the metacognitive literature.

Heuristics and Biases

Although numerous heuristics have been examined in the JDM literature, only two have been widely researched in the metacognitive literature: the fluency heuristic and the availability heuristic. Fluency is arguably the most widely studied of the heuristics, in part because fluency is so easily manipulated by experimenters. As it relates to metacognition, the fluency heuristic relies on the rate or fluency with which the information comes to mind. The availability heuristic relies on or is influenced by the sheer quantity of information that comes to mind. In other words, fluency is associated with process information, and availability is associated with content. Ultimately, both of these heuristics probably fall under the original definition of the availability heuristic as proposed by Tversky and Kahneman (1973).

Fluency of Processing[4]

The objective speed or fluency with which information is processed or comes to mind at the object level has been examined for decades and has been found to vary naturally (e.g., as with word frequency; Howes, 1957) and to vary as a function of experimental manipulation (e.g., as with repetition priming; Warrington & Weiskrantz, 1978). The metalevel's subjective assessment or metaperception of this object-level fluency has also been examined extensively, and fluency can have either positive or negative effects on the magnitude and accuracy of metacognitive judgments, depending on many factors (Benjamin et al., 1998; Briñol, Petty, & Tormala, 2006; Dunlosky, Baker, Rawson, & Hertzog, 2006; Whittlesea & Leboe, 2003).

Although one might think of fluency in absolute terms ("That was fast"), a growing body of research is exploring fluency in subjective and relative terms ("That was faster than I expected it to be").[5] Although most of the metacognitive research of fluency that I present addresses only absolute fluency, some researchers are actively comparing the effects of absolute and relative fluency (e.g., Whittlesea & Williams, 2001a, 2001b).

Feeling-of-Knowing Judgments   Feeling-of-knowing (FOK) judgments involve a cue (e.g., question, word) and a target (e.g., answer, word, trigram). As such, there are two kinds of fluency that have been examined: (1) the fluency with which a cue is processed (a component of cue familiarity; see Whittlesea & Leboe, 2003, for a comprehensive review), and (2) the fluency with which information about the corresponding target is retrieved. The picture is complicated a bit by the fact that there are two kinds of FOKs. FOKs generated very early in the cue-perceptual/target-retrieval processes, but before the target has been fully retrieved, are termed *preliminary FOKs* (e.g., Reder & Ritter, 1992). FOKs generated only after retrieval of the complete target has failed are termed *standard FOKs* or just FOKs (e.g., Connor, Balota, & Neely, 1992).

Cue Fluency   The fluency of cue processing has been examined mostly by experimentally manipulating the cues (e.g., Son & Metcalfe, 2005).

Reder and her colleagues (Reder, 1987, 1988; Reder & Ritter, 1992) used a game show style, speeded-response paradigm. In her 1988 work, some of the words used in the game show's general knowledge questions were preexposed (and thus presumably processed more fluently during the game show phase of the experiment). Reder found that preliminary FOKs were greater for preexposed questions than new questions, even though retrieval of correct answers was unaffected by the preexposure manipulation. Using math problems, Reder and Ritter (1992) found that increases in the frequency of preexposure to components of the math problems, and not to the answers, led to increases in preliminary FOK ratings, even though preexposure had no effect on retrieval of the answers. Schwartz and Metcalfe (1992, Experiment 4) used a different manipulation with cue–target pairs. In this experiment, they preexposed some of the cues and some of the targets via an initial pleasantness rating task. Although they did not measure cue fluency directly, preexposure is known to increase the fluency of item processing on subsequent presentations (e.g., McKone, 1995). Following preexposure, all pairs were presented and studied intact, and then all pairs were tested for cued recall of the target. FOKs were generated for nonrecalled targets and were followed by a recognition test. They found that FOKs were significantly higher in conditions in which only the cue was preexposed despite the fact that in these cases retrieval of the target was unaffected. And, FOKs were unaffected when only the target was preexposed, but preexposed targets were more likely to be recognized than unprimed targets.

Together, these experiments indicated that preliminary and standard FOKs can be increased simply by preexposing the cue so that it is presumably processed more fluently than "normal," even though cue fluency may bear no relationship to actual test performance.

Target Fluency   Target fluency is almost always examined using standard FOKs (i.e., when target retrieval fails). In general, the findings indicate that the stronger the FOK is, the longer one is willing to search memory for the answer before giving up (e.g., Koriat, 1993; Nelson & Narens, 1990). In other words, there is a positive relationship between target retrieval latency and FOK ratings. For example, Costermans, Lories, and Ansay (1992) found that when participants gave the highest FOK ratings (indicating, "I am absolutely sure I know the answer") they spent almost three times longer attempting to retrieve the answer before giving up than they did when they gave the lowest FOK ratings (indicating, "I am absolutely sure I do not know the answer"). When no information comes to mind, or information comes to mind that indicates that the answer is not in memory, people can respond very quickly (Kolers & Palef, 1976).

In summary, two general findings exist. First, there is a positive relationship between the preliminary FOK ratings and the fluency with which the cue is processed regardless of the retrievability of the target. Second, there is a positive relationship between FOK ratings and the amount of time people will search memory before terminating the search due to nonretrieval.

Judgments of Learning   Researchers have established that the amount of time participants spend studying items at encoding (hereafter termed *encoding fluency*) is negatively correlated with the magnitude of both immediate and delayed JOLs, and the negative correlation is stronger for immediate JOLs than for delayed JOLs (Koriat & Ma'ayan, 2005). In other words, the less fluently an item is encoded/learned, the lower the subsequent JOL rating given to that item.

Furthermore, the fluency with which answers are retrieved at (or near) the time of the JOL is negatively correlated with the magnitude of both immediate JOLs (e.g., Serra & Dunlosky, 2005) and delayed JOLs (e.g., Koriat & Ma'ayan, 2005). In other words, the longer it takes to retrieve a target at the time of the JOL, the lower the JOL rating. However, this negative correlation only appears when participants explicitly attempt to retrieve the target. For example, Son and Metcalfe (2005) found that when participants were asked only to generate JOLs and were not instructed to attempt recall, then the relationship between JOL latency (not retrieval latency because no retrieval was required) and JOL rating was an inverted-U function. JOLs were generated most quickly for the lowest and highest JOL ratings and slowest for intermediate JOL ratings.

Not surprisingly, the accuracy of the JOLs depends on when the fluency is measured (at encoding or retrieval) and how diagnostic this fluency is of future test performance. For example, high-frequency (HF) words are processed more fluently at encoding than low-frequency (LF) words, and HF words are given, on average, higher JOL ratings than LF words, regardless of whether testing will be recall (Van Overschelde, 2006) or recognition (Begg et al., 1989). However, actual test performance varies as a function of word frequency between recall and recognition tests and between recall of pure lists and recall of mixed lists. With pure lists, more HF words are recalled than LF words, and under several conditions with mixed lists, fewer HF words are recalled than LF words (e.g., Van Overschelde, 2002). With old–new recognition, recognition performance is almost always better for LF words than for HF words (e.g., Diana & Reder, 2006). Therefore, the accuracy of JOLs will be high when pure lists are used and tested with recall, low when mixed lists are used and tested with recall (Van Overschelde, 2006), and low when either pure or mixed lists are used and tested with recognition (Begg et al., 1989). In these cases, fluency at encoding is predictive of test performance in only one of the three test conditions (pure list recall).

By contrast, Benjamin et al. (1998) measured the time required to retrieve answers to trivia questions. They found that participants gave higher JOL ratings to answers that were retrieved quickly at the time of the JOLs than to those retrieved slowly. However, in contrast to their predictions, the answers retrieved quickly were actually less likely to be recalled at testing than answers retrieved slowly. In this case, participants appear to have assumed that retrieval fluency was positively predictive of future recall when the opposite was true, and the accuracy of their metacognitive judgments suffered as a result.

Lee, Narens, and Nelson (1993, as cited in Narens, Jameson, & Lee, 1994) used paired associates, and immediately prior to the delayed JOLs the targets were subliminally primed. This priming presumably increased the fluency with which the target, or partial information about the target, was retrieved at the time of the JOL. Primed targets were given higher JOLs than unprimed targets. However, this kind of priming was short-lived and resulted in no improvement in final recall. The accuracy of the JOLs was not reported.

Retrospective Confidence Judgments Participants tend to show greater confidence when information is retrieved fluently. Costermans et al. (1992) observed a positive relationship between the fluency of retrieving answers to questions and the subjective confidence in those answers, but this relationship occurred regardless of the accuracy of the answer. Kelley and Lindsay (1993) found that participants had higher confidence in their answers to questions when the answers were presented during a preexposure task, presumably enhancing target fluency. Again, the higher confidence ratings occurred regardless of whether the answer was correct or incorrect. Shaw (1996) found that eyewitnesses to mock crimes became more confident in their answers to questions about the crime the longer they spent thinking about their answers.

Old–New Recognition Judgments Old–new recognition judgments generally occur after studying a list of items and the test involves old, previously studied items and new, unstudied items. Participants must discriminate among old and new items.

Accurately making these judgments seems crucial to so many aspects of life, and numerous experiments have been conducted to evaluate the effect of fluency on the accuracy of these judgments (e.g., Kelley & Jacoby, 1998; Whittlesea & Leboe, 2003). These judgments are metacognitive in nature because people are monitoring available object-level information and deciding whether the information is new or is from a memory of a past experience (for details, see Batchelder & Batchelder, this volume).

Researchers often manipulate item fluency immediately prior to testing and without participants being aware of the manipulation. For example, Jacoby and Whitehouse (1989) enhanced the fluency of item processing in two ways. After studying a list of items, old and new items were presented for an old–new recognition test. In one condition, new items were primed immediately prior to the test, and it was done so that participants were unaware of the priming. In the other condition, new items were primed just prior to the recognition test, and it was done so that participants were aware of the priming. In both priming conditions, retrieval fluency was facilitated by the priming, relative to new, unprimed items, but in the unaware priming condition participants judged the primed new items as old more often than did participants in the aware priming condition. Thus, participants who were aware of the priming appeared to discount the increased fluency caused by the priming when making their recognition judgments, and their metacognitive judgment accuracy was better as a result. In other words, when the sources of fluency are attributed to features of the test condition, and not to prior experience, then participants may discount the validity of fluency when making their judgments (see Kelley & Rhodes, 2002, for an extensive review).

As mentioned, fluency can vary absolutely and relative to expectations. Whittlesea and Leboe (2003) showed that when people are tested with recognition, their judgments are based on absolute fluency when stimuli vary only in fluency. When more meaningful stimuli and contexts are used, then judgments were based more on relative fluency.

Allocation of Study Time   People often allocate their study time based on the fluency with which information is processed or comes to mind. For example, when learners hold the goal of mastery, they will allocate more study time to tasks that require more effort (Eisenberger, 1992) and to items processed less fluently (e.g., Koriat & Ma'ayan, 2005). During learning, the fluency with which items are processed often changes (increases), and people appear to monitor this rate change and use this information to decide when to terminate study. The findings indicated they terminate study when this rate decreases below some threshold (e.g., Koriat, Ma'ayan, & Nussbaum, 2006; Metcalfe & Kornell, 2005; Nelson & Leonesio, 1988).

Liking   Liking has traditionally not been studied as a metacognitive judgment. However, the fact that people often judge fluently processed items as more likeable, more aesthetically pleasing, or as having a more positive effect implies that liking is the result of a judgment about cognitions.[6] Researchers have found that liking of neutral stimuli increases with repeated exposure (for reviews, see Bornstein, 1989; Zajonc, 2000), and this increase in liking is related, in part, to the increase in fluency of processing the stimulus brought about by the repeated exposures (e.g., Whittlesea, 1993; Willems & Van der Linden, 2006). They have also found that people's experience of aesthetic pleasure is increased by increasing the fluency with which stimuli are processed (for a review, see Reber, Schwarz, & Winkielman, 2004). Finally, people's affective response to stimuli has been found to be mediated by the fluency of processing the stimuli (Winkielman & Cacioppo, 2001).

Summary This wealth of research on the influence of fluency on metacognitive judgments and on control decisions leads to two important conclusions. First, our perception and assessment of fluency can affect these metacognitive processes. Second, unfortunately because the subjective assessment of fluency is not always positively correlated with objective test performance, and sometimes it is even negatively correlated, the accuracy of our metacognitive judgments and control decisions can vary substantially and significantly depending on the situation.

Availability of Cues

The sheer quantity of information available at the time one makes a metacognitive judgment or control decision can have strong effects on the accuracy of these control actions. The metalevel's subjective assessment or the metaperception of the availability of this information at the object level has also been examined, and as with fluency, it can have either positive or negative effects on the magnitude and accuracy of metacognitive processes, depending on many factors.

Feeling of Knowing Much research has found that FOKs were influenced by the amount of partial target information accessible at the time of the judgment (Hart, 1965; Koriat, 1993, 1995). For example, FOKs are higher when an affective quality of the target word (i.e., good/bad) can be produced than when it cannot (Schacter & Worling, 1985); when target items are overlearned compared to once-learned items (Nelson, Leonesio, Shimamura, Landwehr, & Narens, 1982); when the target is learned using a deep level-of-processing manipulation than when using a shallow one (Lupker, Harbluk, & Patrick, 1991); when items are studied for 7 seconds compared to items studied for 2 seconds (Schwartz & Metcalfe, 1992); and for commission errors than for omission errors, even when learners are told their answers are incorrect (Krinsky & Nelson, 1985). In addition, Nelson and his colleagues (Nelson et al., 1982) observed a positive correlation between FOK rating and the latency of correct recognition. In other words, FOKs were higher for target items that were recognized more quickly, a finding that implies that more target information had been activated during retrieval attempts for high-FOK items than for low-FOK items. All of these findings indicate that FOKs increase in magnitude as the quantity of available target information increases.

Unfortunately for learners, people are often unaware of the correctness of the partial information currently available in memory. For example, Koriat (1995) varied orthogonally the accessibility and accuracy of answers to questions. He showed that highly accessible answers were associated with higher FOKs, regardless of the accuracy of the answers. Koriat (1995) concluded that "participants base their estimates of future recognition performance on *how much* [italics added] information comes to mind, regardless of its accuracy, when trying to recall the answer" (p. 134).

Even when the quantity of target information available is enhanced by the experimenter, learners do not always monitor or assess this information as relevant. For example, when targets are primed below threshold, the priming manipulation increases retrieval but has no effect on FOKs (Jameson, Narens, Goldfarb, & Nelson, 1990).

Taken together, these results clearly indicate that FOKs are predictive of test performance in some cases and not in others, and that FOKs can be strongly affected by the quantity of information that is available regardless of the accuracy of that information.

Judgments of Learning   The amount of target information available at the time of the JOL is known also to influence the JOL ratings (Dunlosky & Nelson, 1992; see Koriat, 1997, for a comprehensive review). Benjamin and Bjork (1996) showed that the accessibility of information at the time of the JOL was positively related to JOL rating, even though in their experiments accessibility was negatively correlated with eventual test performance. Under some conditions, people also can assess the quality of the accessible information. For example, Dunlosky, Rawson, and Middleton (2005) found that participants evaluated the quality of word definitions that were recalled immediately prior to making JOLs, and they gave higher judgments to correctly recalled definitions than to commission incorrectly recalled definitions.

Forgetting plays a key role in how much information is available at the time of the JOL. For example, immediate JOLs occur after almost no forgetting has occurred, but delayed JOLs can occur after substantial forgetting has occurred. And, because forgetting represents a negatively decelerating function, more forgetting occurs after immediate JOLs than after the typical delayed JOL (e.g., Van Overschelde & Nelson, 2006). Therefore, the amount and kinds of information generally available at the time of immediate JOLs is not highly diagnostic of future test performance, whereas the amount and kinds of information generally available at the time of delayed JOLs is diagnostic (Van Overschelde & Nelson, 2006). As a result of these differences, immediate JOLs are less accurate than delayed JOLs presumably because the information about the target that is accessible at the time of the immediate JOLs is weakly diagnostic of retrieval at test, but with delayed JOLs it is strongly diagnostic of retrieval at test (e.g., Nelson, Narens, & Dunlosky, 2004).

Conclusion

As originally proposed, Nelson and Narens' metacognitive model (Nelson, 1996; Nelson & Narens, 1990, 1994) has been a foundational model for theorizing about metacognition. As reviewed here, extensive evidence supports the claims that metacognitive processes are affected by (1) the quality of the dynamic metamodel of the current state of the object level, (2) the current metalevel goal or goals, (3) the knowledge one has about how the metalevel can control the object level and the consequences of these control actions, and (4) the perceived constraints on these control actions. Here, I proposed that these four general classes of information combine to form a metamodel on which metacognitive JDM processes operate. This idea leads to the conclusion that metacognitive judgments and control actions are made not on the object level per se, but on one's interpretation or assessment of the accessible information about the object level, along with a host of goal-relevant information. This idea has been underemphasized in metacognitive research and theory, and I believe future research along this line will be fruitful.

Notes

1 There have been 2,586 to be exact, according to a PsycINFO search conducted on August 28, 2006, using the search "metacognition" OR "metamemory" OR "metacomprehension."

2 Koriat et al. (2004) referred to the influences of these kinds of constraints as theory-based judgments. However, because I argue that all metacognitive decisions are based on one's interpretations about the available cues, all metacognitive decisions are, in one sense, theory-based decisions.

3 In fact, most of the 12 experiments in Koriat et al. (2004) showed no effect of D_{jt} when manipulated between subjects.

4 Some researchers have labeled fluency as *ease of processing* (EOP; e.g., Begg et al., 1989; Dunlosky et al., 2006); however, because the word *ease* implies a subjective assessment of processing speed (cf. Reber, Fazendeiro, & Winkielman, 2002), I prefer the more objective label of fluency of processing.

5 Because this relative fluency is a comparison between current processing and some normative model of processing, it may be an example, instead, of the use of the representative heuristic.

6 Whittlesea and Price (2001) showed that the increased liking, which they termed pleasantness, was the result of a global, nonanalytical, method of evaluating stimuli that more closely matched the way in which prior stimuli were processed. Therefore, the match in cognitive processing between memory of a prior perception and a current perception resulted in a subjective assessment that was experienced as pleasantness or liking.

References

Aristotle. (2006). *On the soul* (J. A. Smith, Trans.). (Original work published ~350 BCE). Translation available at: http://classics.mit.edu/Aristotle/soul.html.

Ashby, W. R. (1956). *Introduction to cybernetics*. London: Wiley.

Aurobindo, S. (1998). *The Upanishads*. Twin Lakes, WI: Lotus Press.

Begg, I. M., Duft, S., Lalonde, P., Melnick, R., & Sanvito, J. (1989). Memory predictions are based on ease of processing. *Journal of Memory and Language, 28*, 610–632.

Benjamin, A. S., Bjork, R. A., & Schwartz, B. L. (1998). The mismeasure of memory: When retrieval fluency is misleading as a metamnemonic index. *Journal of Experimental Psychology: General, 127*, 55–68.

Benjamin, A. S., & Bjork, R. A. (1996). Retrieval fluency as a metacognitive index. In L. Reder (Ed.), *Implicit memory and metacognition* (pp. 309–338). Hillsdale, NJ: Erlbaum.

Bornstein, R. F. (1989). Exposure and affect: Overview and meta-analysis of research, 1968–1987. *Psychological Bulletin, 106*, 265–289.

Briñol, P., Petty, R. E., & Tormala, Z. L. (2006). The malleable meaning of subjective ease. *Psychological Science, 17*, 200–206.

Carroll, M., Nelson, T. O., & Kirwan, A. (1997). Tradeoff of semantic relatedness and degree of overlearning: Differential effects on metamemory and on long-term retention. *Acta Psychologica, 95*, 239–253.

Clark, E. V. (1978). Strategies for communicating. *Child Development, 49*, 953–959.

Conant, R. C., & Ashby, W. R. (1970). Every good regulator of a system must be a model of that system. *International Journal of Systems Science, 1*, 89–97.

Connor, L. T., Balota, D. A., & Neely, J. H. (1992). On the relation between feeling of knowing and lexical decision: Persistent subthreshold activation or topic familiarity? *Journal of Experimental Psychology: Learning, Memory, and Cognition, 18*, 544–554.

Costermans, J., Lories, G., & Ansay, C. (1992). Confidence level and feeling of knowing in question answering: The weight of inferential processes. *Journal of Experimental Psychology: Learning, Memory, and Cognition, 18*, 142–150.

Craik, K. J. W. (1943). *The nature of explanation.* Cambridge, UK: Cambridge University Press.

Cultice, J. C., Somerville, S. C., & Wellman, H. M. (1983). Preschooler's memory monitoring: Feeling-of-knowing judgments. *Child Development, 54*, 1480–1486.

Diana, R. A., & Reder, L. M. (2006). The low frequency encoding disadvantage: Word frequency affects processing demands. *Journal of Experimental Psychology: Learning, Memory, and Cognition, 32*, 805–815.

Dunlosky, J., Baker, J. M. C., Rawson, K. A., & Hertzog, C. (2006). Does aging influence people's metacomprehension? Effects of processing ease on judgments of text learning. *Psychology and Aging, 21*, 390–400.

Dunlosky, J., & Hertzog, C. (1998). Training programs improve learning in later adulthood: Helping older adults educate themselves. In D. J. Hacker (Ed.), *Metacognition in educational theory and practice* (pp. 249–275). Mahwah, NJ: Erlbaum.

Dunlosky, J., Hertzog, C., Kennedy, M., & Thiede, K. W. (2005). The self-monitoring approach for effective learning. *Cognitive Technology, 10*, 4–11.

Dunlosky, J., Kubat-Silman, A., & Hertzog, C. (2003). Training monitoring skills improves older adults' self-paced associative learning. *Psychology and Aging, 18*, 340–345.

Dunlosky, J., & Nelson, T.O. (1992). How shall we explain the delayed-judgment-of-learning effect? *Psychological Science, 3*, 317–318.

Dunlosky, J., Rawson, K. A., & Middleton, E. L. (2005). What constrains the accuracy of metacomprehension judgments? Testing the transfer-appropriate-monitoring and accessibility hypotheses. *Journal of Memory and Language, 52*, 551–565.

Dunlosky, J., & Thiede, K. W. (2004). Causes and constraints on shift-to-easier-materials effect in the control of study. *Memory & Cognition, 32*, 779–788.

d'Ydewalle, G., Swerts, A., & DeCorte, E. (1983). Study time and test performance as a function of test expectancy. *Contemporary Educational Psychology, 8*, 55–67.

Eisenberger, R. (1992). Learned industriousness. *Psychological Review, 99*, 248–267.

Engle, R. W., & Kane, M. J. (2004). Executive *attention*, working memory capacity, and a two-factor theory of cognitive control. In B. H. Ross (Ed.), *The psychology of learning and motivation: Advances in research and theory* (Vol. 44, pp. 145–199). New York: Elsevier Science.

Flavell, J. H., Friedrichs, A. G., & Hoyt, J. D. (1970). Developmental changes in memorization processes. *Cognitive Psychology, 1*, 324–340.

Gilovich, T., Griffin, D. W., & Kahneman, D. (2002). *Heuristics and biases: The psychology of intuitive judgment.* New York: Cambridge University Press.

Goldsmith, M., Koriat, A., & Pansky, A. (2005). Strategic regulation of grain size in memory reporting over time. *Journal of Memory and Language, 52*, 505–525.

Hart, J. T. (1965). Memory and the feeling-of-knowing experience. *Journal of Educational Psychology, 56*, 208–216.

Howes, D. (1957). On the relation between the intelligibility and frequency of occurrence of English words. *Journal of the Acoustical Society of America, 29*, 296–305.

Jacoby, L. L., & Whitehouse, K. (1989). An illusion of memory: False recognition influenced by unconscious perception. *Journal of Experimental Psychology: General, 118*, 126–135.

Jameson, K. A., Narens, L., Goldfarb, K., & Nelson, T. O. (1990). The influence of near-threshold priming on metamemory and recall. *Acta Psychologica, 73*, 55–68.

Joslyn, C. (2001). The semiotics of control and modeling relations in complex systems. *Biosystems, 60*, 131–148.

Kelley, C. M., & Jacoby, L. L. (1998). Subjective reports and process dissociation: Fluency, knowing, and feeling. *Acta Psychologica, 98*, 127–140.

Kelley, C. M., & Lindsay, D. S. (1993). Remembering mistaken for knowing: Ease of retrieval as a basis for confidence in answers to general knowledge questions. *Journal of Memory and Language, 32*, 1–24.

Kelley, C. M., & Rhodes, M. G. (2002). Making sense and nonsense of experience: Attributions in memory and judgment. In Brian H. Ross (Ed.), *The psychology of learning and motivation: Advances in research and theory* (Vol. 41, pp. 293–320). San Diego, CA: Academic Press.

Kelley, C. M., & Sahakyan, L. (2003). Memory, monitoring, and control in the attainment of memory accuracy. *Journal of Memory and Language, 48*, 704–721.

Kobasigawa, A., & Dufresne, A. (1992). *Differential allocation of study time by Grade 3 children.* Unpublished manuscript.

Kolers, P. A., & Palef, S. R. (1976). Knowing not. *Memory & Cognition, 4*, 553–558.

Koriat, A. (1993). How do we know that we know? The accessibility model of the feeling of knowing. *Psychological Review, 100*, 609–639.

Koriat, A. (1995). Dissociating knowing and the feeling of knowing: Further evidence for the accessibility model. *Journal of Experimental Psychology: General, 124*, 311–333.

Koriat, A. (1997). Monitoring one's own knowledge during study: A cue-utilization approach to judgments of learning. *Journal of Experimental Psychology: General, 126*, 349–370.

Koriat, A., & Bjork, R. A. (2005). Illusions of competence in monitoring one's knowledge during study. *Journal of Experimental Psychology: Learning, Memory, and Cognition, 31*, 187–194.

Koriat, A., Bjork, R. A., Sheffer, L., & Bar, S. K. (2004). Predicting one's own forgetting: The role of experience-based and theory-based processes. *Journal of Experimental Psychology: General, 133*, 643–656.

Koriat, A., Goldsmith, M., Schneider, W., & Nakash-Dura, M. (2001). The credibility of children's testimony: Can children control the accuracy of their memory reports? *Journal of Experimental Child Psychology, 79*, 405–437.

Koriat, A., & Ma'ayan, H. (2005). The effects of encoding fluency and retrieval fluency on judgments of learning. *Journal of Memory and Language, 52*, 478–492.

Koriat, A., Ma'ayan, H., & Nussinson, R. (2006). The intricate relationships between monitoring and control in metacognition: Lessons for the cause-and-effect relation between subjective experience and behavior. *Journal of Experimental Psychology: General, 135*, 36–69.

Koriat, A., Ma'ayan, H., Sheffer, L., & Bjork, R. A. (2006). Exploring a mnemonic debiasing account of the *underconfidence*-with-*practice* effect. *Journal of Experimental Psychology: Learning, Memory, and Cognition, 32*, 595–608.

Kornell, N., & Metcalfe, J. (2006). Study efficacy and the region of *proximal learning* framework. *Journal of Experimental Psychology: Learning, Memory, and Cognition, 32*, 609–622.

Kreutzer, M. A., Leonard, C., & Flavell, J. H. (1975). An interview study of children's knowledge about memory. *Monographs of the Society for Research in Child Development, 40,* 1–60.

Krinsky, R., & Nelson, T. O. (1985). The feeling of knowing for different types of retrieval failure. *Acta Psychologica, 58,* 141–158.

Kuhn, D. (2000). Metacognitive development. *Current Directions in Psychological Science, 9,* 178–181.

Lee, V. A., Narens, L., & Nelson, T. O. (1993). *Subthreshold priming and the judgment of learning.* Unpublished manuscript.

Leonesio, R. J., & Nelson, T. O. (1990). Do different metamemory judgments tap the same underlying aspects of memory? *Journal of Experimental Psychology: Learning, Memory, & Cognition, 16,* 464–470.

Lovelace, E. A. (1984). Metamemory: Monitoring future recallability during study. *Journal of Experimental Psychology: Learning, Memory, and Cognition, 10,* 756–766.

Lundeberg, M. A., & Fox, P. W. (1991). Do laboratory findings on test expectancy generalize to classroom outcomes? *Review of Educational Research, 61,* 94–106.

Lupker, S. J., Harbluk, J. L., & Patrick, A. S. (1991). Memory for things forgotten. *Journal of Experimental Psychology: Learning, Memory, and Cognition, 17,* 897–907.

Mazzoni, G., & Cornoldi, C. (1993). Strategies in study time allocation: Why is study time sometimes not effective? *Journal of Experimental Psychology: General, 122,* 47–60.

McKone, E. (1995). Short-term implicit memory for words and nonwords. *Journal of Experimental Psychology: Learning, Memory, and Cognition, 21,* 1108–1126.

Metcalfe, J. (2002). Is study time allocated selectively to a region of proximal learning? *Journal of Experimental Psychology: General, 131,* 349–363.

Metcalfe, J., & Kornell, N. (2003). The dynamics of learning and allocation of study time to a region of proximal learning. *Journal of Experimental Psychology: General, 132,* 530–542.

Metcalfe, J., & Kornell, N. (2005). A region of proximal learning model of study time allocation. *Journal of Memory and Language, 52,* 463–477.

Narens, L., Jameson, K. A., & Lee, V. A. (1994). Subthreshold priming and memory monitoring. In J. Metcalfe & A. P. Shimamura (Eds.), *Metacognition: Knowing about knowing* (pp. 71–92). Cambridge, MA: MIT Press.

Nelson, T. O. (1996). Consciousness and metacognition. *American Psychologist, 51,* 102–116.

Nelson, T. O., & Dunlosky, J. (1992). How shall we explain the delayed-judgment-of-learning effect? *Psychological Science, 3,* 317–318.

Nelson, T. O., & Leonesio, R. J. (1988). Allocation of self-paced study time and the "labor-in-vain effect." *Journal of Experimental Psychology: Learning, Memory, and Cognition, 14,* 676–686.

Nelson, T. O., & Narens, L. (1990). Metamemory: A theoretical framework and new findings. *The Psychology of Learning and Motivation, 26,* 125–141.

Nelson, T. O., & Narens, L. (1994). Why investigate metacognition? In J. Metcalfe & A. P. Shimamura (Eds.), *Metacognition: Knowing about knowing* (pp. 1–25). Cambridge, MA: MIT Press.

Nelson, T. O., Narens, L., & Dunlosky, J. (2004). A revised methodology for research on metamemory: Pre-judgment recall and monitoring (PRAM). *Psychological Methods, 9,* 53–69.

Nelson, T. O., Leonesio, R. J., Shimamura, A. P., Landwehr, R. S., & Narens, L. (1982). Overlearning and the feeling of knowing. *Journal of Experimental Psychology: Learning, Memory, and Cognition, 8,* 279–288.

Newell, A. (1980). Reasoning, problem solving, and decision processes: The problem space as a fundamental category. In R. S. Nickerson (Ed.), *Attention and performance, VIII* (pp. 693–718). Hillsdale, NJ: Prentice-Hall.

Newell, A., & Simon, H. A. (1972). *Human problem-solving.* Englewood Cliffs, NJ: Prentice-Hall.

Perfect, T. J. (2004). The role of self-rated ability in the accuracy of confidence judgments in eyewitness memory and general knowledge. *Applied Cognitive Psychology, 18,* 157–168.

Pressley, M., Levin, J. R., & Ghatala, E. S. (1984). Memory strategy monitoring in adults and children. *Journal of Verbal Learning and Verbal Behavior, 23,* 270–288.

Rawson, K. A., Dunlosky, J., & McDonald, S. L. (2002). Influences of metamemory on performance predictions for text. *The Quarterly Journal of Experimental Psychology A: Human Experimental Psychology, 55A,* 505–524.

Reber, R., Fazendeiro, T. A., & Winkielman, P. (2002). Processing fluency as the source of experiences at the fringe of consciousness. *Psyche: An Interdisciplinary Journal of Research on Consciousness, 8.*

Reber, R., Schwarz, N., & Winkielman, P. (2004). Processing fluency and aesthetic pleasure: Is beauty in the perceiver's processing experience? *Personality and Social Psychology Review, 8,* 364–382.

Reder, L. M. (1987). Strategy selection in question answering. *Cognitive Psychology, 19,* 90–138.

Reder, L. M. (1988). Strategic control of retrieval strategies. In G. H. Bower (Ed.), *The psychology of learning and motivation: Advances in research and theory* (Vol. 22, pp. 227–259). San Diego, CA: Academic Press.

Reder, L., & Ritter, F. E. (1992). What determines initial feeling of knowing? Familiarity with question terms, not with the answer. *Journal of Experimental Psychology: Learning, Memory, and Cognition, 18,* 435–451.

Schacter, D. L., & Worling, J. R. (1985). Attribute information and the feeling-of-knowing. *Canadian Journal of Psychology, 39,* 467–475.

Scheck, P., & Nelson, T. O. (2005). Lack of pervasiveness of the *underconfidence*-with-*practice* effect: Boundary conditions and an explanation via anchoring. *Journal of Experimental Psychology: General, 134,* 124–128.

Schneider, W., & Bjorklund, D. F. (1998). Memory. In D. Kuhn & R. S. Siegler (Eds.), *Handbook of child psychology: Vol. 2. Cognition, perception, and language* (5th ed., pp. 467–521). New York: Wiley.

Schwartz, B. L. (1994). Sources of information in metamemory: Judgments of learning and feelings of knowing. *Psychonomic Bulletin & Review, 1,* 357–375.

Schwartz, B. L., & Metcalfe, J. (1992). Cue familiarity but not target retrievability enhances feeling-of-knowing judgments. *Journal of Experimental Psychology: Learning, Memory, and Cognition, 18,* 1074–1083.

Serra, M. J., & Dunlosky, J. (2005). Does retrieval fluency contribute to the *underconfidence*-with-*practice* effect? *Journal of Experimental Psychology: Learning, Memory, and Cognition, 31,* 1258–1266.

Shaughnessy, J. J., & Zechmeister, E. B. (1992). Memory-monitoring accuracy as influenced by the distribution of retrieval practice. *Bulletin of the Psychonomic Society, 30,* 125–128.

Shaw, J. S. (1996). Increases in eyewitness confidence resulting from postevent questioning. *Journal of Experimental Psychology: Applied, 2,* 126–146.

Son, L. K., & Metcalfe, J. (2000). Metacognitive and control strategies in study-time allocation. *Journal of Experimental Psychology: Learning, Memory, and Cognition, 26,* 204–221.

Son, L. K., & Metcalfe, J. (2005). Judgments of learning: Evidence for a two-stage process. *Memory & Cognition, 33*, 1116–1129.

Speer, J. R., & Flavell, J. H. (1979). Young children's knowledge of the relative difficulty of recognition and recall memory tasks. *Developmental Psychology, 15*, 214–217.

Thiede, K. W. (1996). The relative importance of anticipated test format and anticipated test difficulty on performance. *The Quarterly Journal of Experimental Psychology, 49A*, 901–918.

Thiede, K. W., & Dunlosky, J. (1994). Delaying students' metacognitive monitoring improves their accuracy in predicting the recognition performance. *Journal of Educational Psychology, 86*, 290–302.

Thiede, K. W., & Dunlosky, J. (1999). Toward a general model of self-regulated study: An analysis of selection of items for study and self-paced study time. *Journal of Experimental Psychology: Learning, Memory, and Cognition, 25*, 1024–1037.

Thorkildsen, T., & Nicholls, J. (1998). Fifth graders' achievement orientation and beliefs: Individual and classroom differences. *Journal of Educational Psychology, 90*, 179–201.

Tversky, A., & Kahneman, D. (1973). Availability: A heuristic for judging frequency and probability. *Cognitive Psychology, 5*, 207–232.

Van Overschelde, J. P. (2002). The influence of word frequency on recency effects in directed free recall. *Journal of Experimental Psychology: Learning, Memory, and Cognition, 28*, 611–615.

Van Overschelde, J. P. (2006). *Are metacognitive control actions affected by normative word frequency?* Unpublished manuscript.

Van Overschelde, J. P., & Nelson, T. O. (2006). Delayed judgments of learning cause both a decrease in absolute accuracy (calibration) and an increase in relative accuracy (resolution). *Memory & Cognition, 34*, 1527–1538.

Warrington, E. K., & Weiskrantz, L. (1978). Further analysis of the prior learning effect in amnesic patients. *Neuropsychologia, 16*, 169–177.

Weinert, F. E. (1986). Developmental variations of memory performance and memory related knowledge across the life-span. In A. Sorensen, F. E. Weinert, & L. R. Sherrod (Eds.), *Human development: Multidisciplinary perspectives* (pp. 535–556). Hillsdale, NJ: Erlbaum.

Whittlesea, B. W. A. (1993). Illusions of familiarity. *Journal of Experimental Psychology: Learning, Memory, and Cognition, 19*, 1235–1253.

Whittlesea, B. W. A. (1997). Production, evaluation, and preservation of experiences: Constructive processing in remembering and performance tasks. In D. L. Medin (Ed.), *The psychology of learning and motivation: Advances in research and theory* (Vol. 37, pp. 211–264). San Diego, CA: Academic Press.

Whittlesea, B. W. A., & Leboe, J. P. (2003). Two fluency heuristics (and how to tell them apart). *Journal of Memory and Language, 49*, 62–79.

Whittlesea, B. W. A., & Price, J. R. (2001). Implicit/explicit memory versus analytic/non-analytic processing: Rethinking the mere exposure effect. *Memory & Cognition, 29*, 234–246.

Whittlesea, B. W. A., & Williams, L. D. (2001a). The discrepancy-attribution hypothesis: I. The heuristic basis of feelings and familiarity. *Journal of Experimental Psychology: Learning, Memory, and Cognition, 27*, 3–13.

Whittlesea, B. W. A., & Williams, L. D. (2001b). The discrepancy-attribution hypothesis: II. Expectation, uncertainty, surprise, and feelings of familiarity. *Journal of Experimental Psychology: Learning, Memory, and Cognition, 27*, 14–33.

Willems, S., & Van der Linden, M. (2006). Mere exposure effect: A consequence of direct and indirect *fluency*-preference links. *Consciousness and Cognition: An International Journal, 15,* 323–341.

Winkielman, P., & Cacioppo, J. T. (2001). Mind at ease puts a smile on the face: Psychophysiological evidence that processing facilitation elicits positive affect. *Journal of Personality and Social Psychology, 81,* 989–1000.

Wolters, C. A. (2003). Understanding procrastination from a self-regulated learning perspective. *Journal of Educational Psychology, 95,* 179–187.

Zabrucky, K., & Ratner, H. H. (1986). Children's comprehension monitoring and recall of inconsistent stories. *Child Development, 57,* 1401–1418.

Zajonc, R. B. (2000). Feeling and thinking: Closing the debate over the independence of affect. In J. P. Forgas (Ed.), *Feeling and thinking: The role of affect in social cognition* (pp. 31–58). New York: Cambridge University Press.

Measurement of Relative Metamnemonic Accuracy

Aaron S. Benjamin and Michael Diaz

Introduction

Evaluating metamnemonic accuracy is an inherently difficult enterprise as the theorist must contend with all of the usual variability inherent to normal memory behavior and additionally consider other sources that are relevant only to the metamnemonic aspects of the task. This chapter reviews the arguments motivating the use of the Goodman-Kruskal gamma coefficient γ in assessing metamnemonic accuracy and pits that statistic against a distance-based metric d_a derived from signal detection theory (Green & Swets, 1966). We evaluate the question of which potential measures of metamnemonic accuracy have the most desirable measurement characteristics and which measures support the types of inference that researchers commonly wish to draw. In doing so, we attempt to make general arguments without providing a detailed account of the underlying mathematics or statistics, but we do place appropriate references should those interested desire a more technical treatment of the issues that arise.

T. O. Nelson was a pioneer of methodologies in the field and a consistent devotee of increasing analytical sophistication and rigorous measurement (see, e.g., Gonzalez & Nelson, 1996; Nelson, 1984). Although not all of the conclusions reached in this chapter are the same as those reached in Nelson's (1984) classic article, we would hope that the work nonetheless is considered a testament to Nelson's legacy of meticulous attention to the quantitative foundations of metacognitive research.

Metamemory Experiments

To begin, let us briefly review the basic substance of metamemory experiments, the data table, and the traditional analytic approaches. Be forewarned that the field is diverse and complicated, and any general portrayal of a metamemory experiment is bound to be a caricature at best. We do not mean to trivialize the many varieties of experiment that do not fit into the mold, but many, if not most, experiments share certain common characteristics:

1. *A manipulation of study or judgment conditions.* Many experiments evaluate metamemory in the context of a manipulation of memory. This manipulation may consist of an orienting instruction (e.g., generating vs. reading; Begg, Vinski, Frankovich, & Holgate, 1991); an ecological (e.g., altitude; Nelson et al., 1990) or pharmacological (e.g., benzodiazepines; Mintzer & Griffiths, 2005) intervention; use of item repetition (Koriat, Sheffer, & Ma'ayan, 2002), list position (e.g., recency vs. primacy; Benjamin, Bjork, & Schwartz, 1998), interference (Diaz & Benjamin, 2008; Maki, 1999; Metcalfe, Schwartz, & Joaquim, 1993), or scheduling (e.g., spacing between repetitions; Benjamin & Bird, 2006; Dunlosky & Nelson, 1992; Simon & Bjork, 2001; Son, 2004); or varying item characteristics (e.g., high- versus low-frequency words; Benjamin, 2003). The intent is to induce a difference in performance between conditions (although this is not necessarily the case), in order to evaluate the degree to which metamnemonic judgments reflect that difference. In other cases, populations of subjects (e.g., older and younger [Hertzog, Kidder, Powell-Moman, & Dunlosky, 2002]; memory impaired and memory intact [Janowsky, Shimamura, & Squire, 1989]), rather than items are compared. Alternatively, the study conditions may be held constant but the conditions of the metacognitive evaluation may be manipulated. Such manipulations might vary, for example, the timing (Nelson & Dunlosky, 1991) or the speed (Benjamin, 2005; Reder, 1987) of the judgment. Note that this aspect of the procedure is often, but not always, experimental: Items are randomly assigned to conditions, and the full force of experimental paradigms can be brought to bear on this part of the design.

2. *A measure of metamemory.* At some point prior to (Underwood, 1966), during, or after study (Arbuckle & Cuddy, 1969; Groninger, 1979), or even after testing (as in, e.g., feelings of knowing [Hart, 1965] or confidence in answers [Chandler, 1994]), subjects are asked to make a deliberate judgment about their memory performance. Mostly, those judgments are made on an item-by-item basis, but they may be for a group of items or for the entire set of items in the experiment. Alternatively, subjects may be asked to make a decision about restudying items (Benjamin & Bird, 2006; Son, 2004; Thiede & Dunlosky, 1999), and it is presumed that such decisions implicitly reflect their judgments of memory (Finn & Metcalfe, 2006). These judgments may take place within a context that allows an interrogation of memory, such as when only the cue term of a cue–target pair is used to elicit the judgment (Dunlosky & Nelson, 1992), or one in which such interrogation is difficult (e.g., if the entire cue–target pair is presented or if responses are speeded; Benjamin, 2005; Reder, 1987).

3. *A test of memory.* After some delay following the judgment procedure, memory is queried. It is rare (cf. Nelson, Gerler, & Narens, 1984) to employ an experimental manipulation at this point because it is uninformative to examine the effects of a manipulation on judgments that precede that manipulation. However, aspects of the test, particularly its relative difficulty, may play a role in evaluating metamnemonic accuracy.

Evaluating Metamemory Accuracy

Now, consider the fundamental question of metamemory experiments: How well does metamemory reflect memory? Metamemory is considered to be accurate when subjects show some sort of a calibrated assessment of their memory's failings and successes. Bear in mind that a useful measure of metamnemonic accuracy should be independent of actual levels of memory performance.

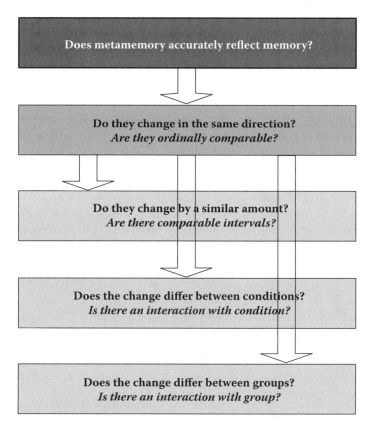

Figure 1   A taxonomy of questions about metamnemonic accuracy.

Figure 1 relates this fundamental question to the typical paradigm used to study metamemory and provides a rough taxonomy of questions ranked in order of measurement complexity. In rare circumstances, it might be informative to assess metamemory with reference to an absolute standard — for example, to evaluate whether a patient group reveals above-chance metamnemonic accuracy — but, more commonly, metamemory is tracked as a function of an experimental manipulation.

Ordinal Evaluation of the Experimental Factor

One straightforward analytic option is to jointly evaluate the effect of that manipulation on average memory performance and average metamemory judgments. Such paradigms are particularly powerful demonstrations when the effects of the variable are opposite for memory and metamemory (e.g., Benjamin, 2003; Benjamin et al., 1998; Diaz & Benjamin, 2008; Kelley & Lindsay, 1993; Metcalfe et al., 1993) but are limited by the inability to make interval-level comparisons between metamnemonic and mnemonic measures. This question is portrayed on the first sublevel of possible research questions in the hierarchy in Figure 1 to emphasize the minimal sophistication it requires on the part of the measurement scales: All that must be assumed is that higher scores indicate superior memory performance and a prediction of superior memory performance compared to lower scores. More complex demands are placed on those scales by the three questions that lie below this level.

Relationships Between Judgments and Performance

More often, the relationship between metamemory judgments and memory performance is assessed as a function of the manipulation. This relationship can be summarized in numerous ways, but the two most commonly used approaches are *calibration curves*, in which mean performance and mean judgments collapsed across a subset of items and conditions are jointly plotted, and *correlations*, in which the association between performance and judgments is evaluated. Calibration curves are used as a metric for *absolute* metamnemonic accuracy, or the degree to which mean rating values accurately estimate mean performance. Consequently, such analyses are only possible when ratings are made on scales isomorphic to probability scales and have certain interpretive (Gigerenzer, Hoffrage, & Kleinbolting, 1991) and analytic (Erev, Wallsten, & Budescu, 1994) difficulties (see also Keren, 1991). Such analyses are not the focus of this chapter and are not considered further here.

Correlational Measures

In contrast to absolute accuracy, *relative* metamnemonic accuracy is measured by the within-subject correlation of performance and predictions. Again, this assessment is usually made across conditions of a manipulation of memory. A good example is the delayed-judgment-of-learning effect (Nelson & Dunlosky, 1991), which is arguably the most robust and important effect in the metamemory literature. Nelson and Dunlosky (1991) showed that judgments about future recallability were much more highly correlated with later performance when a filled interval was interposed between study and judgments.

The consensual analytic tool for such paradigms is γ (Goodman & Kruskal, 1954, 1959), owing mainly to an influential article by Nelson (1984; see also Gonzalez & Nelson, 1996), in which γ was shown to be superior to a number of other measures of association, as well as to scores based on conditional probabilities and differences thereof (Hart, 1965), in terms of permitting a particular probabilistic interpretation of scores: What is the probability that Item X is remembered and Item Y is not given that Item X received a higher metacognitive judgment than Y?[1] Here, we reconsider that conclusion from the perspective of the three research questions at the bottom of Figure 1. For these cases, it is necessary to be in possession of data with relatively advanced metric qualities. To claim, for example, that a manipulation affects memory more than metamemory or that two groups who differ in baseline metamemory skills gain a differential amount from an intervention requires a measure that affords interval-level interpretation. The remainder of this chapter evaluates several candidate statistics for such qualities and reviews a solution based on the isosensitivity function of signal detection theory (SDT; e.g., Green & Swets, 1966; Peterson, Birdsall, & Fox, 1954; Swets, 1986a, 1986b). Nelson (1986, 1987) considered this alternative and rejected it, but we take a closer look at the debate, provide some supportive data for the SDT view with reanalyses of recent work, and demonstrate its metric qualities with simulated data sets. In addition, we show that a relatively simple transformation of γ improves its metric qualities and makes it comparable in certain ways to the measure derived from SDT.

Gamma and Its Use in Metamemory Research

Here, five major arguments in support of the use of γ are considered. These arguments derive primarily from the early work of Goodman and Kruskal (1959) as well as the psychologically motivated papers by Nelson (1984) and Gonzalez and Nelson (1996).

1. γ is easily generalized from the 2×2 case (in which it is equivalent to Q; Yule, 1912) to the $n \times m$ case. Thus, γ is appropriate when there are greater than two choices on the judgment scale.
2. Because there is no evidence concerning the form of the probability distributions relating future memory status (remembered or not) to the underlying judgment dimension, the machinery of SDT is unwarranted, and a purely nonparametric measure such as γ is preferred.
3. To the degree that γ is an efficient estimator, it should have desirably low error variance relative to other estimators. That quality increases the power to detect differences between conditions.
4. The γ coefficient bears a linear relationship to the probabilistic construal mentioned and thus has a transparent psychological interpretation in terms of subject performance (Nelson, 1984).
5. The γ coefficient is independent of criterion test performance, unlike other measures.

We shall consider each of these claims and revisit the adequacy of γ in light of the questions posed in Figure 1. Bear in mind that Nelson (1984) formulated these claims in the context of a search for a superior measure of feeling-of-knowing accuracy; here, we are more concerned with measuring metamemory more generally, and the prototype case we have in mind is in fact more like a typical judgment-of-learning (JOL) paradigm. It is not evident that this difference matters much.

Generalizability Across Experimental Designs

It is true that many alternative measures of association, such as phi, do not generalize coherently beyond the 2×2 case, and that such a limitation is undesirable for measuring metamnemonic accuracy. The γ coefficient is easily generalized to tables of arbitrary size, which makes it clearly superior in experiments in which predictions are more finely grained than binary ones. However, it is not clear that it is much of an advantage to be able to deal with more than two levels of the outcome variable; indeed, only the rare metamemory experiment has a memory outcome with more detail than "remembered" or "not remembered." In any case, the advantage of a measure that handles designs of $n \times m$ ($n,m \geq 2$) over one that effectively treats $2 \times m$ ($m \geq 2$) designs is likely minimal and may be offset by other relevant factors.

Signal Detection Theory Is Unsupported as an Analytic Tool

Unfortunately, it is not possible to do justice to the application of SDT to psychology in the limited space here (for further technical discussions, see Macmillan & Creelman, 2005; Wickens, 2001). Fundamentally, SDT relates performance in choice tasks to probability distributions of evidence conditionalized on the to-be-discriminated factor and decision criteria that partition that space into responses. Given the incredibly wide applicability of SDT to psychological tasks of detection and discrimination in perception (Swets, Tanner, & Birdsall, 1955), memory (Banks, 1970; Egan, 1958), and forecasting (Mason, 1982) and the impressive consistency of support across that wide array of tasks (Swets, 1986a), it certainly deserves a closer look in the case of metamemory. We do so and consider anew the unsupported assumptions pointed out by Nelson (1984, 1987).

Efficiency and Consistency

Measures derived from SDT have either lower error variance or usually lower error variance (that is, lower through a wide range of possible values) than does γ (Swets, 1986b, pp. 113–114). In addition, it has been noted that γ reveals disturbingly low levels of stability across alternative test forms, test halves, and even odd- and even-numbered items (Thompson & Mason, 1996; see also Nelson, 1988). Such low reliability calls into question experiments that fail to find differences between conditions, of which there are many.

A related question is whether γ is a consistent estimator — that is, whether the rate at which it approaches its asymptotic value with increasing sample size is as high as possible. Although we do not consider this property in detail, it is worth making note of one critical property of γ that is likely to influence consistency. As noted by Schwartz and Metcalfe (1994, Table 5.2), the fact that γ treats data purely ordinally — in terms of pairwise ranks — leads to both its desirable properties and perhaps some undesirable ones. A subject who assigns two item ratings of 5% and 95% probability of future recall is likely not making the same claim if the individual assigns those item ratings of 49% and 50%; yet, γ treats the cases equivalently. This property of γ is desirable only insofar as the prediction data are unlikely to have interval-level properties. Yet it discards vast amounts of information in treating them as purely ordinal. We will show that this treatment is overly conservative, and that relaxing that assumption only slightly affords the use of measures that may be more efficient and more consistent.

Psychological Interpretability

It is on the issue of psychological interpretability that much of our discussion centers. Nelson's (1984) argument about the clear relation between γ and the conditional judgment probability mentioned is a strong one, and we have no contention with the claim. However, we do question whether such a probabilistic interpretation affords the types of research questions and interpretations listed as the bottom three in Figure 1. That is, does the use of γ support interval-level analyses and conclusions? The answer is almost certainly no. At the very least, γ belongs to a class of measures (along with probability and other correlation measures) that are bounded on both ends. Measurement error leads to skewed sampling distributions at the margins of bounded scales and renders interpretation of intervals, and consequently interactions, difficult[2] (Nesselroade, Stigler, & Baltes, 1980; Willett, 1988). Schwartz and Metcalfe (1994) noted this problem in the context of between-group comparisons.

To be sure, this criticism is appropriately directed at a very wide range of analyses in the psychological literature (Cronbach & Furby, 1970), and we do not wish to imply any particular fault of researchers in metacognition. The important point is that equal intervals across a scale should not be assumed when treating psychological data, a point emphasized by Tom Nelson throughout much of his work. It is the burden of the theorizer to support such a claim prior to employing analyses that presume such measurement characteristics. To preview, it is on this very point that the application of SDT is most desirable. Measures of accuracy derived from SDT have interpretations rooted in geometry and are straightforwardly defensible as having interval characteristics.

Invariance With Criterion Test Performance

Nelson (1984, Figure 1) illustrated that γ, in contrast with a difference of conditional probabilities (Hart, 1965), was invariant with criterion test performance. However, Schwartz and Metcalfe (1994) noted that γ was not independent of the number of test alternatives in forced-choice recognition. Although we shall not consider the issue further here, it should be noted that γ may, under some conditions, vary with aspects of the task irrelevant to measurement of metamemory.

Signal Detection Theory and Metamemory Tasks

SDT provides an alternative solution to the question of how to summarize performance in contingency tables. The statistics of SDT are derived from a simple model of decision making under stimulus uncertainly, characterized by four basic assumptions (adopted from Benjamin, Diaz, & Wee, 2008):

1. Events are individual enumerable trials on which a signal is presented or not.
2. A strength value characterizes the evidence for the presence of the signal on a given trial.

3. Random variables characterize the probability distributions of strength values for signal-present and signal-absent events.
4. A scalar criterion serves to map the continuous strength variable onto a binary (or *n*-ary) decision variable.

For a metamemory task, it is assumed that stimuli that are later to be remembered (TBR) enjoy greater values of memory strength than stimuli that are later to be forgotten (TBF). The "memory strength" variable is really a variable by proxy; in fact, one of the great benefits of SDT is that, although an evidence axis needs to be postulated, it need not be identified. It simply reflects the evidence that can be gleaned from a stimulus regarding its memorability or, in this case, its perceived memorability.

To the degree that subjects can perform such a discrimination accurately — that is, if they can claim which items they will remember and which they will not at a rate greater than chance — then the distribution for TBR items must have generally higher values of memory strength than the distribution for TBF items. This is shown in the top panel of Figure 2. Evidence values (e_1 and e_2) are experienced by the subject and compared to a criterion C; in the case illustrated in Figure 2, the subject would reject the item yielding e_1 evidence and endorse the item yielding e_2 evidence.

SDT has been used primarily as a tool to aid in the separation of decision components of choice tasks from the actual sensitivity of the judgment. Sensitivity is a function of the overlap of the inferred probability distributions, and the placement of decision criterion (or criteria) represents the decision aspect of the task. As a theoretical device, *isosensitivity* functions can be plotted that relate the probability of a metacognitive hit (claiming that I will remember an item that will in fact be remembered later) to the probability of a metacognitive false alarm (claiming that I will remember an item that will not be remembered later). This function is a plot of how those values vary jointly as the criterion moves from a lenient position to a conservative one (or vice-versa). The bottom left panel for Figure 2 shows the isosensitivity function corresponding to the distributions in the top part of the figure in probability coordinates; the bottom right panel shows that same function in normal-deviate coordinates.

Empirical isosensitivity functions are useful in part because they allow one to evaluate whether the assumptions about the shapes of the probability distributions are valid. Specifically, normal probability distributions yield perfectly linear isosensitivity contours in normal-deviate coordinates, as shown in the bottom right panel of Figure 2 (Green & Swets, 1966). It has been claimed that the linearity of such functions is not a strong test of those assumptions because many different probability functions yield approximately linear forms (Lockhart & Murdock, 1970; Nelson, 1987). This is only partially true. Because the isosensitivity function is constrained to be monotonically increasing, there are many distributional forms that yield functions for which a large proportion of the variance (even above 95% in some cases) is linear. However, all forms except the normal distribution will lead to a nonlinear component as well. Consequently, an appropriate test is whether the addition of a nonlinear component to a linear regression model increases the quality of the fit. We present such a test and show that, contrary to the admonitions of Nelson (1987), SDT provides a viable model of the information representation and decision-making

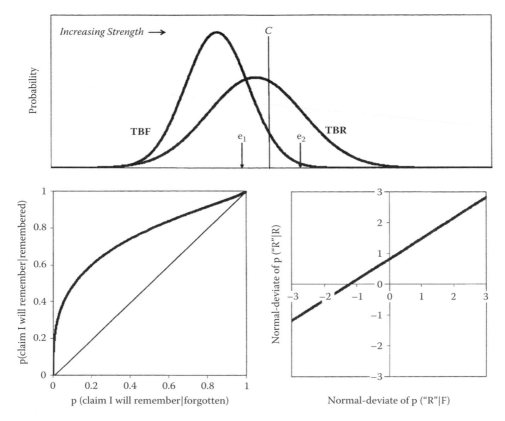

Figure 2 The signal detection theoretic framework and the isosensitivity function. Top panel: Normal probability distributions of strength for eventually forgotten (left) and remembered (right) items. e1 and e2 indicate possible values of experienced strength, or evidence, for future memorability. C indicates the location of a decision criterion. Bottom panels: Isosensitivity functions corresponding to the distributions shown in the top panel in probability coordinates (left) and normal-deviate coordinates (right).

process underlying metacognitive judgments. Let us first turn to the nitty-gritty of computing an isosensitivity function for metamemory data.

The Detection-Theoretic Analysis of a Metamemory Task

SDT analysis requires that our data be tabulated in the form of a contingency table. This requirement is straightforward in the case of a metamemory task, in large part because such a formulation is consistent with the computation of γ. Such a table is shown in the top right of Figure 3. Note that the data must be in a $2 \times m$ table in which there are m rating classes and two potential outcomes — presumably, remembered and forgotten. In the present example, there are six rating classes, with 1 indicating that the subject is very confident that they will *not* remember the stimulus and 6 indicating that they are very confident that they *will* remember it.

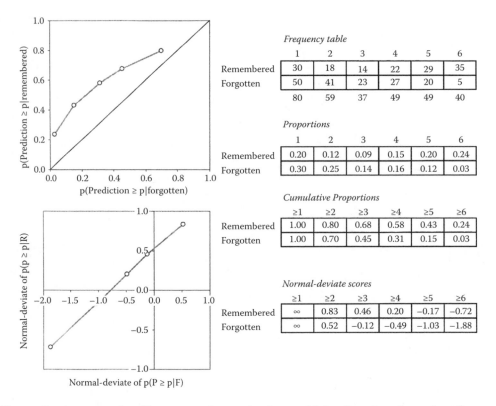

Figure 3 An example of how to estimate the isosensitivity function from data from a metamemory experiment.

Several additional transformations are necessary and are shown vertically on the right of Figure 3. First, frequencies are converted to proportions of each outcome class (shown in the second table on the right side of Figure 3). Those proportions are cumulated from right to left across the rating scale, such that the sixth cell in a row contains the proportion of 6 responses, the fifth cell in a row contains the proportion of a 5 or a 6 response, and so on. These cumulative proportions are treated as increasingly liberal response criteria, and a joint plot of those values yields the isosensitivity function shown in the top left of Figure 3. Note that the most liberal point is always going to be (1,1) since it reflects the cumulative probability of *any* response. The final data table shows the cumulative proportions after an inverse-cumulative normal transformation (i.e., changing from proportions to z scores) and yields the normal-deviate isosensitivity plot shown in the bottom left.

The sensitivity of the ratings can be understood as either the degree to which the theoretical distributions overlap, as mentioned, or as the distance of the isosensitivity function from chance performance, indicated in the top function as the major diagonal and in the bottom function as an unshown linear contour passing through the scale origin. We introduce one measure d_a that corresponds to the shortest possible distance from the origin (scaled by $\sqrt{2}$) to the isosensitivity function in the bottom plot. That value can be easily computed:

$$d_a = \frac{\sqrt{2}y_0}{\sqrt{1+m^2}}$$

in which y_0 and m represent the y-intercept and slope, respectively, of the normal-deviate isosensitivity function. The d_a can be conceptualized in terms of the geometry of the isosensitivity function, as defined above, or in terms of the distributional formulation in the top part of Figure 2; in that case, d_a is the distance between the means of the normal distributions divided by the root-mean-square average of their standard deviations.

Using d_a to measure metamemory accuracy is a novel suggestion to our knowledge. There was some consideration of whether d' — a similar but not equivalent measure — is an appropriate score to measure metamnemonic accuracy (Nelson, 1984, 1987; Wellman, 1977). The d' measures the distance between the probability distributions scaled by a common standard deviation. The assumption of common variance has proven incorrect in most substantive domains (Swets, 1986a) but is nonetheless commonly used because it can be computed on the ubiquitous 2 × 2 data table. At least a 2 × 3 table is required for d_a, and its fit is only testable with a minimum of four columns. Such a characteristic is hardly a limitation in metamemory research, however; it simply implies that subjects' rating scale must contain more than two discrete choices. In fact, it is more commonly necessary to construct judgment quantiles from prediction data to *reduce* the number of points in isosensitivity space (and thus also increase the precision of the estimates). In the next section, we directly address the question of whether the SDT model of metamnemonic judgment is an accurate one.

Analyses of Metamemory Tasks

Nelson (1984) wrote, "Unfortunately, there is no evidence in the feeling-of-knowing literature … to justify the assumption that the underlying distributions are normal" (p. 121). In this section, we present such evidence. We consider two data sets. The first is from our recent work (Diaz & Benjamin, 2008), for which the prediction task is on a scale of 0 to 100, and the criterion task is cued recall. For the second data set (Benjamin, 2003), the prediction is on a 1-to-9 scale, and the criterion tasks are both recognition and free recall. We have deliberately chosen tasks that differ substantively in order to demonstrate the robustness of the analysis.

Analysis of Diaz and Benjamin (2008)

These experiments involved multiple study–test trials with paired-associate terms, over which proactive interference was introduced by reusing cue terms. One condition is reported here in which there were 20 items per studied list (henceforth, the difficult condition), and another condition is reported in which there were 10 or 16 items per list (the easy condition).[3]

TABLE 1   An Example of How to Compute Quantile Frequencies Under Conditions With Tied Boundary Scores

Data Table					
JOL	0	20	40	40	40
Recall	0	1	0	1	1

Frequency Table			
	Q1	Q2	Total
Remembered	$1 + 0.5(2/3) = 1.33$	$2.5(2/3) = 1.67$	3
Forgotten	$1 + 0.5(1/3) = 1.17$	$2.5(1/3) = 0.83$	2
Total	2.5	2.5	5

Because the prediction data were on a 0-to-100 scale, the first step was to convert those data to quantile form. To get a reasonable estimate of the isosensitivity function, there should be a sufficient number of bins to estimate the shape of the function adequately (at least four and ideally five or more) and a sufficient number of observations to avoid very low frequencies in any particular bin. A good rule of thumb is to have subjects try to distribute their judgments more or less evenly across the rating scale and to try to have no fewer than 20 of each rating. In this case, the number of discrete ratings was actually greater than the number of observations, so it was necessary to convert the data to quantiles.

For each subject, individual matrices of performance and JOLs were sorted by JOL magnitude and divided into six bins. The goal was to have each bin contain an equal number of items and to partition those items by whether they were eventually recalled (or recognized). Because the total number of items was not always divisible by six, the column totals were not always integers. In addition, because of numerous ties on the JOL variable, some interpolation was necessary. Table 1 gives a simple example of how this was done. In this example, there are five total items to be divided into two bins. Thus, the marginal total for each (column) quantile bin must be 2.5. Because there are three remembered and two forgotten items, the row totals are also fixed.

In the first quantile, there is one item that is remembered, one that is forgotten (those values are in bold in the table) and half of an item remaining with a value that must be interpolated from the remaining tied scores. Because only one of those three tied scores represents a forgotten item, one third of the remaining half item is allocated to the forgotten bin and two thirds are allocated to the remembered bin. Similarly, for the second quantile, all of the members are tied and lie on the bin boundary. Thus, of the 2.5 total items, one third is allocated to the forgotten bin and two thirds to the remembered bin.

Parameters for the SDT model were estimated individually for each subject using maximum likelihood estimation (Ogilvie & Creelman, 1968). Linear regression accounted for a mean of 97.2% and 96.4% of the individual subject's data in the easy and difficult conditions, respectively. The addition of a quadratic term increased the mean variance accounted for to 99.1% and 98.7%, respectively; this increase was

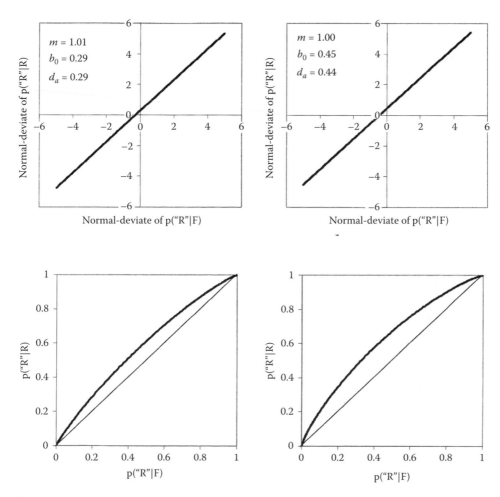

Figure 4   Isosensitivity functions in probability (top) and normal-deviate (bottom) coordinates for the difficult (left) and easy (right) conditions drawn from Diaz and Benjamin (2008).

reliable in only 2% of the subjects in each condition.[4] This value is lower than the chance probability of 5%. In addition, the mean value of the quadratic term in the full model was not reliably different from 0 in either condition. These findings suggest that the assumption of normally distributed evidence holds in these data.

Average isosensitivity functions based on the mean parameters of the linear model across subjects are shown in Figure 4. These data reveal that metamemory performance is in fact superior in the easy condition. The d_a values shown in Figure 4 are for the average functions shown in the figure; mean d_a values based on individual subject performance were similar but revealed an even larger difference (d_a [easy] = 0.51, d_a [difficult] = 0.25). The difference between conditions was reliable (t [169] = 4.23) and confirmed a similar result obtained using γ (γ_{easy} = 0.32, $\gamma_{difficult}$ = 0.19; t [169] = 3.49), but with a larger effect size.

Analysis of Benjamin (2003)

In this experiment (Benjamin, 2003, Experiment 3), subjects made predictions of recognition performance on a 1-to-9 scale, took a test of recognition followed by an additional prediction phase for a test of recall, and then took the recall test. Unlike the case just described, frequencies did not need to be interpolated. However, because performance was so high on the recognition test, there were a number of subjects for whom the fit of isosensitivity functions could not be evaluated; those subjects were dropped from the analysis of the shape of the function.

Linear regression accounted for a mean of 84.7% and 85.8% of the individual subject's data in the recognition and recall conditions, respectively. Quadratic regression increased the mean fit to 89.3% and 93.6%, respectively. Despite the larger increase than in the previous analysis, the magnitude of the increase was reliable in only 3% of the cases. As before, the mean value of the quadratic term in the full model was not reliably different from 0 in either condition. The assumption of normally distributed evidence was thus supported in this data set as well.

Mean values of d_a were 0.44 and 0.51 for recognition and recall, respectively. Corresponding values of γ were 0.29 and 0.38. Neither difference was reliable, but all values were reliably different from 0.

Scale Characteristics of d_a and γ

The analyses reported in the previous section indicate that the application of the machinery of SDT to the traditional metamemory task is valid and thus permits the use of d_a as a measure of metamemory performance. Because d_a is rooted firmly in the geometry of the isosensitivity function, it has interpretive value as a measure of distance and all of the advantages that such an interpretation affords: equal intervals across the scale range and a meaningful 0. Like actual distance, d_a is bounded only at 0 and ∞.[5]

Let us now return to the question of the metric qualities of γ. We claimed that γ could not have interval-level properties because of its inherent boundaries. In the next section, we simulate data based on the confirmed assumptions that were tested and evaluate exactly how well γ performs and whether simple transformations are possible that increase its metric qualities. The strategy we use to evaluate γ and other measures is to generate data based on a population profile with a known metric space and then test the ability of γ, d_a, and other measures to recover that metric space. We use the assumption of normal probability distributions to generate simulated metamemory strengths for recalled and unrecalled items and apply different measures of metamemory accuracy to assess performance in those simulated data.

Simulations

For each of 1,000 sim-subjects, memory performance on 100 test trials was simulated by randomly sampling profiles from a normal distribution with a mean of 50 and

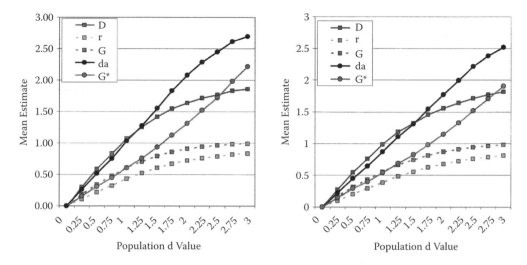

Figure 5   Estimates of *r* (the Pearson correlation coefficient), *D* (the Hart difference score), γ (the Goodman-Kruskal gamma correlation), and d_a (a distance measure based on signal detection theory) as a function of the distance between generating distributions. The degree of linearity of the function reveals the potential of the statistic for use in drawing interval-level inferences on data. Left panel: Signal variability = 1. Right panel: Signal variability = 1.5.

variance of 10. The profile represented the number of items recalled out of 100 for each sim-subject. Then, for each unremembered item, an evidence score was drawn from a normal distribution with mean 0 and variance 1, and for each remembered item an evidence score was drawn from a normal distribution with mean *d* and variance *s*. These scores were transformed into confidence ratings by relation to three criteria that were set for most simulations to lie at the mean of the noise distribution, the mean of the signal distribution, and halfway between the two. This transformation produced a matrix of memory scores (0 or 1) and confidence ratings (1, 2, 3, or 4) that was used to estimate the values of several candidate metamemory statistics, including γ, d_a, *r* (the Pearson correlation coefficient), and *D* (the difference in mean judgments between recalled and unrecalled items; Hart, 1965).

Results

The first important set of results can be seen in Figure 5, in which each statistic is plotted as a function of *d* (with *s* = 1 in the left panel and *s* = 1.5 in the right panel). The major diagonal indicates perfect recovery of the parameter *d*. Several general patterns are evident. First, the correlation measures suffer, as expected, near the boundary of the scale and exhibit a decided nonlinearity. Second, differential variability in the strength distributions (shown in the right portion of the figure) decreases the overall fit of all measures and results in estimates that are biased to be low. Because our estimates of the variability of the signal distribution were in fact quite close to 1, we consider more closely here the case in the left panel.

Because the two correlation statistics r and γ have probabilistic interpretations, they should not be expected to fall on the major diagonal. However, the important aspect of the failure of these measures is the clear nonlinearity. If a statistic is a linear transformation of the population value, then the estimator can be claimed to have interval-level properties. As noted, the boundary on r and γ introduce nonlinearity; consequently, a linear fit accounts for only 91% and 85% of those functions, respectively. The much-maligned Hart difference score statistic D fares better than γ but is also limited by a functional asymptote due to the judgment scale range (89%). However, it performs admirably over a limited range of performance. D_a outperforms the other statistics substantially at 98% linearity, and its failures lie only at the extreme end of the performance scale. D_a is thus the most promising candidate for drawing interval-level inferences from metamemory data.

The correlation measures suffer on this test because of the boundaries at -1 and 1. Thus, to test those measures more fairly, we additionally consider transformations of r and γ that remove the compromising effects of those boundaries. One commonly used function that serves this purpose is the logit, or log odds, which is defined as

$$Logit\ X = \log\left(\frac{X}{1-X}\right)$$

This function only operates validly on positive values; thus, rather than use G, we use the transformation of γ that Nelson (1984) called V and is presented in our footnote 1. Here, we define G^* as the logit of that value. It is related to γ as follows:

$$G^* = \log\left(\frac{\gamma+1}{1-\gamma}\right).$$

The linearity of the relationship between the candidate measures G^* and r^* (the equivalently transformed Pearson correlation coefficient) and the population value from which the data were generated was assessed. This transformation increased the fit of a linear relationship from below 95% to over 99% for both measures under both simulation conditions. It thus appears as though G^* (and r^*, for that matter) is a promising candidate for evaluation of interval-level hypotheses. However, several characteristics are noteworthy. First, G^* is $-\infty$ when $\gamma = -1$ and ∞ at $\gamma = 1$ (i.e., when performance is perfect), which means that it is quite unstable at the margins of performance. The untransformed measure γ does not have this unfortunate property, but this is the price that is paid by the conversion to a more valid measurement scale. Second, it allows for no obvious and immediate interpretation in terms of behavior or theory, although this disadvantage is mitigated by its easy translation to and from γ.

Several other conditions were simulated to assess the robustness of these effects. When the criteria are placed in either nonoptimally conservative or lenient locations, the fit of d_a is decreased by an order of magnitude smaller amount ($\Delta R^2 = 0.003$) than is γ ($\Delta R^2 = 0.03$), but both d_a and G^* are equally linear (~99%). Adding variance to the signal distribution increases linearity slightly; this general effect likely reflects the well-known advantage of rendering the frequency distribution of ratings more uniform. In all cases, d_a, G^*, and r^* all provide excellent fits (~99%). When the numbers of items and subjects are reduced to more validly approximate conditions of a typical experiment on metamemory (20 items for 20 subjects, with a mean performance of 10 and variance of 3), all fits suffer, but r^* outperforms all others (~97%) with G^* not far behind (~95%). Under conditions of relatively low or high mean memory performance (mean of 20 or 80 items remembered out of 100), none of the statistics (d_a, G^*, or r^*) shows an appreciable drop in fit.

The bottom line of these simulations is that the greater linearity of d_a extends over a great variety of conditions, and that a logit transformation of V improves its linearity significantly. The superiority of d_a should not be surprising given that the data were generated using assumptions that are built into signal detection theory. However, the robustness of the effect, as well as the poor performance of γ and quite impressive performance of G^*, should be surprising. It would appear that γ is a poor choice of a statistic for use in interval-level comparisons, such as those indicated in the bottom three lines of Figure 1. Either G^* or d_a should be used in experimental designs that invite interval-level comparison.

Turning to the question of measurement variance, γ fares much better. In fact, across all of the simulated conditions described above, the coefficient of variation (COV; a ratio of the standard deviation to the mean) was consistently lowest for γ. This is especially true at high levels of metamemory performance ($d > 2$). There are three important caveats to this finding. First, it is difficult to know to what extent the boundary at 1 on γ influences this effect. However, this concern has limited practical implications. More worrisome, there is a marked heteroskedasticity in estimates of γ as a function of d, and this effect has the potential to lead to analytic complications. In addition, it appears that at least some of that variability may be legitimate individual-difference variability that is lost by γ: Reducing memory variance in the simulations to 0 reduces (but does not eliminate) the advantage of γ over d_a in terms of COV. It does thus appear that the types of noise introduced in the simulations described here lead to greater variability in estimates of d_a than γ. This finding merited a closer look at empirical comparisons of the two measures.

Empirical Comparisons of Coefficient of Variation

The smaller COV in γ than d_a could reflect an oversimplification in the simulation or an empirical regularity. If it is in fact an empirical regularity, then it might temper our enthusiasm for d_a somewhat. We reexamined the data from Diaz and Benjamin (2008) and Benjamin (2003) and estimated the COV across both experiments. For the Diaz and Benjamin (2008) data, the estimates were equivalent (COV = 0.98). For the Benjamin (2003) data, COV for recognition was lower using d_a (1.25) than γ (1.56), but slightly higher for d_a (0.77) than γ (0.72) on the recall test. This result confirmed the claim that the superiority of γ in the simulations was a combination of devaluing individual-difference variability and the marked simplification of the generating process yielding rating data. Overall, the measures appear to be more or less equivalent in terms of COV.

Summary

Here, we have taken a closer look at the question of what types of measures might best support the types of inferences researchers wish to draw using metamemory data. In doing so, we have taken advantage of the theoretical framework of signal detection theory (Green & Swets, 1966; Peterson et al., 1954) and evaluated whether data from two metamemory experiments (Benjamin, 2003; Diaz & Benjamin, 2008) were consistent with the assumptions of that framework. Because those assumptions were strongly supported, we have advised that d_a and measures like it (MacMillan & Creelman, 2005; Wickens, 2001) can profitably be used as measures of metamemory. Using SDT, we have made our assumptions about the process of making metamemory judgments as explicit as possible. Using data simulated on the basis of those confirmed assumptions, we have shown that γ is unlikely to have those desirable interval-level characteristics, and we thus advise against its use when interactions, between-group comparisons, and across-scale comparisons are used. An alternative is to use G^*, which is a simple monotonic transformation of γ (or r^*, which is the equivalent transformation of Pearson's r), which appears to have superior measurement characteristics. However, these statistics suffer from certain characteristics as well: They are highly variable at their extremes, and they do not have an obvious or transparent interpretation in terms of subject behavior (like γ) or psychological theory (like d_a). Nonetheless, one possibility is to use γ except in analyses that require interval-level data and use G^* for such analyses. The disadvantages of such an approach relative to the use of d_a and signal detection theory are minimized.

With these recommendations, there are a few important details to keep in mind when estimating the isosensitivity function from metamemory data. First, there must be a reasonably large number of both remembered and unremembered items. When there is not, the probability of empty cells in the frequency table is undesirably high, and the isosensitivity function may be underdetermined. This recommendation should be familiar as γ is also notably unstable when there are not sufficient numbers of remembered and unremembered items. Ideal performance is at 50%.

Second, it is important that subjects use the full range of the judgment scale. This recommendation is much more important for the isosensitivity function than for γ because estimating that function takes advantage of the ordering of judgments (i.e., that $1 < 2 < 3 < 4$), whereas γ evaluates judgments only on a pairwise basis. Subjects should specifically be instructed to use the full range of the rating scale if the isosensitivity function is to be estimated.

Third, the rating scale should have at least four options. Bear in mind that m options lead to a curve with $m - 1$ points, and that subjects who perform particularly well or particularly poorly may yield fewer than $m - 1$ usable points. In addition, if the assumption of normal probability distribution functions is to be tested as part of the analysis, then there must be sufficient points to fit and test a quadratic function (i.e., > 3). In that case, the rating scale should have at least five options. We recommend the use of a semicontinuous scale, like the subjective probability scale described in Diaz and Benjamin (2008) and the quantile estimation procedure developed in this chapter and depicted in Table 1. This technique deals well with individual differences in scale use that are more difficult to rectify with a scale with fewer options.

For researchers who wish to evaluate the differential effectiveness of a manipulation on metamnemonic accuracy, either within or between groups, it is critical to have in hand a dependent measure that can be defended as having interval-level properties. The measure reviewed here, d_a, has such qualities to a much greater degree than does the commonly used γ, and we hope that the review provided here helps researchers better evaluate their measurement options and use d_a fruitfully in appropriate cases or use an appropriate transformation of γ under the necessary conditions.

Notes

1. Nelson called the value associated with this interpretation V, and it is related to γ by the following relationship: $V = 0.5\gamma + 0.5$.
2. Remember that "crossover" interactions, which require only an ordinal interpretation, are not subject to such a concern, as noted here.
3. The difficult condition corresponds to Experiment 1 in Diaz and Benjamin (2006) and the easy condition to Experiment 2. Both data sets reported here include additional versions of the experiments not reported in that article.
4. Model fit was tested as,

$$F = \left(\frac{\triangle R^2}{1 - R_{full}^2} \right) \left(\frac{N - K_{full} - 1}{K_{full} - K_{reduced}} \right)$$

in which N represents the number of data points (the number of points on the isosensitivity function) and K the number of parameters in each model (in this case, three in the full model and two in the reduced model). There were five points on the isosensitivity function for all but 6 subjects who had false alarm rates of 0 or hit rates of 1 for one rating range. Those subjects were omitted from this analysis because the F ratio was indeterminate. The test distribution was thus $F(1, 1)$ with $\alpha = .05$, two tailed.
5. Strictly speaking, d_a is bounded at $-\infty$ and ∞ because the mean of the signal distribution can theoretically lie to the left of the mean of the noise distribution. However, values less than 0 reveal below-chance performance and thus should only arise because of measurement noise or perverse subject behavior.

References

Arbuckle, T. Y., & Cuddy, L. L. (1969). Discrimination of item strength at time of presentation. *Journal of Experimental Psychology, 81,* 126–131.

Banks, W. P. (1970). Signal detection theory and human memory. *Psychological Bulletin, 74,* 81–99.

Begg, I., Vinski, E., Frankovich, L., & Holgate, B. (1991). Generating makes words memorable, but so does effective reading. *Memory & Cognition, 19,* 487–497.

Benjamin, A. S. (2003). Predicting and postdicting the effects of word frequency on memory. *Memory & Cognition, 31,* 297–305.

Benjamin, A. S. (2005). Response speeding mediates the contribution of cue familiarity and target retrievability to metamnemonic judgments. *Psychonomic Bulletin & Review, 12,* 874–879.

Benjamin, A. S., & Bird, R. D. (2006). Metacognitive control of the spacing of study repetitions. *Journal of Memory and Language, 55,* 126–137.

Benjamin, A. S., Bjork, R. A., & Schwartz, B. L. (1998). The mismeasure of memory: When retrieval fluency is misleading as a metamnemonic index. *Journal of Experimental Psychology: General, 127,* 55–68.

Benjamin, A. S., Diaz, M., & Wee, S. (2008). *Signal detection with criterial variability: Applications to recognition memory.* Manuscript under review.

Chandler, C. C. (1994). Studying related pictures can reduce accuracy, but increase confidence, in a modified recognition test. *Memory & Cognition, 22,* 273–280.

Cronbach, L. J., & Furby, L. (1970). How we should measure "change": Or should we? *Psychological Bulletin, 74,* 68–80.

Diaz, M., & Benjamin, A. S. (2008). *The effects of proactive interference (PI) and release from PI on judgments of learning.* Manuscript under review.

Dunlosky, J., & Nelson, T. O. (1992). Importance of the kind of cue for judgments of learning (JOL) and the delayed-JOL effect. *Memory & Cognition, 20,* 374–380.

Egan, J. P. (1958). *Recognition memory and the operating characteristic.* USAF Operational Applications Laboratory Technical Note No. 58–51.

Erev, I., Wallsten, T. S., & Budescu, D. V. (1994). Simultaneous over- and underconfidence: The role of error in judgment processes. *Psychological Review, 101,* 519–527.

Finn, B., & Metcalfe, J. (2006). *Judgments of learning are causally related to study choice.* Manuscript in preparation.

Gigerenzer, G., Hoffrage, U., & Kleinbolting, H. (1991). Probabilistic mental models: A Brunswikian theory of confidence. *Psychological Review, 98,* 506–528.

Gonzalez, R., & Nelson, T. O. (1996). Measuring ordinal association in situations that contain tied scores. *Psychological Bulletin, 119,* 159–165.

Goodman, L. A., & Kruskal, W. H. (1954). Measures of association for cross classifications. *Journal of the American Statistical Associations, 49,* 732–764.

Goodman, L. A., & Kruskal, W. H. (1959). Measures of association for cross classifications: II. Further discussions and references. *Journal of the American Statistical Association, 54,* 123–163.

Green, D. M., & Swets, J. A. (1966). *Signal detection theory and psychophysics.* New York: Wiley.

Groninger, L. D. (1979). Predicting recall: The "feeling-that-I-know" phenomenon. *American Journal of Psychology, 92,* 45–58.

Hart, J. T. (1965). Memory and the feeling-of-knowing experience. *Journal of Educational Psychology, 56,* 208–216.

Hertzog, C., Kidder, D. P., Powell-Moman, A., & Dunlosky, J. (2002). Aging and monitoring associative learning: Is monitoring accuracy spared or impaired? *Psychology and Aging, 17,* 209–225.

Janowsky, J. S., Shimamura, A. P., & Squire, L. R. (1989). Memory and metamemory: Comparisons between patients with frontal lobe lesions and amnesic patients. *Psychobiology, 17,* 3–11.

Kelley, C. M., & Lindsay, D. S. (1993). Remembering mistaken for knowing: Ease of retrieval as a basis for confidence in answers to general knowledge questions. *Journal of Memory and Language, 32,* 1–24.

Keren, G. (1991). Calibration and probability judgments: Conceptual and methodological issues. *Acta Psychologica, 77,* 217–173.

Koriat, A., Sheffer, L., & Ma'ayan, H. (2002). Comparing objective and subjective learning curves: Judgments of learning exhibit increased underconfidence with practice. *Journal of Experimental Psychology: General, 131,* 147–162.

Lockhart, R. S., & Murdock, B. B. (1970). Memory and the theory of signal detection. *Psychological Bulletin, 74*, 100–109.

Macmillan, N. A., & Creelman, C.D. (2005). *Detection theory: A user's guide* (2nd ed.). Mahwah, NJ: Erlbaum.

Maki, R. H. (1999). The role of competition, target accessibility, and cue familiarity in metamemory for word pairs. *Journal of Psychology: Learning, Memory, and Cognition, 25*, 1011–1023.

Mason, I. (1982). *On scores for yes/no forecasts.* Paper presented at the Ninth Conference on Weather Forecasting and Analysis, Australian Meteorological Society (pp. 169–174), Seattle, WA.

Metcalfe, J., Schwartz, B. L., & Joaquim, S. G. (1993). The cue-familiarity heuristic in metacognition. *Journal of Experimental Psychology: Learning, Memory, and Cognition, 19*, 851–864.

Mintzer, M. Z., & Griffiths, R. R. (2005). Drugs, memory, and metamemory: A dose-effect study with lorazepam and scopolamine. *Experimental and Clinical Psychopharmacology, 13*, 336–347.

Nelson, T. O. (1984). A comparison of current measures of feeling-of-knowing accuracy. *Psychological Bulletin, 95*, 109–133.

Nelson, T. O. (1986). ROC curves and measures of discrimination accuracy: A reply to Swets. *Psychological Bulletin, 100*, 128–132.

Nelson, T. O. (1987). The Goodman-Kruskal gamma coefficient as an alternative to signal-detection theory's measures of absolute-judgment accuracy. In E. E. Roskam & R. Suck (Eds.), *Progress in mathematical psychology* (pp. 299–306). New York: Elsevier Science.

Nelson, T. O. (1988). Predictive accuracy of the feeling of knowing across different criterion tasks and across different subject populations and individuals. In M. M. Gruneberg (Ed.), *Practical aspects of memory: Current research and issues* (pp. 190–196). New York: Wiley.

Nelson, T. O., & Dunlosky, J. (1991). When people's judgments of learning (JOLs) are extremely accurate at predicting subsequent recall: The "delayed-JOL effect." *Psychological Science, 2*, 267–270.

Nelson, T. O., Dunlosky, J., White, D. M., Steinberg, J., Townes, B. D., & Anderson, D. (1990). Cognition and metacognition at extreme altitudes on Mount Everest. *Journal of Experimental Psychology: General, 119*, 367–374.

Nelson, T. O., Gerler, D., & Narens, L. (1984). Accuracy of feeling-of-knowing judgments for predicting perceptual identification and relearning. *Journal of Experimental Psychology: General, 113*, 282–300.

Nesselroade, J. R., Stigler, S. M., & Baltes, P. B. (1980). Regression toward the mean and the study of change. *Psychological Bulletin, 88*, 622–637.

Ogilvie, J. C., & Creelman, C. D. (1968). Maximum-likelihood estimation of receiver operating characteristic curve parameters. *Journal of Mathematical Psychology, 5*, 377–391.

Peterson, W. W., Birdsall, T. G., & Fox, W. C. (1954). The theory of signal detectability. *Transactions of the IRE Professional Group on Information Theory, PGIT-4*, 171–212.

Reder, L. M. (1987). Strategy selection in question answering. *Cognitive Psychology, 19*, 90–138.

Schwartz, B. L., & Metcalfe, J. (1994). Methodological problems and pitfalls in the study of human metacognition. In J. Metcalfe & A. P. Shimamura (Eds.), *Metacognition: Knowing about knowing* (pp. 93–113). Cambridge, MA: MIT Press.

Simon, D. A., & Bjork, R. A. (2001). Metacognition in motor learning. *Journal of Experimental Psychology: Learning, Memory, and Cognition, 27*, 907–912.

Son, L. K. (2004). Spacing one's study: Evidence for a metacognitive control strategy. *Journal of Experimental Psychology: Learning, Memory, and Cognition, 30*, 601–604.

Swets, J. A. (1986a). Form of empirical ROCs in discrimination and diagnostic tasks: Implications for theory and measurement of performance. *Psychological Bulletin, 99*, 181–198.

Swets, J. A. (1986b). Indices of discrimination or diagnostic accuracy: Their ROCs and implied models. *Psychological Bulletin, 99*, 100–117.

Swets, J. A., Tanner, W. P., Jr., & Birdsall, T. G. (1955). *The evidence for a decision making theory of visual detection.* Technical Report No. 40, University of Michigan, Electronic Defense Group.

Thiede, K. W., & Dunlosky, J. (1999). Toward a general model of self-regulated study: An analysis of selection of items for study and self-paced study time. *Journal of Experimental Psychology: Learning, Memory, and Cognition, 25*, 1024–1037.

Thompson, W. B., & Mason, S. E. (1996). Instability of individual differences in the association between confidence judgments and memory performance. *Memory & Cognition, 24*, 226–234.

Underwood, B. J. (1966). Individual and group predictions of item difficulty for free learning. *Journal of Experimental Psychology, 71*, 673–679.

Wellman, H. M. (1977). Tip of the tongue and feeling of knowing experiences: A developmental study of memory monitoring. *Child Development, 48*, 13–21.

Wickens, T. D. (2001). *Elementary signal detection theory.* London: Oxford University Press.

Willett, J. B. (1988). Questions and answers in the measurement of change. In E. Z. Rothkopf (Ed.), *Review of research in education* (Vol. 15, pp. 345–422). Washington, DC: American Education Research Association.

Yule, G. U. (1912). On the methods of measuring the association between two attributes. *Journal of the Royal Statistical Society, 75*, 579–652.

Measuring Memory and Metamemory:

Theoretical and Statistical Problems with Assessing Learning (in General) and Using Gamma (in Particular) to Do So

Barbara A. Spellman, Aaron Bloomfield, and Robert A. Bjork

Introduction

This chapter addresses the interrelated problems of assessing learning in general and using γ (the Goodman-Kruskal γ correlation), in particular, to do so. We carry out our analysis in the context of the metamemory literature on judgments of learning (JOLs), but we believe that the lessons learned are widely applicable.

Consequences of Assessing Learning

In what has become a classic metamemory paper, Dunlosky and Nelson (1992) had participants study paired associates such as ocean–tree. Later, the experimenters re-presented the same items and asked participants to judge how likely they would be to remember the second word if shown the first word 10 minutes later (i.e., they were asked to make JOLs in the form of predicting their future recall performance). There were two independent variables of interest. The first was delay: JOLs were made either immediately (i.e., the next trial after the words were presented) or after some number of intervening (presentation or JOL) trials. The second was type of presentation at the time of making the JOL: Participants saw either the intact cue–target pair (i.e., ocean–tree) or the cue alone (i.e., ocean–?). As measured by γ, JOLs were far more accurate in the delayed cue-only condition than any other condition. The superiority of the delayed cue-only condition is an important effect (e.g., for evaluating whether one has studied enough) and has been replicated many times (see Narens, Nelson, & Scheck; Weaver, Terrell, Krug, & Kelemen, this volume, for a review).

In a similar study, Nelson and Dunlosky (1991) noted that most of their participants reported trying to silently recall the target word when given a delayed cue-only JOL; that is, they made "covert retrieval attempts." In our comment on that article, we (Spellman & Bjork, 1992) argued that some of the superiority of the delayed cue-only condition might be due to a self-fulfilling prophecy — because covert retrieval attempts could have two important, if unintended, consequences (see Figure 1).

The first consequence is strategic: Participants use the outcome of the covert retrieval as a basis to predict future recall on the final test. That is, if they fail at covert retrieval on the JOL trial, they are likely to assume that they will fail again on the

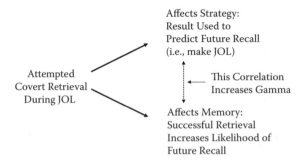

Figure 1 The hypothesized consequences of making a delayed cue-only JOL (Spellman & Bjork, 1992).

distant final recall test; thus, they will give those items a low JOL rating. If they succeed at the covert retrieval, they are likely to assume that they will succeed again on the final recall test, so they will give those items a much higher JOL rating. Evidence for this consequence comes from a different pattern of use of the JOL scale in the delayed cue-only condition (see, e.g., Dunlosky & Nelson, 1992; Kelemen & Weaver, 1997; Kimball & Metcalfe, 2003; Nelson & Dunlosky, 1991; Weaver & Kelemen, 1997). Evidence also comes from studies in which participants are asked to *explicitly* recall the target item when presented with the cue item immediately *before* making the JOL (the PRAM method—pre-judgment recall and monitoring—for studying JOLs developed by Nelson, Narens, & Dunlosky, 2004). When participants make such explicit pre-JOL retrievals they (1) give much higher JOLs to retrieved items than to nonretrieved items (Koriat & Ma'ayan, 2005) and (2) show the same overall pattern of use of the JOL scale as participants who are not instructed to make the explicit retrieval attempts (Nelson et al., 2004).

The second consequence of a covert retrieval is memorial. The act of retrieval is itself a learning event in the sense that the retrieved information becomes more recallable in the future than it would have been otherwise (e.g., Bjork, 1975). A successful retrieval attempt on a JOL trial, therefore, will increase the probability that the judged item is indeed recalled on the later test (Dougherty, Scheck, Nelson, & Narens, 2005; Kelemen & Weaver, 1997; Kimball & Metcalfe, 2003). In other words, by the very act of trying to assess memory, we have changed memory. We argued that those two consequences, and the correlation between them, could account for the superior JOLs in the delayed cue-only condition.

Using Gamma to Assess Learning

We asserted that JOLs in the delayed cue-only condition are far superior to those in the other conditions. But, what do we mean by superior? One way in which judgments could be superior is measured by *calibration*, which is an absolute measure of accuracy. A perfectly calibrated person would, for example, recall none of the items to which she gave a JOL of 0; 20% of the items she gave a JOL of 20; and so forth. In fact, participants in the delayed cue-only condition are better calibrated than in the other conditions (e.g., Nelson & Dunlosky, 1991). However, most JOL studies have focused on relative accuracy (or resolution), as measured by the Goodman-Kruskal γ correlation (or just γ).

The Goodman-Kruskal γ correlation provides a measure of participants' ability to detect which items are more likely to be remembered than which other items. The γ correlation has become the standard index of JOL accuracy, due in large part to Nelson's (1984) extensive review and analysis of the potentially useful statistics and his ultimate endorsement of γ. He wrote: "Of these measures ... the Goodman-Kruskal γ correlation seems best" (p. 124).[1]

Note that γ correlates two observables: JOL ratings and memory performance. Ideally, however, researchers are interested in something unobservable: how well an item was learned in the first place.[2] The problem, as we mentioned, is that in trying to measure learning we might change learning. In fact, we believe that the relatedness of the strategic and memorial consequences of covert retrieval can inflate γ for people who are *not* perfect judges of what they know above what it would be for people who *are* perfect judges of what they know.

Consider, for example, a participant who has learned two pairs of words, with pair A–A′ having been learned slightly better than pair B–B′. When making delayed cue-only JOLs, the participant covertly attempts to retrieve the target word from each pair. Assume, given the probabilistic nature of recall, that the person succeeds at retrieving B′ but not A′ and so, incorrectly, gives B–B′ a higher JOL rating. The successful retrieval of B′ (at a delay) increases the strength of B–B′ in memory, and B′ becomes not only more likely to be recalled on the final test than it was before, but also probably more likely to be recalled than is A′. At final test, B′ might be recalled when A′ is not. Thus, even though the participant was incorrect at assessing the initial relative learning of A–A′ and B–B′, it can appear as if the participant's relative JOLs were accurate. Therefore, as Spellman and Bjork (1992) argued, delayed cue-only JOLs are "predictions [that] create reality."

Chapter Outline

In this chapter we present a mathematical simulation of (what we believe to be) the effects of making a JOL. We show that participants who are less accurate at judging their true state of learning could appear to be more accurate at making JOLs when they base their JOLs on the success or failure of their covert retrieval attempt at the time of the JOL. We examine how much of the improvement in JOL accuracy might be due to the changed use of the JOL scale at a delay and how much might be due to the benefits of successful retrieval. We also use the simulation to illustrate some unsavory properties of the γ statistic and describe experimental design techniques that can help get the most stable γs.

First, we describe a hypothetical participant called the *perfectly insightful participant* — that is, someone who knows exactly what he or she knows — and we illustrate why γ is not "perfect" (i.e., does not equal 1) for such a participant. Second, we introduce our simulation in general terms and describe its assumptions and implementation. Finally, we present the results of hundreds of simulation runs relevant to the issues mentioned.

Evaluation of the Perfectly Insightful Participant Using Gamma

Someone who is perfect at judging his or her initial learning will not generally obtain a γ of 1. Gamma is calculated by comparing performance for each item to performance for each other item and counting up concordances and discordances. A *concordance* occurs when an item with a JOL that is higher than that of another item is recalled while that second item is not recalled. A *discordance* occurs when an item with a JOL that is higher than that of another item is *not* recalled while that second item *is* recalled. Thus, there is no reference to absolute performance; γ is all about judging relative performance.

The γ correlation is computed as follows:

$$(Concordances - Discordances)/(Concordances + Discordances)$$

Note a very important consequence of the definition: Pairs of items that are given identical JOLs and pairs of items that are either both recalled or both not recalled do not contribute to this statistic.[3] Many, sometimes even most, potential comparisons can therefore be irrelevant to the computation of γ.

Consider someone who is perfectly calibrated. Assume further that such a person has learned a list of 60 words with 10 each having a probability of recall of 0, .20, .40, .60, .80, and 1, and that there are not any consequences of making a JOL. In a JOL experiment, then, such a perfect person would then assign JOLs of 0%, 20%, 40%, 60%, 80%, and 100% to the items of each kind, respectively, and at the time of the final test, this person will also recall 0, 2, 4, 6, 8, and 10 items in each JOL category. What is γ for such a "perfect" performance? Because this perfect person sometimes assigns a low JOL to an item that does get recalled (e.g., two of the JOL = 20 items) and a high JOL to an item that does not get recalled (e.g., two of the JOL = 80 items), there are some discordances, and γ is not a perfect 1. For the perfectly calibrated person in this example, γ is .84 — high, but certainly not perfect.

Simulation Overview

The simulation is designed to model participants in an experiment in which they make delayed cue-only JOLs. Readers are encouraged to use the simulation as they read the chapter. (It can be found at http://people.virginia.edu/~bas6g/metamemory. To view all the features described in this chapter, use the "verbose" setting.)

The simulation first generates an initial learning distribution for the items in the study based on a mean, a standard deviation (*SD*), and the number of items entered by the user. During each run, the program simulates two different types of participants.

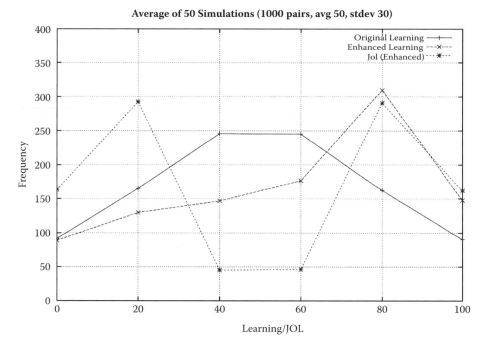

Figure 2 A graph taken from the simulation Web site. The solid line shows initial learning (identical to "perfect" JOLs) and is shown in the Web site in red. For this simulation, the mean is 50, and the standard deviation is 30. The long dashed line (on Web site in green) shows enhanced learning as a result of successful covert retrieval with $d1 = 2$ (moderate learning). The short dashed line (on Web site in blue) shows enhanced JOLs with $d2 = 1.8$ (medium-size scale shift).

- *Perfectly insightful participants.* The JOLs for such participants are exactly equal to the original learning. That is, such participants are assumed to be perfectly accurate assessors of what they know. In addition, the act of making a JOL is assumed to have no consequences for either their actual judgment (i.e., the JOL equals the learning) or the learning of the items.
- *Enhanced participants.* The JOLs are *not* exactly equal to the initial learning. Rather, the act of making a JOL is assumed to have two consequences: (1) a strategic consequence in which such participants draw on the success or failure of covert retrieval attempts to revise their JOLs up or down with respect to their original learning; and (2) a memorial consequence via which the learning of items that were successfully retrieved increases, resulting in such items becoming more likely to be recalled at final test. Simulation users have some control over the functions that modify the shift in JOLs and the learning consequences of successful retrieval.

The simulation presents graphs of the initial learning (red), enhanced learning (green), and enhanced JOLs (blue) (see Figure 2). It computes γs for the perfectly insightful condition and for the enhanced condition (plus two other γs described here). Finally, it gives averages over repeated runs.

Simulation Assumptions and Implementation

Original Learning

The simulation generates a normal distribution for original learning with a mean and standard deviation set by the user. For each simulated participant, the program can simulate the learning of up to 1,000 paired associates. Each pair is represented by a pair number (Simulation Column 1) and has an original learning "strength" from 0 to 100 (Simulation Column 2). This simulation treats recall as probabilistic and an item's strength as reflecting its probability of recall (times 100 for convenience). Items from the generated normal distribution with values greater than 100 are set equal to 100, and those with values less than 0 are set equal to 0. The user can enter a mean (from 0 to 100), a standard deviation, and the number of pairs learned.

For purposes of graphing the original learning (red line), the learning values are placed into six bins: 0–10, 10–30, 30–50, 50–70, 70–90, and 90–100. We selected six to correspond to the number of judgments allowed in most of the early JOL experiments (i.e., participants could make JOLs of 0, 20, 40, 60, 80, or 100; see, e.g., Dunlosky & Nelson, 1992; Kelemen & Weaver, 1997). In some studies, participants, when asked to make a JOL, can respond with any number from 0 to 100 inclusive to represent their estimated probability of recall (Koriat and colleagues tended to use that technique; see, e.g., Koriat & Bjork, 2005; Koriat & Ma'ayan, 2005). In still other studies, the choices were limited to the range of a rating scale (e.g., 0–10, as in Son & Metcalfe, 2005; we address the effects of the choice of JOL scale in Simulations 3 and 4).

Note that all conditions begin with the identical learning strength distribution; that is, initial learning is equated across conditions.

JOLs from Perfect Participants

For participants with perfect insight, JOLs for each item are exact matches to their initial learning. For these participants, the act of making the JOL has no consequences for the JOL or for learning, meaning that their JOLs have the exact same distribution as the initial learning (red line). Thus, the JOLs will be normally distributed because the initial learning is normally distributed. Unlike learning, however, JOLs are observable. Several experiments demonstrated that immediate JOLs are more or less normally distributed (Dunlosky & Nelson, 1994, Experiment 1; Nelson et al., 2004; Weaver & Kelemen, 1997). For purposes of computing γ in most of our simulations, we left the JOLs at their original values (that is, any rational number from 0 to 100 inclusive).

JOLs from Enhanced Participants

Enhanced participants are assumed to make a covert retrieval attempt at the time of JOL. The simulation determines whether that retrieval attempt succeeds and then

TABLE 1   Examples of the Calculations for Revising Strength and Judgments of Learning (JOLs) as a Function of Initial Strength and JOL Retrieval Success (Assuming Default Values $d1 = 2$ and $d2 = 1.8$)

Word Pair (Column 1)	Original Learning (Column 2)	JOL Success? (Column 4)	Enhanced Learning (Column 5)	Enhanced JOL (Column 10)
Pair 1	38	No	38	17
Pair 2	38	Yes	69	72
Pair 3	52	No	52	23
Pair 4	52	Yes	76	79
Pair 5	62	No	62	28
Pair 6	62	Yes	81	83
Pair 7	76	No	76	34
Pair 8	76	Yes	88	89

Note: Column numbers in parenthesis refer to the Web simulation (use the "verbose" setting to view them there). Note that although Pair 2 is learned worse than Pair 3, it is covertly retrieved at JOL, whereas Pair 3 is not. Pair 2 therefore is (incorrectly) given a higher JOL. Because successful covert retrieval also increases the item's learning, Pair 2 is more likely to be recalled than Pair 3 at final test. If that happens, the participant looks correct (i.e., rated Pair 2 higher than Pair 3 and recalled the former but not the latter) but was actually incorrect in judging learning. In the simulation, column 4 reads 0 or 1 which means "no" or "yes," respectively.

modifies the learning and the JOL accordingly. Table 1 gives examples of how the modification works.

Random Value 1 (Simulation Column 3) and Recall at JOL (Simulation Column 4)   For the covert retrieval at JOL, a word pair with an original learning strength of, say, 28, will be retrieved 28% of the time; one with a strength of 57, 57% of the time; and so forth. To implement that probabilistic retrieval, for each word pair a random number from 0 to 100, inclusive, is generated from a flat distribution. This random number is compared to the original learning: If the random number is smaller than the original number, the word is assumed to be retrieved at JOL (and gets a 1 in Column 4); if the random number is larger, then it is assumed not to be retrieved at JOL (and gets a 0 in Column 4).

Enhanced Learning (Simulation Column 5)   One of the consequences of making a JOL is to increase the strength of a successfully retrieved target above its original learning. It has been shown that making a delayed cue-only JOL has consequences for the memorability of the items; we have unpublished data showing that JOLs are like tests in that they (1) enhance recall above that for pairs given only a single study opportunity and (2) mitigate forgetting over time (see Roediger & Karpicke, 2006, for a review of testing effects). The mitigation effect has been seen in both cued recall and recognition measures (see also Dougherty et al., 2005; Kelemen & Weaver, 1997; Kimball & Metcalfe, 2003).

In the simulation, the form of the increase for successfully retrieved items is

$$\text{Enhanced learning} = \text{Original learning} + (100 - \text{Original learning})/d1$$

If items are not successfully retrieved, then original learning is unchanged. Using this type of function (a delta learning rule function), weak items that are successfully retrieved benefit more than do strong items that are successfully retrieved. The minimum $d1$ is 1, which would set learning of all retrieved items to 100. The default is set at 2 because at typical delays between JOL and final recall, the benefit of a successful JOL is only moderate.[4] The effect of enhanced learning can be seen in the Enhanced Learning column of Table 1 and in Figure 2.

Enhanced JOL (Simulation Column 10)   Another consequence of making a delayed cue-only JOL, compared to an immediate one, is a shift in the use of the JOL scale. When participants make immediate JOLs, they tend to use the middle of the JOL scale; when they make delayed JOLs, they more often use the ends of the JOL scale (see Dunlosky & Nelson, 1994; Kimball & Metcalfe, 2003; Nelson et al., 2004; Weaver & Kelemen, 1997). Using a Monte Carlo simulation, Weaver and Kelemen showed that some of the improvement in γ for delayed JOLs is a consequence of that shift in distribution.

In our simulation, the JOL increases if the target was recalled and decreases if it was not. The form of the function is

If recalled: Revised JOL = Original learning + (100 − Original learning)/$d2$

If not recalled: Revised JOL = Original learning − Original learning/$d2$

These functions are presented in the same form as the one for enhancing learning, but there is a more intuitive way of thinking about the JOL functions. Suppose that if an item is retrieved at JOL, the participant first considers giving a JOL of 100 but then modifies that extreme JOL downward by a sense of how well the item had been originally learned. Similarly, suppose that if an item is *not* retrieved at JOL, the participant first considers giving a JOL of 0 but then modifies that extreme JOL upward by a sense of how well the item had been originally learned. Consistent with the notion of adjusting JOLs based on more than just retrieval success or failure, there is evidence that the reaction times for very low and very high JOLs are made fastest, and those in the middle are made slowest (Son & Metcalfe, 2005; but see Kelemen & Weaver, 1996). In that case, the revised JOLs would look like

If recalled: Revised JOL = 100 − Some fraction of (100 − Original learning)

If not recalled: Revised JOL = 0 + Some fraction of original learning

To use the same $d2$ parameter as above, the equations (which now look less intuitive) would be

If recalled: Revised JOL = 100 − ($d2$ − 1)/$d2$ * (100 − Original learning)

If not recalled: Revised JOL = 0 + ($d2$ − 1)/$d2$ * Original learning

In general, these functions give a U-shape pattern to the JOLs, which is consistent with data for delayed JOLs (see Dunlosky & Nelson, 1994; Nelson et al., 2004; Weaver & Kelemen, 1997). The default is set at 1.8 because it tends to give a U shape over a range of learning parameters. It would, of course, be possible to have asymmetric revisions up and down after covert retrieval success and failure, respectively, by using two different $d2$s.

The effect of enhanced JOLs can be seen in the Enhanced JOL column of Table 1 and in Figure 2.

Final Recall

To determine whether final recall succeeds, each pair's strength is compared against a random number.

Random Value 2 (Simulation Column 6)   As for Random Value 1, for each word pair, a random number from 0 to 100, inclusive, is generated from a flat distribution. This random value is used to determine recall for both conditions, thus matching them on "memory ability."

Final Recall Perfect Condition (Simulation Column 9)   Random Value 2 is compared to original learning (Column 2): If the random number is smaller than the original learning, the word is recalled (and gets a 1 in Column 9); if the random number is larger than the original learning, then it is not recalled (and gets a 0 in Column 9).

Final Recall Enhanced Condition (Simulation Column 12)   Random Value 2 is compared to enhanced learning (Column 5): If the random number is smaller than the enhanced learning, the word is recalled (and gets a 1 in Column 12); if the random number is larger than the enhanced learning, then it is not recalled (and gets a 0 in Column 12).

Note that because some pairs in the enhanced condition were strengthened by the covert retrieval practice at JOL, recall in the enhanced condition must be greater than or equal to recall in the perfect condition.

Computing Gamma

The simulation computes four different γs; the two of major interest are the perfect and enhanced conditions (see Table 2).

Perfect Condition   To compute γ for the perfect condition, the simulation uses the perfect JOL (which was equal to the original learning) and the outcome of the final recall. This γ and this JOL are for perfectly insightful participants.

TABLE 2   Four Different Gammas Computed by the Simulation

	Learning/Recall	
JOL	Original (Columns 2 and 6)	Enhanced (Columns 4 and 8)
Perfect (Column 5)	Perfect condition	Learning-only condition
Enhanced (Column 7)	Shift-only condition	Enhanced condition

Note: Column numbers in parenthesis refer to the Web simulation.

Enhanced Condition   To compute γ for the enhanced condition, the simulation uses the enhanced JOL and the outcome of the enhanced final recall. Note that for each pair, if the covert recall at JOL was successful, both of these numbers are above those in the perfect condition; however, if the covert recall was not successful, learning is the same, but the JOL is lower than in the perfect condition. The two other γs of interest represent conditions in which the covert retrieval at the time of JOL has only one of the two hypothesized effects.

Learning-Only Condition   The learning-only condition assumes that in response to covert retrieval attempts at the time of JOL, participants do *not* revise their JOLs but *do* increase the strength of successfully retrieved items. Although we know that JOLs are in fact shifted at a delay, this condition allows us to examine the contribution of the (hypothesized) strength increase alone.

Shift-Only Condition   The shift-only condition is the "opposite" of the learning-only condition: It assumes that in response to covert retrieval attempts at the time of JOL, participants *do* revise their JOLs but do *not* also increase the strength of successfully retrieved items. Weaver and Kelemen (1997) demonstrated that some of the increase in γ in the delayed cue-only condition is due solely to the change in use of the JOL scale from a somewhat normal distribution to a U-shape distribution.

Simulations

Simulation 1: Varying the Mean and Standard Deviation of Original Learning

Simulation 1 varies the two parameters of the original learning (normal) distribution: the mean and the standard deviation. One desirable property of a metacognitive measure is insensitivity to level of memory performance (Nelson, 1984); this insensitivity allows comparison of *metacognitive* performance across groups with a *memory* performance that might differ (e.g., young and elderly; see Schwartz & Metcalfe, 1994). We chose means of 50 (the center of the distribution) and 20 and 80 (representing difficult and easy items, respectively). Although 20 and 80 are symmetrical about 50 and therefore it seems as if they should show equal effects, the function for increasing strength after a successful covert retrieval makes them differ. For standard deviations, we chose 10 (a narrow distribution) and 30 (a wide distribution somewhat mirroring immediate JOL use).

Note that when discussing differences across simulations, standard inferential tests do not make sense because we could easily run large numbers of simulated participants, get very small standard errors, and find significant results.

Effect of Varying the Standard Deviation of the Learning Distribution   Varying the standard deviation of the learning distribution has a huge effect on γ (see Figure 3). In going from a standard deviation of 10 (top panel) to one of 30 (bottom panel), γ substantially increased; bigger standard deviations lead to bigger γs. In addition, standard deviations of γ across simulations (i.e., the equivalent of experiments) were bigger for the narrow learning distribution than for the wide one. Both of these effects point to the importance of having not only study items that vary in difficulty but also sets of items with equal variability if comparing across different stimuli. Thus, the range of item difficulty can have effects both for estimating the calibration of individual participants and for comparing across participants, conditions, or experiments (Schwartz & Metcalfe, 1994).

Effect of Varying the Mean of the Learning Distribution   Varying the learning mean affected γ, although less so than varying the standard deviation. The learning mean of 50 had the lowest γs; changing the mean to 20 or 80 increased γ between .12 and .15, with the one exception described here. Why should the middle of the scale have the lowest γ? We suspect it is because when there are lots of items at the extremes (very poorly or very well learned), those items will behave as expected at final recall — and hence contribute a substantial number of concordances to the γ equation. Items in the middle are less predictable regarding whether they will or will not be recalled at final test and therefore create more discordances, decreasing γ. Note that if γ starts out positive, adding an equal number of concordances and discordances *decreases* γ. For example, suppose that there are 6 concordances and 4 discordances; γ is then

$$\frac{\text{concordances} - \text{discordances}}{\text{concordances} + \text{discordances}} = \frac{6-4}{6+4} = \frac{2}{10} = .20$$

However, if an item or items then contribute both one more concordance and one more discordance, γ becomes

$$\frac{7-5}{7+5} = \frac{2}{12} = .17$$

The exception to the general effect of varying the mean is going from a mean of 50 (medium) to 80 (easy) in the enhanced condition. For that condition, when the mean is 20 or 50, a successful covert retrieval results in a lot of learning, spreading out the learning distribution substantially. However, with a learning mean of 80, there is not much "spreading" left to be done; therefore, the enhanced condition looks like some of the other conditions.

Comparing Conditions   Across all parameters, JOLs are better in the enhanced condition than all three other conditions — including the perfect condition. Thus,

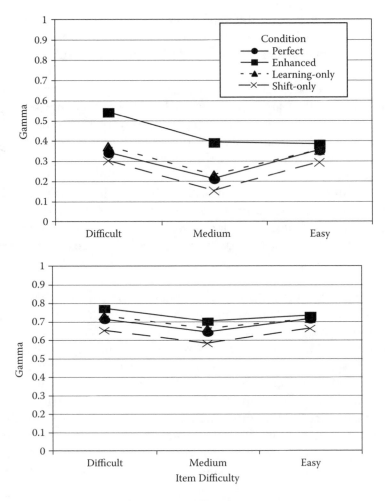

Figure 3 The γs change with changes in mean and variability of learning distribution. Item difficulty refers to means of learning distribution: Difficult = 20; Medium = 50; Easy = 80. Item variability is low in the top panel (standard deviation [SD] = 10) and high in the bottom panel (SD = 30). (For 50 simulated runs with 100 items each. Learning parameter = 2 [moderate]; JOL-shift parameter = 1.8 [medium]).

revising the JOL and learning in tandem causes an increase in γ. Participants who are worse judges of initial learning (because their JOLs do not equal their initial learning) are better predictors of what they will remember in the future than are the perfectly insightful participants — and therefore have higher γs.

What of the conditions in which the covert retrieval at JOL has only one consequence? When only learning changes, γs are nearly the same as in the perfect condition. When only the JOL distribution changes, γ decreases. The latter effect is surprising and a contrast to the simulation results of Weaver and Kelemen (1997). Our main hypothesis for this result has to do with two differences between the simulations. The first is the simulation of the use of the JOL rating scale: In our simulation, JOLs were rational numbers from 0 to 100, whereas in Weaver and Kelemen's study the JOLs were the same as used by the participants (0, 20, 40, 60, 80, 100). In Simulations 3 and 4, we demonstrate how restricting the number of JOLs can artificially inflate γ.

The second difference has to do with the way items are given JOLs. In our simulation, JOL assignment depends on the item's original learning strength. In the perfect and learning-only conditions, the JOL is equal to the original learning; in the shift-only and enhanced conditions, the JOL is revised based on whether the item was retrieved during the covert retrieval at the time of JOL. Thus, an item with an original learning of 20, that randomly is covertly retrieved at JOL, is given a JOL of about 60. If such an item is not recalled at final test (as it probably would not be in the shift-only condition because it still has only a 20% chance of being recalled), many discordances result, reducing γ.

Weaver and Kelemen's approach was quite different. First, they assigned JOLs to items by using the JOL distributions generated by participants in an experiment. So, for example, if participants used a particular JOL rating 20% of the time, then .2 of the items were randomly assigned to that JOL. To determine whether an item was recalled, they used the participants' conditional probability of recall for each JOL. So, for example, if 52% of items with a JOL rating of 40 were recalled by participants at final test, then 52% of the items with JOLs of 40 were randomly assigned to be recalled in the simulation. They could then compare what happens to γ when using the conditional probabilities of either immediate or delayed JOLs and crossing that with the JOL rating distribution of either the immediate or delayed JOLs. Using the probabilities from the delayed JOL condition, they found an increase from .73 to .93 in γ when moving from the immediate to delayed JOL distribution. Of course, those conditional probabilities already have built in (we would argue) the enhanced learning as the result of covert retrieval in the delayed condition.

Simulation 2: Varying the Size of the Consequences of Covert Retrievals at JOL

In our second simulation, we vary the consequences of the covert retrievals for both learning and JOLs (see Table 3).

Effects of Changing the Learning Parameter (d1)   Changing the learning parameter $d1$ affects only the learning-only and enhanced conditions, that is, only the conditions in which original learning is modified by successful covert retrieval at JOL. When $d1 = 1$, a successful covert retrieval changes learning to 100, which guarantees recall on the final test; that is, $d1 = 1$ simulates maximal learning. A $d1$ of 2 simulates moderate learning and of 4 simulates minimal learning. When $d1$ and $d2$ each equal 1, which makes JOLs either 0 or 100, items successfully covertly retrieved will get JOLs of 100 and will definitely be recalled at final test, thus creating a γ of 1.

Effects of Changing the JOL Shift Parameter (d2)   The JOL shift parameter ($d2$) defaults to 1.8, which indicates a moderate shift in JOL use. If $d2$ is set to 1, JOLs become extreme (either 0 or 100); if $d2$ is set to 2.5, JOLs are shifted only slightly as a result of covert retrieval success or failure. In this simulation, if the JOL distribution is shifted, it does not matter how much it is shifted because (1) items are shifted as a

TABLE 3   Mean (and Standard Deviation [*SD*]) of Gammas for 50 Simulated Runs With 100 Items Each and Varying Size of Consequences of Covert Retrievals at Judgment of Learning (JOL)

Parameters				Condition			
Learning Mean	Learning SD	*d1* (Learning)	*d2* (JOL)	Perfect	Enhanced	Learning Only	Shift Only
50	30	1	1.0	.64 (.08)	1.00 (0)	.73 (.06)	.57 (.13)
50	30	1	1.8	.63 (.08)	.89 (.03)	.72 (.07)	.56 (.08)
50	30	1	2.5	.62 (.10)	.89 (.04)	.72 (.07)	.57 (.10)
50	30	2	1.0	.63 (.08)	.78 (.10)	.64 (.07)	.53 (.14)
50	30	2	1.8	.63 (.08)	.69 (.07)	.65 (.09)	.56 (.09)
50	30	2	2.5	.63 (.07)	.69 (.07)	.65 (.08)	.57 (.08)
50	30	4	1.0	.64 (.09)	.68 (.11)	.64 (.09)	.56 (.15)
50	30	4	1.8	.62 (.09)	.63 (.09)	.63 (.08)	.56 (.10)
50	30	4	2.5	.64 (.07)	.64 (.08)	.65 (.07)	.58 (.08)

Note: When $d1 = 1$ a successful covert retrieval changes learning to 100, thus guaranteeing recall at final test (maximal learning); $d1 = 2$ simulates moderate learning (simulation default value); $d1 = 4$ simulates minimal learning. When $d2 = 1.0$, JOLs become extreme (either 0 or 100); if $d2 = 1.8$, JOLs shift as in many delayed JOL studies (simulation default value); if $d2 = 2.5$, JOLs shift only slightly.

function of their current strength, and (2) γ measures relative accuracy. So, if Item Q is recalled at final test and Item R is not, it does not matter whether their JOLs are 57 and 36, respectively, or 81 and 74, respectively; they will still produce a concordance.

Comparing Conditions   Of course, changing these parameters has no effect on the perfect condition because that condition enjoys neither of the consequences of covert retrievals at JOL. The enhanced condition has the highest γ when learning is more than minimal (when $d1 = 4$, the enhanced learning distribution moves very little). The shift-only condition again has the lowest γ.

Simulation 3: Varying the Number of JOL Ratings

Varying the number of JOL ratings that participants can use affects γ in several ways (see Figure 4). First, in almost all conditions, reducing the number of JOL ratings increases γ. The effect was particularly strong in the mean = 20, standard deviation = 10 condition (top left panel), in which, for example, the γ in the perfect condition increased by .16. Second, reducing the number of JOL ratings increases the variability of γ, particularly when the standard deviation is small (top panels).

These effects occur because of how γ deals with "ties." Ties occur when two items are given identical JOL ratings or have the same recall status.

Ties reduce the stability of γ in the following way: Suppose participants study N word pairs. When each pair (its JOL and its recall) is compared to every other pair, there are $(N * (N - 1))/2$ comparisons. However, not every comparison results in a concordance or discordance. If two items are both recalled, they produce neither; if

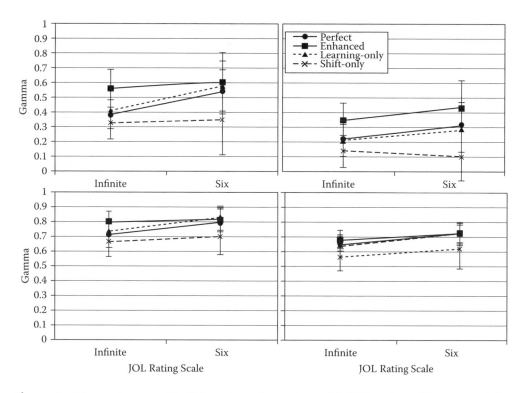

Figure 4 The γs change with different numbers of possible JOL ratings. The mean of the learning distribution is 20 (difficult) in the left panels and 50 (medium) in the right panels. The variability is low in the top panels (standard deviation [SD] = 10) and high in the bottom panels (SD = 30). Infinite is any rational number from 0 to 100; six places each JOL into a bin of 0–10, 10–30, 30–50, 50–70, 70–90, or 90–100.

two items are both not recalled, they produce neither; if two items are given the same JOL rating, they produce neither. Suppose that half of the items are recalled at final test. Now, the maximum total number of comparisons that could result in a concordance or discordance is

$$(\tfrac{1}{2}N * (\tfrac{1}{2}N - 1))/2 + (\tfrac{1}{2}N * (\tfrac{1}{2}N - 1))/2$$

a much smaller number. (For example, if $N = 10$, the equation on top yields 45; the equation on the bottom yields 20.)

When JOL ratings are rational numbers (as generated in our simulations), ties in ratings are unlikely or uncommon. When the JOL scale is limited to 0, 20, 40, and so on or to a 0–10 rating scale, ties are frequent.[5] Increasing the number of options on a scale should decrease the number of ties.

With a limited JOL scale (especially when the standard deviation of learning is small) γ becomes more variable because there are many "tied" JOLs, so γ is based on fewer concordances and discordances and is therefore less stable. With a limited JOL scale, γ becomes inflated because, with a larger scale, items that are close in JOL rating but differ in recall will produce many discordances; however, when the scale is limited, those items will receive the same JOL rating and will not contribute discordances. (And, consistent with these remarks, reducing the number of discordances causes a bigger increase in γ than increasing concordances by the same number.)

Simulation 4: Varying the Number of Study Items

It is, of course, a general rule in experiments to try to get as many observations as possible from each participant. This advice is particularly important when computing γ because, as described, so many potential comparisons are thrown away due to ties in JOL ratings or recall status. Table 4 shows the effects of varying the number of items studied by each participant. Note the huge standard deviations with only 15 observations, especially with a narrow learning distribution (e.g., $SD = 10$). Remember that in a within-subject design, if a participant studies 60 words but the pairs are in four conditions, γ is being computed on (at best) only 15 observations per cell. Note also that, as in Simulation 3, γ generally continues to be higher when the number of ratings is limited.

Discussion

Across variations in many parameters, the enhanced condition, in which covert retrieval at the time of JOL affects both learning and JOL, produces the highest γ, even higher than those for our hypothetical perfectly insightful participant. These high γs do not result when only learning is enhanced or when only JOLs are shifted; rather, they result from the correlation between the two consequences of successful covert retrieval.

Other Factors

Our simulation, of course, does not take into account all factors that could affect γ. For example, we have intentionally left out forgetting from the simulation. How forgetting is modeled could affect the different γs in different ways. One way to model forgetting would be to decrease the learning of all items by the same amount; another would be to decrease the learning of all items by the same percentage. As long as the relative probability of recall of different items does not change, γ should not change (except at very low recall rates in which γ relies on very few concordances and discordances). Another way to model forgetting would be to have some probabilistic forgetting function. Again, however, if that function only inverted learning strengths of a few items, γs might decrease and become more variable, but the conditions should remain relatively the same. Finally, any of those could be implemented but with the addition of different forgetting rates for items that were or were not successfully retrieved at JOL. We believe that successful covert retrievals, like successful tests, slow the rate of forgetting. Therefore, JOLs for items that were enhanced based on

TABLE 4   Mean (and Standard Deviation [*SD*]) of Gammas for 50 Simulated Runs Varying Number of Items and Number of Judgment of Learning [JOL] Ratings (Learning Mean = 50; *d*1 = 2; *d*2 = 1.8)

Number of Items Learning St. Dev		Condition							
		Perfect		Enhanced		Learning Only		Shift Only	
		Infinite	Six	Infinite	Six	Infinite	Six	Infinite	Six
15	30	.63	.71	.66	.73	.64	.74	.53	.58
		(.24)	(.23)	(.22)	(.22)	(.23)	(.24)	(.27)	(.28)
60	30	.61	.70	.68	.73	.63	.72	.55	.62
		(.12)	(.13)	(.11)	(.11)	(.11)	(.12)	(.12)	(.13)
100	30	.61	.69	.67	.71	.63	.71	.55	.59
		(.08)	(.08)	(.08)	(.09)	(.08)	(.09)	(.08)	(.09)
1,000	30	.63	.72	.69	.74	.65	.74	.57	.62
		(.02)	(.03)	(.02)	(.02)	(.02)	(.02)	(.02)	(.02)
15	10	.17	.19	.35	.46	.19	.24	.09	.06
		(.32)	(.50)	(.28)	(.41)	(.34)	(.55)	(.31)	(.42)
60	10	.20	.30	.35	.44	.23	.34	.11	.03
		(.15)	(.25)	(.13)	(.18)	(.15)	(.25)	(.13)	(.24)
100	10	.25	.34	.40	.51	.26	.36	.15	.12
		(.10)	(.15)	(.10)	(.15)	(.09)	(.15)	(.11)	(.14)
1,000	10	.24	.33	.39	.48	.25	.34	.15	.10
		(.04)	(.05)	(.03)	(.05)	(.03)	(.05)	(.04)	(.06)

successful retrievals will remain more accurate over time because those items will be less affected by the forgetting function.

In some recent studies, participants have been asked to make JOLs over longer intervals, ranging from a day to a week (e.g., Koriat, Bjork, Sheffer, & Bar, 2004). Over such long intervals, forgetting would not be the only function to be modeled; there is also the question of whether and how participants strategically factor in the long delay when making JOLs.

The Trouble With Gamma and Finding Relief

We have seen that γ is sensitive to various parameters, sometimes in expected ways and sometimes in unexpected ways. Because γ is a correlation, it is sensitive to the standard deviation of the learning distribution; small standard deviations (i.e., a "restricted range") reduce γ and increase its variability. Also, γ is very variable when there are a small number of items (e.g., 15) going into its computation. The γ correlation does turn out to be sensitive to the mean of original learning. And, reducing the number of possible JOL ratings participants can potentially make (from 101 to 6) can significantly increase γ. All of these consequences occur, at least in part, because in computing γ ties are not counted.

These problems can be ameliorated to some extent through careful experimental design. Study items should have a range of difficulty within conditions and should be equally difficult across conditions. As many observations as possible should go into each computation of γ. And, participants should be allowed to use as wide a JOL rating scale as can be practically and sensibly used in the study.

Conclusions

The results of our simulations demonstrate that the superior γs in the delayed cue-only JOL condition need not reflect more accurate assessments of original learning. Rather, inaccurate assessments might lead to accurate predictions when those assessments and actual recall performance are correlated by virtue of both being based on the outcome of covert retrievals at the time of JOL. We believe that such JOLs irretrievably alter the state of learning, thus making accurate assessments of original learning permanently unrecoverable. But, delayed cue-only JOLs do make people much better at something different and, in fact, something more useful — predicting what they will recall in the future.

The γ correlation has flaws. It is important to recognize those flaws and to try to design studies to minimize their effects. At times, it may be important to use other measures, such as measures of absolute accuracy, along with γ's measure of relative accuracy (see also Masson & Rotello, 2008). Despite the troubles with γ, however, we are not convinced it should be discarded. Perhaps Tom Nelson's (1984) true opinion of γ was similar to that of Winston Churchill's opinion of democracy: "Democracy," said Sir Winston, "is the worst form of government except all those other forms that have been tried from time to time."

Notes

1. Note, however, that he compared it to other statistics useful for analyzing 2×2 feeling-of-knowing data. One of γ's good properties, he noted, is that it could be used for tables larger than 2×2, as is done in JOL studies. However, he did not compare γ to the other statistics for larger tables.
2. Although "judgment of learning" does sound as if it should judge the unobservable learning, many have noted that, "Judgments of learning … are predictions about future test performance" (Nelson & Narens, 1994, p. 16).
3. "Gamma was designed to be unaffected by ties" (Nelson, 1984, p. 116; see Gonzalez & Nelson, 1996, for an explanation). Note, however, as we show below, manipulations that affect the proportion of ties will affect γ.
4. Note that the memorial benefits of delayed cue-only JOLs need not show up when compared to delayed cue-targets JOL (which are, in effect, re-presentations). Cue-only JOLs can only help items that can be successfully retrieved at the time of JOL, but as the time from initial presentation to JOL gets longer, that proportion of items decreases. Cue-target JOLs can help all items at all times. The relevant comparisons to see the benefits of delayed cue-only JOLs are (1) items with single presentations (which will be remembered less frequently) and (2) items that are explicitly recalled at delays matching that of the JOLs (which will be remembered more frequently than single presentation items and as frequently as JOL items).

5. Gonzalez and Nelson (1996, p. 162) noted that such ties are ambiguous — they might be intended (the participant might have wanted to give two items ratings of 20), or they might be limited by the (in)sensitivity of the procedure (the participant might have wanted to give the items ratings of, e.g., 18 and 22 but could not because of the scale).

References

Bjork, R. A. (1975). Retrieval as a memory modifier. In R. Solso (Ed.), *Information processing and cognition: The Loyola Symposium* (pp. 123–144). Hillsdale, NJ: Erlbaum.

Dougherty, M. R., Scheck, P., Nelson, T. O., & Narens, L. (2005). Using the past to predict the future. *Memory & Cognition, 33,* 1096–1115.

Dunlosky, J., & Nelson, T. O. (1992). Importance of the kind of cue for judgments of learning (JOL) and the delayed-JOL effect. *Memory & Cognition, 20,* 374–380.

Dunlosky, J., & Nelson, T. O. (1994). Does the sensitivity of judgments of learning (JOLs) to the effects of various study activities depend on when the JOLs occur? *Journal of Memory and Language, 33,* 545–565.

Gonzalez, R., & Nelson, T. O. (1996). Measuring ordinal association in situations that contain ties scores. *Psychological Bulletin, 119,* 159–165.

Kelemen, W. L., & Weaver, C. A., III. (1997). Enhanced metamemory at delays: Why do judgments of learning improve over time? *Journal of Experimental Psychology: Learning, Memory, and Cognition, 23,* 1394–1409.

Kimball, D. R., & Metcalfe, J. (2003). Delaying judgment of learning affects memory, not metamemory. *Memory & Cognition, 32,* 918–929.

Koriat, A., & Bjork, R. A. (2005). Illusions of competence in monitoring one's knowledge during study. *Journal of Experimental Psychology: Learning, Memory, Cognition, 31,* 187–194.

Koriat, A., Bjork, R. A., Sheffer, L., & Bar, S. K. (2004). Predicting one's own forgetting: The role of experience-based and theory-based processes. *Journal of Experimental Psychology: General, 133,* 643–656.

Koriat, A., & Ma'ayan, H. (2005). The effects of encoding fluency and retrieval fluency on judgments of learning. *Journal of Memory and Language, 52,* 478–492.

Masson, M. E. J., & Rotello, C. M. (2008). Bias in the Goodman-Kruskal Gamma coefficient measure of discrimination accuracy. Unpublished manuscript.

Nelson, T. O. (1984). A comparison of current measures of feeling-of-knowing accuracy. *Psychological Bulletin, 95,* 109–133.

Nelson, T. O., & Dunlosky, J. (1991). When people's judgments of learning (JOLs) are extremely accurate at predicting subsequent recall: The "delayed-JOL effect." *Psychological Science, 2,* 267–270.

Nelson, T. O., & Narens, L. (1994). Why investigate metacognition? In J. Metcalfe & A. P. Shimamura (Eds.), *Metacognition: Knowing about knowing* (pp. 1–26). Cambridge, MA: MIT Press.

Nelson, T. O., Narens, L., & Dunlosky, J. (2004). A revised methodology for research on metamemory: Pre-judgment recall and monitoring (PRAM). *Psychological Methods, 9,* 53–69.

Roediger, H. L., III, & Karpicke, J. D. (2006). The power of testing memory: Basic research and implications for educational practice. *Perspectives on Psychological Science, 1,* 181–210.

Schwartz, B. L., & Metcalfe, J. (1994). Methodological problems and pitfalls in the study of human metacognition. In J. Metcalfe & A. P. Shimamura (Eds.), *Metacognition: Knowing about knowing* (pp. 93–114). Cambridge, MA: MIT Press.

Son, L. K., & Metcalfe, J. (2005). Judgments of learning: Evidence for a two-stage process. *Memory & Cognition, 33*, 116–1129.

Spellman, B. A., & Bjork, R. A. (1992). When predictions create reality: Judgments of learning may alter what they are intended to assess. *Psychological Science, 3*, 315–316.

Weaver, C. A., III, & Kelemen, W. L. (1997). Judgments of learning at delays: Shifts in response patterns or increased metamemory accuracy? *Psychological Science, 8*, 318–321.

Current Directions in Memory Monitoring and Control

Information-Based and Experience-Based Metacognitive Judgments:
Evidence from Subjective Confidence

Asher Koriat, Ravit Nussinson, Herbert Bless, and Nira Shaked

Introduction

Dual-process theories have been very influential in social psychology and cognitive psychology. These theories postulate a distinction between two modes of thought that underlie judgment and behavior (see Chaiken & Trope, 1999; Kahneman & Frederick, 2005). Different labels have been proposed to describe the two modes (see Koriat, Bjork, Sheffer, & Bar, 2004): nonanalytic versus analytic (Jacoby & Brooks, 1984), associative versus rule based (Sloman, 1996), impulsive versus reflective (Strack & Deutsch, 2004), experiential versus rational (Epstein & Pacini, 1999), and heuristic versus systematic (Chaiken, Liberman, & Eagly, 1989; Johnson, Hashtroudi, & Lindsay, 1993). Although each of these labels emphasizes different aspects of the distinction, there is a general agreement that one mode of thought is fast, automatic, effortless, and implicit, whereas the other is slow, deliberate, effortful, and consciously monitored. Several researchers preferred to use the labels proposed by Stanovich and West (2000), System 1 versus System 2, which are more neutral.

A similar dual-process framework has been proposed for the analysis of metacognitive monitoring, focusing on the question of how people know that they know. The distinction is between experience-based (EB) and information-based (IB) metacognitive judgments (Koriat, 2007; Koriat & Levy-Sadot, 1999; Strack, 1992). The conceptualization of this distinction brings to the fore specific features that may have some bearing for dual-process views in general. In the rest of the introduction, we first describe this distinction and then illustrate how it was applied in research on judgments of learning (JOLs) and feelings of knowing (FOKs). In the experimental part of the chapter, we show how reliance on experience-driven and information-driven processes can yield diametrically opposed effects.

Information-Based and Experience-Based Processes in Metacognition

What is the basis of metacognitive judgments? Assuming that these judgments are inferential in nature, what are the cues on which they are based? Cue utilization views assume a distinction between two possible bases of metacognitive judgments. On the one hand, such judgments may be based on a deliberate use of beliefs and memories to reach an educated guess about one's competence and cognitions. On the other hand, they may rely on the automatic application of heuristics that take advantage of various mnemonic cues and result in a sheer subjective feeling. Possibly, both processes may contribute in each case to metacognitive judgments, sometimes operating in collaboration and sometimes acting in opposition (see Kelley & Jacoby, 2000). However, for the sake of exposition, we sharpen the distinction between them as if they represent alternative cognitive processes.

Let us consider IB (or theory-based) judgments first. Clearly, judgments about one's knowledge and competence may be based on similar processes as those underlying many judgments and predictions that people make in everyday life. Thus, when students are asked to judge how well they have done on an exam, their judgments may be based on such data as their preconceived notions about their competence in the domain tested, the amount of time they had spent studying for the exam, their assessment of the difficulty of the exam, and so on. For example, Dunning, Johnson, Ehrlinger, and Kruger (2003) found such retrospective assessments to greatly overestimate performance, partly because people tend to base their assessments on their preconceived, inflated beliefs about their skills rather than on their specific experience with taking the test. Also, retrospective assessments of one's performance in a test have been found to depend on people's beliefs about what the test measures, irrespective of their actual performance on that test (Ehrlinger & Dunning, 2003). The study of "metacognitive knowledge" has figured prominently among developmental psychologists: Children's beliefs about their own memory capacities and limitations, and about the factors that affect memory performance have been found to affect both learning strategies and recall predictions (A. L. Brown, 1987; Flavell, 1999; Schneider & Pressley, 1997).

The FOK judgments may also be based on deliberate inferences from one's own beliefs and knowledge. Consider a person who fails to retrieve the answer to a question and is then asked to assess how likely he or she is to "know" the answer to the extent of being able to choose it among distracters. The person may base this assessment on such beliefs as how much expertise he or she has on the topic, whether he or she recalls having used that information in the past, and so on. In that case, the assessment has the quality of an educated guess, and the person may prefer to phrase his or her judgment as "I ought to know the answer" rather than "I feel that I know the answer" (see Costermans, Lories, & Ansay, 1992).

The EB judgments, in contrast, actually involve a two-stage process (Koriat, 2000), first a process that gives rise to a sheer subjective feeling and second a process that uses that feeling as a basis for memory predictions. Thus, when the person in the previous example searches his or her memory for a solicited target, the person may have the experience of directly detecting the presence of the target, as occurs in the tip-of-the-tongue (TOT) state (see R. Brown & McNeill, 1966). The person may even sense that recall is imminent and may experience frustration for failing to retrieve the elusive target. These feelings may serve as the basis for the reported FOK judgments.

What is the process that gives rise to such metacognitive feelings? It has been proposed that metacognitive feelings are formed on the basis of mnemonic cues that give rise directly to these feelings. For example, JOLs made during study have been assumed to rely on the ease with which to-be-remembered items are encoded or retrieved during learning (Benjamin & Bjork, 1996; Dunlosky & Nelson, 1992; Koriat & Ma'ayan, 2005). Indeed, Hertzog, Dunlosky, Robinson, and Kidder (2003) found JOLs to increase with the success and speed of forming an interactive image between the cue and the target during paired-associate learning. Benjamin, Bjork, and Schwartz (1998) had participants answer general information questions and predict the likelihood of recalling their answers at a later free-recall test. Recall predictions were found to correlate positively with the speed of retrieving an answer, although actual recall exhibited the opposite effect. Also, when participants studied paired associates under self-paced instructions, JOLs were found to decrease with the amount of time invested in the study of each item. These results suggest that learners' JOLs are based on a memorizing effort heuristic that easily learned items are more likely to be remembered than items that require more effort to learn (Koriat, Ma'ayan, & Nussinson, 2006). This heuristic has been found to have some degree of validity because ease of learning is generally diagnostic of recall likelihood (Koriat, in press).

The EB FOK judgments have been assumed to rely on such mnemonic cues as the familiarity of the pointer that serves to probe memory (Metcalfe, Schwartz, & Joaquim, 1993; Reder & Ritter, 1992; Reder & Schunn, 1996) and on the accessibility of pertinent partial information about the solicited memory target (Dunlosky & Nelson, 1992; Koriat, 1993). Indeed, advance priming of the terms of a question (assumed to increase the familiarity of the question) was found to enhance speeded FOK judgments without correspondingly raising the probability of recall or recognition of the answer (Reder, 1988; B. L. Schwartz & Metcalfe, 1992). Other studies support the view that FOK judgments are influenced by the overall accessibility of pertinent information regarding the solicited target (Koriat, 1993; Koriat & Levy-Sadot, 2001). The assumption is that even when recall fails, people may still access a variety of partial clues about the target, and these partial clues may produce the feeling that the target is stored in memory and will be recalled or recognized in the future.

Basic Differences Between Experience-Based and Information-Based Judgments

The foregoing brief review illustrates some of the basic differences between IB and EB metacognitive judgments. The first difference concerns the nature of the cues that are used as the basis of these judgments. IB judgments draw on the *declarative content* of domain-specific beliefs that are retrieved from long-term memory (e.g., "memory declines over time," "I am not very good in geography"). In contrast, EB judgments rely on mnemonic cues that are devoid of declarative content. These cues derive from the very experience of learning, remembering, and deciding rather than from the content of thought. Hence, such cues as the fluency with which information is encoded or retrieved have been referred to as "structural" or "contentless" cues (Koriat & Levy-Sadot, 1999) because they relate to the very quality of processing, that is, to the feedback that one obtains online from one's own processing and performance.

The second difference concerns the quality of the underlying process. In the case of IB judgments, the inferential process is an *explicit*, deliberate process that yields an educated, reasoned assessment. In the case of EB judgments, in contrast, the process that gives rise to a subjective feeling is *implicit* and largely unconscious: Various mnemonic cues act en masse to give rise to a sheer intuitive feeling.

Third, the process that gives rise to IB judgments is a *dedicated* process that is initiated and compiled ad hoc with the goal of producing a metacognitive judgment. In contrast, EB metacognitive judgments are *by-products* of the ordinary processes of learning, remembering, and thinking. Thus, when learners study a new item of information, their immediate intention is normally to master that item rather than to monitor the degree with which it is studied. However, when attempting to study the item, they also detect its encoding fluency, which then gives rise to the feeling of mastery (Koriat, Ma'ayan, et al., 2006). In a similar manner, when people attempt to retrieve an item from memory, their normal intention is that of remembering rather than of judging its ease of access. However, when retrieval fails, the accessibility of partial clues about the elusive item can serve to support FOK judgments (Koriat, 1993). Thus, the processes that give rise to EB judgments can be said to be *parasitic* on the normal cognitive operations and to arise as a fringe benefit from the performance of these operations.

Finally, the accuracy of IB judgments depends on the validity of the beliefs on which they rest. Inflated beliefs about one's competence may lead to unwarranted overconfidence (Metcalfe, 1998). The accuracy of EB judgments, in contrast, depends on the validity of the mnemonic cues utilized. Indeed, in paired-associate learning, delayed JOLs, when cued by the stimulus term, tend to be markedly more accurate in predicting recall than immediate JOLs (Dunlosky & Nelson, 1992; Nelson & Dunlosky, 1991). Presumably, in making delayed JOLs, learners rely heavily on the accessibility of the target, which is an effective predictor of subsequent recall (Nelson, Narens, & Dunlosky, 2004). When JOLs are solicited immediately after study, the target is practically always retrievable, and hence its accessibility has little diagnostic value.

The Distinction Between Information-Based and Experience-Based Judgments in Previous Research

We cite here only a couple of studies to illustrate the usefulness of the distinction between IB and EB metacognitive judgments. Several studies examined the question of how people know that they do not know the answer to a question. The results of Glucksberg and McCloskey (1981; see also Klin, Guzman, & Levine, 1997) suggest that lack of familiarity with the question normally serves as a basis for an EB "don't know" response. When participants were told in an earlier phase of the experiment that the answer to particular questions is not known, this was found to *increase* the latency of a don't know response to these questions when presented later, possibly because now the response tended to be based on information rather than on sheer subjective experience. Presumably, EB judgments are made faster and more automatically than IB judgments.

The remaining examples concern JOLs made during study. Koriat and Bjork (2005) examined the illusion of competence that often arises in studying new information. They proposed that this illusion derives in part from the inherent discrepancy between the learning and testing conditions: On a typical memory test, people are presented with a question and are asked to produce the answer, whereas in the corresponding learning condition both the question and the answer generally appear in conjunction. A failure to discount the answer during learning has the potential of creating a *foresight bias* — an unduly strong feeling of competence. This bias is particularly strong in paired-associate learning when the target (present during study) brings to the fore aspects of the cue that are less apparent when the cue is later presented alone (at test). For example, the pair baby–cradle (in Hebrew) tends to produce inflated JOLs during learning (Koriat & Bjork, 2006a) because the association in the backward direction (cradle–baby) is much stronger than that in the forward direction (baby–cradle): In a word association task, the likelihood of *cradle* eliciting *baby* as the first response is .88, whereas that of *baby* eliciting *cradle* is .00. However, participants estimated that 54% of the people who are presented with the word *baby* would be likely to respond with the word *cradle* as the first word that comes to mind (Koriat, Fiedler, & Bjork, 2006).

Koriat and Bjork (2006b) compared the effectiveness of two procedures in alleviating the foresight bias, a mnemonic-based procedure and a theory-based (or IB) procedure. The mnemonic-based procedure, which involved a repeated presentation of the same list, was based on previous findings suggesting that study–test experience, and particularly test experience, enhances learners' sensitivity to mnemonic cues that are diagnostic of memory performance. The theory-based procedure, in contrast, induced participants to resort to theory-based judgments as a basis for JOLs. Both procedures proved effective in mending the foresight bias. Importantly, however, they yielded differential effects with regard to the transfer of improved monitoring to the study of new items. Only the theory-based procedure exhibited transfer, as reflected in JOLs and self-regulation of study time. Thus, subjective experience can be educated through metacognitive training, but the effect of this training on the accuracy of EB judgments is item specific. In contrast, an effective theory that helps mend IB judgments can ensure generalization to new situations.

Another study that illustrates the importance of distinguishing between EB and IB judgments was based on the idea that EB JOLs should be insensitive to the anticipated retention interval because the processing fluency of an item at the time of encoding should not be affected by when testing is expected (Koriat et al., 2004). Indeed, JOLs were entirely indifferent to the expected retention interval, although actual recall exhibited a typical forgetting function. As a result, participants predicted about a 50% recall after a week, whereas actual recall was less than 20%.

This result is surprising because forgetting is a central part of everyone's naïve beliefs about memory. However, several manipulations that were intended to induce participants to apply their theory about forgetting failed to yield a forgetting curve for JOLs. The only procedures that were successful were when retention interval was manipulated within individuals and when recall predictions were framed in terms of forgetting rather than in terms of remembering. These and other results suggest that participants do not spontaneously apply their theories about memory in making JOLs. Rather, they can access their knowledge about forgetting only when theory-based predictions are solicited and the notion of forgetting is accentuated.

Kornell and Bjork (2006) produced even more dramatic results in comparing subjective and objective learning curves. Participants were presented with one, two, three, or four study–test cycles of a list of paired associates, and during the initial study cycle they were asked to predict their recall performance on the last test in the series. Although actual recall exhibited the typical learning curve, predicted learning curves were essentially flat. In a second experiment, participants made predictions for each of the tests during the initial study cycle. Despite the within-participant manipulation, predicted learning curves hardly increased with study cycle. These results underscore the idea that learners do not spontaneously apply their theories in making recall predictions.

The few studies described above demonstrate the usefulness of the distinction between IB and EB metacognitive judgments and bring to the fore the critical role that experience-driven processes play in influencing these judgments. Whereas the foregoing discussion focused on JOLs made during learning and on FOK judgments made during remembering, the rest of the chapter applies the distinction between IB-driven and EB-driven processes to the analysis of retrospective subjective confidence. The results are intended to show that the two types of processes may sometimes yield diametrically opposed patterns of results. We conclude with several questions that deserve further research.

Information-Based and Experience-Based Confidence Judgments

In the experiments to be reported, we examined the distinction between EB and IB metacognitive judgments with regard to subjective confidence. Some discussions assume that confidence in the answer to a general information question is based on the weight of the evidence that is marshaled in favor of that answer relative to the evidence in support of the alternative answers (e.g., Griffin & Tversky, 1992; Koriat, Lichtenstein, & Fischhoff, 1980; McKenzie, 1997; Yates, Lee, Sieck, Choi, & Price, 2002). These discussions would seem to stress information-driven processes. Other discussions, in contrast, focus on experience-driven processes, emphasizing the contribution of mnemonic cues such as the ease with which the answer is retrieved or selected (Nelson & Narens, 1990). Indeed, confidence in an answer has been found to increase with the speed of reaching that answer. Furthermore, response latency has been found to be generally diagnostic of the correctness of the answer (e.g., Kelley & Lindsay, 1993; Koriat, Ma'ayan, et al., 2006; Robinson, Johnson, & Herndon, 1997).

In the experiments to be reported, we contrast the two hypothesized bases of confidence judgments, borrowing the ease-of-retrieval paradigm introduced by N. Schwarz et al. (1991; see N. Schwarz, 2004, for a review). In that paradigm, participants are required to retrieve many instances or few instances favoring a particular proposition and then make a judgment about that proposition. The requirement to list many instances is assumed to produce a conflict between two potential cues — the content of the information retrieved and the ease of retrieving it: Retrieving many instances provides stronger content-based evidence but is also associated with the experience of greater effort. In a large number of studies, the effects of ease of retrieval on judgment were found to win over the effects of content in affecting judgment (e.g., Aarts & Dijksterhuis, 1999; Haddock, 2002; Wänke & Bless, 2000; Wänke, Bohner, & Jurkowitsch, 1997; Winkielman, Schwarz, & Belli, 1998). For example, participants who were asked to recall many past episodes demonstrating self-assertiveness later reported lower self-ratings of assertiveness than those who were asked to recall fewer such episodes, presumably because of the greater difficulty experienced in recalling many episodes (N. Schwarz et al., 1991).

In our experiments, we examined the relative contribution of informational content and ease of retrieval to confidence judgments by comparing two conditions that differed in report option: In both conditions, participants answered general knowledge questions by choosing one of two alternative answers. They then listed reasons in support of that answer and finally indicated their confidence in that answer. In the free-report condition, participants listed as many reasons as they could, whereas in the forced-report condition they were asked to provide a specified number of reasons. In the free-report condition, we expected confidence to increase with number of reasons. This is because the strength of the supporting evidence can be assumed to increase with number of reasons retrieved and because in the free-report condition, we expect ease of retrieval to increase with the number of reasons listed. This expectation is based on the finding of Koriat (1993) with regard to FOK judgments. Koriat observed that the number of letters that people retrieved (spontaneously) about a memorized target correlated positively with the speed of retrieving the *first* reported letter, and that both number of letters and speed of retrieval contributed to FOK judgments.

In the forced-report condition of our experiments, in contrast, the retrieval of many reasons should be associated with a stronger experience of effort than the retrieval of few reasons. The effects of ease of retrieval are expected to counteract those of the content of the information retrieved to the extent of reversing the relationship between number of reasons and confidence.

Experiment 1

In Experiment 1, each forced-report participant was yoked to a participant in the free-report condition and was required to provide the same number of reasons that the matched free-report participant had provided for each question. Report option was expected to moderate the effects of number of reasons on confidence judgments.

Method

Participants   Eighty 11th- and 12th-grade high school students participated in the experiment as volunteers.

Materials and Procedure   A set of 16 general knowledge questions in Hebrew, each with two alternative answers, was used. The questions covered a wide range of topics (e.g., "How old was Abraham when his son Isaac was born? (a) 100, (b) 75"). All instructions and materials were compiled in booklets, each question appearing at the top of a separate page. Participants were instructed to choose an answer and then list reasons in support of their choice. For the free-report condition, the instruction, "Write down all supporting reasons you can think of:" appeared below the question, followed by five slots. For the forced-report condition, participants were asked to

TABLE 1   The Frequency Distribution of Number of Reasons Across All Participants and Questions and the Number of Participants Who Reported Each Number of Reasons for the Free-Report and Forced-Report Conditions (Experiment 1)

	Free Report					
	Number of Reasons					
	0	1	2	3	4	5
Number of observations	13	375	182	38	6	1
Number of participants	6	40	39	22	4	1
	Forced Report					
	Number of Reasons					
		1	2	3	4	5
Number of observations		388	182	38	6	1
Number of participants		40	39	22	4	1

provide for each question the exact number of reasons as their free-yoked participants gave to that question. The instruction was, "Write down X supporting reasons:" and the number of slots differed from one question to another accordingly. For both conditions, a 19-point confidence scale appeared at the bottom of each page, with one end (1) labeled, "There is a very low chance that the answer I chose is correct," and the other (19) labeled, "There is a very high chance that the answer I chose is correct."

There were 13 instances (of 618) in which free-report participants failed to provide any reason. In these cases, the yoked participants were required to give one reason for the respective items.

Results   Table 1 shows the distribution of number of reasons for the free- and forced-report conditions. The distribution is skewed: Free-report participants provided one reason in about 60% of the cases. In only 7% of the cases did participants provide three or more reasons.

Figure 1 presents mean confidence judgments as a function of number of supporting reasons for each of the two conditions. For this figure, we treated three or more reasons as three reasons. A Condition × Number of Reasons analysis of variance (ANOVA) was conducted to evaluate the interaction suggested in this figure, using only 21 participants who provided one, two, and three reasons at least once. Because of the yoking procedure, we treated report option as a repeated factor, so that the effective number of "participants" was 21. The analysis yielded a nonsignificant effect for report option $F(1, 40) = 1.35$, MSE (mean square error) $= 16.70$, but significant effects for number of reasons, $F(2, 40) = 6.88$, $MSE = 8.87$, $p < .005$, and for the interaction, $F(2, 40) = 5.69$, $MSE = 5.71$, $p < .01$. Separate one-way ANOVAs indicated that confidence increased significantly with number of reasons for the free-report condition (the means were 10.5, 13.4, and 14.5, respectively, for one, two, and three reasons, for the 21 participants), $F(2, 40) = 11.89$, $MSE = 7.53$, $p < .0001$, but not for the forced-report condition, $F < 1$.

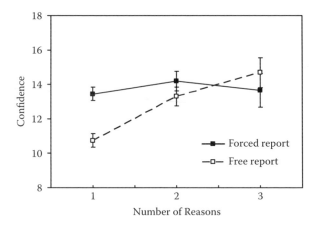

Figure 1 Mean confidence as a function of number of reasons plotted separately for the forced-report and free-report conditions. Error bars represent + 1 standard error of the mean (SEM) (Experiment 1).

Discussion As expected, report option moderated the effects of number of reasons on confidence. The free-report condition yielded the expected increase in confidence with number of reasons, whereas the forced-report yielded no such increase. The pattern observed for the forced-report condition suggests that the effects of ease-of-retrieval counteracted those of the amount of supporting evidence but failed to reverse this effect. One possible reason for this failure is the yoking procedure used. We found that the questions differed reliably in the number of supportive reasons they elicited: When the free-report participants were divided randomly into two groups, mean number of reasons provided by one group to each question correlated .42 ($p < .11$) across the 16 questions with the number of reasons provided by the other group. Assuming that amount (number of reasons) and ease are correlated positively in the free-report condition (see Koriat, 1993), then the questions for which forced-report participants were required to produce many reasons may not induce a sufficiently strong experience of retrieval effort. If so, the item-by-item yoking feature of Experiment 1 underestimates the effects of ease of retrieval in the forced-report condition. To evaluate this possibility, in Experiment 2 we imposed a predetermined number of reasons on forced-report participants independent of the number of reasons provided by the free-report participants. The number of reasons imposed in the forced-report condition was either 1 or 4. We speculated that perhaps retrieving two or three reasons would not produce a sufficiently strong feeling of difficulty that would reverse the impact of amount of evidence. Indeed, in previous studies that contrasted the effects of amount versus ease, the number of reasons (or statements) imposed in the many-reasons condition was sometimes 10 or more (e.g., Tormala, Petty, & Briñol, 2002; Wänke et al., 1997; Winkielman & Schwarz, 2001).

Experiment 2

In Experiment 2, forced-report participants were required to list 1 reason for 8 of the 16 questions and 4 reasons for the remaining questions. We ran twice as many free-report participants as forced-report participants to obtain a sufficient number of free-report participants who provided both one and four reasons. We hypothesized that if indeed amount and ease correlated positively in the case of the free-report condition, then the positive effect of number of reasons on confidence judgments in this condition should be stronger than the respective negative effect in the forced-report condition.

Method

Participants   Sixty University of Haifa undergraduates (43 women and 17 men) participated in the experiment. Participants were assigned randomly to the 2 conditions with the constraint that there were 40 participants in the free-report condition and 20 in the forced-report condition.

Materials and Procedure   The materials were the same as in Experiment 1. The instructions were similar with two exceptions. First, forced-report participants were asked to list either one or four reasons, with number of reasons alternating between questions, and the assignment of number of reasons to questions was counterbalanced across participants. The order of the questions was the same for all participants. Second, participants were specifically instructed that even when they were uncertain, they should avoid such reasons as "just a guess" or "it seems likely."

Results   For the free-report condition (see Table 2), confidence generally increased with number of reasons. Because the means for each category are based on different participants, we compared confidence judgments for 1 and 2 reasons using only 30 participants who provided both 1 and 2 reasons. The respective means were 10.7 and 13.7, $t(29) = 5.74$, $p < .0001$. There were only 10 participants who provided 1, 2, and 3 reasons (the respective means were 8.5, 11.1, and 13.5), yielding $F(2, 18) = 5.92$, $MSE = 10.62$, $p < .05$.

Turning next to the free-forced comparison, only six participants gave both one and four reasons to some of the questions (see Table 2). Figure 2 (top panel) depicts mean confidence as a function of number of reasons for these participants as well as for the 20 forced-report participants. A two-way ANOVA on these means yielded $F <$

TABLE 2   Mean Confidence as a Function of Number of Reasons for the Free-Report Option and the Number of Observations and Participants on Which Each Mean Was Based (Experiment 2)

	Number of Reasons			
	1	2	3	4
Confidence	10.8	13.7	13.5	18.4
Number of observations	310	139	45	11
Number of participants with nonzero observations	40	30	11	6

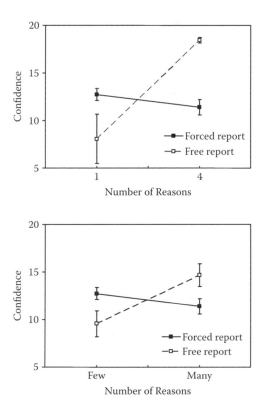

Figure 2   Mean confidence as a function of number of reasons plotted separately for the forced-report and free-report conditions. The free-report means are for participants who gave both 1 and 4 reasons (top panel) and for participants who gave both few (1 or 2) and many (3 or more) reasons (bottom panel). Error bars represent + 1 standard error of the mean (SEM) (Experiment 2).

1 for report option, but number of reasons and the interaction were both significant, $F(1, 24) = 21.07$, $MSE = 8.15$, $p < .0001$, and $F(1, 24) = 38.73$, $MSE = 8.15$, $p < .0001$, respectively. For the free-report condition, confidence increased significantly from one reason to four reasons, $t(5) = 3.63$, $p < .05$, whereas for the forced-report condition, it decreased, $t(19) = 2.16$, $p < .05$.

To ascertain that the results for the free-report participants were not specific to the six participants included in the analysis, we enlarged the sample of free-report participants by combining one and two reasons, treating them as few reasons, and combining three and four reasons, treating them as many reasons. In this manner, we could include 13 free-report participants. Figure 2 (bottom panel) compares the results for these participants with those of the forced-report participants. A two-way ANOVA yielded $F(1, 31) = 0.00$, $MSE = 21.03$, ns (not significant), for report option, but again the effects of number of reasons and the interaction were significant, $F(1, 31) = 6.45$, $MSE = 8.31$, $p < .05$, $F(1, 31) = 19.71$, $MSE = 8.31$, $p < .0001$, respectively.

Here again, confidence increased significantly with number of reasons for the free-report participants, $t(12) = 3.32$, $p < .01$.

Figure 2 also suggests that, indeed, the positive effect of number of reasons on confidence in the free-report condition is stronger than the respective negative effect in the forced-report condition. The mean increase in confidence from one to four reasons in the free-report condition (Figure 2, top panel) was significantly larger than the respective mean decrease in the forced-report condition, $t(24) = 4.79$, $p < .0001$. A similar pattern was observed for the results presented in the bottom panel of Figure 2, $t(31) = 2.59$, $p < .05$.

Discussion   Experiment 2 yielded the expected crossover interaction: Confidence increased significantly with number of reasons under free reporting and decreased significantly under forced reporting. A comparison of these results with those of Experiment 1 supports our suggestion that the extent to which report option moderates the effect of number of reasons on confidence depends on the experienced effort associated with listing many reasons under forced reporting.

The observation that confidence increased more strongly with number of reasons in the free-report condition than it decreased in the forced-report condition is consistent with the idea that whereas amount and ease correlate negatively in the forced-report condition, they correlate positively in the free-report condition. This idea is explored in the next experiment.

Experiment 3

Experiment 3 attempted to obtain support for the hypothesized positive link between amount and ease in the free-report condition. Participants listed reasons in support of their answer, and the time to initiate report of the *first* reason was measured. We examined whether response latency was indeed shorter when more reasons rather than fewer reasons were produced.

Method   Participants were 60 undergraduates (32 women). The materials and procedure were similar to those of the previous experiments except that the experiment was conducted on a personal computer. On each trial, the question and its two alternative answers appeared on the screen. Participants chose an answer by clicking on it with the mouse and then typed in as many supporting reasons as they could, one in each of five blank windows. The latency to type in the first reason — the interval between clicking the chosen answer and starting to type in the first reason — was recorded. After typing in reasons, participants rated their confidence on the 19-point scale, which appeared on the screen.

Results   Across all participants and questions, there were 418, 351, 148, 36, and 7 instances in which participants provided 1, 2, 3, 4, and 5 reasons, respectively.

Figure 3 presents mean latency of providing the *first* reason. It can be seen that latency decreased monotonically with number of reasons, yielding a Spearman rank correlation of 1.00, $p < .05$. We compared the means of ease of retrieval for one or two

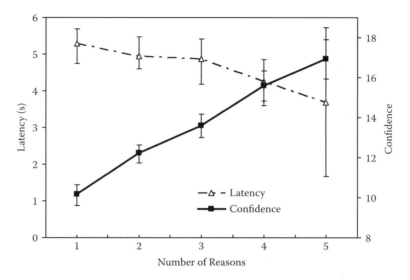

Figure 3 Mean latency and confidence as a function of number of reasons. Error bars represent + 1 standard error of the mean (SEM) (Experiment 3).

reasons versus three or more reasons. Of 42 participants for whom both means were available, 27 exhibited shorter latencies for the many-reasons than for the few-reasons category, $p < .05$, by a binomial test. These results suggest that reasons are more easily retrieved the more of them are available for free reporting.

As in the previous experiments, confidence increased with the number of reasons provided (Figure 3). The rank order correlation (1.00) between confidence and number of reasons was significant at the .05 level. When the analysis was confined to 1, 2, and 3 reasons, using only 39 participants who provided 1, 2, and 3 reasons, mean confidence judgments were 9.8, 12.2, and 13.5, respectively, $F(2, 76) = 21.49$, $MSE = 6.49$, $p < .0001$.

We also examined whether ease of retrieval affected confidence judgments over and above the effects of number of reasons. This examination could be carried out only for the one-reason category for which there was a sufficient number of observations. Using 53 participants who provided 1 reason for at least 2 questions, confidence for slow (above-median) and fast (below-median) responses averaged 10.0 and 11.1, respectively, $t(52) = 1.93$, $p < .06$. Thus, the trend was in the expected direction: A faster retrieval of reasons was associated with higher confidence ratings even when the number of reasons was held constant.

Discussion   The results of Experiment 3 exhibited two trends that are consistent with our expectations. First, ease of retrieval correlated positively with number of reasons; second, ease of retrieval appeared to enhance confidence even when the number of reasons was held constant. These results suggest that the positive correlation observed in all three experiments between number of reasons and confidence in the free-report condition may reflect the joint effects of amount and ease. This may explain in part why the positive effect of number of reasons on confidence was stronger in Experiment 2 than the respective negative effect in the forced-report condition.

General Discussion

The results of this study are consistent with the distinction between IB and EB meta-cognitive judgments. These results suggest that confidence judgments are affected conjointly by the content of declarative information retrieved from long-term memory and by the ease or effort with which that information is retrieved. When reasons in support of an answer are retrieved spontaneously, confidence increases with number of reasons, possibly because of the increased supportive evidence as well as the greater ease of retrieval. In contrast, when number of reasons is experimentally imposed, the two cues conflict, and the greater effort required to retrieve many reasons may tip the balance, producing a negative relationship between number of reasons and confidence.

Studies using the ease-of-retrieval paradigm in social cognition (see N. Schwarz, 2004) have stressed the idea that the two cues — amount and ease — exert conflicting effects in the case of forced reporting. We showed that the two cues go hand in hand in the case of free reporting, consistent with Koriat's (1993) observation in the context of FOK judgments.

We should note, however, that in Koriat's accessibility model (Koriat, 1993) both amount and ease are conceived as nonanalytic mnemonic cues (see Kelley & Jacoby, 1996): They were assumed to enhance immediate FOK regardless of the content and accuracy of the information retrieved and regardless of the compatibility between the various pieces of partial clues retrieved. According to Koriat (1998), only when the computation of FOK judgments becomes more deliberate does the content of the information enter into consideration so that additional clues may sometimes reduce rather than enhance FOK judgments (see also Vernon & Usher, 2003). This assumption differs from that underlying the studies of the ease-of-retrieval paradigm, in which "amount" and "content" are used interchangeably to describe the strength of declarative arguments in favor of a particular judgment. This is understandable because in that paradigm participants are induced to selectively access arguments that have a specific valence (e.g., arguments in support of buying a certain car).

Nevertheless, because the accessibility model has been applied to confidence judgments as well (e.g., Brewer, Sampaio, & Barlow, 2005; Swann & Gill, 1998), it is important to inquire whether the sheer number of arguments retrieved might contribute to the immediate sense of confidence independent of the content of these arguments. If confidence is affected by accessibility, then three cues may act collaboratively to enhance confidence in the free-report condition: amount, ease (both as nonanalytic, mnemonic cues that feed into EB judgments), and content (as a cue for analytic, IB confidence judgments). All three cues may also be operative in the forced-report condition, except that now amount and ease would operate in opposite directions. These speculations deserve further investigation.

Concluding Remarks

This chapter reviewed evidence demonstrating the usefulness of the distinction between IB and EB processes. This distinction has been applied to the study of JOLs, FOK, and confidence judgments, but its ramifications extend beyond the realm of metacognitive judgments. Possibly, the analysis of the distinction between the two processes in metacognition can contribute to the refinement and specification of dual-process theories in general.

In concluding this chapter, we should mention several directions for future research. Throughout this chapter, we treated information-driven and experience-driven processes as if they represent alternative routes to metacognitive judgments. Both processes, however, would seem to operate conjointly, contributing in different degrees to these judgments. The results that we presented on confidence judgments underscore the need to examine the complex interactions that exist between the two processes when they operate in tandem. Future work should examine in greater detail the dynamics of the interaction between these processes as it may vary between different conditions (e.g., free reporting vs. forced reporting) and across time (see Koriat, 1998; Vernon & Usher, 2003).

Research on social cognition suggests several additional directions in which the distinction between IB and EB metacognitive processes may be explored. In reviewing the work on the effects of metacognitive experience on judgments, N. Schwarz (2004) emphasized the point that the effects of metacognitive experiences (e.g., the ease with which ideas come to mind) depend on the naïve theory of mental processes that people use in interpreting these experiences. Indeed, it has been observed that participants can be induced to discount the effects of mnemonic cues by attributing them to irrelevant sources (Jacoby & Whitehouse, 1989; N. Schwarz & Clore, 1983; Strack, 1992). A question of interest is whether this is also true for the effects of mnemonic cues on metacognitive judgments such as JOLs and FOK. Can people be induced to discount the effects of cue familiarity and accessibility on FOK judgments by attributing these effects to a different source? Also, there has been increasing evidence suggesting that the naïve theories underlying the effects of metacognitive experiences are highly malleable to the extent that theories with opposite implications can be successfully induced (Unkelbach, 2006; Winkielman & Schwarz, 2001). Can learners be induced to apply a naïve theory that states that fluently processed items are *less* likely to be remembered than those requiring greater encoding effort (see Koriat, in press)? These are some of the questions that await further research.

Acknowledgment

As I (A. K.) wrote elsewhere (Koriat, 2007), "There has been a surge of interest in metacognitive processes in recent years, with the topic of metacognition pulling under one roof researchers from traditionally disparate areas of investigation" (p. 289). Undoubtedly, Tom was the major driving force behind this development. Personally, Tom helped me in crystallizing my own research identity and in finding my place under that roof.

This work was supported by a grant from the German Federal Ministry of Education and Research (BMBF) within the framework of German-Israeli Project Cooperation (DIP). We are grateful to Rinat Gil for her help in conducting and analyzing the experiments and to Limor Sheffer for her advice in the statistical analyses.

Ravit Nussinson has previously published under the name Ravit Levy-Sadot.

References

Aarts, H., & Dijksterhuis, A. (1999). How often did I do it? Experienced ease of retrieval and frequency estimates of past behavior. *Acta Psychologica, 103,* 77–89.

Benjamin, A. S., & Bjork, R. A. (1996). Retrieval fluency as a metacognitive index. In L. Reder (Ed.), *Implicit memory and metacognition* (pp. 309–338). Hillsdale, NJ: Erlbaum.

Benjamin, A. S., Bjork, R. A., & Schwartz, B. L. (1998). The mismeasure of memory: When retrieval fluency is misleading as a metamnemonic index. *Journal of Experimental Psychology: General, 127,* 55–68.

Brewer, W. F., Sampaio, C., & Barlow, M. R. (2005). Confidence and accuracy in the recall of deceptive and nondeceptive sentences. *Journal of Memory and Language, 52,* 618–627.

Brown, A. L. (1987). Metacognition, executive control, self-regulation, and other more mysterious mechanisms. In F. E. Weinert & R. H. Kluwe (Eds.), *Metacognition, motivation, and understanding* (pp. 95–116). Hillsdale, NJ: Erlbaum.

Brown, R., & McNeill, D. (1966). The "tip of the tongue" phenomenon. *Journal of Verbal Learning and Verbal Behavior, 5,* 325–337.

Chaiken, S., Liberman, A., & Eagly, A. H. (1989). Heuristic and systematic information processing within and beyond the persuasion context. In J. S. Uleman & J. A. Bargh (Eds.), *Unintended thought* (pp. 212–252). New York: Guilford Press.

Chaiken, S., & Trope, Y. (Eds.). (1999). *Dual-process theories in social psychology.* New York: Guilford Press.

Costermans, J., Lories, G., & Ansay, C. (1992). Confidence level and feeling of knowing in question answering: The weight of inferential processes. *Journal of Experimental Psychology: Learning, Memory, and Cognition, 18,* 142–150.

Dunlosky, J., & Nelson, T. O. (1992). Importance of the kind of cue for judgments of learning (JOL) and the delayed-JOL effect. *Memory & Cognition, 20,* 374–380.

Dunning, D., Johnson, K., Ehrlinger, J., & Kruger, J. (2003). Why people fail to recognize their own incompetence. *Current Directions in Psychological Science, 12,* 83–87.

Ehrlinger, J., & Dunning, D. (2003). How chronic self-views influence (and potentially mislead) estimates of performance. *Journal of Personality and Social Psychology, 84,* 5–17.

Epstein, S., & Pacini, R. (1999). Some basic issues regarding dual-process theories from the perspective of cognitive-experiential self-theory. In S. Chaiken & Y. Trope (Eds.), *Dual process theories in social psychology* (pp. 462–482). New York: Guilford Press.

Flavell, J. H. (1999). Cognitive development: Children's knowledge about the mind. *Annual Review of Psychology, 50,* 21–45.

Glucksberg, S., & McCloskey, M. (1981). Decisions about ignorance: Knowing that you don't know. *Journal of Experimental Psychology: Human Learning and Memory, 7,* 311–325.

Griffin, D., & Tversky, A. (1992). The weighing of evidence and the determinants of confidence. *Cognitive Psychology, 24,* 411–435.

Haddock, G. (2002). It's easy to like or dislike Tony Blair: Accessibility experiences and the favourability of attitude judgments. *British Journal of Psychology, 93,* 257–267.

Hertzog, C., Dunlosky, J., Robinson, A. E., & Kidder, D. P. (2003). Encoding fluency is a cue used for judgments about learning. *Journal of Experimental Psychology: Learning, Memory, and Cognition, 29,* 22–34.

Jacoby, L. L., & Brooks, L. R. (1984). Nonanalytic cognition: Memory, perception, and concept learning. In G. H. Bower (Ed.), *The psychology of learning and motivation: Advances in research and theory* (pp. 1–47). New York: Academic Press.

Jacoby, L. L., & Whitehouse, K. (1989). An illusion of memory: False recognition influenced by unconscious perception. *Journal of Experimental Psychology: General, 118,* 126–135.

Johnson, M. K., Hashtroudi, S., & Lindsay, D. S. (1993). Source monitoring. *Psychological Bulletin, 114*, 3–28.

Kahneman, D., & Frederick, S. (2005). A model of heuristic judgment. In K. J. Holyoak & R. G. Morrison (Eds.), *The Cambridge handbook of thinking and reasoning* (pp. 267–293). Cambridge, UK: Cambridge University Press.

Kelley, C. M., & Jacoby, L. L. (1996). Adult egocentrism: Subjective experience versus analytic bases for judgment. *Journal of Memory and Language, 35*, 157–175.

Kelley, C. M., & Jacoby, L. L. (2000). Recollection and familiarity: Process dissociation. In E. Tulving & F. I. M. Craik (Eds.), *The Oxford handbook of memory* (pp. 215–228). Oxford, UK: Oxford University Press.

Kelley, C. M., & Lindsay, D. S. (1993). Remembering mistaken for knowing: Ease of retrieval as a basis for confidence in answers to general knowledge questions. *Journal of Memory and Language, 32*, 1–24.

Klin, C. M., Guzman, A. E., & Levine, W. H. (1997). Knowing that you don't know: Metamemory and discourse processing. *Journal of Experimental Psychology: Learning, Memory, and Cognition, 23*, 1378–1393.

Koriat, A. (1993). How do we know that we know? The accessibility model of the feeling-of-knowing. *Psychological Review, 100*, 609–639.

Koriat, A. (1998). Metamemory: The feeling of knowing and its vagaries. In M. Sabourin, F. Craik, & M. Robert (Eds.), *Advances in psychological science* (Vol. 2, pp. 461–469). Hove, UK: Psychology Press.

Koriat, A. (2000). The feeling of knowing: Some metatheoretical implications for consciousness and control. *Consciousness and Cognition, 9*, 149–171.

Koriat, A. (2007). Metacognition and consciousness. In P. D. Zelazo, M. Moscovitch, & E. Thompson (Eds.), *The Cambridge handbook of consciousness* (pp. 289–325). Cambridge, UK: Cambridge University Press.

Koriat, A. (in press). Easy comes, easy goes? The link between learning and remembering and its exploitation in metacognition. *Memory & Cognition*.

Koriat, A., & Bjork, R. A. (2005). Illusions of competence in monitoring one's knowledge during study. *Journal of Experimental Psychology: Learning, Memory and Cognition, 31*, 187–194.

Koriat, A., & Bjork, R. A. (2006a). Illusions of competence during study can be remedied by manipulations that enhance learners' sensitivity to retrieval conditions at test. *Memory & Cognition, 34*, 959–972.

Koriat, A., & Bjork, R. A. (2006b). Mending metacognitive illusions: A comparison of mnemonic-based and theory-based procedures. *Journal of Experimental Psychology: Learning, Memory and Cognition, 32*, 1133–1145.

Koriat, A., Bjork, R. A., Sheffer, L., & Bar, S. K. (2004). Predicting one's own forgetting: The role of experience-based and theory-based processes. *Journal of Experimental Psychology: General, 133*, 643–656.

Koriat, A., Fiedler, K., & Bjork, R. A. (2006). Inflation of conditional predictions. *Journal of Experimental Psychology: General, 135*, 429–447.

Koriat, A., & Levy-Sadot, R. (1999). Processes underlying metacognitive judgments: Information-based and experience-based monitoring of one's own knowledge. In S. Chaiken & Y. Trope (Eds.), *Dual-process theories in social psychology* (pp. 483–502). New York: Guilford Press.

Koriat, A., & Levy-Sadot, R. (2001). The combined contributions of the cue-familiarity and the accessibility heuristics to feelings of knowing. *Journal of Experimental Psychology: Learning, Memory and Cognition, 27*, 34–53.

Koriat, A., Lichtenstein, S., & Fischhoff, B. (1980). Reasons for confidence. *Journal of Experimental Psychology: Human Learning and Memory, 6*, 107–118.

Koriat, A., & Ma'ayan, H. (2005). The effects of encoding fluency and retrieval fluency on judgments of learning. *Journal of Memory and Language, 52*, 478–492.

Koriat, A., Ma'ayan, H., & Nussinson, R. (2006). The intricate relationships between monitoring and control in metacognition: Lessons for the cause-and-effect relation between subjective experience and behavior. *Journal of Experimental Psychology: General, 135*, 36–69.

Kornell, N., & Bjork, R. A. (2006). *Objective and subjective learning curves.* Talk presented at the 47th annual meeting of the Psychonomic Society, November 2006, Houston, TX.

McKenzie, C. R. M. (1997). Underweighting alternatives and overconfidence. *Organizational Behavior and Human Decision Processes, 71*, 141–160.

Metcalfe, J. (1998). Cognitive optimism: Self-deception or memory-based processing heuristics? *Personality and Social Psychology Review, 2*, 100–110.

Metcalfe, J., Schwartz, B. L., & Joaquim, S. G. (1993). The cue-familiarity heuristic in metacognition. *Journal of Experimental Psychology: Learning, Memory, and Cognition, 19*, 851–864.

Nelson, T. O., & Dunlosky, J. (1991). When people's judgments of learning (JOLs) are extremely accurate at predicting subsequent recall: The "delayed-JOL effect." *Psychological Science, 2*, 267–270.

Nelson, T. O., & Narens, L. (1990). Metamemory: A theoretical framework and new findings. In G. Bower (Ed.), *The psychology of learning and motivation: Advances in research and theory* (Vol. 26, pp. 125–123). San Diego, CA: Academic Press.

Nelson, T. O., Narens, L., & Dunlosky, J. (2004). A revised methodology for research on metamemory: pre-judgment recall and monitoring (PRAM). *Psychological Methods, 9*, 53–69.

Reder, L. M. (1988). Strategic control of retrieval strategies. In G. H. Bower (Ed.), *The psychology of learning and motivation: Advances in research and theory* (Vol. 22, pp. 227–259). San Diego, CA: Academic Press.

Reder, L. M., & Ritter, F. E. (1992). What determines initial feeling of knowing? Familiarity with question terms, not with the answer. *Journal of Experimental Psychology: Learning, Memory, and Cognition, 18*, 435–451.

Reder, L. M., & Schunn, C. D. (1996). Metacognition does not imply awareness: Strategy choice is governed by implicit learning and memory. In L. M. Reder (Ed.), *Implicit memory and metacognition* (pp. 45–77). Mahwah, NJ: Erlbaum.

Robinson, M. D., Johnson, J. T., & Herndon, F. (1997). Reaction time and assessments of cognitive effort as predictors of eyewitness memory accuracy and confidence. *Journal of Applied Psychology, 82*, 416–425.

Schneider, W., & Pressley, M. (1997). *Memory development between 2 and 20* (2nd ed.). Mahwah, NJ: Erlbaum.

Schwartz, B. L., & Metcalfe, J. (1992). Cue familiarity but not target retrievability enhances feeling-of-knowing judgments. *Journal of Experimental Psychology: Learning, Memory, and Cognition, 18*, 1074–1083.

Schwarz, N. (2004). Metacognitive experiences in consumer judgment and decision making. *Journal of Consumer Psychology, 14*, 332–348.

Schwarz, N., Bless, H., Strack, F., Klumpp, G., Rittenauer-Schatka, H., & Simons, A. (1991). Ease of retrieval as information: Another look at the availability heuristic. *Journal of Personality and Social Psychology, 61*, 195–202.

Schwarz, N., & Clore, G. L. (1983). Mood, misattribution, and judgments of well-being: Informative and directive functions of affective states. *Journal of Personality and Social Psychology, 45*, 513–523.

Sloman, S. A. (1996). The empirical case for two systems of reasoning. *Psychological Bulletin, 119*, 3–22.

Stanovich, K. E., & West, R. F. (2000). Individual differences in reasoning: Implications for the rationality debate. *Behavioral and Brain Sciences, 23*, 645–665.

Strack, F. (1992). The different routes to social judgments: Experimental versus informational strategies. In I. I. Martin & A. Tesser (Eds.), *The constructions of social judgments* (pp. 249–275). Hillsdale, NJ: Erlbaum.

Strack, F., & Deutsch, R. (2004). Reflective and impulsive determinants of social behavior. *Personality and Social Psychology Review, 8*, 220–247.

Swann, W. B., Jr., & Gill, M. (1998). Beliefs, confidence, and the Widows Ademosky: On knowing what we know about others? In V.Y. Yzerbyt, G. Lories, & B. Dardenne (Eds.), *Metacognition: Cognitive and social dimensions* (pp. 107–125). London: Sage.

Tormala, Z. L., Petty, R. E., & Briñol , P. (2002). Ease of retrieval effects in persuasion: A self-validation analysis. *Personality and Social Psychology Bulletin, 28*, 1700–1712.

Unkelbach, C. (2006). The learned interpretation of cognitive fluency. *Psychological Science, 17*, 339–345.

Vernon, D., & Usher, M., (2003). Dynamics of metacognitive judgments: Pre- and postretrieval mechanisms. *Experimental Psychology: Learning, Memory, and Cognition, 29*, 339–346.

Wänke, M., & Bless, H. (2000). The effects of subjective ease of retrieval on attitudinal judgments: The moderating role of processing motivation. In H. Bless & J. P. Forgas, (Eds.), *The message within: The role of subjective experience in social cognition and behavior* (pp. 143–161). Philadelphia: Psychology Press.

Wänke, M., Bohner, G., & Jurkowitsch, A. (1997). There are many reasons to drive a BMW: Does imagined ease of argument generation influence attitudes? *Journal of Consumer Research, 24*, 170–177.

Winkielman, P., & Schwarz, N. (2001). How pleasant was your childhood? Beliefs about memory shape inferences from experienced difficulty of recall. *Psychological Science, 12*, 176–179.

Winkielman, P., Schwarz, N., & Belli, R. F. (1998). The role of ease of retrieval and attribution in memory judgments: Judging your memory as worse despite recalling more events. *Psychological Science, 9*, 124–126.

Yates, J. F., Lee, J. W., Sieck, W. R., Choi, I., & Price, P. C. (2002). Probability judgment across cultures. In T. Gilovich & D. Griffin (Eds.), *Heuristics and biases: The psychology of intuitive judgment* (pp. 271–291). New York: Cambridge University Press.

Memory Monitoring and the Delayed JOL Effect

Louis Narens, Thomas O. Nelson, and Petra Scheck

Introduction

Metacognition pertains to people's self-monitoring and self-control of cognitive processes. One of the most highly researched subareas of metacognition is people's self-monitoring of memory processing (Nelson, 1993). A major kind of self-monitoring of memory pertains to people's judgments of personal learning after a study trial, which are called *judgments of learning* (JOLs).

The typical paradigm used to investigate JOLs requires the subject to make predictions of the likelihood of his or her eventual memory performance on each of the studied items, and sometime thereafter a final memory test occurs. Investigators' interest is focused on the accuracy of the JOLs, as defined by the degree of relationship between the predicted memory performance and the subsequently observed memory performance on the final test. Many experiments (e.g., Begg, Duft, Lalonde, Melnick, & Sanvito, 1989; Connor, Dunlosky, & Hertzog, 1997; Dunlosky & Nelson, 1992, 1994, 1997; Kelemen & Weaver, 1997; Nelson & Dunlosky, 1991; Nelson, Narens, & Dunlosky, 2004; Thiede & Dunlosky, 1994; Weaver & Kelemen, 1997) have replicated the robust effect that a relatively brief delay between study and JOLs for items produces a substantial increase in the accuracy of those JOLs for predicting eventual memory performance as compared to JOLs made immediately after study. This is called the *delayed JOL effect*.

Several kinds of theoretical mechanism have been suggested and evaluated in an attempt to explain the delayed JOL effect. These include "polarized judgments" (Weaver & Kelemen, 1997), the "monitoring-dual-memories" hypothesis (Nelson & Dunlosky, 1991), "retrieval fluency" (Benjamin & Bjork, 1996), "products-of-retrieval theory" (Schwartz, 1994), "self-fulfilling prophecy" (Spellman & Bjork, 1992), and "mnemonic cues concerning accessibility" (Koriat, 1997). Our goal here is not to review the literature about those mechanisms; a review of many of them can be found in the work of Schwartz (1994). Instead, we provide a mathematical model that gives considerable insight into what is needed to achieve the delayed JOL effect. Two of the explanations proposed in the literature — the monitoring-dual-memories (MDM) and the self-fulfilling prophecy (SFP) explanations — are examined in detail and evaluated through the mathematical model.

In general, it should be borne in mind that theoretical considerations involving the delayed JOL effect can be evaluated in many ways. We evaluate them in terms of their adequacy for explaining the delayed JOL effect observed in the study of Nelson and Dunlosky (1991) and related paradigms. We recognize that various proposed mechanisms in the literature may be valid in other kinds of paradigms. However, the controversies in the literature involving the delayed JOL effect have centered around the experiment in Nelson and Dunlosky (1991) and their explanation for it.

Monitoring-Dual-Memories Explanation

Nelson and Dunlosky's (1991) Delayed JOL Effect

Nelson and Dunlosky (1991) used a single learning trial paired-associate task using unrelated concrete nouns (e.g., ocean–tree). The learning trial lasted for 8 seconds per item. The items were divided into blocks. For half of the items of a block, the subject was asked to give a JOL for an item immediately after the learning trial (immediate JOLs) and for the other half of the items of the block to give a JOL for an item approximately 30 seconds after the learning trial for it (delayed JOLs). Between the learning of a delayed JOL item and the elicitation of its JOL, the learning of other items or JOLs of other items occurred. A recall test was given for all the items of a given block before the next block was presented. Accuracy was then computed as a γ correlation between each person's JOLs and subsequent test performance (details are provided in this chapter). Nelson and Dunlosky found that items in the immediate JOL condition had JOL accuracy of +.38, whereas items in the delayed JOL condition had JOL accuracy of +.90. Similar effects have been consistently obtained for paired-associated items.

Nelson and Dunlosky (1991) presented a theoretical explanation for the delayed JOL effect. They called their explanation monitoring dual memories or MDM for short. Dunlosky and Nelson (1992) described MDM as follows:

> One explanation for this pattern of finding is that when people assess the likelihood of eventual recall for recently studied information, they may simultaneously monitor both short-term and long-term memory. ... This explanation suggests that for immediate JOLs, information about the stimulus–response pair in short-term memory adds noise or dominates the monitoring (i.e., retrieval) of information in long-term memory. This reduces the accuracy of immediate JOLs because eventual recall will be based on information only in long-term memory. By contrast, delayed JOLs exceed the span of retrieval from short-term memory (i.e., less than 30 seconds, Peterson & Peterson, 1959) and thereby allow better interrogation of long-term memory via the information contained therein, without noise from information about that item in short term memory. (p. 379)

Dunlosky and Nelson (1992) conducted the following experiment as partial confirmation of the MDM explanation. It was similar to that of Nelson and Dunlosky (1991) except for the following manipulation: The kind of cue for the immediate or delayed JOLs was of two types: (1) the stimulus from a stimulus–response item or (2) the full stimulus–response item (Nelson & Dunlosky, 1991, only used stimulus-alone cues). MDM suggests that one should expect to see the delayed JOL effect when JOLs are cued by the stimulus alone but should not see the effect when JOLs are cued by the stimulus–response pair. In fact, this is what was found:

When the cue is the stimulus-alone, the delayed-JOL effect is extremely robust, but when the cue is the stimulus–response pair, the delayed-JOL effect is negligible. (Dunlosky & Nelson, 1992, p. 378)

In terms of MDM, they give the following interpretation for the failure of the stimulus–response cue to produce a delayed JOL effect:

In the case of the delayed JOLs cued by the stimulus–response pair, the stimulus–response may be attended to (e.g., entered into short-term memory and then retrieved) before the person can retrieve the information from long-term memory about that item (see the latencies in Wescourt & Atkinson, 1973). This information from short-term memory about the item would produce the same kind of monitoring problems as those which occur in the case of immediate JOLs. (Dunlosky & Nelson, 1992, p. 379)

Theoretical Assessment of the MDM Explanation

In this section, a theoretical model for the γ-accuracy of JOLs is given. The model expresses γ as a weighted sum of three other γ-accuracies, each corresponding to a different kind of evaluation. The MDM explanation is then evaluated in terms of the theoretical model. In a subsequent section, the theoretical model is used to evaluate the self-fulfilling prophesy (SFP) explanation.

We start by classifying a JOL in terms of the kind of information that is used in making the judgment. The classification is then used to sort dyads of to-be-learned items into three types, each yielding an informative measure of accuracy.

Judgments of Maintenance and Feeling of Knowing

An item is said to be recallable at time of judgment if and only if at the time of the JOL the item would have been recalled if a recall test were presented instead of a JOL. Items that are not recallable at time of judgment are called nonrecallable items at time of judgment.

Recallable items are defined counterfactually; therefore, whether an item is truly recallable at time of judgment is not observable. Thus, a theoretical assumption is needed to link recallable items to observable data for the notions of recallable (or nonrecallable) at time of judgment to have scientific import. For example, in an experiment we described here, a recall test for some items is given just before their JOL. If such an item is correctly recalled in this test, then it is deemed to be recallable at the time of the JOL, which occurs immediately after the recall test. Here, the linking theoretical assumption is that an item that is recalled at a time t is recallable at slightly later times. Other linking theoretical assumptions involving the recallability/nonrecallabilty of items are given later.

A JOL of a recallable item at the time of the judgment is called a *judgment of maintenance* or JOM. We use the term *maintenance* in the same way as Bahrick and his coworkers (e.g., Bahrick, 1979; Bahrick & Hall, 1991) when they discussed "maintenance of knowledge." The key idea is that a currently recallable item must be maintained sufficiently long to be again recalled on a subsequent test of memory for that item. A JOL of a nonrecallable item at the time of the judgment is called a *feeling-of-knowing* (FOK) judgment. This nomenclature is consistent with the literature's use of the term FOK (e.g., Hart, 1967; Nelson & Narens, 1994; Schwartz, 1994). Thus, the JOM is the person's belief that he or she will maintain in memory (i.e., not forget) the retrieved target, and the FOK is the person's belief about his or her subsequent memory performance on a currently nonretrieved item.

Decomposition of γ

This section provides a precise description of JOL accuracy and a method of decomposing a γ accuracy measure into a weighted sum of accuracy measures. The decomposition better accounts for how various cognitive processes influence the size of JOL accuracy than the accuracy measurement generally used in the metamemory literature (i.e., the Goodman-Kruskal γ statistic). The finer analysis provided by the decomposition is used to evaluate theories of the delayed JOL effect. To describe rigorously this decomposition, several definitions and some technical notation are needed.

JOL accuracy is generally measured in terms of the Goodman-Kruskal gamma statistic, called here gamma and denoted by the symbol γ. Gamma is computed in terms of dyads of items. A dyad is just a pair of items {J, K}. {J, K} is said to be concordant, if and only if eiher (i) the JOL rating is higher for Item J than Item K and on the final recall test, Item J is recalled but Item K is not recalled or (ii) the JOL rating is higher for Item K than Item J and on the final recall test, Item K is recalled but Item J is not recalled; {J, K} is said to be discordant if and only if either (i′) the JOL rating is higher for Item J than Item K and on the final recall test, Item J is not recalled but Item K is recalled or (ii′) the JOL rating is higher for Item K than Item J and on the final recall test, Item K is not recalled but Item J is recalled; and {J, K} is said to be tied if and only if the JOL rating is the same for Item J as for Item K or the recall outcome is the same for Item J as for Item K, or both. In the computation of γ, tied dyads are discarded. (See Gonzalez & Nelson, 1996, for the rationale for discarding ties.) The following equation computes γ:

$$\gamma = (c - d)/(c + d) \qquad (1)$$

where c is the number of concordant dyads, and d is the number of discordant dyads. The maximum value of γ is +1.0 (when $d = 0$), and the chance value of γ is 0 (when $c = d$). Other properties of γ are well known in the literature (e.g., for reasons γ is preferable to other measures of metacognitive accuracy, see Nelson, 1984; for mathematical properties of γ, see Gonzalez & Nelson, 1996, and Goodman & Kruskal, 1954, 1959).

Nelson, Narens, and Dunlosky (2004) developed a methodology for JOL research that decomposes JOL γ accuracy into three component measures of accuracy: maintenance, contrast, and FOK gammas. The methodology is called PRAM (prejudgment recall and monitoring) because an additional recall test, called a pre-JOL recall attempt, is inserted just prior to each JOL. In PRAM, these component measures of JOL accuracy are observable. In the present chapter, similarly defined measures are treated more theoretically and are generally unobservable. Nevertheless, it is argued that such measures are essential for evaluating theories of the delayed JOL effect.

In the following, let C and D be respectively the sets of concordant and discordant items of a JOL study yielding the JOL accuracy measure γ. Let S be a subset of $C \cup D$. Then, by definition,

- C_S is the set of concordances in S.
- D_S is the set of discordances in S.
- c_S is the number of elements in C_S.
- d_S is the number of elements in D_S.

Then, the JOL γ accuracy of S, γ_S, is by definition

$$\gamma_S = (c_S - d_S)/(c_S + d_S).$$

The partitioning $C \cup D$ into appropriate sets of dyads S_1, ... , S_k can provide considerable insight into how γ is achieved because γ decomposes mathematically into a weighted sum of JOL accuracies γ_1, ..., γ_k; that is,

$$\gamma = w_1 \cdot \gamma_1 + \ldots + w_k \cdot \gamma_k, \tag{2}$$

where

- γ_1, ..., γ_k are, respectively, the JOL γ accuracies for S_1, ..., S_k.
- w_i is the proportion of items of $C \cup D$ that are in S_i, $i = 1$, ..., k.

For the purposes of analyzing the delayed-JOL effect, $C \cup D$ is partitioned into three sets, with each set defined in terms of an item's state of retrievability at the time of its JOL.

For the computation of γ, JOMs and FOKs yield three kinds of dyads:

- Maintenance dyads that compare JOM items (i.e., dyads composed of two JOM items).
- FOK dyads that compare FOK items (i.e., dyads composed of two FOK items).
- Contrast dyads that compare a JOM item with an FOK item (i.e., dyads composed of a JOM item and an FOK item).

These three kinds of dyads partition the set of dyads and yield the following decomposition of JOL γ accuracy:

$$\gamma = (c - d)/(c + d) = w_m \cdot \gamma_m + w_f \cdot \gamma_f + w_c \cdot \gamma_c, \tag{3}$$

where

c is the number of concordances.

d is the number of discordances.

w_m, w_f, and w_c are, respectively, the proportions of dyads of $C \cup D$ that are maintenance, FOK, and contrast dyads.

γ_m, γ_f, and γ_c are, respectively, γ accuracy measures for the sets consisting of maintenance, FOK, and contrast dyads of $C \cup D$.

We view that the information participants use in making JOMs is fundamentally different from the information they use in making FOKs because JOM items are retrievable, and FOK items are not. As a result, we view JOMs and FOKs as different judgments, and therefore we consider maintenance, FOK, and contrast γs as accuracy measures for fundamentally different judgments. These three γ accuracies allow for a more penetrating analysis of metacognitive accuracy and a sharper evaluation of theories for the delayed JOL effect than is possible through the use of just the overall γ for JOL accuracy.

Mathematical Model

Theoretical Assumptions

We argue that in the Nelson and Dunlosky (1991) paradigm the term $w_m \cdot \gamma_m$ in Equation 3 dominates the size of γ for immediate JOLs, while the term $w_c \cdot \gamma_c$ dominates the size of γ for delayed JOLs. To accomplish this, three theoretical assumptions linking JOL rating behavior to memory performance are made. As discussed next, the three assumptions are plausible for paradigms like that employed in Nelson and Dunlosky (1991). There is empirical support for two of the assumptions, and the third is made to simplify proofs and the form of a mathematical model that approximates delayed JOL accuracy. In the following, each of the assumptions is described, and if relevant, empirical support for the assumption is given.

The assumption of *persistence of forgetting* says that a target that is nonrecallable at a given time remains nonrecallable at later times and thus in particular is not recalled on the final recall test. Persistence of forgetting appears to hold very strongly in the situations that have been investigated using paired associates, even if it may not hold in some other kinds of situations (see Nelson, Gerler, & Narens, 1984). For instance, in the experiment described in Nelson et al. (2004), items that were not recalled on a test given 30 seconds after learning were given another recall test 2 minutes after learning. The median probability of an item being recalled 2 minutes after learning was 0.0. Other experiments on delayed JOLs have also confirmed this assumption. For instance, Kelemen and Weaver (1997, Table 3) reported that the mean percentage of correct final recall for items not recalled on an initial recall test (which occurred in place of, rather than adjacent to, each JOL) was 0% in 10 of the 14 conditions they examined. Across all 14 conditions that they examined, the mean was 3%, indicating that persistence of forgetting occurred for 97% of the items not recalled at the time the JOL would have occurred.

The assumption of *superiority of JOMs* says that people rate a JOM item higher than an FOK item. If the only data obtained from the subject are JOLs, then the empirical validity of this assumption cannot be assessed. Previous research by Shaughnessy and Zechmeister (1992) found that subjects inflated the magnitude of their JOLs for items recallable on an initial test and reduced the magnitude of their JOLs for nonrecallable items. It should be noted that while our research suggests the validity of superiority of JOMs for the vast majority of items in paradigms like that of Nelson and Dunlosky (1991), this assumption may not be valid for every item. Reasons for failures include (1) the subject might retrieve a target that he or she believes may be incorrect (such that the "sought-after item" defined by the experimenter is different from the sought-after item defined by the subject), and (2) the subject may have a nonretrieved item on the tip of the tongue and may believe that it will subsequently become retrievable.

The assumption of *no tied ratings* says that people give each item a unique JOL rating. Although there are valid methods of data collection that produce such unique ratings, they are rarely employed in JOL experiments for practical reasons. Instead, most JOL experiments use a fairly limited number of rating values for a much larger number of to-be-learned items, resulting in some ratings being tied. However, as discussed in the section on impact of tied ratings, the mathematical model given (which assumes no tied ratings) can be extended to accommodate tied ratings. When this is done, it is shown that the addition of tied ratings cannot lower delayed JOL accuracy but can raise it. Because of this, we view the assumption of no tied ratings to be a conservative assumption for explaining the delayed JOL effect, that is, we would expect a stronger delayed JOL effect if the data collection resulted in tied JOL ratings. Our use of the no tied ratings assumption is to simplify calculations of the mathematical model.

The above three theoretical assumptions yield the following mathematical model that provides the basis for our theoretical explanation for the delayed JOL effect:

Theorem 1

Suppose the above theoretical assumptions of persistence of forgetting, superiority of JOMs, and no tied ratings. Let M be the proportion of maintenance items, R be the proportion of items correctly recalled on the final test, and suppose $0 < R < 1$. Then,

$$\gamma = [(M - R)/(1 - R)] \cdot \gamma_m + (1 - M)/(1 - R), \qquad (4)$$

where γ is the gamma for JOL accuracy, and γ_m is the gamma accuracy for the set of maintenance items. *(For the proof of Theorem 1, contact Louis Narens or John Dunlosky.)*

The decomposition of γ in Equation 3 yielded

$$\gamma = w_m \cdot \gamma_m + w_c \cdot \gamma_c + w_f \cdot \gamma_f.$$

The assumption of persistence of forgetting requires that both items of an FOK dyad are not recalled on the final test, and therefore all FOK dyads are tied. Thus, $w_f = 0$ in the above equation. The assumption of superiority of JOMs requires that all maintenance items receive higher ratings than all FOK items, and this together with persistence of forgetting yields that all contrast dyads are concordances, thus yielding

$$\gamma_c = 1.$$

These facts are reflected in Equation 4 by the sum

$$[(M - R)/(1 - R)] \cdot \gamma_m + (1 - M)/(1 - R),$$

which can be rewritten as

$$[(M - R)/(1 - R)] \cdot \gamma_m + [(1 - M)/(1 - R)] \cdot 1 + 0 \cdot \gamma_f,$$

where in terms of the earlier notation, $\gamma_c = 1$, and $w_3 = 0$.

Note that it follows from persistence of forgetting that $M \geq R$. Also, note that the right side of Equation 4 approaches +1.0 as R approaches M, and thus because +1.0 is the highest value obtainable by γ, $\gamma = +1.0$ when $R = M$, and γ is near +1.0 when R is near M. Furthermore, as R monotonically declines from M to approach 0, the right side of Equation 4 monotonically declines to approach the value

$$1 - M (1 - \gamma_m).$$

In providing theoretical analyses of the delayed JOL effect, the following empirically based assumption is often used without explicit reference:

The assumption of relative superiority of maintenance γs is used in the analyses of theoretical models of the delayed JOL effect. It says that immediate JOL accuracy is not larger than maintenance accuracy. Empirical support for this assumption is provided by the experiment in Nelson et al. (2004), which has an immediate JOL accuracy γ_i, of +.23 and maintenance accuracy γ_m of +.46. The relative superiority of maintenance γs allows us to use γ_i, which is observable in JOL paradigms, as a lower estimate of γ_m, which is not observable in almost all the JOL paradigms in the literature. We use this lower estimate of γ_m to illustrate that one can obtain in natural ways robust delayed JOL effects without assuming principles like MDM that require γ_m to be much larger than γ_i. It should be emphasized that our purpose in making the assumption of relative superiority of maintenance γs is to apply our theoretical model to the MDM explanation, which assumes a much stronger principle. We do consider the assumption to be valid in all JOL experiments. The point we make next is that even with this assumption — which is valid in some JOL experiments — the delayed JOL effect is likely to be due to processes different from the one given by the MDM explanation.

Application to the Monitoring-Dual-Memories Explanation

As a concrete example, consider the case where $M = .6$. We first consider the extreme case where $\gamma_m = 0$. Then, γ will be near +1.0 when final recall R is near .6, and γ will always be greater than

$$1 - .6(1 - .0) = .4.$$

Next, consider the more plausible case of $\gamma_m = .38$, the value of immediate JOL accuracy in Nelson and Dunlosky (1991). Then, γ will be near +1.0 when final recall R is near .6, and γ will always be greater than

$$1 - .6(1 - .38) = .63$$

no matter when final recall takes place. This is already a large increase over immediate JOL γ accuracy of .38. Next, consider in addition to $\gamma_m = .38$ that $R = .46$, the proportion of correctly recalled items in the final test in Nelson and Dunlosky (1991). Then, by Equation 4, $\gamma = .84$. Of course, if a reasonable number of maintenance dyads with tied JOL ranks were incorporated, this estimate of +.84 for γ could significantly increase. (The data collection method of Nelson & Dunlosky, 1991, which uses six rating levels, guarantees a reasonable number of such tied dyads.)

The above example shows that the principles of persistence of forgetting and superiority of JOMs are sufficient to provide a plausible explanation of the delayed JOL effect: The effect occurs because from these assumptions it follows that, in Equation 3,

$$w_f = 0$$

that is, FOK dyads have negligible impact on the size of γ;

$$\gamma_c = 1$$

and for reasonable choices of the delay and the time of recall, w_c is much larger than w_m.

With respect to the MDM hypothesis, Theorem 1 suggests that the vast majority of the increase in the delayed versus immediate γ accuracies that occurs in paradigms similar to Nelson and Dunlosky (1991) is likely to result from the impact of the contrast dyads. Such a result does not yield very much information about the mechanisms underlying metamemory processing because it is primarily due to having the difference between M and R small (which is primarily a result of the experimenter's selections of the difficulty of the items and the times for judgment and final recall) combined with the important fact that in such paradigms recallable items at time of JOL robustly receive higher JOL ratings than nonrecallable ones.

An important goal for metacognitive theory is understanding how judgments of recallable items in the study may differ for immediate and delayed JOLs. Dunlosky and Nelson (1992) cued JOLs for items by either presenting an item's stimulus as the cue or an item's stimulus and response as the cue. According to MDM, the presentation of both stimulus and response at time of an item's delayed JOL will interfere with the retrievability of the item from long-term memory, producing less-accurate judgments involving long-term memory than those JOLs cued by the stimulus alone. However, it should also be noted that $M = 1$ for the set of items cued by stimulus–response because all such items are recallable at time of judgment. For such items, Equation 4 degenerates into

$$\gamma = \gamma_m,$$

which is smaller than

$$\gamma = (1 - w) \cdot \gamma_m + w$$

when $w \neq 0$, the latter being the case for the set of items cued by the stimulus alone because for such items $M < 1$. Dunlosky and Nelson (1992) reported the following finding:

> The two kinds of cues for delayed JOLs had different effects on JOL accuracy as opposed to recall. Namely, delayed JOLs cued by stimulus alone yielded much greater JOL accuracy than did delayed JOLs cued by the stimulus–response, whereas recall was somewhat greater for delayed JOLs cued by the stimulus–response pair than for delayed JOLs cued by the stimulus alone. (p. 379)

Thus, in this experiment, the stimulus–response condition when compared to the stimulus-alone condition not only produced a higher M, which by Equation 4 lowers delayed JOL accuracy, but also a higher R, which by Equation 4 raises JOL accuracy. The combination of these two opposing effects, with possibly a contribution of a lowering of γ_m in the stimulus–response condition, produced the observed lowering of JOL accuracy in the stimulus–response condition.

Self-Fulfilling Prophecy (SFP) Explanation

Spellman and Bjork (1992) provided the following explanation for the delayed JOL effect:

> One strategy for making a delayed JOL is to use the presented stimulus as a cue to try to recall the response item, and to base the JOL on whether recall is successful. Given the known effect of such retrieval practice, successful covert recall during the JOL task will in turn increase the likelihood that the subject will successfully recall that item on the later overt recall test... Thus, if delayed JOLs are based on the ability to recall the response, and final recall is also based on the ability to recall the response, it follows that delayed JOLs and final recall will necessarily be correlated. (p. 315)

Spellman and Bjork's (1992) observation can be expressed in terms of the theory of JOL accuracy described by Theorem 1 as follows: Looking at Equation 4,

$$\gamma = [(M - R)/(1 - R)] \cdot \gamma_m + (1 - M)/(1 - R),$$

we see that as R approaches M, γ approaches 1. Spellman and Bjork's explanation is that the delayed JOL judgment increases the strength of the maintenance items to an extent that at the time of the final test these items are more recallable than they would have otherwise been, thus producing a smaller difference between M and R. This is a mechanism that clearly could produce a delayed JOL effect. However, the above equation depends on both M and R. Thus, a modest — or even a large — increase in R alone is not enough to guarantee a large increase in γ; M must be selected in such a manner to capitalize on this increase. For example, using the right-hand side of the above equation and letting $M = .75$, $R = .25$, and $\gamma_m = .38$, we see that doubling the size R to .50 (i.e., increasing R by .25) will produce an increase in the right-hand part of the equation from .58 to .67 — not a substantial enough increase to produce a typical delayed JOL effect. However, for $M = .90$, $R = .65$, and $\gamma_m = .38$, increasing the size of R by 38% (i.e., increasing R by .25) will produce an increase from .55 to 1.0. Thus, the SFP hypothesis can at most only account for the part of the delayed JOL effect that is due to increased R.

The title of Spellman and Bjork's (1992) article is, "When Predictions Create Reality: Judgments of Learning May Alter What They Are Intended to Assess." They summarized this part of their theory as follows:

In our view, Nelson and Dunlosky's findings reflect a psychological analog of the Heisenberg Uncertainty Principle: Any effort to take a reading of a subject's current state of knowledge may alter that state of knowledge. In this specific instance, when subjects measure their own degree of learning after a delay by making covert recall attempts, they alter their degree of learning. The delayed JOL, in effect, creates its own reality; in such happy circumstances, the accuracy of the measurement is assured. (p. 316)

We agree that making a delayed JOL can change the state of the judged item, and thus may not be a good evaluation of the initial learning. However, in this quotation, Spellman and Bjork appear to us to attach more importance to this observation than it deserves.

According to their explanation (Spellman & Bjork, 1992), one makes a JOL by attempting a covert recall of the item. In doing this, one does not affect the recallability state of the item at the time of attempted recall but affects the recallability states of the item for later recall tests, particularly the final recall test. Thus, in particular, persistence of forgetting is not affected for items nonrecalled at the time of the delayed JOL judgment regardless of how they are affected by the judgment; that is, persistence of forgetting is not affected by delayed JOLs. Similarly, items that are recallable are ranked higher than items that are nonrecallable, regardless of how they are affected by the judgment; that is, superiority of JOMs is not affected by delayed JOLs. The only thing that can influence JOL accuracy that is affected by a delayed JOL judgment is possible changes in the strengths of recallable items for final recall. In some circumstances, this can have considerable impact (e.g., it can produce a large increase in final recall); in other circumstances, it can only have a small effect (e.g., when the delay between the times of an item's delayed JOL and its final recall was selected by the experimenter in such a manner that only a small percentage of recallable items at the delayed judgment time are recalled at the final test). Also, the JOL accuracy for recallable items γ_m often makes an important contribution to overall JOL accuracy, and the SFP explanation is silent about how the "analog of Heisenberg's uncertainty principle" affects the size of γ_m.

Experimental Assessment of the Mathematical Model

An experiment presented in Nelson et al. (2004) allows us to assess the mathematical model described by Equation 4. The experiment closely matches the paradigm used by Nelson and Dunlosky (1991), except that a recall test was given to some items just prior to their JOLs. A delayed JOL effect was observed with immediate γ accuracy of +.23 and delayed γ accuracy of +.92.

The additional recall test given for some items just before judgment allowed for the empirical determination of the values of γ, M, R, and γ_m in Equation 4. With these values, we can then use the right-hand side of Equation 4 to approximate γ. The empirical values for the delayed items are

$$M = .53, R = .49, \text{ and } \gamma_m = .50$$

Equation 4 with these values yields

$$\gamma = .96 \text{ (theory)}$$

whereas the data yield

$$\gamma = .92 \text{ (experiment)}.$$

(4% of the items violated persistence of forgetting, producing a slightly lower γ than expected from the theory). Thus, in this case, the theoretical and experimental results for γ differ by .04 — a very small amount for a γ correlation above +.90.

Although in this experiment the γ accuracy of delayed maintenance items, +.50, was much higher than the γ accuracy of immediate maintenance items, +.21, the estimated contribution of maintenance dyads to delayed γ accuracy via Equation 4 is minuscule because $M = .53$ was so close to $R = .49$, which by Equation 4 yields an estimated increase in γ due to maintenance dyads of less than +.02.

Equation 4 can be rewritten as

$$(1 - w) \cdot \gamma_m + w, \tag{5}$$

where

$$w = (1 - M)/(1 - R).$$

Equation 5 is determined by the two parameters γ_m and w. The MDM explanation provides a partial theory of γ_m, namely, γ_m is at least as large as the γ correlation for immediate JOL accuracy and larger than immediate JOL accuracy when JOLs are given after a sufficient delay from learning. It does not, however, have anything to say about w. In contrast, the SFP explanation provides a partial theory of w but has nothing to say about γ_m. Neither explanation explicitly states that the γ for contrast dyads γ_c should be near +1.0 (which allows the second term in Equation 5 to be written as w rather than $w \cdot \gamma_c$), although this is an obvious add-on to both explanations. Thus, the MDM and SFP explanations emphasize complementary aspects of the delayed effect. Neither individually nor together do they provide an adequate explanation for the delayed JOL effect presented in the Nelson and Dunlosky (1991) study because neither expresses the idea that the effect in that study is mostly driven by contrast dyads.

We believe it is likely that one can construct experimental circumstances in which the MDM explanation explains a delayed JOL effect finding, and one can construct other circumstances for which the delayed JOL effect is explained by the SFP explanation. For the empirical study described in Nelson et al. (2004) and analyzed above, the MDM explanation fails to account for a significant part of the observed delayed JOL effect, whereas the SFP could account for a significant part of it; however, whether SFP accounts for the full effect cannot be determined by data collected for this experiment.

Dynamic Monitoring Dual Memories

Equation 4, reformulated as

$$\gamma = (1 - w)\, \gamma_m + w \cdot 1 \tag{6}$$

expresses a law interrelating metamemory and memory processes. It is formulated for ideal situations captured by the hypotheses of Theorem 1. In Equation 6, w is completely determined by memory processes because it is completely determined by the number of items recallable at the delay between learning and JOL M and the number of items recallable at final recall R; that is,

$$w = (1 - M)/(1 - R).$$

Thus, the contribution to JOL accuracy γ that is due to metamemory processing is completely contained in the terms 1 and γ_m. The 1 corresponds to the monitoring accuracy of contrast dyads. Because of the assumptions of Theorem 1, it is maximal and therefore constant. γ_m is maintenance accuracy, that is, the monitoring accuracy of the maintenance dyads. Because the monitoring accuracy for contrast dyads 1 is constant, it cannot play a role in accounting for changes in monitoring accuracy. Therefore, any change in monitoring accuracy is due to a change in maintenance accuracy γ_m, and thus any theories about increasing monitoring accuracy for situations covered by Theorem 1 are necessarily theories about γ_m. Unfortunately, as discussed, the standard data collection methods for JOL experiments do not permit an estimate of γ_m. In our view, this has led to some confusion in the literature about the impact of increased monitoring accuracy because researchers had to do their analysis of increased monitoring accuracy in terms of γ. Because the value of w, which is detached from monitoring, has an impact on γ, this presents serious difficulties for viewing γ as a measure of monitoring accuracy. The following empirical study illustrates this point.

Nelson, Scheck, Dunlosky, and Narens (1999) presented preliminary results from a study in which 147 participants made JOLs for concrete noun–noun pairs after 0, 3, 6, 9, or 30 seconds of filled time following the offset of study. One group of participants made a pre-JOL recall attempt just prior to each JOL, and the other group made JOLs not preceded by a recall attempt. Both groups made a final recall attempt at approximately 2 minutes after studying the items. The following analyses pertain only to the group who made prejudgment recall attempts prior to making JOLs for each item. In accordance with the above notation, M denotes percent of correctly recalled items on the pre-JOL recall test, and R denotes the percent of correctly recalled items on the final recall test.

For recall performance (Table 1), a one-way analysis of variance (ANOVA) showed that the mean M differed significantly depending on the delay between study and JOL, $F(4, 348) = 445.55$, $p < .05$. A series of t tests with Bonferonni correction showed a greater proportion correct pre-JOL recall after a delay of 3 as compared to 6 seconds, $t(87) = 21.63$, $p < .01$, and for 6 as compared to 9 seconds, $t(87) = 2.79$, $p < .01$, but no difference in proportion correct pre-JOL recall between 9- and 30-second

TABLE 1   Results

Delay Between Study and JOL	Empirical				Theoretical
	M	R	γ_m	γ	γ
0 seconds	.96	.22	.39	.42	.42
3 seconds	.96	.22	.47	.58	.50
6 seconds	.48	.29	.33	.73	.82
9 seconds	.44	.28	.40	.81	.87
30 seconds	.40	.30	.20	.79	.89

delays, $t(87) = 2.18$, $p < .01$. The comparison between 0- and 3-second delays could not be made because the standard error of the difference was zero.

The mean R also differed significantly depending on the delay between study and JOL, $F(4, 348) = 11.22$, $p < .05$. A series of t tests with Bonferonni correction showed a smaller R after a delay of 3 as compared to 6 seconds, $t(87) = 3.81$, $p < .01$ but no difference in R between 6 and 9 seconds, $t(87) = .61$, $p < .01$, or 9 and 30 seconds, $t(87) = 1.10$, $p < .01$. Again, the comparison between 0 and 3 seconds could not be made because the standard error of the difference was zero.

Concerning the relationship between JOLs and final recall, the mean overall differed significantly depending on the delay between study and JOL, $F(4, 288) = 18.68$, $p < .05$. There was no significant difference in accuracy between JOLs made at a 0- versus 3-second delay, $t(82) = 2.47$, $p < .01$, at a 6- versus 9-second delay, $t(79) = 1.94$, $p < .01$, or at a 9- versus 30-second delay, $t(80) = .40$, $p < .01$, but there was a significant difference in accuracy between 3 and 6 seconds, $t(78) = 2.80$, $p < .01$. This indicates that a critical point in the difference in predictive accuracy between immediate and delayed JOLs occurs between 3 and 6 seconds. Interestingly, this point is also one at which differences were observed in pre-JOL recall and final recall.

The mean γ_m differed significantly depending on the delay between study and JOL, $F(4, 216) = 3.26$, $p < .05$. However, paired-sample t tests showed no significant difference made at a 0- versus 3-second delay, $t(82) = 1.12$, $p > .01$, at a 3- versus 6-second delay, $t(73) = 1.17$, $p > .01$, at a 6- versus 9-second delay, $t(65) = .17$, $p > .01$, or at a 9- versus 30-second delay, $t(63) = 1.81$, $p > .01$.

The mean γ_c did not differ significantly depending on the delay between study and JOL, $F(4, 112) = 1.59$, $p > .10$. The difference in γ_f across delay between study and JOL could not be computed because of the small number of observations. The empirical means and the theoretical based on M, R, and γ_m are given in Table 1.

Notice in Table 1 the nonmonotonic behavior of γ_m with respect to delay time. This, combined with the decrease in γ_m between the 3- and 30-second delays, is an empirical violation of the MDM theory. Notice that the empirical displays increasing monotonic behavior. (The difference of −.02 between the 30- and 9-second delays is not significant; the difference .15 between the 6- and 3-second delays is significant.) This, combined with the nonmonotonic behavior of γ_m, provides an empirical illustration that one should not rely on increasing γ correlations between JOL and final recall for evaluation of the MDM theory.

In Table 1, the empirical γ are, except for the 3-second delay, less than the corresponding theoretical γs. This can only happen if there are violations of the mathematical model. No tied ratings is violated by the design of the experiment. But as discussed, this cannot lower an empirical γ if the other assumptions of the model hold. Thus, the discrepancy of having smaller empirical γs than theoretical ones is likely due to violations of persistence of forgetting or superiority of JOMs or both. This demonstrates one of the advantages of deriving the model's mathematical equation from qualitative assumptions: When there is a discrepancy between the equation and data, one can often investigate the discrepancy qualitatively in terms of the qualitative assumptions that gave rise to the equation. Such an investigation was not carried out for the preliminary investigation of the dynamic MDM data presented here.

Conclusions

Several explanations of the delayed-JOL effect described by Nelson and Dunlosky (1991) have been put forth in the literature. They all give plausible mechanisms for producing this effect but are deficient in various ways for accounting for it as observed by Nelson and Dunlosky. This chapter gives a mathematical model for the delayed JOL effect that is based on a theoretical classification of items at the time of JOL into recallable and nonrecallable items. The classification is then used to decompose JOL accuracy into the weighted sum

$$\gamma = (1 - v - w) \cdot \gamma_m + w \cdot \gamma_c + v \cdot \gamma_f, \tag{7}$$

where γ_m, γ_c, and γ_f are, respectively, the γ accuracies for maintenance, contrast, and FOK items. Our analysis of the Nelson and Dunlosky paradigm suggests that for this paradigm $v = 0$ and $\gamma_c = 1$. (The mathematical model derives $v = 0$ from the theoretical assumption of persistence of forgetting, and $\gamma_c = 1$ from the assumptions of persistence of forgetting and superiority JOMs. Cited empirical support was given for both assumptions.) This allows Equation 7 to be simplified to

$$\gamma = (1 - w) \cdot \gamma_m + w. \tag{8}$$

The variables γ_m and w in Equation 8 are the foci of the MDM and SFP explanations of the delayed JOL effect. MDM focuses on γ_m, whereas SFP focuses on w. Neither explanation provides an account for the other variable; that is, MDM is silent about the impact of w on delayed γ accuracy, and SFP is silent about the impact of γ_m. Such silences make both explanations incomplete.

In summary, these explanations have two major weaknesses: (1) They fail to integrate their suggested mechanisms for increased accuracy with the structure of their measure of accuracy (in this case, the Goodman and Kruskal γ statistic); and (2) they fail to take into account other mechanisms that also increase γ and thus do not provide cogent arguments regarding why their proposed mechanisms account for the bulk of the delayed JOL effect. Accordingly, other mechanisms should be considered, and importantly, they can be empirically evaluated using the decomposition of γ offered in this chapter.

References

Bahrick, H. P. (1979). Maintenance of knowledge: Questions about memory we forgot to ask. *Journal of Experimental Psychology: General, 108,* 296–308.

Bahrick, H. P., & Hall, L. K. (1991). Lifetime maintenance of high school mathematics content. *Journal of Experimental Psychology: General, 120,* 20–33.

Begg, I., Duft, S., Lalonde, P., Melnick, R., & Sanvito, J. (1989). Memory predictions are based on ease of processing. *Journal of Memory and Language, 28,* 610–632.

Benjamin, A. S., & Bjork, R. A. (1996). Retrieval fluency as a metacognitive index. In L. Reder (Ed.), *Implicit memory and metacognition* (pp. 309–338). Hillsdale, NJ: Erlbaum.

Connor, L. T., Dunlosky, J., & Hertzog, C. (1997). *Aging and metamemory: Performance-level dependence of memory predictions.* Poster presented at the 35th annual meeting of the Psychonomic Society, November, St. Louis, MO.

Dunlosky, J., & Nelson, T. O. (1992). Importance of the kind of cue for judgments of learning (JOL) and the delayed-JOL effect. *Memory & Cognition, 20,* 374–380.

Dunlosky, J., & Nelson, T. O. (1994). Does the sensitivity of judgments of learning (JOLs) to the effects of various study activities depend on when the JOLs occur? *Journal of Memory and Language, 33,* 545–565.

Dunlosky, J., & Nelson, T. O. (1997). Similarity between the cue for judgments of learning (JOL) and the cue for test is not the primary determinant of JOL accuracy. *Journal of Memory and Language, 36,* 34–49.

Gonzalez, R., & Nelson, T. O. (1996). Measuring ordinal association in situations that contain tied scores. *Psychological Bulletin, 119,* 159–165.

Goodman, L. A., & Kruskal, W. H. (1954). Measures of association for cross classifications. *Journal of the American Statistical Associations, 49,* 732–764.

Goodman, L. A., & Kruskal, W. H. (1959). Measures of association for cross classifications: 2. Further discussion and references. *Journal of the American Statistical Associations, 54,* 126–163.

Hart, J. T. (1967). Memory and the memory-monitoring process. *Journal of Verbal Learning and Verbal Behavior, 6,* 685–691.

Kelemen, W. L., & Weaver, C. A., III (1997). Enhanced metamemory at delays: Why do judgments of learning improve over time? *Journal of Experimental Psychology: Learning, Memory, and Cognition, 23,* 1394–1409.

Koriat, A. (1997). Monitoring one's own knowledge during study: A cue-utilization approach to judgments of learning. *Journal of Experimental Psychology: General, 126,* 1–22.

Nelson, T. O. (1984). A comparison of current measures of feeling-of-knowing accuracy. *Psychological Bulletin, 95,* 109–133.

Nelson, T. O., & Dunlosky, J. (1991). The delayed-JOL effect: When delaying your judgments of learning can improve the accuracy of your metacognitive monitoring. *Psychological Science, 2,* 267–270. Findings reprinted in *Science News,* 1991, *140,* 93.

Nelson, T. O., Gerler, D., & Narens, L. (1984). Accuracy of feeling-of-knowing judgments for predicting perceptual identification and relearning. *Journal of Experimental Psychology: General, 113,* 282–300.

Nelson, T. O., & Narens, L. (1994). Why investigate metacognition? In J. Metcalfe & A. Shimamura (Eds.), *Metacognition: Knowing about knowing.* Cambridge, UK: Bradford Books.

Nelson, T. O., Narens, L., & Dunlosky, J. (2004). A revised methodology for research on metamemory: Pre-judgment recall and monitoring (PRAM). *Psychological Methods, 9,* 53–69.

Nelson, T. O., Scheck, P., Dunlosky, J., & Narens, L. (1999). Effects of study-judgment lag on judgment-of-learning accuracy. Unpublished data.

Peterson, L. R., & Peterson, M. J. (1959). Short-term retention of individual verbal items. *Journal of Experimental Psychology, 58,* 193–198.

Schwartz, B. L. (1994). Sources of information in metamemory: Judgments of learning and feelings of knowing. *Psychonomic Bulletin and Review, 1,* 357–375.

Shaughnessy, J. J., & Zechmeister, E. B. (1992). Memory-monitoring accuracy as influenced by the distribution of retrieval practice. *Bulletin of the Psychonomic Society, 20,* 125–128.

Spellman, B. A., & Bjork, R. A. (1992). When predictions create reality: Judgments of learning may alter what they are intended to access. *Psychological Science, 3,* 315–316.

Thiede, K. W., & Dunlosky, J. (1994). Delaying students' metacognitive monitoring improves their accuracy in predicting their recognition performance. *Journal of Educational Psychology, 86,* 290–302.

Weaver, C. A., III, & Kelemen, W. L. (1997). Judgments of learning at delays: Shifts in response patterns or increased metamemory accuracy? *Psychological Science, 8,* 318–321.

Wescourt, K. T., & Atkinson, R. C. (1973). Scanning for information in short-term memory. *Journal of Experimental Psychology, 98,* 95–101.

The Delayed JOL Effect with Very Long Delays:
Evidence From Flashbulb Memories

Charles A. Weaver III, J. Trent Terrell,
Kevin S. Krug, and William L. Kelemen

Introduction

Judgments of learning (JOLs) made immediately after studying typically correlate modestly with future performance. If those judgments are made following a delay, however, the predictions of performance are remarkably accurate, a phenomenon referred to as the *delayed judgment of learning* (d-JOL) effect (Nelson & Dunlosky, 1991). Delays between study and test, however, rarely last longer than a few minutes and usually involve simple paired-associate learning. We investigated very long-term JOLs using a flashbulb memory event, the destruction of the space shuttle *Columbia* in February 2003. Students answered seven typical questions concerning their personal circumstances of learning of the event 2 days, 9 days, or 1 month after the event and provided confidence judgments and JOLs at the same time. All were retested 3 months after the disaster. The γ correlations between JOLs and memory were slightly less than .50, higher than typical immediate JOLs but not as high as d-JOLs observed in the laboratory. Correlations between confidence judgments and memory were considerably higher, especially if the initial report was delayed. To test whether "privileged access" was involved in these judgments, other individuals predicted long-term retention of the memories after reading subjects' reports. Others' predictions were slightly but significantly less accurate, indicating modest effects of privileged access in predicting very long-term memories. We conclude that both mnemonic and metamnemonic processes (Koriat, 1997) are used in making these judgments of future recollection.

At the annual meeting of the Psychonomic Society in 2001, the first author had a conversation with Tom Nelson concerning new research on the d-JOL effect. At that time, Nelson and Dunlosky's (1991) seminal paper had been out around 10 years and had generated a great deal of research, discussion, and disagreement. How was it that after this much time, with so much written and debated about this simple phenomenon, the disagreements persisted? Tom's explanation, as was his style, was simple and to the point: "There's a lot of variance to be explained."

JOLs had been studied for some time (see Arbuckle & Cuddy, 1969, for an early example of similar judgments). In JOL paradigms, subjects are usually presented with a pair of words to study (say, elephant–sunburn) and are told that later they will be given the first word of the pair as a cue and will have to recall the second word — a simple paired-associate learning procedure. After study but before test, subjects are asked to predict their future performance. They are given the cue (elephant) and asked to make a prediction of their ability to recall the target (sunburn, although the target is generally not present at time of JOL). If judgments are made immediately after studying an item, correlations between JOLs and memory performance are modest, with γ correlations usually about .50. Nelson and Dunlosky (1991), however, found remarkably accurate predictions of future performance ($G = .90$) when judgments were delayed by a few minutes, something they called the d-JOL effect.

Nelson and Dunlosky (1991) initially proposed the monitoring-dual-memories (MDM) hypothesis to explain their results. They hypothesized that subjects make their predictions by performing a (covert) retrieval attempt: Given the cue, they simply tested themselves to see if they could recall the target. Successful retrieval of the target item produced a high JOL. With immediate JOLs, though, the target is probably still in short-term memory (STM), increasing the likelihood of successful retrieval (but also producing high JOLs). However, eventual recall of the target word requires retrieval from long-term memory (LTM). Therefore, JOLs that tap only LTM will be more accurate. As a result, retrieval from STM contaminates immediate JOLs but not delayed JOLs.

Nelson and Dunlosky's (1991) explanation was very quickly challenged. Spellman and Bjork (1992, 1997) countered that the d-JOL effect was essentially an artifact, that the delayed judgments actually created the effect being observed: "[The] delayed-JOL procedure used by Nelson and Dunlosky invited covert recall practice. Accordingly, their findings can be explained by the simple assumption that people base delayed JOLs on an assessment of retrieval success, which, in turn, influences their retrieval success on the subsequent recall test" (Spellman & Bjork, 1992, p. 315). More recently, Kimball and Metcalfe (2003) offered a similar explanation. They proposed that delayed (and successful) retrieval attempts function like spaced rehearsal trials: Retrieved items get high JOLs but additional study. Unretrieved items get low JOLs and received no such additional study. When they re-presented word pairs following all JOLs, the d-JOL effect disappeared, consistent with their explanation.

Over the past 15 years, our lab has looked at a number of possible explanations for the d-JOL effect and found problems with all of them. Nelson and Dunlosky's MDM hypothesis, for example, would not necessarily require long delays to produce the d-JOL effect. Essentially, anything that disrupted STM should result in high JOL accuracy. Kelemen and Weaver (1997) used brief but filled delays after studying word pairs. Rather than waiting 10 minutes, subjects were presented word pairs but then were immediately required to perform an STM distraction task, either the classic "counting by 7s" distraction task of Peterson and Peterson (1959) or the "G-word" task of Craik and Watkins (Craik & Watkins, 1973). Both produced improvements in JOL accuracy (Gs increased from about .30 to about .50), but despite clear evidence that the distraction tasks were effective, none produced the accuracy of Gs at longer delays (in our experiments, we observed Gs in delayed conditions of between .70 and .80).

A second potential source of the d-JOL effect was suggested by Schwartz (1994) (see also Dunlosky & Nelson, 1994). He observed that the distribution of JOLs changes over time. That is, subjects are more likely to use the middle range of the JOL scale immediately (producing an inverted U-shaped distribution), but gravitate toward the extremes at delays (a U-shaped distribution). Since γ correlations are computed by comparing all possible pairs of observations, changes in the frequency with which JOLs occur can alter the observed correlations. Weaver and Kelemen (1997) tested this possibility by conducting a series of mathematical simulations. These simulations allowed us to manipulate independently two different factors that might contribute to different Gs. First, we can alter the pattern of JOL distributions, reflecting those observed in either immediate or delayed JOL conditions. We could also manipulate the metamemory functions (e.g., the conditional probability of successful retrieval given an observed JOL, as shown in calibration curves) observed in those two conditions. Changes in metamemory functions accounted for roughly two thirds of the improvements in JOL accuracy at delays, demonstrating that these improvements were not simply artifacts of changes in JOL distributions.

A third potential explanation for the d-JOL effect was proposed by Dunlosky and Nelson (1997), what they called transfer-appropriate monitoring (TAM). This is similar to the well-known transfer-appropriate processing approach to memory (Lockhart, 2002; Morris, Bransford, & Franks, 1977; Roediger, 1990; Roediger, Gallo, & Geraci, 2002), in which memory benefits to the extent that the kind of processing required at retrieval is similar to that required at encoding. TAM proposes that prediction or monitoring of future performance will be accurate to the extent that the conditions at time of prediction are similar to those at the time of test. According to TAM, delayed JOLs are more accurate because the conditions under which they are made mirror those at time of test. To test this, Dunlosky and Nelson moved from a cued-recall to a recognition test, and their evidence was inconsistent with the TAM hypothesis. However, the recognition test used by Dunlosky and Nelson was incomplete because the incorrect alternatives on the final test were not shown during the JOLs, and therefore TAM could not be entirely ruled out as a factor.

A stricter test of the TAM hypothesis of JOL accuracy was conducted by Weaver and Kelemen (2003). All subjects studied cue–target word pairs (such as elephant–sunburn). Weaver and Kelemen manipulated the conditions in which JOLs were made as well as the nature of the memory test (cued recall vs. recognition). At the time of JOL, subjects were shown

1. Cue alone (elephant–?)
2. Cue plus target (elephant–sunburn)
3. Cue alone with future cue–target distracters (elephant–?, elephant–diamond, elephant–macaroni, etc.); this was like Condition 1, but the distracters that would be present at final test were also present during JOL
4. Cue plus target with future distracters, with the correct answer unmarked; this was like Condition 2, but included the distracters that would be present at final test
5. Cue plus target with future distracters, with the correct answer marked at time of JOL

TAM predicted judgments to be most accurate when JOL conditions match test conditions. Therefore, Condition 1 should have produced the most accurate predictions for the cued-recall test as the match between prediction and test conditions was high. Conversely, Condition 4 should have produced the most accurate predictions for the recognition test, again because of the close match between prediction and test conditions. This did not occur. Instead, prediction accuracy was highest when the answers were not presented (or at least not marked) at time of prediction. Failed retrieval attempts are particularly diagnostic of future performance (Dunlosky & Nelson, 1992; Kimball & Metcalfe, 2003; Koriat, Goldsmith, & Pansky, 2000; Nelson, Narens, & Dunlosky, 2004; Son, 2004), and presenting marked answers at time of judgment removes this rich source of information. Weaver and Kelemen concluded, "We see little evidence to support TAM as a viable account of metamemory accuracy" (p. 1064).

Our research, then, has cast doubt on at least three possible theoretical explanations: MDM, shifts in the distributions of judgments over time, and TAM. Unfortunately, we cannot provide a clear alternative explanation. In the remainder of this introduction, we discuss the phenomenon of flashbulb memories and how they may be able to contribute to the possible mechanisms underlying JOL accuracy.

Virtually all the research on the d-JOL effect has used paired associates of some sort. In addition, the "delays" used are seldom more than a few minutes long. Does the d-JOL effect extend to more complicated materials? For example, are similar processes at work when students are preparing for an exam? Those of us who conduct metamemory research tend to tell our students that when preparing for an upcoming exam, they should not test themselves immediately after studying. While this is not unreasonable (and frankly, probably right), d-JOL effects have not been entirely confirmed with complex materials (see, however, Maki, 1998; Thiede, Anderson, & Therriault, 2003; Thiede, Dunlosky, Griffin, & Wiley, 2005).

Likewise, when we are judging our memory in less-constrained situations, we often are more interested in predicting what we will remember in a week, a month, or a year. For example, Hall and Bahrick (1998) did show that judgments of very LTM can be quite accurate, although the material they studied was simple associates, which may be critical for finding such accurate long-term judgments. With more complex and rich memories, personal significance is likely to be a meaningful predictor. However, autobiographical memory research (Linton, 1982; Rubin, 1998; Wagenaar, 1986) suggests that we are not always capable of determining the significance of an event at the time of its occurrence, which would make judgments of future memorability difficult.[1] Can we make predictions about the durability of a LTM of personally significant events? To investigate this, we took advantage of a flashbulb memory event by asking individuals to make predictions about what they would (and would not) remember several months later.

Flashbulb Memory

Flashbulb memories are ones for the personal circumstances surrounding a memorable event. In their now-classic paper, Brown and Kulik (1977) defined these as "memories for the circumstances in which one first learned of a very surprising and consequential (or emotionally arousing) event. … Almost everyone can remember, with an almost perceptual clarity, where he was when he heard, what he was doing at the time, who told him, what was the immediate aftermath, how he felt, and one or more totally idiosyncratic, and often trivial concomitants" (p.73). Flashbulb memories appear to be universal and are one of the more intuitively understood memory experiences; it is not hard to imagine citizens of ancient Rome telling stories to their grandchildren about where they were when they got news that Julius Caesar had been assassinated.

At the risk of oversimplifying, flashbulb memory research has progressed through three phases: the phenomenological phase (1977–1988), the evaluation of special mechanisms phase (1988–1995), and the functional analysis phase (1996–present). During the first phase (1977–1988), the basic phenomenon of flashbulb memory was defined and explored (see Bohannon, 1988; Brown & Kulik, 1977; Neisser, 1982; Pillemer, 1984; Pillemer, Koff, Rhinehart, & Rierdan, 1987; Reynolds & Takooshian, 1988). While there was certainly some discussion and concern regarding possible problems with the accuracy or distortion of the memories, the emphasis was on the concept of flashbulb memory itself. The name was catchy, the explanation of "perfect memory forever" was tempting, and Brown and Kulik even drafted an obscure, speculative hypothetical brain mechanism to explain them: Livingston's (1967) "now print!" hypothesis.

During the late 1980s and early 1990s (the evaluation of special mechanisms phase), the focus changed to one of healthy skepticism. McCloskey and colleagues (McCloskey, Wible, & Cohen, 1988) were among the first to do a prospective study on the accuracy of flashbulb memories. They had subjects complete an initial memory questionnaire within a few hours of the *Challenger* disaster in 1986. When subjects were retested 9 months later, McCloskey et al. were able to compare these reports with what subjects had written down previously. Although subjects' memories were reasonably accurate, they clearly were not photograph-like. The later reports were subject to decay and distortion, just like all episodic memories. Similar studies followed (Christianson, 1989; Loftus & Kaufman, 1993; Neisser & Harsh, 1992; Weaver, 1993; Wright, 1993), until it became clear to most researchers that flashbulb memories were unique in their content but not necessarily in their production.

The current phase of flashbulb memory research, the functional analysis phase, is characterized by the use of flashbulb memories in the study of larger questions in memory research. For example, Tekcan found that flashbulb memories throughout the lifespan display Rubin's reminiscence bump (Tekcan & Demir, 2002; Tekcan & Peynircioglu, 2002). In addition, flashbulb memories appear to go through a consolidation-like process (Christianson & Engelberg, 1999; Niedzwienska, 2003; Weaver & Krug, 2004; Winningham, Hyman, & Dinnel, 2000) and appear to be almost a type of memory illusion. These recollections are characterized by the confidence we hold them with, not by their accuracy (Coluccia, Bianco, & Brandimonte, 2006; Hyman, 1999; Neisser & Harsh, 1992; Talarico & Rubin, 2003; Weaver, 1993; Weaver & Krug, 2004; Winningham et al., 2000; Wright, Gaskell, & Omuircheartaigh, 1997). Flashbulb memories have been used to help investigate traumatic memories such as those that might produce post-traumatic stress disorder (PTSD) (Berntsen & Rubin, 2006; Koss, Tromp, & Tharan, 1995; Nourkova, Bernstein, & Loftus, 2004; Tromp, Koss, Figueredo, & Tharan, 1995); to examine memory loss associated with Korsakoff's syndrome, Alzheimer's disease, and other disorders (Candel, Jelicic, Merckelbach, & Wester, 2003; Guilmette et al., 2004; Thompson et al., 2004); and to examine false or distorted memory (Finkenauer et al., 1998; Greenberg, 2004; Loftus & Kaufman, 1993; Niedzwienska, 2003; Weaver, 1995).

The present investigation falls squarely into the functional analysis phase: We used flashbulb memories to study the question of JOLs in very LTM. On Saturday, February 1, 2003, the space shuttle *Columbia* began reentry. Foam insulation had broken off during launch, damaging the leading edge of the left wing; this wing failed under the heat and stress of reentry, causing the shuttle's catastrophic destruction. The disaster took place at an altitude of less than 50 miles and almost exactly above the campus of Baylor University in Waco, Texas, where all data were collected. In fact, many of us in Waco at the time recalled hearing a loud thunder-like boom at about 9 AM, not knowing at the time the source of the noise. Although less dramatic than the *Challenger* explosion, there is little doubt the *Columbia* disaster was a significant, important event, especially to those in Central Texas.

Method

Two hundred and thirty five subjects were recruited from the Baylor University subject pool and were given course credit for their participation. One hundred twenty four completed a first survey 2 days following the disaster (although only 108 of these completed the follow-up questionnaire), 53 completed it 9 days later, and 74 completed it 30 days later. Ages ranged from 17 to 24, with the vast majority between 18 and 22. Subjects were tested in groups, and all participants within a single group were assigned to the same delay condition.

Two days following the disaster, the first group of participants was asked to complete a questionnaire similar to those used by Weaver (1993), Weaver and Krug (2004), and others, asking

1. How did you hear about the news?
2. What was the exact time?
3. Where were you?
4. What were you doing?
5. Who were you with?
6. What were you wearing?
7. What were your first thoughts?

In addition, subjects were asked, "How certain are you that your answer is correct?" They provided this assessment of their subjective confidence in each answer, using a 0–100 scale. They were also asked to provide a JOL response to the question, "What is the likelihood that you will remember this detail about the destruction of the space shuttle *Columbia* in 3 months?" They answered using the same 0–100 scale. Those in the second and third groups followed an identical procedure, although they received the questionnaire 9 days or 30 days after the disaster, respectively.

All subjects were given a second identical questionnaire during the first week of May 2003, approximately 3 months after the event. They were not asked to make JOLs at this second interval, although they did provide a second confidence rating.

TABLE 1   Mean Self-Reported Memory and Confidence

Time of Initial Report	Initial			3 Month	
	Memory	Confidence	JOL	Memory	Confidence
2 days	99	95	78	88	77
9 days	99	91	75	93	73
1 month	93	90	75	92	83

Results

Self-reported memory scores were computed simply by assigning a 1 if the participant provided an answer and a 0 if the question was left blank or the participant could not remember. This shows respondents' subjective impression of having a memory. They are reported for completeness but are not discussed. *Memory consistency scores* for each participant were computed by comparing later responses to responses given initially, scored using both strict and lenient criteria.[2] To facilitate comparisons with confidence judgments and JOLs, mean "memory" and "consistency" scores are reported using a 0–100 scale (simply proportion correct times 100). To minimize problems of missing data, responses were not nested within subjects; each response was considered as a unit of analysis.[3]

Self-Reported Memory and Confidence   Mean self-reported memory and confidence scores, averaged over the seven flashbulb memory questions for the three groups, are shown in Table 1. Virtually all subjects recalled the information if they were asked within 9 days, although memory declined somewhat after 1- and 3-month intervals. Subjective confidence followed a similar pattern.

Memory Consistency   To score consistency, we followed the system used by Christianson (1989), Weaver (1993), Weaver and Krug (Weaver & Krug, 2004), and others. Consistency was scored using both strict and lenient criteria. To be scored as correct according to the strict criteria, information provided on the later questionnaire must have been identical to that provided on the initial questionnaire. To be scored as correct on the lenient criteria, the same general information would need to be in both responses, but the details need not match. For example, a person may have said initially they were "with Bill and Trent" but at the 3-month interval recalled only "being with friends." This response would be scored as correct using the lenient but not the strict criteria.

Memory consistency is shown in Figure 1. Delaying the time of initial report increased the consistency of the reported memories using both lenient and strict criteria, $Fs(2, 1,876) = 15.9$ and 16.1, respectively, both $ps < .05$. Tukey's HSD confirmed that reports taken initially were less consistent than reports delayed by 1 week or 1 month, but that the latter two did not differ from each other. Mean JOLs did not differ from one another ($ps > .05$).

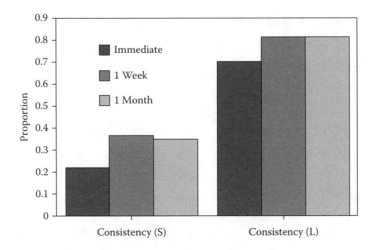

Figure 1   Mean consistency using strict (S) and lenient (L) criteria as a function on time of initial memory assessment.

Correlations Between Judgments of Learning, Confidence, and Memory Consistency   The γ correlations were computed across subjects and items in each of the three conditions, and the results are shown in Figure 2. (The analyses shown here use only data scored using the lenient criteria, although the pattern of results was identical using the strict criteria.) JOL accuracy increased slightly but significantly when the JOLs were delayed either 9 days or 1 month, $F(2, 228) = 3.86$, $p < .05$, although the last two delay conditions did not differ. When comparing initial confidence judgments and memory consistency, correlations increased as delay increased, $F(2, 227) = 11.5$, $p < .05$. Highest correlations were obtained when the initial report was delayed by a month, again suggesting that flashbulb memories go through a process of change and consolidation during the several weeks following a flashbulb event.

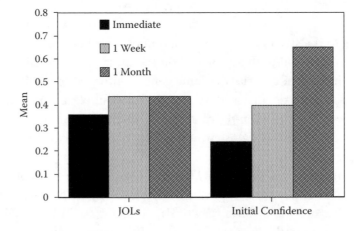

Figure 2   The γ correlations between judgments of learning (JOLs) and initial confidence judgments with memory consistency (using lenient criteria).

Discussion

The flashbulb memory data show a now-familiar pattern: The longer one waits before giving an initial memory report, the more likely later reports will be consistent. Although this seems paradoxical, it is not — delayed reports are not more likely to be *accurate*, just more likely to be consistent. Flashbulb memories appear to take between a week and a month to become stable; during that time, they are subject to postevent information, suggestion, source confusion, and so on, just like other episodic memories. Once they are formed, though, not only are they stable, they are also confidently held (see Coluccia et al., 2006; Talarico & Rubin, 2003; Weaver, 1993; Weaver & Krug, 2004; Wolters & Goudsmit, 2005).

We found small but significant increases in JOL accuracy when JOLs were delayed, although our effects were smaller than are typically seen in the laboratory. Of course, the "immediate" judgments obtained here were made at least 2 days after the actual event, hardly comparable to the "immediate" laboratory condition, usually made just a few seconds after study. Correlations between subjective confidence and memory consistency, on the other hand, did show systematic increases with longer delays. In fact, the γ correlation between confidence and memory when judgments were delayed by a month were nearly .70, comparing favorably to delayed JOLs observed with simpler materials and shorter delays. The general principle — the longer one waits before judging the likelihood of future memory, the better — seems to hold, particularly if one looks at confidence judgments rather than JOLs.

This raises an interesting theoretical challenge for the "memory hypothesis" of Kimball and Metcalfe (2003). First, the memory hypothesis predicts that delayed JOLs function as covert retrieval attempts as well as distributed rehearsal, thus creating their own reality. However, memory at the initial assessment in our data was exceptionally high (see Table 1), meaning that there were few instances of highly diagnostic retrieval failures. Furthermore, because of the way γs are computed, items that are recalled at neither the initial nor the delayed assessments are excluded from the analyses. Thus, the items that drive γ are those that are recalled initially but forgotten later (see Nelson et al., 2004). Can subjects recall an item at the initial test, yet accurately predict that this same item will be forgotten later? If so, this would be evidence against the memory hypothesis. In fact, that is exactly what we found. Despite the fact that recall was nearly perfect at initial assessments — there were almost no memory failures — subjects were reasonably accurate at predicting which items would not be remembered at longer intervals.

What Role Does Privileged Access Play in Predicting the Fate of Long-Term Memories?

Does such a finding mean that people do have access to something like "memory strength"? One could imagine, for example, that metamemory judgments might be made by simply reading off the strength parameter in a model like Search of Associative Memory (SAM) (Raaijmakers & Shiffrin, 1981). During discussions of these data following a conference presentation (T. O. Nelson, personal communication,

November 20, 2004), an interesting question arose: Does the ability to predict the later fate of long-term memories depend on "privileged access" to those memories? That is, can one reliably predict which memories will be retained over a certain interval just by examining the content of the memories, or are those holding the memories personally better able to make this kind of assessment? Ruth's Maki's excellent chapter in this volume looks at the role of privileged access in several ways: by comparing individuals' performance to their own predictions (standard metamemory procedure), by comparing performance to normative performance, and by comparing performance to predictions of other's performance. Other researchers (Jameson, Nelson, Leonesio, & Narens, 1993; Matvey, Dunlosky, & Guttentag, 2001; Vesonder & Voss, 1985) have employed a learner-observer-judge paradigm, in which others may observe a learner's study procedures (observers) or the items being studied (judges). Jameson et al. (1993) found observers made more accurate predictions of future performance than judges, but neither group was as accurate as the subjects themselves, a fairly typical result. Others, using similar procedures, also reported advantages for this with privileged access (see Hertzog, Kidder, Powell-Moman, & Dunlosky, 2002).

We were interested in a slightly different question. Rather than have an observer watch a subject learn new material, can one use the *contents* of a memory as a basis for prediction? One way to test this hypothesis would be to present the initial reports created by one subject, describing their memories of the *Columbia* explosion, to a different group of observers. These observers, then, are asked to predict the likelihood that those memories would be retained over a 3-month interval. The observer would have no information about the subject other than what is written in the flashbulb memory account.

We took a subset (total $n = 110$) of the questionnaires, pseudorandomly drawn from all of the three delay groups, and gave them to a completely different group of subjects. (Five of the questionnaires initially selected included sparse or missing memory reports. They were eliminated and replaced with another report.) For each of the flashbulb memory questions, these naïve subjects were asked to predict the likelihood that the person who wrote down this information would still remember it 3 months later. This would allow us to determine whether the *content* of a memory gave clues to its memorability, say, in the length of the answer or the amount detail provided.

In doing so, we relied on Koriat's (1997) distinction among intrinsic, extrinsic, and mnemonic factors in JOLs (see also Koriat, Sheffer, & Ma'ayan, 2002). *Intrinsic cues* refer to inherent characteristics of the items that suggest difficulty, such as the degree of relationship between paired associates. *Extrinsic cues* refer to the conditions at the time of learning (such as an increase or decrease in study time) or to changes in processing used at the time of learning. In contrast, *mnemonic cues* are subjective, internal cues (see Benjamin, Bjork, & Schwartz, 1998; Koriat & Ma'ayan, 2005) that suggest the degree to which information has been learned.

When judging long-term retention of their own flashbulb memories, individuals may rely on any or all of these. They may use mnemonic cues by judging how quickly the memory can be recalled (retrieval fluency) or evaluate the vividness or perceptual salience of the memory. Extrinsic factors would be used to estimate the effects of delays — knowing that 4 months would pass between the event and subsequent retrieval could be used to predict future performance. Finally, intrinsic cues could be used if one were to judge overall memorability of types of information — knowing that people are more likely to remember who they were with on a given day than what they were wearing that same day, for example.

While any of these might be used to make predictions, not all of them require personal retrieval of the information. Mnemonic cues — like retrieval fluency — demand privileged access and thus could not be used by those simply reading others' reports. Predicting a decline in memory accuracy over time or predicting that "what one was wearing" is more likely to be forgotten and, in contrast, requires no special access.

For each person's memory, then, we had two different sets of yoked predictors: their own JOLs and JOLs made by a person who had just read their initial report. We compared these predictions looking first at resolution. We compared mean JOLs for correct and incorrect responses for both the person writing the memory (self) and one who just read it (others) in a 2 (person making the judgments, self or others) by 2 (accurate vs. inaccurate memories) multivariate analysis of variance (MANOVA). These results are presented in Figure 3. Overall, mean JOLs made by others were significantly lower than JOLs made by self, and mean JOL was higher for accurate than inaccurate memories, $Fs > 12.4$, $ps < .05$. Most importantly, though, there was no interaction between the two: JOLs for accurate memories were about 10 points higher for both self and other. Special access, then, is not required to discriminate memories that are more likely to be incorrect after 3 months.

A second way to compare self- and other predictions is to use relative calibration measures, usually measured by G (Nelson, 1984, 1996). Mean G (relating JOL and memory accuracy, lenient) using JOLs (self) was .44, while mean G for others' JOL was slightly but significantly lower, .32 ($p = .03$). Calibration curves for self- and other's JOLs, as well as confidence judgments, are shown in Figure 4. It should be noted here that while these results suggest underconfidence, this is entirely due to the fact that we used the lenient criteria to construct the calibration curves. For comparison, mean JOL for self using the strict criteria is shown on Figure 4.

General Discussion

Our flashbulb memory results are consistent with recent flashbulb memory research. First, we add these results to the overwhelming consensus that flashbulb memories,

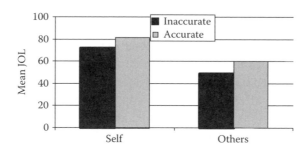

Figure 3   Discrimination scores for correct and incorrect memories, comparing judgments made by self and others.

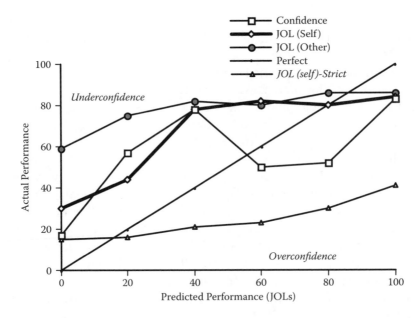

Figure 4   Calibration curves for confidence judgments, judgments of learning (JOLs) made by self, and JOLs made by others, using the lenient scoring criteria. (JOL-self using the strict criteria is shown for comparison.)

despite their name, are not photograph-like. They are not perfectly accurate or immune from forgetting and distortion. Furthermore, like Winningham et al. (2000) and Weaver and Krug (2004), we found strong evidence of initial changes in flashbulb memories, followed by stability. When we assessed memory of the *Columbia* disaster within 2 days of the event, we found significant changes in memories when retested 3 months after the event. Even using the lenient scoring criteria, memories were inconsistent nearly one third of the time; using more strict criteria, fully three fourths of such memories were inconsistent. Although memories first measured 1 week or 1 month after the event were not immune to forgetting and distortion, they were significantly more consistent (although very likely they were no more accurate).

The more interesting questions revolve around the nature of very long-term JOLs. Our data show that individuals can make reliable predictions of LTMs for the distant (3-month) future, although these predictions are not perfect. Since virtually all memories were still accessible at the time of first JOL, subjects could not simply use retrieval success or failure as the basis for predictions — there were not enough retrieval failures to make this useful. Rather, subjects were able to distinguish, *among memories that were currently retrieved*, which of those would be more likely to be retrieved after a 3-month interval. A strictly memory-based explanation of the d-JOL effect (Kimball & Metcalfe, 2002) could not explain these results satisfactorily. On the other hand, predictions of future performance did become more accurate when initial assessment was delayed, thereby increasing the frequency of highly diagnostic retrieval failures — just as the memory hypothesis would predict.

Our data regarding the necessity of privileged access are inconclusive. On the one hand, the discrimination scores showed that those who read the contents of a memory report were just as accurate in their predictions of future performance as those who actually experienced the events. Analysis of the relative calibration, on the other hand, suggests an advantage for privileged access. JOLs made by the people who experienced the event were slightly (although significantly) more accurate than those who only read about those accounts.

Based on those data, privileged access seems marginally necessary for predicting future memory. The *most* accurate predictions of all (Gs of nearly .70), however, involved not JOLs but subjective confidence judgments, which are almost definitionally "mnemonic" in Koriat's (1997) classification system. To keep the research parallel, we briefly considered asking those who read our subjects' memories to provide confidence judgments in addition to JOLs. The more we thought about it, the more absurd it sounded. It is one thing to ask, "How likely it is that the person who wrote this report will remember it 3 months from now?" but something else entirely to ask, "How confident do you think the person who wrote this report was at the time they wrote it?" The first judgment is unfamiliar, maybe, but understandable. The second strains comprehension.

Our data, then, support the notion that for all their apparent simplicity, JOLs require complex cognitive and metacognitive operations. Using present success or failure to predict future success or failure (the memory hypothesis) provides useful information but cannot be used when all information is currently retrievable or when predicting future memory performance of others. In those situations, predicting future performance appears to be a combination of experience- or theory-based judgments — How much will learning be influenced by restudy, or How quickly does memory decline over time? (Koriat, Bjork, Sheffer, & Bar, 2004; Koriat et al., 2002) — and experiential factors: How quickly was I able to retrieve that information, or How familiar did that item appear? (Benjamin et al., 1998; Koriat & Ma'ayan, 2005; Serra & Dunlosky, 2005; Son & Metcalfe, 2005). Tom Nelson was right when he said that the d-JOL effect would continue to be studied because there is a lot of variance to be explained. Implied in his message is the fact that no single explanation should be expected to account for it all. He was right, then, on both counts.

Notes

1. One embarrassing example of this happened to the first author a few years ago, during the course of an office move. I came across some flashbulb memory questionnaires I had collected in 1993 after the United States launched a massive missile attack in January 1993, at 2 years after the start of the Gulf War. Not only did I have no memory of having collected those questionnaires, *I didn't have (and still don't have) any memory of the event itself!* The military attack that seemed to be significant at the time turned out not to be so personally relevant after all.

2. In scoring responses, we might assume that the memory reported initially is accurate. This is a safe assumption when the first questionnaire is completed within a few days of the event in question, but less so when the initial report is delayed. In those cases, we are assessing the consistency of the report rather than the accuracy. Winningham

et al. (2000) and Weaver and Krug (2004) both report greater long-term consistency if the initial report is delayed, suggesting that flashbulb memories proceed through a consolidation-like process during the first few weeks following a flashbulb event.

3. This has no effect on mean values, of course, but eliminates the need to discard all of a subject's responses if one value is missing. From an analysis standpoint, this adds potential within-subject error back to the residual sum of squared errors (SSE), slightly reducing the power of our test.

References

Arbuckle, T. Y., & Cuddy, L. L. (1969). Discrimination of item strength at time of presentation. *Journal of Experimental Psychology Monographs, 81*, 126–131.

Benjamin, A. S., Bjork, R. A., & Schwartz, B. L. (1998). The mismeasure of memory: When retrieval fluency is misleading as a metamnemonic index. *Journal of Experimental Psychology-General, 127*, 55–68.

Berntsen, D., & Rubin, D. C. (2006). Flashbulb memories and posttraumatic stress reactions across the life span: Age-related effects of the German occupation of Denmark during World War II. *Psychology and Aging, 21*, 127–139.

Bohannon, J. N. (1988). Flashbulb memories for the space shuttle disaster: A tale of two theories. *Cognition, 29*, 179–196.

Brown, R., & Kulik, J. (1977). Flashbulb memories. *Cognition, 5*, 73–99.

Candel, I., Jelicic, M., Merckelbach, H., & Wester, A. (2003). Korsakoff patients' memories of September 11, 2001. *Journal of Nervous and Mental Disease, 191*, 262–265.

Christianson, S. A. (1989). Flashbulb memories: Special, but not so special. *Memory and Cognition, 17*, 435–443.

Christianson, S. A., & Engelberg, E. (1999). Memory and emotional consistency: The *MS Estonia* ferry disaster. *Memory, 7*, 471–482.

Coluccia, E., Bianco, C., & Brandimonte, M. A. (2006). Dissociating veridicality, consistency, and confidence in autobiographical and event memories for the *Columbia* shuttle disaster. *Memory, 14*, 452–470.

Craik, F. I. M., & Watkins, M. J. (1973). The role of rehearsal in short-term memory. *Journal of Verbal Learning and Verbal Behavior, 12*.

Dunlosky, J., & Nelson, T. O. (1992). Importance of the kind of cue for judgments of learning (JOL) and the delayed-JOL effect. *Memory and Cognition, 20*, 374–380.

Dunlosky, J., & Nelson, T. O. (1994). Does the sensitivity of judgments of learning (JOLs) to the effects of various study activities depend on when the JOLs occur? *Journal of Memory and Language, 33*, 545–565.

Dunlosky, J., & Nelson, T. O. (1997). Similarity between the cue for judgments of learning (JOL) and the cue for test is not the primary determinant of JOL accuracy. *Journal of Memory and Language, 36*, 34–49.

Finkenauer, C., Luminet, O., Gisle, L., El Ahmadi, A., van der Linden, M., & Philippot, P. (1998). Flashbulb memories and the underlying mechanisms of their formation: Toward an emotional-integrative model. *Memory and Cognition, 26*, 516–531.

Greenberg, D. L. (2004). President Bush's false "flashbulb" memory of 9/11/01. *Applied Cognitive Psychology, 18*, 363–370.

Guilmette, T. J., Carroll, B., Ferreira, J., Magner, E., Mihuta, M., & Kennedy, M. L. (2004). Recall of 9/11/01 as an indicator of cognitive functioning in the elderly. *Aging Neuropsychology and Cognition, 11*, 450–458.

Hall, L. K., & Bahrick, H. P. (1998). The validity of metacognitive predictions of widespread learning and long-term retention. In G. Mazzoni & T. O. Nelson (Eds.), *Metacognition and cognitive neuropsychology: Monitoring and control processes* (pp. 23–36). Mahwah, NJ: Erlbaum.

Hertzog, C., Kidder, D. P., Powell-Moman, A. & Dunlosky, J. (2002). Aging and monitoring associative learning: Is monitoring accuracy spared or impaired? *Psychology and Aging, 17,* 209–225.

Hyman, I. E. (1999). Creating false autobiographical memories: Why people believe their memory errors. In E. Winograd (Ed.), *Ecological approaches to cognition: Essays in honor of Ulric Neisser* (pp. 229–252). Mahwah, NJ: Erlbaum.

Jameson, A., Nelson, T. O., Leonesio, R. J., & Narens, L. (1993). The feeling of another person's knowing. *Journal of Memory and Language, 32,* 320–335.

Kelemen, W. L., & Weaver, C. A., III. (1997). Enhanced memory at delays: Why do judgments of learning improve over time? *Journal of Experimental Psychology: Learning, Memory, and Cognition, 23,* 1394–1409.

Kimball, D. R., & Metcalfe, J. (2002). *Explaining the delayed-JOL effect: Evidence of a Heisenberg effect.* Paper presented at the 43rd annual meeting of the Psychonomic Society, November 2002, Kansas City, MO.

Kimball, D. R., & Metcalfe, J. (2003). Delaying judgments of learning affects memory, not metamemory. *Memory & Cognition, 31,* 918–929.

Koriat, A. (1997). Monitoring one's own knowledge during study: A cue-utilization approach to judgments of learning. *Journal of Experimental Psychology: General, 126,* 349–370.

Koriat, A., Bjork, R. A., Sheffer, L., & Bar, S. K. (2004). Predicting one's own forgetting: The role of experience-based and theory-based processes. *Journal of Experimental Psychology-General, 133,* 643–656.

Koriat, A., Goldsmith, M., & Pansky, A. (2000). Toward a psychology of memory accuracy. *Annual Review of Psychology, 51,* 481–537.

Koriat, A., & Ma'ayan, H. (2005). The effects of encoding fluency and retrieval fluency on judgments of learning. *Journal of Memory and Language, 52,* 478.

Koriat, A., Sheffer, L., & Ma'ayan, H. (2002). Comparing objective and subjective learning curves: Judgments of learning exhibit increased underconfidence with practice. *Journal of Experimental Psychology: General, 131,* 147–162.

Koss, M. P., Tromp, S., & Tharan, M. (1995). Traumatic memories: Empirical foundations, forensic and clinical implications. *Clinical Psychology: Science and Practice, 2,* 111–132.

Linton, M. (1982). Transformations of memory in everyday life. In U. Neisser (Ed.), *Memory observed* (pp. 77–91). New York: Freeman.

Livingston, R. B. (1967). Brain circuitry relating to complex behavior. In C. G. Quarton, T. Melnechuck, & F. O. Schmidt (Eds.), *The neurosciences: A study program* (568–577). New York: Rockefeller University Press.

Lockhart, R. S. (2002). Levels of processing, transfer-appropriate processing, and the concept of robust encoding. *Memory, 10,* 397–403.

Loftus, E. F., & Kaufman, L. (1993). Why do traumatic experiences sometimes produce good memory (flashbulbs) and sometimes no memory (repression)? In E. Winograd & U. Neisser (Eds.), *Affect and accuracy in recall: Studies of "flashbulb" memories* (pp. 212–223). New York: Cambridge University Press.

Maki, R. H. (1998). Predicting performance on text: Delayed versus immediate predictions and tests. *Memory & Cognition, 26,* 959–964.

Matvey, G., Dunlosky, J., & Guttentag, R. (2001). Fluency of retrieval at study affects judgments of learning (JOLs): An analytic or nonanalytical basis for JOLs? *Memory & Cognition, 29,* 222–233.

McCloskey, M., Wible, C. G., & Cohen, N. J. (1988). Is there a special flashbulb-memory mechanism? *Journal of Experimental Psychology: General, 117,* 171–181.

Morris, C. D., Bransford, J. D., & Franks, J. J. (1977). Levels of processing versus transfer appropriate processing. *Journal of Verbal Learning and Verbal Behavior, 16,* 519–533.

Neisser, U. (1982). Snapshots or benchmarks? In U. Neisser (Ed.), *Memory observed: Remembering in natural contexts.* San Francisco: Freeman.

Neisser, U., & Harsh, N. (1992). Phantom flashbulbs: False recollections of hearing the news about the *Challenger.* In E. Winograd & U. Neisser (Eds.), *Affect and accuracy in recall: Studies of "flashbulb memory"* (pp. 9–31). New York: Cambridge University Press.

Nelson, T. O. (1984). A comparison of current measures of the accuracy of feeling-of-knowing predictions. *Psychological Bulletin, 95,* 109–133.

Nelson, T. O. (1996). Gamma is a measure of the accuracy of predicting performance on one item relative to another item, not of the absolute performance on an individual item. *Applied Cognitive Psychology, 10,* 257–260.

Nelson, T. O., & Dunlosky, J. (1991). When people's judgments of learning (JOLs) are extremely accurate at predicting subsequent recall: The "delayed-JOL effect." *Psychological Science, 2,* 267–270.

Nelson, T. O., Narens, L., & Dunlosky, J. (2004). A revised methodology for research on metamemory: Pre-judgment recall and monitoring (PRAM). *Psychological Methods, 9,* 53.

Niedzwienska, A. (2003). Misleading postevent information and flashbulb memories. *Memory, 11,* 549–558.

Nourkova, V., Bernstein, D., & Loftus, E. F. (2004). Altering traumatic memory. *Cognition & Emotion, 18,* 575–585.

Peterson, L. R., & Peterson, M. (1959). Short-term retention of individual verbal items. *Journal of Experimental Psychology, 58,* 193–198.

Pillemer, D. B. (1984). Flashbulb memories of the assassination attempt on President Reagan. *Cognition, 16,* 63–80.

Pillemer, D. B., Koff, E., Rhinehart, E. D., & Rierdan, J. (1987). Flashbulb memories of menarche and adult menstrual distress. *Journal of Adolescence, 10,* 187–199.

Raaijmakers, J. G. W., & Shiffrin, R. M. (1981). Search of associative memory. *Psychological Review, 88,* 93–134.

Reynolds, R. I., & Takooshian, H. (1988). Where were you August 8, 1985? *Bulletin of the Psychonomic Society, 26,* 23–25.

Roediger, H. L. III (1990). Implicit memory: Retention without remembering. *American Psychologist, 45,* 1043–1056.

Roediger, H. L. III, Gallo, D. A., & Geraci, L. (2002). Processing approaches to cognition: The impetus from the levels-of-processing framework. *Memory, 10,* 319–332.

Rubin, D. C. (1998). Knowledge and judgments about events that occurred prior to birth: The measurement of the persistence of information. *Psychonomic Bulletin & Review, 5,* 397–400.

Schwartz, B. L. (1994). Sources of information in metamemory: Judgments of learning and feelings of knowing. *Psychonomic Bulletin & Review, 1,* 357–375.

Serra, M. J., & Dunlosky, J. (2005). Does retrieval fluency contribute to the underconfidence-with-practice effect? *Journal of Experimental Psychology: Learning, Memory, and Cognition, 31,* 1258–1266.

Son, L. K. (2004). Spacing one's study: Evidence for a metacognitive control strategy. *Journal of Experimental Psychology: Learning, Memory, and Cognition, 30*, 601–604.

Son, L. K., & Metcalfe, J. (2005). Judgments of learning: Evidence for a two-stage process. *Memory & Cognition, 33*, 1116–1129.

Spellman, B. A., & Bjork, R. A. (1992). When predictions create reality: Judgments of learning may alter what they are intended to assess. *Psychological Science, 3*, 315–316.

Spellman, B. A., & Bjork, R. A. (1997). *When prophecy succeeds (too well): Inaccurate judgments of learning can produce better-than-perfect predictions.* Paper presented at the 38th annual meeting of the Psychonomic Society, November, 1997, Philadelphia.

Talarico, J. M., & Rubin, D. C. (2003). Confidence, not consistency, characterizes flashbulb memories. *Psychological Science, 14*, 455–461.

Tekcan, A. I., & Demir, C. (2002). *Is there a reminiscence bump for flashbulb memories?* Paper presented at the 43rd annual meeting of the Psychonomic Society, November 2002, Kansas City, MO.

Tekcan, A. I., & Peynircioglu, Z. F. (2002). Effects of age on flashbulb memories. *Psychology and Aging, 17*, 416–422.

Thiede, K. W., Dunlosky, J., Griffin, T. D., & Wiley, J. (2005). Understanding the delayed-keyword effect on metacomprehension accuracy. *Journal of Experimental Psychology: Learning, Memory, and Cognition, 31*, 1267–1280.

Thiede, K. W., Anderson, M. C. M., & Therriault, D. (2003). Accuracy of metacognitive monitoring affects learning of texts. *Journal of Educational Psychology, 95*, 66–73.

Thompson, R. G., Moulin, C. J. A., Ridel, G. L., Hayre, S., Conway, M. A., & Jones, R. W. (2004). Recall of 9.11 in Alzheimer's disease: Further evidence for intact flashbulb memory. *International Journal of Geriatric Psychiatry, 19*, 495–496.

Tromp, S., Koss, M. P., Figueredo, A. J., & Tharan, M. (1995). Are rape memories different? A comparison of rape, other unpleasant, and pleasant memories among employed women. *Journal of Traumatic Stress, 8*, 607–627.

Vesonder, G. T., & Voss, J. F. (1985). On the ability to predict one's own responses while learning. *Journal of Memory and Language. 24*, 363–376.

Wagenaar, W. A. (1986). My memory: A study of autobiographical memory over six years. *Cognitive Psychology, 18*, 225–252.

Weaver, C. A., III. (1993). Do you need a "flash" to form a flashbulb memory? *Journal of Experimental Psychology: General, 122*, 39–46.

Weaver, C. A., III. (1995). The search for "special mechanisms" in memory: Flashbulbs, flashbacks, and other not-so-bright ideas. *False Memory Syndrome Newsletter, 4*, 16–22.

Weaver, C. A., III, & Kelemen, W. L. (1997). Judgments of learning at delays: Shifts in response patterns or increased metamemory accuracy? *Psychological Science, 8*, 318–321.

Weaver, C. A., III, & Kelemen, W. L. (2003). Processing similarity does not improve metamemory: Evidence against transfer-appropriate monitoring. *Journal of Experimental Psychology: Learning, Memory, and Cognition, 29*, 1058–1065.

Weaver, C. A., III, & Krug, K. (2004). Consolidation-like effects in flashbulb memories: Evidence from September 11, 2001. *American Journal of Psychology, 117*, 517–530.

Winningham, R. G., Hyman, I. E., & Dinnel, D. L. (2000). Flashbulb memories? The effects of when the initial memory report was obtained. *Memory, 8*, 209–216.

Wolters, G., & Goudsmit, J. J. (2005). Flashbulb and event memory of September 11, 2001: Consistency, confidence and age effects. *Psychological Reports, 96*, 605–619.

Wright, D. B. (1993). Recall of the Hillsborough disaster over time: Systematic biases of "flashbulb" memories. *Applied Cognitive Psychology, 7*, 129–138.

Wright, D. B., Gaskell, G. D., & Omuircheartaigh, C. A. (1997). The reliability of the subjective reports of memories. *European Journal of Cognitive Psychology, 9,* 313–323.

Privileged Access for General Knowledge and Newly Learned Text Material

Ruth H. Maki

Introduction

Privileged access allows an individual to know about the idiosyncratic or personal contents of his or her own mind (Nelson, Leonesio, Landwehr, & Narens, 1986). The belief that individuals have privileged access to the contents of their minds underlies the study of metacognition. If individuals cannot access the contents of their minds either directly or indirectly, they cannot judge the level of their knowledge, their degree of learning, or the accuracy of their test performance. The research reported in the present chapter investigates privileged access with two types of materials: newly learned text material and general knowledge. In addition, privileged access was investigated both by using normative data as compared to individual data (Underwood, 1966; Nelson et al., 1986) and by comparing predictions about one's own performance with predictions about the performance of others (Lovelace, 1984; Underwood, 1966; Vesonder & Voss, 1985).

Privileged Access

Nelson et al. (1986) directly addressed the question of privileged access by comparing the accuracy of feelings of knowing (FOK) for individuals with the predictive accuracy of normative data. They asked whether individuals' own judgments about future recognition of answers that they could not recall matched their recognition success better than average recognition scores or average judgments. If individuals have privileged access to the idiosyncratic aspects of their knowledge, then individual FOK judgments should predict individual recognition better than overall difficulty or average judgments. Although Nelson et al. found some evidence for privileged access, their study has some limitations by today's standards because privileged access was studied only for answers that could not be recalled. Indeed, Nelson (1996) noted that the findings may be different with a full range of recallable and nonrecallable materials. The research reported in the present chapter expands on Nelson et al.'s (1986) paradigm to investigate privileged access for different types of materials, including correct and incorrect answers in the analysis.

Nelson et al. (1986) investigated the relationship between individuals' performance on general knowledge questions and several potential predictors, including individuals' own FOK judgments, normative FOK judgments, and normative item difficulty. The Nelson and Narens (1980) norms for the general knowledge questions were used to determine normative values. As is commonly done with FOK judgments, participants made predictions of future performance following the inability to recall an answer, and then they took a memory test. Four different types of tests were used: four-alternative and eight-alternative forced-choice recognition, relearning, and identification of briefly flashed answers (perceptual identification).

Nelson et al. (1986) reasoned that if participants have privileged access to their memories, then their own FOK judgments should predict future performance better than either normative FOKs or normative question difficulty. For both recognition tasks and for relearning, individuals' FOKs predicted individuals' performance significantly better than did normative FOKs. For the perceptual identification task, the trend was similar, but it was not significant. Nelson et al. concluded that individuals use idiosyncratic information related to the assessment of their own learning. This results in participants' own predictions being more accurate for their performance than average predictions.

However, normative question difficulty produced a different pattern. In the two recognition groups, normative question difficulty predicted performance better than did individuals' FOK judgments. In the relearning and perceptual identification groups, normative question difficulty and individual FOK judgments did not produce a statistically significant difference in prediction accuracy. Nelson et al. (1986) reported being somewhat surprised by the fact that normative difficulty was as good a predictor as individual FOKs in some tasks and better than individual FOKs in other tasks. In contrast, individual FOKs predicted performance better than normative FOKs, suggesting that idiosyncratic components of memory were used to improve prediction accuracy. Why, then, did the same idiosyncratic components about item difficulty not produce the same type of benefit when individuals' prediction accuracy was compared to normative item difficulty? As mentioned, the FOK paradigm involves judgments only about nonrecallable material. Koriat (1993) argued that requiring judgments only for nonrecalled answers to questions gives information to participants about the correctness of their answers. To avoid this external source of information, he recommended that judgments be made on all items. We asked participants to make judgments about all answers in the present experiment. Whether a full range of recallable and nonrecallable material would produce a stronger case for the superiority of individual judgments over normative difficulty is addressed in this chapter.

In the Nelson et al. (1986) data, the correlation between individuals' FOKs and normative question difficulty was quite low, suggesting that individuals do not know what makes questions difficult in general. Furthermore, questions that were difficult in general were difficult for each individual, as evidenced by a high correlation between individual performance and normative item difficulty. Nelson et al. suggested that underutilization of normative information may be a factor that makes FOKs only moderately accurate. They suggested that this tendency to ignore base rate information in FOK judgments may be another example of this more common error in judgment and decision making (Kahneman & Tversky, 1973).

Calogero and Nelson (1992) asked whether exposure to base rate information would improve FOK accuracy. They also used the Nelson and Narens (1980) norms for general knowledge questions. Half of the participants were informed about the percentage of participants who correctly answered the question in the normative data, and half of the participants were not informed. Participants having base rate information produced higher relationships between their FOK judgments and recognition accuracy than participants who did not have base rate information. However, strength of the relationship between individual FOKs and recognition was still about the same as that between normative question difficulty and individual recognition. That is, privileged access to one's own knowledge did not produce higher accuracy than normative difficulty even when individuals had base rate information.

These results can be viewed in terms of Koriat's (1997) cue utilization approach to judgments of learning (JOLs). Intrinsic factors include the characteristics of the materials, such as difficulty of test questions. Extrinsic factors involve the conditions of learning or the way in which learning material was encoded. Mnemonic factors relate to internal indicators for how well material has been learned. These include accessibility of information in memory and cue familiarity. Calogero and Nelson's (1992) participants did not rely on intrinsic factors related to the difficulty of questions as much as they should have in making FOK judgments even when they were given specific information about the difficulty of the questions. With these general knowledge questions, participants probably could not rely on extrinsic factors related to the original learning of the information. They must have relied on mnemonic factors, such as the number of accessible facts related to the question (Koriat, 1993), but these did not relate to actual performance as strongly as the intrinsic factor of normative difficulty. Privileged access implies that individuals use individual mnemonic factors, and furthermore, it assumes that these factors are more accurate than the more normative intrinsic factors.

Other methods of manipulating the use of individuals' privileged access to their own mental processes include using one individual's ratings to predict another individual's performance (yoking) and having individuals predict others' performances after watching them. An early study investigating the relationship among subjective predictions, normative item difficulty, and individual performance using both recallable and nonrecallable materials was conducted by Underwood (1966). He presented lists of trigrams (strings of three letters that were mostly nonwords) that he scaled according to actual performance in a learning task, participants' expected performance in a learning task, ratings of difficulty, and participants' predictions about their own learning. Underwood found that Pearson r correlations of individual predictions and performance were lower than individual's predictions and normative performance and also lower than normative predictions and normative performance. Although this suggests an absence of an idiosyncratic component in predicting performance, Underwood also yoked participants by randomly pairing them and correlating the ratings of one participant with the performance of another. This produced significant correlations, but these were lower than correlations produced by pairing ratings and performance of the same individuals. Thus, Underwood concluded that there is an idiosyncratic component to judging learning, but there is also a substantial normative component.

Lovelace (1984) also investigated the idiosyncratic and normative components of predictions of learning. He asked participants to predict future recall of paired associates. Following one study trial, Lovelace found a moderate correlation between normative judgments and normative recall. He used a yoking procedure to determine whether there was also an idiosyncratic component to individuals' ratings that predicted their recall. Lovelace found that correlations linking ratings to recall were higher when both values came from the same individual than when one individual's ratings were correlated with another individual's recall. Thus, like Underwood (1966), Lovelace concluded that there is both a normative component to JOLs and an idiosyncratic component.

Vesonder and Voss (1985) took a different tack to study the role of idiosyncratic information in predicting recall. They presented materials for learning, and individuals predicted future recall performance. Predictions were made by the learners who later recalled, by other participants who observed and heard the learners' responses, and by participants who observed the learners but could not hear their responses. Generally, the accuracy of predictions of performance was similar for participants who learned and recalled and for those who watched and heard recall. Those participants who did not hear the recall predicted less well, especially on trials after the first. Vesonder and Voss interpreted these results as showing that the idiosyncratic component that facilitates predictions in multitrial recall is knowledge about performance on the previous trial. This idiosyncratic component of metacognitive judgments was small when items were not previously recalled.

A similar result was reported by Matvey, Dunlosky, and Guttentag (2001), who asked participants to make JOLs for the recall of response words in a paired-associate task. Learners generated targets with deleted letters to either rhymes (cave–s _ _ _) or category cues (animal–b _ _ _). Observers watched the learners generating responses, and judges, who were instructed about the learners' conditions during learning, read the word pairs without deleted letters. Participants in all three groups made a JOL for each pair. Learners' and observers' JOLs were related equally to the speed with which learners generated targets, and this correlation was much larger than for judges who read the word pairs but did not have access to the learners' generation latency. Both this study and that of Vesonder and Voss (1985) suggest that observers and learners rely on similar cues in making JOLs, and that the idiosyncratic component to such judgments is fairly small.

However, Jameson, Nelson, Leonesio, and Narens (1993) repeated Vesonder and Voss's experiment with FOK judgments and general knowledge questions. Judgments were made only for nonrecalled answers to the questions, so the cue of whether an item was previously recalled was not available. Jameson et al. found that individuals predicted their own performance more accurately than other individuals did, even though only nonrecallable items were judged. Participants who heard the recall of learners used several cues in addition to normative difficulty of the questions, including whether the recall failure was an omission or commission, the latency of the recall attempt, and the plausibility of the wrong answer as judged by how many participants in the norming study selected it.

Self- versus Other Judgments

In addition to this cognitive literature on privileged access, there is a social psychology literature in which judgments of self and others are compared. Generally, the results of these studies showed that individuals believe that others are more likely to have knowledge if they themselves have it. Nickerson, Baddeley, and Freeman (1987) used the Nelson and Narens (1980) general knowledge questions. Participants estimated the percentage of college students who would get an answer correct, and then participants answered the question themselves. Nickerson et al. compared judgments for questions that participants answered correctly and incorrectly. Participants estimated that more college students would answer correctly when they themselves answered correctly than when they answered wrong. Nickerson et al. interpreted their data as evidence for the false consensus effect (Ross, Greene, & House, 1977); that is, people assume that other individuals are more similar to themselves than they actually are.

Fussell and Krauss (1991) conducted a similar study in which New York City residents identified landmarks in New York. When participants knew the name of a landmark, they gave higher estimates of the percentage of New York residents who knew the name than when they did not know the landmark. Fussell and Krauss suggested that was either an example of the false consensus effect or selective sampling in that more knowledgeable participants may have friends who actually are more knowledgeable. At any rate, both this study and that of Nickerson et al. (1987) showed that one's own knowledge affects judgments about others' level of knowledge.

Allwood (1994) conducted a study that was similar to Nickerson et al.'s (1987) study with general knowledge questions except that they asked participants to answer the questions and to make confidence judgments both about their own answers and about the answers of another individual. Allwood found that participants' judgments of others' answers were higher and more overconfident than participants' judgments of their own answers. Self-judgments were correlated with each participant's performance, and other judgments were correlated with that same performance. The correlations were not significantly different for self- and other judgments. This suggests that self and other judgments were similar except that participants added a constant to each judgment when the target was another person rather than oneself.

Introduction to the Experiment

Several questions about privileged access and ratings for oneself and others were investigated in the present experiment. In one portion of the experiment, participants predicted their performance on tests over newly studied text materials, and they judged their confidence in those test answers. In another portion of the experiment, the same participants judged their confidence in answers to general knowledge questions. To extend Nelson et al.'s (1986) analysis of FOK ratings, correlations between individual performance and four predictors were compared. The predictors were judgments about self, judgments about others, normative judgments, and normative performance. If participants have privileged access to their memories, self-judgments should relate to individual performance better than other judgments, normative judgments, or normative performance.

The reverse side of this question asks if individuals have knowledge about normative difficulty and if they understand that the performance of other individuals will be equivalent to the normative values. If they understand this, then the relationship between confidence for others and normative difficulty should be higher than the relationship between confidence for self and normative difficulty. In contrast, similar relationships for self and others and normative difficulty would suggest that participants give confidence judgments for others that are too similar to confidence judgments for themselves; that is, they show the false consensus effect.

Participants were also yoked so that one participant's self and other judgments were correlated with another participant's performance. If there is an idiosyncratic component to individual judgments, then judgments and performance for one individual should produce higher correlations than judgments and performance for two different individuals. This should be especially true for self-judgments and less true for judgments about others.

Each of the analyses described was conducted with posttest confidence judgments for general knowledge questions and for predictions and posttest confidence judgments for newly learned text. When participants made predictions or posttest confidence judgments about newly learned text, they had the opportunity to use all three factors described by Koriat (1997), namely, intrinsic, extrinsic, and mnemonic factors. As with posttest confidence judgments for general knowledge questions, they could use intrinsic factors related to difficulty of texts and questions, and they could use mnemonic factors related to accessibility of information. In addition, they could use extrinsic factors related to reading speed, rereading, and amount of attention devoted to reading each text. Because these extrinsic factors can be used in making judgments about text but not in judgments about general knowledge questions, idiosyncratic factors may play more of a role in text judgments than in judgments about general knowledge.

To investigate this, individuals read texts and answered questions about them. They made prediction judgments for themselves and others after reading the texts and after taking the tests over the texts. This procedure allowed the examination of idiosyncratic components in predictions and confidence judgments about a complex learning task. Text difficulty was varied to determine whether idiosyncratic components of judgments are more or less evident with more difficult texts.

Method

Design   Participants were randomly assigned to difficult text or revised text groups. All participants read and made judgments about texts, and they made posttest confidence judgments about general knowledge questions. Half of the participants did the general knowledge task before the text judgment task, and the other half of the participants participated in the reverse order. All participants made posttest confidence judgments both for themselves and for other students after answering general knowledge questions. For the text task, within-subject variables were judgments about self versus other students and prediction versus posttest estimates of performance.

Participants   A total of 137 participants who were volunteers from the general psychology participant pool at Texas Tech University were tested. Of these, 69 were randomly assigned to the revised text group, and the other 68 were randomly assigned to the difficult text group. An additional 89 participants from the same participant pool in an earlier academic year provided the normative data. All participants received partial course credit for participating.

Materials   For the general knowledge test, 25 general information multiple-choice questions that we created were used rather than the more dated Nelson and Narens (1980) normed questions. These questions, which were developed for an earlier study, each had four alternatives (Chavez, 2002). In that earlier study, percent correct ranged from 6% to 87%, with a mean of 49% correct. Examples of easy, moderate, and difficult general knowledge questions are shown in Appendix A.

The six difficult texts were the same texts used by Rawson, Dunlosky, and Thiede (2000) in their Experiment 1. These were taken from practice tests for the Graduate Record Examination (GRE; Branson, Selub, & Solomon, 1987). Rawson et al. used one short practice text, and two were used in the present study. The second practice text was obtained by shortening a text developed by Glenberg and Epstein (1987). This text has produced low performance in our laboratory. Practice texts contained about 75 words each.

For the revised (easier) texts, each difficult text and practice text was modified to improve readability. Low-frequency words were replaced with high-frequency words. Long, complex sentences were broken into simpler, shorter sentences without embedded clauses. Passive sentences were changed into active sentences. Two of the principled revision rules described by Britton and Gülgöz (1991) to be effective in improving text recall were also used. The same term for the same concept was used throughout the text, and anaphoric references (e.g., "it") were replaced with the referenced concept. An example of a difficult and revised practice text is shown in Appendix B.

The average length of the difficult texts was 478 words (358 to 601), and the average length of the revised texts was 441 words (347 to 604). Difficult texts had about 24 words per sentence, and revised texts had about 14 words per sentence. The mean Flesch Reading Ease measure for the difficult texts was 37.5 (range = 19.1 to 49.4), and the mean Flesch score for the revised texts was 50.9 (range = 42.2 to 59.5). The Flesch-Kincaid grade levels for difficult and revised texts were 11.7 (range = 10.9 to 12.0) and 9.8 (range = 7.6 to 12.0), respectively.

Six multiple-choice test questions with five alternatives were used for each text. In the difficult text condition, these were the same questions as those used by Rawson et al. (2000). Half of the test questions tapped details, and half tapped more conceptual material. In the revised text condition, the questions were the same except that words and phrases that were changed in the texts were also changed in the questions. There were two practice questions for each of the two practice texts. The practice questions for one of the hard and revised practice texts are shown in Appendix C.

Procedure

Participants came to the laboratory for a session lasting 1 hour. Materials were presented on a computer monitor located in an individual cubicle. Inquisit (2002) was used to control presentation of the stimuli and to collect data. All participants participated in both the general knowledge and the text portions of the experiment. Half did the general knowledge portion first, and half did the text portion first.

For the general knowledge portion of the experiment, the 25 questions were randomized individually for each participant. Each question was presented on the computer monitor along with the four alternatives. Participants selected an answer and then they responded to the following query: "Judge your confidence in the answer that you just gave. 25% means you're just guessing; 100% means that you're 100% sure your answer was correct. Move the pointer to the number corresponding to your confidence and click the mouse button." The confidence scale was 25% (guessing), 40%, 55%, 70%, 85%, and 100% (very sure). After responding for themselves, participants were asked to respond to the following: "Judge how well you think other people answered the question that you just answered. 25% means that 25% of other students would get the question correct. 100% means that all other students would get the question correct. Move the pointer to the percent of other students and click the mouse button." The same percentages were given beneath the other query as were used beneath the self-query. Except for the judgments for others that were not given, the procedure was exactly the same for the normative participants in an earlier study who answered the questions and gave their confidence.

In the two text conditions, participants first read each practice text. Sentences were presented on the computer monitor one at a time, and participants pressed the space bar for the next sentence in the text to appear on the screen. After reading both practice texts, participants predicted their performance by responding to the following query: "How likely are you to be able to answer six test questions correctly over the text material in about 20 minutes? Move the pointer to the number corresponding to the number of questions you think you'll answer correctly and press the mouse button." The scale was "1 correct, 2 correct, 3 correct, 4 correct, 5 correct, and 6 correct." After responding for themselves, participants were asked to respond to the following: "How many test questions do you think other people will get correct out of six? Move the pointer to the number you think other people will get correct and press the mouse button." The same scale of different numbers correct was used beneath the other query. Participants were given feedback on their answers for the practice texts, so their posttest confidence was not assessed.

After participants read and responded to the two practice texts, they read either the six difficult texts or the six revised texts, depending on the condition to which they were assigned. Texts were presented in a random order for each participant. After participants had read all six texts, they made predictions for themselves and for others for each of the six texts in response to the title of each text. The queries and the alternatives for each prediction were the same as for the practice texts. Next, partici-pants answered six multiple-choice questions per text. The texts were questioned in random order. After answering the questions for a text, participants indicated their confidence in their answer and then indicated the likelihood that other college stu-dents would get the question correct. The two queries were as follows: "How many of the six test questions do you think you answered correctly for this text passage? Respond in terms of the number you think you got correct. Move the pointer to the number corresponding to your percent correct and click the mouse button." "How many of the test questions do you think other people answered correctly out of six? Move the pointer to the number you think other people got correct and press the mouse button." The scale beneath each query ranged from 1 correct to 6 correct. After completing both the general knowledge and the text portions of the experi-ment, participants were debriefed and awarded credit for participation.

Results

Normative Data   For the general knowledge questions, the data from 89 individu-als from the same participant pool who had participated in an earlier study were used to determine normative confidence judgment percentages and normative per-formance for each of the 25 questions. These same participants also read either the difficult or the revised texts used in the present experiment. In addition, they made prediction judgments, answered the multiple-choice questions, and made posttest confidence judgments. Mean percent correct, predictions, and confidence judgments for the 45 participants in the difficult text condition were used as the normative data in that condition, and mean percent correct, predictions, and confidence judgments for the 44 participants in the revised text condition were used as normative data for the revised texts.

Predictions and Postdictions of Individual Performance   The first analysis used data from the general knowledge questions to determine how closely individual performance was related to posttest confidence judgments and to normative perfor-mance. Following Nelson's (1984) recommendation, nonparametric γ correlations[1] were calculated between judgments and test performance. For general knowledge questions, four γs were calculated for each individual. Each γ related a participant's score on each question (correct or incorrect, 0 or 1) to other measures: self-confidence percentage, other confidence percentage, normative confidence percentage, and nor-mative percentage correct. These mean γs are shown in the top row of Table 1.

A 4 (type of γ) by 2 (text difficulty condition) mixed-design analysis of variance (ANOVA) was used to analyze these γs. Pairs of γs were compared in three planned comparisons: self versus other, self versus normative confidence, and self versus nor-mative percentage correct. Text condition (which was not relevant to this specific analysis) produced no significant effects, $Fs(1, 132) \leq 1.45$, MSE (mean square error) $= .048$, $p > .05$.[2] Overall, type of γ produced a significant main effect, $F(3, 396) = 65.02$, $MSE = .033$, $\eta_p^2 = .330$.[3] The γs relating self-confidence to individual perfor-mance were significantly higher than γs relating confidence for others to individual

TABLE 1   Mean Intrasubject γ Correlations Relating Individual Performance to Individual Judgments, Judgments for Others, Normative Judgments, and Normative Item Difficulty for the General Knowledge and Text Conditions (With Standard Errors of the Mean in Parentheses)

	Self-Judgments–Performance	Other Judgments–Performance	Normative Judgments–Performance	Normative Difficulty–Performance
General knowledge	.488 (.024)	.411 (.026)	.257 (.018)	.548 (.017)
Difficult text predictions	.402 (.070)	.234 (.068)	.349 (.055)	.250 (.050)
Revised text predictions	.411 (.073)	.256 (.072)	.326 (.058)	.422 (.053)
Difficult text confidence	.496 (.053)	.356 (.060)	.290 (.053)	.242 (.050)
Revised text confidence	.538 (.055)	.291 (.061)	.307 (.054)	.447 (.051)

performance, $F(1, 132) = 27.53$, $MSE = .029$, $\eta_p^2 = .173$. The γs relating self-confidence to performance were also significantly higher than γs relating normative judgments to performance, $F(1, 132) = 119.35$, $MSE = .060$, $\eta_p^2 = .475$. However, γs relating self-confidence to performance were significantly *lower* than γs relating normative question difficulty to performance, $F(1, 132) = 5.62$, $MSE = .085$, $\eta_p^2 = .041$.

This pattern of data for confidence judgments on general knowledge questions conceptually replicates the pattern found by Nelson et al. (1986) with FOK judgments. This was true even though their participants made judgments only for nonrecallable answers, and the present participants made judgments for all questions. Normative question difficulty predicted individual performance better than did individual predictions. However, normative confidence judgments did not predict performance as well as individual confidence judgments. In addition, predictions about oneself matched individual performance better than did predictions about other individuals. Thus, there was an idiosyncratic component to self-confidence judgments, but this component was not more effective at predicting individual performance than normative question difficulty.

Next γs for prediction judgments for difficult and revised texts were analyzed in a 2 (text difficulty) by 4 (type of γ) mixed-design ANOVA. The mean γs are presented in the middle rows of Table 1. There was no significant effect of text difficulty, $F < 1$, but type of γ produced a significant main effect, $F(3, 342) = 3.48$, $MSE = .146$, $\eta_p^2 = .030$. The γs relating self-predictions to individual performance ($M = .406$) were significantly higher than γs relating predictions about others to individual performance ($M = .245$), $F(1, 114)[4] = 9.22$, $MSE = .328$, $\eta_p^2 = .075$. However, γs relating self-judgments to individual performance ($M = .406$) did not differ significantly from γs relating normative predictions to individual performance ($M = .338$), $F(1, 114) = 1.90$, $MSE = .287$, or from γs relating normative question difficulty to individual performance ($M = .336$), $F(1, 114) = 1.97$, $MSE = .292$. Thus, normative values of predictions and performance predicted individual performance as well as did individual predictions.

These effects did not interact with text difficulty, $Fs(1, 114) \leq 2.62$, $MSE = .292$, so statistically they were similar for revised and difficult texts.

Table 1 also shows the mean γs relating individual performance and posttest confidence judgments. These data were also analyzed in a 2 (text difficulty) by 4 (type of γ) mixed-design ANOVA. Text condition interacted with type of γ, $F(3, 363) = 3.14$, $MSE = .125$, $\eta_p^2 = .025$, so the planned comparisons were conducted separately for the difficult and revised texts. For the difficult texts, individual confidence judgments matched performance better than did confidence judgment for others, $F(1, 62) = 8.19$, $MSE = .151$, $\eta_p^2 = .117$. Individual confidence judgments also matched performance better than did normative confidence, $F(1, 62) = 8.02$, $MSE = .335$, $\eta_p^2 = .115$, and individual confidence matched performance better than normative question difficulty, $F(1, 62) = 10.85$, $MSE = .374$, $\eta_p^2 = .149$. Thus, unlike posttest confidence judgments for general knowledge questions, individual posttest confidence judgments for texts matched individual performance better than did normative difficulty. This may be because semantic knowledge as tapped by the general knowledge questions across participants was reasonably consistent, but learning from the texts may have been more variable across participants.

The pattern for the revised texts was similar to that found with posttest confidence judgments for general knowledge questions. Individual confidence judgments matched individual performance better than did confidence judgments for others, $F(1, 59) = 14.32$, $MSE = .256$, $\eta_p^2 = .107$. Individual confidence judgments matched individual performance better than normative confidence judgments, $F(1, 59) = 17.71$, $MSE = .182$, $\eta_p^2 = .231$, but individual confidence judgments did not match individual performance better than normative question difficulty, $F(1, 59) = 2.65$, $MSE = .190$.

Self versus Other Predictions   The false consensus effect (Ross et al., 1977) suggests that individuals think that their own performance is more similar to the performance of others than it actually is. Supporting this idea, mean individual γ correlations between the judgments made for self and others were high in all conditions, .89 for general knowledge confidence, .81 for text predictions, and .70 for text confidence judgments. However, the correlation for text confidence judgments was significantly lower than the correlation for general knowledge confidence, $t(120) = 4.22$, $SEM = .044$, suggesting more of an idiosyncratic component in the text confidence judgments than in the general knowledge confidence judgments.

Although the correlations between judgments for self and others were fairly high in all conditions, self-judgments matched individual performance better than other judgments for general knowledge questions as well as for text predictions and posttest confidence judgments. To judge others' performance accurately, participants would need to judge mean performance. To see how well they did this, individual and other judgments were each correlated with normative performance. These mean correlations for general knowledge confidence and for text predictions and posttest confidence are shown in Table 2. Each type of judgment was analyzed in a 2 (text difficulty) by 2 (self–other) mixed-design ANOVA. Text difficulty was a dummy variable in the general knowledge ANOVA. Self- and other confidence judgments matched normative performance equally with general knowledge questions, $F(1, 132) = 1.45$, $MSE = .048$. For predictions over text material, self and other predictions also matched

TABLE 2   Mean Intrasubject γ Correlations Relating Normative Performance to Individual Judgments and Judgments for Others in the General Knowledge and Text Conditions (With Standard Errors of the Mean in Parentheses)

	Self-Judgments–Normative Performance	Other Judgments–Normative Performance
General knowledge	.207 (.013)	.190 (.015)
Difficult text predictions	.364 (.057)	.355 (.061)
Revised text predictions	.341 (.055)	.296 (.059)
Difficult text confidence	.455 (.047)	.318 (.053)
Revised text confidence	.321 (.048)	.203 (.054)

normative performance equally, $F < 1$, and this did not depend on text condition, $F < 1$ for the interaction. For confidence judgments on text-related questions, self-judgments matched normative performance better than did judgments about others, $F(1, 118) = 9.55$, $MSE = .102$, $\eta_p^2 = .075$. This did not interact with text condition, $F < 1$. In no case were participants able to predict normative performance better when they made judgments about others than when they made judgments about themselves. Still, self- and other judgments were different in that self-judgments predicted individual performance better than other judgments in all conditions.

Higher overall γs for self than for others suggests that participants used some idiosyncratic knowledge when they judged themselves that they discounted when they judged others. Although they may have been trying to estimate mean performance when they judged others, the preceding analysis indicates that this was not successful. Participants may have simply used the middle of the scale more for others than for themselves. If so, then judgments about the self should include more extreme judgments than judgments about other individuals.

To test this for the general knowledge task, the percentage of judgments at the lower extremes (25% and 40%) and at the upper extremes (85% and 100%) were computed. When self was judged, 75.07% of the judgments were extreme, but only 58.86% of the judgments were extreme when others were judged. A 2 (text condition) by 2 (self vs. other) mixed-design ANOVA showed that this more extreme use of the scale with self- than other judgments was significant, $F(1, 129) = 132.74$, $MSE = 126.45$, $\eta_p^2 = .507$.

For text, the percentage of predictions that were below 50% (judgments of 1 or 2 correct out of 6) or above 67.67% (judgments of 5 or 6 correct out of 6) was determined for self and other. These were analyzed in a 2 (text difficulty) by 2 (self vs. other) mixed-design ANOVA. The only significant effect was that there were more extreme judgments for self ($M = 44.78\%$) than for others ($M = 33.35\%$), $F(1, 135) = 20.47$, $MSE = 436.80$, $\eta_p^2 = .132$. No other effects were significant in the ANOVA, all $Fs < 1$. Posttest confidence judgments showed a similar pattern. The percentage of judgments that were below 50% and above 67.67% for self was 46.84, and the percentage for others was 33.82. This effect was significant in a 2×2 mixed ANOVA, $F(1, 135) = 23.16$, $MSE = 501.36$, $\eta_p^2 = .146$. Other effects were not significant, $Fs < 1$. Both of these analyses support the hypothesis that γs for self were higher than γs for others at least partly because participants gave more extreme judgments for themselves and more midrange judgments for others.

Yoked Judgments and Performance   Another method of determining whether judgments are based on privileged access to idiosyncratic knowledge is to yoke individuals so that one individual's judgments are used to predict another individual's performance (Lovelace, 1984; Underwood, 1966). Evidence for an idiosyncratic component of judgments would be stronger relationships between individuals' judgments and their own performance than between their judgments and the performance of the yoked participant. This difference should be larger for self-judgments than for other judgments if participants are able to discount idiosyncratic effects when making other judgments. To seek such evidence for the general knowledge task, participants were rank ordered according to their overall general knowledge performance. Then, each pair of individuals with similar levels of performance was yoked. The confidence judgments across questions of one pair member were correlated with performance of the other pair member and vice versa.

The mean individual and yoked γ correlations for self- and other judgments are shown in Table 3.[5] These data were analyzed in a 2 (text difficulty) by 2 (individual vs. yoked) by 2 (self vs. other) mixed-design ANOVA. For general knowledge questions, individual correlations were higher than yoked correlations, $F(1, 131) = 76.39$, $MSE = .015$, $\eta_p^2 = .368$. The only other significant effect in the analysis was the interaction between self–other and yoking, $F(1, 131) = 7.56$, $MSE = .015$, $\eta_p^2 = .055$. As can be seen in Table 3, the difference between individual correlations and yoked correlations was greater when self as compared to other was judged. However, the stronger correlation in the individual condition than in the yoked condition was significant both for self, $F(1, 131) = 80.90$, $MSE = .073$, $\eta_p^2 = .382$, and for other, $F(1, 131) = 55.77$, $MSE = .068$, $\eta_p^2 = .299$. Thus, there was an idiosyncratic component to posttest confidence judgments for general knowledge questions both when individuals were judging themselves and when they were judging others.

A similar analysis was conducted for predictions and posttest confidence judgments for text. Similarity in overall text performance was used to pair individuals. The predictions for one pair member were used to predict the performance of the other pair member and vice versa. Mean γ correlations are shown in Table 3. The 2 (text difficulty) by 2 (individual vs. yoked) by 2 (self vs. other) mixed-design ANOVA

TABLE 3   Mean γs Relating Judgments to Performance for Individual and Yoked Participants (With the Standard Error of the Mean in Parentheses)

	Self-Judgments		Other Judgments	
	Individual	Yoked	Individual	Yoked
General knowledge	.485 (.024)	.188 (.028)	.408 (.026)	.169 (.026)
Difficult text predictions	.402 (.069)	.310 (.069)	.234 (.068)	.256 (.070)
Revised text predictions	.433 (.074)	.336 (.074)	.273 (.073)	.289 (.075)
Difficult text confidence	.496 (.053)	.319 (.067)	.356 (.060)	.243 (.073)
Revised text confidence	.538 (.055)	.279 (.068)	.291 (.061)	.236 (.075)

showed no significant difference between individual and yoked correlations, $F < 1$, for predictions. The interaction between yoking and self–other was marginally significant, $F(1, 112) = 3.20$, $MSE = .113$, $\eta_p^2 = .028$, $p = .076$. The difference between individual and yoked γs tended to be greater in the self condition than in the other condition, but neither of these effects was significant, $F(1, 127) = 1.65$, $MSE = .267$ for self, and $F < 1$ for other. Although the pattern of means suggested that there is an idiosyncratic component to predictions, there was not enough statistical power to produce a difference between individual and yoked predictions.

To identify an idiosyncratic component for posttest confidence judgments for texts, the same pairs of individuals described were yoked. The confidence judgments for one pair member were used to predict the other pair member's performance and vice versa. Mean γ correlations for individuals and yoked pairs are shown at the bottom of Table 3. Overall, individual correlations were higher than correlations for yoked pairs, $F(1, 121) = 7.50$, $MSE = .150$, $\eta_p^2 = .118$. However, there was a marginally significant interaction of yoking with self–other, $F(1, 121) = 3.67$, $MSE = .150$, $\eta_p^2 = .029$, $p = .058$ For confidence judgments about oneself, individual judgments matched performance better than did yoked judgments, $F(1, 131) = 11.81$, $MSE = .234$, $\eta_p^2 = .083$, but individual and yoked γs were not significantly different for other judgments, $F(1, 123) = 1.60$, $MSE = .290$. This pattern shows a fairly strong idiosyncratic component for posttest confidence judgments on text material learned in the experiment.

Discussion

The study described in this chapter was designed to extend Nelson et al.'s (1986) finding that individuals have privileged access to their memories when making FOK judgments. Nelson et al. found that individual FOK judgments matched individual recognition performance better than normative FOK judgments, showing that idiosyncratic aspects of memory boosted FOK accuracy. However, Nelson et al. also found that normative question difficulty predicted individual performance better than individual FOKs. This suggested that idiosyncratic aspects of question difficulty were not more predictive of individual performance than normative difficulty. Thus, the conclusion from normative judgments was that individuals have privileged access, but the conclusion from normative question difficulty was that privileged access produces less accurate judgments than mean question difficulty. The FOK paradigm uses judgments only for nonrecalled answers, so conclusions about privileged access may be weaker than when privileged includes the likelihood of item recall. In the present chapter, privileged access was investigated with general knowledge questions and with newly learned text material. The entire range of recallable and nonrecallable questions was judged. In addition, judgments about oneself and judgments about others were compared.

Posttest confidence judgments for general knowledge questions showed the same pattern as that found by Nelson et al. (1986) with FOKs for nonrecalled answers. Individual confidence judgments predicted individual performance better than normative judgments. However, normative question difficulty predicted individual performance better than did individual judgments. Thus, the conclusion with a full range of recallable and nonrecallable answers is the same as Nelson et al.'s conclusion with FOKs. When individual judgments are compared to normative judgments, individuals show privileged access. However, when individual judgments are compared to normative question difficulty, privileged access is not seen. Privileged access was also evident with the yoking procedure. Predictions about one's own performance were more accurate than predictions about another individual's performance, and this was more true for self-judgments than for judgments about others.

The conclusions with newly learned text, however, were somewhat different. Although the mean γs were highest for self-judgments predicting individual performance, there was no statistical difference between these γs and γs relating normative judgments and normative question difficulty to individual performance. The analysis with yoked participants also showed a mean difference in favor of self-judgments relating more strongly to individual performance than yoked judgments, but the difference was not significant for text predictions. These effects may have resulted from too little statistical power for predictions, or they may have resulted from reliance on different factors in predicting text performance than in judging answers to general knowledge questions.

In predicting future performance for text, individuals could have used all three of Koriat's (1997) factors. Predictions could have been based on intrinsic factors related to text difficulty; extrinsic factors related to reading speed, rereading, and attention allocated to reading; and mnemonic factors related to the accessibility of text material. Because normative predictions related as well to performance as individual predictions, participants apparently relied on common intrinsic factors that make texts difficult for all readers and not on the more idiosyncratic extrinsic and mnemonic factors.

Posttest confidence judgments about answers to questions covering newly learned text produced mixed results. With difficult texts, there was strong evidence for privileged access. Self-confidence judgments predicted performance more accurately than either normative confidence judgments or normative question difficulty. Apparently, participants were able to use idiosyncratic aspects of their learning to judge which multiple-choice questions they had answered correctly and which they had answered incorrectly. With revised texts, however, individual judgments matched performance better than normative judgments, but normative question difficulty and individual judgments matched individual performance about equally well. For both revised and difficult texts, however, posttest confidence judgments matched individual performance better than they matched the yoked participant's performance.

Individual posttest confidence judgments matched individual performance better than normative posttest confidence judgments for general knowledge questions and for revised and difficult texts. Thus, like Nelson et al. (1986), participants had privileged access to their knowledge that was more accurate than normative judgments. However, the situation with respect to normative question difficulty was mixed. Like Nelson et al., normative question difficulty predicted performance on general knowledge questions better than did individual judgments. With newly learned revised text, individual judgments were about equivalent in prediction accuracy relative to normative question difficulty. With newly learned difficult text, however, individual judgments predicted individual performance better than normative question difficulty.

This pattern of results with posttest confidence judgments may represent differ-ential emphasis on the three types of cues for JOLs described by Koriat (1997). With general knowledge questions, participants probably relied on mnemonic factors related to the accessibility of answers (Koriat, 1993) in making confidence judgments. However, the intrinsic factors related to normative difficulty were better predictors of their actual performance. For revised texts, participants may have added extrinsic factors related to their learning to mnemonic factors, and this resulted in judgments that were as accurate as normative question difficulty. For difficult texts, the more idiosyncratic extrinsic and mnemonic factors may have played a greater role in per-formance so that reliance on these factors produced higher relationships with indi-vidual performance than did normative question difficulty.

In all cases, self-judgments predicted individual performance better than did judgments about others. However, self- and other judgments were correlated fairly highly, suggesting that individuals made judgments about others that were similar to the judgments they made about themselves. Participants apparently believed that others knew what they did, providing evidence for the false consensus effect (Ross et al., 1977). Self- and other judgments were less well correlated for text than for general knowledge, again suggesting that judgments about new learning from text have a greater idiosyncratic component than judgments about general knowledge.

Judgments about others matched individual performance less well than did judg-ments about self, suggesting that judgments about others had less of an idiosyncratic component than did judgments about self. Although this suggested that other judg-ments may match mean normative performance better than self-judgments, this was not the case for general knowledge questions, predictions about text, or posttest judg-ments about text. In fact, posttest judgments for text for self matched mean norma-tive performance better than did posttest judgments for others. However, judgments about self were more extreme than were judgments about others in each condition. Participants used the middle of the scale more for others than for themselves, but this restricted judgment range did not match their performance, which like judgments for self, was more variable. Unlike Underwood (1966), who reported that participants were good at judging item difficulty, participants in this study did not include enough variance in those judgments. Judgments about themselves were more variable and matched individual performance better.

Nelson (1996) argued that the empirical study of privileged access would help both philosophers and psychologists to understand consciousness better. We asked whether individuals have privileged access to their knowledge using different types of materials and judgments. The answer to the question concerning privileged access is dependent on the task and type of judgment. As is often the case in empirical studies of cognition, an unqualified answer is not possible. People do seem to have privileged access after they have answered a question, although this access may not produce judgments that are more accurate than normative difficulty. Participants showed less evidence for privileged access when they made predictions about future performance over text. Rather than accessing information about their own learning from text, participants may have used common intrinsic factors related to the dif-ficulty of the texts.

Whether such a qualified answer provides insight into the philosophical issue of privileged access is a question best left to philosophers. However, Tom Nelson made a huge contribution to the field of cognition by showing that issues that have interested philosophers for centuries could be studied empirically (Nelson, 1996). Nelson's contributions were methodological (Nelson, 1984), theoretical (Nelson & Narens, 1990), and empirical (Nelson & Dunlosky, 1991). His work was crucial in making the field of metacognition an integral part of the broader field of cognitive psychology.

Acknowledgment

Thanks to Joshua Arduengo, Cynthia Dempsey, Michael Miesner, Amy Pietan, Emily Phillips, Amanda Wheeler, and Tammy Zacchilli for testing participants. Portions of this chapter were presented at the Thomas O. Nelson Memorial Symposium, November 2005, Toronto, Canada.

References

Allwood, C. M. (1994). Confidence in own and others' knowledge. *Scandinavian Journal of Psychology, 35*, 198–211.

Branson, M., Selub, M., & Solomon, L. (1987). *How to prepare for the GRE*. San Diego, CA: Harcourt Brace.

Britton, B. K., & Gülgöz, S., (1991). Using Kintsch's computational model to improve instructional text: Effects of repairing inference calls on recall and cognitive structures. *Journal of Educational Psychology, 831*, 329–345.

Calogero, M., & Nelson, T. O. (1992). Utilization of base-rate information during feeling-of-knowing judgments. *American Journal of Psychology, 105*, 565–573.

Chavez, N. M. (2002). *Individual differences in verbal working memory, visuo-spatial working memory, and metacognition: Learning from text in a hypertext environment*. Unpublished dissertation, Texas Tech University.

Fussell, S. R., & Krauss, R. M. (1991). Accuracy and bias in estimates of others' knowledge. *European Journal of Social Psychology, 21*, 445–454.

Glenberg, A. M., & Epstein, W. (1987) Inexpert calibration of comprehension. *Memory & Cognition, 15*, 84–93.

Inquisit 1.32 [Computer software]. (2002). Seattle, WA: Millisecond Software.

Jameson, A., Nelson, T. O., Leonesio, R. J., & Narens, L. (1993). The feeling of another person's knowing. *Journal of Memory and Language, 32*, 320–335.

Kahneman, D., & Tversky, A. (1973). On the psychology of prediction. *Psychological Review, 80*, 237–251.

Koriat, A. (1993). How do we know what we know? The accessibility model of feeling of knowing. *Psychological Review, 100*, 609–639.

Koriat, A. (1997). Monitoring one's own knowledge during study: A cue-utilization approach to judgments of learning. *Journal of Experimental Psychology: General, 126*, 349–370.

Lovelace, E. (1984). Metamemory: Monitoring future recallability during study. *Journal of Experimental Psychology: Learning, Memory, and Cognition, 10*, 756–766.

Matvey, G., Dunlosky, J., & Guttentag, R. (2001). Fluency of retrieval at study affects judgments of learning (JOLs): An analytic or nonanalytic basis for JOLs? *Memory & Cognition, 29*, 222–233.

Nelson, T. O. (1984). A comparison of current measures of the accuracy of feeling-of-know-ing predictions. *Psychological Bulletin, 95,* 109–133.

Nelson, T. O. (1996). Consciousness and metacognition. *American Psychologist, 51,* 102–166.

Nelson, T. O., & Dunlosky, J. (1991). The delayed-JOL effect: When delaying your judgments of learning can improve the accuracy of your metacognitive monitoring. *Psychological Science, 2,* 267–270.

Nelson, T. O., Leonesio, R. J., Landwehr, R. S., & Narens, L. (1986). A comparison of three predictors of an individual's memory performance: The individual's feeling of know-ing versus the normative feeling of knowing versus base-rate item difficulty. *Journal of Experimental Psychology: Learning, Memory, and Cognition, 12,* 279–287.

Nelson, T. O., & Narens, L. (1980). Norms of 300 general-information questions: Accuracy of recall, latency of recall, and feeling-of-knowing ratings. *Journal of Verbal Learning and Verbal Behavior, 19,* 338–368.

Nelson, T. O., & Narens, L. (1990). Metamemory: A theoretical framework and some new findings. In G. H. Bower (Ed.), *The psychology of learning and motivation* (pp. 125–173). New York: Academic Press.

Nickerson, R. S., Baddeley, A. D., & Freeman, B. (1987). Are people's estimates of what other people know influenced by what they themselves know? *Acta Psychologica, 64,* 245–259.

Rawson, K. A., Dunlosky, J., & Thiede, K. W. (2000). The rereading effect: Metacomprehen-sion accuracy improves across reading trials. *Memory & Cognition, 28,* 1004–1010.

Ross, L., Greene, D., & House, P. (1977). The false consensus effect: An egocentric bias in social perception and attribution processes. *Journal of Experimental Social Psychology, 13,* 279–301.

Underwood, B. J. (1966). Individual and group predictions of item difficulty for free learning. *Journal of Experimental Psychology, 71,* 673–679.

Vesonder, G. T., & Voss, J. F. (1985). On the ability to predict one's own responses while learn-ing. *Journal of Memory and Language, 24,* 363–376.

Appendix A: Examples of General Knowledge Questions

Question	Correct Answer[a]	Normative Proportions	
		Correct	Confidence
What constellation is the North Star in?	Little Dipper	.06	.58
The Transvaal is in what continent?	Africa	.16	.38
What color was Moby Dick?	White	.46	.63
What country other than Israel borders the Dead Sea?	Jordan	.40	.46
What nation created the Statue of Liberty?	France	.86	.82
What disease was called the Black Death?	Bubonic Plague	.91	.81

[a] General knowledge questions were presented as four-alternative multiple-choice questions.

Appendix B: Practice Texts

Hard Text: Global Temperature and Flooding[6]

Scientific investigators of global climate change have warned that there will occur substantial rises in worldwide sea levels if there is a rise of several degrees in global temperature. The projected increase in worldwide temperature is based on the observation that both individual and corporate use of carbon dioxide-producing combustible fuels has been on the rise since the middle of the last century. The carbon dioxide is delivered into the earth's atmosphere where it acts somewhat like the glass in a greenhouse, retaining radiant energy. The carbon dioxide absorbs infrared heat radiation from the earth instead of allowing it to escape into space. Trapping the infrared heat radiation in the air leads to rising temperature. Even a rise of a few degrees of global temperature may cause melting of the polar icecaps and considerable increases in the height of oceans.

Revised Text: Global Temperature and Flooding

Scientists who study change in the world's climate warn that sea levels will increase if the temperature increases throughout the world. An increase of several degrees in temperature would make the sea levels go up quite a lot. The scientists expect worldwide temperature to increase because people and companies use fuels that make carbon dioxide. The amount of carbon dioxide released by these fuels has been increasing since the middle 1800s. When carbon dioxide is released into the air, it acts like the glass in a greenhouse. The carbon dioxide traps heat near the surface of the earth. Carbon dioxide stops the heat from escaping into space. Because the heat can't escape, the temperature of the earth is rising. If the world's temperature goes up only a few degrees, the polar icecaps will melt. This will cause a large increase in the height of the oceans.

Appendix C: Test Questions for Practice Texts

Questions for Hard Texts

Global Temperature and Flooding

The projected increase in worldwide temperature is based on what observation?

*A) both individual and corporate use of carbon dioxide-producing combustible fuels has been increasing.
 B) trapping of infrared radiation in the air is decreasing.
 C) heat radiation is more likely to be trapped in the earth as sea levels rise.
 D) carbon dioxide has been decreasing in the earth's atmosphere.
 E) more greenhouses have been built, increasing the amount of carbon dioxide trapped in the atmosphere.

Global Temperature and Flooding

How would carbon dioxide cause a rise in global temperature?

*A) by absorbing and retaining infrared heat radiation coming from the earth into the atmosphere.
 B) by reflecting infrared heat energy back to the earth once it had come into contact with the atmosphere.
 C) the rise would come directly from heat being emitted from individual and corporate use of carbon dioxide-producing fuels.
 D) by intensifying the heat potential from the sun's rays when they collide with carbon dioxide gases in the atmosphere.
 E) by facilitating the movement of radiation into space.

Questions for Revised Text

Global Temperature and Flooding [Revised]

The projected increase in worldwide temperature is based on what observation?

A) individuals and companies have been using more fuels that produce carbon dioxide
B) the amount of heat trapped near the earth is decreasing
C) the amount of carbon dioxide in the earth's atmosphere has been decreasing

*D) heat is more likely to be trapped by the sea as sea levels rise
 E) more greenhouses have been built, increasing the amount of carbon dioxide trapped
     in the atmosphere

Global Temperature and Flooding [Revised]

How could carbon dioxide cause a rise in global temperature?

*A) by keeping heat close to the earth's surface rather than letting it escape into space
 B) by reflecting heat energy back to the earth once it has escaped into space
 C) the temperature increase would come directly from heat being given off from the
     use of carbon dioxide-producing fuels
 D) by strengthening the heat from the sun's rays when the rays collide with carbon
     dioxide gases in the atmosphere
 E) by facilitating the movement of the heat into space

*Denotes the correct response. The order of the alternatives was randomized for each participant.

Notes

1 The γ correlations are nonparametric correlations. They range from -1.0 for a perfect
   negative relationship to $+1.0$ for a perfect positive relationship. Nelson (1984) argued that
   γ is the best measure for assessing accuracy of judgments in metacognitive studies.
2 The level of significance used in all statistical tests if $p < .05$.
3 ηp^2 is partial eta squared. It is the ratio of the sum of squares effect to sum of squares
   effect plus sum of squares error for the effect.
4 The degrees of freedom differ for γs depending on how many participants gave judgments that varied across the units judged. The γ is indeterminate if participants give the
   same value to all of the units.
5 The mean γ correlations and the df are different in this analysis from the earlier analysis
   of individual judgments predicting individual performance because both members of
   a yoked pair had to be eliminated if one member of the pair gave the same judgment to
   all general knowledge items or all texts.
6 The hard practice text was a short version of a text used by Glenberg and Epstein
   (1987).

Feeling-of-Knowing Accuracy and Recollective Experience

R. Jacob Leonesio

Introduction

Recollections of particular episodes from an individual's past are referred to as *personal memories* (Brewer, 1986, 1988).[1] Key features of personal memories seem to be that they (1) are specific, (2) involve the self, and (3) are accompanied by a strong experience of recognition that the phenomenal experience on which they are based actually occurred. These kinds of memories constitute the "minutiae of memory," and those that survive may be especially linked to more permanent autobiographical memory knowledge structures (Conway, 2002).

Studies in which personal memories are externally verified by objective criteria are rare (see Weaver, Terrell, Koreg, & Keleman, this volume). The central focus of this investigation was to explore possible bases for feeling-of-knowing (FOK) judgments and the accuracy of these bases for verified personal memories.

Feeling of Knowing

The feeling of knowing (FOK) refers to a specific kind of metamemory judgment made on items that are below the threshold of recall. FOK judgments are therefore made on the subset of items that were incorrectly recalled, as determined by a previously administered recall test. Participants are typically instructed that the FOK refers to the likelihood that a participant will be able to recognize the correct answer among several alternatives. It is possible to evaluate the accuracy of participants' FOK judgments by administering a criterion test after the judgments have been made and calculating a nonparametric measure of association (e.g., Goodman-Kruskal γ) between the FOK judgments and the criterion test (Nelson, 1984, 1987; Nelson & Narens, 1980). Although the criterion test has typically been a recognition test, other criterion tests have also been used. For example, FOK judgments have been positively related to perceptual identification and to savings during relearning (Nelson, Gerler, & Narens, 1984) as well as to several other memory tests (for a listing, see Nelson, 1988).

Naturally occurring FOK experiences (Gruneberg, Smith, & Winfrow, 1973) as well as FOK experiences for specific item domains have been investigated. Items tested have included the meaning of words (Eysenck, 1979); the names of entertainers (Read & Bruce, 1982); word definitions (Yaniv & Meyer, 1987); general information facts (Hart, 1965; Nelson & Narens, 1980); previously learned trigrams (Blake, 1973); sentences (Shimamura & Squire, 1986); and various paired associates (Hart, 1967; Leonesio & Nelson, 1990; Nelson, Leonesio, Shimamura, Landwehr, & Narens, 1982). For normal participants, correlations between FOK judgments and various criterion tests have typically been found to be significantly above chance for all items tested except for subsequent performance on unsolved insight problems (Metcalfe, 1986). In Metcalfe's study, the answers to the problems were not stored in the participants' memory but rather were inferred from their progress toward a solution. The difference between stored versus nonstored items may be a factor that affects FOK accuracy.

In the organizational schema proposed by Nelson et al. (1984), theoretical mechanisms that might underlie FOK judgments have been classified as either trace-access mechanisms or inferential mechanisms. *Trace-access mechanisms* referred to knowledge only about the answer and included incorrect recall, partial recall, and subthreshold memory strength. *Inferential mechanisms* referred to other factors and included general knowledge, motivation, episodic information, and cue recognition. Nelson et al.'s organizational schema was based on the analysis of general information questions, which measured participants' FOK for specific semantic information (e.g., What is the name of the brightest star in the sky excluding the sun? Answer: Sirius). The present study measured participants' FOK for a subtype of episodic information (i.e., personal autobiographic) and required a different organizing schema, so that mechanisms based solely on inference could be distinguished from those including remembrance of the answer *or the cue*. In the present schema, underlying mechanisms for FOK judgments that involved recognition or recall for either the answer or the cue are referred to as mechanisms based on remembrance, whereas mechanisms that rely on intuition for either the answer or the cue or on logical analysis of the context in light of the participant's accumulated knowledge are referred to as either intuitive or inferential mechanisms, respectively. The key distinction made is between a participant's FOK based on memory contents that are reexperienced and are therefore directly monitorable (remembrance) and those for which there is no experience of remembrance and so can only be monitored indirectly or not at all (inference or intuition).

Whether FOK judgments are based primarily on inference/intuition or primarily on remembrance would be expected to vary with the type of item studied. For example, Gruneberg et al. (1973) preselected items that participants knew to be in memory but that were unable to be recalled at the time. It would be expected that participants would have remembrances for these items because they were able to freely recall the questions without any external cueing, and they remembered having access to the items in the past. It would therefore be expected that FOK judgments for these items would be largely based on these remembrances. This is in contrast with the items described in this section that were used by Metcalfe (1986) that appeared conducive to FOK judgments based primarily on inference.

A distinction between inference and remembrance as different bases for FOK judgments is akin to the distinction between plausibility and direct retrieval as different strategies for answering questions (Reder, 1987). However, because FOK judgments are made only on nonrecalled items, "direct retrieval" can be only partially successful; that is, only part of the relevant material can be retrieved (e.g., episodic information, cue information, or part of the answer). An important difference, however, between the present conceptualization and that of Reder (1987) is that in the present conceptualization *remembrance* refers to recollective experience (Gardiner, 1988; Gardiner & Java, 1990; Tulving, 1985), which might be conceived as a kind of mental product, whereas *direct retrieval* as described by Reder (1987) is conceived as a strategy. Under the assumption that on a deep level all cognitive and metacognitive judgments are inferred, the essential distinction between the terms *inference* and *remembrance* is that whereas inference is based on our general knowledge and contextual cues alone, remembrance is mediated by the monitoring of a specific memory or memory attribute that was encoded at or near the time of the sought-after information. If only the general context is accessible, then inference processes must be solely relied on. If, however, the participant remembers having learned the answer or any part of the answer, then the participant's judgment will include these specific remembrance components in addition to any inferential components. This implies that recognition of the specific memory context (e.g., memory for the cue statement or for the specific learning situation) can provide a basis for FOK judgments. This is consistent with FOKs based on cue familiarity (Schwartz & Metcalfe, 1992). It is also analogous to participants' reported basis of self-paced "source identification" judgments (Johnson, Kahan, & Raye, 1984). Here, participants reported that they used related supporting memories as a basis for discriminating dream events that they had reported from those told to them by their partners.

Recollective Experience

Tulving (1985) described relationships between awareness and memory. He postulated that a certain type of awareness that he called "autonoetic" was necessary for remembering personally experienced events. We are usually aware of our memories as memories, but is it our state of autonoetic awareness that distinguishes remembering from perceiving, thinking, imagining, and dreaming, or is it by intention and attribution that we make this distinction? Admittedly, our state of awareness must include a self-knowing capability to distinguish remembering from other kinds of awareness (e.g., imagination, dreaming, or perception), but to conceive of this capability as only a "state of mind" does not seem particularly informative. How might such an autonoetic state explain our failures to make such distinctions, such as situations in which we fail to distinguish remembering from thinking (Schooler, Clark, & Loftus, 1988) or from imagining (Johnson, 1988; Johnson & Raye, 1981)? Perhaps it is our evaluation of recollective experience that provides a key basis for making a wide variety of metacognitive judgments. If this is the case, then the term *autonoetic consciousness* might usefully be conceptualized as an integration of a specific memory trace with its spatial and temporal context and our personal identity (cf. Kihlstrom, 1981; Kihlstrom & Cantor, 1984).

At the heart of this proposed relationship between autonoetic awareness and metamemory judgments is James's (1890) emphasis on the phenomenal experience of remembrance, that is, our awareness of remembering. James (1890) characterized memory as

The knowledge of an event, or fact, of which meantime we have not been thinking, with the additional consciousness that we have thought or experienced it before. ... It must be dated in my past. In other words, I must think that I directly experienced its occurrence. It must have that "warmth and intimacy" which were so often spoken of in the chapter on the self, as characterizing all experiences "appropriated" by the thinker as his own. (pp. 648, 650)

This characterization of memory is very similar to Brewer's (1986, 1988) description of personal memories presented in the introduction. That is, they are easily imagined mental occurrences accompanied by a phenomenal sense of having occurred before. James attributed this "phenomenal sense" to the memory's "contiguous associates" and to its close association to the self of the rememberer. Recollective experience and what is now called *source identification* is central to this formulation of memory. The rememberer (1) recalls a piece of information and (2) attributes this information to a previously remembered experience.

Viewed from this perspective, the awareness that our explicit memories are indeed memories is as much a metamemory process as it is an object-level memory process. Our sense of recollective experience might then be conceived as a synergistic interaction between memory and metamemory processes. FOK judgments and perhaps other metacognitive judgments might depend heavily on our sense of recollective experience. Recollective experience in turn may involve a combination of object-level recall, the recall or reconstruction of contextual details and their plausibility, together with the application of metacognitive decision processes that *integrate* all accessible information during the moments of memory retrieval.

To obtain data relevant to these notions, personal memories were gathered, from a participant's own awake and dreamed experiences, over a period of three consecutive days. These items were interspersed with items gathered from matched individuals to create a pool of items for each participant that had a large variation in source of origin (i.e., self/other, awake/dream). Participants were given a free-recall test followed by a cued-recall test. FOK judgments were later made on a subset of their incorrectly answered cued-recall items. FOK accuracy, participants' self-reported bases of their FOK judgments, and the relationship of their FOK judgments (and their accuracy) to participants' self-reported recollective experience were evaluated. Consistent with conceptions of metamemory that emphasize the importance of "accessibility" (e.g., Koriat, 1993, 1994, 1995), it was hypothesized that FOK judgments for personal memories would largely be based on accessible memory experiences (e.g., remembrance for the cue statement and partial answer recall), and that the accuracy of these judgments would increase with the degree of reported recollective experience. Inferential and intuitive processes should be utilized more often for personal memories that are relatively faded (e.g., the self-dream items compared to the self-awake items) or nonexistent (e.g., other-dream or other-awake items).

Method

Participants

The participants were 34 University of Washington undergraduate students who reported recalling at least two dreams per night. They received one psychology course credit (or if they preferred, extra credit toward their psychology course grade) for participating.

Experience Sampling Procedure

Dream Reports   Participants wore a foam mask in which an infrared movement detector was embedded. This REM (rapid eye movement) -sensing mask was connected to a circuit that counted participants' eye movements. The mask, timing, and component coordinating circuitry were designed and built by Ray Horvitz (Fairhaven College). The circuitry included a modified prototype of the DreamLight™ donated by Dr. Stephen LaBerge (Stanford University). *REM sleep* was defined as the occurrence of at least four eye movements for each of three consecutive 30-second intervals (hereinafter referred to as the REM criterion). A programmable timer activated the apparatus 2 hours after bedtime to allow time for the participant to fall asleep. The occurrence of the REM criterion triggered the activation of an acoustic alarm. Dream reports were recorded immediately after awakening from REM sleep for the three consecutive nights that followed participants' awake reports.

Awake Reports   Participants picked three 90-minute periods during each of three consecutive days when it was possible for their experience to be sampled. The experimenter programmed a watch to beep at a time unknown to the participant during each of the nine 90-minute periods. The watch face was painted over with black acrylic paint so that participants could not access the preprogrammed times. When the watch beeped, the participant recorded (on a microcassette) his or her experience (including perceptions, thoughts, feelings, and behaviors) that occurred during the 10 minutes prior to the sound of the beeper.

Testing Procedure

Two weeks after the last experimental night, each participant was brought into the laboratory and was administered the memory and metamemory tests described next.

Free Recall   Each participant was instructed to write down everything that he or she could remember saying into the tape recorder over the three consecutive days of the experiment. They were instructed to label each statement that they recalled as either a dream or an awake experience.

Cued Recall   A list of cue statements was constructed in the following manner: Transcribed awake and dream reports were printed and separated into *idea units* by two research assistants. An idea unit consisted of each unique verb together with its object and associated modifiers. Each cue statement consisted of six consecutive idea units with one key word omitted. Participants of the same gender who were run within 4 days of one another were matched for the purpose of providing cues for the other-awake and other-dream conditions.

Each participant was given a randomly selected list of statements that contained an equal number of statements from each of the four categories (self-awake, self-dream, other awake, and other dream). The total number of statements presented to each participant varied between 32 and 64 (depending on the amount of autobiographic material collected). The order of the cue statements was random for each pair of participants. Each pair of participants received the same list of cue statements. Each participant was given a list of cue statements and a response form. The participant read each statement and filled in his or her best guess regarding the deleted word in each statement. Recall confidence and source-of-origin judgments were also made (data not presented).

Recollective Experience   Next, the participant indicated the amount of the cue statement (0% to 100%) that they remembered or recognized as having been previously reported or experienced.

Feeling of Knowing   The item category (self-awake, self-dream, other awake, other dream) that contained the fewest incorrectly recalled items set the maximum number of items tested from each of the four categories for the FOK stage. Participants categorized the likelihood of recognizing each of the tested incorrectly recalled items as a pure guess or low, medium, or high FOK. Next, the participant indicated the basis of his or her FOK for every item given an FOK rating greater than a pure guess. This was accomplished in the following manner: Each participant divided 100 percentage points between four experimenter-defined bases and one or more participant-defined bases for all above-chance FOK judgments. Each of the following bases was explained to the participant, both verbally and in writing:

> *Remembrance for the Cue Statement.* How much of your judgment was based on your recognizing that the event or the report of the event into the tape recorder was formerly experienced?
>
> *Partial Recall of an Answer.* How much of your judgment was based on your recalling something about the answer, for example, its meaning, or what it looked, sounded, or felt like? Any recalled aspect of an answer, whether it is general or specific, abstract or concrete, semantic or syntactic, may constitute partial recall of an answer.
>
> *Inference of an Answer.* How much of your judgment was based on your logically inferring what the answer was from the context of the statement or from the test as a whole or from your general knowledge or from knowledge of yourself or of others?
>
> *Intuition.* How much of your judgment was based on a feeling that you knew the answer without knowing the reason why you knew?
>
> _____. How much of your judgment was based on some other component? You can specify this component by writing it in the blank labeled "specify." If you wish to specify more than one component, write it below your other responses on the same line as the word *specify*.

Next, the participant ranked the items within each of the four categories (cf. Shimamura & Squire, 1986).

Recognition   One week after FOK judgments were made, each participant was given a seven-alternative forced-choice recognition test on the previously judged (FOK) items. The delay was necessary to allow time for the experimenter to construct and coordinate sets of unique distracters for participants' incorrectly recalled items. Identical distracters were used for items presented to participant pairs.

Results and Discussion

Object-Level Memory

Free Recall   Results from the free-recall test showed that participants could accurately recall, in the absence of any additional cues, only 9% (95% confidence limit = .02) of their reported dream experience and 10% (95% confidence limit = .02) of their reported awake experience after a delay of 2 weeks. This is probably a realistic estimate of participants' free-recall ability for their actual experience because the experiences were not self-sampled. It is, if anything, a generous estimate because reporting the experience would serve to strengthen the memory for that experience. This result is consistent with data obtained by Brewer (1988) for time-cued thought experiences (i.e., it is halfway between his 1-week and 4-week retention estimates). It is somewhat startling to realize just how quickly the bulk of our day-to-day experience is forgotten (in the absence of richer retrieval cues).

We may not especially notice how much we forget because we usually do not systematically test the *accuracy* of our memory for everyday experience. We remember the general gist of an experience and fill in the rest with appropriate schemata-driven assumptions (Neisser, 1981). In this study, it seemed quite easy for participants to forget whole experiences. Whole experiences that shift below the threshold of free recall would be difficult to notice because they leave no accessible clues of their existence. In the absence of a particular recall need (e.g., a friend's query or the recovery of a misplaced object), we seem content with the memory experiences that remain accessible.

Cued Recall   The percentage correct cued recall for the self-awake and self-dream conditions were 56% and 40%, respectively. The correct guessing rates of the other-awake and other-dream conditions were 14%, and 15%, respectively. Participants were more accurate in responding to their own statements than to the statements of others ($t[99] = 16.36$, $p < .05$), and they were able to recall more key details from their awake statements than from their dream statements ($t[99] = 5.33$, $p < .05$). There was no difference in the response accuracy for the awake versus the dream statements of others ($t[99] = 0.33$, $p > .05$). These results indicate that when participants were given relatively rich cues, they were able to recall about half of the selected details from their own awake experience after a 2-week retention interval.

Metamemory

Reported Bases of FOK Judgments   A primary focus of this study was to investigate the distribution of participants' reported basis for their FOK judgments and to
relate recollective experience to FOK accuracy. Figure 1 shows the relative percentages of participants' reported cue utilization for their FOK judgments for the four
kinds of items for low-, medium-, and high-FOK judgments. Reported differences
were significant by sign tests, $p < .05$, two tailed. For self-generated awake items (left
column), the higher participants' FOK, the more likely it was reported to be based on
cue remembrance and the less likely it was reported to be based on either inference or
intuition. Subjects reported using more cue remembrance for high-FOK judgments
than for low-FOK judgments (15, 1, $N = 16$). The difference in cue remembrance
between the low- and the medium-FOK judgments was not significant (6, 4, $N = 12$),
however, there was a significant increase in reported cue remembrance between the
medium- and the high-FOK judgments (18, 3, $N = 24$).

For participants' dreams (third column), cue remembrance was believed to be utilized more for medium-FOK judgments than for low-FOK judgments (13, 3, $N = 21$),
more for high-FOK judgments than for medium-FOK judgments (11, 0, $N = 23$), and
more for high-FOK judgments than low-FOK judgments (11, 1, $N = 16$). Participants
therefore reported basing their FOK judgments on their remembrance for the cue

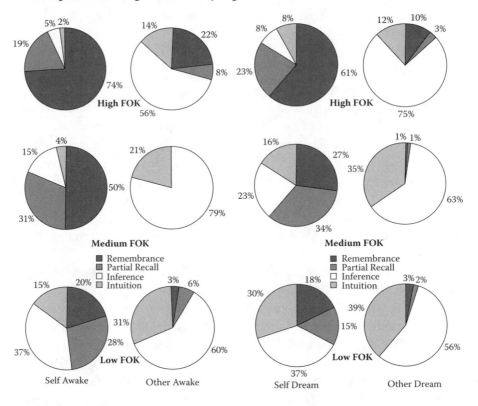

Figure 1   Relative percentages of subjects' reported cue utilization of high-, medium-, and low-
feeling-of-knowing (FOK) judgments for self-awake and other-awake reported experience.

statement, which is what one would expect if they were monitoring recollective experience to determine the relative FOK for a previously nonrecalled item.

One might have expected that reported partial-recall utilization would have increased systematically with the strength of participants' FOK because of its theoretical association with the tip-of-the-tongue state. Figure 1 shows, however, that participants did not believe that partial recall increased with FOK strength. None of these comparisons was significant for either the self-awake or the self-dream items. These findings disconfirm the notion that high FOKs for autobiographic details are *primarily* based on broad aspects of partial recall and support the hypothesis that high FOKs for these items are *primarily* due to monitoring the recollective experience of the context in which the details are embedded.

Comparisons between subjects' reported cue utilization between self-awake and self-dream items were not significant, except for a greater reliance on intuition reported for self-dream items than for self-awake items for low-FOK judgments (10, 0, $N = 13$).

Differences in types of cue utilization for comparisons among the low-, medium-, and high-FOK judgments were not significant within either the other-awake items or within the other-dream items. Medium- and high-FOK judgments were rarely made for other participants' items: For medium FOK other awake, $N = 12$; for high-FOK other awake, $N = 6$; for medium-FOK other dream, $N = 4$; for high-FOK other dream, $N = 3$.

These results support the view that the bases of FOK judgments are multidimensional (Koriat, 1993; Leonesio & Nelson, 1990). It goes beyond previous work in that it measures several specific cues that participants report using. Furthermore, participants report relying on different cues for different kinds of items and report different cues for lower compared to higher FOKs. Remembrance for the cue statement and partial recall of the answer were especially important for participants' higher FOK judgments of their own memories, with the former emerging as participants' dominant reported basis.

Predictive Validity of Reported Bases of Feeling-of-Knowing Judgments   It was possible to evaluate the extent to which participants' reported reliance on each of the aforementioned cues predicted both their FOK judgments and their subsequent recognition performance. This was accomplished by computing γ correlations between the proportional use of each cue and FOK rank and the proportional use of each cue and recognition performance for all items combined (i.e., self-awake, other awake, self-dream, other dream). This analysis showed that these reported judgments had sufficient predictive validity to significantly predict participants' judged FOK. Remembrance for the cue statement and partial recall of the answer predicted higher FOKs (γ = .59 and .24, respectively, $p < .05$), and inference and intuition predicted lower FOKs (γ = −.41 and −.50, respectively, $p < .05$). This confirms the pattern of results across low-, medium-, and high-FOK judgments displayed in Figure 1 and further confirms that participants actually used the strategies they reported. More importantly, these reported strategies also predicted recognition performance. Remembrance for the cue statement and partial recall of the answer significantly predicted correct recognition (γ = .24 and .26, respectively, $p < .05$, two tailed), whereas inference and intuition significantly predicted incorrect recognition (γ = −.19 and −.31, respectively, p < .05). This is what would be expected if these cues were valid predictors of memory knowledge.

This predictive validity (of subsequent recognition performance) did not hold up when item types were analyzed separately. When the self-awake and the self-dream items were analyzed by themselves, none of these reported bases significantly predicted recognition performance (even though reported strategy use was nearly always a significant predictor of FOK). This suggests that participants' strategies were ineffective for these items, which is supported by the FOK accuracy data presented next.

FOK Accuracy   Although FOK accuracy (i.e., FOK and recognition γ) was significantly above chance for the awake items (.32) and for the dream items (.19), it was not significantly above chance for the other-awake (−.10), other-dream (.05), self-awake (.04), or self-dream (.03) items taken separately. The FOK accuracy data were therefore analyzed separately for individuals reporting low recollective experience and individuals reporting high recollective experience (median split). If recollective experience moderates FOK accuracy, then individuals reporting higher recollective experience should have greater FOK accuracy than individuals reporting lower recollective experience.

In contrast to participants with lower recollective experience, Figure 2 shows that participants higher in recollective experience demonstrated above-chance FOK accuracy for all of the item types except others' items and their own awake items. These results support the hypothesis that FOK accuracy is related to individual differences in the degree of recollective experience.

Accurate FOK was not expected for others' items (regardless of individual differences in the degree of recollective experience) because these judgments were largely based on error-prone inferential processes. Although self-awake FOK accuracy was in the predicted direction for individuals reporting high recollective experience, it was not significantly above chance (contrary to expectation). That is, even participants high in recollective experience had difficulty making accurate FOK judgments for these items. This result would occur if the variance in recollective experience or in memory strength among the self-awake items was low. This would be consistent with earlier research that varied the memory strength of items on which FOK judgments were made (Nelson et al., 1982).

To further assess possible effects that the degree of recollective experience might have on FOK judgments and on FOK accuracy, γ correlations were computed to access the predictive validity of recollective experience. Table 1 shows the mean γ correlations between recollective experience and FOK judgments and between recollective experience and recognition performance for the different item types.

It can be seen that although recollective experience predicted participants' *FOK rank* regardless of participants' overall level of recollective experience (Table 1, columns 1 and 3), recollective experience predicted *recognition performance* more strongly for the participants with higher recollective experience (Table 1, columns 2 and 4). For participants reporting lower recollective experience, recollective experience only weakly predicted recognition for all items combined, whereas for participants reporting higher recollective experience, it strongly predicted recognition. For

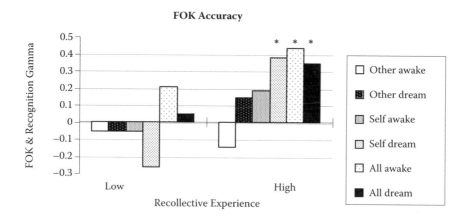

Figure 2   Mean γ correlations between participants' feeling-of-knowing (FOK) judgments and recognition performance for other-generated awake, other-generated dream, self-generated awake, self-generated dream, all awake, and all dream items. Results are shown separately for individuals reporting low recollective experience and for individuals reporting high recollective experience. *Indicates that gamma is above chance expectation, p < .05, two tailed.

TABLE 1   Mean γ Correlations for All Items Combined (i.e., Other Awake, Other Dream, Self-Awake, Self-Dream), Self-Generated Items (i.e., Self-Awake, Self-Dream), Self-Awake Items, and Self-Dream Items Between Recollective Experience and Feeling-of-Knowing (FOK) Rank and Recollective Experience and Recognition Performance for Participants with a Lower or a Higher Degree of Recollective Experience (Median Split)

| | Recollective Experience | | | |
| | Lower | | Higher | |
	FOK Rank	Recognition	FOK Rank	Recognition
All	.71[a]	.23[a]	.72[a]	.75[a]
	(.11)	(.23, 17)	(.38)	(.24, 17)
Self-generated	.42[a]	.03	.55[a]	.43[a]
	(.16)	(.26, 17)	(.12)	(.14, 14)
Self-awake	.04	−.14	.48[a]	.19
	(.23)	(.33, 16)	(.35)	(.47, 12)
Self-dream	.53[a]	−.02	.55[a]	.43[a]
	(.22)	(.38, 10)	(.22)	(.25, 12)

Confidence limit (95%) is in parentheses below each entry. N is equal for each of the two corresponding correlations and follows the second confidence limit.

[a] Indicates that the correlation exceeds chance expectation.

participants reporting higher recollective experience, recollective experience moderately predicted recognition for the combined set of self-generated items and for the self-dream items, but recollective experience did not significantly predict recognition performance for self-awake items. It is especially noteworthy that participants' recollective experience possessed predictive validity for items selected from participants' own experience only for participants with higher overall recollective experience. It is also noteworthy that for the one item set for which participants having greater recollective experience failed to demonstrate above-chance FOK accuracy (i.e., self-awake items) the degree of recollective experience lacked predictive validity.

General Discussion

Metacognitive judgments are introspective evaluations. They are based on our observations of our own mental contents and states. The judgments that participants made in this experiment required them to judge the likelihood that they could give a correct response to questions about their own and others' personal experience. An important aspect of this research was that the accuracy of participants' introspections was not taken for granted but was instead evaluated (Nelson, 1996). This was the case not only for participants' (1) FOK judgments (validated by FOK recognition γs), but also for their (2) reported bases of FOK judgments (validated by proportion-of-reported-cue-utilization and FOK rank γs as well as proportion-of-reported-cue-utilization and recognition γs) and for their (3) degree of recollective experience judgments (validated by recollective-experience and FOK rank and recollective-experience and recognition γs).

The second kind of metajudgments (i.e., the reported-bases-of-FOK judgments) were similar to the introspective judgments investigated by Nisbett and Wilson (1977) and Nisbett and Ross (1980) in that participants were asked, in essence, to introspect about the "causes" of their previous judgments. Causal judgments are especially prone to error because we cannot directly monitor (i.e., access) the mental processes that cause our behavior. There is no guarantee that the mental models that participants construct to explain their behavior correspond to the actual mechanisms causing their behavior (Johnson-Laird, 1983). On the other hand, participants who are actively engaged in an experimental task might have better insight into how they are performing the task than nonparticipants (including the experimenter). In forming theories about the bases of FOK judgments, the systematic collection of participants' causal introspections about their FOK judgments is one potentially important source of information, especially when these causal introspections are made during or immediately after a judgment task (because participants' observations are less subject to forgetting and distortion). Furthermore, if a relationship is found between participants' causal introspections and their original FOK judgments (as was the case here), then new and theoretically relevant information will have been gained.

The third kind of metajudgments gathered requested only that participants report the degree of recollective experience that they presently experienced for each cue statement. This kind of introspective judgment was similar to the introspective judgments reviewed by Ericsson and Simon (1980). These kinds of judgments were expected to be less subject to error because participants were not required to make any causal inferences or to construct models to explain their behavior. These last judgments might therefore be expected to be particularly useful, especially since participants' metamemory judgments were significantly related to their degree of recollective experience for the cue, and these judgments also predicted recognition performance.

In addition, participants having high recollective experience for their cue statements were able to accurately predict recognition performance for their own items across awake and dream items and for the dream items alone. For these same participants, but not for participants with lower recollective experience, their degree of recollective experience generally correlated moderately with degree of FOK and with recognition performance. Recall that for the total set of items, for participants with a higher degree of recollective experience, the correlation between recollective experience and recognition performance was .75 (Table 1, all). By comparison, for this same item set, participants' FOK judgments correlated only .37 ($n = 17$, confidence limit =.16) with recognition performance. This suggests that participants might be able to improve their FOK accuracy by relying more heavily on their recollective experience as a basis for their FOK judgments.

These results demonstrate that recollective experience for the cue statement is a cue that is utilized by participants. This cue is especially useful for individuals who report a high degree of recollective experience because these individuals have the highest FOK accuracy. This finding is consistent with the notion that assessing FOK depends on information that is accessible to the participant (Koriat, 1994; Schwartz & Metcalf, 1992). For these kinds of materials (i.e., reported autobiographic items) and for the retention interval tested, both high recollective experience and heterogeneously sampled experiences (in terms of memory strength or recollective experience) predicted FOK accuracy. FOK accuracy remained indistinguishable from chance for the most homogeneous self-generated items (i.e., self-awake), whereas FOK accuracy was higher for the most heterogeneous items. Heterogeneity would be higher for items sampled across the self–other dimension than for items sampled across the awake–dream dimension. The former pool of items contained both experienced and nonexperienced items, whereas the latter pool of items contained only previously experienced items. Dream items would be more heterogeneous than awake items because an appreciable number of reported dream experiences were later forgotten, resulting in a pool of remembered and nonremembered cues. This was supported by a subsequent analysis that found that after the 2-week retention interval, 21% of participants' previously reported dream cue statements were no longer recognized (compared to only 2% of their awake cue statements).

A relationship between FOK accuracy and item heterogeneity was previously found for paired-associate items by Nelson et al. (1982). In that study, item heterogeneity was manipulated by varying the degree of learning. It was found that the FOK recognition γ correlation for items learned to a criterion of one correct response was −.02, to a criterion of two correct responses was −.03, and to four correct responses was .31. The FOK recognition γ for all items combined was .17. Item heterogeneity was high for the combined item set (because they were composed of different degrees of learning). Item heterogeneity was also high for items learned to four correct responses because overlearning amplifies the effect of interitem heterogeneity (Leonesio & Nelson, 1982).

Future studies might include measures of recollective experience and might manipulate either the heterogeneity of items or participants' recollective experience to observe how these variables affect FOK accuracy and the accuracy of other metamemory judgments. Jameson, Narens, Goldfarb, and Nelson (1990) found that participants' FOK for general information questions was not affected by near-threshold presentation of the answers even though these presentations reliably increased recall. A possible explanation of participants' inability to monitor the increase in memory strength caused by near-threshold presentations is that there was no recollective experience for the briefly presented answers.

Note

1. Although personal memories meet the definition of episodic memory as first defined by Tulving (1972), he and many other researchers have categorized nonautobiographic memories as examples of episodic memory. The term *episodic memory* has come to mean any kind of declarative verbal memory that is not strictly semantic. For example, memory for a list of words learned in a verbal learning experiment would qualify as episodic. Knowledge of a list of words in itself is not personal or autobiographical. If an experimenter is concerned with the words alone and not with the connection between the words and the phenomenal experience of the participant (i.e., the self), the memory data obtained are not appropriately categorized as personal, although it would be episodic.

References

Blake, M. (1973). Prediction of recognition when recall fails: Exploring the feeling-of-knowing phenomenon. *Journal of Verbal Learning and Verbal Behavior, 12,* 311–319.

Brewer, W. F. (1986). What is autobiographical memory? In D. C. Rubin (Ed.), *Autobiographical memory* (pp. 25–49), New York: Cambridge University Press.

Brewer, W. F. (1988). Memory for randomly sampled autobiographical events. In U. Neisser & E. Winograd (Eds.), *Remembering reconsidered: Ecological and traditional approaches to the study of memory* (pp. 21–90). Cambridge, UK: Cambridge University Press.

Conway, M. A. (2002). In A. Baddeley, J. P. Aggleton, & M. A. Conway (Eds.), *Episodic memory: New directions in research* (pp. 53–70). Oxford, UK: Oxford University Press.

Ericsson, K. A., & Simon, H. A. (1980). Verbal reports as data. *Psychological Review, 87,* 215–251.

Eysenck, M. W. (1979). The feeling of knowing a word's meaning. *British Journal of Psychology, 70,* 242–251.

Gardiner, J. M. (1988). Functional aspects of recollective experience. *Memory & Cognition, 16,* 309–313.

Gardiner, J. M., & Java, R. I. (1990). Recollective experience in word and nonword recognition. *Memory & Cognition, 18,* 23–30.

Gruneberg, M. M., Smith, R. L., & Winfrow, P. (1973). An investigation into response blockaging. *Acta Psychologica, 37,* 187–196.

Hart, J. T. (1965). Memory and the feeling-of-knowing experience. *Journal of Educational Psychology, 56,* 208–216.

Hart, J. T. (1967). Memory and the memory-monitoring process. *Journal of Verbal Learning and Verbal Behavior, 6,* 685–691.

James, W. (1890). *The principles of psychology* (Vol. 1) New York: Holt.

Jameson, K. A., Narens, L., Goldfarb, K., & Nelson, T. O. (1990). The influence of near-threshold priming on metamemory and recall. *Acta Psychologica, 73*, 55–68.

Johnson, M. K. (1988). Discriminating the origin of information. In T. F. Oltmanns & B. A. Maher (Eds.), *Delusional beliefs: Interdisciplinary perspectives* (pp. 34–65). New York: Wiley.

Johnson, M. K., Kahan, T. L., & Raye, C. L. (1984). Dreams and reality monitoring. *Journal of Experimental Psychology: General, 113*, 329–343.

Johnson, M. K., & Raye, C. L. (1981). Reality monitoring. *Psychological Review, 88*, 67–85.

Johnson-Laird, P. N. (1983). *Mental models.* Cambridge, MA: Harvard University Press.

Kihlstrom, J. F. (1981). On personality and memory. In N. Cantor & J. F. Khilstrom (Eds.), *Personality, cognition, and social interaction* (pp. 123–149). Hillsdale, NJ: Erlbaum.

Kihlstrom J. F., & Cantor, N. C. (1984). Mental representation of the self. *Advances in Experimental Social Psychology, 17,* 1–47.

Koriat, A. (1993). How do we know that we know? The accessibility model of the feeling of knowing. *Psychological Review, 100,* 609–639.

Koriat, A. (1994). Memory's knowledge of its own knowledge: The accessibility account of the feeling of knowing. In J. Metcalfe and A. P. Shimamura (Eds.), *Metacognition: Knowing about knowing* (pp. 115–135). Boston, MA: Bradford Books.

Koriat, A. (1995). Dissociating knowing and the feeling of knowing; further evidence for the accessibility model. *Journal of Experimental Psychology: General, 124,* 311–333.

Leonesio, R. J., & Nelson, T. O. (1982). Postcriterion overlearning reduces the effectiveness of the method of adjusted learning. *Behavior Research Methods and Instrumentation, 14,* 320–322.

Leonesio, R. J., & Nelson, T. O. (1990). Do different metamemory judgments tap the same underlying aspects of memory? *Journal of Experimental Psychology: Learning, Memory, and Cognition, 16,* 464–470.

Metcalfe, J. (1986). Feeling of knowing in memory and problem solving. *Journal of Experimental Psychology: Learning, Memory, and Cognition, 12,* 288–294.

Neisser, U. (1981). John Dean's memory: A case study. *Cognition, 9,* 1–22.

Nelson, T. O. (1984). A comparison of current measures of the accuracy of feeling-of-knowing predictions. *Psychological Bulletin, 95,* 109–133.

Nelson, T. O. (1987). The Goodman-Kruskal γ coefficient as an alternative to signal-detection theory's measures of absolute-judgment accuracy. In E. E. Roskam & R. Suck (Eds.), *Progress in mathematical psychology* (Vol. 1, pp. 299–306). Amsterdam: Elsevier Science, North-Holland.

Nelson, T. O. (1988). Predictive accuracy of the feeling of knowing across different criterion tasks and across different subject populations and individuals. In M. M. Gruneberg, P. E. Morris, & R. N. Sykes (Eds.), *Practical aspects of memory: Current research and issues* (Vol. 1, pp. 197–202) New York: Wiley.

Nelson, T. O. (1996). Consciousness and Metacognition. *American Psychologist, 51,* 102–116

Nelson, T. O., Gerler, D., & Narens, L. (1984). Accuracy of feeling-of-knowing judgments for predicting perceptual identification and relearning. *Journal of Experimental Psychology: General, 113,* 282–300.

Nelson, T. O., Leonesio, R. J., Shimamura, A. P., Landwehr, R. F., & Narens, L. (1982). Overlearning and the feeling of knowing. *Journal of Experimental Psychology: Learning, Memory and Cognition, 8,* 279–288.

Nelson, T. O., & Narens, L. (1980). A new technique for investigating the feeling of knowing. *Acta Psychologica, 46,* 69–80.

Nisbett, R. E., & Ross, L. (1980). *Human inference: Strategies and shortcomings of social judgment.* New York: Prentice Hall.

Nisbett, R. E., & Wilson, T. D. (1977). Telling more than you can know: Verbal reports on mental processes. *Psychological Review, 84,* 231–259.

Read, J. D., & Bruce, D. (1982). Longitudinal tracking of difficult memory retrievals. *Cognitive Psychology, 14,* 280–300.

Reder, L. M. (1987). Strategy selection in question answering. *Cognitive Psychology, 19,* 19–138.

Schooler, J. W., Clark, C. A., & Loftus., E. F. (1988). Knowing when memory is real. In M. Gruneberg, P. Morris, & R. Sykes (Eds.), *Practical aspects of memory: Current research and issues* (Vol. 1, pp. 83–88). New York: Wiley.

Schwartz, B. L., & Metcalfe, J. (1992). Cue familiarity but not target retrievability enhances feeling-of-knowing judgments. *Journal of Experimental Psychology: Learning, Memory, and Cognition, 18,* 1074–1083.

Shimamura, A. P., & Squire, L. R. (1986). Memory and metamemory: A study of the feeling-of-knowing phenomenon in amnesic patients. *Journal of Experimental Psychology: Learning, Memory, and Cognition, 12,* 452–460.

Tulving, E. (1972). Episodic and semantic memory. In E. Tulving & W. Donaldson (Eds.), *Organization of memory* (pp. 381–403). New York: Academic Press.

Tulving, E. (1985). Memory and consciousness. *Canadian Psychology, 26,* 1–12.

Yaniv, I., & Meyer, D. E. (1987). Activation and metacognition of inaccessible stored information: Potential bases for incubation effects in problem solving. *Journal of Experimental Psychology, 13,* 187–205.

Metacognitive Guessing Strategies in Source Monitoring

William H. Batchelder and Ece Batchelder

Introduction

The purpose of this chapter is to formulate and present evidence for a theoretical approach to metacognitive guessing strategies in source-monitoring experiments. Source monitoring is a type of recognition memory by which one not only has to remember if they have experienced an event in the past but also is required to recognize something about the circumstances under which they encountered the event. An everyday example of source monitoring would be if somebody asked you if you had learned about a particular fact about politics, and if so, whether you heard it on a news program or read it in a daily paper. Another example would be when you have a headache and think that you should take a couple of aspirin. Later in the day, you see the aspirin bottle and wonder if you actually took the aspirin or just thought that you took them (e.g., R. E. Anderson, 1984). This example falls into the subarea of source monitoring called *reality monitoring* (Johnson & Raye, 1981), by which one has to differentiate memories of actions taken in the world from thoughts in one's mind.

In experimental studies of source monitoring (e.g., Bray & Batchelder, 1972; Hintzman, Block, & Inskeep, 1972; Johnson, Hashtroudi, & Lindsay, 1993), participants are exposed to a study list of items from two or more sources, such as words spoken in a male or a female voice or words that are written, spoken, or depicted by pictures. After that, the participants are presented with a test list of old studied items from the various sources mixed with new distracters. The required response to an item on the test list is usually first to indicate whether the item was on the study list and, if so, to indicate its source.

When participants have an incomplete memory about a tested item in source monitoring, they are motivated to bias their responses to optimize the accuracy of their guesses. Selecting a strategy for responding when memory is incomplete necessarily involves metacognitive evaluation. The key assumption explored in this chapter is that when participants are tested on items in a source-monitoring experiment, they utilize metacognitive inferences derived from monitoring their own experimentally induced memory processes as well as extraexperimental experiences and beliefs. These inferences often can be used as a basis for optimizing performance on memory tests; however, when extraexperimental beliefs and experiences are contradicted by the design of the experiment, accuracy may even suffer. The focus of the chapter is on explicating the key assumption in the context of mathematical models of source monitoring. The assumption is formulated within a Bayesian framework in a general enough way that it can serve as a heuristic to suggest how response bias parameters may be calibrated in any type of recognition memory model.

While our approach is quite general, the actual examples presented involve models that fit into the category of multinomial processing tree (MPT) models. MPT models have been developed for many experimental paradigms in the social and behavioral sciences, including ones for recognition memory (Batchelder & Riefer, 1999). Since the original MPT models of source monitoring by Batchelder and Riefer (1990), variations on these models have become popular as a way to disentangle and separately measure latent cognitive processes in a variety of source-monitoring experiments (these are reviewed in Batchelder & Riefer, 1999, 2007). MPT models that have been developed for source monitoring are a form of discrete state threshold models (e.g., Batchelder, 2002). It is true that discrete state models for some recognition memory paradigms are not in favor among many researchers today, and instead theorists are attracted to more complex models such as those that are specified in terms of the theory of signal detection (e.g., Macmillan & Creelman, 2005), hypothetical feature vectors (e.g., McClelland & Chappell, 1998; Shiffrin & Steyvers, 1997), or neural networks (e.g., Sikström, 2001). Even in the area of source monitoring, some theorists have argued that other approaches based on the theory of signal detection are better than discrete state models in fitting data (e.g., Banks, 2000; Slotnick, Dodson, Klein, & Shimamura, 2000).

In our view, there is no "correct model" of source monitoring, and any particular model is at most an approximation to the underlying cognitive activity behind performance. We think that models in this area should be viewed more as measurement tools than correct theories (e.g., Batchelder, 1998), and as such they are viable to the extent that they provide valid and useful interpretations of the data. As with any particular type of model, sometimes discrete state models succeed on this metric, and at other times they do not. We say more about the theory/measurement distinction in the conclusion to this chapter.

This chapter is organized in four main sections. First, a brief review of recognition memory experiments and theories in general is presented along with some formal notation. Many of these theories emphasize that source monitoring is a basic underlying process in all recognition memory experiments because when participants are confronted with an item on test trials, they are required to discriminate experimentally induced sources affecting their memory of the item from various everyday, extraexperimental sources. While this first section is not extensive, it is designed to serve as a reference source for many of the key articles in this area. The second section of the chapter develops a Bayesian approach to formulate theoretical assumptions about metacognitive guessing strategies. These assumptions are formulated as two metacognitive heuristics, and they are used to suggest a basis for several phenomena in simple old/new recognition memory. In the third section, the source-monitoring paradigm is formalized, and a general MPT model is presented that combines the properties of the models of Batchelder and Riefer (1990) and Bayen, Murname, and Erdfelder (1996). Then, the general assumptions about metacognitive guessing are used to derive some formal propositions about response bias calibration in the model, and some supporting data are presented. In the final section, the MPT model is extended to include the possibility of making inferences about source memory derived from extraexperimental sources such as experience in the social world. In one application, some preliminary results of source-monitoring experiments involving ties in a social network are presented.

Review of Recognition Memory

Recognition Memory Experiments

Most experiments in recognition memory involve a sequence of trials of two types. First study items (words, pictures, etc.) are presented for the subject to remember, and after the study trials, test items are presented that require a recognition response.[1] In this chapter, the focus is on study–test paradigms, although the ideas we develop are intended to apply as well in other recognition memory paradigms. The response on a test trial can be dichotomous, for example. "yes" or "no" in a simple old/new recognition memory experiment indicating whether the participant "believes" that a tested item was on the study list. More complex recognition experiments, such as the source-monitoring paradigm (discussed in the introduction) or the process dissociation paradigm (e.g., Jacoby, 1991) involve two or more types of studied items, each corresponding to a unique "correct" response category.

It is easy to develop formal notation that covers most study–test recognition memory experiments. The participant is tested on a set of N items, $S = \{s_1, s_2, ..., s_N\}$. These items include one or more classes of old studied items along with one or more classes of new, distracter items.[2] There are K possible response classes, $R = \{r_1, r_2, ..., r_K\}$, and it is assumed that each of the tested items has a unique correct response class defined by the experimental instructions and study trials. This assumption can be represented by a function f from S to R, where for any item $s_n \in S$, $f(s_n) \in R$ is the correct response for s_n. We denote by C_k the set of all items with correct response r_k. Suppose there are I participants in the experiment, each exposed to the same types of experimentally designed items.[3] Then, the data from the participants can be represented in an $I \times N \times K$ three-way array:

$$\mathbf{D} = (x_{ink})_{I \times N \times K},\tag{1}$$

where

$$x_{ink} = \begin{cases} 1 & \text{if participant } i \text{ responds } r_k \text{ to item } s_n \\ 0 & \text{otherwise} \end{cases}.$$

In many recognition memory experiments, participants are asked to supplement their response to an item with a confidence rating on an ordinal scale indicating the degree to which they believe that their response is accurate (cf. Macmillan & Creelman, 2005), and often response times are recorded as well. In addition, other behavioral measures may be collected, such as second chance responses (e.g., Van Zandt

& Maldonado-Molina, 2004); "remember/know" judgments to recognized items (e.g., Tulving, 1985); speeded responses (e.g., Johnson, Kounios, & Reeder, 1994); metacognitive responses like judgments of learning (JOLs) (e.g., Benjamin, Bjork, & Schwartz, 1998); and event-related brain potentials (e.g., Curran, DeBuse, & Leynes, 2007). Recognition memory experiments have become quite complex as cognitive theorists strive to design paradigms that reveal new empirical phenomena and differentiate various theories and models. Some of the sources of complexity involve experimentally controlled similarity structure among the items (e.g., Clark & Gronlund, 1996); varying the number of item repetitions and item study time within a list (e.g., Hintzman, Curran, & Oppy, 1992); experimental operations that are designed to create receiver operator characteristic (ROC) curves in which memory parameters are assumed to be invariant while guessing parameters vary (e.g., Macmillan & Creelman, 2005); and various priming manipulations (e.g., Lewandowsky, 1986).

Recognition Memory Models

Despite the considerable effort spanning over 50 years on the part of many psychologists, no generally accepted correct theory of recognition memory has emerged, and new models and new theories are still arriving on the scene (many of these were discussed by Dennis, & Humphreys, 2001; Diana, Reder, Arndt, & Park, 2006; Dunn, 2004; and Heathcote, 2003). The theories divide on the issue of whether recognition decisions are made on the basis of a single process, usually called *familiarity*, or instead two processes. Most two-process theories assume that there is a familiarity process like the single-process theories, but in addition there is a process that may result in specific item recollection. Single-process theories evolved from applications motivated by the theory of auditory signal detection (e.g., Egan, 1958; Green & Swets, 1966). The application of signal detection theory to old/new recognition judgments postulates that the familiarity of a tested item is a continuous random variable, for which there is a different probability distribution (usually assumed to be a normal distribution) of familiarity for each type of tested item. Basically, the presentation of an item in the study list tends to boost its familiarity; however, all items have a certain amount of familiarity based on other experimental manipulations, such as priming or extraexperimental sources such as word frequency or recent usage. Decisions are based on a one-dimensional decision axis that is often referred to as a *familiarity axis*, although some theorists regard it as a likelihood ratio axis (e.g., Morrell, Gaitan, & Wixted, 2002) as it is in the original theory of auditory signal detection, for which each point corresponds to the ratio of the likelihood of the observed point given an old item divided by its likelihood given a new item. The decision to respond yes or no to a test item depends on whether the value is above or below a response bias threshold on the decision axis. The location of this threshold is treated as a participant-controlled biasing process that depends on memory monitoring of general properties of the experiment, such as item memorability, the base rate of old to new items, and other experimental or extraexperimental sources. There are also several single-process models based on ideas from the theory of signal detection for more complex recognition memory paradigms (e.g., Banks, 2000; Hilford, Glanzer, Kim, & DeCarlo, 2002; Macmillan & Creelman, 2005).

Dual-process theories of recognition memory were proposed in the early 1970s (e.g., Atkinson & Juola, 1974); however, contemporary dual-process models of old/ new recognition memory have evolved from the ideas of Mandler (1980), which were initially formulated into a model by Jacoby (1991) (see Yonelinas, 2002, for a review). These models assume that correct recognition performance can occur in one of two ways. First, there is explicit memory of aspects of the studied item that are sufficiently strong to cause specific item recollection; second, if item recollection fails, then there is another process based on how "familiar" the item seems. As with single-process theories, familiarity can arise from both experimental and extraexperimental sources. The first two-process model by Jacoby (1991) was a simple MPT threshold model, and later more elaborate two-process MPT models were developed as well (e.g., Buchner, Erdfelder, & Vaterrodt-Plunnecke, 1995). One source of evidence for the dual-process formulation is the ability to experimentally dissociate the two processes, by which an experimental manipulation results in variation in one of the processes without affecting the other (e.g., Gardiner & Richardson-Klavehn, 2000). Another source of support for a dual-process assumption comes from the ability of subjects to make reliable remember/know judgments for items that receive a yes response on the test. Nevertheless, there are efforts to reconcile these results with single-process theory based on ideas from signal detection theory (e.g., Dunn, 2004).

Several single-process models of the simple old/new recognition memory paradigm (e.g., Shiffrin & Steyvers, 1997; Sikström, 2001; McClelland & Chappell, 1998) postulated model specifications considerably more complex than simple variants on the theory of signal detection. They were designed to fit demanding patterns of data, some of which were generated by the advocates of dual-process theorists. To handle the variety of experimental findings with a single-process assumption, the models have postulated very detailed item representations involving hypothetical feature vectors and a variety of computational mechanisms.[4] As with the case for single-process models of recognition memory, dual-process models have begun to invest in elaborate computational specifications (e.g., Diana et al., 2006; Reder et al., 2000).

Metacognitive Inference Assumptions

The participants in most recognition memory experiments are college students complying with psychology course requirements. It is our view that a recognition memory experiment can be viewed productively as a complex "game" between the experimenter and a participant. The setting for such a game is an artificial environment designed by the experimenter, who is attempting to create conditions in which the participant's memory for a tested item is imperfect in controllable ways. In the game, the participant is attempting to optimize performance in some sense on a tested item given knowledge from monitoring the nature of their memory of the item along with online evaluation of the properties of the experiment as well as extraexperimental beliefs and experience. This optimization process requires the participant to make inferences based on these sources of knowledge and to design productive response biasing or guessing strategies from these inferences. Because response bias is an essential component of a recognition memory paradigm, all formal cognitive models of recognition memory have parameters and processes for response bias. Some of the models postulate explicit inferential processes and optimal biasing strategies, whereas others treat biasing as a "nuisance process"[5] that is required to complete the model and allow conclusions about memory to be made.

The goal of this chapter is not to add yet another completely specified recognition memory model to the large population of current models. Instead, the goal is to explore the role of metacognitive inference processes in biasing responses to items when memory is imperfect. We use a Bayesian approach (e.g., Gill, 2002) to suggest how these inferences may be utilized to make response decisions given imperfect memory, and in particular we show how Bayes theorem may be used to derive the probability that a certain response is the correct one given one's memory state for an item and general knowledge of the study and testing sequence. The approach we take is in the spirit of J. R. Anderson's (1990) adaptive analysis of human memory as well as the study of simple human judgmental heuristics by Gigerenzer, Todd, and the ABC Research Group (1999). A Bayesian development similar to ours was presented by Benjamin, Bjork, and Hirshman (1998) for the role of subjective item fluency in old/new recognition memory, and Bayesian formulations have been a part of several completely specified models of recognition memory (e.g., McClelland & Chappell, 1998; Reder et al., 2000; Shiffrin & Steyvers, 1997). In our view, it is possible to make progress in analyzing these inferential processes at a very general metatheoretic level without committing to any completely specified model.

Formal Metatheoretic Representations

Most recognition memory models suppose that when a test item is presented, it can be characterized as being in one of a set of "memory states." Any particular model defines the set of all possible memory states M with each state designed to represent a possible state of memory of an item at the time of its test. Some of these states arise from study events involving old items, and others arise from extraexperimental sources. States may be as simple as detect or nondetect states or very complicated state descriptions such as patterns of activations in a neural network (e.g., Sikström, 2001). In the case of discrete state models such as the various types of threshold models (e.g., Batchelder, 2002), there are only a small number of possible memory states; however, for many models such as those based in signal detection theory, the set of possible memory states is infinite. It is a feature of most models of recognition memory that the memory states of a model contain all the specific information about the state of memory of the tested item that is available for selecting a response, although most models assume that the response probability distribution conditional on a particular memory state may depend on other factors that are independent of the memory state for the tested item. Some of these factors are guessing biases or response thresholds that may be calibrated by global or online knowledge of the composition of the study and test lists (e.g., Brown, Steyvers, & Hemmer, 2007), inferences about the relative difficulty of remembering different classes of items on the study list, and inferences from extraexperimental beliefs and experiences.

It is now possible to state the essential problem setting for this chapter. Given that a tested item is in memory state $m \in M$ of some model, what is the *optimal response* or most likely correct response to make? There are other senses of optimality that might be important, such as maximizing expected utility if there were differential payoffs associated with responses that are hits, false alarms, misses, and correct rejections, (e.g., Green & Swets, 1966), but we do not incorporate them in this chapter. The solution to the problem of optimizing performance in any particular recognition memory setting would be relevant to a participant's response selection process, especially if he or she could monitor their own memory states and make metacognitive inferences about which types of items are likely to give rise to any given memory state. The optimality problem is posed formally as a computation using Bayes theorem in probability theory. For many recognition models, the formal computations implied by our analysis can be carried out in principle; however, in other cases we explore performance optimization to suggest informal metacognitive heuristics for response selection.

The notation developed earlier can be used to formalize the problem of performance optimization. First, the set of tested items needs to be partitioned into correct response classes by defining $C_k = \{s_n | f(s_n) = r_k, n = 1, ..., N\}$, for $k = 1, ..., K$. Thus, C_k denotes the set of all items that have r_k as the correct response. Suppose a particular item is tested, and it gives rise to memory state $m \in M$. To set up the Bayesian computation, it is desirable to define several events; namely, s_n^* is the event that s_n is presented for test, m^* is the event of being in memory state m, and

$$C_k^* = \bigcup_{s_n \in C_k} s_n^*$$

is the event that the tested item is one of the items in C_k. The optimality problem could be solved directly if the values of $\Pr(C_k^* | m^*)$ were known for all $k = 1, 2, ..., K$. The solution would be to pick the response $r_{\hat{k}}$ that corresponds to the most likely response class, where

$$\hat{k} = \arg\max_{k=1}^{K} \{\Pr(C_k^* | m^*)\}. \tag{2}$$

Even if one does not have access to direct knowledge of the probability distribution of the response classes given the memory state, it may still be possible to solve the optimality problem by employing Bayes theorem from probability theory. Bayes theorem states that if A and B are two events with nonzero probability, then

$$\Pr(A | B) = \frac{\Pr(B | A)\Pr(A)}{\Pr(B)}. \tag{3}$$

Equation 3 can be applied to the optimality problem by noting first that

$$\Pr(C_k^*|m^*) = \sum_{s_n \in C_k} \Pr(s_n^*|m^*). \tag{4}$$

Next, substituting the events s_n^* and m^* into Equation 3 yields

$$\Pr(s_n^*|m^*) = \frac{\Pr(m^*|s_n^*)\Pr(s_n^*)}{\Pr(m^*)}. \tag{5}$$

Finally, Equations 4 and 5 can be combined to yield

$$\Pr(C_k^*|m^*) = \sum_{s_n \in C_k} \frac{\Pr(m^*|s_n^*)\Pr(s_n^*)}{\Pr(m^*)}. \tag{6}$$

If the various terms on the right-hand side of Equation 6 were known, the terms on the left-hand side could be calculated, and the optimal response would be obtained from solving Equation 2. In fact, the optimization can be accomplished without knowledge of $\Pr(m^*)$ since $\hat{k}$ that solves Equation 2 is also the $\hat{k}$ that maximizes the expression

$$\sum_{s_n \in C_k} \Pr(m^*|s_n^*)\Pr(s_n^*).$$

To show best how the Bayesian reformulation of the optimization problem is useful, consider the simple case where all $s_n^* \in C_k^*$ are equally likely and equally likely to lead to any particular memory state. This case corresponds to most applications of recognition memory models involving homogeneous items, and it leads to a computational simplification of Equation 6 given by

$$\Pr(C_k^*|m^*) = \frac{\Pr(m^*|C_k^*)\Pr(C_k^*)}{\Pr(m^*)}. \tag{7}$$

In Equation 7, the terms $\Pr(C_k^*)$ can be interpreted as the *base rate* of items with correct response r_k, that is, the likelihood of C_k^* without the evidence given by m^*. These base rates may be known at least approximately by the participant from experimental instructions, logical inference, or experience with early test trials. The base rates may be contrasted with the terms $\Pr(C_k^*|m^*)$, which in Bayesian terms can be referred to as posteriori probabilities of the item classes given the evidence provided by the memory state. The other terms needed to maximize the posterior probabilities are the $\Pr(m^*|C_k^*)$, which may be interpreted as the likelihood of the memory state given the item class.

In the derivation of Equation 7, it was assumed that the set of possible memory states M is given, and of course that is an assumption that is tenable only if there is some explicit memory model behind the supposed game between the experimenter and the participants. As stated, there is no generally accepted memory theory for recognition memory, so one could get different analyses of optimal behavior for different models. Assuming a particular model, exact computations in Equation 7 are possible only in hypothetical situations or in ones involving artificial intelligence. In the case of the participants, the terms might be inferred approximately by metacognitive awareness of the properties of their memory system as well as extraexperimental beliefs. For example, participants may have experienced various things about the study and test items that occurred during the experiment as well as in everyday life, and they may be aware of the effects on memory of such variables as item confusability (e.g., Benjamin & Bawa, 2004), item repetition (e.g., Koriat, Sheffer, & Ma'ayan, 2002), and the forgetting interval from study to test (e.g., Koriat, Bjork, Sheffer, & Bar, 2004). Also we see in the next two sections examples in which participants have false beliefs that could lead to incorrect evaluations of the terms in Equation 7, leading to suboptimal performance. From our point of view, in addition to specifying a formal computation, Equation 7 also suggests the following two heuristics that participants might use in recognition memory experiments and theorists can use to evaluate their models and anticipate experimental phenomena:

Heuristic 1 (Cause)

Given an imperfect state of item memory, consider how likely it is that the memory state would arise from various classes of items that one is encountering in the experiment. Tend to bias responses toward the classes that make the memory state most likely.

Heuristic 2 (Base Rate)

Estimate the relative proportions of items in the various item classes during test trials. Tend to bias responses to the more likely item classes.

There are various ways that participants, memory theorists, or machine algorithms might implement the computations implied by these two heuristics, but they are all facets of using a Bayesian approach to the optimization problem as exhibited in Equation 7. The next two main sections of the chapter show how the two heuristics make predictions in the context of an explicit model of source monitoring applied to specific experiments, but first we take up the simple old/new recognition memory paradigm to get a flavor of how these heuristics work.

Application to Old/New Recognition Memory

In the simplest old/new recognition memory paradigm discussed, the participants study a list of items drawn from a larger item pool, with the items roughly homogeneous in difficulty, and then the participants are tested with some of the old studied items and some unstudied distracter items drawn from the same pool. They are suppose to respond yes (r_y) to old items and no (r_n) to new items, so the data structure in Equation 1 is an $I \times N \times 2$ array, where there are N_1 old items and $N_2 = N - N_1$ new items. Thus, there are two correct classes of items, old items C_y, and new items C_n. Typically, data from an experimental group in old/new recognition are aggregated over participants and items within the two classes[6] and presented as a hit rate (HR) (proportion of yes responses to items in C_y) and a false alarm rate (FAR) (proportion of yes responses to items in C_n).

If a tested item is in memory state $m \in M$, it follows from Equation 7 that the optimal response is r_y if and only if[7]

$$\Pr(m^* \mid C_y^*) \geq \frac{\Pr(m^* \mid C_n^*)\Pr(C_n^*)}{[1 - \Pr(C_n^*)]}. \tag{8}$$

Equation 8 uses the fact that in the case of two response classes,

$$\Pr(C_y^*) + \Pr(C_n^*) = 1.$$

In this case, one can compute a so-called Bayes factor (Gill, 2002) as a measure of the relative strength of the two responses given by

$$BF(r_y : r_n) = \frac{\Pr(m^* \mid C_y^*)\Pr(C_y^*)}{\Pr(m^* \mid C_n^*)\Pr(C_n^*)}, \tag{9}$$

where values of the Bayes factor above one favor response r_y over r_n. If the base rates of old and new items are equal, as they often are in old/new recognition memory experiments, Equation 9 implies the simple rule that one should respond yes to an item if and only if it is more likely that the item's memory state arose from an old item than a new item.

Benjamin, Bjork, and Hirshman (1998) developed a Bayes factor in the form of Equation 9; memory states were assumed to be values on a hypothetical one-dimensional scale of "fluency." They described an experiment by Jacoby and Whitehouse (1989) in which the fluency of both old studied items and new distracters was sometimes enhanced by either rapid subthreshold or slower suprathreshold presentation of an item immediately before its test. One result was that the FAR (saying old to a new distracter) was larger for the subthreshold than the suprathreshold condition. They attributed this finding to the relative ability of the participants to discriminate the source of the boost in fluency due to the manipulations. Benjamin, Bjork, and Hirshman (1998) were able to decompose the terms in their Bayes factor based on fluency into terms that reflect extraexperimental sources, study list sources, and experimental sources other than study. They were able to account for the data in Jacoby and Whitehouse's (1989) experiment by showing that if the participant could discriminate the source of the extrastudy fluency enhancement, as they would in the suprathreshold presentations, then it could be discounted in the Bayes factor. More generally, they argued that if participants' recognition responses are based on fluency, then in addition to direct fluency estimation, they must be able to factor in information about the nature of the study list, the base rates, and explicit recollections from the study episode. Thus, their theory is very close to the general theory proposed here based on Bayesian formulations and our two heuristics that derive from it.

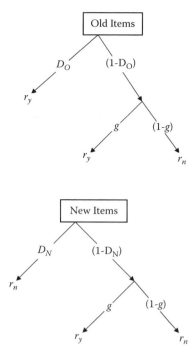

Figure 1 The double high-threshold model for old/new recognition memory in multinomial processing tree (MPT) form. D_O is the probability that an old item is detected as old, D_N is the probability that a new item is detected as new, and g is the probability that an undetected item is biased into the old category.

There is a frequently observed phenomenon in old/new recognition memory called the *mirror effect* (e.g., Glanzer & Adams, 1985, 1990). Basically, the mirror effect is a relationship among HR and FAR across two experimental conditions in an old/new recognition memory experiment. The mirror effect occurs when one of the two conditions produces a higher HR coupled with a lower FAR than the other condition. For example, low-frequency words have a higher HR than high-frequency words, and words repeated several times during study have a higher HR than words presented just once. In both of these cases and many others, the mirror effect reliably occurs. All recent theories of old/new recognition memory that were cited have made the mirror effect one of the main phenomena of interest, and there are now many different types of explanations for the mirror effect, with focus on when it does and does not occur (e.g., Cary & Reder, 2003; Glanzer, Adams, Iverson, & Kim, 1993; Sikström, 2001; Stretch & Wixted, 1998).

The basic mirror effect is quite consistent with our general heuristics for recognition memory responses presented earlier (e.g., Benjamin, 2003). To see this, consider the very simple double high-threshold model of Figure 1 presented as an MPT model (e.g., Macmillan & Creelman, 2005, chapter 4). Most researchers regard the double high-threshold model as an incorrect way to analyze old/new recognition data, but it was selected among several possibilities because it is related to the source-monitoring model of Bayen et al. (1996) discussed in the next section. The model assumes that old items either can be detected as old or, if they are not so detected, then a bias process g determines the response. The threshold for detecting old items D_O is said to be high because new items are not detected as old. An interesting feature of the model is that new items can be detected as new, also with a high threshold D_N. Most current memory theories suppose that new items are judged as new because of a lack of something like familiarity or fluency; although the possibility of detecting new items as new based on metacognitive knowledge was also discussed in several articles (e.g., Strack & Forster, 1998).

In terms of the model in Figure 1,

$$HR = D_O + (1 - D_O)g \qquad (10)$$

and

$$FAR = (1 - D_N)g. \qquad (11)$$

Suppose there are two conditions in an experiment, and let D_{iO}, D_{iN}, and g_i be the threshold for old items, the threshold for new items, and the guessing bias, respectively, for condition i, $i = 1, 2$. Suppose Condition 1 has a higher old item detection rate than Condition 2, so $D_{1O} > D_{2O}$. Knowing this, participants might reason in accord with Heuristic 1 and set the bias g for items that are not detected as old or new to be low, or at least lower than comparable participants in Condition 2, and this suggests the restriction $g_1 < g_2$. One metacognitive way that this might happen was proposed by Greene (1996). Greene assumed a signal detection theory of old/new recognition memory in which the subjects expect that there are about as many old as new items on the test series, and to achieve equal frequencies of yes and no responses, they lower their criterion for yes responses in the harder memory condition, resulting in a higher HR and a lower FAR in the easier condition. Greene's assumption is in accord with both of our heuristics, and in the context of the double high-threshold model in Figure 1 would lead to lowering the guessing rate for the easier condition. To see this, the proportion of r_y responses for the double high-threshold model is given by

$$\Pr(r_y) = \Pr(C_y^*)[D_O + (1 - D_O)g] + [1 - \Pr C_y^*](1 - D_N)g. \qquad (12)$$

If $\Pr(C_y^*) = .5$ and we set $\Pr(r_y) = .5$ in Equation 12, we can solve for the bias $\tilde{g}$ in terms of the detection rates that satisfy the rule suggested by Greene. The result is

$$\tilde{g} = \frac{(1-D_O)}{[(1-D_O)+(1-D_N)]}, \qquad (13)$$

and other things equal, Equation 13 is monotonically decreasing in increasing D_O.

Despite lowering the guessing bias in the easier condition, a mirror effect may or may not occur in the double high-threshold model. Assuming that the guessing probability has not been lowered too much so that $HR_1 > HR_2$, the key to occurrence of the mirror effect depends on the relationship between the two groups on their ability to detect new items as new. From Equation 11, it will occur if and only if $(1 - D_{1N})g_1 < (1 - D_{2N})g_2$, and even assuming $g_1 < g_2$, the mirror effect could fail if D_{2N} was sufficiently larger than D_{1N}. In an experiment in which old item detection was increased by presentation frequency during study, one would expect the detection of new items as new would be about equal between the groups, so the mirror effect would occur, and indeed it does in such an experiment. In the case of higher extraexperimental word frequency, one might even expect that high-frequency words would be harder to detect as new than would low-frequency words because of higher familiarity or fluency. In this case, $D_{1N} > D_{2N}$, and again it is easy to see that a mirror effect would occur even if the bias remained constant between groups. On the other hand, there are cases for which a mirror effect does not occur; for example, in a mixed list of high- and low-frequency words, the detectability of high-frequency words was increased relative to low-frequency words during study by repetitions (e.g., Sikström, 2001). This would result in a higher HR for high-frequency words, and even if the guessing bias is suitably adjusted to be lower by Equation 13 to reflect this, the inability to detect high-frequency distracters as new might keep the FAR for high-frequency words above that for low-frequency words.

Our discussion of the mirror effect in the context of the double high-threshold model is not intended to represent a new theory of this phenomenon. Instead, we wanted to illustrate how our metacognitive heuristics could be used in the context of a specific model to explain an important experimental phenomenon in the simple old/new recognition memory paradigm. Next, we turn to the more complex source-monitoring paradigm, which has several levels of response bias that participants must handle productively.

Analysis of Biases in Source Monitoring

Data Structure

Most source-monitoring experiments in the literature present study lists of items from two sources, C_1 and C_2, and subjects are tested on a series of old studied items and new distracters. When an item is presented for test, the participant has three response options, r_1 for old C_1, r_2 for old C_2, and r_3 for new distracters. After mathematical models for two sources by Batchelder and Riefer (1990) first appeared, variations on their model began to appear, and some of these were for designs involving three or more sources because such designs offer more degrees of freedom in specifying a model (e.g., Batchelder, Hu, & Riefer, 1994; Bayen et al., 1996; Klauer & Wegener, 1998; Meiser & Bröder, 2002; Riefer, Hu, & Batchelder, 1994). The analysis of data in these designs was facilitated by a general algorithm for conducting the statistical analysis of MPT models by Hu and Batchelder (1994), and soon thereafter the algorithm was employed into generally available software described in Hu and Phillips (1999).

This section adopts the general case of $K \geq 2$ sources, where the study list is made up of sets of items from each source. These sets are labeled C_1, C_2, ..., C_K; in addition, C_{K+1} denotes the set (source) of new distracters that appears along with the study sets on the test. Corresponding to these $K + 1$ classes of items are corresponding correct responses r_k, $k = 1, 2, ..., K + 1$. If the items in each source set are assumed to be approximately homogeneous (equally memorable), then it is reasonable to pool data for each participant over items within a source. Therefore, if I participants are run in such an experiment, the data structure in Equation 1 becomes the three-way array given by $\mathbf{D} = (x_{ink})_{Ix(K+1)x(K+1)}$, where x_{ink} is the number of responses to items in class C_n that were assigned to response r_k by participant i, $i = 1, \ldots, I$; $n = 1, \ldots, (K + 1)$; $k = 1, \ldots, (K + 1)$. It is convenient to derive from $\mathbf{D}$ a set of I two-way arrays, one for each participant, given by

$$\mathbf{D}_i = (x_{ink})_{(K+1)x(K+1)}. \tag{14}$$

In most published applications of MPT models for source monitoring, each $\mathbf{D}_i$ is assumed to arise from a product multinomial structure (cf. W. E. Batchelder & Riefer, 1990), where the rows of $\mathbf{D}_i$ are regarded as observations from independent multinomial distributions each with $K + 1$ response categories. This assumption is consistent with the effort to have homogeneous items from each source; however, the independence assumption both within and between rows is a convenient assumption that is rarely addressed in any of the many experiments in recognition memory.[8] Often, participants as well as items within a source are assumed to be homogeneous, and in such cases the data are aggregated over participants and items, yielding a $(K + 1) \times (K + 1)$ aggregated count matrix given by

$$\mathbf{D} = \sum_{i=1}^{I} \mathbf{D}_i.$$

The assumption of participant homogeneity is a strong one, and it has begun to be challenged in the literature; Smith and Batchelder (in press) provided statistical tests for item or participant homogeneity. In cases that participants are not homogeneous, either participants are analyzed separately or the cognitive model should be supplemented with random effects assumptions on participants (e.g., Batchelder & Riefer, 2007; Klauer, 2006; Lee & Webb, 2005: Rouder & Lu, 2005; Smith & Batchelder, 2005). Recognition memory researchers should be aware that if there are participant or item inhomogeneities in an experiment, any group-level phenomena based on aggregated data may well be an artifact of averaging.

A Multinomial Processing Tree Model of Source Monitoring

In this section, the two metacognitive heuristics are applied to an MPT model that combines features of the source-monitoring models of Batchelder and Riefer (1990) and Bayen et al. (1996). Both of these models were initially developed for a two-source experiment, and both have been used to analyze data in many source-monitoring experiments. In the case of $K = 2$ sources, the product multinomial structure in Equation 14 has only six degrees of freedom (two for each row), so there is a restriction on a modeler that, to identify the parameters (uniquely measure them from data), at most six free parameters can be specified in constructing the model. To meet the restriction imposed by the data structure, Batchelder and Riefer (1990) specified their model by making a single "high-threshold" assumption that new distracter items are never "detected" as old or as new items, and responses to them are based entirely on bias processes. Their high-threshold assumption was criticized on theoretical grounds by Kinchla (1994), and Batchelder, Riefer, and Hu (1994) replied by suggesting that in many cases their assumption can serve as a useful approximation that allows one to measure separately the underlying memory and biasing processes in source monitoring.

Bayen et al. (1996) developed a source-monitoring model based on a double high-threshold assumption, where new distracters could be detected as such (see Figure 1). Generally, double high-threshold models of recognition memory are regarded as better approximations to the underlying probabilistic processes in recognition memory than single high-threshold models (e.g., Macmillan & Creelman, 2005, chapter 4). However, to meet the restriction on the number of identifiable parameters in a two-source experiment, the model of Bayen et al. requires the strong restriction that the probability of detecting a new item as new has the same value as the detection probability for one or both of the old item sources.

The MPT model for $K \geq 2$ sources that is presented next has both of the earlier MPT threshold models of source monitoring as special cases. In source-monitoring studies in which the main purpose is to measure the underlying reasons why groups differ, we recommend conducting the experiment with three or more sources. The model is represented as a processing tree in Figure 2. The top tree in Figure 2 considers the case in which an item from any one of the K old sources k is presented for test, $k = 1, 2, \ldots, K$. With probability D_k, the item is detected as being old, and with probability $(1 - D_k)$, it is not so detected. Further, if the item is detected as old, then d_k is the conditional probability that the source of the item is discriminated (remembered). Thus, with probability $D_k d_k$, the item from an old source is both detected and discriminated, and the correct response r_k is given. With probability $D_k(1 - d_k)$, an old item is detected, but the source is not discriminated, and the participant chooses a response from a response bias distribution over the K sources, with $a_j = \Pr(r_j) \geq 0$ and

$$\sum_{j=1}^{K} a_j = 1.$$

Finally, with probability $(1 - D_k)$ the item is not detected as old, and it is nevertheless biased to be one of the K old sources with probability b, and with probability $(1 - b)$ response $r_{(K+1)}$ corresponding to the new distracter item class is made. If a non-detected item is biased to be one of the sources, then the choice is governed by bias probabilities $g_j = \Pr(r_j) \geq 0$, where

$$\sum_{j=1}^{K} g_j = 1.$$

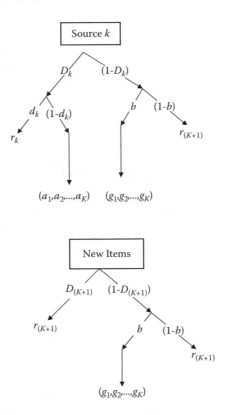

Figure 2 The general source-monitoring model for K sources in multinomial processing tree (MPT) form. Top tree is for old items, and the bottom tree is for new distracters. D_k is the probability of detecting an item from source k as old, $D_{(K+1)}$ is the probability of detecting a distracter as new, d_k is the probability of discriminating the source of an item detected from source k, b is the probability of biasing a nondetected item is from one of the old sources, a_j is the probability a detected but nondiscriminated item is biased into source j, g_j is the probability of a nondetected item that is biased into the old sources is biased to source j, $j = 1, \ldots, K$.

If the tested item is a new item in $C_{(K+1)}$, then the tree at the bottom of Figure 2 applies. With probability $D_{(K+1)}$, the item is detected as new and the correct response $r_{(K+1)}$ is made, and with probability $(1 - D_{(K+1)})$, it is not detected as new. In the latter case, the remaining branches of the tree are the same as in the case of a nondetected item from any of the K old sources.

From the tree in Figure 2, it is possible to derive equations for the probability distribution over the $K + 1$ response classes for each of the $K + 1$ classes of items. For example, a correct response to an item from old source k can occur in three ways in the top tree in Figure 2, and these combine to yield

$$\Pr(r_k | C_k{}^*) = D_k d_k + D_k (1 - d_k) a_k + (1 - D_k) b g_k,$$

for $k = 1, 2, \ldots, K$. On the other hand, an incorrect old source response to an old item can occur in two ways in the top tree, and they combine to yield

$$\Pr(r_j | C_k^\star) = D_k(1 - d_k)a_j + (1 - D_k)bg_j,$$

for $1 \leq k, j \leq K$, $k \neq j$. Finally, a correct response to a new item can occur in two ways, and its probability is given from the lower tree in Figure 2 by

$$\Pr(r_{(K+1)} | C_{(K+1)}^\star) = D_{(K+1)} + (1 - D_{(K+1)})(1 - b).$$

The other response probabilities can be calculated in a similar fashion. The model in Figure 2 has $K + 1$ detection parameters (the Ds), K discrimination parameters (the ds), and $2K - 1$ bias parameters (b, $K - 1$ a_j, and $K - 1$ g_j), $4K$ parameters in all, and the product multinomial structure has $K(K + 1)$ df, namely, K for each of the $K + 1$ stimulus classes. So, as long as $K \geq 3$, there are as many degrees of freedom as parameters.[9]

Applying the Metacognitive Heuristics

For the model in Figure 2, there are a total of $K + 4$ possible memory states that can arise. These include $K + 1$ memory states for which the optimal response is clear, namely, K memory states corresponding to detected and discriminated items from the K old sources and an additional one for new items that are detected as new. The other three memory states are characterized by states that involve imperfect memory, and to select an optimal response, various bias processes must be calibrated. First, there is the case for which an item was not detected as either old or new; in this case, one must decide whether to attribute it to one of the K old sources anyway. Denote this state by m_1, and parameter b is set to handle this situation. Second, there is the state for which an undetected item has been biased to be one of the old K sources (with probability b), and one of them must be selected for the response. Denote this state by m_2, and in this case, the old source is selected from the probability distribution given by $\langle g_j \rangle_{j=1}^{K}$. Finally, there is the case for which an item was detected as old but the source was not discriminated. Denote this state by m_3, and in this case, the bias distribution represented by $\langle a_j \rangle_{j=1}^{K}$ applies. We use the Bayesian approach in Equation 7 to compute the optimal response from the model in Figure 2 for each of these three imperfect memory states.

First, consider the decision to attribute an undetected item in state m_1 to one of the old sources, which has probability b in the model. From Equation 7 and noting that

$$\Pr(m_1^*) = \sum_{j=1}^{K+1}(1 - D_j)\Pr(C_j^*),$$

we obtain

$$\Pr(C_k^*|m_1^*) = \frac{(1-D_k)\Pr(C_k^*)}{\sum_{j=1}^{K+1}(1-D_j)\Pr(C_j^*)}. \tag{15}$$

In most source-monitoring experiments, the base rate of items in each of the $K + 1$ classes is equal, although in cases of $K > 2$, some experimenters match the number of old and new items, distributing the old items evenly over the K sources. If we assume that the base rates of the $K + 1$ classes are equal, the most likely class of the item is C_k, where from Equation 2

$$\hat{k} = \arg\min_{k=1}^{K+1}[D_k]. \tag{16}$$

In other words, the most likely class is the class for which detection has the least probability. From a strictly optimal standpoint, the model should set $b = 1$ if $k \in \{1, 2, \ldots, K\}$ and $b = 0$ if $k = K + 1$.

There are good psychological reasons to suspect that participants would not behave in this optimal way even if they had full knowledge of their detection probabilities. For one, many studies of human decision making have revealed suboptimal decision-making strategies that are characteristic of human decision makers even if they are informed about the relevant information (e.g., Tversky & Kahneman, 1974). Perhaps the case that is most applicable to the current situation is the phenomenon of probability matching (e.g., Estes, 1964): Instead of the optimal strategy of always predicting the more probable of two alternatives in a series of Bernoulli trials, participants tend to use the information in a suboptimal way by matching their response probabilities to the objective probabilities. This way of using base rate information is consistent with tendencies noted in old/new recognition memory to set biases so that the proportion of responses in various classes tends to match the objective proportions. This approach is also consistent with a number of psychological theories of categorization that assume items are assigned to categories with probabilities determined by the relative evidence of each category rather than by selecting the category with the most evidence with probability one (e.g., Nosofsky, 1990). Perhaps the safest conclusion to draw from our two heuristics is that participants who can monitor their own detection probabilities of old items and distracters will tend to bias undetected items into the old source categories to the extent that they are successful in detecting new items and to the extent that the base rate of old items is large.

In the case of memory state m_2, an item is not detected as old but is biased into the old sources. Clearly, in this case the optimal response to pick is the one associated with the old source with the smallest detection probability. While we do not expect to observe optimal response selection based on the arguments given, it is reasonable to predict from Equation 16 that the rank order of the estimated guessing biases g_k for nondetected old items from different sources would match the rank order of the estimated nondetect probabilities $(1 - D_k)$.

This prediction was confirmed in studies of source monitoring involving the "generation effect" (e.g., Slamecka & Graf, 1978), in which the two sources consist of acts the participant did and acts that another did. For example, Voss, Vesonder, Post, and

TABLE 1   Comparison of Estimates of the Memory and Bias Parameters in Experiment 1 of Riefer et al. (1994)

Source	Recalled by Self	Recalled by Other	Not Recalled
$(1 - D)$	.05	.08	.29
g	.03	.19	.78
$D(1 - d)$	.28	.41	.16
a	.30	.46	.24

Note: D is the detection parameter for a source, d is the source discrimination parameter, g is the guessing probability for a source when the item is nondetected, and a is the guessing probability for a detected item when the source is not discriminated.

Ney (1987) ran yoked pairs of participants in a source-monitoring study. First, both members of the pair were exposed to a long list of words on a study list. Subsequently, they took turns alternating recalls of as many words as they could until neither partner could recall any more words. Finally, they were given a $K = 2$ source-monitoring task in which the experimenter presented words in three categories: words recalled by self, words recalled by other, and words not recalled by either (these were treated as the distracters). Voss et al. (1987) found, as expected, that self-generated words were detected better than words recalled by other; however, using conventional operational measures of source memory, they did not find an expected difference between self-generated words and other generated words on source discrimination ability. The researchers suggested that a bias for participants to attribute nondetected words to the other person might have masked the expected source-monitoring difference. This bias is consistent with the metacognitive inference that one would better remember words that they recalled than words that another person recalled, essentially the heuristic, "One of us did it, but I can't remember who did it, so it must have been you."

In a subsequent study, Riefer et al. (1994) used their source-monitoring model (Batchelder & Riefer, 1990) to show that the data of Voss et al. (1987) could not in principle differentiate the hypothesis of equal source memory for self and other from the possibility of a bias to attribute nondetected words to other. Riefer et al. (1994) conducted a new $K = 3$ source-monitoring experiment by making unrecalled words a third source and adding new distracter words. They found reliable detection D and source discrimination d advantages of self over other as well as reliable biases for attributing nondetected items to other over self. Table 1 reports estimated values of the nondetection rates $(1 - D)$ and corresponding guessing biases g for all three sources. In fact, the three g parameters were ordered exactly as predicted by the optimal response rule in Equation 16, that is, the higher the detection probability for a source, the lower the nondetection guessing probability. These estimates reveal a phenomenon in source monitoring that follows from Heuristic 1 to bias items with weak memory states toward the categories of items that have poorer memorability. This result is similar to the mirror effect, for which items with the higher HRs have the lower FAR.

In another study, Durso and Johnson (1980) presented items visually either as words or pictures (where the word corresponding to the picture was obvious) in a source-monitoring study with $K = 2$ sources. They expected to find a source memory

TABLE 2   Comparison of Memory and Bias Parameters in Experiment 2 of Riefer et al. (1994)

Source	Pictures	Visual Words	Spoken Words
$(1 - D)$	.09	.28	.22
g	.16	.34	.50
$D(1 - d)$	.13	.38	.25
a	.22	.41	.37

Note: D is the detection parameter for a source, d is the source discrimination parameter, g is the guessing probability for a source when the item is nondetected, and a is the guessing probability for a detected item when the source is not discriminated.

advantage for pictures following many other experimental paradigms comparing the memory for words and pictures in which a "picture superiority effect" was found (e.g., Nelson, Reed, & Walling, 1976). They used conventional operational definitions of source memory to conclude that there was a picture superiority effect. Batchelder, Hu, and Riefer (1994) argued that it was not possible using the conventional measure to separate a response bias favoring pictures from a source memory advantage of pictures in the Durso and Johnson (1980) study because there were only two sources, so they replicated the study by adding a third source, namely, spoken words (Riefer et al., 1994). A version of the model in Figure 2 was applied to the new data, and they discovered that the detection and discrimination probability for pictures was higher for visual words than pictures, confirming the original expectations of Durso and Johnson. Of interest was the fact shown in Table 2 that the estimate of the guessing biases g for undetected picture items was the smallest, and the detection probability for that class was the highest. This is in accord with that expected from Equation 16. Thus, this result as well as those found in the previous study supports the prediction of an inverse relationship between the detectability of a source and the tendency to bias items toward that source. There is one reversal of this prediction in Table 2 because the lowest detectability is for visual words and the estimate of the guessing probability for undetected visual words is the middle of the guessing estimates rather than being the highest value.

In a series of experiments, Meiser, Sattler, and von Hecker (2007) conducted source-monitoring studies in which they controlled the item detection rates by experimental manipulations, for instance, of frequency and study time. Their study used $K = 4$ sources with the sources constructed by varying two factors, each having two levels (e.g., items in red or green on either the left or the right side of the screen). Meiser and Bröder (2002) developed an MPT source-monitoring model for this paradigm (basically a natural extension of the model in Figure 2 for sources created by crossing the two factors) that has several levels of guessing parameters depending on the various imperfect memory states that might occur (the model was also used in a related study by Riefer, Chien, & Reimer, 2007). The studies of Meiser and coresearchers strongly supported the heuristics that participants bias their guesses to nondetected items toward the sources that have lowest detection rates. In one of their experiments, they manipulated the participants' belief about the relative detectability of the sources even when prior studies established that there were no differences in detectability.

Analysis of their data revealed no differences in detection rates, as expected, and the bias parameter was higher for the source that the participants believed was the harder one to detect; that is, the belief manipulation had the expected effect.

The third imperfect memory state in the model in Figure 2 is m_3, for which an item is detected as an old one, but its source is not discriminated. From Equation 7, the probability that the correct source is C_k given memory state m_3 is given by

$$\Pr(C_k^*|m_3^*) = \frac{D_k(1-d_k)\Pr(C_k^*)}{\sum\limits_{j=1}^{K} D_j(1-d_j)\Pr(C_j^*)}. \tag{17}$$

Assuming that the base rates are equal, it is easy to see from Equation 17 that the optimal response is $r_{\hat{k}}$, where

$$\hat{k} = \arg\max_{k=1}^{K}\{D_k(1-d_k)|k=1,2,...,K\}. \tag{18}$$

Equation 17 is interesting in that it trades off high detection rates with low discrimination rates in such a way that the source with the highest probability of detection but not discrimination is the one that should be selected for optimal responding. Tables 1 and 2 report these values for the two experiments by Riefer et al. (1994) we discussed. In both cases, the rank order of the estimated biases for detected but not discriminated items is exactly the order predicted by Equation 17. Of particular interest in the model is the possibility that the two classes of guessing biases in the model may not be ordered in the same way. This is likely to happen when high detection probabilities are coupled with moderate discrimination probabilities, and in Table 1 there is a noticeable reversal in estimated biases for the self-recalled words and the unrecalled words, illustrating the 'it had to be you' phenomenon discussed earlier.

Metacognitive Inferences From Social Beliefs in Source Monitoring

Thus far, we have considered how various experimental factors within a source-monitoring experiment, such as relative differences in source memory and base rates of distracters, should affect the setting of bias parameters to optimize performance. In this section, we consider cases for which extraexperimental social beliefs can affect the bias parameters. For example, if one remembered reading a news story about politics but failed to remember the source, the political content of the story on a liberal/conservative dimension might be used to make a reasonable guess regarding the source. For another example, suppose one were asked whether two particular people in a social network had a friendly relationship. Absent direct knowledge, indirect knowledge about the positive and negative relationships of each of these two people with others in the social network might influence the response. Stahl (2006) provided a review of applications of MPT models in the area of social psychology, and versions of the source-monitoring model in Figure 2 are seen in many of these applications.

Klauer and Wegener (1998) conducted source-monitoring experiments to better understand the origin of social stereotyping in the so-called "Who said what?" paradigm (e.g., Taylor, Fiske, Etcoff, & Ruderman, 1978). In the original version of this paradigm, participants are exposed to a study series of statements from each of a set of speakers along with an attribution of the group affiliation of the speaker. Then, on test trials old statements are presented to the participant, who is required to assign each of the statements to one of the speakers. The speakers come from two distinct groups (e.g., African American persons and Caucasian persons or pro-life or pro-choice speakers about abortion), and the main purpose of the experiment is to assess whether there is social stereotyping (bias) in the misattributions of speakers to statements. Klauer and Wegener (1998) reviewed 50 studies of the "Who said what?" paradigm, and they argued that there was a need in these studies to disentangle different memory processes from bias processes, and to accomplish this they added distracter items and applied an MPT model to a source-monitoring version of the paradigm.

The test items for the model are a series of statements, some of which were made by various speakers during the study phase and others are new distracters. The speakers come from two distinctive groups, and these groups are considered as the sources, so that coupled with the distracters, there are three categories of test items. Because there are multiple speakers within a group, it is possible to classify responses to old items into one of four categories: (1) correctly attributed to the speaker, (2) attributed to the wrong speaker in the correct group, (3) attributed to a speaker in the wrong group, and (4) classified as a new distracter. In the case of distracters, all but the first response category are possible. In total, there are eight degrees of freedom in the resulting product multinomial structure, and that allowed the researchers to define more parameters than for the usual $K = 2$ source-monitoring study. The model Klauer and Wegener created can be viewed as related to the one in Figure 2 with $K = 2$, except in the case of detected old items that are not discriminated [with probability $D_k(1 - d_k)$ for statements from a person in group k], there is an additional parameter for the possibility that the correct group of the speaker is discriminated even if the speaker is not. In that case, the guesses are confined to the correct group, with equal probability of attribution to each speaker in the group.

Klauer and Wegener (1998) validated their model in a series of between-group experiments in which each experiment varied a factor that should have an effect on the value of a specific parameter and no strong effects on the others. They were successful in dissociating all of the processes in their model, therefore achieving their goal of providing a model-based method of disentangling confounded processes in the "Who said what?" paradigm. One of their validation studies involved a simple manipulation of the number of new distracters relative to the number of old items. In that study, the probability of attributing an undetected item to one of the old sources (the parameter b in Figure 2) was decreased by increasing the number of new distracters, and none of the other parameters differed significantly due to this manipulation. This is a direct indication of the importance of Heuristic 2 in showing the role of base rate in the setting of guessing parameters in the model. Subsequently, Klauer and his colleagues used the model to address a variety of issues in this paradigm, such as the effect of statement content on bias (Klauer & Wegener, 1999); the role of small group size in promoting stereotyping (Klauer, Wegener, & Ehrenberg, 2002);

the role of cognitive load in increasing stereotyping (Klauer & Ehrenberg, 2005); and the impact of social expectancies on stereotyping (Ehrenberg & Klauer, 2005).

Another area involving social inference that was examined with a source-monitoring paradigm was the phenomenon of "illusory correlation" (e.g., Hamilton & Gifford, 1976). In this paradigm, there are two distinct groups of people, and the experimenter presents items consisting of a person's name, the person's group membership, and a single positive (admirable) or negative behavioral act that the person did. Each person is named just once, and the experimenter presents more statements about members of one group than the other. There are more positive than negative statements presented in both groups, but the ratio of positive to negative behavioral acts is the same for both groups. The experimental finding was that the group with the fewer statements receives lower evaluative ratings, more than expected misattributions of negative behaviors, and a higher frequency estimate of negative behaviors than the group with more statements. This phenomenon is called illusory correlation because participants respond as though there is a correlation between the incidence of negative behaviors and the minority group, and this finding is taken by some researchers as indication of a source of the cause of discrimination toward minority groups. Early explanations of the phenomenon were based on the notion that attention and memory storage and retrieval factors would be enhanced for negative behavioral acts in the minority group because they are very infrequent.

Klauer and Meiser (2000) argued that it is difficult to disentangle memory factors and response bias processes in the standard illusory correlation paradigm. For this reason, they created an MPT model of a source-monitoring version of the paradigm. Basically, they added to the test trials new distracter statements that were not presented to the participants. During the test phase, the participants were exposed to five types of items, positive and negative items from the majority and minority groups as well as new distracters. The participants' job was to classify each item as from the majority group, from the minority group, or a new distracter. In essence, their model was a $K = 2$ version of the model in Figure 2, except that there were five rather than three types of items as described. The extra classes of items lead to 10 rather than 6 degrees of freedom in the product multinomial structure, and this allowed the researchers to estimate different detection, discrimination, and bias parameters for each class of items.

In one study, Klauer and Meiser (2000) varied the number of new distracters, and they found that this manipulation only affected the estimate of the parameter b. This was a result that contributed to validating the model since the proportion of distracters should only affect the bias to attribute an undetected item to one of the old sources. Klauer and Meiser (2000) also found that negative statements were better detected as old than positive statements. The most interesting finding, however, was that bias processes (the a_k and g_k in Figure 2) and not memory differences (the D_k and d_k) were behind the tendency to attribute negative behaviors to the minority group. In particular, they found that detected and not discriminated negative items as well as nondetected negative items were attributed more than positive items to the minority group. Further studies (e.g., Meiser & Hewstone, 2001) have reinforced the view that the illusory correlation is due to biasing phenomena rather than memory differences between items from the majority and minority groups. These studies provide strong arguments for using models to disentangle and separately measure confounded processes in complex memory paradigms.

In a series of four experiments, we studied social memory using the source-monitoring paradigm (E. Batchelder & Batchelder, 2005). Research in social (relational) perception and cognition has a long history. In both laboratory experiments and fieldwork, researchers have shown that people have a tendency to perceive and cognitively represent social ties as symmetric, transitive, and balanced (e.g., DeSoto, 1960; Freeman, 1992; Kumbasar, Romney, & Batchelder, 1994; Newcomb, 1961; Picek, Sherman, & Shiffrin, 1975). One of our goals was to examine and measure this tendency toward balance. To pursue this, a social network structure was formulated as a signed graph in which nodes represent actors embedded in the network, and signed edges (lines connecting nodes with positive or negative signs attached to them) represent relations (ties) between pairs of actors, the sign indicating the nature of the relation (friendly or unfriendly). The concept of balance was introduced by Heider (1946) and later formulated by Cartwright and Harary (1956) and Davis (1967) using signed graphs. A signed graph is "balanced" if its nodes can be partitioned into two subsets in such a way that all ties within each subset are positive and all ties between subsets are negative. In case the positive tie represents "friends" and the negative one "enemies," the balance concept supports the informal social heuristics, "A friend of a friend is a friend," and "An enemy of an enemy is a friend."

In each of 4 experiments, 2 groups of participants read a short story describing a subset of the 15 dyadic relations (some positive and some negative) within a network of 6 people. In each experiment, the two groups were set up to have corresponding numbers of positive and negative ties reported in the story, but in one group the ties were consistent with a balanced social structure, and in the other they were not. The signed graphs in Figure 3 are balanced and unbalanced versions of the social structure used in the story in Experiment 2. In the balanced structure, satisfying balance theory are two subsets, ABCDF, and E. The edges present in the graphs were described in the story, the solid line as a friendly (positive) relation, and the dashed line as an unfriendly (negative) relation. The story did not mention anything about the missing edges (e.g., the relation between actors A and D was not specified). Three of the experiments had four positive ties and two negative ties in the story, and the fourth experiment had three ties of each type presented in the story.

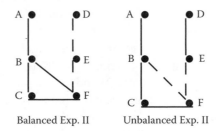

Balanced Exp. II   Unbalanced Exp. II

Figure 3 Two social networks, each with six actors; a solid line between two actors indicates a positive relationship, a dotted line indicates a negative relationship, and no line leaves the status of the relationship unknown.

In the test phase, participants were first asked to recall, for each of the 15 dyadic relations, whether the relationship was presented in the story. Then, they were asked to identify the nature of the detected relationship, whether it was friendly (positive) or unfriendly (negative). For the relationships that were not detected (new), the participants were asked to "guess" the nature of the relationship (positive or negative) based on all the dyadic information given in the story. To follow up on the structure given in the left side of Figure 3, a participant in the balanced group, when asked to report (guess) the relational tie between A and D, would be expected to report a positive tie under the balance hypothesis since this type of tie would push the structure toward balance. In this manner and using the same heuristic, the missing ties would be "filled in" with BD as positive, BE and CE as negative, and so on. Note that in the unbalanced structure, it is not possible to fill in all the missing ties using the same strategy leading to a balanced structure. Studies have shown that people, when presented with a similar problem, tend to make errors in the direction of balance (DeSoto, 1960; Freeman, 1992). For example, in Figure 3, if the sign of the BF tie in the unbalanced structure is "switched" to positive, then the structure can be balanced.

The study–test sequence was repeated twice in each of the four experiments, and this created eight cases for which balanced and unbalanced groups could be compared. This design is a $K = 2$ source-monitoring design in which old positive ties and old negative ties were the two sources, and the unpresented dyads were the distracters. Since the participants must attribute a positive or a negative tie to the dyads they did not detect as old, the product multinomial structure has an additional category, so there are a total of nine rather than six degrees of freedom open to the modeler. The extra degrees of freedom allowed the addition of two 'inference parameters' to the model, one for detected but not discriminated old items and the other for new items in the model in Figure 2. There were three main purposes in doing the experiments: (1) to see if there were differences between the memorability of positive and negative ties, (2) to see if overall memory for balanced social structures was higher than for unbalanced ones, and (3) to see if participants could make metacognitive inferences about the attribution of unremembered or unpresented ties in the direction of balance. In addition, the experiments allowed us to see if the bias parameters reflected metacognitive Heuristics 1 and 2 derived from the Bayesian formulation.

In four experiments, we found that negative ties in the story had significantly higher detection D and discrimination d parameters than old positive ties. Perhaps this was due to the fact that negative relations in a group of actors are salient both in a fictional story and in real life, perhaps because they are relatively rare and play a differentially more important role than positive ties in understanding and predicting the structure of a group. In fact, a related difference in favor of the memorability of negative behavioral acts of group members over positive acts was found in Klauer and Meiser's (2000) source-monitoring studies of illusory correlation.

There was evidence for a memory advantage of balanced stories from ones that were not balanced. For example, over 16 comparisons of the estimates of the 2 detection probabilities between balanced and unbalanced groups, the balanced group's detection parameter was larger in 12 cases, smaller in 3 cases, and tied in 1 case ($p <$ .05, sign test). In 16 comparisons of the estimates of the discrimination parameter d, the balanced group had the larger value in 12 of 16 cases ($p < .05$, sign test). Despite the overall significant differences in comparisons across experiments, the magnitude of the difference in many of the cases was quite small.

Examining the bias parameters, we found that in the first three experiments, with four positive ties and two negative ties in the story, guessing probabilities for positive ties were always larger than .50; further, they clustered around the value of .67, which represents probability-matching behavior as discussed in this chapter. This result is consistent with the base rate heuristic, and similar to the mirror effect, since the detection and discrimination parameters are higher for negative ties but the relationship reverses for the guessing probabilities. Another result in all experiments was that on the second reading in which performance was better, the probability of classifying a new dyad as an old one, essentially a false alarm measured by b in Figure 2, decreased. Again, this result can be viewed as a version of the mirror effect.

The addition of the inference parameters improved the fit over the source monitoring without inference parameters, but this was highly significant only in one of the four experiments. The lack of strong inference effects may have been due in part to memory factors and inadequate attention paid to global structural features when "filling in" missing ties or recalling existing ones. Instead, strategies focusing on local structures might be employed more frequently (e.g., when guessing the AD tie, focusing on A's reported ties and D's reported ties only rather than considering the group as a whole) than those that use the balance heuristic for the entire structure. Also, participants might be more successful in employing this strategy when there is more information available (i.e., inference might be effective when two of the three ties within a triad are known and only one tie has to be filled in, rather than when more than one dyadic tie has to be filled in). To investigate this further, we examined the participants' reported triads for both balanced and unbalanced structures. There were 20 triads in both structures; in the balanced structure condition and using the balance heuristic, any new tie can be specified in such a way that it makes all its triadic relations balanced, whereas in the unbalanced structure condition only those triads with two dyadic ties mentioned in the story can be "completed" as balanced using the same heuristic (e.g., BFE is balanced if BE is positive). We classified all triads that could be classified in this way as balanced or unbalanced. The data revealed that in both the balanced and the unbalanced conditions there was a significant tendency to bias new ties toward balance.

Conclusion

In the first part of the chapter, we reviewed recognition memory paradigms and models, and it was shown that each involves source monitoring in the sense that correct responding requires participants to be able to discriminate experimental and extra-experimental sources of the memory state of a tested item. We argued that recognition memory experiments can be viewed as a game between the experimenter and a participant, with the participant attempting to optimize performance given imperfect item memory that has been engineered in various ways by the experimenter. The optimization process involves a participant's effort to use metacognitive inferences to bias response selection toward the most likely response class of the tested item. These inferences are drawn from metacognitive knowledge obtained from monitoring one's own memory state for a tested item along with knowledge and beliefs acquired from other experimental and extraexperimental sources. It was shown that Bayes theorem was the key to bringing these factors together. In particular, Equation 7 was used to calculate the probability that a response class is correct given a particular memory state, from knowledge of the likelihood of reaching that memory state from each type of item along with its base rate on the test. The Bayesian formulation suggests two heuristics that a participant can use to play the game: Heuristic 1 is to bias responses toward classes likely to have caused the memory state, and Heuristic 2 is to bias responses to classes that occur frequently in the test sequence. These heuristics are used along with a simple double high-threshold MPT model to suggest a basis for the well-studied mirror effect in old/new recognition memory in which groups with high HRs tend to have low FARs.

In the last two main sections of the chapter, we showed how the general MPT model for source monitoring in Figure 2 could be used as a measurement tool to show that metacognitive knowledge has predictable effects in source-monitoring experiments. In particular, the two heuristics that we derived from the Bayesian formulation were consistent with the effect on estimated bias parameters of a number of experimental manipulations. For example, in the cases of the picture superiority effect and the generation effect, a phenomenon similar to the mirror effect occurred in which nondetected items were biased toward the sources with low detection probabilities. In the case of detected items with a source that was not discriminated, biasing was explained by Equation 17, which was derived for the MPT source-monitoring model directly from the Bayesian formulation in Equation 7. These findings were strongly supported in a series of experiments by Meiser et al. (2007) in a source-monitoring design involving sources defined by factorial combinations of attributes. All these studies revealed that the tendency to bias a response toward a particular source is often inversely correlated with the source's memory strength, and this means that to measure memory effects in source monitoring it is important to use a valid model to disentangle latent memory and biasing factors from manifest responses.

The importance of separating memory factors and biasing factors turned out to be particularly important in three applications of the source-monitoring paradigm to understand the role of social perceptions in memory. The first application was to the "Who said what?" paradigm. In this paradigm, it was well established that errors in attributing a statement to a person often result in misattributions to a person in the same social category; however, until the development and application of Klauer and Wegener's (1998) MPT model of source monitoring, there was no way to disentangle and separately measure the roles of memory and biasing processes. The second application was the development of an MPT model of source monitoring for the phenomenon of illusory correlation. After validating their MPT model, Klauer and Meiser (2000) showed that the effect was due to different response biases rather than memory processes as many theorists had thought.

The final application was to our experiments on the memory for friendship ties in a social network. Previous studies had shown that participants tend to fill in missing ties in accord with structural balance; however, these studies were not designed to separate the relative roles of response bias and memory in this phenomenon. We designed an MPT model that allowed for an inference process, and we showed that both detection and source discrimination were better for balanced than for unbalanced social structures. In addition, participants had a tendency toward balance when filling in missing (either nondetected or new) ties.

Throughout the chapter, we stressed the importance of using recognition memory models as measurement tools. In our view, it is an unproductive if not impossible task to discern the "correct" model of source monitoring from a series of behavioral experiments no matter how clever and complex. Instead, we view recognition memory models as ways to measure latent factors that underlie manifest response processes. Viewed in this way, it is important not only to show the model can fit data but to validate the model before it is used for measurement in any particular research paradigm. The validation process involves conducting experiments in which standard manipulations of experimental factors have different and predictable experimental effects on each of the model's parameters. It is the ability of validation experiments to dissociate the parameters of a model that makes it eligible to be a measurement tool. If an experimental variation in a recognition memory paradigm comes along with data that a model cannot account for, a frequent happening in the history of recognition memory models, our strategy is not to invent more hypothetical mechanisms to account for the new data. Instead, our recommendation would be to be careful not to use the model to measure latent processes in experiments that might involve that variation. We believe that successful measurement in science involves both pragmatic approximation and standardized conditions for applicability. It is certainly true that, in the case of natural sciences like physics and chemistry, there is deep and generally accepted theory behind various successful measurement methods. However, in the area of recognition memory we doubt that it is possible to find such theory, at least based on experiments like the current models are based on involving standard behavioral measures.

Acknowledgment

We acknowledge research support from the Alzheimer's Association (IIRG-03-6262 to W. H. Batchelder and E. Batchelder, Co-Principal Investigators) and the National Science Foundation (SES-00136115 to A. K. Romney and W. H. Batchelder, Co-Principal Investigators; and SES-0616657 to X. Hu and W. H. Batchelder, Co-Principal Investigators).

Notes

1. Most recognition memory paradigms are of the study–test variety in which the study list appears before the test list; however, in a continuous recognition memory paradigm (e.g., Shepard & Teghtsoonian, 1961), each trial is both a study and a test trial. The subject is presented with a series of items that mix old items appearing at various lags since last study with items appearing for the first time.
2. In some recognition experiments, the "same" physical item is tested several times at various stages of the experiment, and in such cases it is necessary in the representation that it appear as several different members of S, each differentiated by the trial number of its test.

3. It is usual that the actual items on the study and test lists vary over participants, but they are selected at random from larger item pools of various types that are assumed to be homogeneous on the relevant factors affecting recognition performance.

4. Indeed, in our view many current models of recognition memory are overly invested in specifications of complex and arbitrary hypothetical processes that are motivated more by the desire to fit data patterns than to understand human memory. While fitting data cannot be faulted in itself, most of the applications of these models to data have made strong and untested statistical assumptions about the data, namely, that the observations for a participant arise from independent random variables, that data can be aggregated over homogeneous participants, that items within a given type are homogeneous, and that a fixed set of model parameters can account for the aggregated data (see Batchelder & Riefer, 2007; Rouder & Lu, 2005; and Smith & Batchelder, in press, for some discussion concerning these statistical assumptions).

5. A *nuisance* parameter or process is a technical term in statistical modeling that refers to aspects of the specification of the model that are not of direct interest but are necessary to complete the description of the probability distributions of the model.

6. See footnote 3. In this case, if participants are not homogeneous, HRs and FARs are still valid estimates of the means of these quantities over participants. However, if they are inserted into a formula for estimating parameters of a recognition memory model, for example, d' and β of the signal detection theory, these nonlinear transforms can produce estimates that depart significantly from the mean of parameter estimates taken over participants. This is especially true if there are correlations between the measures on a participant-by-participant basis.

7. Equation 8 assigns ties in the maximum to the yes response for convenience. Such ties are usually improbable or have zero probabilities in specified models.

8. For models of list memory experiments, the assumption of independence of the responses of a participant over a series of test trials is rarely addressed by modelers. This omission in the memory literature stands in strong contrast to the modeling of absolute judgment (e.g., Staddon, King, & Lockhead, 1980) and choice response time (e.g., Thornton & Gilden, 2005; Wagenmakers, Farrell, & Ratcliff, 2004), for which there is a well-recognized autocorrelation structure across a series of trials.

9. Actually, for $K = 3$ sources not all parameters can be identified. Basically, if the parameter b is set to a particular value, the rest of the parameters can be identified. If one has data in the three-source case, one can achieve identification in several ways, such as by equating the new item detection parameter D_4 to any of the other detection parameters, equating the two guessing parameter vectors, or by investigating the model for selected values of the parameter b.

References

Anderson, J. R. (1990). *The adaptive character of thought*. Hillsdale, NJ: Erlbaum.

Anderson, R. E. (1984). Did I do it or did I only imagine doing it? *Journal of Experimental Psychology: General, 113*, 594–613.

Atkinson, R. C., & Juola, J. F. (1974). Search and decision processes in recognition memory. In D. H. Krantz, R. C. Atkinson, & R. D. Luce (Eds.), *Contemporary developments in mathematical psychology: Vol. 1. Learning, memory, thinking* (pp. 243–293). San Francisco: Freeman.

Banks, W. P. (2000). Recognition and source memory as multivariate decision processes. *Psychological Science, 11*, 267–273.

Batchelder, E., & Batchelder, W. H. (2005). *Multinomial models for social information processing.* Paper presented at Cognitive Psychometrics: Cognitive Models as Measurement Tools, January 2005, University of California, Irvine (prepublication paper available on request).

Batchelder, W. H. (1998). Multinomial processing tree models and psychological assessment. *Psychological Assessment, 10,* 331–344.

Batchelder, W. H. (2002). Discrete state models of information processing. In N. J. Smelser & P. B. Baltes (Eds.), *International encyclopedia of the social and behavioral sciences,* (Vol. 6, pp. 3746–3751). Oxford, UK: Pergamon.

Batchelder, W. H., Hu, X., & Riefer, D. M. (1994). Analysis of a model for source monitoring. In G. H. Fischer & D. Laming (Eds.), *Contributions to mathematical psychology, psychometrics, and methodology* (pp. 51–65). New York: Springer.

Batchelder, W. H., & Riefer, D. M. (1990). Multinomial models of source monitoring. *Psychological Review, 97,* 548–564.

Batchelder, W. H., & Riefer, D. M. (1999). Theoretical and empirical review of multinomial process tree modeling. *Psychonomic Bulletin & Review, 6,* 57–86.

Batchelder, W. H., and Riefer, D. M. (2007). Using multinomial processing tree models to measure cognitive deficits in clinical populations. In R. Neufeld (Ed.). *Advances in clinical cognitive science: Formal modeling of processes and symptoms* (pp. 19–50). Washington, DC: American Psychological Association Books.

Batchelder, W. H., Riefer, D. M., & Hu, X. (1994). Measuring memory factors in source monitoring. *Psychological Review, 101,* 172–176.

Bayen, U. J., Murname, K., & Erdfelder, E. (1996). Source discrimination, item detection, and multinomial models of source monitoring. *Journal of Experimental Psychology: Learning, Memory & Cognition, 22,* 197–215.

Benjamin, A. S. (2003). Predicting and postdicting the effects of word frequency on memory. *Memory & Cognition, 31,* 297–305.

Benjamin, A. S., & Bawa, S. (2004). Distractor plausibility and criterion placement in recognition. *Journal of Memory and Language, 51,* 159–172.

Benjamin, A. S., Bjork, R. A., & Hirshman, E. (1998). Predicting the future and reconstructing the past: A Bayesian characterization of the utility of subjective fluency. *Acta Psychologica, 98,* 267–290.

Benjamin, A. S., Bjork, R. A., & Schwartz, B. L. (1998). The mismeasure of memory: When retrieval fluency is misleading as a metacognitive index. *Journal of Experimental Psychology: General, 127,* 1–14.

Bray, N. W., & Batchelder, W. H. (1972). Effects of instructions and retention interval on memory of presentation mode. *Journal of Verbal Learning and Verbal Behavior, 11,* 367–374.

Brown, S. D., Steyvers, M., & Hemmer, P. (2007). Modeling experimentally induced strategy shifts. *Psychological Science, 18,* 40–45.

Buchner, A., Erdfelder, E., & Vaterrodt-Plunnecke, B. (1995). Unbiased measurement of conscious and unconscious memory processes within the process dissociation framework. *Journal of Experimental Psychology: General, 124,* 137–160.

Cartwright, D., & Harary, F. (1956). Structural balance: A generalization of Heider's theory. *Psychological Review, 63,* 277–293.

Cary, M., & Reder, L. M. (2003). A dual-process account of the list-length and strength-based mirror effects in recognition. *Journal of Memory and Language, 49,* 231–248.

Clark, S. E., & Gronlund, S. D. (1996). Global matching models of recognition memory: How do the models match the data? *Psychonomic Bulletin & Review, 3,* 37–60.

Curran, T., DeBuse, C., & Leynes, P. A. (2007). Conflict and criteria setting in recognition memory. *Journal of Experimental Psychology: Learning, Memory, & Cognition, 33,* 2–17.

Davis, J. A. (1967). Clustering and structural balance in graphs. *Human Relations, 20,* 181–187.

Dennis, S., & Humphreys, M. S. (2001). A context noise model of episodic word recognition. *Psychological review, 108,* 452–478.

DeSoto, C. B. (1960). Learning a social structure. *Journal of Abnormal and Social Psychology, 60,* 417–421.

Diana, R. A., Reder, L. M., Arndt, J., & Park, H. (2006). Models of recognition: A review of arguments in favor of a dual-process account. *Psychonomic Bulletin & Review, 13,* 1–21.

Dunn, J. C. (2004). Remember-know: A matter of confidence. *Psychological Review, 111,* 524–542.

Durso, F. T., & Johnson, M. K. (1980). The effect of orienting tasks on recognition, recall, and modality confusions of pictures and words. *Journal of Verbal Learning and Verbal Behavior, 19,* 416–429.

Egan, J. P. (1958). *Recognition memory and the operating characteristic* (AFCRC-TN-58-51). Bloomington: Indiana University Hearing and Communication Laboratory.

Ehrenberg, K., & Klauer, K. C. (2005). The flexible use of source information: processing components of the inconsistency effect in person memory. *Journal of Experimental Social Psychology, 41,* 369–387.

Estes, W. K. (1964). Probability learning. In A. W. Melton, (Ed.), *Categories of human learning* (pp. 89–128). New York: Academic Press.

Freeman, L. C. (1992). Filling in the blanks: A theory of cognitive categories and the structure of social affiliations. *Social Science Quarterly, 55,* 118–127.

Gardiner, J. M., & Richardson-Klavehn, A. (2000). Remembering and knowing. In E. Tulving & F. I. M. Craik (Eds.), *The Oxford handbook of memory* (pp. 229–244). Oxford, UK: Oxford University Press.

Gigerenzer, G., Todd, P., and the ABC Research Group (1999). *Simple heuristics that make us smart.* New York: Oxford University Press.

Gill, J. (2002). *Bayesian methods: A social and behavioral sciences approach.* New York: Chapman & Hall.

Glanzer, M., & Adams, J. K. (1985). The mirror effect in recognition memory. *Memory & Cognition, 13,* 8–20.

Glanzer, M., & Adams, J. K. (1990). The mirror effect in recognition memory: Data and theory. *Journal of Experimental Psychology: Learning, Memory, and Cognition, 16,* 5–16.

Glanzer, M., Adams, J. K., Iverson, G. J., & Kim, K. (1993). The regularities of recognition memory. *Psychological Review, 100,* 546–567.

Green, D. M., & Swets, J. A. (1966). *Signal detection theory and psychophysics.* New York: Wiley.

Greene, R. L. (1996). Mirror effect in order and associative information: Role of response strategies. *Journal of Experimental Psychology: Learning, Memory, and Cognition, 22,* 687–695.

Hamilton, D. L., & Gifford, R. K. (1976). Illusory correlation in interpersonal perception: A cognitive basis of stereotypic judgments. *Journal of Experimental Social Psychology, 12,* 392–407.

Heathcote, A. (2003). Item recognition memory and the receiver operating characteristic. *Journal of Experimental Psychology: Learning, Memory, and Cognition, 29,* 1210–1230.

Heider, F. (1946). Attitudes and cognitive organization. *Journal of Psychology, 21,* 107–112.

Hilford, A., Glanzer, M., Kim, K., & DeCarlo, L. T. (2002). Regularities of source recognition: ROC analysis. *Journal of Experimental Psychology: General, 131,* 494–510.

Hintzman, D. L., Block, R. A., & Inskeep, N. R. (1972). Memory for mode of input. *Journal of Verbal Learning and Verbal Behavior, 11,* 741–749.

Hintzman, D. L., Curran, T., & Oppy, B. (1992). Effects of similarity and repetition on memory: Registration without learning? *Journal of Experimental Psychology: Learning, Memory, amd Cognition, 18,* 667–680.

Hu, X., & Batchelder, W. H. (1994). The statistical analysis of general processing tree models with the EM algorithm. *Psychometrika, 59,* 21–47.

Hu, X., & Phillips, G. A. (1999). GPT.EXE: A powerful tool for the visualization and analysis of general processing tree models. *Behavior Research Methods, Instruments, and Computers, 31,* 220–234.

Jacoby, L. L. (1991). A process dissociation framework: Separating automatic from intentional uses of memory. *Journal of Memory and Language, 30,* 513–541.

Jacoby, L. L., & Whitehouse, K. (1989). An illusion of memory: False recognition influenced by unconscious perception. *Journal of Experimental Psychology: General, 118,* 126–135.

Johnson, M. K., Hashtroudi, S., & Lindsay, D. S. (1993). Source monitoring. *Psychological Bulletin, 114,* 3–28.

Johnson, M. K., Kounios, J., & Reeder, J. A. (1994). Time-course studies of reality monitoring and recognition. *Journal of Experimental Psychology: Learning, Memory, and Cognition, 20,* 1409–1419.

Johnson, M. K., & Raye, C. L. (1981). Reality monitoring. *Psychological Review. 88,* 67–85.

Kinchla, R. A. (1994). Comments on Batchelder and Riefer's multinomial model of source monitoring. *Psychological Review, 101,* 166–171.

Klauer, K. C. (2006). Hierarchical multinomial processing tree models: A latent-class approach. *Psychometrika, 71,* 1–31.

Klauer, K. C., & Ehrenberg, K. (2005). Categorization and fit detection under cognitive load: Efficient or effortful? *European Journal of Social Psychology, 35,* 493–516.

Klauer, K. C., & Meiser, T. (2000). A source-monitoring analysis of illusory correlations. *Personality and Social Psychological Bulletin, 26,* 1074–1093.

Klauer, K. C., & Wegener, I. (1998). Unraveling social categorization in the "who said what" paradigm. *Journal of Personality and Social Psychology, 75,* 1155–1178.

Klauer K. C., & Wegener, I. (1999). Die Salienz sozialer Kategorien: Ein Modell der sozialen Kategorisierung im "Who said what?"-Paradigma. In W. Hacker & M. Rinck (Eds.), Schwerpunktthema "Zukunft gestalten" (pp. 366–72). Lengerich, Germany: Pabst.

Klauer, K. C., Wegener, I., & Ehrenberg, K. (2002). Perceiving minority members as individuals: The effects of relative group size in social categorization, *European Journal of Social Psychology, 32,* 223–245.

Koriat, A., Bjork, R. A., Sheffer, L., & Bar, S. (2004). Predicting one's own forgetting: The role of experience-based and theory-based processes. *Journal of Experimental Psychology: General, 133,* 643–656.

Koriat, A., Sheffer, L., & Ma'ayan, H. (2002). Comparing objective and subjective learning curves: Judgments of learning exhibit increased underconfidence with practice. *Journal of Experimental Psychology: General, 131,* 147–162.

Kumbasar, E, Romney, A. K., & Batchelder, W. H. (1994). Systematic biases in social perception. *American Journal of Sociology, 100,* 477–505.

Lee, M. D., & Webb, M. R. (2005). Modeling individual differences in cognition. *Psychonomic Bulletin & Review, 12,* 605–621.

Lewandowsky, S. (1986). Priming in recognition memory for categorized lists. *Journal of Experimental Psychology: Learning, Memory, and Cognition, 12*, 562–574.

Macmillan, N. A., & Creelman, C. D. (2005). *Detection theory: A user's guide* (2nd ed.). Mahwah, NJ: Erlbaum.

Mandler, G. (1980). Recognizing: the judgment of previous occurrence. *Psychological Review, 87*, 368–374.

McClelland, J. L., & Chappell, M. (1998). Familiarity breeds differentiation: A subjective-likelihood approach to the effects of experience in recognition memory. *Psychological Review, 105*, 724–760.

Meiser, T., & Bröder, A. (2002). Memory for multidimensional source information. *Journal of Experimental Psychology: Learning, Memory, and Cognition, 28*, 116–137.

Meiser, T., & Hewstone, M. (2001). Crossed categorization effects on the formation of illusory correlations. *European Journal of Social Psychology, 31*, 443–466.

Meiser, T., Sattler, C., & von Hecker, U. (2007).Metacognitive inferences in source monitoring: The role of perceived differences in item recognition. *Quarterly Journal of Experimental Psychology, 60*, 10115–1040.

Morrell, H. E. R., Gaitan, S., & Wixted, J. T. (2002). On the nature of the decision axis in signal-detection based models of recognition memory. *Journal of Experimental Psychology: Learning, Memory, and Cognition, 28*, 1095–1110.

Nelson, D. L., Reed, U. S., & Walling, J. R. (1976). Picture superiority effect. *Journal of Experimental Psychology: Human Learning and Memory, 2*, 523–528.

Newcomb, T. M. (1961). *The acquaintance process.* New York: Holt, Rinehart, and Winston.

Nosofsky, R. M. (1990). Relations between exemplar-similarity and likelihood models of classification. *Journal of Mathematical Psychology, 34*, 393–418.

Picek, J. S., Sherman, S. J., & Shiffrin, R. M. (1975). Cognitive organization and storage of social structures. *Journal of Personality and Social Psychology, 31*, 758–768.

Reder, L. M., Nhouyvanisvong, A., Schunn, C. D., Ayers, M., Angstadt, P., & Hiraki, K. (2000). A mechanistic account of the mirror effect for word frequency: A computational model of remember-know judgments in a continuous recognition paradigm. *Journal of Experimental Psychology: Learning, Memory, and Cognition, 26*, 294–320.

Riefer, D. M., Chien, Y., & Reimer, J. F. (2007). Positive and negative generation effects in source monitoring. *Quarterly Journal of Experimental Psychology, 60*, 1389–1405.

Riefer, D. M., Hu, X., & Batchelder, W. H. (1994). Response strategies in source monitoring. *Journal of Experimental Psychology: Learning, Memory, and Cognition, 20*, 680–693.

Rouder, J. N., & Lu, J. (2005). An introduction to Bayesian hierarchical models with an application in the theory of signal detection. *Psychonomic Bulletin & Review, 12*, 573–604.

Shepard, R. N., & Teghtsoonian, M. (1961). Retention of information under conditions approaching a steady state. (1961). *Journal of Experimental Psychology, 62*, 302–309.

Shiffrin, R. M., & Steyvers, M. (1997). A model for recognition memory: REM-retrieving effectively from memory. *Psychonomic Bulletin & Review, 8*, 408–438.

Sikström, S. (2001). The variance theory of the mirror effect in recognition memory. *Psychonomic Bulletin & Review, 8*, 408–438.

Slamecka, N. J., & Graf, P. (1978). The generation effect: Delineation of a phenomenon. *Journal of Experimental Psychology: Human Learning and Memory, 4*, 592–604.

Slotnick, S. D., Dodson, C. S., Klein, S. A., & Shimamura, A. P. (2000). An analysis of signal detection and threshold models of source memory. *Journal of Experimental Psychology: Learning, Memory, and Cognition, 26*, 1499–1517.

Smith, J. B., and Batchelder, W. H. (2005). *Hierarchical multinomial processing tree models.* Paper presented at the annual meeting of the Society for Mathematical Psychology, August 2005, Memphis, TN.

Smith, J. B., & Batchelder, W. H. (in press). *Assessing individual differences in categorical data.* Unpublished manuscript available on request.

Staddon, J. E. R., King, M., & Lockhead, G. R. (1980). On sequential effects in absolute judgment experiments. *Journal of Experimental Psychology: Human Perception and Performance, 6,* 290–301.

Stahl, C. (2006). Multinomiale verarbeitungs-baummodelle in der socialpsychologie (Multinomial processing tree models in social psychology). *Zeitschrift für Sozialpsychologie, 37,* 161–171.

Strack, F., & Forster, J. (1998). Self-reflection and recognition: The role of metacognitive knowledge in the attribution of recollective experience. *Review of Personality and Social Psychology, 2,* 111–123.

Stretch, V., & Wixted, J. T. (1998). On the difference between strength-based and frequency-based mirror effects in recognition memory. *Journal of Experimental Psychology: Learning, Memory, and Cognition, 24,* 1379–1396.

Taylor, S. E., Fiske, S. T., Etcoff, N. J., & Ruderman, A. J. (1978). Categorical and contextual bases of person memory and stereotyping. *Journal of Personality and Social Psychology, 36,* 778–793.

Thornton, T. L., & Gilden, D. L. (2005). Provenance of correlations in psychological data. *Psychonomic Bulletin & Review, 12,* 409–441.

Tulving, E. (1985). Memory and consciousness. *Canadian Psychologist, 26,* 1–22.

Tversky, A., & Kahneman, D. (1974). Judgment under uncertainty: Heuristics and biases. *Science, 185,* 1124–1131.

Van Zandt, T., & Maldonado-Molina, M. M. (2004). Response reversals in recognition memory. *Journal of Experimental Psychology: Learning, Memory, and Cognition, 30,* 1147–1166.

Voss, J. F., Vesonder, G. T., Post, T. A., & Ney, L. G. (1987). Was the item recalled and if so, by whom? *Journal of Memory and Language, 26,* 466–479.

Wagenmakers, E.-J., Farrell, S., & Ratcliff, R. (2004). Estimation and interpretation of 1/f noise in human cognition. *Psychonomic Bulletin & Review, 11,* 579–615.

Yonelinas, A. P. (2002). The nature of recollection and familiarity: A review of 30 years of research. *Journal of Memory and Language, 46,* 441–517.

Implicit Memory Tests:
Techniques for Reducing Conscious Intrusion

Colin M. MacLeod

Introduction

The universally acknowledged point of origin for empirical research on memory is the classic treatise of Ebbinghaus (1885/1964). Being first, he had to develop materials to be learned and remembered — the now-famous nonsense syllables. But, he also had to develop a way to probe his own memory, and this contribution is less often highlighted. The paradigm that he created was the method of relearning. He measured how many trials it required on a first occasion for him to learn a set of materials to a fixed criterion and then noted the reduction in number of trials to relearn that set of materials on a second occasion after some retention interval. That reduction was evidence of residual information in memory, or savings, for the originally learned material.

The relearning/savings paradigm was the only tool that Ebbinghaus (1885/1964) used to study his memory. Intriguingly, his paradigm did not rely on conscious recollection at all: Savings can and does occur even when the subject has no recollection of the targeted item from the originally learned material. Ebbinghaus was quite cognizant of this feature of his memory measure, saying at the outset that, "Most of the experiences remain concealed from consciousness and yet produce an effect which is significant and which authenticates their previous existence" (p. 2). He had created a test of memory that does not rely on conscious remembering almost a century before the use of such tests would return to center stage in the study of memory.

In the intervening 100 years, the emphasis of virtually all research on memory was on tests that do require awareness that remembering is occurring (see Bower, 2000). Dominant among these have been recall and recognition: In each case, the task is to consciously bridge the present to some past learning episode. It was not until the 1980s (see Graf & Schacter, 1985) that this distinction between tests that do require conscious remembering (*explicit tests*) and those that do not (*implicit tests*) was expressly made, and the comparison of the two types of test became the subject of intensive investigation. We now know a vast amount about a wide variety of implicit tests of memory (for reviews, see Bowers & Marsolek, 2003; Roediger & Geraci, 2005; Roediger & McDermott, 1993), and our understanding of memory has benefited greatly from examining memory implicitly. It is certainly the case that our day-to-day functioning relies much more heavily on unconscious than on conscious uses of memory. Of course, it is the conscious probing of memory of which we are aware, which probably leads us to overestimate the proportion of memory use that is conscious — a metamemory error in its own right.

The Problem of Conscious Intrusion in Implicit Memory Tests

Framed in the way just described, the explicit/implicit contrast may sound quite straightforward: You simply need to inform (an explicit test) or not inform (an implicit test) subjects that their memory is being tested. In fact, though, separating these two uses of memory is considerably more complicated than might first appear. There is one overriding reason why this is the case: the problem of *conscious intrusion*. A thumbnail sketch of the problem goes like this. You choose some nominally implicit test, such as one of the first to be used as these tests began to be studied in the 1980s: word fragment completion (Tulving, Schacter, & Stark, 1982; cf. Warrington & Weiskrantz, 1970). Here, having earlier studied a list of words, the subject is given a series of partially obliterated words, such as d-n-sa--, and is asked to complete each of them with a word. The probability of successful completion (dinosaur) is greater for studied words than for unstudied words, despite no instruction to make reference to the studied words. This advantage for studied words is called *priming* and is seen as evidence of the expression of implicit memory processes.

But what assurance do we have that implicit memory processes are (solely) responsible for the observed priming? Faced with such a difficult problem-solving task, the astute subject may well reason that the recently studied list could provide assistance in completing the fragments. Efforts to consciously retrieve studied words might ensue, perhaps not immediately and perhaps not for all test fragments, but any such conscious retrieval would constitute an instance of conscious intrusion. In the absence of any index of when such retrieval had occurred, we would be at a loss to know whether an observed advantage for studied over unstudied words was truly priming of an implicit nature. This is particularly problematic when a manipulation that improves performance on an explicit memory test also improves performance on an implicit test in that, if conscious retrieval were occurring during the nominally implicit test, this correlated improvement is precisely what would be expected. But it is actually a problem any time that conscious retrieval could be occurring.

The goal of this chapter is to examine ways to deal with the problem of conscious intrusion on implicit memory tests. To measure what we want to measure — what we think we are measuring — it is crucial to minimize the probability of conscious intrusion on implicit tests. By now, a quite wide variety of strategies for optimizing the "implicitness" of implicit tests has been offered. In this chapter, these strategies are described and their relative utility and success are evaluated. Table 1 presents the set of research strategies to be considered here.

Before discussing the measurement issues, it would be remiss not to consider the theoretical and applied issues. Implicit memory, whether viewed as a unique memory system or as an isolable processing mode in a unified memory, is an important theoretical idea, one that has dramatically changed our conception of memory. It is now quite uncontroversial to say that we use memory without consciousness much or even most of the time, yet this certainly was not the case even 25 years ago. Indeed,

TABLE 1 Strategies for Minimizing Conscious Intrusion in Implicit Memory Tests

1.	Test amnesic individuals.
2.	Obtain a (double) dissociation.
3.	Equate retrieval cues and vary only task instructions (retrieval intentionality).
4.	Disguise the test via diversionary instructions or items.
5.	Ensure absence of awareness during testing.
6.	Minimize the value of conscious recollection.
7.	Measure processes, not tasks (process dissociation procedure).
8.	Use speeded tests that do not require problem solving.
9.	Employ relearning and savings techniques.

the concept has had an impact on all areas of psychology, notably clinical and social psychology. It has been a leading topic in bringing consciousness front and center in the discipline, and it has deep implications for the understanding and even the possible rehabilitation of memory disorders (see, e.g., Glisky & Schacter, 1987, 1988; Glisky, Schacter, & Tulving, 1986). Given the sweeping influence of implicit memory, we want to be able to measure it well, and it is to that goal that the rest of this chapter is dedicated.

Test Amnesic Individuals

From the beginning of research on implicit memory, evidence deriving from the study of individuals with organic amnesias has played a crucial role. Indeed, looking far back, Claparède (1907; see Nicolas, 1996, for a translation) even demonstrated the presence of unconscious memory in a Korsakoff patient using Ebbinghaus's relearning/savings technique and noted that this preserved unconscious memory was apparent despite the patient's almost total failure in conscious memory, whether by recall or by recognition. This nicely presaged the work of the most recent quarter century.

Taking the earlier work of Warrington and Weiskrantz (1970, 1974) as the point of departure, Graf, Squire, and Mandler (1984; see also Graf, Shimamura, & Squire, 1985) demonstrated that amnesic individuals showed quite normal priming on a visual implicit word completion test (e.g., "Say the first word that comes to mind that begins with def") while showing a dramatic deficit on an explicit recall or recognition test. Schacter, Church, and Treadwell (1994) showed similar preservation on an auditory test of implicit memory in the face of explicit memory loss. Jacoby and Witherspoon (1982) reported an analogous finding: Amnesic subjects exhibited the same bias toward the studied meaning of a homonym (e.g., reed vs. read) as did normal subjects on their implicit homonym spelling test, despite the amnesic subjects showing very poor explicit recognition of the words as having been studied. Corresponding results were reported for the preservation of skill memory (Musen, Shimamura, & Squire, 1990; Musen & Squire, 1991).

If the explicit memory of an amnesic subject is effectively inaccessible, then it seems axiomatic that the performance of that subject on an implicit test cannot be contaminated by conscious recollection. This logic has led to the frequent reports of intact (or even just reliable) implicit memory in amnesic individuals being treated as the definitive corroboration that there can be "pure" implicit priming, and that the loss of explicit memory in amnesic individuals is independent of their preserved implicit memory, such that the two expressions of memory must rely on different neural circuitry. But, sometimes implicit memory does suffer in amnesic subjects (e.g., Jernigan & Ostergaard, 1993). As well, there is ongoing debate in the literature regarding whether amnesic individuals learn new associations as well as normal individuals do. Some reports — beginning with the groundbreaking study of Graf and Schacter (1985) — suggested that they do (e.g., Gabrieli, Keane, Zarella, & Poldrack, 1997; see also Goshen-Gottstein, Moscovitch, & Melo, 2000). Others questioned the generality of this claim (Paller & Mayes, 1994; Rajaram & Coslett, 2000), arguing that learning of new associations is impaired in amnesic individuals. The resolution may have come from Gooding, Mayes, and van Eijk (2000), whose meta-analysis indicated that amnesic individuals show intact implicit memory for new associations involving familiar but not novel materials, and that the structures damaged in amnesia may be essential for handling novelty.

The evidence derived from the study of amnesic individuals is quite compellingly in favor of distinct implicit and explicit memory processes (or perhaps systems, but that debate is beyond the scope of this chapter; see Moscovitch, Vriezen, & Goshen-Gottstein, 1993, for a review). It is persuasive evidence, but it is nonetheless limited. Not every task has been or could be investigated in the context of amnesia, and the amnesias that individuals suffer certainly are not all the same. Also, it is not always the case that implicit memory is entirely preserved when explicit memory is decimated, making the contrast more complicated. Thus, as compelling as the amnesia evidence is, we cannot rely on it as providing complete assurance that all nominally implicit tasks are completely implicit. Indeed, even if a given test were to appear fully implicit in one study, a small change in procedure or materials or the like could overturn this in another study.

Finally, of course, there is the predicament that we cannot await an amnesia-based certification of every conclusion that we wish to draw about implicit memory based on research with nonamnesic individuals. Cases of amnesia are too rare for that. Moreover, the extent of damage to cognitive processes outside memory is often not known, making the comparability of amnesic individuals to nonamnesic individuals more complicated.

Obtain a (Double) Dissociation

In behavioral studies as in neuropsychological studies, a powerful argument for distinct processes is the identification of a task dissociation, the more so if it forms half of a double dissociation (see Dunn & Kirsner, 2003; Shallice, 1988). If a manipulation affects performance on one task (T1) but not on another task (T2), that is a single dissociation; the pattern just described of intact implicit but sharply diminished explicit memory in amnesia represents a single dissociation. If a second manipulation has the opposite effect (i.e., it affects performance on T2 but not on T1), that is a second single dissociation, and the co-occurrence of these two opposite single dissociations constitutes a double dissociation. Under such circumstances, it is generally seen as extremely difficult to argue that performance on one task mediates performance on the other, given their opposite directions of effect.

A good illustration of a double dissociation in behavioral data involving implicit and explicit memory was provided by Jacoby (1983b). Subjects read isolated words or generated them from antonym cues during study. On an explicit recognition test, the generated words were remembered much better than the read words (the familiar generation effect; Slamecka & Graf, 1978). But, on an implicit perceptual identification test, in which masked words had to be identified, the words read at study were better identified than those generated at study. Although this pattern is not entirely general (see Masson & MacLeod, 1992), it is a particularly striking example because it is not just that each task is affected by one level of encoding while the other is not, but that the effects on the two tasks are actually opposite to each other. Dunn and Kirsner (1988), Shallice (1988), and others have distinguished this "crossed" double dissociation from the basic "uncrossed" double dissociation described in the preceding paragraph. There are many examples of double dissociations in the cognitive literature (e.g., Gabrieli et al., 1995). How could priming on the implicit task be the covert result of contamination by conscious recollection when conscious recollection would have produced the opposite pattern?

Dunn and Kirsner (1988, 2003) argued that, despite their widespread use and plausibility, the logic behind dissociations is not unassailable. Single dissociations can reflect a single process with a level of function that is not apparent in a given task. They extended this analysis to both types of double dissociation as well, concluding that, "In summary, functional dissociation, whether single or double, is not logically inconsistent with the single-process model. By varying the transformation relating process function to task performance while retaining a monotonic mapping, it is possible to derive single-process accounts that are consistent with all kinds of dissociation" (1988, p. 96). Add to this the problem that implicit memory tests are often considerably less reliable indices than are explicit memory tests (Buchner & Brandt, 2003; Buchner & Wippich, 2000), and the problem becomes a complex one, especially given that it is most often the explicit test that shows an effect and the implicit test that does not.

Van Orden, Pennington, and Stone (2001) took a different tack — questioning the logic of underlying modularity that they saw as fundamental to the logic of dissociation — in reaching a similarly skeptical conclusion about dissociations. This is related to Reingold's (2003) argument that the tasks that give rise to a (double) dissociation may not be as comparable as the often strongly made contrast assumes: Frequently in memory experiments, the cues available on the implicit and explicit tasks differ considerably (see the discussion concerning the retrieval intentionality criterion), the response measurement is dissimilar, and the role of response bias is not or cannot be equated. Reingold also pointed out the too-often-overlooked problem that a different class of processes (e.g., retrieval vs. decision) may be affected in two tasks that appear to dissociate. To the extent that tasks are difficult to compare directly, the interpretation of a dissociation becomes less straightforward.

A recent issue of *Cortex* featured a target paper by Dunn and Kirsner (2003) and a series of reactions by other researchers. In broad summary, the contributors agreed that dissociations are not definitive but also for the most part agreed with Baddeley (2003), who saw dissociations as useful statistical tools in that they can place quite strong constraints on our process theories. Dissociations force us to think about the underlying processes and, in the case of dissociations between implicit and explicit memory tests, do sometimes provide comfort that conscious intrusion is not a salient factor in implicit test performance because such intrusion would have worked against the observed effect.

Equate Retrieval Cues and Intentionality

The fact that the retrieval cues on the implicit and explicit memory tests are so often very different is itself a quite fundamental problem. Contrast explicit recognition, for which the entire studied word is (re)presented, to implicit fragment completion, for which only some of the letters of the studied word are shown, as was the case in Tulving et al. (1982). Or, compare explicit recognition, for which the test items are fully exposed, to perceptual identification, for which the mask sharply limits perceptual analysis, as was the case in Jacoby (1983b). Not only are there stimulus differences, but also those stimulus differences bring into play different processes — decision making in the case of recognition and visual problem solving in the case of fragment completion and perceptual identification, as illustrations. Such comparisons are not straightforward and direct.

It was with this problem in mind that Schacter, Bowers, and Booker (1989) put forward the retrieval intentionality criterion, invoking this logic: "If the external cues are held constant on two tasks and only the retrieval instructions are varied, then differential effects of an experimental manipulation on performance of the two tasks can be attributed to differences in the intentional versus unintentional retrieval processes that are used in task performance" (p. 53).

Graf and Mandler (1984) reported just such a comparison. They gave subjects three-letter word stems as retrieval cues under two sets of instructions: implicit (stem completion: produce the first word that comes to mind) and explicit (stem-cued recall: produce a studied word). Their results revealed a dissociation: Semantic processing at study resulted in a substantial advantage over nonsemantic processing on the explicit test (a levels-of-processing effect; cf. Craik & Lockhart, 1972) but had no effect on the implicit test. Given the identical stem cues on the two tests and only a difference in instruction, this study fits the retrieval intentionality criterion. Numerous other examples exist (e.g., Richardson-Klavehn & Gardiner, 1996; Roediger, Weldon, Stadler, & Riegler, 1992).

If possible, having identical stimuli presented on the explicit and implicit tests certainly is preferable because this eliminates one task difference. Results can also be impressive, as in Java's (1994) finding of a double dissociation when only instructions differed between otherwise identical implicit and explicit tests. But using identical stimuli is not a perfect solution, either. As Reingold (2003) argued, although the problems of cue difference and response measure difference are solved by the retrieval intentionality criterion, the problem of bias differences in the two types of test remains. So, there must be a higher goal — to equate the tests on as many elements as possible. Butler and Berry (2001, p. 194) pointed out that equating the stimuli alone "does not solve the more intractable issue of phenomenological awareness," citing the findings of Richardson-Klavehn, Clarke, and Gardiner (1999), who showed that performance on a nominally implicit test was driven exclusively by an unintentional retrieval strategy (see also Seamon, McKenna, & Binder, 1998).

Finally, of course, the proximal stimulus on which the subject operates may not coincide with the distal stimulus actually presented and may well differ between the explicit and implicit tasks. It must also be noted that requiring strict adherence to the retrieval intentionality criterion would rule out many conceivable and potentially informative variations in test format, in particular for implicit tests. Critically, it remains possible that subjects could still opt to engage in conscious recollection on the nominally implicit test, the implicit instructional set notwithstanding.

Disguise the Test via Diversionary Instructions or Items

Closely related to the preceding strategy is another one, one that was prevalent early in the effort to compare implicit and explicit memory tests and to identify the processes underlying them. Researchers attempted to disguise the fact that their implicit tasks were actually memory tests (see Schacter, 1987, p. 510). One approach was to use incidental study, the goal being to conceal the study–test relation, thereby preventing subjects from realizing, first, that there had in fact been a study phase and, second, that the test was actually a test. Thus, for example, Jacoby (1983a) represented his study phase for a list of words as a measure of reading speed, what he called a "cover task." However, Greene (1986; see also Bowers & Schacter, 1990) demonstrated that incidental versus intentional learning instructions really did not matter with respect to priming on an implicit test.

A more frequently used approach has been not to try to conceal the study–test relation but rather to disguise that the implicit test is actually a memory test. Sometimes, this has been done using diversionary instructions. Thus, Bowers and Schacter (1990) recruited subjects for a "study of picture and word perception." MacLeod (1989a) informed subjects that an implicit word fragment completion test was part of the research of a colleague, and that it was not the promised memory test. Others represented the implicit test as a "filler task" before the memory test. To avoid concerted efforts at retrieval, it was also quite common to emphasize quick responding, and to highlight that what was sought as a response was "the first word that came to mind" (see Schacter & Graf, 1986). Careful consideration of the task instructions is always important in cognitive psychology; nowhere is this more true than in the case of implicit tests of memory.

More often, the test has been disguised by the inclusion of diversionary distracters. Schacter and Graf (1986) constructed a set of filler items for their implicit test "to disguise the fact that the completion test included previously studied pairs" (p. 434). In a concerted attack on this approach, Challis and Roediger (1993; see also Jacoby, 1983a) systematically varied from 0% to 100% the ratio of studied to unstudied items on a word fragment completion test. One would expect the implicit nature of the test to be better hidden when there were fewer studied items on the test (or less study–test overlap; see Fujita, 1994), but variation in the studied-to-unstudied ratio had no effect on priming. Although this outcome can be seen as good news for the assumption that the test was implicit, it also suggests that such diversionary tactics may not be effective.

A related approach that might occur to an investigator would be to bury the studied material in some kind of larger context, for example, to put the critical words in sentences or passages. This would reduce the isolation of the items and make conscious retrieval less tempting and presumably less successful. Relatively early studies showed, however, that this tactic resulted in substantially reduced priming (e.g., MacLeod, 1989b; Oliphant, 1983). Of course, this could be in part because such contextual embedding foiled subsequent efforts to consciously retrieve the studied items. More likely, though, it is because the integration of the critical items into context makes them less distinctive and accessible for subsequent, usually perceptual, implicit tests (for more on distinctiveness, see Hunt & Worthen, 2006).

Ensure Absence of Awareness During Testing

It would seem logical that if a subject were unaware that his or her memory was being tested, then conscious intrusion should be unlikely: Why use memory strategically if you do not even know that it is being interrogated? This logic has been used with some success in conjunction with perceptual implicit tests. Thus, priming on such tests has been obtained even when subjects report no awareness that the implicit test is in fact a test (i.e., that it is related to the preceding study phase). Following study and test, Bowers and Schacter (1990) had subjects respond to a series of questions that first generally and then more pointedly probed whether they had made the connection between study and test. They then separated their subjects into those who were test aware versus those who were not. Both subsets showed reliable priming, but consistent with their confession that they were aware of the test, test-aware subjects showed more priming on semantically encoded relative to structurally encoded items, whereas this was not the case for test-unaware subjects. Using awareness questions and the remember/know procedure, Java (1994) showed that even when subjects became aware that some test items were studied, they still showed a dissociative pattern on the implicit and explicit tests for the items that they were not aware of having studied. She essentially evaluated awareness on an individual item basis, which is unusual: Typical awareness indices follow the entire test so as not to disrupt it.

Indices of awareness often do show, however, that subjects had at least some awareness of studied items reappearing on the test by the end of the test (see, e.g., Richardson-Klavehn, Lee, Joubran, & Bjork, 1994). The difficulty is in knowing when they became aware and how much this awareness influenced their performance. Were only a couple of items affected, or were most affected? Did this start early in the test or only later? The problem is that a stringent criterion that required elimination of all data for which there was any hint of postexperiment awareness would eliminate much of the literature. Furthermore, this only results in the elimination of data for which subjects remember and report being aware: It must be kept in mind that on such posttest awareness evaluations there is always the possibility of subjects forgetting the degree of their earlier awareness, or of subjects reporting no awareness when in fact they were aware. Awareness measures certainly do tell us, though, that subjects can be quite exquisitely tuned to the study–test relation despite our best efforts to prevent (and to measure) such tuning.

Minimize the Value of Conscious Recollection

Data elimination because of reported awareness is a problem with respect to many studies using perceptual implicit tests, but it is especially problematic in the case of conceptual implicit tests. Thus, using a general knowledge test, Thapar and Greene (1994) found that all of their subjects were aware of the study–test connection, and that they were aware very soon after beginning the test. When Mulligan and Hartman (1996) required subjects to produce category members, more than 90% of their subjects indicated awareness of the study–test relation. This represents a very serious concern in the case of implicit conceptual tests, particularly given the frequently coinciding influences of conceptual processing on conceptual explicit and implicit tests. Are the effects the same because these two types of tests, when functioning as intended, respond similarly or because the implicit tests are being (heavily) contaminated?

The logic of conceptual implicit tests typically requires that a meaningful probe be used to elicit the studied target, whether the probe be for general knowledge (e.g., having studied "Jacques Plante" and subsequently being asked "Which NHL goalie won the most Vezina trophies?") or category exemplar generation (having studied "hockey" and subsequently being given the probe "Name sports"). The problem is that such probes require a quite demanding retrieval involving extended search thereby inviting conscious recollection, perhaps particularly when the answer does not spring immediately to mind. And, of course, retrieval probability is good when information has been encoded semantically, increasing the likelihood of success.

What is required is a task that makes conscious retrieval of little value. Hourihan and MacLeod (2007) have proposed and tested an alternative form of conceptual implicit test. The task is a modified version of implicit word association (e.g., Vaidya et al., 1997) in which ordinarily the subject must produce the first associate that comes to mind to a probe word (e.g., the subject might produce the studied word "saddle" with heightened probability in response to the probe word "horse"). The problem is, once again, the need to produce a studied word in response to a new probe: Subjects could try to consciously retrieve the studied item. Hourihan and MacLeod simply switched from probing with a new word to elicit the studied target to probing with the studied target to elicit a new word — any new word. This rendered conscious recollection useless.

Because subjects would produce a response on every trial, Hourihan and MacLeod (2007) switched from an accuracy measure to a latency measure, measuring time to produce the associate on the reasonable assumption that associates should be produced faster to primed items than to unprimed items, especially when encoding had been conceptual. To determine the contribution of repetition priming for the probe, given that it was studied, they included a separate block of trials in which subjects

were timed while they simply read the probes aloud. Even when repetition priming was subtracted out of associative priming, there was still substantial conceptual
priming remaining, and that conceptual priming benefited from prior conceptual
processing but not from prior nonconceptual processing. It seems very unlikely that
such priming could result from conscious recollection.

Probably the Hourihan and MacLeod (2007) technique is not "pure," either, and
subsequent research will reveal its difficulties. But, the main message is that we need
to develop paradigms that help to reduce the utility of and contribution of conscious
recollection, on the "ounce of prevention is worth a pound of cure" platform. Making the studied information the probe instead of the target is just one of the possible
ways to do so.

Measure Processes, Not Tasks (Process Dissociation Procedure)

Calling a test implicit or explicit suggests that the test is *only* implicit or *only* explicit
— that it involves only unconscious or only conscious processes. Indeed, this sometimes seems to be the assumption underlying contrasts in the literature between
these two categories of tests. Yet, the very recognition that a nominally implicit test
might be contaminated by conscious recollection makes clear that such task purity
is highly questionable. Jacoby (1991, 1997) brought this assumption of purity under
close scrutiny with the introduction of his process dissociation procedure (PDP). He
argued that all processing involves both automatic and intentional influences, and
crucially, that there is no existing way to completely isolate these two processing elements in individual tasks. His emphasis on processes, not tasks, is absolutely correct.
As a solution, he offered a novel and intriguing approach to separating processes.

In Jacoby's initial — and prototypical — PDP experiment (Jacoby, 1991, Experiment 3), subjects studied two lists. In List A, the words were studied in one of two
ways: as anagrams to be solved or as printed words to be read aloud, with all items
presented visually. In List B, all words were presented auditorily. There were two
groups tested under different instructions. In the *inclusion* group, subjects were to
respond "old" to any previously studied item from either list. In the *exclusion* group,
subjects were to respond "old" only to words heard in List B, excluding the anagram
and read words from List A. Conscious processing could then be estimated by subtracting performance in the exclusion condition from that in the inclusion condi-
tion: $C = E - I$. Automatic processing could be estimated by the equation $A = E/(1 - C)$. (In a dual-process model of recognition [Yonelinas, 2002], conscious processing
is equated with recollection, and automatic processing is equated with familiarity.)
Jacoby carefully noted that two key assumptions underlie this approach: The automatic and conscious processes are independent, and the two processes do not change
as a function of instruction.

Using the PDP procedure, Jacoby (1991) demonstrated that dividing attention at
test produced a decrement in performance that was largely restricted to conscious
processing with little influence on automatic processing. This opened the floodgates
for studies using this new approach to separate processes within task, rather than
between tasks. Thus, for example, Jacoby, Toth, and Yonelinas (1993) used PDP to

show that automatic influences on an explicit stem-cued recall test were very sensitive to perceptual manipulations that had little effect on the conscious influences but not to attentional manipulations that strongly affected the conscious influences. There are by now at least 200 published articles using the PDP method, representing domains of study as diverse as decision making (Ferreira, Garcia-Marques, Sherman, & Sherman, 2006) and depression (Jermann, Van der Linden, Adam, Ceschi, & Perroud, 2005).

From the perspective of minimizing conscious recollection in implicit memory tests, the PDP method seems ideal: Separating conscious from unconscious processes is its raison d'être. And, indeed it has been put to widespread and revealing use in the service of this goal. But, it is not the last word, and critics have expressed concerns with its major assumptions. Thus, among others, Graf and Komatsu (1994) and Curran and Hintzman (1997) questioned whether automatic and conscious processes are ever truly independent (see Jacoby, Yonelinas, & Jennings, 1997, for a defense of the independence assumption, and Hirshman, 1998, for more on the logic of testing this assumption). Dodson and Johnson (1996) argued that the influence of familiarity is not fully automatic, and that recollection is not all or none, which they saw as conflicting with core assumptions of the PDP approach. So, the method is not iron clad, but it has been and continues to be very valuable in focusing research on the fundamental processes rather than the tasks. Moreover, the introduction of exclusion instructions as a technique has by itself been important (see, e.g., Merikle, Joordens, & Stolz, 1995).

Use Speeded Tests That Do Not Require Problem Solving

What would lead a subject to invoke conscious recollection during an implicit test? Certainly, awareness of the study–test relation could promote this strategy, but even such awareness might not precipitate recollection if the implicit test is easy enough. As it happens, though, many implicit tests are not at all easy, requiring solution of difficult fragments (e.g., Tulving et al., 1982), or identification under distinctly suboptimal perceptual conditions (e.g., Jacoby, 1983a). Faced with such demanding tasks, for which success is quite limited, subjects may resort to trying to remember the studied material, thereby converting the nominally implicit test into an explicit test. This situation suggests that one way to limit conscious recollection would be to make the subject's task on the implicit test as easy as possible. Why would one use conscious recollection when it is actually easier not to do so?

Possibly the word-based task that requires the least problem solving is speeded reading (also known as *naming* or *pronunciation*; see Scarborough, Cortese, & Scarborough, 1977), which makes it an interesting candidate as a possible implicit test. All the subject need do is say a common single word aloud into a microphone, so it is difficult to imagine that conscious recollection would seem like a worthwhile strategy. MacLeod (1996) showed that subjects were faster to read aloud words that they had studied than words that they had not studied, and this pattern has since been observed in several other studies (MacDonald & MacLeod, 1998; MacLeod & Daniels, 2000; MacLeod & Masson, 2000). In particular, MacLeod and Masson (2000) conducted a series of experiments exploring priming in speeded reading and observed patterns similar to another well benchmarked implicit test: masked word identification (see Masson & MacLeod, 1992). Speeded reading also showed the familiar modality effect in implicit memory, with more priming for words studied visually than auditorily, given the visual presentation of the test items. Moreover, there were no alterations in the data pattern when an effort was made to encourage conscious recollection by alternating speeded reading trials and recognition trials, despite improved explicit memory on the recognition test relative to when the entire recognition test followed the entire speeded reading test. The overall conclusion was that speeded reading is a good measure of repetition priming, likely not very contaminated by conscious recollection.

In a series of studies, Horton and his colleagues (Horton, Wilson, & Evans, 2001; Horton, Wilson, Vonk, Kirby, & Nielsen, 2005; Vonk & Horton, 2006; Wilson & Horton, 2002) have made a more concerted effort to examine response time as a measure of automatic retrieval. They began (Horton et al., 2001) by comparing a speeded implicit task with two other "bracketing" conditions; all tests used word stems as cues. In the speeded implicit test, conscious recollection was discouraged both by having a long initial set of stems that were all unstudied and by instructions to respond as quickly as possible with the first word that came to mind. One of the other conditions was otherwise identical to the implicit test but was explicit, requiring conscious retrieval of studied items. The final condition provided a baseline in that it did not permit conscious retrieval because all test cues were new. Their core idea was that if the implicit test involved conscious retrieval, then latencies on the implicit test should be longer than those on the "all-new" test for which conscious retrieval was not possible, and more like the latencies on the explicit test, for which conscious retrieval was required. In fact, response time data indicated no slowing relative to baseline for the implicit test, evidence that conscious retrieval was not occurring.

From there, Wilson and Horton (2002), Horton et al. (2005), and Vonk and Horton (2006) went on to contrast their speeded method to the PDP (Jacoby, 1991) and argued from their experiments that the PDP underestimated automatic retrieval, whereas the speeded measure provided an accurate estimate. Indeed, Vonk and Horton summarized by saying that the speeded measure represents "a purely automatic retrieval strategy" (p. 505). Although claims for the purity of any measure are suspect, and the speeded measure may not suit every situation, the consistent evidence across the studies by Horton and colleagues does point to this approach as valuable. If it is possible to measure speeded responding in a situation that does not require much in the way of problem solving, this method holds considerable promise for at least minimizing the intrusion of conscious recollection.

Employ Relearning and Savings Techniques

At the beginning of this chapter, the classic work of Ebbinghaus (1885/1964) was described, including his savings technique for studying memory (for more on this, see Nelson, 1985; Slamecka, 1985a, 1985b). In closing the discussion of how to handle contamination of implicit tests by conscious recollection, it seems fitting to return to Ebbinghaus's approach. The relearning/savings method was rarely used in research on human learning and memory after Ebbinghaus, with the occasional notable exception (e.g., Bunch, 1941). This limited use may stem in part from the demands of the procedure, often including extensive original learning together with a delayed retention test requiring a second session. But, Thomas O. Nelson (1971b) revived the technique, modifying it to optimize the procedure. Nelson then proceeded to employ relearning/savings in a series of studies that explored the residue in memory for information that could not be consciously remembered (see Nelson, 1971a, 1978; Nelson, Fehling, & Moore-Glascock, 1979; Nelson & Rothbart, 1972; Nelson & Vining, 1978).

Nelson's version of the relearning/savings paradigm involved a series of stages. During original learning, subjects intentionally learned a series of number–noun paired associates, typically to the stringent criterion of errorless performance on the entire list. After a retention interval of 1 or more weeks, they returned to take part in the remaining phases. First, they were tested for their ability to consciously remember the original pairs, permitting division of the items into a forgotten and a remembered set. Subjects next completed a single learning trial in which Nelson contrasted relearning of pairs that were either identical to original learning or related in some way (e.g., acoustically, Nelson & Rothbart, 1972; semantically, Nelson et al., 1979) to the baseline learning of unrelated new pairs on the subsequent test. To the extent that pairs shown to be forgotten on the pre-relearning test were relearned better than baseline unrelated pairs, there was evidence of savings. That savings was seen as necessarily unconscious given that an immediately preceding test failed to show conscious recollection of the target items.

The relearning/savings paradigm is therefore an implicit one. From the standpoint of the intrusion of conscious recollection, its advantage is that inability to consciously recollect the target information is demonstrated prior to relearning either by recall (e.g., MacLeod, 1976; Nelson, 1971b) or by recognition (MacLeod, 1988; Nelson, 1978). Thus, conscious recollection appears not to be the basis for relearning. Indeed, MacLeod (1976) pushed this analysis a step farther by including a post-relearning measure of whether relearned items had reinstated the originally learned items: Did relearning work by making what had been unconscious become conscious (i.e., by reminding)? Examination of only the items forgotten on the initial test after the retention interval showed that there was reliable savings for these items even when subjects could not recall the originally learned items after relearning.

Despite the difficulty of conducting relearning/savings studies, this method would appear to be worthy of further use and exploration in the context of the problem of conscious recollection contaminating implicit tests.[1] Using this method, we can be considerably more certain of what subjects remember consciously prior to an implicit test. At the very least, although likely also not a perfect solution to the problem, this tool is one that should be considered more often in trying to rule out contamination of implicit tests, thereby adding to the arsenal of methods considered in this chapter.

The Big Picture

There are no doubt other ways that we might try to address the problem of conscious processes and content intruding on what are intended to be unconscious measures.[1] A notable possibility not addressed here is to augment cognitive studies of memory with various forms of brain imaging that may be able to reveal when there is activity in regions associated with conscious processing, especially on tasks intended to be unconscious. But, the goal here has been to cover the major approaches that have been and currently are used to minimize conscious intrusion and to illustrate their advantages and disadvantages. Jacoby (1991) was certainly right in noting that process-pure tests are impossible, so we must try to develop ways to deal with the problems that this creates.

New strategies and paradigms will emerge, but at this juncture, just as it is hard to imagine a process-pure task, it is hard to imagine a process-pure solution. The optimal strategy, as always in experimental research, is a combination of replication and convergence. New measures must be put to stringent test, and their relations to existing measures must be better established than is often the case. When an interesting pattern is observed on a nominally implicit test, it is then appropriate to bring to bear some of the methods described here to enhance the likelihood that the pattern is indeed occurring implicitly, without the intrusion of conscious recollection. Perhaps it is in their very nature that subtle changes in implicit paradigms can produce quite dramatic changes. For that reason, these tests must be examined thoroughly and used with care.

Acknowledgment

It was my great privilege to be Tom Nelson's first graduate student (1971–1975). I owe my career to him, and I deeply miss both his mentorship and his friendship. Whenever I play pool, drive my sports car, listen to "oldies," … or design an experiment, I will remember Tom.

Preparation of this chapter was supported by discovery grant A7459 from the Natural Sciences and Engineering Research Council of Canada. I thank Peter Graf for helpful literature pointers and Kathleen Hourihan and Nigel Gopie for thorough critical readings.

Note

1. In considering contamination of implicit tests, it may also be important to discriminate the intrusion of conscious retrieval from the intrusion of conscious content. Testing amnesic individuals, using the process dissociation procedure, and using relearning and savings paradigms all seem to reduce the likelihood of conscious content intruding. The other techniques described here seem more aimed at reducing the likelihood of a conscious retrieval strategy being applied. This distinction between process and content warrants further consideration as we develop our methods and theories relating to implicit memory.

References

Baddeley, A. (2003). Double dissociations: Not magic, but still useful. *Cortex, 39*, 129–131.

Bower, G. H. (2000). A brief history of memory research. In E. Tulving and F. I. M. Craik (Eds.), *The Oxford handbook of memory* (pp. 3–32). New York: Oxford University Press.

Bowers, J. S., & Marsolek, C. J. (Eds.). (2003). *Rethinking implicit memory*. New York: Oxford University Press.

Bowers, J. S., & Schacter, D. L. (1990). Implicit memory and test awareness. *Journal of Experimental Psychology: Learning, Memory, and Cognition, 16*, 404–416.

Buchner, A., & Brandt, M. (2003). Further evidence for systematic reliability differences between explicit and implicit memory tests. *Quarterly Journal of Experimental Psychology, 56A*, 193–209.

Buchner, A., & Wippich, W. (2000). On the reliability of implicit and explicit memory measures. *Cognitive Psychology, 40*, 227–259.

Bunch, M. E. (1941). The measurement of retention by the relearning method. *Psychological Review, 48*, 450–456.

Butler, L. T., & Berry, D. C. (2001). Implicit memory: Intention and awareness revisited. *Trends in Cognitive Sciences, 5*, 192–197.

Challis, B. H., & Roediger, H. L., III. (1993). The effect of proportion overlap and repeated testing on primed word fragment completion. *Canadian Journal of Experimental Psychology, 47*, 113–123.

Claparède, E. (1907). Expériences sur la mémoire dans un cas de psychose de Korsakoff. *Médicale de la Suisse Romande, 27*, 301–303.

Craik, F. I. M., & Lockhart, R. S. (1972). Levels of processing: A framework for memory research. *Journal of Verbal Learning and Verbal Behavior, 11*, 671–684.

Curran, T., & Hintzman, D. L. (1997). Consequences and causes of correlations in process dissociation. *Journal of Experimental Psychology: Learning, Memory, and Cognition, 23*, 496–504.

Dodson, C. S., & Johnson, M. K. (1996). Some problems with the process-dissociation approach to memory. *Journal of Experimental Psychology: General, 125*, 181–194.

Dunn, J. C., & Kirsner, K. (1988). Discovering functionally independent mental processes: The principle of reversed association. *Psychological Review, 95*, 91–101.

Dunn, J. C., & Kirsner, K. (2003). What can we infer from double dissociations? *Cortex, 39*, 1–7.

Ebbinghaus, H. (1964). *Memory*. New York: Dover. (Original work published 1885)

Ferreira, M. B., Garcia-Marques, L., Sherman, S. J., & Sherman, J. W. (2006). Automatic and controlled components of judgment and decision making. *Journal of Personality and Social Psychology, 91*, 797–813.

Fujita, T. (1994). [Generation effect on implicit and explicit memory tasks: Influence of instructions and proportion overlap of lists]. *Japanese Journal of Psychology, 65*, 181–189.

Gabrieli, J. D. E., Fleischman, D. A., Keane, M. M., Reminger, S. L., & Morrell, F. (1995). Double dissociation between memory systems underlying explicit and implicit memory in the human brain. *Psychological Science, 6*, 76–82.

Gabrieli, J. D. E., Keane, M. M., Zarella, M. M., & Poldrack, R. A. (1997). Preservation of implicit memory for new associations in global amnesia. *Psychological Science, 8*, 326–329.

Glisky, E. L., & Schacter, D. L. (1987). Acquisition of domain-specific knowledge in organic amnesia: Training for computer-related work. *Neuropsychologia, 25*, 893–906.

Glisky, E. L., & Schacter, D. L. (1988). Long-term retention of computer learning by patients with memory disorders. *Neuropsychologia, 26,* 173–178.

Glisky, E. L., Schacter, D. L., & Tulving, E. (1986). Computer learning by memory-impaired patients: Acquisition and retention of complex knowledge. *Neuropsychologia, 24,* 313–328.

Gooding, P. A., Mayes, A. R., & van Eijk, R. (2000). A meta-analysis of indirect memory tests for novel material in organic amnesics. *Neuropsychologia, 38,* 666–676.

Goshen-Gottstein, Y., Moscovitch, M., & Melo, B. (2000). Intact implicit memory for newly formed verbal associations in amnesic patients following single study trials. *Neuropsychology, 14,* 570–578.

Graf, P., & Komatsu, S. (1994). Process dissociation procedure: Handle with caution. *European Journal of Cognitive Psychology, 6,* 113–129.

Graf, P., & Mandler, G. (1984). Activation makes words more accessible, but not necessarily more retrievable. *Journal of Verbal Learning and Verbal Behavior, 23,* 553–568.

Graf, P., & Schacter, D. L. (1985). Implicit and explicit memory for new associations in normal and amnesic subjects. *Journal of Experimental Psychology: Learning, Memory, and Cognition, 11,* 501–518.

Graf, P., Shimamura, A. P., & Squire, L. R. (1985). Priming across modalities and priming across category levels: Extending the domain of preserved function in amnesia. *Journal of Experimental Psychology: Learning, Memory, and Cognition, 11,* 386–396.

Graf, P., Squire, L. R., & Mandler, G. (1984). The information that amnesic patients do not forget. *Journal of Experimental Psychology: Learning, Memory, and Cognition, 10,* 164–178.

Greene, R. L. (1986). Word stems as cues in recall and completion tasks. *Quarterly Journal of Experimental Psychology, 38A,* 663–673.

Hirshman, E. (1998). On the logic of testing the independence assumption in the process-dissociation procedure. *Memory & Cognition, 26,* 857–859.

Horton, K. D., Wilson, D. E., & Evans, M. (2001). Measuring automatic retrieval. *Journal of Experimental Psychology: Learning, Memory, and Cognition, 27,* 958–966.

Horton, K. D., Wilson, D. E., Vonk, J., Kirby, S. L., & Nielsen, T. (2005). Measuring automatic retrieval: A comparison of implicit memory, process dissociation, and speeded response procedures. *Acta Psychologica, 119,* 235–263.

Hourihan, K. L., & MacLeod, C. M. (2007). Capturing conceptual implicit memory: The time it takes to produce an association. *Memory & Cognition, 35,* 1187–1196.

Hunt, R. R., & Worthen, J. B. (Eds.). (2006). *Distinctiveness and memory.* New York: Oxford University Press.

Jacoby, L. L. (1983a). Perceptual enhancement: Persistent effects of an experience. *Journal of Experimental Psychology: Learning, Memory, and Cognition, 9,* 21–38.

Jacoby, L. L. (1983b). Remembering the data: Analyzing interactive processes in reading. *Journal of Verbal Learning and Verbal Behavior, 22,* 485–508.

Jacoby, L. L. (1991). A process dissociation framework: Separating automatic from intentional uses of memory. *Journal of Memory and Language, 30,* 513–541.

Jacoby, L. L. (1997). Invariance in automatic influences of memory: Toward a user's guide for the process-dissociation procedure. *Journal of Experimental Psychology: Learning, Memory and Cognition, 24,* 3–26.

Jacoby, L. L., & Witherspoon, D. (1982). Remembering without awareness. *Canadian Journal of Psychology, 36,* 300–324.

Jacoby, L. L., Toth, J. P., & Yonelinas, A. P. (1993). Separating conscious and unconscious influences of memory: Measuring recollection. *Journal of Experimental Psychology: General, 122,* 139–154.

Jacoby, L. L., Yonelinas, A. P., & Jennings, J. M. (1997). The relation between conscious and unconscious (automatic) influences: A declaration of independence. In J. D. Cohen & J. W. Schooler (Eds.), *Scientific approaches to consciousness* (pp. 13–47). Hillsdale, NJ: Erlbaum.

Java, R. I. (1994). States of awareness following word stem completion. *European Journal of Cognitive Psychology, 6,* 77–92.

Jermann, F., Van der Linden, M., Adam, S., Ceschi, G., & Perroud, A. (2005). Controlled and automatic uses of memory in depressed patients: Effect of retention interval lengths. *Behaviour Research and Therapy, 43,* 681–690.

Jernigan, T. L., & Ostergaard, A. L. (1993). Word priming and recognition memory are both affected by mesial temporal lobe damage. *Neuropsychology, 7,* 14–26.

MacDonald, P. A., & MacLeod, C. M. (1998). The influence of attention at encoding on direct and indirect remembering. *Acta Psychologica, 98,* 291–310.

MacLeod, C. M. (1976). Bilingual episodic memory: Acquisition and forgetting. *Journal of Verbal Learning and Verbal Behavior, 15,* 347–364.

MacLeod, C. M. (1988). Forgotten but not gone: Savings for pictures and words in long-term memory. *Journal of Experimental Psychology: Learning, Memory, and Cognition, 14,* 195–212.

MacLeod, C. M. (1989a). Directed forgetting affects both direct and indirect tests of memory. *Journal of Experimental Psychology: Learning, Memory, and Cognition, 15,* 13–21.

MacLeod, C. M. (1989b). Word context during initial exposure influences degree of priming in word fragment completion. *Journal of Experimental Psychology: Learning, Memory, and Cognition, 15,* 398–406.

MacLeod, C. M. (1996). How priming affects two speeded implicit tests of remembering: Naming colors versus reading words. *Consciousness and Cognition, 5,* 73–90.

MacLeod, C. M., & Daniels, K. A. (2000). Direct versus indirect tests of memory: Directed forgetting meets the generation effect. *Psychonomic Bulletin & Review, 7,* 354–359.

MacLeod, C. M., & Masson, M. E. J. (2000). Repetition priming in speeded word reading: Contributions of perceptual and conceptual processing episodes. *Journal of Memory and Language, 42,* 208–228.

Masson, M. E. J., & MacLeod, C. M. (1992). Reenacting the route to interpretation: Enhanced perceptual identification without prior perception. *Journal of Experimental Psychology: General, 121,* 145–176.

Merikle, P. M., Joordens, S., & Stolz, J. A. (1995). Measuring the relative magnitude of unconscious influences. *Consciousness and Cognition, 4,* 422–439.

Moscovitch, M., Vriezen, E., & Goshen-Gottstein, Y. (1993). Implicit tests of memory in patients with focal brain lesions or degenerative brain disorders. In H. Spinnler and F. Boller (Eds.), *Handbook of neuropsychology* (Vol. 8, pp. 133–173). Amsterdam: Elsevier.

Mulligan, N. W., & Hartman, M. (1996). Divided attention and indirect memory tests. *Memory & Cognition, 24,* 453–465.

Musen, G., Shimamura, A. P., & Squire, L. R. (1990). Intact text-specific reading skill in amnesia. *Journal of Experimental Psychology: Learning, Memory, and Cognition, 16,* 1068–1076.

Musen, G., & Squire, L. R. (1991). Normal acquisition of novel verbal information in amnesia. *Journal of Experimental Psychology: Learning, Memory, and Cognition, 17,* 1095–1104.

Nelson, T. O. (1971a). Recognition and savings in long-term memory: Related or independent? *Proceedings of the Annual Convention of the American Psychological Association, 6,* 15–16.

Nelson, T. O. (1971b). Savings and forgetting from long-term memory. *Journal of Verbal Learning and Verbal Behavior, 10,* 568–576.

Nelson, T. O. (1978). Detecting small amounts of information in memory: Savings for non-recognized items. *Journal of Experimental Psychology: Human Learning and Memory, 4,* 453–468.

Nelson, T. O. (1985). Ebbinghaus's contribution to the measurement of retention: Savings during relearning. *Journal of Experimental Psychology: Learning, Memory, and Cognition, 11,* 472–479.

Nelson, T. O., Fehling, M. R., & Moore-Glascock, J. (1979). The nature of semantic savings for items forgotten from long-term memory. *Journal of Experimental Psychology: General, 108,* 225–250.

Nelson, T. O., & Rothbart, R. (1972). Acoustic savings for items forgotten from long-term memory. *Journal of Experimental Psychology, 93,* 357–360.

Nelson, T. O., & Vining, S. K. (1978). Effect of semantic versus structural processing on long-term retention. *Journal of Experimental Psychology: Human Learning and Memory, 4,* 198–209.

Nicolas, S. (1996). Experiments on implicit memory in a Korsakoff patient by Claparède (1907). *Cognitive Neuropsychology, 13,* 1193–1199.

Oliphant, G. W. (1983). Repetition and recency effects in word recognition. *Australian Journal of Psychology, 35,* 393–403.

Paller, K. A., & Mayes, A. R. (1994). New-association priming of word identification in normal and amnesic subjects. *Cortex, 30,* 53–73.

Rajaram, S., & Coslett, H. B. (2000). New conceptual associative learning in amnesia: A case study. *Journal of Memory and Language, 43,* 291–315.

Reingold, E. M. (2003). Interpreting dissociations: The issue of task comparability. *Cortex, 39,* 174–176.

Richardson-Klavehn, A., & Gardiner, J. M. (1996). Cross-modality priming in stem completion reflects conscious memory, but not voluntary memory. *Psychonomic Bulletin & Review, 3,* 238–244.

Richardson-Klavehn, A., Clarke, A. J. B., & Gardiner, J. M. (1999). Conjoint dissociations reveal involuntary "perceptual" priming from generating at study. *Consciousness and Cognition, 8,* 271–284.

Richardson-Klavehn, A., Lee, M. G., Joubran, R., & Bjork, R. A. (1994). Intention and awareness in perceptual identification priming. *Memory & Cognition, 22,* 293–312.

Roediger, H. L., III, & Geraci, L. (2005). Implicit memory tasks in cognitive research. In A. Wenzel & D. C. Rubin (Eds.), *Cognitive methods and their application to clinical research* (pp. 129–151). Washington, DC: American Psychological Association.

Roediger, H. L., III, & McDermott, K. B. (1993). Implicit memory in normal human subjects. In H. Spinnler and F. Boller (Eds.), *Handbook of neuropsychology* (Vol. 8, pp. 63–131). Amsterdam: Elsevier.

Roediger, H. L., III, Weldon, M. S., Stadler, M. L., & Riegler, G. L. (1992). Direct comparison of two implicit memory tests: Word fragment and word stem completion. *Journal of Experimental Psychology: Learning, Memory, and Cognition, 18,* 1251–1269.

Scarborough, D. L., Cortese, C., & Scarborough, H. S. (1977). Frequency and repetition effects in lexical memory. *Journal of Experimental Psychology: Human Perception and Performance, 3,* 1–17.

Schacter, D. L. (1987). Implicit memory: History and current status. *Journal of Experimental Psychology: Learning, Memory, and Cognition, 13*, 501–518.

Schacter, D. L., Bowers, J., & Booker, J. (1989). Intention, awareness, and implicit memory: The retrieval intentionality criterion. In S. Lewandowsky, J. C. Dunn, & K. Kirsner (Eds.), *Implicit memory: Theoretical issues* (pp. 47–65). Hillsdale, NJ: Erlbaum.

Schacter, D. L., Church, B., & Treadwell, J. (1994). Implicit memory in amnesic patients: Evidence for spared auditory priming. *Psychological Science, 5*, 20–25.

Schacter, D. L., & Graf, P. (1986). Effects of elaborative processing on implicit and explicit memory for new associations. *Journal of Experimental Psychology: Learning, Memory, and Cognition, 12*, 432–444.

Seamon, J. G., McKenna, P. A., & Binder, N. (1998). The mere exposure effect is differentially sensitive to different judgment tasks. *Consciousness and Cognition, 7*, 85–102.

Shallice, T. (1988). *From neuropsychology to mental structure.* Cambridge, UK: Cambridge University Press.

Slamecka, N. J. (1985a). Ebbinghaus: Some associations. *Journal of Experimental Psychology: Learning, Memory, and Cognition, 11*, 414–435.

Slamecka, N. J. (1985b). Ebbinghaus: Some rejoinders. *Journal of Experimental Psychology: Learning, Memory, and Cognition, 11*, 496–500.

Slamecka, N. J., & Graf, P. (1978). The generation effect: Delineation of a phenomenon. *Journal of Experimental Psychology: Human Learning and Memory, 4*, 592–604.

Thapar, A., & Greene, R. L. (1994). Effects of level of processing on implicit and explicit tasks. *Journal of Experimental Psychology: Learning, Memory, and Cognition, 20*, 671–679.

Tulving, E., Schacter, D. L., & Stark, H. A. (1982). Priming effects in word-fragment completion are independent of recognition memory. *Journal of Experimental Psychology: Learning, Memory, and Cognition, 8*, 336–342.

Vaidya, C. J., Gabrieli, J. D. E., Keane, M. M., Monti, L. A., Gutiérrez-Rivas, H., & Zarella, M. M. (1997). Evidence for multiple mechanisms of conceptual priming on implicit memory tests. *Journal of Experimental Psychology: Learning, Memory, and Cognition, 23*, 1324–1343.

Van Orden, G. C., Pennington, B. F., & Stone, G. O. (2001). What do double dissociations prove? *Cognitive Science, 25*, 111–172.

Vonk, J., & Horton, K. D. (2006). Automatic retrieval in directed forgetting. *Memory & Cognition, 34*, 505–517.

Warrington, E. K., & Weiskrantz, L. (1970). Amnesic syndrome: Consolidation or retrieval? *Nature, 228*, 628–630.

Warrington, E. K., & Weiskrantz, L. (1974). The effect of prior learning on subsequent retention in amnestic patients. *Neuropsychologia, 12*, 419–428.

Wilson, D. E., & Horton, K. D. (2002). Comparing techniques for estimating automatic retrieval: Effects of retention interval. *Psychonomic Bulletin & Review, 9*, 566–574.

Yonelinas, A. P. (2002). The nature of recollection and familiarity: A review of 30 years of research. *Journal of Memory and Language, 46*, 441–517.

Investigating Metacognitive Control in a Global Memory Framework

Kenneth J. Malmberg

Introduction

How does one learn? How does one remember? These are the broad questions that the Nelson and Narens (1990) research program addressed. Of course, they were not the first to ask these questions, but they did approach these questions in a novel way.

The Nelson and Narens approach to understanding learning and memory can be viewed as an extension of Atkinson and Shiffrin's (1968) proposal that memory consists of a set of memory structures and control processes. The memory structures are assumed to be used to support the performance of all learning and memory tasks, whereas control processes (e.g., rehearsal) are assumed to be strategically used to perform particular tasks. Many researchers have sought to understand the nature of the structural aspects of learning and memory, and this has led to several formal models. Nelson and Narens, on the other hand, organized the prevalent measures and developed a framework that describes how the structural aspects of memory are monitored and controlled. It is a testament to the empirical richness of the Nelson and Narens *metamemory* framework that those modern researchers who investigate metamemory do so largely independently of those who investigate the structural aspects of memory (and vice versa). In this chapter, I consider how these two approaches to understanding learning and memory might be jointly used to build better models of learning and memory.

Retrieval and Matching in Memory

Global theories of memory attempt to explain a large number of memory phenomena with just a few central assumptions. They often describe remembering as an interaction between retrieval cues and memory. That is, memory is queried by probing it with a set of information that represents the nominal stimulus and the result of the probe depends on the nature of the information in the retrieval cue. Typically it is assumed that memory traces are activated or accessible to the extent that they contain information that is similar to the contents of the retrieval cue and to the extent that they are well encoded.

Most theories of episodic memory propose that two types of processes access the information stored in memory (e.g., Gillund & Shiffrin, 1984; Hintzman, 1987;

Humphreys, Bain, & Pike, 1989; Murdock, 1993; Shiffrin & Steyvers, 1997). I refer to these as *retrieval* and *global-matching* processes, and they produce qualitatively different types of information (cf. Humphreys et al., 1989). A retrieval process provides information about the contents of a memory trace, while a global-matching process provides information about the familiarity of a retrieval cue. The latter process is referred to as *global matching* because the retrieval cue is compared to the contents of a large number of (perhaps all) traces in memory. Thus, familiarity is assumed to be a positive function of the similarity between these memory traces and the retrieval cue.

For instance, let us assume that one has studied a pair of words: trout and pint. If subsequently presented with trout, one might probe memory with the orthographic, phonologic, and semantic information associated with it. The probability of then retrieving pint would be a positive function of how well encoded trout and pint were during study. In addition, having been presented with trout, one almost certainly would have some sense that it was recently encountered (i.e., it seems familiar) independently of the ability to retrieve pint, and the longer trout was studied or the more times trout was studied, the better encoded it would be and hence the more familiar it would seem.

Accordingly, free or cued recall tasks are generally assumed to involve a retrieval process, while recognition tasks are often assumed to involve a global-matching process (Gillund & Shiffrin, 1984; Hintzman, 1987; Humphreys et al., 1989; Malmberg, Zeelenberg, & Shiffrin, 2004; Murdock, 1993; Shiffrin & Steyvers, 1997). In some theories of recognition memory, output from the global-matching process (e.g., familiarity) serves as the input to a decision mechanism that is modeled by a version of signal detection theory to produce a response. Other theories of recognition assume that recognition is based on the operation of both retrieval and a global-matching process (e.g., Atkinson & Juola, 1973; Malmberg, Holden, & Shiffrin, 2004; Mandler, 1980; Reder et al., 2000; see Clark, 1998; Mandler, 1991; Yonelinas, 2002, for reviews). A major topic of research has been to empirically test these two models of recognition. Less attention has been given to what role, if any, familiarity plays in free or cued recall, although I discuss some relevant findings here. One reason for this comparative lack of interest by memory researchers is that familiarity alone is insufficient for successfully performing a recall task; recall demands a response that names an item, and the matching process does not produce items as output. A second reason concerns the limited scope of many memory theories.

Search Permission and Familiarity

Memory control processes generally produce the input for the retrieval process, and they make use of the output from the retrieval process to govern the completion of a memory task. With several exceptions (e.g., Atkinson & Shiffrin, 1968; Malmberg & Xu, 2007; Raaijmakers & Shiffrin, 1981), memory control processes have not been modeled in great detail. Consideration of a range of possible control processes provides a rich field of possibilities for the use of familiarity in recall.[1] For example, Diller, Nobel, and Shiffrin (2001) assumed in their REM model of cued recall that the amount of time subjects are willing to search memory is a positive function of the familiarity of the retrieval cue.

Does familiarity affect the amount of time one is willing to search memory in a cued recall task? Convergent empirical support for the hypothesis that the familiarity produced by the retrieval cue is used to control memory search comes from several investigations of metacognitive feeling-of-knowing judgments (Koriat, 1993; Metcalfe, 1993; Reder, 1987; Schwartz & Metcalfe,1992; also see Glucksberg & McCloskey, 1981). For instance, some have proposed that the length of a search is based on a chain of events beginning with memory access (Nelson & Narens, 1990; Reder, 1987). A feeling-of-knowing judgment is made when retrieval fails, and additional attempts to remember are likely when feeling-of-knowing judgments are positive (Nelson & Narens, 1990). Several investigators have proposed that feeling-of-knowing judgments are informed, at least in part, by the familiarity produced by the retrieval cue (Koriat, 1993; Metcalfe, 1993; Nelson, Gerler, & Narens, 1984; Reder 1987).

Schwartz and Metcalfe (1992) and Metcalfe, Schwartz, and Joaquim (1993) confirmed a straightforward prediction of this hypothesis: Directly priming a cue produces greater feeling-of-knowing judgments. Nelson et al. (1984) reported a positive correlation between feeling-of-knowing judgments and the length of a search for answers to general knowledge questions. Reder (1987) reported longer search times in response to primed normatively difficult general knowledge questions but shorter search times in response to primed normatively easy questions (Reder, 1987, Experiment 6). Thus, there is some evidence that cue familiarity does inform the decision of when to terminate a search of semantic memory. It remains, however, an open question regarding whether the familiarity of the retrieval cue affects the length of search for episodic memory tasks, like paired-associate cued recall, and whether there are any empirical limitations to such a model.

Hypotheses and Predictions

Here, I report the results of four paired-associate cued recall experiments. Pairs of words were studied, and one word was presented as a cue to recall the other word at test. The responses were divided into two categories for the present analyses: correct responses and "don't know" responses. The interests here are how cue familiarity affects the willingness to search memory (or length of search) and how this might affect recall performance. The first interest is inherently a metamemory issue, and the latter is primarily a structural memory issue.

To address these issues, I measured both the accuracy and the latency of cued recall performance. The latencies of correct responses do not provide a good indicator of maximum search time because a search may have continued longer if not for the retrieval of an item deemed worthy of reporting (cf. Gillund & Shiffrin, 1984; Nelson & Narens, 1990; Raaijmakers & Shiffrin, 1981). Rather, the amount of time subjects were willing to search memory is assumed to be indicated by the latency of the don't know responses (cf. Glucksberg & McCloskey, 1981; Reder, 1987). Generally speaking, if familiarity is a factor that positively affects the decision to search, the average don't know latency for cues that produce a high degree of familiarity should be longer than the average don't know latency for cues that produce a low degree of familiarity. There are, however, several specific hypotheses to consider concerning the effect of familiarity on cued recall performance.

Null Hypothesis

The output of the global-matching process has no significant effect on the decision of when to terminate a search, and the familiarity manipulation does not produce interference. If the null hypothesis is correct, the familiarity manipulation should not have a significant effect on the mean proportions of a correct response or on the mean response latencies for either correct or don't know responses. For example, Diller et al.'s (2001) REM model does not predict a list-strength effect for cued recall (Shiffrin & Steyvers, 1997; also see Ratcliff, Clark, & Shiffrin, 1990, for the relevant findings concerning list-strength effects for cued recall). Thus, storing relatively strong memory traces does not interfere with retrieval of relatively weak traces.

Effective-Search Hypothesis

The output of the global-matching process affects the decision of when to terminate a search, additional retrieval attempts increase the chance of success, and either the familiarity manipulation does not produce interference or the additional time spent searching improves recall to a greater extent than interference harms recall. The effective-search hypothesis assumes the additional time spent searching memory will increase the probability of success either because subsequent retrieval attempts with the same set of cues are independent or because cues are changed on subsequent attempts, producing additional opportunities to find an effective retrieval cue (cf. Diller et al., 2001). If the effective-search hypothesis is correct, don't know latencies should be longer for cues that produce a relatively high degree of familiarity, and the additional time spent searching memory should produce higher probabilities of correct responses.

There are two possible scenarios involving the latencies of the correct responses that are consistent with the effective-search hypothesis. One is that relatively familiar cues produce longer average latencies for correct responses because some of the extra searches will result in the retrieval of the target. Another result that is consistent with the effective-search hypothesis is that cue familiarity may have a countervailing effect on the time course of retrieval by producing some relatively fast correct responses in addition to some relatively slow correct responses. That is, the average latency for the earliest correct responses may be shorter for functionally stronger than for functionally weaker cue–target pairs. If so, an increase in correct recall may be observed even though the latencies of correct responses appear to be independent of the familiarity of the cue.

Ineffective-Search Hypothesis

The output of the matching process affects the decision of when to terminate a search, additional retrieval attempts do not increase the chance of success, and the familiarity manipulation does not produce interference (see preceding section). If the ineffective-search hypothesis is correct, don't know latencies should be longer for cues that evoke a relatively high degree of familiarity. In addition, the longer time spent searching memory should have no significant effect on either the probabilities or latencies of correct responses because the extra searches are being carried out with ineffective retrieval cues. For example, access to memory is direct in many composite memory models (e.g., TODAM2, Murdock, 1993; the matrix model, Humphreys et al., 1989). For this reason, repeatedly probing with the same retrieval cue would not increase the probability of correct recall because the state of memory does not change. If, however, subjects vary the contents of the retrieval cue from one probe to the next, then additional probes may produce an increase in the likelihood of successful retrieval.

Even in a separate-trace global memory model like SAM or REM, in which multiple searches are carried out and different traces may be retrieved due to the stochastic nature of retrieval, additional searches may not necessarily produce a large increase in the probability of correct recall if subjects do not change retrieval cues from one probe to the next. Why might subjects be reluctant to change retrieval cues? In cued recall, the task is to remember the word that was paired with the experimenter-provided cue at study. One variant of the ineffective-search hypothesis assumes that additional memory probes use the same ineffective retrieval cues as earlier probes and that probing memory with the same ineffective retrieval cue produces the same result (Gillund & Shiffrin, 1984; Raaijmakers & Shiffrin, 1981). It would make little sense from the subject's point of view to abandon the experimenter-provided retrieval cue given the nature of the task.

Interference Hypotheses

The familiarity manipulations may produce interference that makes it more difficult to retrieve the target item from memory. Interference is often thought of as a form of response competition that occurs when two or more possible responses are associated with, and produced by, the information in the retrieval cue (see M. C. Anderson & Neely, 1998, for a review). On this basis, interference is expected to produce longer latencies for correct responses because resolving the competition between responses takes time (cf. Anderson, 1981; Goebel & Lewandowsky, 1991) and lower proportions of correct responses because sometimes the incorrect item that is producing the interference will be chosen. However, interference will not affect the latencies of don't know responses.

Experiment 1

An extra-list direct-priming procedure was used to manipulate the familiarity of the cues (Metcalfe et al., 1993). Subjects carried out a series of word fragment completion trials prior to the presentation of the paired-associate study list. Half of the words designated to be cues at test appeared during the word fragment completion trials (*primed cues*), and the remaining cues only appeared on the study list (*unprimed cues*). If familiarity is a factor influencing the length of search and to the extent that the episodic traces stored during the priming phase take part in the global-matching process, then the latencies of don't know responses to the primed cues will be longer than those in response to the unprimed cues.

Method

Subjects, Design, and Materials   Forty-six introductory psychology students participated in exchange for course credit. A single within-subject factor, primed versus unprimed cue, was varied. Eighty words were randomly drawn for each subject from a pool of 100 words used for word fragment completion tasks by Rajaram and Roediger (1993). Forty paired associates were formed for each subject by randomly pairing two words, and one of the words from each pair was randomly selected to be a cue at test.

For each subject, 20 paired associates were randomly assigned to the primed condition, and the remaining 20 pairs were assigned to the unprimed condition. *Priming* was operationally defined as the presentation of cues prior to study during word fragment completion trials. The 20 words serving as cues in the primed condition were decomposed into word fragments by removing one letter such that each fragment could be completed to form exactly one word.

The dependent variables of interest were the latencies and probabilities of correct and don't know responses. Latencies of correct responses were measured from the time the cue appeared on the monitor to the time the subject entered the first letter of a response. Don't know latencies were measured from the time the cue appeared on the monitor to the time the subject pressed a key signaling he or she did not remember the target item. With a single exception, the frequencies of incorrect responses were too low to enable meaningful data analyses. Therefore, with the one exception, these data are not discussed further.

Procedure   The experiment was conducted on personal computers in individual subject booths. Subjects were first given standard instructions about the cued recall phase of the experiment and were told that they had as long as they wanted to try to remember the target response. They were also told that if they could not remember the word paired with the cue, they could end the current trial at any time and move on to the next trial by entering a don't know response.

After receiving instructions for the cued recall portion of the experiment, subjects were given instructions for the word fragment completion task. They were told that the purpose of the word fragment completion task was to become familiar with entering responses using the computer keyboard. On each priming trial, a word fragment was displayed in the center of the computer monitor. After the letter that correctly completed the word fragment was entered by the subject, the next priming trial began.

After finishing the word fragment completion trials, subjects were reminded of the cued recall instructions. During the learning phase of the experiment, paired associates were presented side by side in the center of a computer monitor for 5 seconds. On completion of the study phase, subjects performed a distracter task lasting at least 30 seconds. The distracter task consisted of adding 10 random digits that were presented 1 at a time at a rate of 1 every 3 seconds. Cued recall testing followed the distracter task.

On each cued-recall trial, one word from a studied pair was displayed in the center of the monitor. Below the cue, a prompt was displayed where subjects would type in their response to the cue. When subjects thought they knew the word that had been paired with the cue, they typed the word on the computer keyboard and pressed "Enter." When subjects thought they did not know the answer, they pressed the question mark key on the keyboard. As soon as either response was made by the subject, the next test trial began. The same procedure was used in the remaining three experiments.

Results and Discussion

The standard of significance is .05, and the statistical analyses of the latencies were performed on the log-transformed latencies of the correct and don't know responses to control for outliers (Ratcliff, 1993). It was not possible to guarantee that each subject would produce every possible type of response in every condition of the experiment; thus, the degrees of freedom that are reported may vary from condition to condition.

The mean proportions and latencies of the various responses are reported in Table 1. The don't know latencies for primed cues were significantly greater than for unprimed cues [$t(44) = 2.16$]. Priming did not significantly affect the proportion of don't know responses [$t(45) = .65$]. Priming the cue did not have a statistically significant effect on the proportion of correct responses [$t(45) = .20$] or on their latencies [$t(43) = .11$].

Longer don't know latencies for primed cues suggest that the familiarity produced by the retrieval cue affected the search permission control process. The failure to observe statistically reliable effects of priming on either the proportion or latency of

TABLE 1   Mean Proportions and Latencies of Correct Responses and Don't Know Responses for Experiment 1

| | Response Type | | | |
| | Correct Responses | | Don't Knows | |
Priming Condition	Proportion	Latency (s.)	Proportion	Latency (s.)
Primed cue	.42	3.8	.45	7.1
Unprimed cue	.42	3.5	.47	6.1

Note: The proportions of correct and don't know responses do not sum to 1.0 because commission errors were sometimes made.

correct responses indicates that interference did not differentially affect the priming conditions and is inconsistent with the effective-search hypothesis. The pattern of data is consistent with the ineffective-search hypothesis. Subjects conducted longer searches in response to the relatively familiar cues, but the extra searches did not produce successful recall.

Experiment 2

The semantic similarity of retrieval cues was used in Experiment 2 to manipulate familiarity. For some cue–target pairs (A–C), a related cue–target pair was studied (A′–D). I refer to these as *similar cues*. The cues of the remaining cue–target pairs were chosen randomly, and hence they are only incidentally similar to the rest of words comprising the study list. I refer to these as *dissimilar, nonsimilar,* or *randomly similar cues.* Assume that similar cues have more semantic features in common than nonsimilar cues (Estes, 1994; Hintzman, 1987). According to global-matching theories of recognition, the level of familiarity produced by matching a retrieval cue against the contents of memory is a positive function of the similarity between the retrieval cue and the memory set (Clark & Gronlund, 1996). Dissimilar cues will only tend to match their own trace stored during study. However, similar cues not only will match their own trace, but also will partially match the memory trace corresponding to the study trial with the semantically similar cue. Thus, global-matching models predict that the similar cues will elicit higher levels of familiarity than nonsimilar cues (Hintzman, Caulton, & Levitin, 1994). If familiarity positively affects the length of search, then the don't know latencies for similar cues will be longer than for dissimilar cues.

Method

Forty-three students from introductory psychology courses participated in the experiment in exchange for course credit. A single-factor (semantically similar versus nonsimilar cues) within-subject design was used. *Semantic similarity* was operationally defined as two exemplars from the same semantic category according to the Battig and Montague (1969) norms. Sixty paired associates were randomly formed for each subject. Half of the cues were semantically similar to other cues, and half were not. For each subject, 60 target words were randomly assigned to the 60 cues.

Results and Discussion

Four subjects' data were not included in the statistical analysis because of failure to understand the instructions or computer malfunction. The mean proportion and latencies of the different responses are presented in Table 2. Subjects searched longer in response to similar cues than to nonsimilar cues [$t(38) = 2.67$]. In addition, subjects made significantly fewer don't know responses to similar cues [$t(38) = 2.56$]. The

TABLE 2   Mean Proportions and Latencies of Correct Responses and Don't Know Responses for Experiment 2

	Response Type			
	Correct Responses		Don't Knows	
Priming Condition	Proportion	Latency (s.)	Proportion	Latency (s.)
Similar cue	.21	3.5	.62	5.5
Dissimilar cue	.20	3.7	.68	4.8

Note: The proportions of correct and don't know responses do not sum to 1.0 because commission errors were sometimes made.

similarity of the cue did not significantly affect the proportions [$t(38) = .70$] or the latencies of correct responses [$t(36) = .98$]. Higher levels of familiarity were associated with longer searches, and the additional searches did not produce successful retrievals. In fact, cue similarity increased the number of incorrect responses at the expense (i.e., commission errors) of the don't know responses but had no effect on the correct responses. Thus, the additional time spent searching did not improve the accuracy of cued recall; in fact, it was correlated with a lower level of accuracy.

Experiment 3

In Experiment 3, the familiarity produced by the retrieval cue was manipulated by controlling the amount of time the cue was available for study during the learning phase of the experiment. This was accomplished using an offset study design (see Benjamin, 2005); conditions in which the cue and target appear together for t seconds are compared with conditions in which a t-second pairing of the cue and target was preceded by an s-second presentation of the cue alone. Increasing the amount of time that a cue is studied should increase its familiarity. The design is shown in Figure 1.

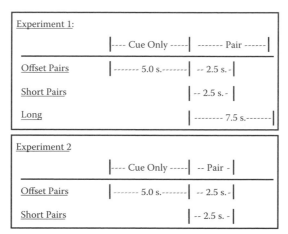

Figure 1   Pair types that were used in the design of Experiment 1 versus 2.

For the "short pairs," the cue and target appeared simultaneously and remained on screen together for 2.5 seconds. For the "long pairs," the cue and target also appeared simultaneously and remained on screen together for 7.5 seconds. For the "offset pairs," the cue appeared on the screen alone for 5 seconds. after which it was joined by the target, and the pair remained onscreen together for an additional 2.5 seconds. Thus, the offset cues were presented for the same amount of time as the long cues, but the offset cues and targets were presented as a pair for the same amount of time as the short pairs.

If cues that evoke higher levels of familiarity produce longer search times, don't know should be longer for offset and long pairs than for short pairs because the offset and long cues should be more strongly encoded. The effective-search hypothesis predicts that the additional time searching will increase the proportion of correct responses in these conditions. The ineffective-search hypothesis predicts that the additional time spent searching will not increase the proportion of correct responses. The interference hypothesis predicts that the proportion of correct responses will be greater in the short than in the offset and long conditions.

Method

Subjects, Design, and Materials   Sixty volunteers from introductory psychology courses participated in exchange for course credit. For each subject, 90 nouns with normative frequencies between 20 and 50 per million were randomly selected from the Kucera and Francis (1967) pool of words used in Experiment 1 and formed into 45 pairs. Pair type was the single within-subject factor manipulated at three levels: short, long, and offset. For each subject, 15 pairs were randomly selected to serve in each condition, and one word from each pair was randomly selected for each subject to serve as the cue.

Cues were presented simultaneously with the target in both the short and long study conditions. Short pairs were studied for 2.5 seconds, and long pairs were studied for 7.5 seconds. Offset cues were presented 5.0 seconds prior to the presentation of the target, after which the cue and the target were studied for 2.5 seconds together. Study order was completely randomized for each subject to control for lag. The dependent variables of interest were the latencies and probabilities of correct and don't know responses.

Results and Discussion

The mean latencies and response probabilities are presented in Table 3. The pair-type manipulation had a significant effect on both the latencies [$F(2, 114) = 3.70$] and the proportion [$F(2, 118) = 7.04$] of don't know responses. Subjects searched longer with offset [$t(57) = 2.41$] and long cues [$t(57) = 2.60$] than with short cues, but the don't know latencies for the offset and long cues did not differ significantly [$t(57) = .29$]. Thus, subjects searched longer to relatively familiar cues.

TABLE 3   Mean Proportions and Latencies for Correct and Don't Know Responses for Experiment 3

| | Response Type | | | |
| | Correct Responses | | Don't Know Responses | |
Pair Type	Proportion	Latency (s.)	Proportion	Latency (s.)
Short	.32	3.3	.60	4.2
Offset	.37	3.1	.53	4.9
Long	.39	3.0	.53	5.0

Note: The proportions of correct and don't know responses do not sum to 1.0 because commission errors were sometimes made.

Subjects made significantly fewer don't know responses in the offset [$t(59) = 2.19$] and long conditions [$t(59) = 3.68$] than in the short condition. The proportions of don't know responses for the offset and long cues did not differ significantly [$t(57) = .33$]. The difference in proportions of don't know responses is complemented by a difference in the proportion of correct responses [$F(2,118) = 4.10$] but not on their latencies [$F(2,114) = 1.49$]. The proportion of correct responses for short pairs was significantly less than for long [$t(59) = 2.70$] and offset pairs [$t(59) = 2.20$], and the last two conditions did not differ significantly [$t(59) = .70$]. The longer subjects searched memory, the greater the proportion of correct responses and the lower the proportion of don't know responses.

The finding that don't know latencies for long and offset pairs were greater than for short pairs provides evidence that the search permission control process was positively affected by the familiarity of the retrieval cue. These longer latencies to respond don't know were also associated with increased proportions of correct responses, which suggests that the willingness to spend additional time searching was somewhat effective. The fact that the latencies of correct responses did not differ significantly suggests that increasing the strength with which the cue is encoded decreases the amount of time it takes to access at least some traces in memory, offsetting the increased amount of time associated with retrieving other traces from memory.

Experiment 4

In the prior experiments, the familiarity manipulation produced longer memory searches. Experiment 4 examined the question, in an a priori manner, of whether the use of familiarity to control search time can be strategically overridden when the subject has reason to believe that familiarity may not be a reliable indicator of memorability. It was identical to Experiment 3 with the exception that the long pairs were eliminated in Experiment 4, leaving only the short and offset pairs.

In Experiment 3, the link between increases in familiarity and study time was salient, but the presence of the long pairs gave subjects reason to believe that familiarity was a reliable indicator of target memorability. Eliminating the long pairs may lead subjects to disregard familiarity as an indicator of memorability because subjects note the amount of time studying the cue is not correlated with the amount of time studying the pair. That is, in Experiment 4, the reason why some cues produced higher levels of familiarity than others is salient, but there is also reason to believe that familiarity is not a reliable indicator of the memorability of the target. On these assumptions, removing the long cues in Experiment 4 should result in equivalent don't know latencies for short and offset pairs. As a result, the proportion correct for the short and offset pairs should also be equivalent.

Method

Subjects, Design, and Materials   Thirty-four volunteers from introductory psychology courses participated in exchange for course credit. A single within-subject factor (short pairs vs. offset pairs) was manipulated in the paired-associate cued recall procedure used in the previous experiments. For each subject, 80 words were randomly drawn from the same pool of words used in Experiment 3 and randomly formed into 40 paired associates for each subject. One of the items from each pair was randomly selected to be a cue at test, and the other member of the pair served as the target for the cue. Pairs were randomly divided between the short and offset conditions for each subject. Each short pair of words was studied together for 2.5 seconds. The offset cues appeared on the computer screen for 5 seconds prior to the presentation of the target, after which the cue and the target were studied together for 2.5 seconds.

Results and Discussion

The mean latencies and response probabilities are presented in Table 4. The results are easy to describe: The amount of time the cue was studied did not have a significant effect on any of the dependent measures. The importance of these null results can best be understood in comparison with the results of Experiment 3. The sole difference between Experiments 3 and 4 was the presence of long pairs during the learning phase of Experiment 3, and the absence of these long pairs had two important consequences. The familiarity of the cue did not affect how long subjects were willing to search memory, and hence the proportion of correct responses was the same for the short and the offset conditions. Apparently, subjects judged that the additional time spent studying the cues in the offset condition relative to the short condition would

TABLE 4   Mean Proportions and Latencies for Correct and Don't Know Responses for Experiment 4

	Response Type			
	Correct Responses		Don't Know Responses	
Pair Type	Proportion	Latency (s.)	Proportion	Latency (s.)
Short	.33	3.1	.56	4.2
Offset	.35	3.3	.54	4.2

Note: The proportions of correct and don't know responses do not sum to 1.0 because commission errors were sometimes made.

help them remember the targets, and hence length of search was based on something other than cue familiarity.

I hypothesized that familiarity would be overridden in Experiment 4 for two reasons. First, the source of the familiarity was salient because they knew they had studied the cue by itself during the time it appeared by itself in the offset condition. Second, subjects believed the familiarity was not a good indicator of memorability because the time spent studying the pairs together was the same regardless of how long they studied the cue. One might have expected that improving the encoding of the cues by increasing the amount of time that they were studied would have improved memory in the offset condition regardless of whether subjects were willing to search longer. However, during the time when the cue was presented by itself in the offset condition it might not been encoded in a manner that strengthened the cue–target association. For instance, the representations of the cue and the cue–target association may have been stored in separate traces (Murdock, 1993), and without additional search time, access to the associative trace was not improved.

General Discussion

Other Factors That Might Influence Length of Search

As a package, the results of these experiments suggest that cue familiarity can affect but does not always affect the amount of time one is willing to search memory. When the familiarity of the cue is thought to be correlated with the memorability of the target, relatively familiar cues can produce longer average length of searches and better recall performance. On the other hand, Experiment 2 showed that even when the additional time spent searching produced lower accuracy due to interference, cue familiarity positively affected the length of search. Last, when the familiarity of the cue was not thought to be correlated with the memorability of the target, it appeared to play little or no role in determining the length of search.

The final conclusion begs the question: When cue familiarity is not affecting length of search, what is affecting the length of search? It is, of course, quite possible that feeling-of-knowing judgments are at times influenced by factors other than cue familiarity. In fact, a large number of variables have been posited to possibly affect feeling-of-knowing judgments (Nelson et al., 1984).

Koriat (1993) made the general distinction between information provided by an *internal monitor* and *trace accessibility*. The internal monitor is assumed to provide information about the presence versus the absence of an item in memory based on processes that are independent of those used to access memory when performing a recall task, whereas information produced by structural retrieval processes provides clues to the subject regarding how accessible an item is. Without further specification of the nature of the internal monitor, this assumption concerning the basis of feeling-of-knowing judgments is rather unsatisfactory on a metatheoretical basis, and it has been said to be rejected on empirical grounds (Koriat, 1993). Indeed, Koriat preferred the hypothesis that the by-products of unsuccessful retrieval attempts influence feeling-of-knowing judgments. Namely, the amount and intensity of the information retrieved from memory are the basis for feeling-of-knowing judgments, and these constructs map nicely onto the global memory framework that assumes that retrieval processes produce information about specific items in memory, and global-matching processes produce information about an item's familiarity (cf. Hintzman, 1987).

This particular trace accessibility hypothesis comes up short, however, when applied to the present results. First, it is unclear why the extra-list cue-priming manipulation used in Experiment 1 would enhance the amount of target information retrieved. Second, the results of Experiment 3 might be explained by assuming that the intensity of the information retrieved from memory only corresponded to that information associated with the cue (i.e., cue familiarity), and that only the intensity of the information retrieved from memory was used to guide length of search. If one assumes that accessibility of the target trace is what governs length of search, then one would have expected longer average length of searches in the long-pair condition relative to the offset-pair condition since the targets were studied much longer in the long-pair condition and hence more information about them should have been accessible. Moreover, this cue familiarity version of the trace accessibility hypothesis cannot explain why eliminating the long pairs from the study list, as was done in Experiment 4, produced similar search durations for relatively familiar and unfamiliar cues.

It appears that length of search, at least at times, can be influenced by factors that have little to do with how accessible items are. For instance, given the results of Experiment 3, we would have expected for recall to be better in the offset condition of Experiment 4 if subjects had been willing to search longer. Nelson et al. (1984) discussed several other factors that could affect feeling-of-knowing judgments and perhaps length of search. They made a distinction between *trace access* mechanisms and *inferential* mechanisms. According to Nelson et al., "trace-access mechanisms share the characteristic that the person is presumed to have access to nonrecalled item during feeling of knowing judgments," (295) whereas for inferential mechanisms "the feeling of knowing does not monitor the nonrecalled target item." (297) Nelson et al. assigned a large number of possible mechanisms to one or the other classes that could give rise to a feeling-of-knowing judgment. For instance, the retrieval of different types of partial information was classified as a trace access mechanism, whereas cue familiarity was classified as an inferential mechanism.

Several other trace access and inferential mechanisms were discussed by Nelson et al. (1984), but given the current state of the science of structural memory theory, some of the distinctions between trace access and inferential mechanisms are a bit blurry. For instance, producing cue familiarity involves access to the contents of trace representing the cue, even if those contents are not available to the subject. More generally, one might define a trace access mechanism as one that provides information about a particular aspect of an item in memory, whereas an inferential mechanism provides information that is not specific to any particular item. The latter type of information could be used to affect the length of search for a particular cue based on what is known or believed about the typical item or class of items. Such a conceptualization of trace access is more consistent with Koriat's (1993) model while preserving Nelson et al.'s (1984) notion of the possibility that other factors can affect feelings of knowing or length of search.

In the present case, for instance, it seems plausible that subjects learned some-thing about the nature of the study list as a whole in addition to the individual word pairs that comprised it. That is, in Experiment 3 subjects might have noticed that cue strength was positively (if not perfectly) correlated with target strength, whereas in Experiment 4 they were independent of each other. When combined with a heuristic that states that the familiarity of the cue is a valid predictor of successful recall only when it is positively correlated with strength with which the target is encoded, sub-jects may choose to utilize cue familiarity as a determinant of length of search.

On the Accuracy of Feeling-of-Knowing Judgments

In addition to the factors that affect feeling-of-knowing judgments and length of search, a critical question has to do with why feeling-of-knowing judgments are only moderately predictive of subsequent criterial testing performance (cf. Nelson & Narens, 1990). Koriat (1993) proposed that trace access mechanisms might provide information that leads to either correct or incorrect feeling-of-knowing judgments. Because subjects have no direct way of assessing the validity of the information retrieved from memory, feeling-of-knowing judgments can be misleading. On the other hand, memory strength or familiarity has no direct influence on feeling-of-knowing judgments but is simply assumed to be correlated with the amount of par-tial information that is retrieved about the target such that increases in memory strength produce more correct partial information and less incorrect partial infor-mation, leading to a positive correlation between feeling-of-knowing judgments and recognition performance.

The assumption that memory strength and the retrieval of partial information are correlated is called into question by factors that have opposite effects on recogni-tion and recall, such as word frequency (Gillund & Shiffrin, 1984). In addition, two findings from Experiments 1 and 2 call into question the assumption that familiar-ity does not have a direct effect on feeling-of-knowing judgments. In Experiment 1, some of the cues used in the cued recall phase were presented prior to the study list as a part of a word fragment completion task. Later, when cued recall was tested, subjects were willing to search longer when cued with a previously primed word. In Experiment 2, the study list consisted of some cues that were only randomly similar to the other cues on the study list, whereas the remaining cues were semantic asso-ciates of another cue on the study list. Because familiarity is assumed to be a posi-tive function of the similarity between a retrieval cue and the contents of memory (i.e., the target trace and the traces of other studied items) semantically similar cues should have seemed more familiar at test than randomly similar cues. The finding that semantically similar cues produced longer average lengths of search confirmed these assumptions. While these findings are consistent with a cue familiarity hypoth-esis, it is difficult within a global memory framework to explain why these operations would have led to increases in the amount of partial target information retrieved.

Here, I propose that the relatively moderate correlations between feeling-of-know-ing judgments and recognition accuracy might be the result of at least three factors. First, methodological factors can negatively affect feeling-of-knowing judgments.

Typically, feeling-of-knowing judgments are only obtained after unsuccessful attempts to recall. However, subjects presumably had access to the types of information used to make feeling-of-knowing judgments even when recall was successful. In these cases, one would expect that the feeling-of-knowing judgments are much better predictors of recognition performance.

Second, feeling-of-knowing judgments based on inferential mechanisms might be misleading, or the heuristic used might not be valid. For instance, one might expect that feeling-of-knowing judgments made in the offset condition in Experiment 2 would be less predictive of recognition than those made in the same condition of Experiment 1. Confirmation of this rather speculative hypothesis must wait for further experimentation.

Last, the accuracy of feeling-of-knowing judgments might be negatively influenced by cue familiarity. As mentioned in the introduction to this chapter, structural theories of memory typically assume that a global-matching process is responsible for producing a sense of familiarity associated with the nominal cue. The global-matching assumption assumes that the retrieval cue is compared to many traces in memory in addition to the target trace. This produces a somewhat noisy result as the spurious matches or mismatches influence the familiarity that results from memory access. To the extent that spurious matches provide misleading levels of cue familiarity, one expects that feeling-of-knowing judgments are inaccurate predictors of subsequent recognition performance.

Conclusions

This endeavor was relatively unusual because it acknowledged the contributions of both structural and metamemory research by combining them in a single project that investigated the controlled use of human memory. There remain many issues to investigate concerning the interaction of structural and metamemory processes, and I hope that this research provides a reasonable example of how they might be addressed.

The present experiments were jointly motivated by common assumptions made by structural memory and metamemory theories. I was particularly intrigued by the possibility of gathering relevant observations that could help extend extant memory models to the temporal dynamics associated with retrieval, an issue that is usually ignored for sake of simplicity. I was also intrigued by the possibility of constraining several hypotheses concerning length of search made in the metamemory literature by several well-supported assumptions made by structural memory models. Based on these assumptions, the present results supported the notion that cue familiarity can affect how long one is willing to search memory, but only when cue familiarity is not attributed to spurious factors. In addition, the length of search appears to be only incidentally related to its effectiveness.

Note

1. Although the use of familiarity in recall has not been widely examined, it has not been ignored. Some composite storage memory models like composite holographic associative recall model (CHARM) (Eich, 1982) and theory of distributed associative memory (TODAM) (Murdock, 1982) posit that a matching process is involved in a postretrieval deblurring process that is used to eliminate noise from the retrieved content in cued recall (see Goebel & Lewandowsky, 1991; and Snodgrass, 1987, for critiques). The noisy output is matched against a lexicon of possible responses, and the highest match is chosen as the response. In search of associative memory (SAM) and retrieving effectively from memory (REM) (Diller, Nobel, & Shiffrin, 2001; Gillund & Shiffrin, 1984; Raaijmakers & Shiffrin, 1981), sampling probability for recall is based on the similarity of the retrieval cues and traces relative to the normalized to global-match strength.

References

Anderson, J. R. (1981). Interference: The relationship between response latency and response accuracy. *Journal of Experimental Psychology: Human Learning and Memory, 7,* 326–343.

Anderson, M. C., & Neely, J. H. (1996). Interference and inhibition in memory retrieval. In E. L. Bjork & R. A. Bjork (Eds.), *Memory handbook of perception and cognition* (pp. 237–313). San Diego, CA: Academia Press.

Atkinson, R. C., & Juola, J.F. (1973). Factors influencing speed and accuracy of word recognition. In S. Kornblum (Ed.), *Attention and performance* (Vol. 4, pp. 583–612). New York: Academic Press.

Atkinson, R. C., & Shiffrin, R. M. (1968). Human memory: A proposed system and its control processes. In W. E. Spence & J. T. Spence (Eds.), *The psychology of learning and motivation* (Vol. 2, 89–195). New York: Academic Press.

Battig, W. F., & Montague, W. E. (1969). Category norms for verbal items in 56 categories: A replication and extension of the Connecticut norms. *Journal of Experimental Psychology, 80,* 1–46.

Benjamin, A. S. (2005). Response speeding mediates the contribution of cue familiarity and target retrievability to metamnemonic judgments. *Psychonomic Bulletin & Review, 12,* 874–879.

Clark, S. E. (1998). Recalling to recognize and recognizing recall. In C. Izawa (Ed.), *On human memory: Evolution, progress, and reflections on the 30th anniversary of the Atkinson-Shiffrin model* (pp. 215–244). Hillsdale, NJ: Erlbaum.

Clark, S. E., & Gronlund, S. D. (1996). Global matching models of recognition memory: How the models match the data. *Psychonomic Bulletin & Review, 3,* 37–60.

Diller, D. E., Nobel, P. A., & Shiffrin, R. M. (2001). An ARC-REM model for accuracy and response time in recognition and recall. *Journal of Experimental Psychology: Learning, Memory, and Cognition, 27,* 414–435.

Eich, J. M. (1982). A composite holographic associative recall model. *Psychological Review, 89,* 627–661

Estes, W. K. (1994). *Classification and cognition.* New York: Oxford University Press.

Gillund, G., & Shiffrin, R. M. (1984). A retrieval model for both recognition and recall. *Psychological Review, 91,* 1–67.

Glucksberg, S., & McCloskey, M. (1981). Decision about ignorance: Knowing that you don't know. *Journal of Experimental Psychology: Human Learning and Memory, 7,* 311–325.

Goebel, R. P., & Lewandowsky, S. (1991). Retrieval measures in distributed memory models. In E. Hockley & S. Lewandowsky (Eds.), *Relating theory and data: Essays on human memory in honor of Bennet B. Murdock* (pp. 509–528). Hillsdale, NJ: Erlbaum.

Hintzman, D. L. (1987). Recognition and recall in MINERVA2: Analysis of the "recognition failure" paradigm. In P. Morris (Ed.), *Modeling cognition: Proceedings of the international workshop on modeling cognition* (215–229). London: Wiley.

Hintzman, D. L., Caulton, D. A., & Levitin, D. J. (1994). Retrieval dynamics in recognition and list discrimination: Further evidence of separate processes of familiarity and recall. *Memory & Cognition, 26*, 449–462.

Humphreys, M. S., Bain, J. D., & Pike, R. (1989). Different way to cue a coherent memory system: A theory of episodic, semantic, and procedural tasks. *Psychological Review, 96*, 208–233.

Koriat, A. (1993). How do we know what we know? The accessibility model of the feeling of knowing. *Psychological Review, 100*, 609–639.

Kucera, H., & Francis, W. (1967). *Computational analysis of present-day American English.* Providence, RI: Brown University Press.

Malmberg, K. J., Holden, J. E., & Shiffrin, R. M. (2004). Modeling the effects of repetitions, similarity, and normative word frequency on judgments of frequency and recognition memory. *Journal of Experimental Psychology: Learning, Memory, and Cognition, 30*, 319–331.

Malmberg, K. J., & Shiffrin, R. M. (2005). The "one-shot" hypothesis for context storage. *Journal of Experimental Psychology: Learning, Memory, and Cognition, 31*, 322–336.

Malmberg, K. J., & Xu, J. (2007). On flexibility and on the fallibility of associative memory. *Memory & Cognition, 35*, 545–556.

Malmberg, K. J., Zeelenberg, R., & Shiffrin, R.M. (2004). Turning up the noise or turning down the volume? On the nature of the impairment of episodic recognition memory by midazolam. *Journal of Experimental Psychology: Learning, Memory, and Cognition, 30*, 540–549.

Mandler, G. (1980). Recognizing: The judgment of previous occurrence. *Psychological Review, 87*, 252–271.

Mandler, G. (1991). Your face looks familiar but I can't remember your name: A review of dual-process theory. In W. E. Hockley & S. Lewandowsky (Eds.), *Relating theory and data: Essays on human memory in honor of Bennet B. Murdock* (pp. 207–226). Hillsdale, NJ: Erlbaum.

Metcalfe, J. (1993). Novelty monitoring, metacognition, and control in a composite holograph associative recall model: Implication for Korsakoff amnesia. *Psychological Review, 100*, 3–22.

Metcalfe, J. M., Schwartz, B. L., & Joaquim, S. G. (1993). The cue-familiarity heuristic in metacognition. *Journal of Experimental Psychology: Learning, Memory, and Cognition, 19*, 861–861.

Murdock, B. B. (1993). TODAM2: A model for the storage and retrieval of item, associative, and serial-order information. *Psychological Review, 100*, 183–203.

Nelson, T. O., Gerler, D., & Narens, L. (1984). Accuracy of feeling of knowing judgments for predicting perceptual identification and relearning. *Journal of Experimental Psychology: General, 113*, 282–300.

Nelson, T. O., & Narens, L. (1990). Metamemory: A theoretical framework and new findings. In G. Bower (Ed.), *The psychology of learning and motivation: Advances in research and theory* (pp. 125–173). New York: Academic Press.

Raaijmakers, J. G. W., & Shiffrin, R. M. (1981). Search of associative memory. *Psychological Review, 88*, 93–134.

Rajaram, S., & Roediger, H.L. III (1993). Direct comparison of four implicit memory tests. *Journal of Experimental Psychology: Learning, Memory, and Cognition, 9*, 765–776.

Ratcliff, R. (1993). Methods for dealing with reaction time outliers. *Psychological Bulletin, 114*, 510–532.

Ratcliff, R., Clark, S. E., & Shiffrin, R. M. (1990). The list-strength effect I: Data and discussion. *Journal of Experimental Psychology: Learning, Memory, and Cognition, 16*, 162–178.

Reder, L. M. (1987). Strategy selection in question answering. *Cognitive Psychology, 12*, 90–138.

Reder, L. M., Nhouyvanisvong, A., Schunn, C. D., Ayers, M. S., Angstadt, P., & Hiraki, K. (2000). A mechanistic account of the mirror effect for word frequency: A computational model of remember–know judgments in a continuous recognition paradigm. *Journal of Experimental Psychology: Learning, Memory, and Cognition, 26*, 294–320.

Schwartz, B. L., & Metcalfe, J. M. (1992). Cue familiarity but not target retrievability enhances feeling-of-knowing judgments. *Journal of Experimental Psychology: Learning, Memory, and Cognition, 18*, 1074–1083.

Shiffrin, R. M., & Steyvers, M. (1997). A model for recognition memory: REM: retrieving effectively from memory. *Psychonomic Bulletin & Review, 4*, 145–166.

Snodgrass, J. G. (1987). Discussion of chapter by Murdock. In D. S. Gorfein & R. R. Hoffman (Eds.), *Memory and learning: The Ebbinghaus centennial conference* (pp. 311–318). Hillsdale, NJ: Erlbaum.

Yonelinas, A. P. (2002). The nature of recollection and familiarity: A review of 30 years of research. *Journal of Memory and Language, 46*, 441–517.

Tales from the Crypt ... omnesia

Timothy J. Perfect and Louisa J. Stark

Introduction

Consider the problems facing a research student trying to think of a novel experiment to test a theoretical idea that forms the core of her doctoral thesis. Given the limitations of time and energy, it is likely that the student is working in constrained circumstances. She probably has not read everything she should have and is unlikely to have understood everything she has read. Unless she is particularly assiduous, she will not have made notes on everything she has read or discussed with her adviser, and it is certain that she will not have perfect recall for the material to which she has been exposed. Nevertheless, our hypothetical student is determined to excel, and as the midnight oil burns away, she suddenly has a creative insight, and the next experiment comes to her in a flash. Eureka! The next day she proudly presents her idea to her adviser, convinced that suitable praise will be lavished on her.

Now imagine her disappointment when the adviser (wise and all-knowing as this hypothetical adviser is) tells her that it is an excellent idea. So good in fact, that it was published by John Doe 5 years ago. Worse, the adviser told them to go and read Doe's work 3 months ago, or perhaps worse yet, the adviser is John Doe. The student's apparent flash of creative genius was in fact a memory but was not experienced as such. In fact, the student appears to have *unconsciously plagiarized* the prior event, mistaking something old for something new. She thought someone else's idea was her new idea, a rather disturbing metacognitive error.

Informal discussion with colleagues indicates that such experiences are not uncommon. It is not just struggling students who make such errors; the literature contains a number of anecdotal accounts of how famous academics have unwittingly plagiarized others. Freud's "discovery" that everyone starts life initially bisexual was in fact a plagiarized idea. His colleague Fliess had suggested this to him 2 years earlier. Freud initially denied that Fliess had told him this, claiming the idea as his own, before later recollecting the original exchange and acknowledging his plagiarism (Taylor, 1965). Skinner (1983), in a review of his own experience as an older academic, acknowledged that a dispiriting experience of his later life had been to generate seemingly novel and insightful ideas, only to discover that they were old ideas that he had published many years before. In the creative industries, there are numerous cases in which successful prosecutions have been based on the notion of unconscious plagiarism. Perhaps the most famous case is that of George Harrison, who was found guilty of copyright infringement (i.e., plagiarism) of the Chiffons' hit "He's So Fine" with his own song "My Sweet Lord" (*Bright Tunes Music Corp v. Harrisongs Music Ltd.*, 1976).

The court ruled that he had not intentionally plagiarized the song but had copied what was in his unconscious mind (Self, 1993) and so found him guilty.

In the hypothetical scenario, the student confused a memory for the act of creativity. Another case of plagiarism is when two (or more) people claim to be the source of an original idea. That is, the people concerned acknowledge that the idea is a memory, but they dispute whose memory it is. Examples of such errors might be two scientists arguing over which of them was responsible for a particular discovery, spouses arguing over whose idea it was to take a holiday in Mexico, or siblings arguing over which of them had given the cat a haircut when they were 4 years old. In each case, the partners may remember the event, but each remembers it differently and claims the memory as their own. Assuming that they both did not have the same experience, one has plagiarized the other.

In this chapter, we explore some metacognitive aspects of unconscious plagiarism errors. In the first section, we review the original laboratory studies of unconscious plagiarism, detailing the methodology by which unconscious plagiarism has been studied and outlining the factors that influence the rate of unconscious plagiarism that is observed in laboratory tasks. In the appendix, we tabulate the results of the major studies we discuss to enable the reader to get a feel for the overall pattern of findings in the literature. We introduce some of our work exploring how the way people think about ideas can influence the likelihood of plagiarizing. In the final section, we review the issue of the degree to which people believe that a plagiarized idea is their own, presenting new data on this topic.

The Brown and Murphy (1989) Paradigm

The first laboratory research on unconscious plagiarism was conducted by Brown and Murphy (1989), and their paradigm has come to dominate the field, so we describe it in detail here. Their first two studies involved a three-stage paradigm, beginning with a group problem-solving session. In groups of four, each participant was asked in turn to orally generate a member of a semantic category (e.g., fruits) without repeating an answer given previously. In this manner, the group generated 16 items for each of 4 conceptual categories. Following this initial generation phase, participants were later asked to recall the items that they had originally generated to each category cue (the recall-own task) and finally to generate four completely new members of the category that no one had previously generated (the generate-new task).

Brown and Murphy (1989) reported plagiarized errors in all stages of the experiment. That is, during the generation phase, 3.4% of generated items were repetitions of an idea generated earlier in the sequence of responses. During the recall-own phase, 7.3% of items were claimed as memories when in fact they had been generated by someone else, and during the generate-new phase, 8.6% of items purported to be new were in fact repetitions of previously presented ideas. Analysis across all tasks revealed that the overwhelming majority of people plagiarized. When plagiarism errors did occur, they tended to be higher-frequency items, and they were more likely to have been an idea generated by the member of the group that preceded the plagiarizer during the generation phase. In Experiment 2, two additional factors were manipulated, and a measure of confidence was taken. We return to the confidence data later, but for now, the two factors of interest were the nature of the categories used to cue generation, with semantic categories contrasted with orthographic categories (e.g., words beginning with *be*). The second factor was the extent to which members of the group initially generated answers to the same category cue at the same time. In the whole condition, which replicated the first experiment, all participants generated members of each category at the same time, until 16 items had been produced, and then all moved on to the next category cue. In contrast, the quarter condition had the group generate four items from a category before moving on to the next category. This was cycled through four times to obtain the same number of exemplars. The single condition completely intermixed the four categories and had each participant give an answer to a different cue on each trial in randomized order. In the control condition, each participant generated exemplars to a different category. As before, plagiarism was observed in all three phases of the experiments (generation phase, 8.8%; recall-own phase, 10.3%; generate-new phase, 14.0%). For the generation phase, there was a main effect of group, with participants in the single condition more likely to repeat a response already given than in the other conditions, but these errors did not differ across category type. For the recall-own phase, there was no effect of group, but plagiarism errors were more likely for the orthographic category cues. Neither factor was significant for the analysis of plagiarism errors in the generate-new phase.

In the final experiment, participants were tested individually, with the other group members replaced by cue cards with (semantic) category members on them. Participants were required to read through these cards, interjecting their own responses to the cue every fourth item. Testing proceeded as before. Again, participants repeated previously seen items during generation (3.9%), recalled visually presented items as having been generated by themselves (3.9%), and generated old items when asked to think of new exemplars (9.8%).

While the Brown and Murphy (1989) paradigm has proven enormously influential and has been taken up by a number of subsequent researchers, it is worth considering whether the evidence above truly constitutes evidence that unconscious plagiarism has been captured in the laboratory. We consider three potential critiques: (1) base rate, (2) plagiarism or output-monitoring error, and (3) confidence.

What Is the Appropriate Base Rate?

Brown and Murphy (1989) spent a good deal of time discussing the appropriate rate of repetition errors one would expect to see in the recall-own and generate-new phases of the experiment in the absence of unconscious plagiarism. However, it is worth dwelling for a moment on what exactly is meant by the claim that particular errors are caused by *unconscious plagiarism*. In the generate-new phase, unconscious plagiarism for previously studied items occurs because those items have residual activation from the study phase that increases the likelihood of item selection for output, while insufficiently strong for the participants to classify the item as old. In essence, this reduces unconscious plagiarism in the generate-new task to a form of implicit memory, under exclusion instructions (e.g., Jacoby, 1996). That is, participants are instructed to generate items to a cue, excluding any that are recollected as having been experienced in the previous session. However, with a restricted set of possible responses, such as types of fruit, there is always the possibility that people will reproduce an old item by chance in the absence of any implicit memory for the old item. The question then is whether the rate of repeated responses (e.g., 8.6% in Experiment 1) reflects implicit memory or chance.

To estimate the likelihood of repetitions by chance, Brown and Murphy (1989) used the likelihood of self-repetition on a recall attempt or in a semantic generation task. On the basis of a brief review of the literature, they argued that the likelihood of self-repetition was on the order of 1.6%. That is, when attempting to produce a list of items to demand, participants accidentally repeat themselves on 1.6% of occasions. Brown and Murphy (1989) argued that rates of repetition errors higher than this represent an influence of the generation phase and hence are evidence of unconscious plagiarism. However, as others have argued (e.g., Tenpenny, Keriazakos, Lew, & Phelan, 1998) this rate may be an underestimate because self-generated items are particularly strong in memory relative to other-generated items. While weaker memory may result in unconscious plagiarism due to partial activation of an old memory, it also raises the likelihood of duplication of previous responses by chance. To understand why, think of a truly naïve participant who is asked to generate fruits in the generate-new phase having not been part of the study phase. In the absence of any memory, the participant is most likely to generate more frequent category members (apple, banana) and thus reproduce responses given previously. Brown and Murphy (1989) acknowledged this point since they reported that a control group who, having not been exposed to the initial generation phase, produced 17.5% "plagiarisms" by chance at test. But, crucially, this is not unconscious plagiarism since it is not mistaking a memory for a new idea. The question is whether the 8.6% of occasions that participants repeated old ideas (in Experiment 1) represents plagiarism or less-than-perfect memory for the original episode. Put another way, perfect memory for the generation phase should lead to no repetitions of old ideas, and no memory for the past leads to 17.5% repetitions by chance. How then is the rate of 8.6% repetitions to be interpreted? To support the case that this is unconscious plagiarism, one must rule out the possibility that it represents chance performance associated with forgetting half the original event.

Fortunately, in subsequent research the focus moved away from absolute levels of unconscious plagiarism to relative levels of such errors across experimental conditions. If these changes are uncorrelated with absolute levels of performance on the recall task, this enables us to draw firmer conclusions about evidence for unconscious plagiarism. That is, given the same level of memory for the past event, the same opportunities for chance repetitions should be observed. However, if recall performance is inversely correlated with plagiarism rate, the problem of differential effects of guessing remains. Examples of this include demonstrations that plagiarism increases with delay (Bredart, Lampinen, & Defeldre, 2003; Brown & Halliday, 1991; Marsh & Bower, 1993; Marsh, Landau, & Hicks, 1996; Marsh, Ward, & Landau, 1999) or with poorer initial encoding (Macrae, Bodenhausen, & Calvini, 1999). A situation that would overcome this potential criticism is if observed plagiarism rates exceed chance levels of repetition. For instance, if Brown and Murphy (1989) had reported an unconscious plagiarism rate of 50%, this would clearly have exceeded the 17.5% repetition rate seen by chance and so would have constituted strong evidence of plagiarism. While subsequent studies have reported levels of plagiarism higher than 17.5% (e.g., Stark & Perfect, 2006, in press), we are not aware of any study that has explicitly contrasted unconscious plagiarism rates with a no-study control group. If levels of recall vary across conditions, this might be a worthwhile procedural innovation to adopt in the future, although it will require careful implementation. The instructions to the control group would have to be carefully worded. Instructions to generate four fruits is likely to produce high base levels of repetitions, whereas instructions to generate four fruits that were unlikely to have been thought of by four other people may produce a different set of responses, with lower repetition levels. It is the latter that more closely mimics the instructions given to participants in the generate-new phase.

All the foregoing applies to plagiarism in the generate-new task, but what about the recall-own task? In the recall-own task, the unconscious plagiarism account is that the item is regarded as old, but participants confuse the source of the oldness to themselves. This is a different kind of error compared to the mistaken duplication of a previous response when attempting to be novel, and yet the same base rate of 1.6% was used by Brown and Murphy (1989) to establish that the observed plagiarism rate was reliable. This appears rather an arbitrary figure since it was not derived from the source-monitoring literature. On the one hand, it could reasonably be argued that no intrusions should occur in a recall task since participants are free to report what they wish, and so any intrusion represents a plagiarism error. However, because participants were instructed to write down four responses to each category cue at test, there is a strong implication that they were encouraged to reduce their report criterion, and in so doing they reproduced ideas previously generated by others. However, they did so with very low confidence (see the discussion of confidence), so again it is hard to argue that this represents strong evidence for unconscious plagiarism because participants may not have *believed* that these items were originally their own.

An additional interpretational difficulty with data from the recall-own task is that participants not only err by plagiarizing old ideas. Sometimes, participants claimed that other people generated ideas that they had in fact generated themselves (i.e., reverse plagiarism). Plus, they also attributed source to entirely new items, either to others or to themselves (the "it had to be you" and "it had to be me" effects; Bink, Marsh & Hicks, 1999; Hoffman, 1997). But, because these items are entirely new within the context of the experiment, partial activation as a result of experimental exposure cannot be the basis for the attribution to self for the "it had to be me" ideas. Of course, random variation in strength, perhaps due to extraexperimental exposure, could explain such errors, but such variation would be expected for all ideas, including those generated initially. Consequently, rates of "it had to be me" errors for new items provide an alternate baseline against which to evaluate plagiarism for old items. Brown and Murphy (1989) made this comparison in each of four data sets in their article. Two showed higher rates of unconscious plagiarism than "it had to be me" errors (Experiments 1 and 2, semantic task), one showed no difference (Experiment 2, orthographic task), and one showed the reverse effect (Experiment 3). In addition, they reported the degree of confidence in the two forms of error. Experiment 2 showed that people were just as confident in the ownership of new ideas as they were plagiarized ideas, while Experiment 3 showed people were more confident in the ownership of new ideas. Collectively, these data do not provide compelling evidence that people routinely mistake prior exposure for a strong sense of ownership of an idea within this paradigm.

Plagiarism or Output-Monitoring Error?

One possibility, not acknowledged by Brown and Murphy (1989) but discussed in the follow-up study by Brown and Halliday (1991), is that plagiarism errors in this paradigm represent items that participants had intended to say but had been usurped by another group member, most likely the person speaking directly before them. Recent work by Parks (Parks, 1997; Parks & Strohman, 2005) supported this interpretation. They manipulated intention to speak in a mock debate paradigm and showed that intending to make a debating point but being prevented from doing so led people to later believe that they had in fact said the key phrase. This interpretation is also consistent with Landau and Marsh's (1997) observation that attempting to guess one's (computer) partner's responses inflated the rate of subsequent plagiarism. So, it is possible in the Brown and Murphy paradigm that participants are not so much plagiarizing others' efforts as misremembering that they were beaten to the punch in saying a particular exemplar. People may have misremembered the intention to say "pineapple" with actually having said it.

A critic might argue that this is a trivial point because participants are still plagiarizing others who originally presented the idea. However, at the time the person originally thought of the idea, it was novel (within the context of the experiment), and so the plagiarism charge is less easy to press. More important, though, is the fact that this criticism potentially undermines the whole paradigm as a model for real-world cases of plagiarism because the causal mechanism of intention to speak an idea requires that the plagiarizer and the victim be planning responses concurrently. In real-world cases, this is never the case: If the Chiffons' hit had not been in the public domain before George Harrison wrote his song, he would have had no case to answer.

Confidence

George Harrison was so convinced in the originality of his composition that he was prepared to release it as a single and then defend its originality in court. Similarly, Freud was willing to jeopardize his friendship with Fliess over the ownership of the idea of original bisexuality. Real-world plagiarists then can be convinced that an idea is their own. By contrast, however, participants in Brown and Murphy's (1989) original studies did not seem quite so confident in their plagiarized responses. Confidence was only measured in the final two studies, but in both, confidence was lower for plagiarized items than correctly recalled items or correctly generated new items. In one case, 100% of plagiarized items in the recall-own task of Experiment 3 were given the lowest possible confidence rating. Thus, participants may have mistakenly reproduced others'

ideas in the experiment, but they did not seem very convinced that the idea was originally theirs. We return to the issue of belief in the final section of this chapter.

Because one of our motivations is to understand real-world plagiarism, one point
is worth dwelling on before we continue the review of previous research using this
paradigm. Brown and Murphy (1989) provided two operationalizations of unconscious plagiarism: errors in the generate-new task and in the recall-own task. Which
provides the better model for real-world plagiarism? We believe that the answer is
actually a mixture of the two. Although the generate-new task seems to capture best
the intention to be creative in the face of past experience, reflection soon reveals that
this is only a superficial resemblance to what happens in real life. Unlike our experiments, the real world is a messy, uncontrolled environment in which people ruminate,
recollect, and mentally rehearse their past. Previous events and ideas are rehearsed
and revamped so that they are fit for future purpose. So, while George Harrison's
original error may have been in strumming an old tune when attempting to write a
new one (a generate-new failure), his final belief that the tune was his is unlikely to
have been fixed at that point in time. No doubt, part of his subsequent belief stemmed
from recalling the many occasions in which he developed the work rather than his
previous encounters with the Chiffons' hit. Thus, while he was trying to generate a
new product, his belief in the ownership of that product was based in part on recall.

Developments of the Unconscious Plagiarism Paradigm

On the basis of their data, Brown and Murphy (1989) argued that their paradigm provides a robust methodology for measuring unconscious plagiarism and suggested a
number of potential ways in which researchers could follow-up their initial findings.
Although we are less convinced about the original methodology, the paradigm has
been widely adopted. Fortunately, many of these subsequent studies have addressed
some of the problems with the original demonstration of unconscious plagiarism.

Brown and Halliday (1991) extended the work of Brown and Murphy (1989) in two
key ways. First, they demonstrated that introducing a delay between generation and
test phases substantially increased unconscious plagiarism; in the recall-own phase,
the increase was from 4.3% to 13.1%, and in the generate-new phase, the increase
was from 6.7% to 13.3%. Several subsequent studies have confirmed the inflation in
plagiarism following a delay (Bredart et al., 2003; Landau & Marsh, 1997; Marsh &
Bower, 1993; Marsh & Landau, 1995; Marsh, Landau, & Hicks, 1996; Marsh, Ward, &
Landau, 1999). Plus, Brown and Halliday (1991) included a source recognition condition that replaced the recall-own and generate-new phases for a separate group of participants. In this task, participants were presented with a series of category exemplars
and were asked to indicate whether they had been previously generated by themselves
(own ideas), by someone else (other's ideas), or were entirely new. They found that,
with immediate testing, only 2.1% of old ideas were called new, while 4.8% of old
ideas were associated with the wrong source. However, 1 week later, 6.1% of old ideas
were called new, but 19.4% of old items were associated with the wrong source. Thus,
these data suggest that memory for source is forgotten more rapidly than memory
for the item itself, in line with other research on source memory (Schacter, Harbluk,

& McLachlan, 1984), and they strongly refute an explanation for differential levels of plagiarism due to differential guessing based on no memory for the item. However, the study did not report whether the source memory errors were more likely to result in more plagiarism (other's ideas being claimed as own on a source recognition test) or less (own ideas being claimed as other's on the source recognition test).

Marsh and Bower (1993) found the same effects of delay on plagiarism rates in their study, which used a different initial task and social setting. Their participants engaged individually with a computer partner in four games of a version of the game Boggle. In each game, players saw a 4 × 4 grid of letters and had to type in words that could be completed from adjacent letters in the grid. They alternated with the computer in generating such words, which had been programmed to generate words in a normative fashion. Either immediately afterward or 1 week later, participants attempted to recall their own Boggle solutions and generate new solutions to the task. Like Brown and Halliday (1991), Marsh and Bower (1993) found that a delay significantly increased plagiarism in both a recall-own task (immediate, 7.5%; delayed, 31.8%) and the generate-new task (immediate, 17.5%; delayed, 28.1%). Thus, plagiarism was not restricted to tasks in which groups of participants attempted to generate answers to a single cue. In a second experiment, Marsh and Bower (1993) added an evaluative judgment to the generation phase of the Boggle game. After each generation (by the computer or by the participant), the participant was prompted to either judge whether the word had more than four letters (shallow encoding) or was associated with something positive (deep encoding) in a between-subject design. For the recall-own task, this encoding manipulation had no impact on plagiarism (shallow encoding, 25.4%; deep encoding, 20.7%). However, for the generate-new task, participants were much more likely to plagiarize the computer's solutions that had been subject to shallow encoding (19.1%) than those subject to deep encoding (8.2%). In a follow-up study, Marsh and Bower used the same source recognition task as had been used by Brown and Halliday (1991) and found that 16.5% of the computer's ideas were attributed to the self. This source error ("it had to be me") occurred about the same as the rate at which participants judged their own solutions as having been originally generated by the computer ("it had to be you," 14.7%). When participants mistakenly claimed a new solution was old, they were more likely to say it came from the computer (23.2%) than themselves (14.0%), that is, an "it had to be you" effect (Hoffman, 1997; Johnson & Raye, 1981).

An outcome of the work of Marsh and Bower (1993) was a two-threshold model that was tested more formally by Marsh and Landau (1995) (see also Marsh & Hicks, 1998; Hicks & Marsh, 1999). A schematic representation of this model is shown in Figure 1. This is essentially a strength-based signal detection model, with self-generated memories having higher average strength than items generated by others, which in turn are more active than new ideas. To simulate plagiarism in the recall-own and generate-new tasks, it was assumed that two thresholds pertain at test. The lower threshold distinguishes between old ideas and new ideas. A higher threshold distinguishes between self-generated ideas and other ideas. Thus, at test, if an idea passes the higher threshold, it is deemed to have been self-generated. If an idea falls below this threshold but above the lower threshold, it is deemed to have been other generated. Within this framework, it is easy to explain dissociations between generate-new

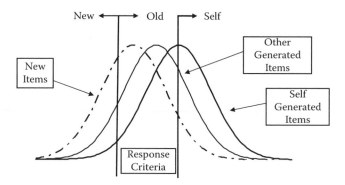

Figure 1   A schematic representation of the Marsh and Bower (1993) strength model of unconscious plagiarism.

and recall-own plagiarism. Generating old items in a generate-new task is driven by the relative strength of the other-generated distribution and the placement of the lower threshold. More errors will be seen if the lower threshold is raised or if the other-generated ideas are relatively weak. In contrast, plagiarism in the recall-own phase is influenced by the placement of the higher threshold and by having stronger other-generated ideas.

Marsh and Landau (1995) provided support for the claim that new ideas and other-generated and self-generated ideas differ in strength by means of a lexical decision task added to the paradigm. Participants made lexical decision judgments for words that had appeared in the generation phase (self or other) or were new, and participants were faster to judge self-generated words than other-generated words, which in turn were judged faster than new words. Moreover, other-generated words that were later plagiarized were recognized faster than other-generated words that were not later plagiarized, consistent with the view that these ideas represent the stronger end of the other-generated distribution and are likely to cross the higher threshold.

Since the pioneering research by Alan Brown, Richard Marsh, and their colleagues, the basic paradigm has been modified in a number of ways to determine the conditions under which plagiarism is more or less likely, and this evidence in turn has been used to inform theorizing about the causes of unconscious plagiarism. In the next section, we give a brief overview of this work, classified under a number of loose headings.

Who Plagiarizes Whom?

To date, there has been remarkably little work on who is more likely to unconsciously plagiarize or who is likely to be plagiarized. The original studies demonstrated that in a group setting, a person is more likely to plagiarize the person who speaks before he or she speaks, although this effect was not replicated in a study in which the order of generation was randomized (Linna & Gülgöz, 1994). Whether this effect (and non-replication) is due to momentary inattention as people contemplate their upcoming turn in generation or the effects of speech planning remains uncertain.

Macrae et al. (1999) manipulated the similarity of members of the group who initially generated responses to orthographic cues by having either same-gender dyads or mixed-gender dyads. Those in the same-sex dyad showed higher subsequent plagiarism rates in a recall-own task, but there was no effect of group membership on plagiarism in the generate-new task. Thus, participants were more likely to recall as their own the ideas from a partner who was more similar to them (i.e. the same sex) than dissimilar to them. However, the similarity of the group members had no impact on the generate-new phase because all that is required to prevent plagiarism is a sense of familiarity. The propensity to plagiarize from members of the same sex was replicated in a real-world study by Defeldre (2005a) using a self-report questionnaire about occasions when people had discovered themselves unconsciously plagiarizing in everyday life. However, because of the self-report nature of the plagiarism errors in this study, it is hard to establish whether such discovered plagiarisms represented occasions on which people thought they were being truly novel or thought they were remembering one of their own former ideas. Interestingly, Landau and Marsh (1997) reported a pattern that is at odds with the idea that partner similarity drives plagiarism rate. They compared rates of plagiarism on a Boggle task when a person played with a computer partner or a human partner. Like Macrae et al., they found no impact of the kind of partner on plagiarism in the generate-new task. However, for the recall-own task, participants were more likely to plagiarize the computer than their human partner. Landau and Marsh (1997) argued that this is because the human partner leads to more differentiated memories, but the source-similarity argument favored by Macrae et al. (1999) would have predicted the reverse pattern.

Macrae et al. (1999) also studied the effect of the presence or absence of the partner at final test and found that people were more likely to plagiarize their partner in the recall-own phase if the partner were absent at test than if present. The presence or absence of the partner had no such effect on rates of plagiarism in the generate-new phase. Macrae et al. argued that the presence of the partner made source more salient at final test and thereby reduced plagiarism, although they acknowledged that fear of social sanctions might have caused people to change their report criteria.

In a laboratory study using an orthographic generation task, Defeldre (2005b) examined the rate of plagiarism in younger and older adults using the rationale that because older adults have a documented source-monitoring deficit, they should show higher rates of plagiarism in a recall-own task. One week after the generation task, participants attempted to recall their own answers. While older adults recalled slightly fewer of the original ideas, there was no evidence of the expected increase in recall-own plagiarism, although older adults did intrude new items (i.e., items never generated in Phase 1) at twice the rate of their younger counterparts. More recently, McCabe, Smith, and Parks (2007) used the standard laboratory paradigm to explore the propensity of older adults to plagiarize. Unlike Defeldre, they did find that older adults were more likely than their younger counterparts to plagiarize, both in a generate-new task (Experiments 1 and 2) and in a recall-own task (Experiment 2). Moreover, they found that generate-new plagiarism errors were predicted by measures of episodic recall and working memory capacity, and that once these factors were controlled for, no variance was associated with age. Because they only tested recall-own plagiarism in one study, they did not attempt a similar analysis for such errors. This is a pity given the theoretical claims about the differential basis for generate-new and recall-own plagiarism. Clearly, given the different results shown by the two aging studies and the novel regression approach taken by McCabe et al. (2007), age-related change in unconscious plagiarism is an area worthy of further exploration.

In Which Tasks Does Plagiarism Occur?

A number of authors have striven to expand the range of tasks for which plagiarism can be generated, beyond semantic and orthographic category generation and Boggle task solutions. Defeldre's (2005a) survey of everyday plagiarism errors found that plagiarism can indeed be experienced in a range of domains, from the anticipated attempts at creativity in the domains of literature and music, to more prosaic activities such as thinking of a nickname, thinking of new games for scouts, and inventing a cocktail. In the laboratory, researchers have shown plagiarism both in extended verbal tasks and in pictorial tasks.

The extended verbal tasks used are ones in which participants hear or generate solutions to problems such as ways to reduce traffic accidents rather than generating members of semantic categories. Marsh et al. (1997) used this initial task to explore rates of unconscious plagiarism in subsequent generate-new and source recognition tasks. Across four experiments testing generate-new plagiarism, participants reliably reproduced old solutions to the problems when attempting to generate new solutions between 6.3% and 24.5% of the time. However, when re-presented with a mixture of old and new ideas and asked to judge the source, participants attributed other's ideas to themselves (i.e., plagiarized on a source-monitoring test) on less than 2% of occasions. We return to this issue in the final section, where we discuss belief in plagiarized errors. Similarly, Bink et al. (1999) demonstrated that participants plagiarized previously heard solutions to problems when attempting to generate new ones. Interestingly, participants were more likely to plagiarize credible sources of solutions to traffic problems (town planners) than less-credible sources (undergraduates), even though the ideas were identical. More recently, we (Stark & Perfect, 2006, 2007, 2008; Stark, Perfect, & Newstead, 2005) have shown plagiarism in both generate-new and recall-own tasks following an initial generation of alternate uses for common objects, such as a brick or a paperclip.

A modified version of the Brown and Murphy (1989) paradigm involves exposing participants to "example" solutions to problems rather than being involved in a generation phase. This procedure has been adopted in a series of studies looking at plagiarism in the attempted production of novel pictures. For instance, in a study when participants were asked to draw space creatures from their wildest imaginations, they tended to conform to more earthly stereotypes such as having standard body shapes, two eyes, one mouth, and so forth (Ward, 1994). Marsh, Landau, and Hicks (1996) gave participants three exemplars of space creatures that all contained antennae, a tail, and four legs. Despite instructions to avoid basing answers on the exemplars, participants' attempted new creations were more likely to contain these key features than those of a control group given the same instructions but who had not seen the examples.

What Encoding Factors Influence Plagiarism Rates?

Because the Brown and Murphy (1989) paradigm necessarily begins with a generation phase in which idea ownership is established, it is perhaps not surprising that
encoding factors have been little explored. Only two studies have been reported in
which the quality of the initial encoding was related to the subsequent propensity to
plagiarize. The first was that of Marsh and Bower (1993), as discussed, who reported
that shallow encoding led to more generate-new plagiarism than deeper encoding but
had no impact on recall-own plagiarism. Macrae et al. (1999) investigated the dis-
tracting effects of a radio playing during the generation task. Distraction at encoding
had no impact on plagiarism in a generate-new task but reliably increased the propensity to falsely recall a partner's answers as theirs compared to the no-distraction
control. Thus, regarding the two tasks, Marsh and Bower found encoding quality to
predict plagiarism in the generate-new task but not the recall-own task, while Macrae
et al. found the reverse.

Marsh and Bower (1993) interpreted their data in terms of a strength model. They
argued that stronger representations in memory, due to deeper encoding, were more
likely than weaker ones to cross the threshold of partial activation and so be plagiarized in the generate-new task. However, to explain why no similar increase in
recall-own plagiarism occurred requires some additional assumptions. One, which
the authors argued for, is that the strengthening effects of deeper encoding would be
greater for self-generated ideas. Given the known benefits of generation, this seems
unlikely; unfortunately, Marsh and Bower did not provide the correct recall data to
support (or refute) their claim. In any case, without a concomitant change in report
threshold, which Marsh and Bower did not argue for, it is hard to see why deeper
encoding should not lead to more correct recall and more plagiarism, in their model,
since any increase in strength to partner-generated ideas should cause more items to
cross the higher threshold as well as the lower one. Indeed, a problem with a simple
strength model is that generate-new plagiarism errors occur when one threshold is
crossed, but another is not. Judicious placement of thresholds can explain why deeper
processing leads to more plagiarism (more items cross the lower threshold) or less
(more items cross the higher threshold). Without other data to constrain the model,
clear predictions about the impact of memory strength on generate-new plagiarism
are not always possible.

Macrae et al. (1999) argued that their data speak to a source-monitoring account
of unconscious plagiarism in which both stronger and weaker items at encoding
have sufficient strength to make an undifferentiated judgment of oldness and hence
to reject the items in a generate-new task. However, they argued that distraction at
encoding leads to memory representations that are qualitatively poorer and so less
informative regarding the source of the event. Still, they did not specify what the
nature of this information might be beyond the ability to differentiate between stored
memories. However, why greater differentiation should affect only source judgments
(the high threshold in the strength model) and not old/new recognition (the low
threshold) is unclear.

Which Factors During the Retention Interval Influence Plagiarism Rates?

We (Perfect & Stark, in press; Stark & Perfect, 2006, 2007, 2008; Stark et al., 2005) have been exploring the effects of different kinds of mental activity during the retention interval between the initial generation phase and the subsequent generate-new and recall-own phases of the Brown and Murphy (1989) paradigm. Our rationale for expanding the three-stage paradigm into a four-stage one was that real-world plagiarists are unlikely to have thought about the idea they come to plagiarize only on a single occasion. George Harrison is unlikely to have conceived of the final version of "My Sweet Lord" in a single sitting. Rather, it is more likely that he worked on it extensively, perhaps trying different rhythms or tempos, different keys, different arrangements, and so forth, as well as working on the basic tune and lyrics to his song over an extended period. Could it be that this extended mental work is what led Harrison to be so convinced that the original idea was his own and to deny the influence of the Chiffons' hit? After all, his memory for the more recent effort would be much clearer than his memory for the original song, so this could provide a plausible basis for ownership of the finished piece.

Rather than have our undergraduate volunteers try to create novel songs, we decided to use a modified version of the Brown and Murphy (1989) paradigm in which the original generation task involved finding alternate uses for common objects, such as paperclips or shoes (Christensen, Guilford, Merrifield, & Wilson, 1960). In all other respects, our generation phase matched the standard paradigm, as did our subsequent recall-own and generate-new phases 1 week later. The key manipulation was an additional phase in which participants were invited to think about the ideas again (Stark et al., 2005). A within-subject design was used in which participants were asked to think about previously generated ideas in one of three ways, which were contrasted with a final control condition. Each condition utilized a quarter of the ideas — one from each group member for each object. One quarter of previously generated ideas were re-presented, with no instructions on how they should be processed. A further quarter were re-presented, and participants were asked to rate how easy it was to form an image of the idea in use and to rate the effectiveness of the idea (imagery elaboration). The next quarter of the ideas were re-presented with the instruction that participants try to think of three ways of improving the idea (generative elaboration). All these re-presented ideas were contrasted with control ideas that had previously been generated but were not included in this additional phase.

Our interest was in the effects of these different forms of elaboration on the subsequent rates of plagiarism in the generate-new and recall-own tasks. Fortunately, the results across a number of replications and minor variants of the paradigm have been remarkably consistent, so the data from Stark et al.'s (2005) Experiment 1 can serve as illustration. For the generate-new task, both imagery elaboration and generative elaboration reduce the likelihood of subsequent plagiarism relative to control. Simple re-presentation of the ideas had no impact on this measure.

For successful recall of participants' own ideas, imagery and generation also had the same effect, increasing successful recall relative to control. Re-presentation also led to higher levels of recall than control. These data, together with the generate-new data, led to a simple interpretation of the effects of elaboration in the additional phase of our experiment. Both imagery elaboration and generative elaboration led to stronger representations of the original ideas, and so consequently better correct recall, and lower levels of plagiarized intrusions in the generate-new phase.

However, performance on the recall-own phase revealed a substantially different pattern. Relative to control, neither re-presentation nor imagery increased the likelihood that participants subsequently appropriated someone else's idea as their own. However, those ideas that were subject to improvement were subsequently plagiarized much more often than control. How much more depends on how one measures plagiarism rate. One can take an input-bound measure and reason that, because of the design, participants had equal likelihood of plagiarizing each kind of item when attempting to recall their own ideas. The fact that participants plagiarized an average of 0.53 control ideas, 0.63 re-presented ideas, 0.55 imagined ideas, and 1.7 improved ideas suggests that they plagiarized generatively improved ideas roughly three times as often as the other ideas. However, one can take an output-bound measure and ask what proportion of ideas produced when attempting to recall are plagiarized. Because recall was unequal across conditions, this produces a different pattern. For control, 28.6% of recalled ideas were plagiarized. Recall of re-presented ideas included 22.0% that were plagiarized, and recall of imagined ideas included 17.3% that were plagiarized. However, when attempting to recall improved ideas, 41.3% of ideas were plagiarized, thus showing roughly twice the rates seen in other conditions. Thus, whichever measure one takes, this is both a substantial level of plagiarism and a substantial effect across conditions.

This pattern was subsequently replicated in Experiment 2 of the same article and has been replicated many times since (Stark & Perfect, 2006, 2008; Perfect & Stark, in press). Across this series of studies, we have shown that the effect is revealed both in recall-own measures and with a source-monitoring measure, and the effect is magnified by repeating the improvement phase in the interval or by further delaying the final test phase. However, neither repeating the imagery elaboration nor forming an image of an idea that has been improved by someone else have an impact on subsequent plagiarism.

This within-subject design has much to commend it. Because the focus is on relative levels of unconscious plagiarism across conditions, it is not subject to the previous arguments about chance levels of reproduction of old ideas. Even if one were to accept that all the reproductions of old ideas in the control condition reflect chance, one cannot make the same argument about the higher rate that is seen in the idea improvement condition. In addition, because memory performance is matched across imagery and idea improvement conditions, again one cannot explain away the difference in plagiarism rates on the recall-own task as a function of different absolute memory strength. This in turn is helpful in determining what kinds of information are used by individuals in deciding on the source of previously experienced ideas when attempting to recall their own ideas.

Because the data from this series of experiments firmly refute a simple strength-based account of unconscious plagiarism in the recall-own task, we have argued that there are two avenues worthy of future exploration. These can broadly be classed as a memory content-based account and a memory process-based account. The memory process account is essentially an extension of the source-monitoring framework (Johnson, 1988; Johnson, Hashtroudi, & Lindsay, 1993; Johnson & Raye, 1981). That framework argues that people attribute the source of a mental event by reference to different qualitative aspects, such as perceptual detail, emotional detail, and records of cognitive operations. In these terms, people plagiarize improved ideas because the act of improvement produces mental events that resemble those that are produced by generation. Because both initial generation and subsequent improvement involve the task of generating elements, we have argued (Stark & Perfect, 2006; Stark et al., 2005) that it is this generative element that causes the confusion over source.

However, we have also acknowledged that there is a memory content account that cannot yet be ruled out. It may be that when attempting to generate improvements to an idea, people do so in an idiosyncratic manner. So, perhaps they may be asked to improve someone else's idea of using a shoe as a flowerpot. In so doing, they may bring to mind the idea of decorating the shoe, waterproofing it, and placing it on a shoe box as a stand. But, perhaps when they do this, it is their shoe that they are decorating and their choice of colors with which they mentally decorate it, and in their house they mentally imagine it placed on its stand. Perhaps it is these personal details that are later misremembered as evidence that the original idea of using a shoe as a flowerpot was their own. Unfortunately, at time of writing, we are unable to distinguish between these two potential accounts of the generative elaboration effect, although our efforts are ongoing (Perfect & Stark, in press).

Because we are discussing a potential memory content account, it is worth spending a moment discussing an issue that always arises when we discuss these data with colleagues. They, legitimately, ask whether recalling an improved idea is plagiarism if the content of the idea is different. We have two answers. First, our experimental instructions are very clear. We ask participants to recall the original ideas, and it is these ideas that they do recall, and these ideas that they plagiarize. In the source-monitoring version, it is the original version of the ideas that they misattribute to themselves. Thus, experimentally, we feel that we are on strong ground in saying that it is plagiarism. From an applied perspective, the issue is less black and white because in some areas one person's plagiarism is another's homage. However, legally, the courts are concerned about the underlying similarity of two ideas rather than the surface form. It is not possible to change the lyrics, add a brass section and some backing vocals, and claim authorship of an entirely new song. If "Your Way" is too close to "My Way," you have plagiarized.

Which Factors at Test Influence Plagiarism Rates?

A recurrent theme throughout this discussion is the pattern of findings with the recall-own and generate-new test formats. However, some studies have used other manipulations at test, and other test formats, to explore the practical and theoretical basis of unconscious plagiarism errors. One such study was by Marsh et al. (1997), who explored a range of factors across four experiments that utilized the problem-solving task at generation. One week later, participants returned to be tested on their memory for the previous session. In Experiment 1, participants asked to generate new ideas plagiarized at a rate of 21%. However, a group who were presented with previous statements and asked to judge the source only plagiarized (claimed someone else's idea as their own) on 0.8% of occasions. This discrepancy between performance in a generate-new task and a source-monitoring task was replicated across three subsequent studies. In addition, Experiment 2 showed lower rates of plagiarism on the generate-new task if participants were reminded of the original source of the ideas by means of a response sheet that encouraged them to think back to the source of the original events (7.8%) than a control group (21.2%). Experiment 3 showed that requiring rapid responses on the generate-new task increased plagiarism (24.5%) relative to control (11.5%). Experiment 4 manipulated two factors. One was the degree to which the instructions stressed the need to avoid plagiarism. Lenient instructions (equating to those used in the previous experiments) led to higher rates of plagiarism (16.1%) than stricter instructions (8.3%). The other factor was group versus individual testing, although this was confounded with oral versus written responding. They found higher rates of plagiarism in the generate-new task for the group (15.7%) than the individual testing (8.7%), which is the opposite effect (albeit with a different task) to that reported by Macrae et al. (1999), who found less plagiarism with group testing on a recall-own task and no effect of group on the generate-new task.

In contrast to the effects of the different test factors (speed, instructions, group vs. individual testing) on the rates of plagiarism in the generate-new task, there were no reliable effects of these manipulations in the source recognition test formats. Plagiarism errors on the source-monitoring task were numerically lower than such errors in the generate-new task in every case and reliably lower on five of eight comparisons.

In Landau, Marsh, and Parsons' (2000) study, participants initially read solutions to the problem of how to reduce traffic accidents. Half the (bilingual) participants were asked to translate each idea, while the remainder just read them. Subsequently, both participant groups were asked to generate new ideas. Following this, participants were re-presented with each of the original ideas and asked to rate how long they had known that idea. Landau et al. found a dissociation across these two tasks. Translating the ideas significantly reduced the likelihood of plagiarizing it in the generate-new task (5%) compared to the read-only condition (15%). However, the reverse effect was apparent for the length-of-knowing rating; translating the ideas led people to believe that they had known the idea for longer than if they had merely read the idea.

Belief in Plagiarism

In this final section, we return to the issue of the degree to which participants truly believe that a plagiarized idea is their own. One measure of the success, or otherwise, of the laboratory model of unconscious plagiarism is the extent to which we can explain how people can come to be utterly convinced that a memory is a novel creation or that an event happened to them when it happened to someone else.

At least two criteria need to be met for the laboratory paradigm to be successful in explaining the behavior of people like George Harrison. First, we ought to have a paradigm in which participants plagiarize with confidence. That is, participants really should believe that they thought of using a shoe as a flowerpot rather than having a vague feeling about the idea and giving that as a response to fill up a response sheet. The second criterion is that plagiarism should be evident under different test

TABLE 1   Percentage of Responses Associated with Each Level of Confidence in the Recall-Own Tasks Reported by Brown and Murphy (1989) and Marsh and Bower (1993) for Ideas That Were Originally Generated by the Participant (Correct Recall), by Someone Else (Plagiarized Ideas), or Were Entirely New (Intrusions)

Measure	Confidence Level		
	Positive	Somewhat Sure	Guess
Brown and Murphy (1989) Experiment 2			
Correct recall	94.4	4.4	1.2
Plagiarized ideas	25.3	26.6	48.1
New intrusions	24.5	19.4	56.1
Brown and Murphy (1989) Experiment 3			
Correct recall	90.4	8.2	1.4
Plagiarized ideas	0.0	0.0	100.0
New intrusions	10.4	20.6	69.0
Marsh and Bower (1993) Immediate Testing			
Correct recall	94.1	4.0	1.8
Plagiarized ideas	16.0	20.8	62.5
New intrusions	25.0	20.8	54.2
Marsh and Bower (1993) Delayed Testing			
Correct recall	71.4	18.9	9.7
Plagiarized ideas	12.5	33.0	54.5
New intrusions	10.8	20.0	69.2

conditions. In particular, plagiarism should be evident both when people attempt to generate new ideas (or recall their own ones) and when people are asked explicitly to judge the source of a previous idea. It is one thing for someone to pick out some notes on a guitar and think they are being original; it is another thing entirely to go to court, having been confronted with the original hit record, and still to claim that the second tune is original. Thus, we see this metacognitive element of belief in the ownership of the memory as a core element of unconscious plagiarism. With this in mind, the minimal requirement in the laboratory equivalent then should be a propensity to plagiarize, whether measured by a generative task (recall-own/generate-new) or a recognition task for source. However, as we discuss, the literature on the issue of belief in plagiarism is neither extensive nor compelling.

Brown and Murphy (1989) included a measure of confidence in their second and third experiments, albeit in the slightly idiosyncratic form of a 3-point scale from positive, through somewhat sure, to guess. This scale was replicated in the study by Marsh and Bower (1993), using the Boggle task with a computer partner, as described. For illustrative purposes, the proportion of each confidence level associated with recall-own plagiarism is reproduced in Table 1 for these two studies, although other studies measuring confidence could have been used in their place because they show largely the same pattern. Several points are noteworthy. First is the degree of concurrence in the pattern of confidence ratings across studies both within each article and across articles, which given the methodological differences in studies is reassuring. The second point to note is that participants were much more confident in those items they correctly recalled as their own compared to items they plagiarized and compared to entirely new items that they intruded. This was true for all studies, although confidence dropped somewhat across delay in the Marsh and Bower (1993) study, as one might expect.

The next point one could make is that plagiarized responses are sometimes experienced with high confidence. As Marsh and Bower (1993) optimistically stated, "Approximately 40% of their plagiarisms received a positive or somewhat confident rating" (p. 678). However, as inspection of Table 1 soon reveals, this cannot be taken as evidence of confidence in unconscious plagiarism because confidence for items that were reproduced from the test phase was no higher than confidence for items that were entirely new. If the plagiarized ideas had been reproduced on the basis of some partial activation, one might reasonably have expected higher confidence in those responses than in entirely new responses, but this was not so. How then are these high-confidence plagiarisms to be interpreted? One possibility is that high-confidence responses for both new intrusions and plagiarized responses represent items that were initially thought of but not produced by anyone (intrusions) or that were thought of but produced by the partner first (plagiarisms), along the lines of the suggestion by Parks (Parks, 1997; Parks & Strohman, 2005) already discussed. This, however, reduces unconscious plagiarism to faulty output monitoring. From an applied perspective, this is not a trivial point. The likelihood of concurrently duplicating a category member in an experimental setting is quite high, but the likelihood of concurrently creating the same complex idea in a real-world task, such as writing a song, is very low.

In addition to examining confidence in the recall-own tasks, both Brown and Murphy and Marsh and Bower reported confidence distributions for the generate-new tasks. The patterns were not dissimilar to those seen for the recall-own task. Correct responses (i.e., ideas not presented previously) were associated with higher confidence levels than plagiarized ideas. However, a substantial proportion of plagiarized items (between 30% and 52%) was associated with the highest confidence rating. However, whether this represents evidence for high-confidence plagiarism or evidence that some previous items are truly forgotten and so duplicated with high confidence is harder to ascertain, as we discussed.

The second way in which strong belief can be demonstrated in the ownership of plagiarized ideas is to demonstrate that participants maintain their belief in the face of different criterion tests. That is, they not only generate the item in a free-recall test, but they also judge themselves to be the original source when reminded of the existence of the original source, either by means of retrieval cues or by use of a source-monitoring test, or maintain the belief in the face of penalties associated with making plagiarism errors.

A number of lines of evidence that we have already discussed converge in suggesting that the rates of plagiarism observed in recall-own and generate-new tasks perhaps are an overestimate of the number of ideas that a participant believes he or she actually generated. One line is the demonstrations that manipulations of report criterion led to differential rates of unconscious plagiarism. Free report gives lower rates of plagiarism than forced report, in which participants have to give a fixed number of responses (Tenpenny et al., 1998). Instructing people to be careful to avoid plagiarism or financially rewarding them for not plagiarizing (Stark, Perfect, & Newstead, 2005) likewise varies the observed rates. Presumably, the presence of a partner (Macrae et al., 1999) similarly acts on the report criterion. The demonstrations by Landau, Marsh, and colleagues (Landau & Marsh, 1997; Landau et al., 2000) that rates of plagiarism errors are influenced by the form of the final test also speak to this same issue. The rate at which people attribute past events to themselves depends on which question is asked.

Theoretically, the source-monitoring framework offers a means by which these effects can be interpreted, with the idea that people subject different kinds of evidence to different levels of scrutiny to solve their current cognitive demands for source-specifying information. Limitations of space prevent a full discussion of this theoretical framework, so those interested should consult the original articles for fuller accounts (but in particular, see Marsh & Landau, 1995; Landau et al., 2000). However, we note in passing that the framework remains frustratingly difficult to pin down since it has been used to account for different patterns of results, in particular the effects of partner similarity (contrast Macrae et al., 1999, with Landau & Marsh, 1997) and the effects of stronger versus weaker encoding (compare Marsh & Bower, 1993, with Macrae et al., 1999) on the patterns of plagiarism across recall-own and generate-new tasks.

Instead, the point we wish to make about these demonstrations is the applied one: If rates of plagiarism can be moved around by means of instructional manipulations or test format, what does this imply for the degree of belief held by our experimental plagiarists in the ideas that they espouse to be their own? For instance, Experiment 1 of Landau and Marsh (1997) showed a rate of 21.1% plagiarism for other's ideas, which melts away to an error rate of 0.8% in a source recognition test. Theoretically, this discrepancy can be explained in terms of a differential application of monitoring or monitoring based on qualitatively different information, but what does this distinction mean in terms of *metacognitive belief* in those plagiarized ideas? On face value, the data appear to suggest that participants did not strongly believe that they were the source of these plagiarized ideas at all because they were prepared to concede that the ideas were not their own when asked the appropriate question. But, George Harrison was not so easily budged in his belief. Surely, at some point before appearing in court, George carefully considered the two potential sources of his tune. And yet, he went on to court.

For the Brown and Murphy (1989) paradigm to begin to explain behavior like this, we need a demonstration of plagiarism that survives changes in test format and that leads to high confidence in the ownership of those ideas. Given our success in inflating rates of unconscious plagiarism in the recall-own phase by means of a generative elaboration phase, we wondered whether such a manipulation would also increase the confidence in the ownership of these ideas.

In a recent study (Stark & Perfect, 2006), we replicated the basic procedure of Stark et al. (2005), which involved the basic Brown and Murphy (1989) paradigm with an additional elaboration phase. However, instead of final recall-own and generate-new tests, participants were given a source recognition test for the originally generated ideas. Two aspects of the results were noteworthy. First, like Landau and Marsh

(1997), we found overall reduced levels of plagiarism in the source-monitoring task relative to the recall-own task used previously. However, we also replicated the elaboration effects found in Stark et al. (2005). Relative to control ideas and imagined ideas, elaborating ideas by improving them led to three times the rate of plagiarism errors, measured this time by a source recognition test. Thus, it seems that our elaboration manipulation may begin to suggest a way in which people come to believe that they originated an idea, even when forced explicitly to consider the origin of the idea.

But, do people really believe in these ideas as measured by a confidence measure? We explored this question in a series of four experiments, which included a measure of degree of confidence in the ownership of ideas. Each experiment differed along different dimensions, but for present purposes, these are unimportant. All four experiments were essentially replications of Stark et al. (2005), using different materials, but with a confidence judgment for the ownership of each idea recalled. All four experiments had an initial generation phase, an elaboration phase involving both imagery and generative elaboration, and a final recall-own phase.

The previous effects were replicated in all studies, so here they are collapsed for purposes of analysis. Adding study as a factor to these overall analyses produced no significant main or interactive effects, so we do not focus on the cross-task differences any further. Compared to control ideas, both imagery elaboration and idea improvement led to more correct recall of a person's original ideas (control, 41.4%; imagery, 63.0%; generation, 62.3%). However, as before, only idea improvement increased unconscious plagiarism rates in the recall-own task. On average, participants plagiarized 0.38 of the control ideas, 0.47 of the imagery ideas, and 1.38 of the improved ideas. Using the output-based measure of plagiarism, based on the total number of responses recalled by each participant, it was found that 18% of control ideas were plagiarized compared to 16% of imagined ideas, but 36% of improved ideas. But, how confident were people in the ownership of the ideas they had plagiarized?

We examined this in two analyses. The first, illustrated in Figure 2a, looked at the number of plagiarized responses at each level of confidence (1 = low confidence, 5 = high confidence). There was a main effect of elaboration status, in line with the main effect on overall rates of plagiarism, but no interaction between confidence level and elaboration status. Thus, the increase in the number of plagiarized responses was equal at all levels, so elaboration is not associated with a higher number of low-confidence or guess responses. This was confirmed in a second analysis, shown in Figure 2b, in which we calculated the proportion of plagiarized responses seen at each level of confidence. Here, there was no main effect of elaboration (since we had conditionalized on this factor) and no interaction. Thus, in terms of the distribution of confidence, generative elaboration does not apparently increase confidence in plagiarized responses. However, in absolute terms, generative elaboration significantly increases the number of plagiarized items associated with high confidence in ownership. Because it only takes one plagiarized idea to result in a dispute with a rival, spouse, sibling, or fellow creative artist, it is clear that generative elaboration is a dangerous process to undertake. The fact that scientific developments are almost inevitably the product of developing other peoples' ideas through elaboration should give us all pause for thought the next time we have a "Eureka!" moment.

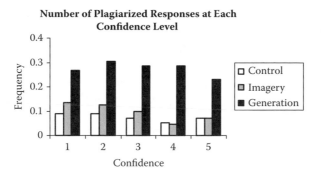

Figure 2a The effects of elaboration status on the frequency of different ratings of confidence given to plagiarized ideas.

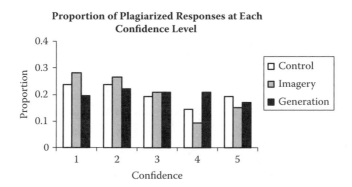

Figure 2b The effects of elaboration status on the proportion of different ratings of confidence given to plagiarized ideas.

Acknowledgments

We wish to thank the ESRC for financial support of the project described in this chapter (ESRC R000221647). We would also like to thank Lisa Son for helpful comments on an earlier draft of this chapter.

References

Bink, M. L., Marsh, R. L., & Hicks, J. L. (1999). An alternate conceptualization to memory "strength" in reality monitoring. *Journal of Experimental Psychology: Learning Memory & Cognition, 25,* 804–809.

Bink, M. L., Marsh, R. L., Hicks, J. L., & Howard, J. D. (1999). The credibility of a source influences the rate of unconscious plagiarism. *Memory, 7,* 293–308.

Bredart, S., Lampinen, J. M., & Defeldre, A. C. (2003). Phenomenal characteristics of cryptomnesia. *Memory, 11,* 1–11.

Brown, A. S., & Halliday, H. E. (1991). Cryptomnesia and source memory difficulties. *American Journal of Psychology, 104,* 475–490.

Brown, A. S., & Murphy, D. R. (1989). Cryptomnesia: Delineating unconscious plagiarism. *Journal of Experimental Psychology: Learning Memory & Cognition, 15,* 432–442.

Christensen, P., Guilford, J., Merrifield, R., & Wilson, R. (1960). *Alternate uses test.* Beverly Hills, CA: Sheridan Psychological Service.

Defeldre, A. C. (2005a). Inadvertent plagiarism in everyday life. *Applied Cognitive Psychology, 19,* 1033–1040.

Defeldre, A. C. (2005b). *The study of phenomenological characteristics and appearing conditions of unconscious plagiarism attribution errors.* Unpublished PhD thesis, University of Liege, Belgium.

Hicks, J. L., & Marsh, R. L. (1999). Attempts to reduce the incidence of false recall with source monitoring. *Journal of Experimental Psychology: Learning Memory and Cognition, 25,* 1195–1209.

Hoffman, H. G. (1997). Role of memory strength in reality monitoring decisions: Evidence from source attribution biases. *Journal of Experimental Psychology: Learning, Memory, and Cognition, 23,* 371–383.

Jacoby, L. L. (1996). Dissociating automatic and consciously controlled effects of study/test compatibility. *Journal of Memory and Language, 35,* 32–52.

Johnson, M. K. (1988). Reality monitoring: An experimental phenomenological approach. *Journal of Experimental Psychology: General, 117,* 390–394.

Johnson, M. K., Hashtroudi, S., & Lindsay, D. S. (1993). Source monitoring. *Psychological Bulletin, 114,* 3–28.

Johnson, M. K., & Raye, C. L. (1981). Reality monitoring. *Psychological Review, 88,* 67–85.

Landau, J. D., & Marsh, R. L. (1997). Monitoring source in an unconscious plagiarism paradigm. *Psychonomic Bulletin and Review, 4,* 265–270.

Landau, J. D., Marsh, R. L., & Parsons, T. E. (2000). Dissociation of two kinds of source attributions. *American Journal of Psychology, 113,* 539–551.

Linna, D. E., & Gülgöz, S. (1994). Effect of random response generation on cryptomnesia. *Psychological Reports, 74,* 387–392.

Macrae, C. N., Bodenhausen, G. V., & Calvini, G. (1999). Contexts of cryptomnesia: May the source be with you. *Social Cognition, 17,* 273–297.

Marsh, R. L., Bink, M. L., & Hicks, J. L. (1999). Conceptual priming in a generative problem-solving task. *Memory and Cognition, 27,* 355–363.

Marsh, R. L., & Bower, G. H. (1993). Eliciting cryptomnesia: Unconscious plagiarism in a puzzle task. *Journal of Experimental Psychology: Learning Memory and Cognition, 19,* 673–688.

Marsh, R. L., & Hicks, J. L. (1998). Test formats change source-monitoring decision processes. *Journal of Experimental Psychology: Learning Memory and Cognition, 24,* 1137–1151.

Marsh, R. L., & Landau, J. D. (1995). Item availability in cryptomnesia: Assessing its role in two paradigms of unconscious plagiarism. *Journal of Experimental Psychology: Learning, Memory, and Cognition, 21,* 1568–1582.

Marsh, R. L., Landau, J. D., & Hicks, J. L. (1996). How examples may (and may not) constrain creativity. *Memory & Cognition, 24,* 669–680.

Marsh, R. L., Landau, J. D., & Hicks, J. L. (1997). Contributions of inadequate source monitoring to unconscious plagiarism during idea generation. *Journal of Experimental Psychology: Learning, Memory, and Cognition, 23,* 886–897.

Marsh, R. L., Ward, T. B., & Landau, J. D. (1999). The inadvertent use of prior knowledge in a generative cognitive task. *Memory and Cognition, 27,* 94–105.

McCabe, D., Smith, A. D., & Parks, C. M. (2007). Inadvertent plagiarism in young and older adults: The role of working memory capacity in reducing memory errors. *Memory & Cognition, 35,* 231–241.

Parks, T. E. (1997). False memories of having said the unsaid: Some new demonstrations. *Applied Cognitive Psychology, 11,* 485–494.

Parks, T. E., & Strohman, L. K. (2005). False memories of having said the unsaid: On the importance of a prior intention to speak. *American Journal of Psychology, 118,* 115–121.

Perfect, T. J., & Stark, L.-J. (in press). Why do I have the best ideas? The role of idea quality in unconscious plagiarism. *Memory.*

Schacter, D. L., Harbluk, J. L., & McLachlan, D. R. (1984). Retrieval without recollection: An experimental analysis of source amnesia. *Journal of Verbal Learning and Verbal Behavior, 23,* 593–611.

Self, J. (1993). The "My Sweet Lord"/"He's So Fine" plagiarism suit. Retrieved June 23, 2005, from http://abbeyrd.best.vwh.net/mysweet.htm.

Skinner, B. F. (1983). Intellectual self-management in old age. *American Psychologist, 38,* 239–244.

Stark, L.-J., & Perfect, T. J. (2006). Elaboration inflation: How your ideas become mine. *Applied Cognitive Psychology, 20,* 641–648.

Stark, L.-J., & Perfect, T. J. (2007). Whose idea was that? Source monitoring for idea ownership following elaboration. *Memory, 15,* 776–783.

Stark, L.-J. & Perfect, T. J. (2008). The effects of repeated idea elaboration on unconscious plagiarism. *Memory & Cognition, 36,* 65–73.

Stark, L.-J., Perfect, T. J., & Newstead, S. (2005). When elaboration leads to appropriation: Unconscious plagiarism in a creative task. *Memory, 13,* 561–573.

Taylor, F. K. (1965). Cryptomnesia and plagiarism. *British Journal of Psychiatry, 111,* 1111–1118.

Tenpenny, P. L., Keriazakos, M. S., Lew, G. S., & Phelan, T. P. (1998). In search of inadvertent plagiarism. *American Journal of Psychology, 111,* 529–559.

Ward, T. B. (1994). Structured imagination: The role of category structure in exemplar generation. *Cognitive Psychology, 27,* 1–40.

APPENDIX: Rates of Plagiarism (%) Observed in Studies of Recall-Own and Generate-New Plagiarism That Have Used the Brown and Murphy (1989) Paradigm to Measure Unconscious Plagiarism

Study	Initial Generation Cues	Condition	Delay	Recall-Own Plagiarism	Generate-New Plagiarism		Notes
					Other	Self	
Brown and Murphy (1989)							
Experiment 1	Semantic categories		Immediate	7.3	8.1	0.5	Original paper discussed total plagiarism rate, including self-plagiarism
Experiment 2	Semantic categories	Whole	Immediate	5.5	10.9	0.8	
		Quarter	Immediate	4.7	5.5	0	
		Single	Immediate	9.4	13.3	0	
		Control	Immediate		21.1	2.3	
	Orthographic categories	Whole	Immediate	13.3	10.2	0.8	
		Quarter	Immediate	12.5	16.4	2.3	
		Single	Immediate	16.4	18.0	2.3	
		Control	Immediate		16.0	1.2	
Experiment 3	Semantic categories		Immediate	3.9	9.8	0	
Brown and Halliday (1991)							
Experiment 1	Semantic categories	Recall-own and generate-new	Immediate	4.3	6.7		3 people per group, generating 6 exemplars per category; at test, forced recall, but for only 4 items; no data presented on self-plagiarism
			1 week	13.1	13.3		
		Source-monitoring and generate-new	Immediate	3.1	3.1		
			1 week	6.2	6.2		

Marsh and Bower (1993)

	Material	Procedure	Delay				Notes
Experiment 1	Boggle words		Immediate	7.5	17.5	2.5	Individuals played Boggle with a computer partner; data are collapsed across item difficulty manipulation; no data on self-plagiarism in generate-new reported in Experiment 3
			1 week	31.8	28.1	7.4	
Experiment 2a	Boggle words	Vowel counting after generation.	1 week	25.4	19.1	4.7	
		Semantic judgment after generation	1 week	20.7	8.2	4.3	
Experiment 2b	Boggle words	Stem completion of partner's item at generation	1 week	31.9	14.1	6.9	
Experiment 3	Boggle words	Source monitoring added at end of standard procedure	1 week	22.8	18.0		

Linna and Gülgöz (1994)

	Material	Procedure	Delay				Notes
Experiment 1	Semantic categories	Random order generation	Immediate	6.5	11.2		Generate new data not broken down into self versus other plagiarism

Marsh and Landau (1995)

	Material	Procedure	Delay				Notes
Experiment 1	Boggle words	LD before tests	Immediate	20.8	18.7	4.9	LD = lexical decision task, conducted before or after standard recall-own and generate-new tests
		LD after tests	Immediate	21.5	19.4	4.2	
Experiment 2	Semantic categories	Recognition group	Immediate	21.3	18.1	3.1	
		LD before tests	Immediate	5.9	13.6	1.7	
Experiment 3	Boggle words	Computer first	Immediate	16.7	21.7	1.7	At generation, participant, or computer partner generate all their answers in a single block
		Participant first	Immediate	27.5	15.0	5.0	

APPENDIX: Rates of Plagiarism (%) Observed in Studies of Recall-Own and Generate-New Plagiarism That Have Used the Brown and Murphy (1989) Paradigm to Measure Unconscious Plagiarism (Continued)

Study	Initial Generation Cues	Condition	Delay	Recall-Own Plagiarism	Generate-New Plagiarism		Notes
					Other	Self	
Marsh, Landau, and Hicks (1997)							
Experiment 1	Brainstorming		Immediate		5.7		Initial task in all studies is to generate solutions to real-world problems; in first three experiments, this occurred in large groups, with no control over who generated the solutions; self-plagiarism not reported, but unlikely to high given group size
			1 week		21.0		
Experiment 2	Brainstorming/ problem solving	Standard	1 week		21.2		
		Source focus during generation phase	1 week		7.8		
Experiment 3	Brainstorming/ problem solving	Standard	1 week		11.5		
		Speeded final test	1 week		24.5		
Experiment 4	Brainstorming/ problem solving	Group/lenient	1 week		21.2		Group size of 4 at generation; instructions varied the importance of not making a plagiarism error, with either lenient or strict instructions; participants were tested in groups or individually
		Group/strict	1 week		10.2		
		Individual/lenient	1 week		11		
		Individual/strict	1 week		6.3		

Landau and Marsh (1997)

Experiment 1	Boggle words	Read	Immediate	46	38	In Experiment 1, the computer partner's initial generations were read or guessed from word stems as the word was revealed one letter at a time (generate); in Experiment 2, the Boggle partner was a human or a computer
		Generate	Immediate	56	34	
Experiment 2	Boggle words	Human	Immediate	42	36	The test phase was forced, with 4 answers per item required (i.e., 100% of generated responses)
		Computer	Immediate	50	42	Self- and other plagiarism in generate-new phase were pooled

Tenpenny, Keriazakos, Lew, and Phelan (1998)

Experiment 1	Semantic categories	Real	Immediate	4.8	21.1	Participants were asked to generate either real members of a category or fictional ones for a "made-up language"
		Fictional	Immediate	0	0	
Experiment 2	Semantic categories	Real	Immediate	1.6	24.4	10% error rate was a single response
		Fictional + definitions	Immediate	10	0	

Bink, Marsh, Hicks, and Howard (1999)

Experiment 1	Reading solutions to problems	Student's ideas	Immediate	8.0	No initial generation phase means no recall-own plagiarism or self-plagiarism possible
		Expert's ideas	Immediate	15.0	
Experiment 3	Reading solutions to problems	Student's ideas + implication	Immediate	11.0	At study, participants provided one implication of each idea presented to them
		Expert's ideas + implication	Immediate	13.0	

APPENDIX: Rates of Plagiarism (%) Observed in Studies of Recall-Own and Generate-New Plagiarism That Have Used the Brown and Murphy (1989) Paradigm to Measure Unconscious Plagiarism (Continued)

Study	Initial Generation Cues	Condition	Delay	Recall-Own Plagiarism	Generate-New Plagiarism		Notes
					Other	Self	
Macrae, Bodenhausen, and Calvini (1999)							
Experiment 1	Orthographic categories	Same sex	Immediate	24.4	4.6	2.6	Partnerships consisted of same-sex or mixed-sex dyads
		Mixed sex	Immediate	14.5	6.2	2.6	
Experiment 2	Orthographic categories	Control	Immediate	12.7	3.5	2.0	Mixed-sex dyads either worked in silence or worked with a distracting radio in the room
		Distraction	Immediate	23.5	5.2	2.3	
Experiment 3	Orthographic categories	Partner present	Immediate	9.7	3.8	1.1	Test phase was either tested alone or tested in presence of original partner; this occurred in a different room from initial encoding
		Partner absent	Immediate	21.4	3.1	2.3	
Landau, Marsh, and Parsons (2000)							
Experiment 1	Reading solutions to problems	Read only	Immediate		15.0		Participants were bilingual; in translation condition, participants translated from Spanish to English; because no generation phase, no recall-own or self-plagiarism data
		Translate	Immediate		5.0		
Defeldre (2005b)							
Experiment 1	Orthographic categories	Younger adults	1 week	23.1			Recall was forced; no generate-new phase
		Older adults	1 week	22.8			
Experiment 2	Orthographic categories	Younger adults	1 week	19.8			
		Older adults	1 week	24.9			

Stark, Perfect, and Newstead (2005)

Experiment	Task	Condition	Delay			Notes
Experiment 1	Alternate uses test	Control	1 week	27.2	23.8	Recall not forced; self-plagiarism not reported in generate-new plagiarism phase
		Hear again	1 week	22.0	25.8	
		Imagined ideas	1 week	17.3	22.0	
		Improved ideas	1 week	41.3	15.3	
Experiment 2	Alternate uses test	Control	1 week	12.5	14.5	Financial inducement not to plagiarize
		Hear again	1 week	10.0	11.8	
		Imagined ideas	1 week	16.0	7.0	
		Improved ideas	1 week	26.3	14.5	

Stark and Perfect (2006)

Experiment	Task	Condition	Delay			Notes
Experiment 1	Alternate uses test	Control	1 week	10.9	25.8	Recall not forced; self-plagiarism not reported in generate-new plagiarism phase
		Imagery elaboration	1 week	25.6	14.8	
		Improvement of ideas	1 week	38.8	21.0	
		Imagery for ideas improved by others	1 week	29.6	15.8	

McCabe, Smith, and Parks (2007)

Experiment	Task	Condition	Delay			Notes
Experiment 1	Semantic generation	Younger adults	Immediate	3.9		Recall-own errors not measured; self-plagiarism errors not reported formally; in Experiment 1, they are described as "one self-plagiarism for each age group on the task"; in Experiment 2, they are described as < 2% for each age group
		Older adults	Immediate	10.9		
Experiment 2	Semantic generation	Younger adults	Immediate	1.8	6.3	
		Older adults	Immediate	7.8	10.4	

APPENDIX: Rates of Plagiarism (%) Observed in Studies of Recall-Own and Generate-New Plagiarism That Have Used the Brown and Murphy (1989) Paradigm to Measure Unconscious Plagiarism (Continued)

Study	Initial Generation Cues	Condition	Delay	Recall-Own Plagiarism	Generate-New Plagiarism Other	Generate-New Plagiarism Self	Notes
			Stark and Perfect (2008)				
Experiment 1	Alternate uses test	Control	1 week	10.4	10.3		Separate control groups were used for the idea imagery and idea improvement conditions; self-plagiarism not reported
		Imagine once	1 week	14.4	14.3		
		Imagine twice	1 week	16.0	7.0		
		Control	1 week	19.0	17.5		
		Improve once	1 week	29.1	10.3		
		Improve twice	1 week	48.0	13.0		

Metacognitive Processes in Creating
False Beliefs and False Memories:
The Role of Event Plausibility

Giuliana Mazzoni

Introduction

This chapter represents an extension of my interest in metacognitive control to the area of false memories, in which I have been working for the past decade or so. The distinction between monitoring and control processes in metacognition, as proposed by Nelson and Narens (1990), is crucial in helping understand what happens when false memories are created.

I once had an animated discussion with a clerk at a car rental office because, when I returned the car, he could not find the slip with my credit card number. I had provided my credit card a few days before, when my partner and I had rented the car to visit the Olympic peninsula. Now, alone, I was returning the car. It took all his patience to convince me that maybe I had *not* given my credit card to him because that idea was conflicting with my very clear and vivid memory of taking the card out of my purse and handing it to him. Memories cannot lie. But, I was wrong, as I found out when I finally allowed the clerk to look under my partner's name. I had had a false memory. The clerk was right; it had been my partner's credit card that was used to rent the car.

False memories are not rare phenomena. Considerable research has established that they are relatively common (see Mazzoni & Scoboria, 2007, for a recent review) and can be created with relative ease. People can come up with false memories as a consequence of several types of procedures. Some of them involve suggestion, which includes suggestive procedures such as hypnosis (Lynn, Lock, Loftus, Krackow, & Lilienfeld, 2003; Mazzoni & Lynn, 2007; McConkey & Sheehan, 1995); dream interpretation (Mazzoni, Loftus, Seitz, & Lynn, 1999); and presentation with false information about the past, either verbally (Sharman, Manning, & Garry, 2005; Garry & Wade, 2005; Loftus & Pickrell, 1995) or visually (Lindsay, Hagen, Read, Wade, & Garry, 2004; Wade, Garry, Read, & Lindsay, 2002). In other cases, however, the degree of suggestion is minimal or nil. This occurs, for example, when false memories are created via the activation of mental processes such as visual imagery (Garry, Manning, Loftus & Sharman, 1996; Mazzoni & Memon, 2003) or automatic semantic activation (Roediger & McDermott, 1995). False memories can be developed about phenomena of varying degrees of complexity, from simple items, such as words (Roediger & McDermott, 1995), to complex life scenes, such as spilling punch on the dress of the bride's mother at a wedding (Hyman & Pentland, 1996) or having a school nurse remove a small piece of skin from one's little finger (Mazzoni & Memon, 2003).

A major question about false memories refers to how these "memories" are created. Although researchers have proposed a number of models of false memory creation, most seem to agree that, independent of the specific way in which they are created, they all entail some common processes. In particular, false memories, as well as true memories, are the result of a series of evaluative and decisional processes. It is through such processes that the "goodness" of retrieved information is evaluated, and the decision is made whether the content of mental events can be considered a memory of an experienced event. The retrieved information will be output only if the decision is positive (Koriat & Goldsmith, 1996; Mazzoni & Kirsch, 2002).

There are some important theoretical differences among the various models proposed to explain the development of false memories, even when there is agreement that they involve some basic evaluative processes. These evaluative and decisional mechanisms have been framed in terms of source-monitoring processes (e.g., Johnson, Hashtroudi, & Lindsay, 1993; Johnson & Raye, 2000); attributional processes (Kelley & Jacoby, 1996; Whittlesea & Williams, 2001); or more generic monitoring processes (Roediger, Watson, McDermott, & Gallo, 2001), among others. However, they all can be subsumed under the more general label of metacognitive processes (Koriat & Goldsmith, 1996; Mazzoni & Kirsch, 2002). Indeed, the decision regarding whether a mental event is a memory is by definition metamemorial.

In the present chapter, the role of metacognition in the *creation* of false memories is briefly reviewed. The focus of the chapter is the analysis of one specific type of information used for metacognitive decisions: event plausibility. The chapter is divided into two sections. In the first section, some false memory phenomena are briefly introduced, and a distinction between false memories and false beliefs is drawn. The role of metacognitive processes is then briefly outlined, and the Mazzoni and Kirsch (2002) metacognitive model of false memory creation is summarized. The following section is devoted to analyzing the role of event plausibility in the creation of false memories, and the results of some recent studies are reported. A model of false memory creation based on event plausibility is proposed.

The Creation of False Memories

Consider first some examples of false memory creation. False memories can be created for events of varying degrees of complexity. For example, in the well-known Deese-Roediger-McDermott (DRM) paradigm, false memories can be created for single words. In this paradigm, people are presented with lists of words that are all associated to a target word that is not presented. During recall and recognition tests, the target word is remembered with the same probability as the words presented in the middle of the list and sometimes with even greater probability (up to .87) (Roediger & McDermott, 1995; Stadler, Roediger, & McDermott, 1999). This phenomenon is attributed to an unaware activation of semantic connections between each presented word and the target word (Seamon, Luo, & Gallo, 1998). This results in high levels of activation of the target word, which in turn leads to its retrieval, which in the present context is incorrect. Activation, however, is not sufficient to explain the results, and data have shown that a monitoring component needs to be added. According to the monitoring activation explanation (Roediger et al., 2001; Watson, McDermott, & Balota, 2004), in addition to activation, ineffective monitoring of what was actually presented is crucial to creating the effect. Indeed, studies have shown that enhancing monitoring of the presented words can substantially reduce the probability of remembering the nonpresented target word (Watson et al., 2004).

False memories can also be created for simple actions and for more complex life events via a number of different techniques. In particular, imaginative techniques have been used to that aim. Imagination can create false memories for simple common actions, such as breaking a pencil or brushing one's teeth (Goff & Roediger, 1998), and even for simple but bizarre actions, such as sitting on dice (Thomas & Loftus, 2002). In the Goff and Roediger study, participants either performed, watched, or imagined a common action. On a subsequent recognition test, imagined actions were falsely recognized to a relatively high degree as having been performed by the participants themselves. These studies on the effect of imagination in creating false memories for recent actions represent an extension of prior work showing the effect of imagination on memory for more complex childhood events. In the so-called imagination inflation effect (e.g., Garry et al., 1996), asking participants to imagine a complex past event (e.g., breaking a window with one's hand, giving a friend a haircut, spilling punch on the dress of the bride's mother at a wedding) leads people to believe that the event had actually occurred.

Single (Garry et al., 1996; Heaps & Nash, 1999) or repeated (e.g., Hyman & Pentland, 1996) imagery can be used to make people believe and "remember" false events. In the repeated imagery studies, participants were asked to imagine a target event of some complexity over three consecutive days. The event was quite specific (e.g., spilling punch on the bride's mother's dress at a wedding before age six). Participants were asked to imagine this made-up event among a series of real events that had been reported by their parents. Real events included events that participants remembered and events that participants did not remember. After the third act of imagination, some people reported remembering the event with some degree of detail. The effectiveness of imaginative techniques seems to be quite extensive. For example, in the Hyman and Pentland study, approximately 25% of participants reported spilling punch at a wedding.

Although participants presumably never did spill punch at a wedding, given that their parents did not remember such event, in many of the imagination studies, one cannot be completely certain that the earlier newly remembered event had not in fact happened to the person. However, the fact that imagination can create memories that are clearly false has been definitively demonstrated by Mazzoni and Memon (2003), who showed that people can falsely remember in incredible detail a rather complex and certainly nonoccurring event, in this case having a school nurse remove a slice of skin from the participants' little finger for diagnostic purposes. We first made sure that none of the participants had ever had such procedure performed on them by ascertaining that this procedure is never done in the country where participants lived (the national and local health system was contacted as well as the national and local school administration). In this way, it was clear that any memory of the event was certainly false. Participants were simply asked to close their eyes and imagine the event as well as they could, imagining themselves as they were at the target age. Imagination lasted only 5 minutes and was then reported and written down. Memories were collected days later. That 5 minutes of pure imagination and the passing of time can create such vivid memories is a rather striking outcome.

Past events of various degrees of complexity can come to be falsely remembered via a number of variably suggestive techniques. For example, hypnosis and age regression can easily create false memories for complex autobiographical events (for a review, see Mazzoni & Lynn, 2007). Indeed, these procedures have even been used to intentionally create false memories for therapeutic purposes (e.g., Janet, 1889; McConkey & Sheehan, 1995). Since the inception of hypnosis and age regression as therapeutic techniques, some therapists have age regressed patients to intentionally create what they called "pseudomemories" of traumatic events (i.e., positive, soothing, and clearly false memories that could replace unpleasant, traumatic memories). A relatively large number of studies have shown that via hypnosis and age regression, people can falsely remember events of various levels of complexity, ranging from remembering a nonexistent noise that allegedly occurred at night in the previous week (Laurence & Perry, 1983) to remembering a mobile hanging from the crib very early in infancy, when participants were only a few months old (Spanos, Burgess, Burgess, Samuels, & Blois , 1999) to remembering one's first birthday (Malinoski, Lynn, & Sivec, 1998).

A series of studies showed that dream interpretation, another therapeutic technique that is substantially less suggestive than hypnosis and age regression, can create in the participants the false belief that complex events had happened to them early in life (Mazzoni & Loftus, 1998; Mazzoni, Loftus, et al., 1999). In the dream interpretation studies, participants reported a dream, which received a bogus interpretation. The aim of the interpretation was to convey the idea that a certain target event had happened to the participants in their early childhood. After the dream interpretation, at least 25% of the people came to believe that they had almost drowned, that they were abandoned by their parents, or that other similar mild traumatic events had occurred.

Doctored photos have been used as an innovative method for inducing false memories of childhood events that never occurred. Wade et al. (2002), for example, showed that participants believed and sometimes remembered details of a hot air balloon ride that had not occurred but for which a doctored photo had been produced. In a subsequent study (Lindsay et al., 2004), it was found that even showing an undoctored photo (e.g., of classmates) related to the period of a false childhood event can enhance the belief that the event had occurred and, along with other suggestive information, can increase the likelihood of reporting memories of the false event, which in this study consisted of putting a slimy substance on the chair of a teacher.

Although visual information is particularly effective in creating false beliefs and memories of complex autobiographical events, verbal information can also have a strong influence on the belief that an event had occurred when in fact it had not. For example, reading made-up passages (allegedly from magazines) reporting the occurrence of a false event increased the belief that the event had indeed occurred during childhood. For example, Mazzoni and Vannucci (1999) showed that reading bogus articles made some participants claim that they believed classical music was aired in the hospital nursery when they were just a few days old. In fact, classical music has never been aired in hospital nurseries in Italy, where these individuals were born, and hence these beliefs were false. False reports presented by relatives can be even more effective. In one study (Loftus & Pickrell, 1995), siblings falsely told participants that they had gotten lost in a shopping mall in their early childhood. This false information increased the participants' belief that they had indeed gotten lost and led them to remember additional details of the event.

The studies described, as well as many others not mentioned here, clearly demonstrate the degree to which memory is malleable and show the relative ease with which false memories can be created, even for rather complex autobiographical events. The main puzzle has been to understand how these false memories are created and which conditions facilitate or hinder the appearance of this phenomenon. One major theoretical explanation proposed to explain how false memories are created refers to the coexistence of two parallel memory traces for an event (which could be created by an act of imagination), one with verbatim information and one with nonverbatim, "gist" information. When an event happens or is imagined, both traces are created, but while the verbatim trace fades quickly, the gist trace lasts longer. Therefore, the attempt to remember the event soon comes to rely almost exclusively on the gist trace, which has no information about the details of its presentation or initial creation. This theory, called fuzzy trace theory (FTT; Brainerd & Reyna, 2002, 2005), seems to explain rather nicely most, if not all, false memory phenomena.

Despite its successes, FTT has a hard time explaining how people come to believe that a false event has occurred to them even in the absence of any hint of a memory of it, or how they create false memories for really bizarre autobiographical events (such as being abducted by aliens; see Newman & Baumeister, 1998). The "core meaning" of bizarre events such as alien abduction and ritualistic satanic worship seem too extreme to argue that these false memories derive from the activation of previous gist traces. Before considering other possible explanations, one should notice that it is rather common for people to believe in the occurrence of some events, even in the complete absence of any possible memory of them (Scoboria, Mazzoni, Kirsch, & Relyea, 2004). People believe they were born, for example, without remembering their birth. In the false memories arena, many studies that purportedly deal with the creation of false *memories* instead examine only whether people *believe* that the event occurred. Thus, at times, the term *false memory* is a misnomer for a phenomenon that should more appropriately be called *false belief*. If one accepts a subjective phenomenological approach to memory (e.g., as in the distinction between "remember" and "know" judgments; Tulving, 1985), in which a mental event is a memory when it evokes in the individual the *sense* of being a memory (e.g., the ability to "see" and relive the event, to "feel" that it is a memory), the logical conclusion is that in many false memory experiments, what the participants develop is not a memory for the event in question, but rather the conviction (belief) that the event has occurred without any specific recollective experience of its occurrence. For example, the original imagination inflation studies (Garry et al., 1996; see also Heaps & Nash, 1999), as well as several studies on the creation of false memories via dream interpretation

(Mazzoni, Lombardo, Malvagia, & Loftus, 1999) or via solving anagrams (Bernstein, Whittlesea, & Loftus, 2002), did not examine whether these procedures had created false memories. Instead, they only asked participants whether they believed that the target event had happened.

The distinction between false beliefs and false memories is quite important (Mazzoni & Kirsch, 2002; Smeets, Merckelbach, Horselenberg, & Jelicic, 2005) as it suggests that partly different processes might be responsible for the creation of the two phenomena. For example, as proposed by Mazzoni and Kirsch (2002), one could hypothesize a greater influence of inferential mechanisms when false beliefs are created in the absence of any (also false) memory. According to the Mazzoni and Kirsch model, the first cognitive act that is undertaken when deciding whether an event has actually happened is to initiate a memory search to assess whether a candidate memory is available for it (in other words, whether a related mental content is present and possesses the subjective quality of a memory). If a "memory-like" candidate is available, one relies on source monitoring and other attributional processes to decide whether the memory candidate is good enough to be considered a memory, thereby confirming that the event had in fact occurred. However, when a sufficiently good candidate is not available or no candidate is available at all, one has to rely on other types of information and draw conclusions based on them. These conclusions are based mostly on additional inferential processes that are not needed when a "good" memory candidate is found.

The distinction between false memories and false beliefs, first posed on logical grounds, has been confirmed empirically. In one of the few studies in which both false beliefs *and* false memories were tested, Mazzoni, Loftus et al. (1999) showed that dream interpretation substantially increased false beliefs in the occurrence of an event, whereas it produced very few false memories. False beliefs were assessed by asking, "How likely is it that you personally, before the age of six, did in fact lose a toy?" whereas to examine false memories participants were asked, "Do you actually remember losing a toy before you were the age of six?" Results showed that responses to the two questions were different and partially independent. This indicates that one can create false autobiographical beliefs without having to rely on false memories to obtain the effect.

Although the role played by metacognitive processes in the creation of false beliefs is particularly clear, especially when a good memory candidate is not found, these processes are also involved in the creation of false memories. The extent to which the characteristics people use to decide that a mental event is a memory or a belief are the same or are different has not been explored yet. Whether a memory candidate is good enough to be reported as a memory of the event and even whether a memory candidate is found in the first place rely on metacognitive factors. For example, one has to know (metacognitive knowledge) what a memory is. Although intuitively most of us know and can identify certain mental events as memories, this type of knowledge (i.e., a memory is a mental event that possesses a recollective quality, that contains perceptual details, and that conveys the sense of reliving an experience) should not be taken for granted. Indeed, it can be deficient in confabulating patients, who might mistake a sense of familiarity for a sense of recollection and hence call a memory something that only conveys a great sense of familiarity. Metacognitive knowledge also includes knowledge of what a good memory is. In other words, to decide that a mental event is a memory, one has to know not only that it includes knowledge about the extent to which a mental event needs to possess perceptual-like qualities and evoke emotions and subjective feelings, but also that the content of the mental event has to refer to the right time when the event was experienced, have the right people involved in it, and so on.

The source-monitoring framework proposed by Marcia Johnson (Johnson et al., 1993) brilliantly illustrates this type of metacognitive knowledge and explores and explains the metacognitive processes that allow the individual to evaluate the source of the information and make the distinction between mental events that have been previously experienced from an external source and mental events that had been internally produced. According to this framework, a failure in source monitoring is responsible for the creation of false memories for complex events (Henkel, Franklin, & Johnson, 2000) and may be an important process in the creation of all false memories.

The metacognitive knowledge that is used in deciding whether an unremembered event has occurred is different from that involved in deciding that one remembers the event. In the former case, the metacognitive knowledge refers to event memorability, one's memory ability, other autobiographical events, one's family background, level of familiarity of the event, relevance of recently acquired information, and event plausibility. The plausibility of the event is the focus of the next section of this chapter. Here, some space is devoted to the description of an initial metacognitive model of false memories and belief creation that takes into account these various types of knowledge and their metacognitive evaluation.

All these elements have been integrated in a metacognitive model of the creation of false autobiographical memories and beliefs by Mazzoni and Kirsch (2002). The model relies on the assumption that the decision to report an autobiographical memory and the belief that an event has occurred are partly independent and occur sequentially, with search for an autobiographical memory coming first. In other words, when answering the question "Did event X happen to you?" people first search their memory and assess whether a good memory is available for the event. The search triggers the activation of various possible memory candidates, and metacognitive processes help decide about their goodness as memories of the specified event (Koriat & Goldsmith, 1996). Only candidates that pass a certain preset criterion are considered good enough candidates and are volunteered as memories for the event. Source monitoring (Johnson et al., 1993) can play a major role in this phase. For example, elements that are in memory because they have been imagined shortly before can trick the source-monitoring process into deciding that they are good memory candidates as they possess a high degree of the visual-perceptual details that are usually typical of really experienced events (see also Hyman & Kleinknecht, 1999; Mazzoni, Loftus, & Kirsch, 2001). If imagination is accompanied by the activation of emotional reactions, the likelihood of considering these mental creations as good memories is even greater.

But, when no good candidate is found? Should an individual, not finding any memory, conclude that the event has not happened? The model proposes that, in such cases, the decision is not immediate but depends on how the lack of memory is evaluated. This evaluation is genuinely metacognitive in nature. If lack of memory is considered to be diagnostic of nonoccurrence (i.e., no memory means nonoccurrence), then the conclusion is that the event had not occurred. Conversely, if lack of memory is not considered to be completely diagnostic of nonoccurrence (i.e., even if there is no memory, the event might still have happened), then additional metacognitive inferential processes come into play, and their results will eventually determine the final decision (the event has happened vs. the event has not happened).

To illustrate this point, consider the case in which people are asked whether they had eaten breakfast on a particular date when they were four years old. Unless the date represents a very special moment in the person's life, no good memory for that specific breakfast is likely to be retrieved, but this lack of memory would not be considered diagnostic of nonoccurrence since metacognitive knowledge tells us that (1) the event is definitely plausible; (2) usually one does not remember such a mundane event as breakfast (memorability check); and (3) if the event happened, then it happened too many years before to be still in memory (time-related forgetting). Therefore, the event might have happened. Furthermore, knowledge about oneself, one's habits, and one's history might suggest that it probably happened (e.g., it was customary for my family to eat breakfast in the morning). People can also take into account their knowledge about their memory ability, so that knowing to have a poor memory increases the chances to consider the absence of a memory as uninformative about the occurrence of an event. Lack of memory in the case just mentioned is definitely nondiagnostic. Conversely, a situation in which lack of memory is considered to be diagnostic of nonoccurrence is the following: Did you ever see the president of the United States hit your secondary school teacher while riding a white horse in your classroom? The immediate answer is no, and it is based on the same set of inferences from the same forms of knowledge used in the previous example (plausibility, memorability, time-related forgetting, etc.). This time, however, the inferences simply go in the opposite direction.

This diagnostic process represents a crucial moment in the decision about whether an event had occurred. The individual's estimate of event memorability is fundamental in this phase. Bizarre events are usually considered more memorable than common events, as are more rare events or events that evoke stronger emotional reactions. How event memorability influences the creation of false memories (of simple events) has been explored by Strack and Bless (1994) in adults and by Ghetti and Alexander (2004) in children. Both groups of authors demonstrated that people tend to make false alarms more often for items that they consider less memorable, whereas fewer false items are recognized when items are more memorable. Although these studies used recognition tasks (i.e., memory), the same mechanisms ought to be at play in the creation of false beliefs.

As people vary greatly in their esteem for their memory, this individual metacognitive element interacts with knowledge about the memorability of the event itself. For example, by extrapolating from data reported by Hertzog, Dixon, and Hultsch (1990a, 1990b), one can predict that lack of memory would be more likely to be interpreted as nondiagnostic of an event by people with low memory esteem than by people with high memory esteem. People who believe that they easily forget will tend to consider lack of memory as a normal condition and, as such, uninformative about the occurrence of an event. Conversely, people who believe that they are very good at remembering consider *lack* of memory as a more reliable indicator that the event *had not* occurred.

If lack of memory is considered diagnostic of the nonoccurrence of an event, then a relatively quick "no" response should follow in answer to the question, "Did the event happen to you?" If lack of memory is considered to be nondiagnostic, however, then the final response will be much slower as it is necessary to take more information into account before the final decision is made. The final decision can be either yes or no, depending on the content of the additional information examined. This additional information can be of various types. It can refer to the event's frequency, its familiarity, the degree of activation of related information, and to a series of elements that are part of knowledge about the self. In this last group of elements, one can find knowledge about one's history, habits, behaviors, tastes, emotions, reactions, and so on, all of which enter in determining the event's personal plausibility. False beliefs (as well as false memories) are more easily created for events that are plausible than for events that are not plausible (Pezdek, Blandon-Gitlin, Lam, Hart, & Schooler, 2006; Pezdek, Finger, & Hodge, 1997; Pezdek & Hodge, 1999). This factor is important enough to warrant further exploration and is the focus of the final section of this chapter.

Event Plausibility

Kathy Pezdek and her collaborators (Pezdek et al., 1997; Pezdek & Hodge, 1999) were among the first to raise the issue of event plausibility in the creation of false memories. Their claim that one can develop false memories only for plausible events was supported by the results of two groups of studies in which the authors showed that it is virtually impossible to implant false memories for events that are highly infrequent and highly unlikely. In one series of studies, Jewish and Catholic children were asked to imagine either a Jewish Sabbath or a Catholic Mass. The results showed that it was virtually impossible to implant a false memory of attending a Mass in Jewish children, and that only a very small minority of Catholic children developed a false memory of attending a Jewish Sabbath. In another study, the authors tried to implant the memory of a rectal enema, with no success. They claimed that it is impossible to implant a memory for an event that is very infrequent and virtually unknown to people (American students usually have only a very vague idea of what a rectal enema is).

These results, which seem rather reasonable, conflict with some real-world facts. For example, there are people who hold a very strong conviction that they were abducted by aliens (Newman & Baumeister, 1998). Some of them are even able to remember the abduction in unusually gruesome detail. As it is highly unlikely that aliens (if they exist at all) waste their time in abducting, testing, and having sex with humans, these beliefs and memories can be considered false. But, people who hold them are adamant about the occurrence of these events. It is, then, possible to have false beliefs and false memories of highly implausible events. The same comments apply to beliefs and memories of other events, such as satanic ritual sexual abuses. In the United States, where this phenomenon peaked a few decades ago, the Federal Bureau of Investigation launched a formal investigation into occult satanic sects and found no evidence whatsoever of ritual sexual abuse. Nonetheless, some people hold with a high degree of certainty the belief and the memory of these rather implausible events, to the extent of bringing alleged perpetrators to court (see a recent well-known Italian case, the Mirandola case, in which many children accused many adults of satanic ritual abuse).

These real-world facts demonstrate that people can falsely believe and remember even highly implausible events. How can these data be reconciled with the experimental results showing the difficulty of implanting a false memory for implausible events? Mazzoni et al. (2001) addressed this issue by hypothesizing plausibility to be pliable and malleable, as are other event characteristics. In three experiments, they demonstrated that event plausibility can be increased by providing convincing (though false) information, and that by virtue of this increase, people can also come to develop a false belief in the occurrence of an initially implausible event. Witnessing demonic possession was the target implausible event. Participants were students at a university in southern Italy, where demonic possession is not considered to be as impossible as, for example, having one's body turn forest green. Nonetheless, all students rated the event as highly implausible for people like themselves; this means that even if demonic possession might exist, it was not conceivable that they or others in their own cultural environment had witnessed it. Students in the experimental group then read passages that described more in detail what demonic possession entails and contained some narratives about the occurrence of demonic possession in families like theirs. The passages also reported the alleged experiences of some people (e.g., priests) who narrated first-person accounts of their encounters with demonic possession. These passages aimed to provide a script for demonic possession and information about the relatively high frequency with which such events occur, particularly in the participants' social environment. Plausibility ratings increased substantially and significantly after reading the passages. When a personalized suggestion was added (i.e., they received a bogus interpretation of their responses to a fear questionnaire, indicating a relatively high probability of having witnessed events similar to demonic possession), participants' belief that the event had occurred to them in their childhood increased substantially (18% of the participants jumped to a score higher than 5 on an 8-point rating scale) and significantly. The authors concluded that plausibility is easily malleable. They also suggested that the increase in plausibility then opens the possibility for the development of the belief in the occurrence of the event. Transposed to alien abduction, the point is that, although this is a highly implausible event for most of the readers of this chapter, it might have become a much more plausible event for the people who claim they went through that experience, and this might have occurred by exposing these people to convincing information.

Mazzoni et al. (2001) proposed a three-stage model of the development of false beliefs and false memories in which plausibility played a major role. First, the event must be perceived to be sufficiently plausible, both in terms of general plausibility, which refers to the belief that the event occurs at least to some people, and in terms of personal plausibility, which is the belief that an event is plausible for the individual, and not only in general. Second, individuals must have the autobiographical belief that the event is likely to have happened to them. Third, they must interpret their thoughts and fantasies about the event as memories. If the event is initially implausible, the provision of plausibility-enhancing information is required as a first step. Although it is intriguing to consider that the creation of a very compelling false memory might in itself help to enhance the degree of plausibility of an event, this possibility has not been explored as yet. In psychotherapy, this might occur by having clients read books about the incidence of events that had not happened to them (e.g., child abuse). If it is personally unbelievable, information aimed at establishing an autobiographical belief must be provided. In therapy, this might consist of feedback about supposed sequelae abuse that fits the client's behavior. Finally, the occurrence of the event might be imagined as a means of providing a memory of its occurrence.

Important for this chapter is the idea that plausibility is a relative concept. Plausibility is relative in two ways. First, it is a continuous, modifiable variable that can be enhanced or diminished. Second, events are plausible in relation to an individual's culture and history, so that different people will have different assessments of the plausibility of the same event. The Mazzoni et al. (2001) study clearly demonstrated both of these aspects of plausibility. Personal plausibility was significantly enhanced, but only when the plausibility-enhancing information pertained to the participant's culture. People would not accept that something has ever happened to them if it is absolutely implausible that it could happen to anyone. In addition, the event must be plausible for them personally. But, what is implausible for a skeptical intellectual individual might be plausible for a more gullible person. Beliefs about facts also differ, and plausibility directly depends on them.

The distinctions among general plausibility, personal plausibility, and belief have been most fully explored by Scoboria et al. (2004; see also Scoboria, Mazzoni, Kirsch, & Jimenez, 2006). General plausibility refers to the possibility of an event occurring to anyone, whereas personally plausible events are not only possible in principle, but also for a specific individual in relation to his or her social environment, family background, and culture. Scoboria et al. (2004) noted that an event may be plausible both generally and personally without the person believing that it has occurred. In other words, the event could easily have happened to me, but I do not think it has. The distinction is based on the reference to one's own actual life experiences (autobiographical belief) versus one's potential experiences.

Scoboria et al. (2004) demonstrated empirically that general plausibility, personal plausibility, belief in occurrence, and memory of an event are partially independent, but nested constructs, with measures of the superordinate constructs being almost always greater than those of the subordinate ones. In other words, for any given event, general plausibility ratings are almost always greater than personal plausibility ratings, which in turn are greater than the beliefs in occurrence, which are greater than memory ratings. The nested model implies (and the data demonstrate) that if an event is personally plausible, it is almost always considered to be plausible in general, that believed-in events are considered to be generally and personally plausible, and that remembered events are believed in and hence generally and personally plausible. On the contrary, generally plausible events might not be personally plausible, plausible events might not be believed in, and events that are believed to have occurred might not be remembered.

How does plausibility influence the development of beliefs about the occurrence of events? What role does it play when a person seeks to answer the question, "Did event X happen to you?" Based on the ideas proposed by Mazzoni et al. (2001) and Mazzoni and Kirsch (2002), I proposed that the first step in this process is to assess whether a memory exists for the target event (Mazzoni, 2007; see also Pezdek et al., 1997). However, this search is warranted only if the event is considered to be plausible. In other words, it would be a waste of cognitive resources to search for the memory of an event that is highly implausible and that is highly unlikely to have occurred. Plausibility assessment thus represents a preliminary step, the result of which will then determine the type of ensuing processes that are activated. If the event is deemed implausible, then no memory search is triggered, and a very quick "No" response is output. Only when the event is deemed plausible is a search in memory activated.

This process is illustrated in Figure 1. The left branch represents the case in which the event is deemed implausible; the right branch represents the case in which the event is considered sufficiently plausible to deserve a memory search. As the figure shows, in case of a clearly implausible event, no further processes are activated, and the response to the question "Did the event happen to you?" should be a very quick "No." In case of a plausible event, the response could be of either type (yes or no), and more important, it should be much slower because many more processes are activated. One of these is a search in memory. If the memory is not found, then several evaluative processes are activated, by which it is decided whether the lack of memory

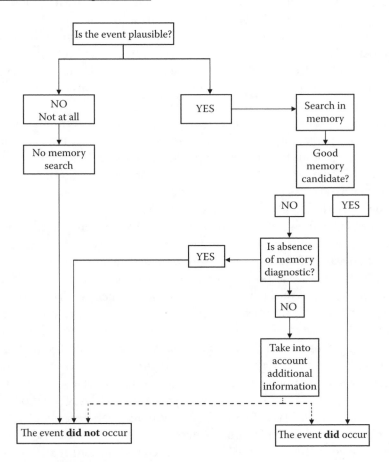

Figure 1 The effect of plausibility: a metacognitive model.

is diagnostic of nonoccurrence. If lack of memory is not diagnostic, then additional information is taken into account and the final decision (yes or no) depends on the outcome of the evaluation of this additional information.

The hypothesis described in Figure 1 bears some similarity to hypotheses about the amount of time people take in giving "don't know" responses to questions (Gentner & Collins, 1981; Glucksberg & McCloskey, 1981; Klin, Guzman, & Levine, 1997; Koriat & Lieblich, 1977). In these studies, it was found that very fast responses are obtained when no relevant information is present in memory, whereas the provision of information slows response times, even if the information is irrelevant and uninformative. The results have been explained by postulating the presence of metacognitive processes that provide a fast preliminary evaluation of the stimulus or the content of memory. Whether further search in memory or other cognitive processes are activated depends on the output of these fast preliminary monitoring processes (also see Metcalfe, 1993). Similarly, preliminary plausibility judgments may precede slower memory retrieval in sentence verification tasks (Reder, 1982).

In answering the question, "Did event X happen to you?" monitoring the plausibility of the event constitutes a similar preliminary screening that allows a parsimonious and efficient use of cognitive resources. Recent data (Mazzoni, 2007) have provided support for this model. This study was the first in which an opaque behavioral measure (surreptitiously assessed response time) was used to examine the relationship between plausibility and beliefs in the occurrence of autobiographical events. Previous studies examining this relationship have been limited to self-report measures, which are susceptible to various artifactual influences (e.g., compliance with perceived demand characteristics of the experimental situation). Surreptitiously assessed response time is less susceptible to these influences.

In the Mazzoni (2007) study, the latency of response to the question, "How likely is it that this event happened to you before the age of six?" was recorded. The prediction was that this measure of processing time would be significantly associated with the self-reported plausibility of the event, even when belief in its occurrence is held constant. One might expect that the response time for making a decision would be more highly associated with the decision itself (it occurred vs. it did not occur) than with plausibility. The study confirmed the exact opposite prediction. The time required to decide whether an event had happened was more closely related to the perceived plausibility of the event than to the decision itself. In other words, plausibility ratings were significantly better than rated belief in occurrence in predicting the response times for the belief ratings. As predicted, response time was very short when the event was deemed highly implausible and increased sharply when the event was deemed at least somewhat plausible, followed by significant but less-pronounced increases in response time as plausibility increased further. This pattern of results had been predicted because a determination that an event is implausible should preclude the initiation of a memory search. It is worth emphasizing that the association between plausibility and response time held regardless of the decision made about the occurrence of the event. In other words, response times increased with increasing perceived plausibility, even when insufficient corroborating information was found in memory and the final decision was that the event had not happened.

Conclusion

False beliefs and false memories represent a striking but rather common phenomenon. In this chapter, I reviewed evidence demonstrating the importance of metacognitive information and processes in their creation. Although monitoring processes have been invoked in major theoretical explanations of the creation of false memories (activation plus monitoring for the DRM paradigm; Roediger et al., 2001) or false memories and false beliefs (source-monitoring framework; Johnson & Raye, 2000), the model presented here is the only one that explicitly accounts for the large role of event plausibility in the creation of false beliefs and memories. In addition, I (2007) showed a more specific mechanism by which plausibility affects the decision about the occurrence of events in a person's life.

Studying the creation of false memories and false beliefs within the framework of metacognitive mechanisms put these phenomena into a broader picture in which not only "pure" memory processes are involved, but also inferential and decisional processes that make use of information other than what is provided by memory search. This helps link research on typical false memories phenomena with research on other forms of memory distortions (e.g., hindsight bias; Mazzoni & Vannucci, 2007), which for the moment have pertained to completely different areas of investigation.

References

Bernstein, D. M., Whittlesea, B. W. A., & Loftus, E. F. (2002). Increasing confidence in remote autobiographical memory and general knowledge: Extension of the revelation effect. *Memory & Cognition, 30*, 432–438.

Brainerd, C. J., & Reyna, V. F. (2002). Fuzzy-trace theory and false memory. *Current Directions in Psychological Science, 11*, 164–169.

Brainerd, C. J., & Reyna, V. F. (2005). *The science of false memories*. New York: Oxford University Press.

Garry, M., Manning, C., Loftus, E. F., & Sherman, S. J. (1996). Imagination inflation. *Psychonomic Bulletin and Review, 3*, 208–214.

Garry, M., & Wade, K. A. (2005). Actually, a picture is worth less than 45 words: Narratives produce more false memories than photographs do. *Psychonomic Bulletin & Review, 12*, 359–366.

Gentner, D., & Collins, A. (1981). Studies of inference from lack of knowledge. *Memory & Cognition, 9*, 434–443.

Ghetti, S., & Alexander, K. W. (2004). "If it happened, I would remember it": Strategic use of event memorability in the rejection of false autobiographical events. *Child Development, 75*, 542–561.

Glucksberg, S., & McCloskey, M. (1981). Decisions about ignorance: Knowing that you don't know. *Journal of Experimental Psychology: Human Learning & Memory, 7*, 311–325.

Goff, L. M., & Roediger, H. L., III (1998). Imagination inflation for action events: Repeated imaginings lead to illusory recollection. *Memory & Cognition, 26*, 20–33.

Heaps, C., & Nash, M. R. (1999). Individual differences in imagination inflation. *Psychonomic Bulletin & Review, 6*, 313–318.

Henkel, L. A., Franklin, N., & Johnson, M. K. (2000). Cross-modal source monitoring confusions between perceived and imagined events. *Journal of Experimental Psychology: Learning, Memory, and Cognition, 26*, 321–335.

Hertzog, C., Dixon, R. A., & Hultsch, D. F. (1990a). Metamemory in adulthood: Differentiating knowledge, belief, and behavior. In T. H. Hess (Ed.), *Aging and cognition: Knowledge organization and utilization* (pp. 161–212). Amsterdam: North Holland, Elsevier Science.

Hertzog, C., Dixon, R. A., & Hultsch, D. F. (1990b). Relationships between metamemory, memory predictions, and memory task performance in adults. *Psychology and Aging, 5*, 215–227.

Hyman, I. E., & Kleinknecht, E. E. (1999). False childhood memories: Research, theory and applications. In L. Williams & V. Banyard (Eds.), *Trauma and memory* (pp. 175–188). Thousand Oaks, CA: Sage.

Hyman, I. E., & Pentland, J. (1996). The role of mental imagery in the creation of false childhood memories. *Journal of Memory and Language, 35*, 101–117.

Janet, P. (1889/1973). *L'automatisme psychologique*. Paris: Alcan.

Johnson, M. K., Hashtroudi, S., & Lindsay, D. S. (1993). Source monitoring. *Psychological Bulletin, 114*, 3–28.

Johnson, M. K., & Raye, C. L. (2000). Cognitive and brain mechanisms of false memories and beliefs. In D. L. Schacter & E. Scarry (Eds.), *Memory, brain, and belief* (pp. 35–86). Cambridge, MA: Harvard University Press.

Kelley, C. M., & Jacoby, L. L. (1996). Memory attributions: Remembering, knowing, and feeling of knowing. In L. M. Reder (Ed.), *Implicit memory and metacognition* (pp. 287–307). Mahwah, NJ: LEA.

Klin, C. M, Guzman, A. E., & Levine, W. H. (1997). Knowing that you don't know: Metamemory and discourse processing. *Journal of Experimental Psychology: Learning, Memory, and Cognition, 23*, 1378–1393.

Koriat, A., & Goldsmith, M. (1996). Monitoring and control processes in the strategic regulation of memory accuracy. *Psychological Review, 103*, 490–517.

Koriat, A., & Lieblich, I. (1977). A study of memory pointers. *Acta Psychologica, 41*, 151–164.

Laurence, J. R., & Perry, C. (1983). Hypnotically created memory among highly hypnotizable subjects. *Science, 222*, 523–524.

Lindsay, D. S., Hagen, L., Read, J. D., Wade, K. A., & Garry, M. (2004). True photographs and false memories. *Psychological Science, 5*, 149–154.

Loftus, E. F., & Pickrell, J. E. (1995). The formation of false memories. *Psychiatric Annals, 25*, 720–725.

Lynn, S. J., Lock, T., Loftus, E. F., Krackow, E., & Lilienfeld, S. O. (2003). The remembrance of things past: Problematic memory recovery techniques in psychotherapy. In S. O. Lilienfeld, S. J. Lynn, & J. M. Lohr (Eds.), *Science and pseudoscience in clinical psychology* (pp. 205–239). New York: Guilford Press

Malinoski, P. T., Lynn, S. J., & Sivec, H. (1998). The assessment, validity and determinents of early memory reports: A critical review. In S. J. Lynn & K. M. McConkey (Eds.), *Truth in memory* (pp. 109–136), New York: Guilford Press.

Mazzoni, G. (2007). "Did you witness demonic possession?" A response time analysis of the relationship between event plausibility and autobiographical beliefs. *Psychonomic Bulletin & Review, 14*, 277–281.

Mazzoni, G., & Kirsch, I. (2002) Autobiographical memories and beliefs: A preliminary metacognitive model. In T. Perfect & B. Schwartz (Eds.), *Applied metacognition* (pp. 121–145). Cambridge, UK: Cambridge University Press.

Mazzoni, G., & Loftus, E. F. (1998). Dreaming, believing, remembering. In J. Rivera & T. R. Sarbin (Eds.), *Believed-in imaginings: The narrative construction of reality* (pp. 145–156). Washington, DC: APA Press.

Mazzoni, G., Loftus, E. F., & Kirsch, I. (2001). Changing beliefs about implausible autobiographical events: A little plausibility goes a long way. *Journal of Experimental Psychology: Applied, 7,* 51–59.

Mazzoni, G., Loftus, E. F., Seitz, A., & Lynn, S. J. (1999). Changing beliefs and memories through dream interpretation. *Applied Cognitive Psychology, 13,* 125–144.

Mazzoni, G., Lombardo, P., Malvagia, S., & Loftus, E. F. (1999). Dream interpretation and false beliefs. *Professional Psychology: Research and Practice, 30,* 45–50.

Mazzoni, G., & Lynn, S.J. (2007). Using hypnosis in eyewitness memory: Past and current issues. In R. C. L. Lindsay, M. Toglia, D. Ross, & J. D. Read (Eds.), *Handbook of eyewitness psychology: Memory for events* (Vol. 1). Mahwah, NJ: LEA.

Mazzoni, G., & Memon, A. (2003). Imagination can create false memories. *Psychological Science, 14,* 2, 186–188.

Mazzoni, G., & Scoboria, A. (2007). False memories. In F. D'Urso et al. (Ed.), *Handbook of applied cognition.* New York: Wiley.

Mazzoni, G., & Vannucci, M. (1999). *The provision of new information can change beliefs and memories about autobiographical events.* Paper presented at the meeting of the Society of Applied Research in Memory and Cognition, July, 9–11, Boulder, CO.

Mazzoni, G., & Vannucci, M. (2007). False memories and the hindsight bias phenomenon. *Social Cognition, 25,* 203–220

McConkey, K., & Sheehan, P. W. (1995*). Hypnosis, memory, and behavior in criminal investigation.* New York: Guilford.

Metcalfe, J. (1993). Novelty monitoring, metacognition, and control in a composite holographic associative recall model: Implications for Korsakoff amnesia. *Psychological Review, 100,* 3–22

Nelson, T. O., & Narens, L. (1990). Metamemory: A theoretical framework and new findings. In G. H. Bower (Ed.), *The psychology of learning and motivation* (Vol. 26, pp. 125–173). New York: Academic Press.

Newman, L. S., and Baumeister, R. F. (1998). Abducted by aliens: Spurious memories of interplanetary masochism. In S. J. Lynn & K. M. McConkey (Eds.), *Truth in memory* (pp. 284–303). New York: Guilford Press.

Pezdek, K., Blandon-Gitlin, I., Lam, S., Hart, R., & Schooler, J. (2006). Is knowing believing? The role of event plausibility and background knowledge in planting false beliefs about the personal past. *Memory & Cognition, 34,* 1628–1635.

Pezdek, K., Finger, K., & Hodge, D. (1997). Planting false childhood memories: The role of event plausibility. *Psychological Science, 8,* 437–441.

Pezdek, K., & Hodge, D. (1999). Planting false childhood memories in children: The role of event plausibility. *Child Development, 70,* 887–895.

Reder, L. M. (1982). Plausibility judgments versus fact retrieval: Alternative strategies for sentence verification. *Psychological Review, 89,* 250–280.

Roediger, H. L., III, & McDermott, K. B. (1995). Creating false memories. Remembering words not presented in lists. *Journal of Experimental Psychology: Learning, Memory, and Cognition, 21,* 803–814.

Roediger, H. L., III, Watson, J. M., McDermott, K. B., & Gallo, D. A. (2001). Factors that determine false recall: A multiple regression analysis. *Psychonomic Bulletin and Review, 8,* 385–407.

Scoboria, A., Mazzoni, G., Kirsch, I., & Jimenez, S. (2006). The effects of prevalence and script information on plausibility, belief, and memory of autobiographical events. *Applied Cognitive Psychology, 20*, 8, 1049–1064.

Scoboria, A., Mazzoni, G., Kirsch, I., & Relyea, M. (2004). Plausibility and belief in autobiographical memory. *Applied Cognitive Psychology, 18*, 791–807.

Seamon, J. G., Luo, C. R., & Gallo, D. A. (1998). Creating false memories of words with and without recognition of list items: Evidence for non-conscious processes. *Psychological Science, 9*, 20–26.

Sharman, S. J., Manning, C. G., & Garry, M. (2005). Explain this: Explaining childhood events inflates confidence for those events. *Applied Cognitive Psychology, 19*, 67–74.

Smeets, T., Merckelbach, H., Horselenberg, R., & Jelicic, M. (2005). Trying to recollect past events: Confidence, beliefs and memories. *Clinical Psychology Review, 25*, 917–934.

Spanos, N. P., Burgess, C. A., Burgess, M. F., Samuels, C., & Blois, W. O. (1999). Creating false memories of infancy with hypnotic and nonhypnotic procedures. *Applied Cognitive Psychology, 13*, 201–218.

Stadler, M. A., Roediger, H. L., III, & McDermott, K. B. (1999). Norms for word lists that create false memories. *Memory & Cognition, 27*, 494–500.

Strack, F., & Bless, H. (1994). Memory for non-occurrence. Metacognitive and presuppositional strategies. *Journal of Memory and Language, 33*, 203–217.

Thomas, A. K., & Loftus, E. F. (2002). Creating bizarre false memories through imagination. *Memory & Cognition, 30*, 423–431.

Tulving, E. (1985). Memory and consciousness. *Canadian Psychologist, 26*, 1–12.

Wade, K. A., Garry, M., Read, J. D., & Lindsay, D. S. (2002). A picture is worth a thousand lies: Using false photographs to create false childhood memories. *Psychonomic Bulletin & Review, 9*, 597–603.

Watson, J. M., McDermott, K. B., & Balota, D. A. (2004). Attempting to avoid false memories in the Deese/Roediger-McDermott paradigm: Assessing the combined influence of practice and warnings in young and old adults. *Memory & Cognition, 32*, 135–141.

Whittlesea, B. W. A., & Williams, L. D. (2001). The discrepancy-attribution hypothesis I: The heuristic bases of feeling of familiarity. *Journal of Experimental Psychology: Learning, Memory and Cognition, 27*, 3–13.

www.alessandrab.org/articoli%20forno/tempiforno/Gli%20abusologi%20.

Research on the Allocation of Study Time:
Key Studies From 1890 to the Present (and Beyond)

Lisa K. Son and Nate Kornell

Introduction

Time has always been a fascinating concept. Many great philosophers, physicists, and psychologists have pondered the definition, and the very existence, of time. Is time inside the mind or external to it? Is time a fourth dimension on a space–time continuum? Is time real or just an illusion? The answers to each of these questions, themselves, are worthy of a book (or stack of books). It is easier to agree with other aspects of time, however, for instance, "Lost time is never found again" (Benjamin Franklin, who also said "Time is money"); and "Time is God's way of keeping everything from happening at once" (anonymous). Time cannot be repeated, skipped, or replaced, and no commodity is more valuable. How time is allocated may determine the effectiveness of our behaviors; thus, time is a central element of life itself. In this chapter, we present a history of research on the topic of how people allocate time during study, beginning with its roots prior to the cognitive revolution and stopping at key points throughout the psychological literature. In doing so, we aim to answer the question of whether people achieve optimality when allocating the limited time that is available.

A History of Time Allocation

William James, the father of modern psychology, was one of the earliest to describe various aspects of time from a psychological perspective (1890). In Figure 1, we begin with James on our "timeline" of time allocation. Pastness, he said, is time on which memory and history builds. He wrote of pastness as "that to which every one of our experiences in turn falls a prey" (p. 605). Immediate, or present, time was more complicated — although present time has a "duration … we do not first feel one end and then feel the other after it, and from the perception of the succession feel the interval of time in between, but we seem to feel the interval of time as a whole, with its two ends embedded in it" (p. 610). James also sorted out the difference between how we perceive time and space, two concepts that may be analogous to a physicist but are quite different to someone looking at his or her watch. He described the difference between space and time as follows:

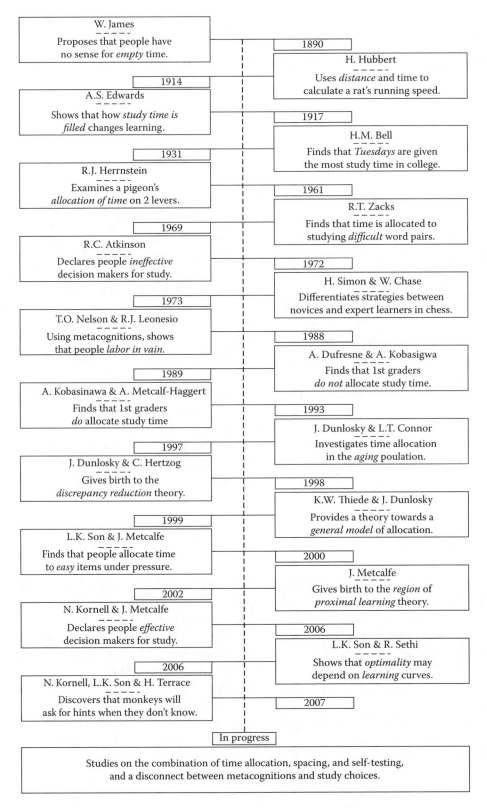

Figure 1 A timeline of time allocation.

To realize a quarter of a mile we need only to look out the window and *feel* its length by an act which, though it may in part result from organized associations, yet seems immediately performed. To realize an hour, we must count "now! — now! — now! — now! —" indefinitely. Each "now" is the feeling of a separate *bit* of time, and the exact sum of the bits never makes a very clear impression on the mind." (p. 611)

James went on to propose that people cannot accurately estimate how much time is available: "To be conscious of a time interval at all is one thing; to tell whether it be shorter or longer than another interval is a different thing" (p. 615). Finally, James wisely explained that time that is "filled" is easily approximated — for example, if time is filled with a song, we can estimate how long the time was based on the beat of the song. On the contrary, time that is empty, "We have no sense for" (p. 619).

James's characterization of time perception is accurate — which is unfortunate because decisions about time allocation become critical precisely when time is available, or empty, not filled. And, if one has "no sense for" the amount of time that is available, then how can it be allocated appropriately? In some sense, James foreshadowed doubt that would be cast decades later on the idea that time allocation could ever be optimal.

But, the question of people's optimal allocation of empty time was put on hold for almost 80 years. Instead, behavioral and psychological researchers focused on the contents of filled time. In fact, the time that was required to complete a task, *reaction time*, quickly became one of the key dependent variables in experimental psychology. In 1914, for instance, Helen Hubbert measured how far rats could run in a maze as a function of a range of time durations. Using a stopwatch to keep track of time, Hubbert was able to calculate the running speed of each of her subjects.

A few years later, in 1917 — still decades before the cognitive revolution — in a collection of articles bound together and titled, *Studies in Psychology Contributed by Colleagues and Former Students of Edward Bradford Titchener*, Edwards was the first to show that even equal times (times that are equally filled, that is) could result in vast learning differences when tested later. In his experiment, students were told to study, but during study, one group was given a review period, while the other was not. Edwards's results showed superior learning in the review group over the non-review group. Thus, in the early 1900s it became known that the type of time filler used can significantly change learning and retention in study situations. (But still, it remained to be seen whether people would choose the right strategy on their own, that is, whether people would allocate study time to review, a question that has begun to be answered only recently; Kornell & Bjork, 2006; Kornell & Son, 2006.)

Some years later, Bell (1931) examined the study habits of a population that could be characterized as having difficulty allocating time — college students. By recording the distribution of students' study time over the course of a week, Bell showed that most studying was done on Tuesday, and the least studying was done on Friday. Interestingly, in what was perhaps the first hint of a *labor-in-vain effect* (see Nelson & Leonesio, 1988, described in the next section), time spent studying was not diagnostic of scholastic success. That is, school grades did not increase as study time did. Other explanations were not tested; for instance, students might have chosen to study just enough to achieve a certain level of performance (e.g., a B+ average grade) and devoted just enough time to studying to do so (and a student's goals play an important role in their study decisions; Dunlosky & Thiede, 1998; Thiede & Dunlosky, 1999). More evidence of labor in vain surfaced 2 years later: Eurich (1933) recorded how much time college students spent reading each day, along with the number of pages they read. He found that seniors read more pages than did the sophomores, but no significant difference appeared regarding the issue of test performance (although, again, other factors were not tested; for example, selection effects may have been responsible or perhaps students who read more, especially the seniors, were taking more difficult classes than those who studied less).

In the years between the mid-1930s and the late 1960s, researchers took on a diverse range of topics with respect to time. For instance, studies were conducted on how much time was needed to learn a specific vocation or to become an expert in a specialized field, such as dentistry, medicine, automobile driving, and aviation piloting (e.g., Toops & Kuder, 1935). It would be decades before researchers concluded that it takes approximately 10 years to develop expertise in any area, including chess, painting, piano playing, neuropsychology, and music composition — even Mozart was unable to produce world-class music until the age of 17 (Bloom, 1985; Ericsson, 1996; Ericsson, Krampe, & Tesch-Römer, 1993; Hayes, 1989; H. A. Simon & Chase, 1973). Witnessing the fruits of one's labor can require enormous patience; even in the presence of prodigious talent, the rewards of optimal study time allocation can be very long term, which makes it all the harder for students to learn to make optimal decisions about how to regulate their study time.

The cognitive revolution arrived in the 1960s, with new ideas and uses for time. Following on Broadbent's (1958) introduction of the idea of the human brain as an information processor, Melton (1963) proposed that our short-term processing abilities were limited by time, and the time it took to scan one's own memories was even recorded (Sternberg, 1966). More importantly for the present purposes, researchers began to take interest in how people (and animals) *chose* to allocate their time, spurring a new era of research on learner-controlled time allocation.

Learner-Controlled Time Allocation

How is time allocated? This question, which James foreshadowed in the 19th century, was asked again almost 80 years later, in both pigeons (Herrnstein, 1961) and humans (Zacks, 1969). In the pigeon study, there were two levers, both releasing food on variable-interval schedules, and the amount of time that the pigeon allocated to each of the levers was recorded. The results suggested that the pigeons seemed to have a systematic and virtually optimal allocation strategy. The amount of time that they allocated to each lever matched the lever's reinforcement value. In a study by Zacks asking a similar time allocation question — except with college undergraduates — participants were presented with word pairs on a computer and were told that they could study each pair for as long as they wished. They could also take test trials whenever they chose. The results of this first-of-its-kind experiment showed that (1) there was a controlled method by which researchers could measure time allocation strategies, and (2) when allowed to allocate their time freely, people spent more time on pairs that were objectively more difficult to learn.

Around the same time, Atkinson (1972) focused on perhaps the most important issue in the examination of study time allocation: Do people allocate their study time *effectively*? He based his research on a Markov model of human learning in which items could be in one of three states: L (or permanently learned), T (or transitional), and U (or unlearned). According to this theory, the learning objective is to bring as many items as possible into the L state, which is a "safe" state (i.e., learned items are not in danger of being forgotten). To arrive at the L state, an item must pass through first the U state and then the T state. Using a computer algorithm, Atkinson was able to categorize which of the items — English–German vocabulary pairs — were in each of the three states for each participant. The computer (or the participants themselves, in one condition) then allocated study time to each item based on its current state of learning. There were four time allocation conditions: (1) random order, in which all items, including those that were already in L, were presented for an equal amount of time; (2) self-selection, in which the participants were allowed to choose for themselves which items they would study (and they tended to choose the unlearned items); (3) optimal strategy with equal parameters, in which items that were in either T or U were given equal time; and (4) optimal strategy with unequal parameters, in which those items that were determined to be in the intermediate T state were given the most study time. On a delayed test, as expected, the random sequence produced the worst performance. Both the equal parameter and the self-selection conditions produced intermediate and comparable performances. The most impressive finding was that when the computer devoted the most study time to the intermediate T items — in the unequal parameters condition — learning was greatly enhanced (there was a 108% performance gain over the random strategy). Interestingly, the self-selection strategy yielded a gain that was much smaller, only 53% over the random strategy. Atkinson concluded that the most effective strategy is to allocate study time to items of intermediate difficulty, not to the items that are the most difficult or to those that are already learned. On a pessimistic note, he also concluded that, "My data, and the data of others, indicate that the learner is not a particularly effective decision maker" (p. 930). This bold claim has been challenged by more recent evidence, which we consider in detail in this chapter.

Still, learners usually have control over their learning, and over the next 15 years or so, cognitive psychologists investigated people's time allocation strategies using paradigms that were similar to the one Zacks used in 1969 (see Son & Metcalfe, 2000, for a review). In general, experimental participants were given items that varied in objective difficulty to study, one at a time, for as long as they wished. The majority of studies showed that people had a systematic strategy, in line with Zacks' and Atkinson's findings: They allocated most of their time to relatively difficult items.

During this time period, primarily throughout the 1980s, research on learner-controlled study time allocation became more and more intertwined with research on *metacognitive* knowledge. Rather than testing people's allocation strategies on items at various levels of *objective* difficulty, experimental participants were asked to make their own *subjective* assessments of difficulty prior to making study time allocation decisions — the same way they would have to in real life, making metacognitive judgments to guide study time allocation. In one important instance, Nelson and Leonesio (1988) tested college students in three distinct stages: (1) a judgment stage, in which they were presented with a series of items and had to assess how difficult it would be to learn each one; (2) a study stage, in which participants spent as much time as they wanted studying each item (as in previous time allocation studies); and (3) a recall stage, in which participants' memories for the items were tested. Consistent with previous research, people allocated more study time to the *judged* difficult items. Furthermore, in one condition participants were encouraged to study until they had mastered every item; in another, they were not. The former condition yielded large increases in study time but almost no improvement in later recall — the first laboratory evidence for what was called the labor-in-vain effect (see also Mazzoni & Cornoldi, 1993; Mazzoni, Cornoldi, & Marchitelli, 1990; Nelson, 1993).

Models of Study Time Allocation

A preponderance of time allocation studies in the 1980s and 1990s showed that people preferred to allocate study time to relatively difficult items (Son & Metcalfe, 2000). The *discrepancy-reduction* hypothesis was proposed as an explanation for those findings (Dunlosky & Hertzog, 1998). The hypothesis stated that the allocation of study time is related to the discrepancy between an item's actual and desired knowledge state, which needs to be reduced if learning is to occur. According to the model, the most study time should be allocated to items that have the largest discrepancy. The discrepancy-reduction hypothesis is both descriptive and prescriptive; it proposes that what people do is the same as what they should do — focus on the hardest items.

Virtually all study time allocation studies conducted in the 20th century shared certain unnatural elements. For example, most experiments presented to-be-learned materials one at a time and allowed people to study for as long as they wanted, *but only once.* Under those conditions, people were able to determine how much time they spent on a given item, but they could not choose which items they wanted to study (and the two types of decisions can lead to different outcomes; see Metcalfe & Kornell, 2005). Furthermore, the items were usually presented sequentially, not simultaneously (which also leads to different outcomes; see Thiede & Dunlosky, 1999). A second constraint was that because participants were given unlimited time to study, they might have believed — perhaps rightly in the laboratory context — that time pressure was not an issue, and that there was ample available time to learn all of the items. In real life, though, time pressure is common during study (just ask anyone who has ever run out of time studying for an exam or turned in a paper late). More important, taking time to study one topic or item often leaves less time to study others. These issues — of simultaneous presentation and of the total time available — were investigated in a series of studies (e.g., Son & Metcalfe, 2000; Thiede & Dunlosky, 1999; also see Dunlosky & Thiede, 2004). Thiede and Dunlosky, for example, found that people's allocations shifted to easier materials when items were presented *simultaneously* instead of sequentially. This shift to studying the easier materials also occurred when time pressure increased (e.g., Metcalfe, 2002; Son & Metcalfe, 2000).

In light of the new procedures and resultant findings, a new theory was put forth, arguing for the importance of a "region" of difficulty in which items are most amenable to learning, which consists of items just beyond the learner's grasp. This region does not necessarily include the most difficult items, but rather items that are *almost learned* — a region of difficulty comparable to Atkinson's (1972) transitory (*T*) state. The items that inhabit this region could also depend on the specific learning situation: For instance, changes in study format or increases in time pressure could shift the region toward easier items, which can be learned in a relatively short amount of time. Thiede and Dunlosky (1999) first reported such a shift, calling this strategy a shift to easier materials (STEM), and soon thereafter Metcalfe (2002) proposed the term *region of proximal learning* to refer to the most learnable items. Metcalfe and Kornell (2003; see also Kornell & Metcalfe, 2006; Metcalfe & Kornell, 2005) tested this new time allocation theory and found that when people were asked to select easy, medium, and difficult items under varying time availabilities (5, 15, and 60 seconds), they tended to study the easy items when very little time was available and moved to the medium and difficult items only as time availability increased. Like discrepancy reduction, the region of proximal learning framework is prescriptive as well as descriptive, and there is evidence suggesting that, by using it, people increase their learning (see "Optimal Time Allocation" below). Although, as described, the region of proximal learning model and the discrepancy reduction model make different predictions in some circumstances, their predictions are the same under other conditions (when there is no time pressure, and there is not a tradeoff in time between studying one item and another), and since it is under those conditions that most study time allocation experiments have been conducted, both theories are consistent with Zacks's (1969) study time allocation findings and most everything that followed (Son & Metcalfe, 2000).

It seems clear today that the allocation decisions people make are driven metacognitively, and that allocations depend on factors like whether items are presented simultaneously or sequentially, how much total study time is available, and the personal goals a student sets. The fact that people use a certain strategy is by no means proof that they *should* use that strategy, however, as every psychology student knows (especially students studying the use of heuristics in judgment and decision making). In the words of Metcalfe and Kornell (2005), "We still do not know whether what [people] do enhances their learning, or is in any way optimal" (p. 476). The issue of which allocation strategies are optimal is the next focus in our timeline.

Optimal Time Allocation

How might one go about testing what is optimal? One way is to pit people against a computer, as Atkinson (1972) did over 30 years ago; as described, he showed that people were better than random but far from optimal. Nelson, Dunlosky, Graf, and Narens (1994) took a similar approach; they asked people to make metacognitive judgments of learning (JOLs) about a set of word pairs and then to choose which of the items they wanted to restudy. Following the study choice, participants were allowed to restudy in one of four conditions: self-control, in which participants studied the items they had selected; high JOL, in which they studied the items they had rated as easiest; low JOL, in which they studied the items they had rated as hardest; and objectively difficult, in which they studied the objectively most difficult items based on norms.

Recall performance on a test that followed restudy showed that the best performance occurred in the self-control and low-JOL conditions, followed by the objectively difficult condition. Performance was worst in the high-JOL condition. Recall in the self-control and low-JOL conditions were the same because participants in the self-control condition chose to study the low-JOL items (so participants studied essentially the same items in both cases). It appears as though the basic strategy participants used was to study the items they did not already know (a seemingly universal strategy). This experiment showed that people can, and do, help themselves when studying by choosing to study items they do not know instead of items they do know.

Kornell and Metcalfe (2006) further investigated the potential benefits of self-regulated study time allocation. After replicating Nelson et al.'s (1994) findings, Kornell and Metcalfe presented participants with a more difficult problem: What would people do if they had to decide which items to study when they could not simply reject items they already knew, that is, when all of the items were unknown? Participants were asked to study and make JOLs on Spanish–English pairs, and then they were tested on all of the pairs; any pair they answered correctly was dropped from the rest of the experiment. Participants were then asked to select half of the remaining items for further study. After making their choices, participants were divided into four independent conditions: high JOL, in which they studied the subjectively easiest items; low JOL, in which they studied the subjectively hardest items; honor, in which they studied the items that they had selected; and dishonor, in which they studied the items that they had not selected. The results showed that people chose to study the *easiest* items when selecting among items they did not know. Moreover, test performance was the highest when people's choices were honored. Thus, in contrast to what Atkinson (1972) found but similar to what Nelson et al. (1994) found, people seemed to use strategies that were effective and, in this procedure, optimal for learning (see also Son, under revision).

Another way to investigate optimal strategies is to derive theoretical predictions about which study strategies should work best by numerically simulating the types of allocations that would result in the highest levels of learning. One of the challenges in doing this is to include all of the major factors that might influence the learning of any particular item. Based on the existing data on time allocation strategies, the following seem to be important: (1) the learning curve, or how incremental increases in learning change over time; (2) where on the learning curve a particular item currently is, or how much prior allocation has already been invested; and (3) the total time that is available for study. Son and Sethi (2006) compared concave and S-shaped learning curves, two potential learning functions (see Figure 2), and defined as a possible goal of the learner to maximize the learning "score," or extent of learning, summed across all items that are to be learned, for all time availabilities. Optimality depended on the item's learning curve: When the items followed the path of a concave function, then regardless of time availability, optimality entailed that people allocate more time to the less-well-learned items (with learning gains that will be greater than those that are more fully learned and at a plateau). When the learning curves were S shaped, however, optimality looked more complicated. With little time availability, one should allocate time to the items closer to a learned state, but as time availability increased, items at a lower state of learning should receive more

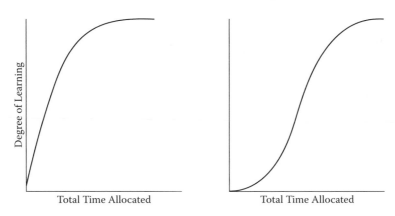

Figure 2   Two learning functions: concave and S shaped.

study. These findings suggested that optimal time allocations will depend highly on the structure of the learning function: With one type of curve, a discrepancy-reduction strategy is favored; with another learning curve, the region of proximal learning strategy seems beneficial.

Under this framework, whether people can achieve optimality is still unanswered. To be optimal, the learner would need to know two things: (1) the shape of the learning curves for the items that need to be learned and (2) how much time was available for study. How realistic is it to assume that these factors are known during study? There is evidence to suggest that, as a rule, people wholly misunderstand the shape of the learning curve (Kornell & Bjork, 2006). One might, however, have a fairly realistic sense of how much learning would be gained during a *short* and *present* time. If people did not consider the entire learning curve and instead based their decisions on knowledge of this "limited region" learning gain, might optimality still be attained? Sethi and Son (data collected in 2007, manuscript under revision) tested this idea and calculated when optimality would occur if time were allocated preferentially for the item with the highest current gain in learning. What they found was that, using these adaptive strategies based on limited knowledge, again it would depend on the shape of the item's entire learning curves: When learning was concave, people would always be optimal; when learning was S shaped, there would be regions of time availability where optimality would not be attained.

The question of optimal time allocations is obviously a complicated one, which makes modeling it virtually impossible without a number of simplifying assumptions. One such assumption, which may be relaxed in future investigations, is the use of learning score, or extent of learning, summed across all items as a metric of learning. In reality, summed learning level and the number of items that can be retrieved (i.e., the number of items that are above a retrievability threshold) are not necessarily the same; for example, by strengthening a set of weak items, summed learning level increases, but if those items do not become recallable, then recall rates do not increase. This is especially important in the current context because ignoring such weak items is one of the reasons studying according to the region of proximal learning framework is advantageous in terms of rates of recall — even when it might not be advantageous in terms of summed learning level. Of course, how optimal one is will depend on what goal one has in mind. Another assumption that greatly simplifies the predictions, but may be relaxed at some point, is that studying an item does not change the shape of its learning curve but instead simply moves an item along a fixed curve. Son and Sethi (2006) assumed that the processes of forgetting and learning could be represented as items moving up and down a fixed curve. In other models, however, learning is accompanied by two changes; the item moves up a learning curve, but at the same time, the actual shape of the learning curve itself changes (as does the shape of the forgetting curve). Indeed, the strength of a given item in memory can be represented by two indices, corresponding to current retrievability and long-term storage (see Bjork & Bjork, 1992).

In summary, findings from the last dozen years show that people appear to have systematic time allocation strategies and benefit from using them. Two models of study time allocation, discrepancy reduction and region of proximal learning, are able to account for most of the research from the 20th century, and the latter is able to account for some of the more ecological research that has occurred in the 21st century as well. The scope of the research has continued to broaden as new methods of research have been designed, and efforts to increase generality (e.g., Thiede, Anderson, & Therriault, 2003) have raised new questions and answered others.

Beyond the Classroom

In a classroom, the importance of metacognitive monitoring and self-regulated study is limited somewhat by the fact that part of a teacher's job is to help students make study choices (or to tell them outright what and when to study). But, not all study decisions occur in a classroom. Self-regulated study may play its most important role when students are on their own. Students constantly face time allocation choices during homework, for example, what topic to study next, for how long, and when to move on to the next topic. Students also face decisions about *how* to study; there are innumerable study techniques that students use, some of which are very effective (e.g., creating an integrated summary of a textbook chapter) and some probably not very effective at all (e.g., trying to read a chapter for the first time while half asleep the night before an exam). In some cases, a workbook leads students through exercises during homework but is primarily for younger students; older students are largely left to decide on their own.

In our experience, the majority of students have had little or no training in how to study. The second author often reads a children's book (*My Friends*, by Taro Gomi, 2005) containing the line, "I learned to study from my friends the teachers." If only it were true. In a survey of University of California at Los Angeles undergraduates, 80% answered "No" when asked whether a teacher taught them to study the way they do (Kornell & Bjork, 2007). Perhaps this state of affairs was reasonable in William James's time, when the knowledge base about which study techniques work was relatively small — but as this chapter illustrates, that is no longer the case.

Not all study choices occur in an educational context. To take a unique example, Kornell, Son, and Terrace (2007) investigated a completely different type of study choice, one that *never* occurs in a classroom: the study choices of nonhuman primates.

Instead of asking undergraduates to study for an exam, they trained monkeys to make "study" choices that allowed them to earn food rewards. The monkeys were presented with a list-learning task in which they had to touch a set of photographs in a certain order. They could ask for a "hint," representing an "I don't know enough" state, during the task by touching an icon on the right side of a touch-sensitive computer monitor mounted in their testing chambers (see Figure 3). When they requested a hint, blinking lines appeared on the screen surrounding the next correct response in the list of photographs. To constrain hint taking, there was a penalty for taking hints—the monkeys earned only a food pellet when they used a hint to arrive at a correct answer, but they earned a more desirable M&M for correct answers made without hints.

Requesting a hint was similar to a study choice in the sense that, like a choice to restudy versus not restudy, a monkey had to decide whether to complete the list by asking for a hint (i.e., by studying) or whether to complete the list without a hint (i.e., by not studying). Making that decision required that the monkey monitor whether it knew the answer — that is, it required metacognition. The result was that the monkeys learned to take hints at high rates when a list was new (and they had not yet learned the sequence of photographs well) and to decrease their hint taking as they gained more experience with the list. This finding demonstrated that monkeys, by using their metacognitive abilities to control their behavior, engage in self-regulated learning.

NO HINT AVAILABLE

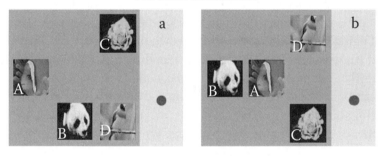

HINT AVAILABLE

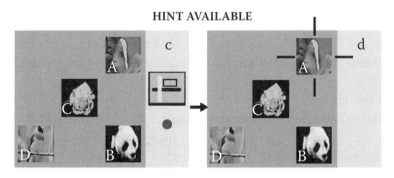

Figure 3   Sample trials of a monkey list-learning task in which the monkeys had to touch a set of photographs in a certain order. On the right of the screen there was a "hint" icon that, when pressed, represented an "I don't know" state. If the hint icon was pressed, blinking lines appeared on the screen surrounding the next correct response in the list of photographs. (Originally published in Kornell, Son, & Terrace, 2007.)

Factors That Affect Study Time Allocation

Almost all previous research on study time allocation has focused on what people chose to study as a function of item difficulty. (The central variable controlling study decisions in both discrepancy reduction and the region of proximal learning model is difficulty.) However, other factors affect study time allocation as well. For example, Dunlosky and Thiede (1998) showed that a range of factors affect study decisions (e.g., the number of points awarded for remembering a given item and the likelihood that an item would be tested), each illustrating the importance of motivation in study decisions. In 1999, Thiede and Dunlosky took a first step toward a general model of study time allocation by focusing on the role of goals in study decisions. Participants were either told to set a low performance goal (remember 6/30 items) or a high performance goal (remember 24/30 items). They chose to study easier items in the former condition than in the latter. This was only true when the items were displayed simultaneously, however, which led to the hypothesis that working memory constraints, which were greater with sequential than simultaneous presentation, are also a factor in time allocation decisions (also see Dunlosky & Thiede, 2004). Thus, in addition to the difficulty of an item, when people make time allocation decisions they consider their learning goals and their level of extrinsic motivation (as well as intrinsic motivation; see Son & Metcalfe, 2000).

There are also interpersonal factors that can affect study time. One example is aging. In general, aging brings with it memory deficits. Dunlosky and Connor (1997) showed that aging is also associated with metacognitive deficits in that older adults' allocation of study time is less entrained by item difficulty. Older adults are still able to monitor fairly well, however, and as Dunlosky and Hertzog (1997) showed, at least in some situations, older and younger adults use essentially the same heuristic to select items for study.

At the other end of the aging spectrum is a group of people who study a lot and can probably use help: children. A more detailed description of some of our research on study time allocation in children is presented, but in general, children are remarkably metacognitive at a young age, and their patterns of study time allocation reflect that (Dufresne & Kobasigawa, 1989; Metcalfe, 2002). Dufresne and Kobasigawa were the first to examine children's time allocation abilities and tested children in Grades 1, 3, 5, and 7. The children were told to study two booklets, one hard and one easy, of paired associates for as long as they wanted until they could remember all of the pairs perfectly. Although the children in Grades 5 and 7 spent more time studying the difficult booklet, those in Grades 1 and 3 spent approximately equal amounts of time on each, suggesting a lack of self-regulation. However, in a subsequent study, Kobasigawa and Metcalf-Haggert (1993) found that when the materials were pictures of familiar objects rather than verbal paired associates, even first graders used a self-regulating strategy: They allocated more study time to materials that were more difficult. In summary, the study choices of both children and older adults show some impairment but mostly adeptness.

Choices About Study Techniques

As mentioned, most study time allocation research has focused on item difficulty; perhaps more important, it has also involved essentially two measures: which items participants choose to study and for how long they study (see Kornell & Metcalfe, 2006). Is self-regulated learning confined to those two decisions, made based on item difficulty? Far from it. There are any number of study techniques that people use (e.g., flash cards, underlining, summarizing their notes, practice quizzes), and each has some degree of overlap (or nonoverlap) with factors that are known to influence memory (e.g., spaced practice, deep semantic processing, knowledge integration, testing effects). Research on which techniques people fill their study time with, what they believe about those techniques, and how effective their choices are is just beginning in the realm of study time allocation research. These questions were foreshadowed by Edwards (1917), who showed (see section on history of time allocation) that studying efficiently (by reviewing) was more effective than studying without review, even if the amount of study time was held constant. In this section, we describe three sets of experiments concerning how people study but in which the variable of primary interest is not item difficulty.

William James believed, as described, that people have "no sense" for "empty time" but can accurately perceive time when it is "filled" with something like beats. In a study we conducted (Son & Kornell, in preparation), participants were asked to plan out a study schedule, and beats were provided in the form of visual slots on a computer screen, each of which represented a 3-second study event that participants could fill with any item they chose to study. With a nod to historical research on time allocation, two questions were asked: What time allocation strategy would be used? Would people's allocation strategies be *in vain*? We also asked a new question: Would people spontaneously space their practice?

The method was as follows: Participants were first presented with a list of 16 synonym pairs (e.g., saturnine–gloomy) to study for a later test. After a pair was presented, participants made a judgment, on a scale from 0 to 10, indicating how confident they were that they would be able to recall the synonym when given only the cue word on a later memory test. After the presentation/judgment phase, all 16 words (without synonyms) were shown on the left side of a computer screen simultaneously. On the right side of the screen, there was a list of study slots. The participant's task was to click on a cue that they wanted to restudy and drag it from the left-hand side of the computer screen into one of the slots on the right-hand side. Participants were told that each slot represented 3 seconds of study time. There were three conditions: We provided 8, 16, or 24 slots for study. In the 8-slot condition, for instance, at most half of the 16 items could be restudied. In the 8-, 16-, and 24-slot conditions, participants had a total of 24, 48, and 72 seconds, respectively, of total study time to allocate.

Participants were told that they would study the pairs in their list of slots from top to bottom, in whatever order they created. They were also told that they could study pairs as many (or few) times as they wanted. For instance, a participant could study one item zero times and another three times, and those three could be spaced apart or massed together. Thus, participants fully controlled the number of times every item was studied and the study schedule. The only constraint was that all of the slots had to be filled. Once the restudy list had been created, there was a restudy period during which the cue–target pairs were shown sequentially in the exact order that the participant had chosen. After a 3-minute distracter task, participants were given a cued recall test.

The data showed that the more difficult a participant judged a pair to be, the more study time was allotted to it. This is consistent with the discrepancy-reduction model and, because the participants' perception was that they could (for the most part) potentially learn most or all of the items they did not know, with the region of proximal learning model. The most important finding was that the amount of spacing was significantly greater than would be expected by chance (although it was also significantly smaller than the maximum possible spacing). In other words, participants chose to space their study. Although this is good news from a practical standpoint, it is also surprising in light of previous experiments showing that people give higher (or equivalent) ratings to massed than spaced practice (Baddeley & Longman, 1978; Dunlosky & Nelson, 1994; D. A. Simon & Bjork, 2001; Zechmeister & Shaughnessy, 1980; although delayed JOLs result in the opposite pattern, see Dunlosky & Nelson, 1994) and given one study showing that children prefer to mass practice (Son, 2005). A basic assumption of research on self-regulated learning is that study choices are guided by metacognitive judgments. That assumption may need to be reexamined, at least in this case, given that people choose to space but rate massing as more effective (also see Koriat, Ma'ayan, & Nussinson, 2006; Kornell & Son, 2006).

There has also been research on how spacing choices are related to item difficulty. In one set of experiments, people chose to space relatively easy items (Son, 2004), and in another case they chose to space relatively difficult items (Benjamin & Bird, 2006). In the Kornell and Son (under revision) study described here, the amount of spacing was approximately equal for easy and difficult items.

Like spacing, self-testing is an effective — if somewhat counterintuitive (Bjork, 1994) — study technique. When do people self-test? Son (2005) examined first-grade children's study decisions and found two things; first, they chose to self-test, and second, they did so especially for information they felt they knew. College students seem to do the same. Son and Kornell (under revision) asked participants to choose whether they wanted to (1) view word pairs intact or (2) see the cue first, test themselves, and then see the target. The first time through the list, participants chose presentation mode, but after going through the list two or three times and reaching the point at which they began to know the pairs, they switched to self-testing.

Thus, when making study decisions, people choose to space practice and self-test, both very effective strategies (e.g., Cepeda, Pashler, Vul, Wixted, & Rohrer, 2006; Roediger & Karpicke, 2006a). There appears to be a disconnect, in both cases, between metacognitive judgments and study choices. As mentioned, people choose to space practice but tend to give higher JOLs following massed practice. The same appears to be true of self-testing; people choose to self-test, but there is some evidence, although it is mixed, that they give higher JOLs following re-presentation (Roediger & Karpicke, 2006b), although others have reported higher ratings following testing (Begg, Vinski, Frankovich, & Holgate, 1991; Mazzoni & Nelson, 1995).

We (Son & Kornell, in preparation) conducted a direct test of the disconnect between JOLs and study choices in the domain of self-testing. In that preliminary experiment, participants studied a list of 12 word pairs one at a time. Then, they were given a chance to study the list a second time, but this time they were given a choice: They could either have the list re-presented, or they could take a practice quiz, during which the cue would be presented, they would type in the answer (if they could remember it), and then they would be shown the correct answer. After making their choice and studying the list for the second time, participants were asked how many of the items they would be able to recall on a later test (i.e., "I will remember __/12," an aggregate JOL). There were four lists, and at the end of the last list, all four lists were tested.

The results showed that people strongly favored testing over re-presentation in their study choices, but JOL ratings were approximately the same in the two conditions. Thus, there was indeed a disconnect, even within single individuals, between study choices and JOLs. Furthermore, recall rates were higher after self-testing than presentation, demonstrating that self-testing was an effective strategy. If JOLs had not been recorded, one might have concluded that the reason people chose to test was because doing so improved learning. Paradoxically, it appears that, instead, people chose self-testing in spite of the fact that they believed — incorrectly — that testing and straight presentation work equally well. A postexperimental questionnaire further revealed that, in fact, rather than thinking that self-testing helps them *learn,* people instead think — rightly — that it helps them *monitor* their learning. That is, they realized that self-testing improves metacognitive accuracy (which it does; see Dunlosky & Nelson, 1992; Nelson & Dunlosky, 1991). Thus, people think self-testing sharpens their ability to monitor their learning but not their learning itself, and therefore they choose to self-test, not based on metacognitive monitoring, but instead to *serve* metacognitive monitoring.

Conclusion and Overview

Many pieces have been put together, but the puzzle of time allocation is far from solved. Learners seem to be systematic about their allocation decisions with respect to item difficulty. A virtually universal finding is that people do not study information they think they already know (Metcalfe & Kornell, 2005). In some situations, people allocate time to the most difficult items. In other situations, such as when they are pressed for time, they focus on easier items. As far as optimality, in some instances people make allocation decisions that significantly improve competence (e.g., Kornell & Metcalfe, 2006). In other situations, however, increases in time allocation appear to be labor in vain (Nelson & Leonesio, 1988). In some situations, such as when making decisions about spacing and self-testing — context in which time allocation is just beginning to be explored — people seem to make effective decisions (by choosing to space and self-test; see Son & Kornell, in preparation; and Son, 2005, respectively), even when they do not seem to realize that their decisions are effective (see Zechmeister & Shaughnessy, 1980, and Roediger & Karpicke, 2006b, respectively).

Part of the reason for the disconnect between metacognitive ratings and study choices is the wide array of factors that influence study decisions that are not directly related to metacognitive monitoring and vice versa. Many are commendable, like self-testing to monitor one's learning, or studying information that one finds interesting (Son & Metcalfe, 2000). But, others may be equally important. For example, which study technique is the most fun? What makes one *feel* like one is learning (which is often different from what makes one actually learn). What grade is one studying for (e.g., "studying for a B")? What is on TV? Finally, the question that seems to be the main determiner of which topic a student chooses to study next: What is the most overdue (Kornell & Bjork, in press)? These touch on what we consider to be the three general factors that are important for optimizing study, in particular the allocation of time: goals, motivation, and efficiency. Goals, of course, are the very foundation of study, and it is impossible to overestimate the importance of motivation. The most important objective of research on study time allocation, however, is to uncover ways of improving efficiency. As Benjamin Franklin said, "Do not squander time, for that is the stuff life is made of."

References

Atkinson, R. C. (1972). Optimizing the learning of a second-language vocabulary. *Journal of Experimental Psychology, 96*, 124–129.

Baddeley, A. D., & Longman, D. J. A. (1978). The influence of length and frequency of training session on the rate of learning to type. *Ergonomics, 21*, 627–635.

Begg, I., Vinski, E., Frankovich, L., & Holgate, B. (1991). Generating makes words memorable, but so does effective reading. *Memory & Cognition, 19,* 487–497.

Bell, H. M. (1931). Study habits of teacher's college students. *Journal of Educational Psychology, 22,* 538–543.

Benjamin, A. S., & Bird, R. (2006). Metacognitive control of the spacing of study repetitions. *Journal of Memory and Language, 55,* 1, 126–137.

Bjork, R. A. (1994). Memory and metamemory considerations in the training of human beings. In J. Metcalfe & A. Shimamura (Eds.), *Metacognition: Knowing about knowing* (pp. 185–205). Cambridge, MA: MIT Press.

Bjork, R. A., & Bjork, E. L. (1992). A new theory of disuse and an old theory of stimulus fluctuation. In A. F. Healy, S. M. Kosslyn, & R. M. Shiffrin (Eds.), *From learning processes to cognitive processes: Essays in honor of William K. Estes* (Vol. 2, pp. 35–67). Hillsdale, NJ: Erlbaum.

Bloom, B. (1985). *Developing talent in young people.* New York: Ballantine.

Broadbent, D.E. (1958). *Perception and communication.* London: Pergamon.

Cepeda, N. J., Pashler, H., Vul, E., Wixted, J. T., & Rohrer, D. (2006). Distributed practice in verbal recall tasks: A review and quantitative synthesis. *Psychological Bulletin, 132,* 354–380.

Dufresne, A., & Kobasigawa, A. (1989). Children's spontaneous allocation of study time: Differential and sufficient aspects. *Journal of Experimental Child Psychology, 47,* 274–296.

Dunlosky, J., & Connor, L.T. (1997). Age differences in the allocation of study time account for age differences in memory performance. *Memory & Cognition, 25,* 691–700.

Dunlosky, J., & Hertzog, C. (1997). Older and younger adults use a functionally identical algorithm to select items for restudy during multitrial learning. *Journal of Gerontology: Psychological Science, 52,* 178–186.

Dunlosky, J., & Hertzog, C. (1998). Training programs to improve learning in later adulthood: Helping older adults educate themselves. In D. J. Hacker, J. Dunlosky, & A. C. Graesser (Eds.), *Metacognition in educational theory and practice* (pp. 249–275). Mahwah, NJ: Erlbaum.

Dunlosky, J., & Nelson, T. O. (1992). Importance of the kind of cue for judgments of learning (JOL) and the delayed JOL effect. *Memory & Cognition, 20*, 374–380.

Dunlosky, J., & Nelson, T. O. (1994). Does the sensitivity of judgments of learning (JOLs) to the effects of various study activities depend on when the JOLs occur? *Journal of Memory and Language, 33*, 545–565.

Dunlosky, J., & Thiede, K. W. (1998). What makes people study more? An evaluation of factors that affect people's self-paced study and yield "labor-and-gain" effects. *Acta Psychologica, 98,* 37–56.

Dunlosky, J., & Thiede, K. W. (2004). Causes and constraints of the shift-to-easier-materials effect in the control of study. *Memory & Cognition, 32*, 779–788.

Edwards, A. S. (1917). The distribution of time in learning small amounts of material. In *Studies in psychology: Titchener commerative volume* (pp. 209–213). Worcester, MA: Wilson.

Ericsson, K. A. (1996). The acquisition to expert performance: An introduction to some of the issues. In K. A. Ericsson (Ed.), *The road to excellence: The acquisition of expert performance in the arts and sciences, sports and games* (pp. 1–50). Mahwah, NJ: Erlbaum.

Ericsson, K. A., Krampe, R. T., & Tesch-Römer, C. (1993). The role of deliberate practice in the acquisition of expert performance. *Psychological Review, 100*, 363–406.

Eurich, A. C. (1933). The amount of reading and study among college students. *School and Society, 37,* 102–104.

Gomi, T. (2005). *My friends.* San Francisco: Chronicle Books.

Hayes, J. R. (1989). *Complete problem solver.* Mahwah, NJ: Erlbaum.

Herrnstein, R. J. (1961). Relative and absolute strength of response as a function of frequency of reinforcement. *Journal of the Experimental Analysis of Behavior, 4*, 267–272.

Hubbert, H. B. (1914). Time versus distance in learning. *Journal of Animal Behavior, 4*, 60–69.

James, W. (1890). *The principles of psychology* (Vol. 1, pp. 605–642). New York: Holt.

Kobasigawa, A., & Metcalf-Haggert, A. (1993). Spontaneous allocation of study time by first- and third-grade children in a simple memory task. *The Journal of Genetic Psychology, 154*, 223–235.

Koriat, A., Ma'ayan, H., & Nussinson, R. (2006). The intricate relationships between monitoring and control in metacognition: Lessons for the cause-and-effect relation between subjective experience and behavior. *Journal of Experimental Psychology: General, 135*, 36–69.

Kornell, N., & Bjork, R. A. (2006). Predicted and actual learning curves. Paper presented at the 47th annual meeting of the Psychonomic Society, November 2006, Houston, TX.

Kornell, N., & Bjork, R. A. (2007). The promise and perils of self-regulated study. *Psychonomic Bulletin & Review, 14*, 219–224.

Kornell, N., & Metcalfe, J. (2006). Study efficacy and the region of proximal learning framework. *Journal of Experimental Psychology: Learning, Memory, and Cognition, 32,* 609–622.

Kornell, N., & Son, L. K (2006). *Self-testing: A metacognitive disconnect between memory monitoring and study choice.* Poster presented at the 47th annual meeting of the Psychonomic Society, Houston, TX.

Kornell, N., & Son, L. K. (under revision). Choosing self-testing at the (imagined) expense of learning: A metacognitive dissociation.

Kornell, N., Son, L. K., & Terrace, H. (2007). Transfer of metacognitive skills and hint seeking in monkeys. *Psychological Science, 18,* 64–71.

Mazzoni, G., & Cornoldi, C. (1993). Strategies in study-time allocation: Why is study time sometimes not effective? *Journal of Experimental Psychology: General, 122,* 47–60.

Mazzoni, G., Cornoldi, C., & Marchitelli, G. (1990). Do memorability ratings affect study-time allocation? *Memory & Cognition, 18,* 196–204.

Mazzoni, G., & Nelson, T. O. (1995). Judgments of learning are affected by the kind of encoding in ways that cannot be attributed to the level of recall. *Journal of Experimental Psychology: Learning, Memory, and Cognition, 21,* 1263–1274.

Melton, A. W. (1963). Implications of short-term memory for a general theory of memory. *Journal of Verbal Learning and Verbal Behavior, 2,* 1–21.

Metcalfe, J. (2002). Is study time allocated selectively to a region of proximal learning? *Journal of Experimental Psychology: General, 131,* 349–363.

Metcalfe, J., & Kornell, N. (2003). The dynamics of learning and allocation of study time to a region of proximal learning. *Journal of Experimental Psychology: General, 132,* 530–542.

Metcalfe, J., & Kornell, N. (2005). A region of proximal learning model of study time allocation. *Journal of Memory and Language, 52,* 463–477.

Nelson, T. O. (1993). Judgments of learning and the allocation of study time. *Journal of Experimental Psychology: General, 122* 269–273.

Nelson, T. O., & Dunlosky, J. (1991). When people's judgments of learning (JOLs) are extremely accurate at predicting subsequent recall: The "delayed-JOL effect." *Psychological Science, 2,* 267–270.

Nelson, T. O., Dunlosky, J., Graf, A., & Narens, L. (1994). Utilization of metacognitive judgments in the allocation of study during multitrial learning. *Psychological Science, 5,* 207–213.

Nelson, T. O., & Leonesio, R. J. (1988). Allocation of self-paced study time and the "labor-in-vain effect." *Journal of Experimental Psychology: Learning, Memory, and Cognition, 14,* 676–686.

Roediger, H. L., III, & Karpicke, J. D. (2006a). The power of testing memory: Basic research and implications for educational practice. *Perspectives on Psychological Science, 1,* 181–210.

Roediger, H. L., III, & Karpicke, J. D. (2006b). Test-enhanced learning: Taking memory tests improves long-term retention. *Psychological Science, 17,* 249–255.

Sethi, R., & Son, L. K. (data collected in 2007, manuscript under revision). *Adaptive learning and the allocation of time.*

Simon, D. A., & Bjork, R. A. (2001). Metacognition in motor learning. *Journal of Experimental Psychology: Learning, Memory, and Cognition, 27,* 907–912.

Simon, H. A., & Chase, W. G. (1973). Skill in chess. *American Scientist, 61,* 391–403.

Son, L. K. (2004). Spacing one's study: evidence for a metacognitive control strategy. *Journal of Experimental Psychology: Learning, Memory, and Cognition, 30,* 601–604.

Son, L. K. (2005). Metacognitive control: Children's short-term versus long-term study strategies. *Journal of General Psychology, 132,* 347–363.

Son, L. K. (under revision). Monitoring, control, and heightened performance: A metacognitive progression. *Psychonomic Bulletin & Review.*

Son, L. K., & Kornell, N. (in preparation). Metacognitive organization of a study schedule.

Son, L. K., & Metcalfe, J. (2000). Metacognitive and control strategies in study-time allocation. *Journal of Experimental Psychology: Learning, Memory, and Cognition, 26*, 204–221.

Son, L. K., & Sethi, R. (2006). Metacognitive control and optimal learning. *Cognitive Science, 30*, 759–774.

Sternberg, S. (1966). High-speed scanning in human memory. *Science, 153*, 652–654.

Thiede, K. W., Anderson, M. C. M., & Therriault, D. (2003). Accuracy of metacognitive monitoring affects learning of texts. *Journal of Educational Psychology, 95*, 66–73.

Thiede, K. W., & Dunlosky, J. (1999). Toward a general model of self-regulated study: An analysis of selection of items for study and self-paced study time. *Journal of Experimental Psychology: Learning, Memory, and Cognition, 25*, 1024–1037.

Toops, H., & Kuder, G. F. (1935). Measures of aptitude. *Review of Educational Research, 5*, 215–228.

Zacks, R. T. (1969). Invariance of total learning time under different conditions of practice. *Journal of Experimental Psychology, 82*, 441–447.

Zechmeister, E. B., & Shaughnessy, J. J. (1980). When you know that you know and when you think that you know but you don't. *Bulletin of the Psychonomic Society, 15*, 41–44.

Contemporary Issues Involving the Metamemory–Memory Framework

Metacognitive Neuroscience

Bennett L. Schwartz and Elisabeth Bacon

Introduction

Metacognition can be defined as the awareness, experience, and control of our cognitive processes. Despite the obvious importance of metacognition to our sense of self (Metcalfe & Kober, 2005), there has been little research concerning the neuroscience of metacognition. However, those studies that have been conducted do show some common findings. It is clear the frontal lobes, particularly prefrontal areas, are essential to metacognition. Neuroimaging studies showed that prefrontal cortex is active during judgments of learning (JOLs), feeling-of-knowing (FOK) judgments, and tip-of-the-tongue (TOT) states. Neuropsychological patients with prefrontal damage show deficits in monitoring accuracy. Equally important, some drugs selectively impair metacognition. Studies have now demonstrated that benzodiazepines impair global metamemory assessments; that is, users of the drug are unaware of the amnesia induced by the drugs. However, benzodiazepines do not seem to affect relative accuracy in FOK judgments and JOLs. We speculate on the relation of metacognition to other tasks associated with the prefrontal lobes.

Nelson and Narens (Nelson, 1984, 1996; Nelson & Narens, 1980, 1990, 1994) made numerous contributions to the science of memory and psychology in general, but none more important than the development of both theories and methodologies to bring issues of metacognition to the experimentalists' table. In 1990, Nelson and Narens introduced their model of monitoring and control, which revolutionized the way in which metacognition was studied (see Nelson & Narens, 1990, 1994). They conceived of metacognition in terms of two interactive processes: a monitoring function, which provided consciously accessible information for introspection, and a control function, which allowed the person to direct learning or retrieval in adaptive (or maladaptive) ways (Nelson, 1996; Nelson & Narens, 1990). In addition, they postulated that the processes used in monitoring and control varied depending on the memory process in question. Thus, JOLs at encoding will tap different memory processes than do FOK judgments at retrieval (Nelson & Narens, 1990; also see Dunlosky & Nelson, 1994; Koriat, 1993, 1995; Metcalfe, 1993; Metcalfe, Schwartz, & Joaquim, 1993). For a quarter century, Nelson's contribution to the field led the way, and the rest of us followed. This chapter is no different. In particular, we connect Nelson and Narens's (1990) monitoring/control framework and the distinction between different forms of metacognitive judgments to the burgeoning literature on neuroscience and metamemory.

Although a steady stream of studies have examined the effects of brain damage on metamemory, only in the last few years has there been a serious attempt to look at metamemory from the standpoint of brain imaging and on the relation between psychopharmacology and metamemory. Although we will touch on the neuropsychological patient literature, our goal is to concentrate on neuroimaging and psychopharmacology work. Pannu and Kaszniak (2005) wrote an excellent review of the neuropsychological literature, which we do not attempt to duplicate here. Our goal is to make some generalizations about the neuroscience of metacognition.

In this chapter, we first review the Nelson and Narens (1990) framework with an eye to how it might be applied to neuroscience. Second, we advance some hypotheses, based on the Nelson/Narens framework, about which patterns we may expect to see in the neuroscience data. Third, we review the data on metamemory in three distinct areas: neuroimaging, psychopharmacology, and neuropsychology (the study of brain-damaged patients). Finally, we attempt to reconcile what we know about the brain with theories of metacognition.

The Nelson and Narens (1990) Framework

Nelson and Narens (1990) framework is, at its core, a functional one; that is, it focuses on the question, What purpose does metacognition serve the individual? Essential to the framework are the concepts of monitoring and control. Monitoring processes involve the assessment of the progress or success of a particular memory process. It provides the individual with feedback regarding the success or failure of a particular mnemonic (or cognitive) process (see Figure 1). We measure it by asking participants to report judgments. Ease of learning (EOL), JOLs, FOKs, TOT states, and retrospective confidence judgments (RCJs) all represent judgments that reveal aspects of the monitoring process. Each of these judgments taps into a different phase of the mnemonic process (see Figure 2). For the acquisition of information, Nelson and Narens provided us with EOLs for before study and JOLs for during study. For retrieval, we have FOKs and TOT states during retrieval and RCJs to assess the accuracy of that retrieval after it has occurred.

In the Nelson and Narens framework, monitoring is useless without the ability to use it to direct the ongoing cognitive processes, known as *control*. Control involves

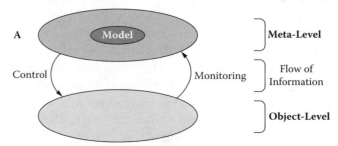

Figure 1   Nelson and Narens (1990) model of monitoring and control. (Adapted from Nelson & Narens, 1990, as adapted by Dunlosky, Serra, and Baker, 2007.)

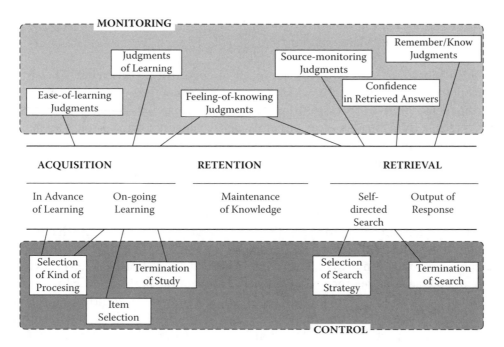

Figure 2   The stages of metamemory as they relate to memory. (Adapted from Nelson & Narens, 1990, as adapted by Dunlosky, Serra, & Baker, 2007.)

the decisions and behaviors we choose to do that may enhance (or sabotage) our chance of retrieving a particular memory later. That is, if we know we know something already, it requires no further study; if we do not know it, we ought to study it more. If we are confident we can recall something later that we cannot recall now, we may continue to search memory for that item. Thus, control behaviors include study time allocation, search strategy selection, and search termination.

Nelson and Narens (1990) argued that monitoring and control are highly interactive. They envisioned the system as one of constant feedback from one process to the other. Subsequent study of difficult items would lead to higher JOLs, which might result in the termination of study. Koriat, Ma'ayan, and Nussinson (2006) expanded on this idea, suggesting that the output of the control system is a major input for the monitoring system. In Koriat et al.'s view, one source of information for monitoring is the control behavior itself. In one way, this new approach turns all of metacognition on its head. Koriat et al. argued that we observe our control behaviors, and this provides us the information to make our judgments (monitoring). However, from the point of Nelson and Narens, the consequences of control are one more source of information to inform the metacognitive process of monitoring.

We think that there is now sufficient data to argue that the Nelson and Narens framework is more than a framework; it represents a model of the behavioral data. It is our goal here to demonstrate that different processes underlie monitoring and control at different stages of the learning and retrieval processes. We also suggest that a helpful avenue of research would be to examine the monitoring/control distinction using neuroscience methods (Izaute & Bacon, 2005).

Current Theory in Neuroscience: The Role of the Prefrontal Cortex in Metacognition

In this chapter, we start with the approach of cognitive neuroscience. That is, we attempt to construct a model of which large-scale areas of the human brain are active during metacognitive processes. To preface one of the obvious conclusions, converging evidence from various areas of neuroscience suggest a critical role for the prefrontal cortex in most aspects of metacognition (see Pannu & Kaszniak, 2005, for a review). Although this conclusion is not new (see Janowsky, Shimamura, & Squire, 1989; Shimamura, 2000, and the chapter, "A Neurocognitive Approach to Metacognitive Monitoring and Control," in this volume), neuroimaging data have been able to pinpoint function within the prefrontal cortex and to distinguish between how different monitoring processes differentially tap areas of the brain. That is, with the advent of functional magnetic resonance imaging (fMRI) and neuroimaging, researchers are beginning to uncover a more detailed correlation between brain function and metacognitive processes. We discuss areas of the brain specific to monitoring (at present, we could find no fMRI studies addressing metacognitive control) and if activity in some areas of the brain correlates with specific judgments but not others. Although we suspect that most of these areas will be found within the prefrontal cortex, it is important to note that it is never easy with the brain. The prefrontal cortex is large and has numerous subdivisions. Furthermore, metacognitive deficits have been observed after temporal damage (Prevey, Delaney, Mattson, & Tice, 1991), and some fMRI studies showed selective activation of areas of the brain other than the prefrontal cortex. Moreover, data from psychopharmacology on the selective effects of some drugs on metamemory further complicate the picture. Nonetheless, some consistent patterns have been clearly emerging.

Neuroimaging and Metamemory: JOLs, FOKs, and TOT States

There has been a paucity of fMRI studies concerning metamemory considering the enormous bulk of memory research now using fMRI. Those studies that have used fMRI to examine metamemory have examined FOKs or TOT states. We could identify only one article that examined JOLs using fMRI technology (Kao, Davis, & Gabrieli, 2005), which we review here. A handful of studies have used the technology to examine TOT states and FOKs, which we focus on here.

Kao et al. (2005), using fMRI technology, examined people's ability to predict their ability to later recognize visual pictures. Using this paradigm, Kao et al. examined both areas of the brain involved in encoding (medial temporal lobes) and those involved in monitoring. Consistent with the crucial role of prefrontal cortex in metacognition, Kao et al. found that left ventromedial prefrontal cortex was associated with JOLs but not memory performance. This left hemisphere preference was found even though the stimuli were visual. Kao et al. also found areas of the prefrontal cortex, lateral and dorsomedial, that were associated with both JOLs and successful recall. Thus, in the first fMRI study of JOLs, there are data that support the fundamental role of prefrontal cortex in metacognitive judgments. We now turn to FOKs and TOT states.

Most researchers have assumed a close correlation between TOT states and FOKs (i.e., Yaniv & Meyer, 1987; Schwartz, Travis, Castro, & Smith, 2000; but see Nelson, 2000). Most operational definitions of TOT states involve asking participants to judge if they feel like they can recall a target answer that is not currently recallable, whereas definitions of FOKs center on a feeling that one can recognize the target answer. Thus, one difference between the judgments is the criterion task judged (see Schwartz, 2002). Indeed, most behavioral studies have found strong correlations between FOKs and TOT states (Metcalfe et al., 1993; Schwartz et al., 2000; Yaniv & Meyer, 1987), although some data have been published to suggest that TOT states and FOKs are not always identical (Widner, Otani, & Winkelman, 2005; Widner, Smith, & Graziano, 1996). Interestingly, the neuroimaging data suggest differences between TOT states and FOKs that had previously been missed in the behavioral data.

The neuroimaging data show potential differences between TOT states and FOKs. It appears that, despite their verbal component, TOT states are dominated by right hemisphere prefrontal processes, whereas FOKs are carried out by the left prefrontal cortex. This counterintuitive finding has appeared in several studies. For example, using general information questions, both Maril, Wagner, and Schacter (2001) and Kikyo, Ohki, and Sekihara (2001) found mostly right prefrontal activity during TOT states. These areas included the anterior cingulate, the right dorsolateral prefrontal cortex and right inferior prefrontal cortex. These areas of the brain appeared unique to TOT states and were not as strongly activated during either know or don't know responses (Maril et al., 2001).

In contrast, Maril, Simon, Mitchell, Schwartz, and Schacter (2003) examined fMRI data during FOK judgments. With respect to FOKs, the unique activity appeared to be in areas in the left prefrontal cortex, notably the inferior frontal gyrus and in areas of the parietal lobe (Brodmann area [BA] 7). Similarly, Jing, Niki, Xiaoping, and Yuejia (2004) found left prefrontal activity (BAs 8 and 47) during FOKs for paired associates. Along similar lines, Schnyer, Nicholls, and Verfaellie (2005) found that the left ventral medial prefrontal cortex was uniquely activated during FOKs for the last word of a previously studied sentence. Kikyo, Ohki, and Miyashita (2002) also found mostly left prefrontal activity during FOKs, although they did find some activity bilaterally in the inferior and medial prefrontal cortex. Kikyo and Miyashita (2004) found bilateral prefrontal activity for FOKs when retrieving names from face–name pairs. They also found activity in the temporal lobe. Nonetheless, these studies paint a picture in which TOT states tend to be produced in the right prefrontal cortex and anterior cingulate, and FOKs tend to be produced in the left prefrontal cortex.

The comparison between FOKs and TOT states is compromised by the difference in materials used in each of the studies described. In the TOT studies, Maril et al. (2001) and Kikyo et al. (2001) asked participants to retrieve information from their existing semantic memory. Although Kikyo et al. (2001, 2002) used the same stimuli, it is difficult to compare the two studies because the 2001 study inferred the presence of TOT states rather than asked for them directly. That is, TOT states were assumed to have occurred if a participant could not recall the item but recognized it later. For many reasons, this logic is suspect (see Schwartz, 2002). In the studies examining FOKs, Maril et al. (2003) and Jing et al. (2004) asked participants to retrieve newly learned word pairs. Schnyer et al. (2005), examining FOK as well, used sentence completion. Thus, in these studies, the type of judgment (TOT vs. FOK) is confounded with the stimuli used to assess the judgments.

To resolve this discrepancy, Maril, Simons, Weaver, and Schacter (2005) compared TOT states and FOKs in the same study using the same stimuli. The stimuli were similar to those of Maril et al. (2001). The experimenters gave the participant two cue words (e.g., Carmen, composer), and the participants had to recall the name of the composer of the opera *Carmen* (Bizet). If participants could not recall the target, they had the opportunity to press a button that either meant FOK or that meant TOT. Consistent with their earlier work, Maril et al. (2005) found that TOT states, but not FOKs, were associated with activity in the anterior cingulate, right dorsolateral prefrontal cortex, and right inferior cortex. They did not find, however, activity uniquely associated with FOKs.

Thus, this study is suggestive that TOT states and FOKs may be qualitatively different psychological states as areas of the brain were activated during TOT states but not during FOKs. However, because the participants in Maril et al. (2005) could only choose to indicate a TOT or an FOK, it is likely that the task demands suggested that TOT states marked stronger states of knowing for the participants than did FOKs. Thus, participants may have used the FOK judgment to indicate that they likely knew the target but were not as confident as when they indicated a TOT. Thus, the areas of the brain that were activated for TOT states but not for FOKs may simply reflect this greater strength or confidence rather than any qualitative differences between FOKs and TOT states. Indeed, it would have been revealing if, using the same stimuli but different participants, fMRIs could be collected while only a TOT or an FOK is requested. Nonetheless, the Maril et al. (2005) study combined with the other studies suggest that there may in fact be qualitative differences between TOT states and FOKs, but each study alone is not adequate to argue for different underlying processes. Although any such conclusions are premature simply because not enough data have been collected, it is worth noting that, like JOLs, the FOKs appear to show up in the left ventromedial cortex, whereas the TOT states appear to show up in the right dorsolateral cortex. This may suggest that FOKs and JOLs share more in common than do FOKs and TOT states (see Table 1).

In contrast to FOKs and TOT states, which seem to be based on processes in the prefrontal cortex, regardless of their placement in the left and right hemisphere, a new study suggested that not all metamemory may be directed by prefrontal processes (Chua, Schacter, Rand-Giovannetti, & Sperling, 2006). Chua et al. examined RCJs after recognition judgments in a face–name paradigm. Following recognition, participants judged their confidence in the correctness of their answer. During this decision, Chua et al. found activity in the parietal lobe (both medial and lateral) when comparing RCJs to recognition. Comparing high confidence to low confidence revealed activity in the hippocampus and cingulate as well as other limbic regions. Thus, although the cingulate is active in both TOT states and retrospective confidence, the other regions are greatly different. Future studies must be done to confirm the role of the parietal lobe in RCJs.

Neuroimaging holds great promise in the understanding of human cognitive processes. We look forward to updating this section in 10 years with not a handful of studies but a torrent of them. We encourage those researchers with access to

TABLE 1 Neuroimaging Studies, Metamemory Measurement, and the Regions of Brain Uniquely Associated with Metamemory Judgments

Study	Metamemory Measure	Left or Right Hemisphere	Region of Cortex
Kao et al. (2005)	JOL	Left	Ventromedial PF
			Lateral and dorsomedial PF
Maril et al. (2001)	TOT	Right	Anterior cingulate
			Dorsolateral PF
			Inferior PF
Kikyo et al. (2001)	TOT[a]	Right	Anterior cingulate
			Dorsolateral PF
			Inferior PF
Maril et al. (2005)	TOT	Right	Anterior cingulate
			Dorsolateral PF
			Inferior PF
Maril et al. (2005)	FOK		No unique activity
Maril et al. (2003)	FOK	Left	Inferior PF
			Parietal
Jing et al. (2004)	FOK	Left	Inferior PF
Kikyo et al. (2002)	FOK	Bilateral	Inferior and medial PF
Kikyo & Miyashita (2004)	FOK	Bilateral	PF, temporal lobe
Schnyer et al. (2005)	FOK	Left	Ventromedial PF
Chua et al. (2006)	RCJ	Bilateral	Parietal (medial and lateral)

Note: FOK, feeling of knowing; JOL, judgment of learning; PF, prefrontal cortex; RCJ, retrospective confidence judgment; TOT, tip of the tongue.

[a]TOTs were inferred by the researchers, not provided by the participants.

neuroimaging tools to investigate metacognitive processes. Comparisons across metamemory judgments that equate on procedures and stimuli may be especially useful. In addition, examining metacognitive control using fMRI techniques should bear fruit.

Drugs and Metamemory

A number of psychopharmacological agents have been used in studies examining metamemory. These drugs include alcohol (Nelson, McSpadden, Fromme, & Marlatt, 1986; Nelson et al., 1998); amphetamines (Mintzer & Griffiths, 2003); caffeine (Lesk & Womble, 2004); nitrous oxide (Dunlosky et al., 1998); scopolamine (Mintzer & Griffiths, 2005); methadone (Mintzer & Stitzer, 2002); and benzodiazepines (Bacon et al., 1998; Bacon, Schwartz et al., 2007; Izaute & Bacon, 2005; Massin-Krauss, Bacon, & Danion, 2002; Merritt, Hirshman, Hsu, & Berrigan, 2005; Mintzer & Griffiths, 2005; Roy-Byrne et al., 1987; Wolkowitz et al., 1987). Although most of these drugs have wide and diverse effects on the brain, they can be used to probe cognitive function. In particular, because of the profound amnesic effects of benzodiazepines (Bacon, Schwartz et al., 2007), this class of drugs has been investigated in a number of metamemory paradigms. We focus on the literature on the effects of benzodiazepines on metamemory.

Benzodiazepines, such as diazepam, lorazepam, triazolam, and midazolam, are the most commonly consumed drugs in the Western world because of their effects on anxiety, insomnia, and muscle relaxation (Kaplan, 2005). However, they are also strong amnesia-inducing drugs, especially within the episodic memory domain (Buffet-Jerrott & Stewart, 2002; Curran, 1991, 1999, 2000; Danion, 1994). The benzodiazepines that are the most commonly studied in cognitive research are diazepam, lorazepam, and midazolam. The pattern of memory impairment differs slightly from one benzodiazepine to another, as for example, lorazepam impairs priming, whereas diazepam does not (Buffet-Jerrott & Stewart, 2002). All the benzodiazepines impair episodic memory, but their effects on short-term memory and semantic memory are mixed, depending on the task (Bacon, Izaute, & Danion, 2007; Izaute & Bacon, 2006).

Clinical observations indicated that patients who develop a transient amnesia following an acute administration of benzodiazepine are grossly unaware that they are currently experiencing an episodic memory deficit (Hinrichs, Mewaldt, Ghoneim, & Berie, 1982; Curran et al., 1987; Roache & Griffith, 1985; Weingartner et al., 1993). For example, Roache and Griffith (1985) observed that subjects under the influence of benzodiazepine consistently underestimated the degree of their impairment relative to their predrug performance. These observations suggest that metamemory, as measured by FOKs, JOLs, or RCJs, might also be impaired.

However, there is preliminary evidence from a few experimental studies that some aspects of metamemory are preserved during benzodiazepine-induced amnesia. Wolkowitz et al. (1987) considered that diazepam-treated subjects were able to retrospectively estimate their level of performance in a free-recall task, with their confidence ratings declining as a function of the diazepam dose. In another study of diazepam, Roy-Byrne et al. (1987) reported that subjects experienced a subjective sense of cognitive impairment; when the subjects were asked to rate their confidence for recalled words, there was no impairment of their ability to judge how well they had performed the task.

However, these studies with diazepam have investigated metamemory on the basis of global memory performance and not on the basis of correspondence between each individual metamemory rating and each individual answer. In the meantime, the possibility cannot be excluded that metamemory is impaired by some, but not all, benzodiazepines.

The question that has concerned metamemory researchers is whether participants display metamemory deficits when explored with the standard tools of metamemory (see Nelson & Narens, 1990). Most of the studies arrive at similar conclusions. Benzodiazepines leave participants globally unaware that their memory has become weaker, although they may remain aware of which items they are learning or remembering and which items they are not learning or remembering; that is, benzodiazepines do not impair relative judgment accuracy (for details on measuring relative accuracy, see Benjamin & Diaz, this volume). Thus, global confidence and calibration tend to be inaccurate while participants are under the influence of benzodiazepines, whereas relative accuracy is unaffected by benzodiazepines.

Izaute and Bacon (2006) investigated the effects of lorazepam on recall of both complete and partial information of recently learned material as well as on the effects of the retrieved partial information on FOK ratings (i.e., Koriat, 1993). The material to be learned consisted of four-letter nonsense tetragrams, with each letter providing partial information with regard to the four-letter target. They observed that, under the influence of lorazepam, participants presented an impairment of episodic short-term memory performance, and that the drug reduced FOK magnitudes, which were lower than the estimations of the placebo participants. However, the predictive value of the FOK remained accurate.

With respect to the retrieval of partial information, Izaute and Bacon (2006) showed that, in both the lorazepam and control condition, FOKs increased with the amount of partial information retrieved. This increase in FOK and partial information was also diagnostic of final recognition. High γ correlations were observed in both groups between the FOKs and partial retrieval, and both FOK and partial retrieval were highly correlated with recognition performance (Izaute & Bacon, 2006). Thus, this study supported the accessibility hypothesis as a source of information for FOK judgments (Koriat, 1993).

Bacon et al. (1998) and Merritt et al. (2005) examined the role of lorazepam and midazolam, respectively, on FOKs in tasks assessing episodic memory. Bacon et al. used a sentence completion task. Participants studied sentences and later had to recall the last word from each sentence. In case of no recall (omissions), they gave FOK judgments regarding the retrievability of the target answer in a future recognition task. The accuracy of FOK was measured by the γ coefficient. The results showed that FOK ratings of the lorazepam-treated participants were slightly but not significantly lower than those expressed by the placebos. Indeed, the lorazepam group's FOK accuracy was at chance (0.06), whereas that of the placebo group, albeit low (0.29), was significantly above chance. However, one cannot really conclude that metamemory accuracy was impaired by lorazepam because differences between groups were not statistically significant. Merritt et al. (2005) used paired associate learning, and a forced recall step was followed by a recognition stage. Participants were asked to give immediate JOLs in the course of the learning stage, and they had to judge FOKs for the incorrect recall answers (commissions). The measure of metamemory accuracy was here obtained by Hart's difference score as the γ correlation could not be obtained due to floor memory effect in the midazolam group. Here, the mean FOKs were significantly lower under midazolam, but the accuracy of the judgments was not affected by midazolam. Thus, both studies found that benzodiazepines lowered the mean FOK rating but did not affect accuracy. Furthermore, in tasks assessing semantic memory, Bacon et al. (1998) and Bacon, Izaute and Danion (2007), using general information questions, found that FOK accuracy was not impaired by lorazepam. Thus, individual metacognitive judgments made at the time of retrieval and regarding future retrievability of memory targets were not affected adversely by benzodiazepines. Participants were aware on an item-by-item basis of which targets they would not remember.

Three studies have examined the effect of benzodiazepines on JOLs (Izaute & Bacon, 2005; Merritt et al., 2005; Mintzer & Griffiths, 2005). The three studies revealed converging findings. First, both Izaute and Bacon (2005) and Mintzer and Griffiths (2005) found that the relative accuracy of JOLs was not affected by the benzodiazepines. Merritt et al. did not have enough participants who produced measurable γ correlations to determine JOL accuracy. Second, Izaute and Bacon (2005) and Mintzer and Griffiths (2005) found that although relative accuracy was unimpaired, absolute accuracy was impaired. JOLs tended to be overconfident (Mintzer & Griffiths, 2005), not different from the placebo condition, even though memory was impaired (Merritt et al., 2005). Mintzer and Griffiths suggested, and we concur, that although participants may be able to order items in relative strength of memory, they are globally unaware that the benzodiazepines are affecting their memory. Thus, they do not lower their JOLs, leading to overcalibration and poor study time decisions.

Four studies have closely examined the effects of benzodiazepines on post-answer confidence or RCJs (Bacon et al., 1998; Massin-Krauss et al., 2002; Mintzer & Griffiths, 2003, 2005). In tasks assessing episodic memory, the data are quite equivocal. Mintzer and Griffiths (2003) found that the benzodiazepine triazolam lowered γ correlations of RCJs after recognition judgments for a list of words. In the sentence completion task from Bacon et al. (1998), γ correlations between RCJs and recall were lower in the lorazepam condition than in the control condition, whereas Mintzer and Griffith did not find decreases in γ correlations between RCJs and recall between the lorazepam and control conditions in a cued recall task with word pairs. Two studies explored RCJs in tasks assessing semantic memory using general information questions. Bacon et al. (1998) and Massin-Krauss et al. (2002) did not find decreases in γ correlations between RCJs and recall between the lorazepam and control conditions. Thus, we have a picture of RCJs that suggest accurate relative accuracy, if sometimes impaired. However, it is difficult to draw definite conclusions as the memory test and general procedures and benzodiazepines used differed in various studies.

The general pattern that emerges from these studies is the following: The benzodiazepines do not affect a person's ability to discriminate items in memory, that is, relative accuracy. Under lorazepam, participants know which items are more or less difficult to learn or retrieve. However, they do not seem to be aware of the general amnesic-producing effects of the benzodiazepines. Thus, on global measures, they tend to overestimate confidence (Mintzer & Griffiths, 2005), to increase the number of commission errors (Bacon et al., 1998; Bacon, Schwartz et al., 2007), or to fail to study items for longer to compensate for the drug-induced amnesia (Izaute & Bacon, 2005).

The question can be asked: Does this mean that benzodiazepines affect metamemory at all? The answer to this is somewhat oblique. They do not affect discrimination or relative accuracy, the ability to distinguish those items that are better or more poorly learned, stored, or retrieved. For those who approach metacognition from the perspective of cognitive psychology, this is what is central to metacognition. However, benzodiazepines fail to induce a metamnemonic awareness of the amnesic deficit, sometimes known as *absolute accuracy*. This, then, is indeed a failure of metacognition to notice what is a robust effect on memory. So, from this perspective, benzodiazepines can be considered to induce a deficit in metacognition.

Metamemory and Neuropsychology

Metamemory has now been investigated across a wide range of patients in a wide range of tasks (see Pannu & Kaszniak, 2005, for a recent review). Although there are exceptions, much of this work supports the idea that the prefrontal areas of the frontal lobe are important for metacognition, and metacognitive deficits arise when these areas are damaged. In this section, we review the data that support this conclusion.

In an early article that examined metamemory in patient populations, Shimamura and Squire (1986) compared two classes of amnesic patients, a mixed group of patients with amnesia compared with a group of Korsakoff patients. The patients were tested with respect to both episodic and semantic memory. FOK judgments were the criterion metacognitive judgment. They found that, despite poor memory on the part of the mixed-etiology amnesia group, there was intact FOK accuracy. However, the Korsakoff group was significantly lower in relative FOK accuracy, as measured by γ correlations, than the mixed-etiology amnesia group (and the control). Moreover, the Korsakoff group FOK accuracy did not differ from chance.

Janowsky et al. (1989) compared FOK accuracy in patients with frontal lobe damage and patients with damage to their temporal lobe in both semantic and episodic memory tasks. In the episodic task, the patients with frontal lobe damage showed a deficit in FOK accuracy only after long retention intervals. However, in RCJs, there were no significant differences across groups, suggesting that RCJs tap into a different set of neurocognitive processes than do other metacognitive judgments. Schnyer et al. (2004) also found lower FOK accuracy among patients with prefrontal damage, and similar to Janowsky et al. (1989), they also did not find differences between patients and controls in RCJ accuracy. Schnyer et al.'s study suggested a greater involvement of the right medial prefrontal cortex, consistent with their later neuroimaging study (Schnyer et al., 2005).

Pinon et al. (2005) also looked at patients with frontal lesions classified as having dysexecutive syndrome (defined as a "failure to control the selection of information in temporary storage"; Shimamura, 2000, p. 208). The patients were asked to study word pairs for a later memory test. Relative to healthy controls, the patients with frontal lesions showed impaired FOK accuracy as measured by γ correlations. Indeed, these patients' γ correlations were considerably below zero; that is, they mispredicted their future retrieval. Despite the strong deficit in FOK accuracy, JOL accuracy did not significantly differ between patients with frontal lesions and healthy controls.

Widner et al. (2005) looked at normal participants but screened them for frontal lobe functioning. They then divided the participants into those who scored low on frontal functioning and those who scored high. Consistent with other studies, Widner et al. found lower FOK accuracy among those who scored low on frontal functioning relative to those who scored high. This effect was present for FOKs but not TOT states. There was no difference among the groups in terms of number and accuracy of TOT states. Of course, these were normal functioning people, so it is not clear what to make of the null effects on TOT states. Nonetheless, the FOK data are consistent with the claim that prefrontal lobes are important to metacognitive monitoring.

Two studies examined the effect of frontal damage on a prediction of global recall. Vilkki, Servo, and Surma-aho (1998) asked participants to remember lists of words. Afterward, the patients and controls were asked to predict how many words they would recall from each list. The patients with left frontal lobe damage showed impaired recall and predictive ability relative to the patients with impaired right frontal lobe and controls. Similarly, Vilkki, Surma-aho, and Servo (1999) found that when predicting which faces people would recognize, patients with damaged right frontal lobes showed a deficit in both retrieval and prediction. In both studies, the patients tended to be markedly overconfident in their predictions. Although these studies required more global judgments and neither of these studies required JOLs specific to each item, they further reinforce the centrality of the prefrontal lobes to metamemory.

Vilkki et al.'s studies (1998, 1999) also required participants to make FOKs and RCJs. Like the predictions of recall, FOKs were impaired in the patients with frontal damage (as in Janowsky et al., 1989; Schnyer et al., 2004). However, RCJs showed no differences between patients with frontal lobe damage and controls. This parallels the neuroimaging findings from Chua et al. (2006) that showed that parietal areas of the brain appear to be associated with RCJs rather than the prefrontal areas involved in other metamemory judgments.

However, as is typical when examining brain damage, the story is not that neat. Pannu, Kaszniak, and Rapcsak (2005) looked at FOKs and RCJs for face stimuli in patients with damaged frontal lobes and in controls. In contrast to all the previously reviewed studies, when making FOKs for faces, the patients with impaired frontal lobes did not differ from controls. However, again in contrast with other studies, RCJs were impaired for the patients with impaired frontal lobes relative to controls. This suggests that the neural bases of metacognition are at least partially dependent on the material that is being processed.

RCJs appear to have different bases than other memory judgments, perhaps because they are made retrospectively, that is, after a memory has been retrieved, rather than prospectively (before the memory is retrieved), as in FOKs, TOT states, and JOLs. Interestingly, RCJ accuracy is somewhat impaired in schizophrenia (Moritz, Woodward, & Chen, 2006). First-episode schizophrenics showed higher confidence for errors and lower confidence for correct answers when asked to express confidence in retrieved words (Moritz et al., 2006). In patients with chronic schizophrenia, the accuracies of either JOLs (Bacon et al., 2007) or the FOKs for episodic (Souchay, Bacon, & Danion, 2006) or semantic tasks (Bacon, Danion, Kauffmann-Muller, & Bruant, 2001) were preserved. This pattern is opposite of what was described here for patients with frontal lobe impairment.

However, across a host of other neurological conditions, Pannu and Kaszniak (2005) found little evidence for impaired metacognition relative to other cognitive functions. That is, metacognition may be impaired, as in Alzheimer's, but so are all other functions. They reviewed the literature on metamemory in multiple sclerosis, traumatic brain injury, temporal lobe epilepsy, Alzheimer's disease, Parkinson's disease, Huntington's disease, and HIV infection. Only when the studies they reviewed cited evidence of compromised frontal function did they see evidence of selective impaired metamemory. The exception may be temporal lobe epilepsy. Prevey et al. (1991) found that temporal lobe epileptics showed lower FOK accuracy than did normal controls. We note here that there are many studies examining metacognition in Alzheimer's, which are not reviewed here. We refer those interested to the review of Pannu and Kaszniak (2005).

Based on these studies, Pannu and Kaszniak (2005) concluded that the data "across metamemory studies in neurological populations are consistent with the conclusion that the frontal lobes play a central role in the production of accurate metamemory judgments" (p. 122). They continued to argue that this effect may be exacerbated in patients who have memory deficits and compromised frontal function. Thus, they did not think of the prefrontal lobes as the only area involved in metacognition, just one of the important components.

Putting Things Together

There is good reason to argue that the neuroscience data on metacognition are consistent with the Nelson and Narens (1990) framework. First, the neuroscience data support the idea that each judgment (JOLs, EOLs, FOK, etc.) is a unique expression of the monitoring system. That is, it appears that different circuits in the brain are involved in different judgments and with respect to different kinds of stimuli. Thus, JOLs are different from FOKs in the way the judgment is made, the kinds of information that it draws on, and in the areas of the brain responsible. Although both appear mediated by the left ventromedial cortex, FOKs also appear to draw on inferior prefrontal cortex. Moreover, Maril and her colleagues (Maril et al., 2001, 2003, 2005) showed that subtle differences between TOT states and FOKs can be traced to different neural circuits. TOT states are based on the right dorsolateral prefrontal cortex, whereas FOKs show up in the left ventromedial cortex. Finally, some judgments, in particular RCJs, appear to have a different neural basis, in the parietal lobe rather than the frontal lobe.

The second major component of the Nelson-Narens (1990) model is the distinction between monitoring and control. *Monitoring* refers to the processes that allow us to assess and become aware of our cognitive processes, *whereas* control refers to the processes we use to affect change in our cognitive processes. Much behavioral data support this distinction that we can control our cognitive processes in complex and often-helpful ways (but see Koriat et al., 2006). However, at present, although the neuroscience data on monitoring are increasing rapidly, there are only a few studies that examined metacognitive control from the point of view of neuroimaging, psychopharmacology, or neuropsychology. Izaute and Bacon (2005) found that benzodiazepines interfered with the relation between JOLs, which were accurate at predicting recall, and study time decisions. This article suggests that it may be possible to find neural distinctions between monitoring and control, but at present the data just are not there from other judgments and other methodologies. We urge those researchers with access to neuropsychological patients, fMRI machines, and other neuroscience methodologies to begin to address the issue of metacognitive control. Metacognitive control is the means by which people can consciously affect change in their rapid ongoing cognitive processes. Discovering its neural basis would indeed be important.

Acknowledgment

Both of us have been profoundly influenced by the thinking and writing of Tom Nelson. His works are the "bedside" reading of our own research; like all of us, we miss him greatly. We would like to thank Arthur Shimamura and Leslie Frazier for comments on earlier drafts of this chapter.

References

Bacon, E., Danion, J.-M., Kauffmann-Muller, F., & Bruant, A. (2001). Consciousness in schizophrenia: A metacognitive approach to semantic memory. *Consciousness and Cognition, 10*, 473–484.

Bacon, E., Danion, J.-M., Kauffmann-Muller, F., Schelstraete, M-A., Bruant, A., Sellal, F., et al. (1998). Confidence level and feeling of knowing for episodic and semantic memory: An investigation of lorazepam effects on metamemory. *Psychopharmacology, 138*, 318–325.

Bacon, E., Izaute, M., & Danion, J.-M. (2007) Preserved memory monitoring but impaired memory control during episodic encoding in patients with schizophrenia. *Journal of the International Neuropsychological Society, 13*, 219–227.

Bacon, E., Schwartz, B. L., Paire-Ficout, L., & Izaute, M. (2007). Dissociation between the cognitive process and the phenomenological experience of TOT: Effect of the anxiolytic drug lorazepam on TOT states. *Consciousness and Cognition, 16*, 360–373.

Buffet-Jerrott, S. E., & Stewart, S. H. (2002). Cognitive and sedative effects of benzodiazepine use. *Current Pharmaceutical Design, 8*, 45–58.

Chua, E. F., Schacter, D. L., Rand-Giovannetti, E., & Sperling, R. A. (2006). Understanding metamemory: Neural correlates of the cognitive process and subjective level of confidence in recognition memory. *NeuroImage, 29*, 1150–1160.

Curran, H. V. (1991). Benzodiazepines, memory and mood: A review. *Psychopharmacology, 105*, 1–8.

Curran, H. V. (1999). Effects of anxiolytics on memory. *Human Psychopharmacology, 14*, 72–79.

Curran, H. V. (2000). Psychopharmacological approaches to human memory. In M. S. Gazzaniga (Ed.), *The new cognitive neurosciences* (2nd ed., pp. 797–804). Boston: MIT Press.

Curran, H. V., Schiwy, W., & Lader, M. (1987). Differential amnesic properties of benzodiazepines: A dose-response comparison of two drugs with similar elimination half-lives. *Psychopharmacology, 92*, 358–364.

Danion, J.-M. (1994). Drugs as a tool for investigating memory. *European Neuropsycho-pharmacology, 4*, 179–180.

Dunlosky, J., Ishikawa, T., Nelson, T. O., Domoto, P. K., Wang, M.-L., Roberson, I., et al. (1998). Inhalation of 30% nitrous oxide impairs people's learning without impairing people's judgments of learning of what will be remembered. *Experimental and Clinical Psychopharmacology, 6*, 77–86.

Dunlosky, J., & Nelson, T. O. (1994). Does the sensitivity of judgments of learning (JOLs) to the effects of various study activities depend on when JOLs occur? *Journal of Memory and Language, 33*, 545–565.

Dunlosky, J., Serra, M. J., & Baker, M. C. (2007). Metamemory. In F. Durso et al. (Eds.), *Handbook of applied cognition* (2nd ed., pp. 137–162). New York: Wiley.

Hinrichs, J. V., Mewaldt, S. T., Ghoneim, M. M., & Berie J. L. (1982). Diazepam and learning: Assessment of acquisition deficits. *Pharmacology, Biochemistry, and Behavior, 17,* 165–170.

Izaute, M., & Bacon, E. (2005). Specific effects of an amnesic drug: Effects of lorazepam on study time allocation and on judgment of learning. *Neuropsychopharmacology, 30,* 196–204.

Izaute, M., & Bacon, E. (2006). Effects of the amnesic drug lorazepam on complete and partial information retrieval and monitoring accuracy. *Psychopharmacology, 188,* 472–481.

Janowsky, J. S., Shimamura, A. P., & Squire, L. R. (1989). Memory and metamemory: Comparisons between patients with frontal lobes damage and amnesic patients. *Psychobiology, 17,* 3–11.

Jing, L., Niki, K., Xiaoping, Y., & Yue-jia, L. (2004). Knowing that you know and knowing that you don't know: A fMRI study on feeling-of-knowing (FOK). *Acta Psychologica Sinica, 36,* 426–433.

Kao, Y.-C., Davis, E. S., & Gabrieli, J. D. E. (2005). Neural correlates of actual and predicted memory formation. *Nature Neuroscience, 8,* 1776–1783.

Kaplan, M. (2005). Benzodiazepines and anxiety disorders: A review for the practicing physician. *Current Medical Research and Opinion, 6,* 941–950.

Kikyo, H., & Miyashita, Y. (2004). Temporal lobe activation of "feeling-of-knowing" induced by face-name associations. *NeuroImage, 23,* 1348–1357.

Kikyo, H., Ohki, K., & Miyashita, Y. (2002). Neural correlates for feeling-of-knowing: An fMRI parametric analysis. *Neuron, 36,* 177–186.

Kikyo, H., Ohki, K., & Sekihara, K. (2001). Temporal characterization of memory retrieval processes: an fMRI study of the "tip of the tongue" phenomenon. *European Journal of Neuroscience, 14,* 887–892.

Koriat, A. (1993). How do we know that we know? The accessibility account of the feeling of knowing. *Psychological Review, 100,* 609–639.

Koriat, A. (1995). Dissociating knowing and the feeling of knowing: Further evidence for the accessibility model. *Journal of Experimental Psychology: General, 124,* 311–333.

Koriat, A., Ma'ayan, H., & Nussinson, R. (2006). Metacognition: Lessons for the cause-and-effect relation between subjective experience and behavior. *Journal of Experimental Psychology: General, 135,* 36–69.

Lesk, V. E., & Womble, S. P. (2004). Caffeine, priming and tip of the tongue: Evidence for plasticity in the phonological system. *Behavioral Neuroscience, 118,* 453–461.

Maril, A., Simon, J. S., Mitchell, J. P., Schwartz, B. L., & Schacter, D. L. (2003). Feeling-of-knowing in episodic memory: An event-related fMRI study. *NeuroImage, 18,* 827–836.

Maril, A., Simons, J. S., Weaver, J. J., & Schacter, D. L. (2005). Graded recall success: an event-related fMRI comparison of tip of the tongue and feeling of knowing. *NeuroImage, 24,* 1130–1138.

Maril, A., Wagner, A. D., & Schacter, D. L. (2001). On the tip of the tongue: An event-related fMRI study of semantic retrieval failure and cognitive conflict. *Neuron, 31,* 653–660.

Massin-Krauss, M., Bacon, E., & Danion, J.-M. (2002). Effects of the benzodiazepine lorazepam on monitoring and control processes in semantic memory. *Consciousness and Cognition, 11,* 123–137.

Merritt, P., Hirshman, E., Hsu, J., & Berrigan, M. (2005). Metamemory without the memory: Are people aware of midazolam-induced amnesia. *Psychopharmacology, 177,* 336–343.

Metcalfe, J. (1993). Novelty monitoring, metacognition, and control in a composite holographic associative recall model: Interpretations for Korsakoff amnesia. *Psychological Review, 100*, 3–22.

Metcalfe, J., & Kober, H. (2005). Self-reflective consciousness and the projectable self. In H. Terrace & J. Metcalfe (Eds.), *The missing link in cognition: Origins of self-reflective consciousness* (pp. 57–83). Oxford, U.K.: Oxford University Press.

Metcalfe, J., Schwartz, B. L., & Joaquim, S. G. (1993). The cue familiarity heuristic in metacognition. *Journal of Experimental Psychology: Learning, Memory, and Cognition, 19*, 851–861.

Mintzer, M. Z., & Griffiths, R. R. (2003). Triazolam-amphetamine interaction: Dissociation of effects on memory versus arousal. *Journal of Psychopharmacology, 17*, 17–29.

Mintzer, M. Z., & Griffiths, R. R. (2005). Drugs, memory, and metamemory: A dose-effect study with lorazepam and scopolamine. *Experimental and Clinical Psychopharmacology, 13*, 336–347.

Mintzer, M. Z., & Stitzer, M. L. (2002). Cognitive impairment in methadone maintenance patients. *Drug and Alcohol Dependence, 67*, 41–51.

Moritz, S., Woodward, T. S., & Chen, E. (2006). Investigation of metamemory dysfunctions in first-episode schizophrenia. *Schizophrenia Research, 81*, 247–252.

Nelson, T. O. (1984). A comparison of measures of the accuracy of feeling-of-knowing predictions. *Psychological Bulletin, 95*, 109–133.

Nelson, T. O. (1996). Consciousness and metacognition. *American Psychologist, 51*, 102–116.

Nelson, T. O. (2000). Consciousness, self-consciousness, and metacognition. *Consciousness and Cognition, 9*, 220–223.

Nelson, T. O., Graf, A., Dunlosky, J., Marlatt, A., Walker, D., & Luce, K. (1998). Effect of acute alcohol intoxication on recall and on judgments of learning during the acquisition of new information. In G. Mazzoni & T. O. Nelson (Eds.), *Metacognition and neuropsychology: Monitoring and control processes* (pp. 161–180). Mahwah, NJ: Erlbaum.

Nelson, T. O., McSpadden, M., Fromme, K., & Marlatt, G. A. (1986). Effects of alcohol intoxication on metamemory and on retrieval from long-term memory. *Journal of Experimental Psychology: General, 115*, 247–254.

Nelson, T. O., & Narens, L. (1980). Norms of 300 general-information questions: Accuracy of recall, latency of recall, and feeling-of-knowing ratings. *Journal of Verbal Learning and Verbal Behavior, 19*, 338–368.

Nelson, T. O., & Narens, L. (1990). Metamemory: A theoretical framework and new findings. In G. H. Bower (Ed.), *The psychology of learning and motivation* (pp. 1–45). New York: Academic Press.

Nelson, T. O., & Narens, L. (1994). Why investigate metacognition. In J. Metcalfe & A. Shimamura (Eds.), *Metacognition: Knowing about knowing* (pp. 1–26). Cambridge, MA: MIT Press.

Pannu, J. K., & Kaszniak, A. W. (2005). Metamemory experiments in neurological populations: A review. *Neuropsychological Review, 15*, 105–130.

Pannu, J. K., Kaszniak, A. W., & Rapcsak, S. Z. (2005). Metamemory for faces following frontal-lobe damage. *Journal of the International Neuropsychological Society, 11*, 668–676.

Pinon, K., Allain, P., Kefi, M. Z., Dubas, F., & Le Gall, D. (2005). Monitoring processes and metamemory experience in patients with dysexecutive syndrome. *Brain and Cognition, 57*, 185–188.

Prevey, M. L., Delaney, R. C., Mattson, R. H., & Tice, D. M. (1991). Feeling-of-knowing in temporal lobe epilepsy: Monitoring knowledge inaccessible to conscious recall. *Cortex, 27*, 81–92.

Roache, J. D., & Griffith, R. G. (1985). Comparison of triazolam and pentobarbital: performance impairment, subjective effects and abuse liability. *The Journal of Pharmacology and Experimental Therapeutics, 234,* 120–133.

Roy-Byrne, P. P., Uhde, T. W., Holcomb, H., Thompson, K., King, A. K., & Weingartner, H. (1987). Effects of diazepam on cognitive processes in normal subjects. *Psychopharmacology, 91,* 30–33.

Schnyer, D. M., Nicholls, L., & Verfaellie, M. (2005). The role of VMPC in metamemorial judgments of content retrievability. *Journal of Cognitive Neuroscience, 17,* 832–846.

Schnyer, D. M., Verfaellie, M., Alexander, M., LaFleche, G., Nicholls, L., & Kaszniak, A. W. (2004). A role for right medial prefrontal cortex in accurate feeling-of-knowing judgments: Evidence from patients with lesions to frontal cortex. *Neuropsychologia, 42,* 957–966.

Schwartz, B. L. (2002). *Tip-of-the-tongue states: Phenomenology, mechanism, and lexical retrieval.* Mahwah, NJ: Erlbaum.

Schwartz, B. L., Travis, D. M., Castro, A. M., & Smith, S. M. (2000). The phenomenology of real and illusory tip-of-the-tongue states. *Memory & Cognition, 28,* 18–27.

Shimamura, A. P. (2000). The role of the prefrontal cortex in dynamic filtering. *Psychobiology, 28,* 207–218.

Shimamura, A. P., & Squire, L. (1986). Memory and metamemory: A study of the feeling-of-knowing phenomenon in amnesic patients. *Journal of Experimental Psychology: Learning, Memory, and Cognition, 12,* 452–460.

Souchay, C., Bacon, E., & Danion J.-M. (2006). Episodic feeling-of-knowing in schizophrenia. *Journal of Clinical and Experimental Neuropsychology, 28,* 828–840.

Vilkki, J., Servo, A., & Surma-aho, O. (1998). Word list learning and prediction of recall after frontal lobe lesion. *Neuropsychology, 12,* 268–277.

Vilkki, J., Surma-aho, O., & Servo, A. (1999). Inaccurate prediction of retrieval in a face matrix learning task after frontal lobe lesions. *Neuropsychology, 13,* 298–305.

Weingartner, H. J., Joyce, E. M., Sirocco, K. Y., Adams, C. M., Eckardt, M. J., George, T., et al. (1993) Specific memory and sedative effects of the benzodiazepine triazolam. *Journal of Psychopharmacology, 7,* 305–315.

Widner, R. L., Otani, H., & Winkelman, S. E. (2005). Tip-of-the-tongue experiences are not merely strong feeling-of-knowing experiences. *The Journal of General Psychology, 132,* 392–407.

Widner, R. L., Smith, S. M., & Graziano, W. G. (1996). The effects of demand characteristics on the reporting of tip-of-the-tongue and feeling-of-knowing states. *American Journal of Psychology, 109,* 525–538.

Wolkowitz, O. M., Weingartner, H., Thompson, K., Pickar, D., Paul, S. M., & Hommer, D. W. (1987). Diazepam-induced amnesia: A neuropharmacological model of an "organic amnestic syndrome." *American Journal of Psychiatry, 144,* 25–28.

Yaniv, I., & Meyer, D. E. (1987). Activation and metacognition of inaccessible stored information: Potential bases for incubation effects in problem solving. *Journal of Experimental Psychology: Learning, Memory, Memory, and Cognition, 13,* 187–205.

A Neurocognitive Approach to Metacognitive Monitoring and Control

Arthur P. Shimamura

Introduction

To what extent can brain-based investigations inform research on metacognition? Most view metacognition as a set of intricately complex and dynamic processes — such as those involved in insight, cognitive control, and mnemonic strategies. As such, metacognitive research has been thoroughly interdisciplinary, influencing educational, cognitive, developmental, and clinical investigations (see Hacker; Schneider, & Lockl; Mazzoni & Nelson, 1998; Metcalfe & Shimamura, 1994; Schwartz & Bacon, this volume). It may seem rather premature to consider the brain mechanisms that underlie metacognition. Yet, there have been significant advances in neurobehavioral investigations, most notably the advent of functional magnetic resonance imaging (fMRI). Specifically, we have learned a great deal about the role of the prefrontal cortex (PFC) in cognitive control (see Fletcher & Henson, 2001; Koechlin, Ody, & Kouneiher, 2003; E. K. Miller & Cohen, 2001; Shimamura, 2000). In this chapter, I review neurocognitive findings related to metacognitive monitoring and control. These findings are described within the framework of the Nelson and Narens model of metacognition (1990, 1994) and its neurocognitive counterpart, dynamic filtering theory (Shimamura, 1996, 2000).

The Nelson and Narens Model of Metacognition

According to the influential model developed by Nelson and Narens (1990, 1994), metacognition is defined as the monitoring and control of cognitive processes. By this view, metacognition is essential for the supervision of our perceptions, thoughts, memories, and actions. Nelson and Narens described *metacognition* as the interplay between two levels of information processing — an object level and a metalevel. *Object-level processing* refers to specific components of cognitive function, such as object recognition, phonological coding, spatial representation, and semantic processing. These processors are presumed to operate as functionally distinct modules, often running in parallel and relatively independently from one another. They are, however, *monitored* by metalevel processors that receive information flow from object levels. The role of the metalevel is to evaluate object-level activations and, based on this evaluation, initiate feedback control (see Figure 1).

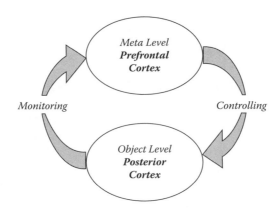

Figure 1   Based on the Nelson and Narens metacognitive model, object-level processes are monitored and controlled by feedforward and feedback loops with metalevel processors. This model provides a useful characterization of prefrontal-posterior cortex interactions, as described by dynamic filtering theory (Shimamura, 2000), a neural description of the Nelson and Narens model.

Nelson and Narens (1994) directed their metacognitive model specifically to the kinds of cognitive processes important for student learning. They proposed that metacognition makes learning more efficient by influencing behavior at various stages of memory processing, from stimulus encoding to the ultimate retrieval of information. For example, metacognitive monitoring at the time of acquisition could be instantiated as *judgments of learning* (JOLs), in which students evaluate (i.e., monitor) the degree to which recently presented information is learned. Such monitoring could suggest that the information was not well learned, and appropriate control would be to engage in further studying. Similar monitoring processes may be initiated just before the time of retrieval, at which time learned material is assessed by *feelings of knowing* (FOKs). Finally, monitoring one's knowledge after taking a test may be assessed by retrospective analysis of feelings of success (or failure), defined in memory research as *confidence ratings*.

To the extent that metacognition imposes top-down regulation of information processing — as is described by the Nelson and Narens model (see Figure 1) — this concept is centrally linked to aspects of *executive control*, such as selective attention, working memory, conflict resolution, and task switching. Abundant neurobehavioral findings implicate the PFC as having a critical role in top-down control of information processing (see Fernandez-Duque, Baird, & Posner, 2000; E. K. Miller & Cohen, 2001; Shimamura, 2002a; Smith & Jonides, 1999). Moreover, some theorists have made explicit links between PFC functions and metacognitive processes (Fernandez-Duque et al., 2000; Pannu & Kaszniak, 2005; Shimamura, 1996; Stuss, Gallup, & Alexander, 2001). In an attempt to delineate a neural mechanism of metacognition, I (1996, 2000) proposed dynamic filtering theory, a neural mechanism drawn from the Nelson and Narens model. It is proposed that the PFC, with its extensive projections to and from many cortical regions, regulates posterior cortical circuits by way of a filtering or gating mechanism. By this view, object-level processors are distributed in posterior cortical regions and are controlled by metalevel processors in PFC regions. The PFC implements metacognitive control by dynamic filtering, that is, by the selection of appropriate signals and suppression of inappropriate signals. Thus, the PFC acts to refine or amplify neural activity by increasing signals and reducing extraneous noise.

When one considers the cacophony of neural activity at any given moment, it becomes rather clear why the brain requires a mechanism for orchestrating cognitive processes. It is particularly important for metacognitive processes to implement inhibitory control as task situations often result in object-level processors interfering with one another. When conflicts occur, decisions must be made to suppress some activity while allowing others to progress. This "filtering" mechanism is thus most critical when monitoring reveals conflicts among object-level processors. Based on dynamic filtering theory, it is the interplay between PFC and posterior regions that implements both selective and suppressive control. Importantly, there is segregation of PFC-posterior projections (Petrides & Pandya, 2001), which suggests that there is not one homunculus-like metacognitive controller but instead a distributed set of controllers or feedback loops. Without PFC control, object-level processors are subject to greater interference from extraneous signals elicited by other processors.

Findings from neuroimaging studies have pointed to regional specificity in the kinds of information that are processed within the PFC. These regions (see Figure 2) can be identified both spatially and by anatomical features (e.g., Brodmann areas [BAs]). They include the anterior PFC (BA10 or frontopolar PFC); dorsolateral PFC (BA9, BA46); ventrolateral PFC (BA44, BA45, BA47); dorsomedial PFC (BA24, BA32, or anterior cingulate gyrus); and ventromedial PFC (BA11, BA12 or orbitofrontal cortex). A sixth region, BA8, is also part of the PFC and includes the frontal eye fields. These regions are intricately connected to cortical and subcortical regions outside the PFC and have interconnections among themselves (Petrides & Pandya, 2001; Simons & Spiers, 2003). They are distinct both in terms of anatomical and functional characteristics, and some of these distinctions are outlined in the following sections.

Monitoring and Controlling Stimulus Encoding

An inordinate load on our cognitive system would occur if we attempted to consider the entire sensory environment at any given moment. Because of this perceptual overload, control over stimulus selection and suppression becomes a necessity. Physiological evidence suggests that even at early stages of sensory encoding, the PFC monitors activity and acts to prepare for or modulate incoming information. For example, in studies using electrophysiological scalp recordings, such as event-related potentials (ERPs), PFC activity initiates a "readiness" signal when individuals are given a warning cue to prepare for an upcoming response. This readiness potential includes the contingent negative variation (CNV) and is thought to help individuals focus attention on specific stimulus features (Walter, Cooper, Aldridge, McCallum, & Winter, 1964). Patients with dorsolateral PFC lesions exhibit a reduction of the CNV and have difficulty attending to relevant stimulus features (Rosahl & Knight, 1995). The finding of a preparatory top-down signal in response to a precue suggests that PFC control can occur even *before* a stimulus appears and thus calls into question the term *late processing*, which has been used to describe top-down control.

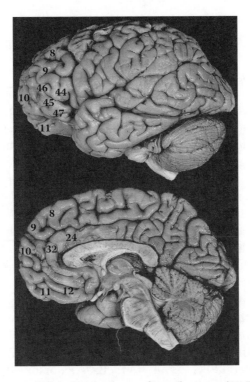

Figure 2 Brodmann areas (BAs) within the prefrontal cortex (PFC) are shown on the lateral surface (top image) and on the medial surface (bottom image) of the neocortex. PFC regions include the anterior PFC (BA10); dorsolateral PFC (BA9, BA46); ventrolateral PFC (BA44, BA45, BA47); dorsomedial PFC (BA24, BA32); and ventromedial PFC (BA11, BA12). Also part of the PFC is BA8, which includes the frontal eye fields. (Brain images reprinted with permission from *Digital Anatomist Interactive Atlas,* University of Washington, Seattle, WA, copyright 1997.)

To the extent that metacognition is a dynamic process that influences stimulus encoding, it should be involved in rather early stages of sensory processing. In ERP studies of patients with dorsolateral PFC lesions, the amplitude of "middle latency" ERPs (70–100 milliseconds), which are presumed to be generated in primary sensory cortex, is heightened as a result of PFC lesions (Knight, Scabini, & Woods, 1989; Yamaguchi & Knight, 1990). Thus, as a result of PFC damage there is a disinhibition or failure to modulate posterior cortical activity (Knight, Staines, Swick, & Chao, 1999). It is as if PFC lesions disrupt cortical processing in the posterior cortex by failing to gate or filter activations. Likewise, in fMRI studies of normal individuals (Frith, Friston, Liddle, & Frackowiak, 1991; Garavan, Ross, Murphy, Roche, & Stein, 2002; Hester, Murphy, & Garavan, 2004; Konishi et al., 1999), both the dorsolateral and ventrolateral PFC are active in tasks involving inhibitory control of sensory information.

As proposed by dynamic filtering theory, metacognitive control is particularly important when object-level processors interfere with one another. In such situations, control must be implemented to resolve the conflict. Stroop or flanker tasks have been used to study conflict in which two simultaneously presented stimuli or features interfere with each other. For example, in a flanker task (Botvinick, Nystrom, Fissell,

Carter, & Cohen, 1999) subjects indicate the direction of a central arrowhead (point-ing left or right) when flanked by congruent (<< < <<) or incongruent (>> < >>) arrow-heads. In fMRI analyses, the dorsomedial PFC (BA32) is particularly active during incongruent trials compared to congruent trials (see Botvinick, Cohen, & Carter, 2004). In Stroop tasks, the dorsomedial PFC, dorsolateral PFC, and parietal cortex are particularly active during conflict conditions (see Zysset, Muller, Lohmann, & von Cramon, 2001). In such conditions, parietal regions are presumed to represent and process spatial locations of the arrowheads. Botvinick, Braver, Barch, Carter, and Cohen (2001) proposed that the dorsomedial PFC (i.e., anterior cingulate cortex) monitors cognitive conflict, whereas the dorsolateral PFC controls these modules. Thus, according to Botvinick et al. (2001) the processes of monitoring and controlling conflict are dissociable functions, being processed by different PFC regions.

Another form of stimulus conflict occurs as cross-trial interference effects. Jonides, Smith, Marshuetz, Koeppe, and Reuter-Lorenz (1998) developed a probe recognition task in which a stimulus array of four letters was followed by a single-letter probe. On each trial, subjects determined whether the probe letter was in the stimulus array. For some trials, the probe letter was not presented during the current trial but had been presented in the just-preceding trial. Thus, on these "recent negative" trials, conflict occurred because subjects must suppress the urge to respond "yes" to a probe letter that had been recently presented, but not in the current trial. Jonides et al. (1998) showed that the left ventrolateral PFC was particularly active in recent negative trials (see also Badre & Wagner, 2005; D'Esposito, Postle, Jonides, & Smith, 1999; Postle & Brush, 2004). These findings are consistent with neuropsychological findings in which patients with PFC lesions exhibit failure to suppress recently activated but irrelevant responses (Thompson-Schill et al., 2002). They suggest that the ventrolateral PFC is involved in response selection, particularly in the face of conflicting responses.

Even at early stages of information processing, such as stimulus encoding and selection, metacognition is required to monitor and control conflicting object-level processors. Findings suggest that the dorsomedial, ventrolateral, and dorsolateral PFC are involved in preparing for upcoming stimuli (e.g., readiness potential), select-ing task-relevant stimulus features, and suppressing extraneous or irrelevant features. Without PFC involvement, information processing is subject to reduced selective attention and heightened interference from extraneous or irrelevant processing.

Monitoring and Controlling Learning Processes

Once stimulus information is selected, efficient learning requires the integration of new information into existing knowledge representations. This interplay between newly encoded information and preexisting knowledge involves the online mainte-nance and manipulation of information in memory. Indeed, our ability to integrate new information into semantic knowledge stands as a hallmark feature of *elaborative encoding*. With respect to metacognitive processes, it is presumed that object-level processes associated with learning (e.g., semantic access, associative binding) are facilitated by metalevel controllers involved in the coordination and guidance of new information into existing memory. In addition, it is critical for metalevel controllers

to suppress extraneous or irrelevant information. Indeed, one critical feature of efficient learning is the mitigation of proactive interference, that is, the ability to suppress recently presented information that is now irrelevant or extraneous.

Our ability to maintain and manipulate information in working memory depends
on the PFC. Patients with dorsolateral PFC lesions exhibit reduced immediate
memory span for a variety of stimuli, including digits, spatial locations, colors, and
sounds (Baldo & Shimamura, 2000; Chao & Knight, 1998; Janowsky, Shimamura,
Kritchevsky, & Squire, 1989). Neuroimaging studies have confirmed the role of the
PFC in maintaining information in working memory (D'Esposito et al., 1999; Smith
& Jonides, 1999). Interestingly, different prefrontal regions are responsible for maintaining different kinds of information. For example, increased activity in the left ventrolateral PFC is observed when individuals are asked to hold names of objects in
mind, whereas increased activity in the right ventrolateral PFC is observed when
individuals are asked to keep spatial locations in mind (Awh & Jonides, 2001). In
many instances, these prefrontal activations are linked to activations in posterior
regions of the brain, suggesting that the maintenance of information in working
memory requires a neural circuit that includes the information to be activated (presumed to be stored in posterior cortex) and the executive control process that keeps
the information active (presumed to be established by the PFC).

Whereas maintaining information in working memory depends on the ventrolateral PFC, manipulating information also recruits the dorsolateral PFC. In an fMRI
study, D'Esposito, Postle, and Rypma (2000) asked individuals to maintain a string
of letters or to manipulate the letters by reordering them in alphabetical order. The
dorsolateral PFC was particularly active when subjects were asked to reorder the letters compared to simply maintaining the string in its presentation order. Another
working memory paradigm, the "n-back" task, has also been used to assess stimulus manipulation and updating (Cohen et al., 1997; for review, see Owen, McMillan,
Laird, & Bullmore, 2005). The simplest n-back task is a 1-back task in which subjects
determine if the stimulus on the current trial (i.e., n trial) matches that of the just
preceding trial (i.e., $n - 1$ trial). The task is made more difficult by having subjects
monitor and coordinate multiple trials. For example, for a trial in a 2-back task, subjects must encode the current stimulus, determine if it matches the $n - 2$ stimulus
(i.e., the stimulus two trials earlier), maintain the $n - 1$ stimulus for the next trial,
and maintain the current trial for the $n + 2$ trial. As evidenced by this example, substantial metacognitive control is required to select, maintain, update, and reroute
stimuli across multiple n-back trials. Neuroimaging studies demonstrate that many
PFC regions, including the ventrolateral, dorsolateral, posterior, and dorsomedial
PFC regions, are recruited when 2- and 3-back tasks are compared with a 1-back task
(see Owen et al., 2005).

To what extent does metacognitive control during learning influence long-term
memory? It is clear from early cognitive investigations that our capacity to encode
and organize information in a meaningful manner significantly facilitates learning
and memory (Bower, Clark, Lesgold, & Winzenz, 1969; Mandler, 1980; G. A. Miller,
1956). These studies suggested that our ability to reorganize or chunk information
meaningfully reduces the load on working memory and facilitates associative binding. Interestingly, patients with PFC damage exhibit poor organizational strategies

during learning, and they fail to elaborate stimuli and group them into meaningful categories (Gershberg & Shimamura, 1995). Neuroimaging studies corroborated the role of the PFC in elaborative encoding. For example, the left ventrolateral PFC has been shown to be particularly active when individuals are asked to consider the meaning of items, such as determining whether a word is concrete (e.g., dollar) or abstract (e.g., freedom) compared to conditions in which they determine superficial features, such as the number of vowels in a word (see Wagner, 2002).

During learning, brain activation in prefrontal regions predicts the success of later retrieval. In fMRI analyses, activation during learning was analyzed on the basis of whether items were later remembered or forgotten (Brewer, Zhao, Desmond, Glover, & Gabrieli, 1998; Wagner et al., 1998; for review, see Paller & Wagner, 2002). Remembered items were associated with greater left ventrolateral PFC activity during learning compared to forgotten items. In other words, if you recruited the PFC during the encoding of an item, you increased your chances of later remembering that item. This method of backsorting brain activations during learning in terms of whether items are subsequently remembered or forgotten offers a useful means by which to relate efficient encoding strategies to long-term memory retrieval (Paller & Wagner, 2002). These findings — taken together with previously cited findings on the role of the ventrolateral PFC in working memory (Awh & Jonides, 2001; Owen et al., 2005; Wagner, 2002) — suggest that successful learning depends on a host of metacognitive control processes, including selection, maintenance, updating, and chunking.

As described, *proactive interference* refers to instances in which previously learned information impedes or interferes with the encoding of new information. For example, in the paired-associate learning task, individuals are presented word pairs (e.g., thief–crime) and are then tested by presenting the first word in a pair and asking for the second word (thief–?). Proactive interference is assessed by presenting a second learning phase involving the same cues but different responses (e.g., thief–bandit). Patients with PFC damage exhibit particular impairment when they try to recall the second set of responses (Shimamura, Jurica, Mangels, & Gershberg, 1995). That is, they exhibit heightened proactive interference from the learning of the first set of associates and make many intrusion errors — as they use words from the first set during testing of the second set. These problems can be explained by a lack of controlling or suppressing the activation of related but now irrelevant information. Neuroimaging studies have shown that the dorsolateral PFC is particularly active in conditions of high proactive interference. For example, when individuals are asked to learn word associates such as dog–boxer then later dog–Dalmatian, they exhibit increased left dorsolateral PFC activity when attempting to learn the second related word pair (Dolan & Fletcher, 1997; see also Fletcher, Shallice, & Dolan, 2000).

The finding that the PFC contributes to the mitigation of proactive interference suggests that this brain region is involved in inhibitory or suppressive control. The combined role of the enhancement of relevant stimuli and the suppression of extraneous stimuli is consistent with dynamic filtering theory (Shimamura, 2000) in that this neural mechanism acts to amplify neural signals by both increasing signal and decreasing noise. In fMRI analyses, such forms of dynamic filtering occur when subjects must attend to target stimuli and ignore distracters. In an fMRI study, Gazzaley, Cooney, McEvoy, Knight, and D'Esposito (2005) used a probe recognition test in which subjects were shown a series of stimuli (two faces, two scenes) and then were asked to determine if a probe stimulus had been presented in the series. Prior to each trial set, subjects were cued regarding whether they should attend to the faces or scenes. Thus, subjects could ignore one type of stimulus and focus attention on the other. Posterior cortical regions sensitive to these two types of stimulus (namely, the fusiform gyrus for faces and parahippocampal gyrus for scenes) were analyzed. Interestingly, when compared to a baseline condition (passive viewing), these brain regions exhibited enhanced activity on trials when the stimuli were task relevant *and* reduced activity when they were to be ignored. Such top-down modulations of selective attention have been shown to be initiated by the PFC (Barcelo, Suwazono, & Knight, 2000; Pessoa, Kastner, & Ungerleider, 2002).

In metacognitive studies, monitoring during learning occurs as JOLs, in which individuals determine the degree to which a study item has been learned and will be remembered at a later time. For example, Nelson and Dunlosky (1991) asked individuals to learn word pairs (e.g., ocean–tree) and then showed the individuals the first word (ocean–) and asked them to determine how likely they would be able to recall the second word if tested 10 minutes later. Nelson and Dunlosky (1991) found that the accuracy of JOLs increased substantially if judgments were delayed for a few minutes after initial presentation. Various explanations have been proposed to account for the delayed JOL effect, although one viable account concerns the negative influence of having study information currently in working memory and thus easily accessible while making JOLs. That is, when study material has just been presented, it may be difficult to assess long-term memory retrieval because the information is so readily available in working memory. Indeed, in other paradigms, memory retrieval is significantly disrupted when information in working memory conflicts with to-be-retrieved information (see Dodson & Shimamura, 2000).

To the extent that JOLs depend on memory monitoring (e.g., selecting and updating stored information) and the suppression of irrelevant information (e.g., disregarding information readily accessible in working memory), the PFC should play a vital role in accurate JOLs. Pinon, Allain, Kefi, Dubas, and Le Gall (2005) assessed both JOL and FOK in patients with frontal lobe lesions. Subjects were shown word pairs, and they made JOL responses for each pair. Following a 20-minute retention interval, they were shown the first word in the pair and asked to recall the second word. If recall was not possible, they made an FOK judgment, which was followed by a recognition test. JOL accuracy was based on recall performance, whereas FOK accuracy was based on recognition performance. Pinon et al. (2005) found that patients with PFC lesions were not significantly impaired on JOL accuracy but were impaired on FOK judgments.

Impaired FOK in PFC patients have been observed in other studies (Janowsky, Shimamura, & Squire, 1989a; Schnyer et al., 2004). The failure to observe a deficit in JOL accuracy may suggest that the PFC is not as dependent on metacognitive monitoring during the learning stage compared to the retrieval stage. However, it may be that JOL accuracy in the patients actually benefited by poor working memory. That is, as a result of having just been exposed to the word pairs, control subjects may have had better working memory access to the stimuli than the patients. As it has been shown that having readily accessible information in working memory *disrupts* JOL accuracy, the control subjects may have actually been disadvantaged in making JOLs compared to the PFC patients with reduced working memory capacity.

In an fMRI study, JOLs for pictorial scenes (photographs) were elicited by asking subjects to determine for each scene whether they would remember it later in a memory test (Kao, Davis, & Gabrieli, 2005). Brain activations during JOL predictions were assessed for scenes given positive JOLs (i.e., predict remember) compared to activations for scenes given negative JOLs (i.e., predict will not remember). Activations in the dorsomedial and anterior PFC were greater for scenes given positive JOLs compared to negative JOLs. Furthermore, across-subject JOL accuracy was correlated with activation in the ventromedial PFC. Thus, these neuroimaging findings suggest a significant role of the PFC in metacognitive judgments during learning. These findings are in contrast to the failure to observe a deficit in JOL accuracy in patients with PFC lesions (Pinon et al., 2005). The discrepancy may have been due to poor test sensitivity in the patient study (e.g., within-group variability in patient groups can be high), or as suggested, the very nature of a working memory deficit in patients could have led to an advantage over control subjects as the facility of working memory access to recently presented information can act to disrupt JOLs (i.e., the delayed JOL effect of Nelson & Dunlosky, 1991).

Monitoring and Controlling Retrieval Processes

Can you name the seven dwarfs in the movie *Snow White*? Successful retrieval of this information will involve a host of metacognitive control and monitoring processes (Shimamura, 2002a). In particular, it is necessary to search for, maintain, update, and reroute retrieved items from memory so that the desired information comes to mind. Neurocognitive findings suggest that such self-generated or directed retrievals depend on the PFC. Thus, memory retrieval requires metacognitive processes similar to those needed for the encoding and learning of new information. In particular, the online selection, maintenance, and manipulation of memory are critical for efficient memory retrieval.

In studies of neurological patients, the verbal fluency task has been used to assess retrieval of semantic knowledge (Benton & Hamsher, 1976). In this task, individuals are given 1 minute to retrieve words that begin with a specific letter or a specific semantic category (e.g., animals). Efficient retrieval requires the use of strategies to monitor and control retrieval paths. For instance, after trying to come up with just any animal, it would be useful to cue oneself with subcategories, such as pets, farm animals, or reptiles. Such strategies are efficient because they facilitate the selection of different items and prevent the reporting of items already generated. Patients with dorsolateral PFC lesions have difficulty controlling their retrieval searches on verbal fluency tasks (Baldo, Shimamura, Delis, Kramer, & Kaplan, 2001; Benton & Hamsher, 1976). They tend to report only 5 to 10 items in a minute, whereas most individuals would be able to retrieve two or three times as many responses. Moreover, patients with dorsolateral PFC lesions tend to make perseverative errors — that is, they repeat the same items, as if they fail to suppress the activation of prior responses.

In neuroimaging studies, the ventrolateral PFC is particularly active during the generation and selection of semantic knowledge (Thompson-Schill et al., 2002; Wagner, Pare-Blagoev, Clark, & Poldrack, 2001). One often-used task to assess semantic retrieval is the verb generation task, in which individuals are presented a noun cue (e.g., nail) and asked to generate an associated verb (e.g., pound). As in the verbal fluency task, verb generation requires one to search for and select information in semantic memory. Also, it is necessary to suppress competing or interfering information. Interestingly, ventrolateral PFC activity increases with increases in the number of competing responses (Wagner et al., 2001). Such regulation of semantic retrieval extends to other linguistic tasks, such as making decisions about the conceptual relatedness between items or interpreting difficult or ambiguous sentences (see Wagner et al., 2001).

Extensive metacognitive processes are also required for episodic recollection. Retrieving events and experiences in one's life depends on the ability to retrieve contextual information, such as remembering where, when, and with whom one experienced a past event. As with semantic retrieval, the retrieval of contextual or source information involves selecting, maintaining, and manipulating information. Neuroimaging studies have implicated the ventrolateral, dorsolateral, and anterior PFC as critical for the top-down control of autobiographical recollection (Gilboa, 2004; Levine, 2004; Maguire, 2001). In the laboratory, tests of source memory are used to assess memory for specific contextual features, such as remembering the color, location, or voice associated with a previously presented item. Patients with PFC lesions do not exhibit severe amnesia for past events, but they are impaired on tests of source recollection (Janowsky, Shimamura, & Squire, 1989b). In neuroimaging studies, the dorsolateral and anterior PFC are particularly involved in source recollection (Burgess, Maguire, Spiers, & O'Keefe, 2001; Henson, Rugg, Shallice, & Dolan, 2000; King, Hartley, Spiers, Maguire, & Burgess, 2005; Ranganath, Johnson, & D'Esposito, 2000; Rugg, Fletcher, Chua, & Dolan, 1999). In tests of source memory, both the right and the left PFC are activated in conjunction with a set of other brain regions, including parietal, medial temporal, and retrosplenial cortex (King et al., 2005; Simons & Spiers, 2003). Consistent with the Nelson and Narens model, it is generally viewed that posterior cortical regions represent stored memory sites and object-level processors, whereas PFC regions monitor and control the activation of these memory sites.

Metacognitive monitoring during retrieval has been assessed in both neurological patients and neuroimaging studies. In particular, FOK responses have been assessed. For such responses, subjects are asked to make predictions about the success of recognizing an item when full recall is not available. For example, subjects may be asked to recall general knowledge information, such as "What is the name of the ship on which Darwin made his famous voyage?" If recall of the answer is not available (i.e., *Beagle*), subjects are asked to predict their FOK by determining the likelihood of recognizing the answer if given some choices. Such judgments depend on an accurate assessment of partial information that is available and an assessment about the degree to which the answer can be inferred (e.g., by familiarity with the topic or cue). Patients with frontal lobe lesions exhibit extremely poor FOK judgments (Janowsky et al., 1989a; Pannu & Kaszniak, 2005; Schnyer et al., 2004).

Neuroimaging studies of FOK and related metacognitive monitoring judgments — such as tip-of-the-tongue (TOT) responses and confidence ratings — have implicated PFC regions (Chua, Schacter, Rand-Giovannetti, & Sperling, 2006; Kikyo, Ohki, & Miyashita, 2002; Maril, Simons, Mitchell, Schwartz, & Schacter, 2003; Maril, Simons, Weaver, & Schacter, 2005; Maril, Wagner, & Schacter, 2001; Schnyer et al., 2004; see also Schwartz & Bacon, this volume). TOT responses refer to the common experience of exceptionally high FOKs without the ability to recall the information. Anterior, dorsolateral, and dorsomedial (i.e., anterior cingulate) regions are particularly active during these metacognitive judgments (Kikyo et al., 2002; Maril et al., 2003, 2005; Schnyer et al., 2004). As expected, FOK and TOT states exhibit similar neural activations, although there often appears to be a graded response such that activation in PFC regions (ventrolateral, anterior, dorsomedial PFC) is greater for TOT states than for FOK judgments in the absence of a TOT state (Maril et al., 2005). In addition, parietal regions are active during both TOT states and FOK judgments, as well as when subjects have successfully recalled information (Maril et al., 2003, 2005; Schnyer et al., 2004). Parietal activations may index object-level processors associated with the access of stored information (see Shannon & Buckner, 2004; Wagner, Shannon, Kahn & Buckner, 2005).

In summary, the PFC is intricately involved in metacognitive control during all stages of learning and memory. The ventrolateral and dorsolateral PFC are most frequently associated with such control processes. The ventrolateral PFC is important for selecting and maintaining information in working memory, whereas the dorsolateral PFC is important for more complex control such as manipulating and updating information in working memory (D'Esposito et al., 2000; Petrides, 1998). Dynamic filtering theory describes such monitoring and control processes in terms of neural enhancement (selection) and suppression (inhibitory control). Depending on the particular memory (i.e., object-level) process involved, different PFC regions control different aspects of memory.

A Multilevel Model of Dynamic Filtering Theory and Extension of the Nelson and Narens Metacognitive Model

As suggested by the findings presented, the Nelson and Narens model of metacognition offers a useful characterization of interactions between PFC and posterior cortex. Both metacognitive monitoring and control depend critically on the PFC in assessing conflict and enabling top-down control of object-level processes. Neuroimaging findings suggest that different PFC regions serve different control functions. The ventrolateral PFC is integral in selecting semantic information and maintaining that information in working memory (Wagner et al., 2001; Thompson-Schill et al., 2002). The dorsomedial PFC (e.g., anterior cingulate cortex) is involved in monitoring cognitive conflict in object-level processors (Botvinick et al., 1999, 2004). The dorsolateral PFC facilitates the manipulation of information in working memory by updating and rerouting information processing (Shimamura, 2000; Simons & Spiers, 2003). Thus, rather than one metacognitive controller, there appear to be numerous controllers that monitor and control different aspects of information processing, such as stimulus selection, conflict monitoring, updating, and rerouting.

The ventromedial PFC (i.e., orbitofrontal cortex) has been less implicated in meta-cognitive processes associated with learning and memory. This brain region has been associated with regulation of emotions, as evidenced by the often-cited neurological case of Phineas Gage (see Macmillan, 2000) and other patients with similar disorders of emotional disinhibition (see Shimamura, 2002b). I (2000) suggested that the ventromedial PFC enables the same kind of monitoring and control as other PFC regions, only it regulates affective processes rather than cognitive processes. As evidence of this possibility, in an ERP analysis, patients with ventromedial PFC lesions exhibited a failure to suppress neural responses to emotionally laden stimuli, such as a loud sound or wrist shock (Rule, Shimamura, & Knight, 2002). Specifically, these patients exhibited heightened (i.e., disinhibited) ERP responses in the posterior cortex, as if they were unable to monitor and control the arousing stimuli. Such patients exhibit problems in decision-making tasks that involve high-risk gambles (Bechara, Tranel, Damasio, & Damasio, 1996) and the ability to inhibit strong prepotent responses (Konishi et al., 1999). Thus, the ventromedial PFC may be viewed as a metalevel processor of emotionally laden or highly prepotent responses.

Taken together, one could view the PFC as a board of executives, with each one responsible for monitoring and controlling a particular part of the business. On occasion — such as problematic situations or conflicts in scheduling — these executives must work in concert to make operations more efficient. It is known that adjacent PFC regions are connected to each other as well as to distinct regions in the posterior cortex (Petrides & Pandya, 2001; Ramnani & Owen, 2004; Semendeferi, Armstrong, Schleicher, Zilles, & Van Hoesen, 2001). By way of these multiple interconnections, the PFC has the capability of influencing many object-level processes in the posterior cortex and coordinating processing among metalevel processors.

If one construes the PFC as comprising a board of metalevel processors, does the brain have a chief executive officer? That is, is there a chief executive officer controlling other controllers? It is unlikely that any single cortical region would be essential for massively controlling the rest of the brain. This formulation comes much too close to postulating a homunculus-like entity that oversees all processing and initiates ultimate control. However, it is not out of the question that there exist multiple levels of control, such that metalevel processors are themselves monitored and controlled by higher-level controllers. Nelson and Narens (1994) suggested this possibility as an extension of their model. The anterior PFC (BA10) may be a worthy candidate for a superordinate level of metacognitive control. This PFC region is particularly involved in tasks that involve complex processing, such as rational decision making, analogical reasoning, and self-generated retrieval from memory (Bunge, Wendelken, Badre, & Wagner, 2005; Christoff & Gabrieli, 2000; Simons, Owen, Fletcher, & Burgess, 2005).

In summary, the PFC plays a significant role in metacognition. Rather than being the storehouse of semantic knowledge or autobiographical memories, the PFC monitors and controls object-level processes associated with the selection, encoding, updating, and retrieval of memories. As one attempts to learn new material, the PFC is involved in accessing semantic memory, maintaining information in working memory, mitigating proactive interference, and updating memory for efficient elaborative encoding. At retrieval, the PFC again facilitates semantic access, organizes retrieved information, and suppresses unwanted or extraneous retrieval paths. Without PFC control, memories are poorly encoded, disorganized, and subject to heightened interference from extraneous activations. According to dynamic filtering theory (Shimamura, 2000), a distribution of metalevel controllers resides in the PFC, with each controller servicing a specific object-level processor. Here, it is proposed that the anterior PFC acts as a superordinate level of control that monitors and controls activity in nearby PFC regions that themselves monitor and control activity in the posterior cortex.

Acknowledgment

This chapter is dedicated to the memory of Thomas O. Nelson. Tom treated me as a colleague and friend. He instilled in me the importance of having a philosophical and methodological understanding of what I was doing. He also showed me how to reef a mainsail in the midst of a windstorm.

References

Awh, E., & Jonides, J. (2001). Overlapping mechanisms of attention and spatial working memory. *Trends in Cognitive Sciences, 5*, 119–126.

Badre, D., & Wagner, A. D. (2005). Frontal lobe mechanisms that resolve proactive interference. *Cerebral Cortex, 15*, 2003–2012.

Baldo, J. V., & Shimamura, A. P. (2000). Spatial and color working memory in patients with lateral prefrontal cortex lesions. *Psychobiology, 28*, 156–167.

Baldo, J. V., Shimamura, A. P., Delis, D. C., Kramer, J., & Kaplan, E. (2001). Verbal and design fluency in patients with frontal lobe lesions. *Journal of the International Neuropsychological Society, 7*, 586–596.

Barcelo, F., Suwazono, S., & Knight, R. T. (2000). Prefrontal modulation of visual processing in humans. *Nature Neuroscience, 3*, 399–403.

Bechara, A., Tranel, D., Damasio, H., & Damasio, A. R. (1996). Failure to respond autonomically to anticipated future outcomes following damage to prefrontal cortex. *Cerebral Cortex, 6*, 215–225.

Benton, A. L., & Hamsher, K. D. (1976). *Multilingual aphasia examination*. Iowa City, IA: University of Iowa Press.

Botvinick, M. M., Braver, T. S., Barch, D. M., Carter, C. S., & Cohen, J. D. (2001). Conflict monitoring and cognitive control. *Psychological Review, 108*, 624–652.

Botvinick, M., Nystrom, L. E., Fissell, K., Carter, C. S., & Cohen, J. D. (1999). Conflict monitoring versus selection-for-action in anterior cingulate cortex. *Nature, 402*, 179–181.

Botvinick, M. M., Cohen, J. D., & Carter, C. S. (2004). Conflict monitoring and anterior cingulate cortex: an update. *Trends in Cognitive Science, 8*, 539–546.

Bower, G. H., Clark, M. C., Lesgold, A. M., & Winzenz, D. (1969). Hierarchical retrieval schemes in recall of categorized word lists. *Journal of Verbal Learning and Verbal Behavior, 8*, 323–343.

Brewer, J. B., Zhao, Z., Desmond, J. E., Glover, G. H., & Gabrieli, J. D. (1998). Making memories: Brain activity that predicts how well visual experience will be remembered. *Science, 281*, 1185–1187.

Bunge, S. A., Wendelken, C., Badre, D., & Wagner, A. D. (2005). Analogical reasoning and prefrontal cortex: evidence for separable retrieval and integration mechanisms. *Cerebral Cortex, 15*, 239–249.

Burgess, N., Maguire, E. A., Spiers, H. J., & O'Keefe, J. (2001). A temporoparietal and prefrontal network for retrieving the spatial context of lifelike events. *Neuroimage, 14*, 439–453.

Chao, L. L., & Knight, R. T. (1998). Contribution of human prefrontal cortex to delay performance. *Journal of Cognitive Neuroscience, 10*, 167–177.

Christoff, K., & Gabrieli, J. D. E. (2000). The frontopolar cortex and human cognition: Evidence for a rostrocaudal hierarchical organization within the human prefrontal cortex. *Psychobiology, 28*, 168–186.

Chua, E. F., Schacter, D. L., Rand-Giovannetti, E., & Sperling, R. A. (2006). Understanding metamemory: Neural correlates of the cognitive process and subjective level of confidence in recognition memory. *Neuroimage, 29*, 1150–1160.

Cohen, J. D., Perlstein, W. M., Braver, T. S., Nystrom, L. E., Noll, D. C., Jonides, J., et al. (1997). Temporal dynamics of brain activation during a working memory task. *Nature, 386*, 604–608.

D'Esposito, M., Postle, B. R., Jonides, J., & Smith, E. E. (1999). The neural substrate and temporal dynamics of interference effects in working memory as revealed by event-related functional MRI. *Proceedings of the National Academy of Sciences of the United States of America, 96*, 7514–7519.

D'Esposito, M., Postle, B. R., & Rypma, B. (2000). Prefrontal cortical contributions to working memory: evidence from event-related fMRI studies. *Experimental Brain Research, 133*, 3–11.

Dodson, C. S., & Shimamura, A. P. (2000). Differential effects of cue dependency on item and source memory. *Journal of Experimental Psychology: Learning, Memory, and Cognition, 26*, 1023–1044.

Dolan, R. J., & Fletcher, P. C. (1997). Dissociating prefrontal and hippocampal function in episodic memory encoding. *Nature, 388*, 582–585.

Fernandez-Duque, D., Baird, J. A., & Posner, M. I. (2000). Executive attention and metacognitive regulation. *Consciousness and Cognition, 9*, 288–307.

Fletcher, P. C., & Henson, R. N. A. (2001). Frontal lobes and human memory: Insights from functional neuroimaging. *Brain, 124*, 849–881.

Fletcher, P. C., Shallice, T., & Dolan, R. J. (2000). "Sculpting the response space" — an account of left prefrontal activation at encoding. *Neuroimage, 12*, 404–417.

Frith, C. D., Friston, K. J., Liddle, P. F., & Frackowiak, R. S. (1991). A PET study of word finding. *Neuropsychologia, 29*, 1137–1148.

Garavan, H., Ross, T. J., Murphy, K., Roche, R. A., & Stein, E. A. (2002). Dissociable executive functions in the dynamic control of behavior: inhibition, error detection, and correction. *Neuroimage, 17*, 1820–1829.

Gazzaley, A., Cooney, J. W., McEvoy, K., Knight, R. T., & D'Esposito, M. (2005). Top-down enhancement and suppression of the magnitude and speed of neural activity. *Journal of Cognitive Neuroscience, 17*, 507–517.

Gershberg, F. B., & Shimamura, A. P. (1995). Impaired use of organizational strategies in free recall following frontal lobe damage. *Neuropsychologia, 33*, 1305–1333.

Gilboa, A. (2004). Autobiographical and episodic memory — one and the same? Evidence from prefrontal activation in neuroimaging studies. *Neuropsychologia, 42*, 1336–1349.

Henson, R. N., Rugg, M. D., Shallice, T., & Dolan, R. J. (2000). Confidence in recognition memory for words: dissociating right prefrontal roles in episodic retrieval. *Journal of Cognitive Neuroscience, 12*, 913–923.

Hester, R., Murphy, K., & Garavan, H. (2004). Beyond common resources: The cortical basis for resolving task interference. *Neuroimage, 23*, 202–212.

Janowsky, J. S., Shimamura, A. P., & Squire, L. R. (1989a). Memory and metamemory: Comparisons between patients with frontal lobe lesions and amnesic patients. *Psychobiology, 17*, 3–11.

Janowsky, J. S., Shimamura, A. P., & Squire, L. R. (1989b). Source memory impairment in patients with frontal lobe lesions. *Neuropsychologia, 27*, 1043–1056.

Janowsky, J. S., Shimamura, A. P., Kritchevsky, M., & Squire, L. R. (1989). Cognitive impairment following frontal lobe damage and its relevance to human amnesia, *Behavioral Neuroscience, 103*, 548–560.

Jonides, J., Smith, E. E., Marshuetz, C., Koeppe, R. A., & Reuter-Lorenz, P. A. (1998). Inhibition in verbal working memory revealed by brain activation. *Proceedings of the National Academy of Sciences of the United States of America, 95*, 8410–8413.

Kao, Y. C., Davis, E. S., & Gabrieli, J. D. (2005). Neural correlates of actual and predicted memory formation. *Nature Neuroscience, 8*, 1776–1783.

Kikyo, H., Ohki, K., & Miyashita, Y. (2002). Neural correlates for feeling-of-knowing: an fMRI parametric analysis. *Neuron, 36*, 177–186.

King, J. A., Hartley, T., Spiers, H. J., Maguire, E. A., & Burgess, N. (2005). Anterior prefrontal involvement in episodic retrieval reflects contextual interference. *Neuroimage, 28*, 256–267.

Knight, R. T., Scabini, D., & Woods, D. L. (1989). Prefrontal cortex gating of auditory transmission in humans. *Brain Research, 504*, 338–342.

Knight, R. T., Staines, W. R., Swick, D., & Chao, L. L. (1999). Prefrontal cortex regulates inhibition and excitation in distributed neural networks. *Acta Psychologica, 101*, 159–178.

Koechlin, E., Ody, C., & Kouneiher, F. (2003). The architecture of cognitive control in the human prefrontal cortex. *Science, 302*, 1181–1185.

Konishi, S., Nakajima, K., Uchida, I., Kikyo, H., Kameyama, M., & Miyashita, Y. (1999). Common inhibitory mechanism in human inferior prefrontal cortex revealed by event-related functional MRI. *Brain, 12*, 981–991.

Levine, B. (2004). Autobiographical memory and the self in time: Brain lesion effects, functional neuroanatomy, and lifespan development. *Brain Cognition, 55*, 54–68.

Macmillan, M. (2000). *An odd kind of fame: Stories of Phineas Gage*. Cambridge, MA: MIT Press.

Maguire, E. A. (2001). Neuroimaging studies of autobiographical event memory. *Philosophical Transactions of the Royal Society of London: Series B, Biological Sciences, 356*, 1441–1451.

Mandler, G. (1980). Recognizing: The judgment of previous occurrence. *Psychological Review, 87*, 252–271.

Maril, A., Simons, J. S., Mitchell, J. P., Schwartz, B. L., & Schacter, D. L. (2003). Feeling-of-knowing in episodic memory: An event-related fMRI study. *Neuroimage, 18*, 827–836.

Maril, A., Simons, J. S., Weaver, J. J., & Schacter, D. L. (2005). Graded recall success: An event-related fMRI comparison of tip of the tongue and feeling of knowing. *Neuroimage, 24*, 1130–1138.

Maril, A., Wagner, A. D., & Schacter, D. L. (2001). On the tip of the tongue: An event-related fMRI study of semantic retrieval failure and cognitive conflict. *Neuron, 31*, 653–660.

Mazzoni, G., & Nelson, T. O. (1998). *Metacognition and cognitive neuropsychology: Monitoring and control processes*: Mahwah, NJ: Erlbaum.

Metcalfe, J., & Shimamura, A. P. (1994). *Metacognition: Knowing about knowing.* Cambridge, MA: MIT Press.

Miller, E. K., & Cohen, J. D. (2001). An integrative theory of prefrontal cortex function. *Annual Review of Neuroscience, 24*, 167–202.

Miller, G. A. (1956). The magical number seven, plus or minus two: some limits on our capacity for processing information. *Psychological Review, 63*, 81–97.

Nelson, T. O., & Dunlosky, J. (1991). When people's judgments of learning (JOLs) are extremely accurate at predicting subsequent recall: The "delayed-JOL effect." *Psychological Science, 2*, 267–270.

Nelson, T. O., & Narens, L. (1990). Metamemory: A theoretical framework and new findings. In G. H. Bower (Ed.), *The psychology of learning and motivation* (pp. 1–45). New York: Academic Press.

Nelson, T. O., & Narens, L. (1994). Why investigate metacognition? In J. Metcalfe & A. P. Shimamura (Eds.), *Metacognition: Knowing about knowing* (pp. 1–25). Cambridge, MA: MIT Press.

Owen, A. M., McMillan, K. M., Laird, A. R., & Bullmore, E. (2005). *N*-Back working memory paradigm: A meta-analysis of normative functional neuroimaging studies. *Human Brain Mapping. Special Issue: Meta-Analysis in Functional Brain Mapping, 25*, 46–59.

Paller, K. A., & Wagner, A. D. (2002). Observing the transformation of experience into memory. *Trends in Cognitive Science, 6*, 93–102.

Pannu, J. K., & Kaszniak, A. W. (2005). Metamemory experiments in neurological populations: a review. *Neuropsychology Review, 15*, 105–130.

Pessoa, L., Kastner, S., & Ungerleider, L. G. (2002). Attentional control of the processing of neural and emotional stimuli. *Brain Research: Cognitive Brain Research, 15*, 31–45.

Petrides, M. (1998). Specialized systems for the processing of mnemonic information within the primate frontal cortex. In A. C. Roberts, T. W. Robbins, & L. Weiskrantz (Eds.), *The prefrontal cortex: Executive and cognitive function* (pp. 103–116). Oxford, UK: Oxford University Press.

Petrides, M., & Pandya, D. N. (2001). Comparative cytoarchitectonic analysis of the human and the macaque ventrolateral prefrontal cortex and corticocortical connection patterns in the monkey. *European Journal of Neuroscience, 16*, 291–310.

Pinon, K., Allain, P., Kefi, M. Z., Dubas, F., & Le Gall, D. (2005). Monitoring processes and metamemory experience in patients with dysexecutive syndrome. *Brain and Cognition, 57*, 185–188.

Postle, B. R., & Brush, L. N. (2004). The neural bases of the effects of item-nonspecific proactive interference in working memory. *Cognitive Affective Behavior Neuroscience, 4*, 379–392.

Ramnani, N., & Owen, A. M. (2004). Anterior prefrontal cortex: Insights into function from anatomy and neuroimaging. *Nature Reviews: Neuroscience, 5*, 184–194.

Ranganath, C., Johnson, M. K., & D'Esposito, M. (2000). Left anterior prefrontal activation increases with demands to recall specific perceptual information. *Journal of Neuroscience, 20*, RC108.

Rosahl, S. K., & Knight, R. T. (1995). Role of prefrontal cortex in generation of the contingent negative variation. *Cerebral Cortex, 5*, 123–134.

Rugg, M. D., Fletcher, P. C., Chua, P. M., & Dolan, R. J. (1999). The role of the prefrontal cortex in recognition memory and memory for source: An fMRI study. *Neuroimage, 10*, 520–529.

Rule, R. R., Shimamura, A. P., & Knight, R. T. (2002). Orbitofrontal cortex and dynamic filtering of emotional stimuli. *Cognitive Affective Behavior Neuroscience, 2*, 264–270.

Schnyer, D. M., Verfaellie, M., Alexander, M. P., LaFleche, G., Nicholls, L., & Kaszniak, A. W. (2004). A role for right medial prefrontal cortex in accurate feeling-of-knowing judgements: Evidence from patients with lesions to frontal cortex. *Neuropsychologia, 42*, 957–966.

Semendeferi, K., Armstrong, E., Schleicher, A., Zilles, K., & Van Hoesen, G. W. (2001). Prefrontal cortex in humans and apes: A comparative study of area 10. *American Journal of Physical Anthropology, 114*, 224–241.

Shannon, B. J., & Buckner, R. L. (2004). Functional-anatomic correlates of memory retrieval that suggest nontraditional processing roles for multiple distinct regions within posterior parietal cortex. *Journal of Neuroscience, 24*, 10084–10092.

Shimamura, A. P. (1996). The control and monitoring of memory functions. In L. Reder (Ed.), *Metacognition and implicit memory* (pp. 259–274). Mahwah, NJ: Erlbaum.

Shimamura, A. P. (2000). The role of the prefrontal cortex in dynamic filtering. *Psychobiology, 28*, 207–218.

Shimamura, A. P. (2002a). Memory retrieval and executive control processes. In D. T. Stuss & R. T. Knight (Eds.), *Principles of frontal lobe function* (pp. 210–220). New York: Oxford University Press.

Shimamura, A. P. (2002b). Muybridge in motion: Travels in art, psychology, and neurology. *History of Photography, 26*, 341–350.

Shimamura, A. P., Jurica, P. J., Mangels, J. A., & Gershberg, F. B. (1995). Susceptibility to memory interference effects following frontal lobe damage: Findings from tests of paired-associate learning. *Journal of Cognitive Neuroscience, 7*, 144–152.

Simons, J. S., Owen, A. M., Fletcher, P. C., & Burgess, P. W. (2005). Anterior prefrontal cortex and the recollection of contextual information. *Neuropsychologia, 43*, 1774–1783.

Simons, J. S., & Spiers, H. J. (2003). Prefrontal and medial temporal lobe interactions in long-term memory. *Nature Reviews: Neuroscience, 4*, 637–648.

Smith, E. E., & Jonides, J. (1999). Storage and executive processes in the frontal lobes. *Science, 283*, 1657–1661.

Stuss, D. T., Gallup, G. G., Jr., & Alexander, M. P. (2001). The frontal lobes are necessary for "theory of mind." *Brain, 124*(part 2), 279–286.

Thompson-Schill, S. L., Jonides, J., Marshuetz, C., Smith, E. E., D'Esposito, M., Kan, I. P., et al. (2002). Effects of frontal lobe damage on interference effects in working memory. *Cognitive Affective Behavior Neuroscience, 2*, 109–120.

Wagner, A. D. (2002). Cognitive control and episodic memory: Contributions from prefrontal cortex. In L. R. S. Squire & L. Daniel (Eds.), *Neuropsychology of memory* (3rd ed., pp. 174–192). New York: Guilford Press.

Wagner, A. D., Pare-Blagoev, E. J., Clark, J., & Poldrack, R. A. (2001). Recovering meaning: Left prefrontal cortex guides controlled semantic retrieval. *Neuron, 31*, 329–338.

Wagner, A. D., Schacter, D. L., Rotte, M., Koutstaal, W., Maril, A., Dale, A. M., et al. (1998). Building memories: Remembering and forgetting of verbal experiences as predicted by brain activity. *Science, 281*, 1188–1191.

Wagner, A. D., Shannon, B. J., Kahn, I., & Buckner, R. L. (2005). Parietal lobe contributions to episodic memory retrieval. *Trends in Cognitive Sciences, 9*, 445–453.

Walter, W. G., Cooper, R., Aldridge, V. J., McCallum, W. C., & Winter, A. L. (1964). Contingent negative variation: An electric sign of sensorimotor association and expectancy in the human brain. *Nature, 203*, 380–384.

Yamaguchi, S., & Knight, R. T. (1990). Gating of somatosensory input by human prefrontal cortex. *Brain Research, 521*, 281–288.

Zysset, S., Muller, K., Lohmann, G., & von Cramon, D. Y. (2001). Color-word matching Stroop task: Separating interference and response conflict. *Neuroimage, 13*, 29–36.

Procedural Metacognition in Children:
Evidence for Developmental Trends

Wolfgang Schneider and Kathrin Lockl

Introduction

Research on metacognitive development was initiated in the early 1970s by Ann Brown, John Flavell, and their colleagues (for reviews, see Brown, Bransford, Ferrara, & Campione, 1983; Flavell, Miller, & Miller, 1993). At the very beginning, research focused on knowledge about memory, which was coined *metamemory* by Flavell (1971). Later, the concept was broadened and termed *metacognition* (Flavell, 1979). Metacognition was defined as any knowledge or cognitive activity that takes as its cognitive object, or that regulates, any aspect of any cognitive activity (Flavell et al., 1993, p. 150). Obviously, this very broad conceptualization includes people's knowledge of their own information-processing skills, as well as knowledge about the nature of cognitive tasks and about strategies for coping with such tasks. Moreover, it also includes executive skills related to monitoring and self-regulation of one's own cognitive activities. Although most developmental studies classified as metacognitive have explored children's metamemory, that is, their knowledge about memory, the term has also been applied to studies investigating children's comprehension, communication, and problem-solving skills (Flavell, 2000; Schneider & Pressley, 1997).

Early Conceptualizations of Metacognitive Knowledge

Flavell and Wellman (1977) came up with a taxonomy of metamemory that distinguished between two main categories: sensitivity and variables. The sensitivity category included knowledge of when memory activity is necessary, for instance, awareness that a particular task in a particular setting requires the use of memory strategies. This category corresponds to procedural metacognitive knowledge and indicates mostly implicit and unconscious memory activities. In contrast, the variables category corresponds to declarative metacognitive knowledge and refers to explicit, conscious, factual knowledge that performance in a memory or problem-solving task is influenced by a number of different factors or variables, such as the child's mnemonic self-concept as well as task and strategy knowledge.

The taxonomy of metamemory was not intended to be exhaustive. A number of other theorists have since contributed to the development of metacognitive theory (for useful reviews and critiques, see Joyner & Kurtz-Costes, 1997; Schneider &

Lockl, 2002). For instance, Paris and colleagues (e.g., Paris & Lindauer, 1982; Paris & Oka, 1986) introduced a component called *conditional metacognitive knowledge* that referred to children's ability to justify or explain their decisions concerning memory actions. Whereas declarative knowledge as defined by Flavell and coworkers focuses on "knowing that," the component added by Paris and colleagues deals with "knowing why" information.

Subsequent research also focused on procedural metacognitive knowledge that was not sufficiently described in Flavell and Wellman's taxonomy. Ann Brown and her colleagues (Brown, 1978; Brown et al., 1983) elaborated on Flavell and Wellman's work. The frame of reference used by Brown and colleagues was the competent information processor, one possessing an efficient "executive" that regulated cognitive behaviors. In their view, this regulatory component is responsible for selecting and implementing strategies, monitoring their usefulness, and modifying them when necessary. It was assumed that children do not monitor and regulate their performance well, as compared to metacognitively mature adults. Overall, Brown et al. (1983) took the perspective that memory-monitoring and regulation processes play a large role in complex cognitive tasks such as comprehending and memorizing text materials. They also argued that the two aspects of metamemory (i.e., the declarative and procedural components) complicate its definition (see also Joyner & Kurtz-Costes, 1997). That is, they are not only closely related but also fundamentally different in nature. Whereas the declarative knowledge component is primarily statable, stable, and late developing, the procedural knowledge component is not necessarily statable, rather unstable, relatively age independent, and dependent on the specific task or situation.

Pressley, Borkowski, and their colleagues (e.g., Pressley, Borkowski, & Schneider, 1989) proposed an elaborate model of metacognition, the good information processor model, that not only includes aspects of procedural and declarative metacognitive knowledge but also links these concepts to other features of successful information processing. According to this model, sophisticated metamemory is closely related to the learner's strategy use, motivational orientation, general knowledge about the world, and automated use of efficient learning procedures. All of these components are assumed to interact. For instance, specific strategy knowledge influences the adequate application of memory strategies, which in turn affects knowledge. As the strategies are carried out, they are monitored and evaluated, which leads to expansion and refinement of specific strategy knowledge.

Assessment of Children's "Theory of Mind"

In the early 1980s, a second wave of studies focused on young children's knowledge about the mental world, better known as *theory-of-mind research*. This wave is still very much in motion and may have produced more than 1,000 publications within the last 25 years or so. It deals with very young children's understanding of mental life and age-related changes in this understanding, for instance, their knowledge that mental representations of events need not correspond to reality. In a now-classic study, Wimmer and Perner (1983) tested young children's understanding of false belief, confirming the assumption that children below the age of about four find it impossible to believe that another person could hold an assertion that the child knows to be false. A little later, beginning at about age four, children come to recognize assertions as the expression of someone's belief that is not necessarily true. Subsequent theory-of-mind research has addressed young children's understanding of mental states such as desires, intentions, emotions, attention, consciousness, and so on.

Differences Between the Metacognitive and Theory-of-Mind Approach

Although researchers in both traditions share the same general objective, that is, to explore children's knowledge about and understanding of mental phenomena, the research literatures have been distinct and unconnected because they focused on different developments. For instance, whereas theory-of-mind researchers have investigated children's initial knowledge about the existence of various mental states such as desires and intentions, metacognitive researchers have focused more on task-related mental processes such as strategies for improving performance on various tasks or on attempts to monitor improvements. Flavell (2000) conceived of this approach as *problem centered* and suggested that it may be labeled *applied theory of mind*.

A second distinction between the two research paradigms concerns the age groups under study. Because theory-of-mind researchers are mainly interested in the origins of knowledge about mental states, they predominantly study infants and young children. On the other hand, metacognitive researchers investigate knowledge components and skills that already require some understanding of mental states and thus mainly test older children and adolescents. A further distinction concerns the fact that developmental research on metacognition deals with what a child knows about his or her own mind rather than somebody else's. As noted by Flavell (2000), how and how often other people use their minds in similar situations is not of primary interest. In contrast, it is the participant's understanding of some other person's mind that is usually of central concern in theory-of-mind studies.

Clarification of the terminology issue seems important. Figure 1 contains an overview of the various theoretical perspectives on metacognitive knowledge popular in the field of developmental psychology, making links between the various taxonomies and terminologies that were used by different research lines. It should be noted that conceptualizations of metacognitive knowledge in other fields of psychology such as gerontology and general cognitive psychology are narrower in scope. For example, several questionnaires assessing declarative metamemory in adults and the elderly focus on participants' beliefs about their memory and thus restrict the concept to the person variable of Flavell and Wellman's taxonomy (e.g., Dixon & Hertzog, 1988; Herrmann, 1982). In contrast, conceptualizations of metamemory in the field of cognitive psychology exclusively elaborate on the procedural knowledge component (e.g., Metcalfe & Shimamura, 1994; Nelson, 1996; Nelson & Narens, 1990, 1994). In fact, as noted by Joyner and Kurtz-Costes, most of the current work on metamemory comes from cognitive psychologists, who focus on monitoring and self-regulation processes in adults. In the remainder of this chapter, we describe the contributions of developmental psychology to our understanding of metacognitive processes in children and adolescents.

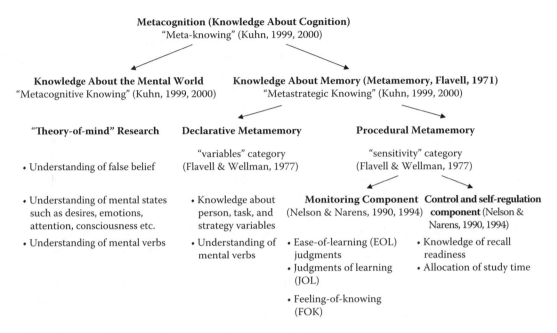

Figure 1   Taxonomy of metacognition components.

The Development of Self-Monitoring and Self-Control

According to Nelson and Narens (1990, 1994), self-monitoring and self-regulation correspond to two different levels of metacognitive processing that interact very closely. *Self-monitoring* refers to keeping track of where you are with your goal of understanding and remembering (a bottom-up process). In comparison, *self-regulation* or *self-control* refers to central executive activities and includes planning, directing, and evaluating your behavior (a top-down process).

What are the determinants of metacognitive judgments and their accuracy? Most researchers adopt a *cue utilization* view, according to which metacognitive judgments are inferential in nature, based on a variety of heuristics and cues that have some degree of validity in predicting memory performance (e.g., Benjamin & Bjork, 1996; Dunlosky & Nelson, 1992; Koriat, 2006). An important distinction is that between theory-based and experience-based metacognitive judgments (Koriat, 1997). Whereas theory-based judgments rely on the deliberate application of metacognitive beliefs or theories about one's competences and skills, experience-based judgments are assumed to rely on mnemonic cues that derive from online information processing. So far, developmental research on procedural metacognition has hardly examined the contributions of mnemonic cues and heuristics to children's judgments. Given that even among adults the contribution of one's theories and knowledge to monitoring and control seems to be quite limited (see Koriat, Bjork, Sheffer, & Bar, 2004), there is reason to assume that children's judgments are predominantly guided by online, implicit utilization of subtle experiential cues.

Self-Monitoring in Children

The most studied type of procedural metamemory is that of self-monitoring, evaluating how well one is progressing (cf. Borkowski, Milstead, & Hale, 1988; Brown et al., 1983; Schneider, 1998a). The developmental literature has focused on monitoring components such as ease-of-learning (EOL) judgments, judgments of learning (JOLs), and feeling-of-knowing (FOK) judgments and explored some aspects of control and self-regulation, such as allocation of study time and termination of study.

Ease-of-Learning Judgments   Ease-of-learning judgments occur in advance of the learning process, are largely inferential, and refer to items that have not yet been learned (Nelson & Narens, 1994). The corresponding memory paradigm is performance prediction. A form of performance prediction first introduced by Flavell, Friedrichs, and Hoyt (1970) refers to the prediction of one's own memory span. Individuals are presented incrementally longer lists of materials to be learned, such as pictures, words, or figures, and are asked to indicate whether they could still recall a list that long. Children's memory is than tapped using the same lists. Comparisons of the predictor value with actual memory span yields the metamemory indicator. Performance prediction accuracy can be measured for a variety of memory tasks, including list-learning paradigms and text-learning tasks (cf. Schneider, Körkel, & Weinert, 1990).

Almost all of the studies on EOL judgments that used list-learning paradigms found that preschool and kindergarten children overestimate their memory performance, whereas elementary school children are much more accurate (e.g., Worden & Sladewski-Awig, 1982; Yussen & Levy, 1975). Although this phenomenon has been repeatedly observed, the underlying mechanisms are not yet clear. Several studies tried to identify young children's difficulties in making accurate performance predictions. It was found that their predictions tended to be more accurate in familiar than in unfamiliar, laboratory-type situations (Justice & Bray, 1979). Moreover, young children's predictions were more accurate when they were tested using nonverbal as opposed to more traditional verbal measures (e.g., Cunningham & Weaver, 1989). Also, preschoolers and kindergarteners were found to be more accurate in predicting other children's performance than their own (Schneider, 1998b; Stipek, 1984).

Overall, the evidence does *not* support the original assumption that young children's overestimations of future performance are due to metacognitive deficiencies, as indicated by more recent work on the issue (Schneider, 1998b; Visé & Schneider, 2000). For instance, the study by Visé and Schneider explored possible reasons for young children's unrealistic predictions. In particular, the study examined whether overestimation in performance prediction is due to deficits in metacognitive monitoring or to motivational factors, for instance, wishful thinking. Four-, six-, and nine-year-old children were asked to predict their own performance in motor tasks (ball throwing and jumping) and memory tasks (memory span and hide-and-seek tasks). Children in the wish condition were asked to declare which performance they wished to achieve in the next trial; children in the expectation condition were asked to indicate which scores they expected to achieve in the next trial. A comparison of children's performance and their postdictions (i.e., their estimates of performance assessed after completion of the task) indicated that all children were well able to monitor their performance, regardless of task, even though they did not use this knowledge for further predictions. Accordingly, the memory-monitoring deficiency hypothesis could not account for the overestimation phenomenon. Furthermore, four- and six-year-old children did not differentiate between their wishes and their expectations, thus replicating and extending the findings by motivational researchers (e.g., Stipek, 1984).

Taken together, findings gave at least partial support for the wishful thinking hypothesis and clear evidence that overestimation in preschoolers and kindergarteners was linked to their belief (causal attribution) that effort has a powerful effect on performance. However, because such motivational processes are not similarly influential in schoolchildren, performance on EOL tasks indeed reflects memory monitoring in this population. Although EOL judgments can be already accurate in young elementary schoolchildren, there are subtle improvements over the elementary school years (see Pressley & Ghatala, 1990; Schneider et al., 1990).

A few other studies also evaluated children's postdictions (Bisanz, Vesonder, & Voss, 1978; Pressley, Levin, Ghatala, & Ahmad, 1987). For instance, Pressley et al. compared 7- and 10-year-olds' postdictions for entire word lists and individual items. There were two major findings: (1) Although rather accurate postdictions were found even for the younger age group, the older children were significantly better; and (2) those children who were most accurate with regard to estimating performance on individual items were not similarly accurate when asked to postdict performance on the entire list and vice versa. Overall, the findings of these studies are in accord with those obtained by Visé and Schneider (2000), indicating that even young children are able to monitor their performance.

Judgments of Learning   Whereas numerous developmental studies have addressed differences in memory performance prediction, only a few studies have dealt with JOLs that occur during or soon after the acquisition of memory materials and are predictions about future test performance on recently studied (and probably still recallable) items. The database concerning children's performance in JOL tasks is particularly small compared to the large body of literature addressing JOLs in adults. Clearly, the tools developed by cognitive psychologists that were brought into developmental research helped to investigate important questions concerning memory monitoring in a developmental context. We are especially grateful to Tom Nelson for providing us with a comprehensive introduction into the JOL methodology as well as the relevant literature and his valuable advice with regard to planning and conducting developmental JOL studies during his stay as a visiting professor (Humboldt awardee) at our department a little more than 10 years ago.

In the first study that explicitly addressed developmental trends in children's JOLs, Schneider, Visé, Lockl, and Nelson (2000) used a paired-associate learning task to assess JOL judgments in 6-, 8-, and 10-year-old children. A major goal of the study was to explore whether the delayed JOL effect that has been repeatedly confirmed in the adult literature could be observed in children of different ages. The children were asked to study 24 pairs (presented in two trials of 12 pairs) of unrelated objects presented on picture cards. In the immediate condition, children were shown the stimulus picture immediately after studying the item pair and were asked whether in about 10 minutes they would still be able to recall the second picture of the pair when prompted with the stimulus picture. In the delayed condition, children first studied all item pairs. Next, they were presented with the stimuli of each item pair and made their JOLs. The average delay between studying and making JOLs was about 2 minutes. As a main result, findings indicated that the delayed JOL effect did also operate in children, regardless of age. That is, JOL accuracy was significantly higher when JOLs were delayed than when they were assessed immediately after studying the items, indicating that even six-year-old children show accurate metacognitive monitoring under delayed conditions.

A second goal of the study (Schneider et al., 2000) was to compare individual-item JOLs with aggregate JOLs based on all items of a given list. To assess children's aggregate JOLs, they were asked at the end of studying the entire list how many of the 12 items they would be able to remember correctly. It was found that overconfidence was typically larger for item-by-item JOLs than for aggregate item JOLs for all age groups, thus replicating the aggregation effect obtained with adults. As a matter of fact, the pattern of findings for the older schoolchildren was very similar to that found for adults. In accord with the findings reported by Pressley et al. (1987), however, only low-to-moderate correlations were found between the two estimation procedures, which leads one to assume that they are tapping different aspects of the estimation process (see also Mazzoni & Nelson, 1995; Nelson & Narens, 1994).

Taken together, the findings of the study (Schneider et al., 2000) suggest that even young children can effectively monitor their learning progress under certain circumstances. On the one hand, they showed that immediate JOLs are typically inaccurate and also represent overestimations of actual performance. Remarkably, this is true not only for children of different ages but also for adults. Immediately after studying new information, judgments about its future recall seem severely biased by the false belief that information currently in short-term memory can be easily recalled some minutes later (e.g., Nelson & Dunlosky, 1991). Obviously, this bias operates similarly in participants of different ages. On the other hand, however, even young children can make rather accurate assessments of the subsequent recallability of items when this judgment is somewhat delayed, that is, when it takes place about 2 minutes after studying the item. In other words, even young children seem to have a good feeling for which items will be recallable and which will not be when long-term memory information has to be accessed for the JOL. Our findings showed not only that developmental trends are negligible but also that the accuracy of young children's delayed JOLs is close to that of adults.

In a more recent study concerning JOLs in children, Koriat and Shitzer-Reichert (2002) addressed the question of the basis of JOLs in children. Based on the cue utilization model of JOLs proposed by Koriat (1997), the study aimed to examine whether different classes of cues that affect JOLs in adults also influence children's metacognitive judgments. In particular, Experiment 1 focused on two different factors: item difficulty, which is regarded as an intrinsic factor, and practice, which is viewed as an extrinsic factor according to the cue utilization model (Koriat, 1997). Second and fourth graders were instructed to study easy and hard pairs of words so that they would be able to recall the response word when cued with the stimulus word. After studying each word pair for 5 seconds, children rated their JOLs on a 5-point scale. To investigate the effect of practice, the study–test cycle was administered four times. Concerning the effect of item difficulty, it was found that children gave higher JOLs to easy than to hard word pairs. However, there was an Age × Difficulty interaction, indicating that the fourth graders more strongly differentiated between easy and hard pairs and showed less overconfidence than the second graders. Moreover, the results revealed that children's JOLs increased with practice for both age groups. Thus, two factors that were found to influence adults' JOLs (namely, item difficulty and practice) similarly affected children's metacognitive judgments. With regard to JOL accuracy, the results were not entirely consistent with those reported by Schneider et al. (2000). Significant age effects emerged with a reliably higher mean γ correlation between JOLs and recall for the fourth graders than for the second graders.

In a second experiment, Koriat and Shitzer-Reichert (2002) aimed to replicate the delayed JOL effect in second- and fourth-grade children by comparing the delayed JOL effect to the effect of practice on JOLs. It was assumed that both delaying JOLs and sufficient practice with the learning material may result in an improved JOL accuracy, but that combining both may have few effects beyond those that are due to delaying JOLs. The elicitation of the JOLs was varied in two ways. First, JOLs were cued either by the stimulus alone or by the intact stimulus–response pair. Second, for half of the items the JOLs had to be given immediately after studying; for the other half of the items, the JOLs were delayed. As a main result, for the stimulus-only condition, the delayed JOL effect could be confirmed; that is, the mean γ correlation between JOL and recall was higher for delayed than for immediate JOLs. Interestingly, the delayed JOL effect did not occur when the JOLs were cued by the intact stimulus–response pair. This finding suggests that the attempt to retrieve the information at the time when a JOL is made is critical for its accuracy.

Furthermore, contrary to Experiment 1 (Koriat & Shitzer-Reichert, 2002), no significant age effects on JOL accuracy emerged. Concerning the effect of practice, JOL accuracy improved with practice. However, this was not the case when JOLs were delayed and cued by the stimulus alone. In this condition, the JOL accuracy was very high from the beginning, and the high accuracy levels remained stable across the presentation trials. These findings led Koriat and Shitzer-Reichert to conclude that delaying JOLs and practice are two different means that lead to the same result of enhanced JOL accuracy.

Whereas developmental research on JOLs reported so far has been limited to paired-associate learning tasks, a study by Roebers, von der Linden, Howie, and Schneider (2007) aimed to investigate children's monitoring abilities in the context of a complex, everyday memory task. Important goals of this study were to explore developmental differences in children's JOLs and to examine the effects of delay and the role of retrievability on JOLs. The sample consisted of 8- and 10-year-old children as well as adults who all watched a short event on a video. Afterward, participants rated on a 7-point-scale how certain they were that they would later be able to recall specific details about the event correctly. The memory test took place 2 weeks after the video presentation and the JOL interview. To investigate the role of retrievability, the JOL interview as well as the memory test not only included answerable questions about details that really occurred in the video but also unanswerable questions that could not be answered on the basis of the video. For example, participants were asked, "What do the boys have in their backpacks when they arrive at the farm-house?" whereas in the video, no information was given about the contents of the backpacks. Roebers at al. assumed that, if JOLs are partly based on the retrievability of information, JOLs about details that were not encoded should be lower than JOLs for encoded information. In other words, individuals should be able to make a meta-cognitive distinction between answerable and unanswerable questions.

As can be seen from Figure 2, JOLs clearly differed as a function of the appropriate-ness of the answer, and JOLs were also influenced by the question type (Roebers et al., 2007). JOLs were highest for answerable questions that were correctly answered in the memory test. In comparison, JOLs were significantly lower before incorrect answers to answerable questions, which in turn were significantly higher than JOLs before incor-rect answers to unanswerable questions. The lowest level of JOLs was found for unan-swerable questions, which subsequently were appropriately answered with "I don't know." Remarkably, the three age groups did not differ in their mean level of JOLs, and no interactions between age and appropriateness of answer or question type emerged. Thus, even children in the youngest age group were able to appropriately differenti-ate between correct and incorrect answers. The same applies for the differentiation between answerable and unanswerable questions. JOL accuracy was also comparable across age groups, with mean γ correlations between JOLs and recall performance ranging between .53 and .70, thus indicating moderate-to-high interrelations.

Furthermore, the comparison of JOLs for answerable and unanswerable questions showed that JOLs were higher for potentially answerable than for unanswerable ques-tions. This suggests that participants based their JOLs on the evaluation of informa-tion retrievability, regardless of age. Thus, the amount of information that comes to mind during the retrieval process seems to have an impact on children's and adults' JOLs. Overall, the results are in accord with the view that JOLs are among others

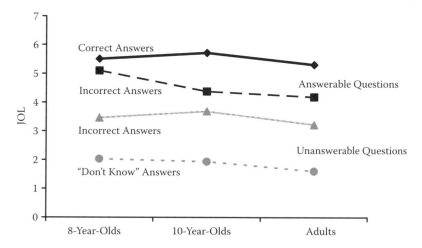

Figure 2 Mean judgments of learning (JOLs) before correct and incorrect answers to answerable questions (upper lines) and before incorrect answers and appropriate don't know answers to unanswerable questions (lower lines) as a function of age group. (Data from Roe-bers, von der Linden, Howie, & Schneider, 2007.)

based on memory characteristics or mnemonic cues, such as the ease with which information is retrieved or the accessibility of pertinent partial information about the memory target (Koriat, 1993).

Feeling-of-Knowing Judgments A number of developmental studies explored children's FOK accuracy (e.g., Cultice, Somerville, & Wellman, 1983; DeLoache & Brown, 1984; Wellman, 1977). FOK judgments occur either during or after a learning procedure and are judgments about whether a currently unrecallable item will be remembered at a subsequent retention test. Typically, children are shown a series of items and asked to name them. When children are shown a picture and cannot recall the name of an object in that picture, they are asked to indicate whether the name could be recognized if the experimenter provided it. These FOK ratings are then related to subsequent performance on the recognition test.

Overall, most of the available evidence on FOK judgments suggests that FOK accuracy improves continuously across childhood and adolescence (e.g., Wellman, 1977; Zabrucky & Ratner, 1986). However, the pattern of developmental trends is not entirely clear. In a study that avoided a methodological problem apparent in previous research on FOK judgments, Butterfield, Nelson, and Peck (1988) showed that 6-year-olds' FOK judgments were actually more accurate than those of 10-year-olds and 18-year-olds. Obviously, this finding did not square well with the results of previous research.

A study by Lockl and Schneider (2002a) was based on a methodologically improved design similar to that used by Butterfield et al. (1988) but included different age groups (i.e., 7-, 8-, 9-, and 10-year-olds). Although the major goal of this study was to replicate the findings of Butterfield and colleagues, another aim was to explore the basis of FOK judgments by comparing the traditional "trace-based" view with the trace accessibility model developed by Koriat (1993). Whereas the former assumes a two-stage process of monitoring and retrieval, the latter proposes that FOK judgments are based on retrieval attempts and determined by the amount of information that can be spontaneously generated, regardless of its correctness. A prediction derived from the trace accessibility view is that FOK judgments for correctly recalled items and incorrect answers (commission errors) should be comparably high and also considerably higher than FOK judgments for omission errors.

As a main result regarding the first goal, no developmental trends in the accuracy of FOK judgments were found (Lockl & Schneider, 2002a). Overall, FOK accuracy was low but significantly above chance for all age groups. The main difference between these findings and those by Butterfield and colleagues concerned the performance of the youngest age group (i.e., first graders). Whereas FOK accuracy was rather high for the American first graders, it was lower in the case of the German first graders. Although there is no truly convincing reason for the differences between both studies regarding their youngest age groups, the findings suggest that there are no significant developmental trends in FOK accuracy over the course of the elementary school years. However, given the inconsistency in findings for the young elementary schoolchildren, more research is needed here.

Furthermore, Lockl and Schneider's (2002a) findings provided support for the trace accessibility view and the assumption that feeling of knowing can be dissociated from knowing. That is, the magnitude of FOK judgments given after commission errors did not differ much from that of FOK judgments provided after correct recall. In comparison, FOK judgments were considerably higher after commission than after omission errors. This contrasts sharply with the finding that recognition performance was comparable in the case of commission and omission errors (about 50% correct), whereas it was nearly perfect when items had been already correctly recalled before.

Taken together, more recent studies assessing monitoring abilities in JOL or FOK tasks demonstrated negligible developmental progression in children's monitoring skills (Butterfield et al., 1988; Koriat & Shitzer-Reichert, 2002; Lockl & Schneider, 2002a; Roebers et al., 2007; Schneider et al., 2000). Thus, these studies contributed to a modification of the view that children are generally overconfident and possess deficient monitoring abilities. In contrast, previous work on procedural metamemory that was largely based on the performance prediction paradigm indicated that young children tend to be overoptimistic and overestimate their memory performance (e.g., Flavell et al., 1970; Schneider, Borkowski, Kurtz, & Kerwin, 1986; Worden & Sladewski-Awig, 1982; Yussen & Levy, 1975). The discrepancy between these two lines of studies may for the most part be due to the fact that different indicators of metacognitive abilities were used (e.g., Koriat & Goldsmith, 1996): On the one hand, studies including performance prediction tasks address *absolute* metacognitive accuracy or calibration, that is, the match between the predicted and actual overall memory performance. On the other hand, studies based on the JOL or FOK paradigm focus on *relative* accuracy or resolution, that is, the accuracy in monitoring the relative recallability of different items. This aspect of monitoring accuracy is especially important in self-paced learning situations when students have to allocate their study time differentially on the to-be-learned materials. JOL or FOK studies typically used γ correlations as indicators of relative accuracy and found no (e.g., Lockl & Schneider, 2002a; Schneider et al., 2000) or only small age differences (e.g., Koriat & Shitzer-Reichert, 2002, Experiment 1). A closer look at the data obtained in these studies reveals that younger children tend to be more optimistic about their future recall. That is, they seem to have a more liberal response criterion and produce more false alarms than older children (and presumably also adults). Because both types of errors (i.e., overestimation and underestimation) are similarly taken into account when γ correlations are computed, the resulting magnitude of the γ correlations may be comparable even though the types of underlying errors are rather different for younger and older children. In sum, there is converging evidence that younger children are more optimistic than older children and adults and often overestimate their future memory performance. This tendency to be overconfident, however, does not seem to affect children's relative monitoring accuracy, which seems comparable across age groups. Besides, other studies concerning children's overconfidence (Schneider, 1998a; Visé & Schneider, 2000) did not support the original assumption that young children's overestimations of future performance are due to metacognitive deficiencies. Rather, they suggest that motivational factors such as wishful thinking and effort attribution biased the recall estimates of young children. Bjorklund and Bering (2002) interpreted the general overestimation of one's competencies as a protective factor for cognitive development in general, helping individuals to maintain motivation and task persistence and thereby fueling developmental progression in a broader sense.

Overall, it could be demonstrated that applying experimental designs already frequently used in general cognitive psychology in developmental studies not only added to our knowledge about age differences in children's monitoring proficiency but also provided important insights into the origins of metacognitive judgments in children.

The Relation Between Monitoring and Control Processes in Children

An important reason to study metacognitive monitoring processes is because monitoring is supposed to play a central role in directing how people study. Numerous studies including adult participants showed that individuals use memory monitoring, especially JOLs, to decide which items to study and how long to spend on them (e.g., Metcalfe, 2002; Nelson, Dunlosky, Graf, & Narens, 1994; Nelson & Narens, 1990; Son & Metcalfe, 2000). However, little is known about how children use monitoring to regulate their study time.

Allocation of Study Time   A classic paradigm suited to further explore this issue refers to the allocation of study time. Research on study time allocation observes how learners deploy their attention and effort. As already noted by Brown et al. (1983), the ability to attend selectively to relevant aspects of a memory task is a traditional index of learner's understanding of the task. Developmental studies on the allocation of study time examined whether schoolchildren and adults were more likely to spend more time on less-well-learned material. A few studies examined whether schoolchildren are more likely to spend more time on less-well-learned material. For example, Masur, McIntyre, and Flavell (1973) asked seven-year-olds, nine-year-olds, and college students to learn a list of pictures for free recall. After the first study trial, participants were instructed to select half the pictures for additional study. Whereas nine-year-olds and college students tended to select items not recalled correctly on the first trial, seven-year-olds did not seem to consider first-trial performance in selecting items for additional processing. However, children in this study were forced to be selective. Thus, we do not know how young children might behave in a spontaneous study situation.

A study by Dufresne and Kobasigawa (1989) investigated how children of different ages spontaneously allocated their study time. In this study, 6-, 8-, 10-, and 12-year-old children were asked to study booklets containing either "easy" (highly related) or "hard" (unrelated) paired-associate items until they were sure they could remember all pairs perfectly. As a main result, Dufresne and Kobasigawa reported an age-related improvement in the efficient allocation of study time. That is, 10- and 12-year-olds spent more time studying the hard items than they spent studying the easy items. However, six- and eight-year-olds spent about the same amount of time on hard pairs as they spent on easy pairs. At the same time, young schoolchildren were more optimistic about their readiness for a test, although only a small number of participants achieved perfect recall. Children's subsequent answers to metacognitive knowledge questions showed that even many of the six-year-old children were able to distinguish between hard and easy pairs. They were aware which materials were easy or hard to learn. Thus, developmental differences were not so much observed in the metacognitive knowledge itself but in its efficient application to self-regulation strategies. This finding was also confirmed in a more recent study in which the items were presented via computer (Lockl & Schneider, 2002b). Again, young schoolchildren spent about the same amount of time on easy pairs as they spent on hard pairs, whereas older schoolchildren devoted more time to studying the hard items than the easy ones.

A study by Kobasigawa and Metcalf-Haggert (1993) indicated that young children's use of regulatory skills depends on the difficulty and complexity of the memory task. First- and third-grade children were asked to learn the names of familiar and unfamiliar objects until they were sure they could name all the items correctly. Both first- and third-grade children spontaneously spent more time studying the unfamiliar items than they spent studying the familiar items. According to Kobasigawa and Metcalf-Haggert, differences in item difficulty were particularly salient, which was probably necessary for young children to adjust their use of study time. The assumption that performance on study time apportionment tasks strongly depends on the difficulty of the task is also confirmed by studies using text materials. For example, Brown, Smiley, and Lawton (1978) demonstrated that sophisticated selection of text material for further study develops somewhat later than the grade-school years.

Although there is evidence that there are clear increases in self-regulation skills from middle childhood to adolescence, the existing database does not provide us with any detailed information about the relation between monitoring and control processes. Accordingly, we do not know exactly whether children use the output of monitoring processes to regulate their study time. For instance, Dufresne and Kobasigawa (1989) demonstrated that many of the younger children were able to discriminate between hard and easy pairs (see also Lockl & Schneider, 2002b). However, in this study, different materials for the metacognitive knowledge questions and for measuring study times were used. Thus, it remains unclear whether a particular item that is judged as difficult to recall will be studied for a longer time than an item that is judged as rather easy to recall.

To investigate the relation between monitoring processes and self-regulation processes more analytically, Lockl and Schneider (2003) asked seven- and nine-year-old children to study easy (highly related) and difficult (unrelated) paired associated pictures. After a first learning phase with a fixed presentation time (3 seconds), JOLs were assessed on a 5-point-scale. Subsequently, the same pairs were presented again for self-paced study. As a first result, it was found that both seven- and nine-year-old children were able to differentiate between easy and difficult pairs. For seven-year-olds, JOLs were $m = 4.63$ and 3.96 for easy and hard item pairs, respectively. Similarly, for nine-year-olds, JOLs were $m = 4.76$ and 3.94 for easy and hard item pairs, respectively. Thus, the age groups did not differ in their mean level of JOLs, and there was no Age group × Difficulty interaction. When JOLs were made, children of both age groups seemed to consider the degree of associative relatedness between the members of the pairs. Put differently, item difficulty as an intrinsic cue affected children's JOLs regardless of age (see also Koriat & Shitzer-Reichert, 2002). To examine whether children used the output of monitoring to guide their learning, γ correlations between JOLs and subsequent study time were computed. The resulting mean γ correlations were $G = -.22$ for seven-year-olds and $G = -.40$ for nine-year-olds, with both values significantly different from zero. Thus, even though children of both age groups studied item pairs with lower JOLs for a longer period of time than item pairs with higher JOLs, the relation between monitoring and control was significantly stronger for nine-year-olds than for seven-year-olds. Accordingly, nine-year-olds regulated their study times more in accordance with their preceding JOLs than seven-year-olds. To examine the impact of self-regulation on recall performance, subgroups were formed within each age group that included children with either high or low self-regulation. It was found that recall performance was significantly better for the children with high self-regulation than for those with low self-regulation, regardless of age. Overall, the data indicated that the ability to translate monitoring into adequate self-regulation strategies reliably improved with age. Furthermore, the quality of self-regulation significantly contributed to the learning outcome. However, because JOLs in this study were generally high and the task was relatively easy, further research including different and maybe more complex learning materials is needed to analyze the relation between monitoring and control in children and adolescents in more detail.

Interestingly, similar patterns of results were found in studies including older adults (e.g., Dunlosky & Connor, 1997; Murphy, Schmitt, Caruso, & Sanders, 1987). For instance, Dunlosky and Connor (1997) found that although older adults (M age = 67 years) and younger adults (M age = 22 years) showed equivalent monitoring accuracy, the magnitude of the correlations between JOLs or recall on one trial and study times on the next trial was less for older than for younger adults. The results of this study indicated that older adults may not optimally utilize the output from monitoring to control study. Furthermore, the study revealed that age-related differences in people's allocation of study time reliably mediated age-related differences in recall performance (see also Hertzog, 2002). Thus, the findings of this study are similar to those obtained with younger children.

The observation that both younger children and older adults seem to experience difficulties with translating monitoring into adequate self-regulation does not imply that the causes are similar in both age groups. In fact, the causes could be quite different. As for older adults, Dunlosky and Connor (1997) discussed the possibility that the older participants in their study may have tried to compensate for possible declines in memory. That is, older adults may have spent too much time studying already well-known items, thereby neglecting less-well-known items.

A promising line of research to explain age differences during childhood (and maybe also during old age) might be to link the ability to translate monitoring into adequate self-regulation to individual differences in working memory capacity. Apparently, metacognitive activities such as self-monitoring and self-regulating require valuable processing capacity. Accordingly, limitations of working memory capacity may undermine decisions on how to allocate study time. In a first study to investigate this issue, Dunlosky and Thiede (2004, Experiment 3) compared low-span and high-span adult participants in a self-regulated learning task in which participants were asked to make JOLs on paired associates and subsequently to select some of them for restudy. Dunlosky and Thiede (2004) found that the mean γ correlation between JOLs and item selection was significantly less for participants with low memory spans than for those with high memory spans, indicating that individual differences in working memory capacity can influence the allocation of study time across items.

Although this study (Dunlosky & Thiede, 2004) was carried out with adults and did not provide any information about developmental progression in metacognitive control processes, it opened a fruitful area for further research. There is no doubt that working memory capacity considerably increases with age. Numerous studies demonstrated developmental differences in each of the three major components of the working memory model developed by Baddeley (1986), that is, phonological loop, visuospatial sketchpad, and central executive (e.g., Gathercole, 1999; Logie & Pearson, 1997). Because the central executive is supposed to be responsible for planning and control processes involved in higher-level cognition, this component might be particularly crucial with respect to self-paced learning situations. Future research will be essential to our understanding of how age-related differences in working memory capacity influence self-regulated learning.

Concluding Remarks

One of the major outcomes of developmental studies on procedural metacognition concerns the lack of clear-cut developmental trends in children's monitoring skills. Although monitoring accuracy tends to improve over the school years, even preschoolers show remarkable monitoring in learning situations with which they are familiar. In contrast, the available evidence on the development of self-regulation skills shows that there are clear increases from middle childhood to adolescence. Effective self-regulation occurs only in highly constrained situations during the elementary school years and continues well into adolescence. Obviously, one of the major developmental trends concerns the integration of monitoring outcomes and self-regulation skills. Whereas young children may be able to monitor comprehension problems accurately, they usually do not know how to cure them. In comparison, older schoolchildren and adolescents know how to benefit from monitoring by implementing effective control strategies.

References

Baddeley, A. D. (1986). *Working memory.* Oxford, UK: Oxford University Press.

Benjamin, A. S., & Bjork, R. A. (1996). Retrieval fluency as a metacognitive index. In L. M. Reder (Ed.), *Implicit memory and metacognition* (pp. 309–338). Hillsdale, NJ: Erlbaum.

Bisanz, G. L., Vesonder, G. T., & Voss, J. F. (1978). Knowledge of one's own responding and the relation of such knowledge to learning. *Journal of Experimental Child Psychology, 25,* 116–128.

Bjorklund, D. F., & Bering, J. M. (2002). The evolved child applying evolutionary developmental psychology to modern schooling. *Learning and Individual Differences, 12,* 1–27.

Borkowski, J. G., Milstead, M., & Hale, C. (1988). Components of children's metamemory: Implications for strategy generalization. In F. E. Weinert & M. Perlmutter (Eds.), *Memory development: Universal changes and individual differences* (pp. 73–100). Hillsdale, NJ: Erlbaum.

Brown, A. L. (1978). Knowing when, where and how to remember: A problem of metacognition. In R. Glaser (Ed.), *Advances in instructional psychology* (Vol. 1, pp. 77–165). Hillsdale, NJ: Erlbaum.

Brown, A. L., Bransford, J. D., Ferrara, R. A., & Campione, J. C. (1983). Learning, remembering, and understanding. In J. H. Flavell & E. M. Markham (Eds.), *Handbook of child psychology: Vol. 3. Cognitive development* (pp. 77–166). New York: Wiley.

Brown, A. L., Smiley, S. S., & Lawton, S. Q. C. (1978). The effects of experience on the selection of suitable retrieval cues for studying texts. *Child Development, 49*, 829–835.

Butterfield, E. C., Nelson, T. O., & Peck, V. (1988). Developmental aspects of the feeling of knowing. *Developmental Psychology, 24*, 654–663.

Cultice, J. C., Somerville, S. C., & Wellman, H. M. (1983). Preschoolers' memory monitoring: Feeling-of-knowing judgments. *Child Development, 54*, 1480–1486.

Cunningham, J. G., & Weaver, S. L. (1989). Young children's knowledge of their memory span: Effects of task and experience. *Journal of Experimental Child Psychology, 48*, 32–44.

DeLoache, J. S., & Brown, A. L. (1984). Where do I go next? Intelligent searching by very young children. *Developmental Psychology, 20*, 37–44.

Dixon, R. A., & Hertzog, C. (1988). A functional approach to memory and metamemory development in adulthood. In F. E. Weinert & M. Perlmutter (Eds.), *Memory development: Universal changes and individual differences* (pp. 293–330). Hillsdale, NJ: Erlbaum.

Dufresne, A., & Kobasigawa, A. (1989). Children's spontaneous allocation of study time: Differential and sufficient aspects. *Journal of Experimental Child Psychology, 47*, 274–296.

Dunlosky, J., & Connor, L. T. (1997). Age differences in the allocation of study time account for age differences in memory performance. *Memory & Cognition, 25*, 691–700.

Dunlosky, J., & Nelson, T. O. (1992). Importance of the kind of cue for judgments of learning (JOL) and the delayed-JOL effect. *Memory & Cognition, 20*, 374–380.

Dunlosky, J., & Thiede, K. W. (2004). Causes and constraints of the shift-to-easier-materials effect in the control of study. *Memory & Cognition, 32*, 779–788.

Flavell, J. H. (1971). First discussant's comments: What is memory development the development of? *Human Development, 14*, 272–278.

Flavell, J. H. (1979). Metacognition and cognitive monitoring. A new area of cognitive-developmental inquiry. *American Psychologist, 34*, 906–911.

Flavell, J. H. (2000). Development of children's knowledge about the mental world. *International Journal of Behavioral Development, 24*, 15–23.

Flavell, J. H., Friedrichs, A. G., & Hoyt, J. D. (1970). Developmental changes in memorization processes. *Cognitive Psychology, 1*, 324–340.

Flavell, J. H., Miller, P. H., & Miller, S. A. (1993). *Cognitive development.* Englewood Cliffs, NJ: Prentice-Hall.

Flavell, J. H., & Wellman, H. M. (1977). Metamemory. In R. V. Kail & J. W. Hagen (Eds.), *Perspectives on the development of memory and cognition* (pp. 3–33). Hillsdale, NJ: Erlbaum.

Gathercole, S. E. (1999). Cognitive approaches to the development of short-term memory. *Trends in Cognitive Science, 3*, 410–419.

Herrmann, D. J. (1982). Know thy memory: The use of questionnaires to assess and study memory. *Psychological Bulletin, 92*, 434–452.

Hertzog, C. (2002). Metacognition in older adults: Implications for application. In T. J. Perfect & B. L. Schwartz (Eds.), *Applied metacognition* (pp. 169–196). Cambridge, UK: Cambridge University Press.

Joyner, M., & Kurtz-Costes, B. (1997). Metamemory development. In N. Cowan (Ed.). *The development of memory in childhood* (pp. 275–300). Sussex: Psychology Press.

Justice, E. M., & Bray, N. W. (1979). The effects of context and feedback on metamemory in young children. *Unpublished manuscript*, Old Dominion University, Norfolk, VA.

Kobasigawa, A., & Metcalf-Haggert, A. (1993). Spontaneous allocation of study time by first- and third-grade children in a simple memory task. *Journal of Genetic Psychology, 154*, 223–235.

Koriat, A. (1993). How do we know what we know? The accessibility model of the feeling of knowing. *Psychological Review, 100*, 609–639.

Koriat, A. (1997). Monitoring one's own knowledge during study: A cue-utilization approach to judgments of learning. *Journal of Experimental Psychology: General, 126*, 349–370.

Koriat, A. (2006). Metacognition and consciousness. In P. D. Zelazo, M. Moscovitch, & E. Thompson (Eds.), *Cambridge handbook of consciousness*. New York: Cambridge University Press.

Koriat, A., & Goldsmith, M. (1996). Memory metaphors and the real-life/laboratory controversy: Correspondence versus storehouse conceptions of memory. *Behavioral and Brain Sciences, 19*, 167–228.

Koriat, A., & Shitzer-Reichert, R. (2002). Metacognitive judgments and their accuracy. Insights from the processes underlying judgments of learning in children. In P. Chambres, M. Izaute, & P.-J. Marescaux (Eds.), *Metacognition: Process, function, and use* (pp. 1–18). Boston: Kluwer.

Koriat, A., Bjork, R. A., Scheffer, L., & Bar, S. K. (2004). Preducting one's own forgetting: The role of experience-based and theory-based processes. *Journal of Experimental Psychology: General, 133*, 643–656.

Kuhn, D. (1999). Metacognitive development. In L. Balter & C. S. Tamis-LeMonda (Eds.), *Child psychology: A handbook of contemporary issues* (pp. 259–286). Philadelphia: Psychology Press.

Kuhn, D. (2000). Theory of mind, metacognition, and reasoning: A life-span perspective. In P. Mitchell & K. J. Riggs (Eds.), *Children's reasoning and the mind* (pp. 301–326). Hove, UK: Psychology Press.

Lockl, K., & Schneider, W. (2002a). Developmental trends in children's feeling-of-knowing judgements. *International Journal of Behavioral Development, 26*, 327–333.

Lockl, K., & Schneider, W. (2002b). Zur Entwicklung des selbstregulierten Lernens im Grundschulalter: Zusammenhänge zwischen Aufgabenschwierigkeit und Lernzeiteinteilung [The development of self-regulated learning in elementary school children: Associations between task difficulty and allocation of study time]. *Psychologie in Erziehung und Unterricht, 49*, 3–16.

Lockl, K., & Schneider, W. (2003). Metakognitive Überwachungs- und Kontrollprozesse bei der Lernzeiteinteilung von Kindern [Monitoring and control processes in children's allocation of study time]. *Zeitschrift für Pädagogische Psychologie, 17*, 173–183.

Logie, R. H., & Pearson, D. G. (1997). The inner eye and the inner scribe of visuo-spatial working memory: Evidence from developmental fractionation. *European Journal of Cognitive Psychology, 9*, 241–257.

Masur, E. F., McIntyre, C. W., & Flavell, J. H. (1973). Developmental changes in apportionment of study time among items in a multitrial free recall task. *Journal of Experimental Child Psychology, 15*, 237–246.

Mazzoni, G., & Nelson, T. O. (1995). Judgments of learning are affected by the kind of encoding in ways that cannot be attributed to the level of recall. *Journal of Experimental Psychology: Learning, Memory, and Cognition, 21*, 1263–1274.

Metcalfe, J. (2002). Is study time allocated selectively to a region of proximal learning? *Journal of Experimental Psychology: General, 131*, 349–363.

Metcalfe, J., & Shimamura, A. P. (1994). *Metacognition: Knowing about knowing*. Cambridge, MA: MIT Press.

Murphy, M. D., Schmitt, F. A., Caruso, M. J., & Sanders, R. E. (1987). Metamemory in older adults: the role of monitoring in serial recall. *Psychology and Aging, 2*, 331–339.

Nelson, T. O. (1996). Consciousness and metacognition. *American Psychologist, 51*, 102–116.

Nelson, T. O., & Dunlosky, J. (1991). When people's judgments of learning (JOLs) are extremely accurate at predicting subsequent recall: The "delayed-JOL effect." *Psychological Science, 2*, 267–270.

Nelson, T. O., Dunlosky, J., Graf, A., & Narens, L. (1994). Utilization of metacognitive judgments in the allocation of study during multitrial learning. *Psychological Science, 5*, 207–213.

Nelson, T. O., & Narens, L. (1990). Metamemory: A theoretical framework and new findings. In G. Bower (Ed.), *The psychology of learning and motivation: Advances in research and theory* (Vol. 26, pp. 125–173). New York: Academic Press.

Nelson, T. O., & Narens, L. (1994). Why investigate metacognition? In J. Metcalfe & A. P. Shimamura (Eds.), *Metacognition. Knowing about knowing* (pp. 1–25). Cambridge, MA: MIT Press.

Paris, S. G., & Lindauer, B. K. (1982). The development of cognitive skills during childhood. In B. Wolman (Ed.), *Handbook of developmental psychology* (pp. 33–349). Englewood Cliffs, NJ: Prentice Hall.

Paris, S. G., & Oka, E. R. (1986). Children's reading strategies, metacognition, and motivation. *Developmental Review, 6*, 25–56.

Pressley, M., Borkowski, J. G., & Schneider, W. (1989). Good information processing: What it is and what education can do to promote it. *International Journal of Educational Research, 13*, 857–867.

Pressley, M., & Ghatala, E. S. (1990). Self-regulated learning: Monitoring from text learning. *Educational Psychologist, 25*, 19–33.

Pressley, M., Levin, J. R., Ghatala, E. S., & Ahmad, M. (1987) Test monitoring in young children. *Journal of Experimental Child Psychology, 43, 96–111*.

Roebers, C., von der Linden, N., Howie, P., & Schneider, W. (2007). Children's metamemorial judgments in an event recall task. *Journal of Experimental Child Psychology, 97*, 117–137.

Schneider, W. (1998a). The development of procedural metamemory in childhood and adolescence. In G. Mazzoni & T. O. Nelson (Eds.), *Monitoring and control processes in metacognition and cognitive neuropsychology* (pp. 1–21). Mahwah, NJ: Erlbaum.

Schneider, W. (1998b). Performance prediction in young children: Effects of skill, metacognition and wishful thinking. *Developmental Science, 1*, 291–297.

Schneider, W., Borkowski, J. G., Kurtz, B. E., & Kerwin, K. (1986). Metamemory and motivation: A comparison of strategy use and performance in German and American children. *Journal of Cross-Cultural Psychology, 17*, 315–336.

Schneider, W., Körkel, J., & Weinert, F. E. (1990). Expert knowledge, general abilities, and text processing. In W. Schneider & F. E. Weinert (Eds.), *Interactions among aptitudes, strategies, and knowledge in cognitive performance* (pp. 235–251). New York: Springer.

Schneider, W., & Lockl, K. (2002). The development of metacognitive knowledge in children and adolescents. In T. J. Perfect & B. L. Schwartz (Eds.), *Applied metacognition* (pp. 224–257). Cambridge, UK: Cambridge University Press.

Schneider, W., & Pressley, M. (1997). *Memory development between 2 and 20*. Hillsdale, NJ: Erlbaum.

Schneider, W., Visé, M., Lockl, K., & Nelson, T. O. (2000). Developmental trends in children's memory monitoring: Evidence from a judgment-of-learning (JOL) task. *Cognitive Development, 15,* 115–134.

Son, L. K., & Metcalfe, J. (2000). Metacognitive and control strategies in study-time allocation. *Journal of Experimental Psychology: Learning, Memory, and Cognition, 26,* 204–221.

Stipek, D. J. (1984). Young children's performance expectations: Logical analysis or wishful thinking? In J. G. Nicholls (Ed.), *The development of achievement motivation* (pp. 121–142). Greenwich, CT: JAI Press.

Visé, M., & Schneider, W. (2000). Determinanten der Leistungsvorhersage bei Kindergarten- und Grundschulkindern: Zur Bedeutung metakognitiver und motivationaler Einflussfaktoren [Determinants of performance prediction in kindergarten and school children: The importance of metacognitive and motivational factors]. *Zeitschrift für Entwicklungspsychologie und Pädagogische Psychologie, 32,* 51–58.

Wellman, H. M. (1977). Tip of the tongue and feeling of knowing experiences: A developmental study of memory monitoring. *Child Development, 48,* 13–21.

Wimmer, H., & Perner, J. (1983). Beliefs about beliefs: Representation and constraining function of wrong beliefs in young children's understanding of deception. *Cognition, 13,* 103–128.

Worden, P. E., & Sladewski-Awig, L. J. (1982). Children's awareness of memorability. *Journal of Educational Psychology, 74,* 341–350.

Yussen, S. R., & Levy, V. M. (1975). Developmental changes in predicting one's own memory span of short-term memory. *Journal of Experimental Child Psychology, 19,* 502–508.

Zabrucky, K., & Ratner, H. H. (1986). Children's comprehension monitoring and recall of inconsistent stories. *Child Development, 57,* 1401–1418.

Metacognition in the Classroom

Marie Carroll

Introduction

This chapter is about how we can better apply metacognitive findings to formal classroom learning. The aim of such an endeavor is not only to construct more complete theoretical models but also to better meet the needs of our students, who have, on the whole, not benefited from at least 20 years of metacognitive research in cognitive psychology.

In calling for natural targets for cognitive research, that is, having concrete situations to which one can apply one's efforts, Nelson and Narens (1994) said:

> We believe with Neisser (1976) that our goal should be "to understand cognition in the context of natural purposeful activity. This would not mean an end to laboratory experiments but a commitment to the study of variables that are ecologically important rather than those that are easily manageable." (p. 4)

Nelson and Narens argued further that the target of such research was

> To explain (and eventually improve) the mnemonic behaviour of a student who is studying for and taking an exam. We chose this target in part for the following reasons: It is relevant (who spends more time memorising for and taking exams than college students?), naturalistic, practical, concrete, and challenging in terms of theory. (p. 6)

The notion that metacognition should be investigated in classroom practice is a theme that is particularly attractive as a research path. We pay lip service, on the whole, to bringing cognitive psychology out of the laboratory, but we have not been as diligent about this as we could be (with several notable exceptions). As Jamshed Bharucha, provost of Tufts University and professor of psychology, said:

> Current knowledge about cognition (specifically, our understanding of active learning, memory, attention, and implicit learning) has not fully penetrated our educational practices, because of inertia as well as a natural lag in the application of basic research. (2006)

Metacognition research in classroom settings affords us the opportunity to know, in a unique way, whether our teaching methods are optimal because metacognition allows us to look at the constructed understanding of our classroom teaching. Metacognition research also informs educators about other important issues that educators frequently fail to grasp, for example, that subjective mastery can be very different from objective mastery of learned material. Koriat, Sheffer, and Ma'ayan (2002) and many others have made the point that differences between subjective knowing and objective performance can give rise to illusions of knowing, with serious consequences for students' grades. Teaching for objective mastery can be greatly enhanced by a concomitant understanding of what the learner understands about the learning process.

In this chapter, I draw on research in metamemory over two decades that shows the importance of understanding what the learner believes or thinks he or she knows about his or her own learning, about what works in the process of memorizing. When this is set alongside objective memory outcomes, the results can be very surprising for educators. I am very selective in the experiments I describe, choosing some of those that exemplify earlier metacognitive studies that also have direct relevance to the classroom. The topics covered are the relativity of metacognitive judgments and their dependence on context; illusions of learning; metacognitive judgments about memory for text; and a new metacognitive judgment — the judgment of source. I conclude with some general implications for classroom practice.

Metacognitive Judgments Are Improved by Having Comparative Information Available

The last 20 or so years saw increased understanding of the methodological issues relating to metacognition and new ways of measuring it (e.g., ease of learning, judgments of learning [JOLs], feeling of knowing [FOK]). One example is our understanding of the theoretical basis of the FOK, that familiarity-based heuristic that arises from being unable to recall information while knowing that it is recognizable. Recent studies have shown FOK can tap not only future recognition but also the state of awareness that was associated with that recognition, that is, whether it was "remembered" or "known" (Hicks & Marsh, 2002).

This remarkable ability — of knowing with some accuracy about information currently not accessible — can be used by learners in test situations for which recognition tests are anticipated. A student, exposed initially to a body of material, with limited study time to undertake conscientious self-testing may rely on the FOK with some confidence in a multiple-choice setting. This knowledge illustrates the limits of considering learning as evident only from what a person can output there and then; rather, it taps into a fundamental self-monitoring ability all students can recruit. They know that some outputs depend on the type of test (e.g., recognition vs. recall) and adjust their learning accordingly (Thiede, 1996).

Whether students understand how the amount of learning affects performance is more complicated because the particular method chosen to elucidate this moderates the relevant effects. Nelson, Leonesio, Shimamura, Landwehr, and Narens (1982) showed that FOK is sensitive to the degree of prior learning of items. After learning word pairs to one, two, or four correct recalls and when tested 4 weeks later, people reported a higher FOK for items learned four times than for once-learned items. In contrast, Carroll and Simington (1986) found something rather different: Greater degrees of learning did not affect FOK ratings but did improve the ability to recall information. Could this mean that people are not, in fact, metacognitively sensitive to the amount of learning they are doing?

In 1993, we reported work that showed why the discrepancy in the findings occurred (Carroll & Nelson, 1993). In one experiment, we compared directly people's

FOK ratings when they had learned *all* items to the *same* criterion (a between-subject design) with their FOK ratings when they learned *subsets* of items to *different* criteria (within-subject design). So, in the between-subject design one group learned all items to a criterion of one correct recall, while a different group had to correctly retrieve the answers six times. In the within-subject group, the same subjects learned some items once and other items six times. We then asked people to rate their likelihood of recognizing the answers to those items they were unable to recall when they came back 4 weeks later for a recognition test.

Those subjects in the between-subject design did not rate their FOKs higher for items learned six times (53%) than they did for once-learned items (47%) — the difference of 6% was not significant. By contrast, in the within-subject design, the FOK ratings were significantly higher for the overlearned items (49%) than for the once-learned items (39%). This in no way reflected their later test performance: At test 4 weeks later, the actual recognition rates for the unrecalled items were higher for overlearned than for once-learned items, as might be expected, for *both* the within- and between-subject designs. Thus, the FOK ratings were sensitive to the amount of learning only in the within-subject condition and allowed us to explain the previous research finding discrepancy. Now, why should this be? Our proposed explanation is illustrated by comparing subjective reports to a telescope (see Nelson & Narens, 1994, p. 18) with a focus that can be adjusted to improve accuracy. When the design is within subjects, people turn their internal ratings telescope to low power and focus on big differences, such as that some items are overlearned and some not. In Koriat's grain size terminology (Koriat & Goldsmith, 1996), they are considering the grain size of the comparisons they are making; this is a coarse-level comparison. (To use another of Koriat's [1997] terms, they are making a comparison on the basis of extrinsic cues: the experimenter-determined variable of number of learning trials). On the other hand, when they experience only one criterion of learning condition (one time *or* six times), they turn the telescope to high power and focus on fine-grain size comparisons at the level of individual items. Thus, they would be using as the basis for their judgments intrinsic cues such as the meaningfulness of, or semantic associations to, individual items.

This finding of grain size differences has since become a theme in the metacognition literature, and it has important implications in the classroom. It shows that students monitoring their learning are highly influenced by the types of comparisons they have to make: When required to make large-group comparisons such as between different classes of items or between different conditions of learning, they adjust to a coarse grain size and focus less on the (perhaps important) differences between individual items or facts. They are perfectly able to see whole classes of items as comparable or to differentiate between individual items as the task requires. For example, a whole body of text that has been relearned may be treated as a single item for some purposes, such as an essay exam. By contrast, the assessment of how well the individual propositions in that text have been learned may be quite different if a different type of test, such as short answer, is anticipated.

What was also interesting about the Carroll and Nelson study (1993) was that the JOL ratings behaved quite differently from the FOK ratings, a finding consistent with Nelson's earlier work (Leonesio & Nelson, 1990). JOL ratings are predictions made immediately after learning about the future memorability of the target given the cue alone. Unlike the FOK ratings, they are usually elicited for all items, not just those that were unable to be recalled. They are probably even more ubiquitous in the classroom; there is evidence that people constantly adjust their learning on the basis of ongoing JOLs (e.g., Koriat & Bjork, 2006a, 2006b). Carroll and Nelson found that in *both* the between- and within-subject conditions, the items learned six times received significantly higher JOL ratings than the items learned once, and this was consistent with the later actual performance. JOLs are highly influenced by the information available when the judgment is made, particularly the cue and target associative information (e.g., Hertzog, Dunlosky, Robinson, & Kidder, 2003).

Koriat and Bjork (2005) showed that the factors surrounding learning ease, such as the fluency with which the answer comes to mind given the cue, is a major factor influencing the judgment of how easily the answer will be retrieved at a later date. This fluency may give rise to many mistaken judgments or illusions of learning because the judgment is based — sometimes erroneously — on the factors surrounding learning rather than the factors that will actually influence later retrieval. In the Carroll and Nelson (1993) study, the conditions surrounding learning were extremely salient, so that what would be expected to dominate the judgments was the condition of learning (six times or once) that produced a higher or lower fluency of response. In the between-subject condition, this swamped any tendency to compare individual items; the poor feeling of fluency following items learned once and the high feeling of fluency following items learned six times dominated the ratings.

Illusions of Knowing

One of the most interesting applications of metamemory research concerns the illusions of knowing just mentioned, and much has been written about these (Benjamin, Bjork, & Schwartz, 1998; Koriat & Bjork, 2006a; Simon & Bjork, 2001). Carroll, Nelson, and Kirwan (1997) showed how JOLs and FOKs track memory for two different kinds of items: (1) overlearned unrelated items and (2) poorly learned (i.e., just once learned or "criterion learned") related items. We traded off the two variables — degree of learning and semantic association — by deliberately confounding them in the design. Both are variables well known to affect both memory performance (*objective memory* as the Nelson and Narens model, 1990, termed it) and metamemory (*subjective memory*). So, we were interested in what happened to the rate of forgetting for small amounts of learning for preexisting weak semantically associated items and for large amounts of learning for semantically unrelated item pairs. Alongside this, we wanted to know about the magnitude and accuracy of metamemory predictions (JOLs, FOKs) about future performance people would make. We knew, for example, that JOLs can tap both item difficulty (relatedness) and degree of learning; when these two are traded off against one another, which do people consider more important an influence on their future memory performance?

In Experiment 1, (Carroll, Nelson, & Kirwan, 1997) people *overlearned* pairs of unrelated items (cue: *cabbage*; target: *shoe*) and criterion-learned weakly semantically related pairs (cue: *spear*; target: *needle*). About 3 minutes after the end of learning for each pair, the subjects had to judge how likely it would be that they would remember the target in response to the cue some time in the future (either 2 weeks or 6 weeks later). As expected, those recalling after 6 weeks recalled only half as well (mean target recall = .35) as those recalling after 2 weeks (.61). And, those who had overlearned the items recalled more than those who had criterion learned them (.53 vs. .42). This was the same for both conditions of test delay. So, in terms of objective memory, the overlearning was more important to the outcome than the degree of relatedness of the items.

Our primary interest was in whether people could predict that this was the way their performance would go. Would their judgments reflect that overlearning would be such a major determinant of what they would remember? The answer, to our surprise, was no, they did not know this. In fact, they believed the opposite: They believed that items that were related would be better remembered than unrelated, even though the amount of learning for these was much less, and this occurred whether the test was 2 or 6 weeks later. They had overweighted a variable that turned out not to be very important for memory at all in this instance. Why? We believe that again they were so influenced by the conditions surrounding learning — in particular, the fluency with which they could retrieve the related target in response to the cue presented alone — while they were learning, that they failed to imagine the future and the conditions surrounding retrieval, when that fluency would have dissipated.

This was a true illusion of learning because it led to people predicting the complete opposite of their memory performance. In the classroom, the consequences might be that students confidently skip over relearning material that seems to "go down easily," assuming that the same feeling will prevail when the exam is administered in a month's time. Educators simply must take steps to prevent the fluency illusion, and they can do this in a number of ways (see Koriat & Bjork, 2005), by, for example, delaying their judgments until some time has elapsed since learning, practicing retrieval (testing) rather than rereading the material as a way of studying, not overweighting the familiarity of the material, and in general imagining themselves in the situation of retrieval rather than encoding.

As well, the Carroll, Nelson, and Kirwan study investigated the FOK for items that were unrecalled at the time of test. Unlike JOL, FOK was more sensitive to overlearning than to semantic relatedness, particularly at the 2-week test, and this makes sense in terms of the fluency heuristic notion. The FOK judgment is made when the conditions surrounding learning have dissipated and when the conditions surrounding the test prevail. After 2 weeks, the effect of overlearning on memory is likely to be stronger than after 6 weeks.

An interesting outcome is the finding of the importance of overlearning for good memory performance. Overlearning (as experimentally defined in the study) was not just a rereading of the cue–target pair; it was a genuine retrieval of the target given the cue. This type of learning by testing is the type shown by some researchers to improve memory performance (Roediger & Karpicke, 2005), and it also should be encouraged as the learning method of choice in the classroom. Carroll and Nelson (1993) demonstrated that even after a very long time (6 weeks), with no intervening practice and only one relearning using the testing method, that single act of retrieval ensured that 35% of the material (randomly paired words) was remembered. The improvement to

61% after the material was learned six times was extremely impressive evidence of the testing effect's efficacy.

In the Carroll, Nelson, and Kirwan study, the misdiagnosis of what would be remembered was so marked that we wondered if we could improve predictions by including in a second experiment a mechanism that has been shown to improve accuracy of prediction. This mechanism was delaying JOL in a very extreme fashion; this time, we had a group making the judgments well after learning had taken place, 24 hours after learning. This meant that judgments were now well separated from the context of learning and the compelling influence of fluency arising from relatedness of the cue and target. We found that delaying the JOLs did indeed eliminate the strong effect of semantic association. People were better able to assess what they would know in some weeks' time because they now rated the likelihood of overlearned unrelated material as about the same as that of the criterion learned related material. The actual recall was 55% correct for the overlearned and unrelated and significantly less for the once-learned and related material (46%). So, while not being able to predict this advantage for overlearning, they were at least no longer overweighting the importance of relatedness as they had in Experiment 1.

Another illusion of knowing was the absence of sensitivity to the retention interval of the JOLs. One might expect that everyone would predict their memory to be worse after 6 weeks than after 2 weeks (as indeed it proved to be), yet the JOLs did not reflect this; average ratings were 62% for the 2-week group and 59% for the 6-week group — a serious overestimation of what they actually remembered. Even delaying the JOLs did not change this insensitivity to test interval. Given that retention interval was manipulated between subjects, these outcomes may again indicate the need for within-subject designs in this sort of research. If people had had to predict their memory for *both* 2- and 6-week intervals, they would have fine-tuned the grain size of their judgments to reflect this. Instead, they made judgments only about their performance after *either* 2 or 6 weeks and overestimated their performance on the long delay. So, although delaying JOLs helped overcome the overweighting of relatedness, it is not the only mechanism for improving accuracy of prediction.

In formal learning, students study different subjects for tests that will occur at different times, and it is more likely that they will be able to discriminate between long and short retention intervals. However, it is unclear whether most students know that delaying JOLs significantly improves prediction. Many previous studies (e.g., Nelson & Dunlosky, 1991; Nelson, Narens, & Dunlosky, 2004) have shown that making a JOL immediately after learning something can result in quite misleading illusions of knowing, whereas delaying them for a day or two can overcome the illusions.

Allocation of Study Time

Judgments made about the memorability of sentences varying in complexity show monitoring influences self-regulation (the allocation of time to rereading) in an optimal way (Miles & Stine-Morrow, 2004). Allocation of increased study time can usually increase students' recall, but this depends on what activities are performed; sometimes, their study habits are suboptimal (Dunlosky & Thiede, 1998) for achieving the required goals (or norms of study). Sometimes, they adopt a low-performance goal and change their study habits to restudying the easier material rather than the harder material, and this can depend on individual differences in cognitive capacity (Dunlosky & Thiede, 2004).

The link between metacognitive monitoring and control of learning is now being examined in studies investigating the "region of proximal learning" (Kornell & Metcalfe, 2006; Metcalfe, 2002), and here it is demonstrated that people can be quite strategic in allocating their study time. When allowed to study material they do not know, people adjust their learning to maximize their performance, such as choosing to study the easiest items. And, indeed, such strategies can maximize outcomes: When given a free choice of what to study, people devote time to items that empirically are shown to produce the best performance.

The Testing Effect

Pervading discussions about allocation of study time are the issue of what constitutes effective "study." A major illusion of knowing is students' erroneous beliefs that certain types of study activities are generally useful. Many studies (e.g., Butler & Roediger, 2007; Carrier & Pashler, 1992; Glover, 1989; McDaniel & Fisher, 1991; McDaniel & Masson, 1985; Wheeler & Roediger, 1992) have demonstrated that the most beneficial activity to allocate time to is self-testing rather than rereading material (or indeed any other activity such as highlighting main points) — an advantage that has come to be called the testing effect. This research was exemplified by Roediger and Karpicke (2005, Experiment 1), who gave university students passages of text to learn. During learning, the students could either restudy (reread) the passage for 7 minutes or do self-testing (title at the top and write as much as you can for 7 minutes). Participants then took a final test either immediately or 2 or 7 days later on these passages. At the 5-minute final test, the restudy group improved recall relative to the self-testing group (81% vs. 75%). However, on final tests of 2 days or 1 week, the reverse effect occurred: The self-testing group produced substantially greater retention than the restudy group: After 2 days, the restudy group got 54% correct compared to self-testing of 69%, and after 1 week, the restudy group performed at 42% compared to 58% for the self-testing group.

In Experiment 2 (Roediger & Karpicke, 2005), the authors addressed the issue of whether repeated testing as a study activity would improve final test performance even more than just one episode of self-testing. What illustrates the illusion of knowing in this experiment is the incorporation of participants' own judgments about which activities — repeated self-testing or repeated restudy — would best improve final test performance. Consistent with Experiment 1, a single episode of self-testing produced better final test performance after 1 week than did rereading. In addition, repeated episodes of self-testing conferred more of an advantage than repeated episodes of rereading. Also consistent with Experiment 1, the reversal effect occurred: Self-testing produced a final test advantage only after long durations, while rereading produced a final test advantage when the final test followed immediately.

But, what did the participants predict would happen (Roediger & Karpicke, 2005)? Their judgments were inversely proportional to the actual test outcome: They believed that repeated study episodes would produce better performance after 1 week than would repeated testing. Something about repeated rereading made the students believe that they would be better able to remember the material.

Why should an opportunity for a test trial produce so much of an advantage over a study trial in long-term retention? The favored explanation involves the learners' state of access to the to-be-learned material. In testing themselves, they are putting themselves into the future context of the test, removing themselves from the context of learning, and making their judgments about future performance accordingly. In studying, they are still in the context of the learning situation, still subject to the illusions of knowing that accompany easy access to the answer — a phenomenon known as the *foresight bias* (Koriat & Bjork, 2005). The processing fluency that they experience during learning through rereading is reflected in their metacognitive judgments, which then turn out to be inaccurate.

Studying Texts

In formal learning situations, students are most likely to be studying texts, not pairs of words. Metacognitive research should, and has, focused on more naturalistic classroom material of this type. In 1997, Shaddock and Carroll reasoned that if JOLs are governed by processing fluency during encoding, they should be insensitive to anticipated retention intervals. This is quite a concern for students studying for exams that will occur at different times. Here, we deliberately tried to use materials that would be used in classroom situations; our subjects read textual extracts from a history book about the living conditions, customs, and events in Edwardian England. In one condition, which we called the coherent condition, they read the following type of text:

> Although the term "idle rich" was often heard, in fact the rich were not idle at all. Members of Edwardian society toiled harder than overworked clerks or warehousemen. A gentleman would have to go down to Cowes for the first week in August, then go up North to shoot grouse or stalk the deer. A woman invited for the weekend at one of the great houses would have to take several large trunks, and then would have to be changing clothes half a dozen times a day.

In another condition of the experiment (the Unconnected condition), subjects read unconnected sentences from the same story, such as

> The Edwardian age was an age of tension between two extremes: Some people were far too rich and others far too poor.

> A gentleman would have to go down to Cowes for the first week in August.

> Weekend parties were organized like small expeditionary forces: Toiling away at pleasure, these drones and butterflies might as well have been worker ants.

> A woman invited for the weekend at one of the great houses would have to take several large trunks.

People read these (quite lengthy) texts in either the coherent or the unconnected format, and some of the sentences were underlined (Shaddock & Carroll, 1997). These underlined sentences, they were told, had to be remembered because they contained ideas that might be tested. This is exactly what a student studying for an exam might do — underline relevant sentences they think are salient and devote extra attention to them.

Then, some test questions, such as the following, were given (Shaddock & Carroll, 1997):

> *Question:* What did this society insist upon? *Answer:* Keeping up appearances

> *Question:* What would a woman invited to one of the great houses for a weekend have to take? *Answer:* Several large trunks

> *Question:* Where would a gentleman go for the first week in August? *Answer:* Cowes

The question only was given and subjects had to make JOL decisions about their likelihood of remembering the answer either immediately after the study session or 24 hours after learning. The JOLs were made in relation to an upcoming test either 2 or 6 weeks later. Some learned the critical sentences twice only and others six times, and overlearning was manipulated within subjects, so that they knew that some of the items were better learned than others. Overlearned items received higher JOLs than twice-learned items (72% vs. 60%), and overlearned items were indeed remembered better than twice-learned items (72% vs. 61% correct), confirming again that subjects were very accurate indeed in their overall memory predictions in a within-subject design.

Shaddock and Carroll's (1997) critical finding was that, when making the judgments after a delay of 24 hours, subjects predicted they would recall 80% after 2 weeks and 57% after 6 weeks, but when they made JOLs in the original learning session, they thought they would remember the same amount (64%) at both delays. What did they actually remember? After 2 weeks, they remembered 80% of the material, and after 6 weeks, they remembered 54% of the material. So, there is a definite benefit in delaying JOL because it makes people more sensitive to the effect of the passage of time on their subsequent recall.

What about the effect of presenting material in a coherent or unconnected fashion? One might expect that recall would be better for the coherent material since it is better supported by the context at encoding (Shaddock & Carroll, 1997). In Experiment 2, in which this variable was manipulated within subjects, the effect of coherence was significant for recall but not for JOLs: They remembered (at a 4-week delay) 56% of the coherently presented test material but only 48% of the material presented in the unconnected format (a significant difference). However, all JOLs in Experiment 2 were elicited in the same session, and they were quite inaccurate. Participants believed that they would recall the same amount of coherent (60%) and unconnected (59%) material. Although delayed JOLs were not explicitly elicited here, a reasonable conclusion is that that JOLs made about normal classroom material should be substantially delayed to take account of important factors that affect memory (such as learning in the presence or absence of a narrative context), and such findings were replicated in other studies (Thiede, Anderson, & Therriault, 2003).

As mentioned, it is a reasonable assumption that JOLs are based on acquisition factors, and these are most likely factors specific to each underlined sentence (opportunities for elaborative encoding, difficulty, distinctiveness). Learners probably fail to take account of more general acquisition factors like semantic linkages or integration between sentences. For example, they fail to notice that the term *idle rich* in the passage above provides a linkage to both the gentleman going to Cowes and the lady requiring several trunks. However, at retrieval some weeks later, these factors become salient (Shaddock & Carroll, 1997).

As a matter of interest, there are several studies that achieved, surprisingly, better memory performance when a text is *less* well structured than when it is well structured (e.g., Mannes & Kintsch, 1987). One of these is work by Harten (2000), whose dissertation work reported giving undergraduate students high- or low-coherence history texts to read. She found that *increased* reading processing that results from having to integrate initially poorly integrated text seemed to enhance readers' ability to evaluate their own comprehension. There was higher JOL prediction accuracy among the readers who read the low-coherence text, which seems to have led students to engage in more evaluative strategies that allowed them to assess better their text comprehension. One could assume that more effort and engagement, brought about by any means, including effortfulness of reading (or in Bjork's terminology, a "desirable difficulty"), would give people more realistic diagnostic information about their future performance. The contrast with the Shaddock and Carroll (1997) finding, in which JOL ratings of more- and less-coherent text did not differ, is most likely caused by degrees of difficulty in text linkages.

While there is a wealth of material showing that material coherently ordered is better understood and remembered than material not in sequence (e.g., Bransford & Johnson, 1972; Mannes, 1994; Muramoto, 1996; Thorndyke, 1977), there are no previous studies examining the sensitivity of metamemory judgments to this variable, except for the Shaddock and Carroll (1997) study that failed to find that people could monitor this superiority. However, there is some evidence that judgments of how well a text has been learned are based on how easily each text was processed; easier processing results in higher judgments (Dunlosky, Baker, Rawson, & Hertzog, 2006).

Failure to monitor the advantage of coherence should be of concern for educators and deserving of further investigation. So, we followed with an experiment (Carroll & Korukina, 1999) that gave us some clue to what might be the problem. The main departure from the Shaddock and Carroll (1997) study was the use of narrative rather than expository texts. These were more "story-like" texts, arranged as before into ordered and disordered versions. As before, the sentences on which they were to be tested were underlined, so that if they had wanted to completely ignore contextual influences in preparation for testing, they could do so. The test was conducted 2 weeks after learning; people made JOLs shortly after learning in response to the question form of each underlined sentence, after having learned each to a criterion of four correct recalls. For example, they learned the sentence: "Below the panel glowed the switches for the robot butler and the maids," and the question form was, "What were the switches below the panel for?" (Answer: The robot butler and the maids.) After 2 weeks, they were tested on the key questions, and as expected, they recalled more of the answers in the ordered mode (58%) than in the disordered mode (52%).

The key finding here was that they also could predict the ordered advantage: They gave JOL ratings of 47% for ordered text items and 41% for disordered text items. We suggested that text genre is an important factor in determining people's sensitivity to the monitoring of coherence.

Wiley, Griffin, and Thiede (2005) also argued for the critical role of the nature of the texts used in determining how well students can gauge their comprehension. Expository texts are written with the goal of trying to communicate information to readers, whereas narrative texts are written more to entertain than to inform (Weaver & Bryant, 1995). Narrative texts may encourage readers to attend to more global ideas concerning the theme, whereas expository texts encourage attention to the details of the passage (McDaniel, Einstein, Dunay, & Cobb, 1986). Attention to global ideas and the text as a whole, more salient in the case of narratives, may be just another instance of grain size influencing metamemorial judgments. This idea was elaborated in work by Lefevre and Lories (2004).

The key point, then, is that monitoring of context depends on which factors of the text seem salient to the reader. If the reader readily sees an advantage of using context, in that it helps memory at the time of learning and at the time of predicting future memorability, the reader will predict the almost-certain advantage that coherence affords to memory. If, however, the reader is focusing more on individual facts, in a text that does not so readily support learning of those facts, the reader will fail to appreciate text coherence as a factor that will later assist recall of those facts.

A further noteworthy aspect of the Harten (2000) study is that more knowledgeable readers benefited more from low-coherence text in making accurate JOLs, whereas less-knowledgeable readers benefited more from the high-coherence text. This is similar to the results of the Shaddock and Carroll (1997) experiment, in which people who overall recalled more items correctly were also better at predicting their later memory performance accurately. So, it is not only text coherence interacting with the type of text (narrative or expository) that affects the JOLs, but also the person's ability and expertise with the material. We know that such individual differences certainly influence objective memory performance: A study by McNamara, Kintsch, Songer, and Kintsch (1996) found that those with expert background knowledge of the content benefited more from text with low coherence than from text with high coherence because they had to draw inferences and fill in gaps (and were able to do so). Those with no background knowledge (the material was technical in nature) were simply not able to do this. The area of individual differences in JOL research is quite ripe for further investigation (see, for instance, Dunlosky & Thiede, 2004), yet has yielded mixed results.

Judgments of Source

In many formal learning situations, people have to make predictions not only about the future memorability of the material itself — the JOL — but also about their likelihood of remembering the origin of the information. Carroll, Mazzoni, Andrews, and Pocock (1999) asked subjects to predict not only whether they would remember material itself but also whether they would remember the origin or source of the

information. An ability such as this is very relevant when one is faced with information from sources that are both internally and externally generated. In formal
learning, there are external sources of information (textbooks, teachers, other students, Web sites), and there are internal sources of information (past knowledge,
inferences generated from material that may or may not be accurate, imagination). In
Western learning traditions, we put value on acknowledgment of source and give a
special status to external sources. We do all we can to eliminate unconscious plagiarism, but not a lot of research has been devoted to how well we are capable of predicting our discrimination of source, and if so, whether we adjust our learning behavior
accordingly. Do people make judgments of source (JOSs) in the way that they do
JOLs? For example, do they use intrinsic factors (Koriat, 1997), such as the a priori
difficulty or memorability of the material, as a basis for judgments about source ("I'll
remember that because it was such a complex idea")? Or do they use internal mnemonic cues to make such judgments ("That is not the sort of thing I would have
thought up myself, so the teacher must have said it")?

In Experiment 1 (Carroll et al., 1999), we asked people to view pictures of objects
and to merely imagine another group of objects given their names, so that there were
clearly two different sources of information: seen or imagined. Our results showed
that people were unable to predict their source discrimination ability for seen and
imagined items at a rate above chance (the mean γ correlations did not differ from
zero). They probably based their source judgments on their judgments of learning
because there was a significant correlation between JOL and JOS: People made similar judgments for memory and source discrimination regardless of presentation format — in effect, the implication was "If I think I will recall it, I will recall its source."
This is a troublesome heuristic because they tended to underestimate their learning
of seen items and overestimate their learning of imagined items. We speculated that
perhaps the poor monitoring of source was due to poor discriminability between the
two sources, and that perhaps we needed to use material with greater difference in
source information, such as motor information versus visual information or self-generated versus other-generated information.

In a second experiment (Carroll et al., 1999), then, the different sources of information were made more salient; subjects now performed an action or imagined performing it, or they watched someone else perform or imagined the other performing
it. Thus, there were two factors manipulated: The Enactment factor (doing vs. imagining) and the Focus factor (self vs. other). Subjects made JOL and JOS predictions
about what they would remember and were tested through free recall of the action
and its source 1 week later. The study showed that in predicting source memory, the
self plays a very important role. People were highly confident they would remember
the source when they performed the action themselves compared to when someone
else performed it. However, in making these judgments they were misled: What they
actually remembered best was the source of actions that others performed. On the
other hand, when they had to discriminate between actions that they had imagined
themselves or someone else performing, they did not give higher source judgments
to the self; there was no difference in source ratings given to self and other. The JOL
findings here were rather different, leading us to suspect that there are different variables influencing JOS and JOL.

When the real-versus-imagined manipulation is replaced by two real sources and the subject has to make source memory predictions about two types of actual events, such as capital cities or hobbies generated by oneself or a partner (Carroll, Davis, & Conway, 2001), JOS ratings were fairly accurate. People knew that the self had a special status, and that they would better recognize the self-generated items.

Do learners have an appreciation of the effect that study modality will have on later recall? It may be important to be able to predict an ability to discriminate whether one learned something in an auditory modality (e.g., through a classmate's verbal comment in a learning group) or in a visual modality (e.g., information read in a textbook). Carroll and Korukina (1999) examined JOSs for key facts in textual material presented in either a visual or auditory mode. In a cued recall test 2 weeks after learning, subjects were more accurate for material learned in an auditory mode (61%) than in a visual mode (49%). They also gave significantly higher JOS ratings to auditorily presented material (45%) than to visually presented material (42%). Although the magnitude of the judgments does not reflect the big difference in recall, they are certainly sensitive to the auditory advantage at test.

The consequences of monitoring source have not been studied in the way that the consequence of monitoring the quality of learning have been (an exception is work by Cook, Marsh, & Hicks, 2006). Yet, they are of interest in their own right, and they may also affect actual memory performance just as JOLs affect, for example, the amount of time allocated to different items in a list as well as the selection of items for restudy (e.g., Dunlosky & Hertzog, 1998; Mazzoni & Cornoldi, 1993; Nelson & Leonesio, 1988; Thiede & Dunlosky, 1999).

Summary

Drawing out some of the implications for classroom learning from the discussion, one could conclude that

1. Students monitoring their learning are highly influenced by the types of comparisons they have to make: When required to see the bigger picture, they adjust to a coarse grain size and focus less on the (perhaps important) differences between individual items or facts. They can make judgments about whole classes of items or differentiate between individual items as the task requires. Their metacognitive judgments reflect this grain size discrimination and may differ as a result. Given what we know about monitoring affecting regulation of learning, the performance outcomes can be very different.
2. Illusions of knowing regularly occur. They need to be understood and countered by educators. We know a great deal about how to do this now, including delaying the JOL and discounting the current ease of access state that accompanies learning by employing testing as a study technique.
3. Judgments of learning about text depend on the grain size the learner apprehends. Using the richness that text affords would be expected to improve not only objective memory but also the accuracy of monitoring. But, this depends very much on what the learner believes is salient at the time of learning. Taking advantage of the richness of text means that judgments must be made at some point later, when the text,

with all its linkages, can be viewed as a whole. And, some texts, such as expository texts, are inherently less supportive of the formation of linkages.

4. Individual differences in metacognitive accuracy belong to an area that should be given more attention, as perhaps should prospective JOS memory.

Conclusion

There is now a wealth of metamemory research that can be applied to the classroom, and I touched on only a small fraction of it here. It is not an overstatement to say that part of Tom Nelson's legacy to us is his appreciation of the application of theoretical work in metacognition to classroom practice.

In the 1980s, metacognitive research was far from the mainstream of interest in cognitive psychology. It is now. An important practical goal in this decade is to translate the findings of metacognition research to the classroom; to ensure that it informs educational practice; to make school educators, university academic teaching units, and rank-and-file faculty aware of what should be done to improve learning. As a university administrator who has for some years attended countless meetings on "teaching and learning," it seems that educators have not progressed much beyond talking about "learning styles," "deep and surface learning," and graduate attributes (which always include references to the enduring and flexible nature of knowledge and its transfer to new contexts). As psychologists, we can contribute much more than we do to such discussions. Knowing what we know (or do not know), understanding the way that this knowledge influences our regulation of learning, and knowing the eventual outcome of that learning — what could be more important than this in how we teach students?

References

Benjamin, A. S., Bjork, R. A., & Schwartz, B. L. (1998). The mismeasure of memory: When retrieval fluency is misleading as metamnemonic index. *Journal of Experimental Psychology: General, 127*, 55–68.

Bharucha, J. (2006). Education as we know it does not accomplish what we believe it does. Retrieved February 27, 2007 from http://www.edge.org/q2006/q06_10.html#bharucha

Bransford, J. D., & Johnson, M. K. (1972). Contextual prerequisites for understanding: some investigations of comprehension and recall. *Journal of Verbal Learning and Verbal Behavior, 4*, 717–726.

Butler, A. C., & Roediger, H. L., III. (2007). Testing improves long-term retention in a simulated classroom setting. *European Journal of Cognitive Psychology, 19*, 514–527.

Carrier, M., & Pashler, H. (1992). The influence of retrieval on retention. *Memory & Cognition, 20*, 633–642.

Carroll, M., Davis, R., & Conway, M. (2001). The effects of self-reference on recognition and source attribution. *Australian Journal of Psychology, 53*, 140–145.

Carroll, M., & Korukina, S. (1999). The effect of context and modality on metamemory judgments. *Memory, 7*, 309–322.

Carroll, M., Mazzoni, G., Andrews, S., & Pocock, P. (1999). Monitoring the future: Object and source memory for real and imagined events. *Journal of Applied Cognitive Psychology, 13*, 373–390.

Carroll, M., & Nelson, T.O. (1993). Effects of overlearning on the feeling of knowing are more detectable in within-subject than between-subject designs. *American Journal of Psychology, 106*, 227–235.

Carroll, M., Nelson, T. O., & Kirwan, A. (1997). Trade-off of semantic relatedness and degree of overlearning: Differential effect on metamemory and long-term retention. *Acta Psychologica, 95*, 239–253.

Carroll, M., & Simington, A. (1986). The effects of degree of learning, meaning, and individual differences on the feeling-of-knowing. *Acta Psychologica, 61*, 3–16.

Cook, G., Marsh, R., & Hicks, J. (2006). Source memory in the absence of successful cued recall. *Journal of Experimental Psychology: Learning, Memory, and Cognition, 32*, 828–835.

Dunlosky, J., Baker, J., Rawson, K., & Hertzog, C. (2006). Does aging influence people's metacomprehension? Effects of processing ease on judgments of text learning. *Psychology and Aging, 21*, 390–400.

Dunlosky, J., & Hertzog, C. (1998). Training programs to improve learning in later adulthood: Helping older adults educate themselves. In D. J. Hacker (Ed.), *Metacognition in educational theory and practice* (pp. 249–275). Mahwah, NJ: Erlbaum.

Dunlosky, J., & Thiede, K. W. (1998). What makes people study more? An evaluation of factors that affect self-paced study. *Acta Psychologica, 98*, 37–56.

Dunlosky, J., & Thiede, K. W. (2004). Causes and constraints of the shift-to-easier-materials effect in the control of study. *Memory & Cognition, 32*, 779–788.

Glover, J. A. (1989). The "testing" phenomenon: Not gone but nearly forgotten. *Journal of Educational Psychology, 81*, 392–399.

Harten, A. C. M. (2000). An investigation of calibration of comprehension: Text processing variables that affect college students' evaluation of their comprehension. *Dissertation Abstracts International Section A: Humanities and Social Sciences, 60* (9-A) 3270.

Hertzog, C., Dunlosky, J., Robinson, A. E., & Kidder, D. P. (2003). Encoding fluency is a cue used for judgments about learning. *Journal of Experimental Psychology: Learning, Memory, and Cognition. 29*, 22–34.

Hicks, J., & Marsh, R. L. (2002). On predicting the future states of awareness for recognition of unrecallable items. *Memory & Cognition, 30*, 60–66.

Koriat, A. (1997). Monitoring one's own knowledge during study: A cue-utilization approach to judgments of learning. *Journal of Experimental Psychology, General, 126*, 582–590.

Koriat, A., & Bjork, R. A. (2005). Illusions of competence in monitoring one's knowledge during study. *Journal of Experimental Psychology: Learning, Memory, and Cognition, 31*, 187–194.

Koriat, A., & Bjork, R. A. (2006a). Illusions of competence during study can be remedied by manipulations that enhance learners' sensitivity to retrieval conditions at test. *Memory and Cognition, 34*, 959–972.

Koriat, A., & Bjork, R. A. (2006b). Mending metacognitive illusions: A comparison of mnemonic-based and theory-based procedures, *Journal of Experimental Psychology: Learning, Memory, and Cognition, 32*, 1133–1145.

Koriat, A., & Goldsmith, M. (1996). Monitoring and control processes in the strategic regulation of memory accuracy. *Psychological Review, 103*, 490–517.

Koriat, A., Sheffer, L., and Ma'ayan, H. (2002). Comparing objective and subjective learning curves: Judgments of learning exhibit increased underconfidence with practice. *Journal of Experimental Psychology: General*, 131, 147–162.

Kornell, N., & Metcalfe, J. (2006). Study efficacy and the region of proximal learning framework. *Journal of Experimental Psychology: Learning, Memory, and Cognition, 32*, 609–622.

Lefevre, N., & Lories, G. (2004). Text cohesion and metacomprehension: Immediate and delayed judgments. *Memory & Cognition, 32*, 1238–1254.

Leonesio, R. J., & Nelson, T. O. (1990). Do different metamemory judgments tap the same underlying aspects of memory? *Journal of Experimental Psychology: Learning, Memory, and Cognition, 16*, 464–470.

Mannes, S. (1994). Strategic processing of text. *Journal of Educational Psychology, 86*, 577–588.

Mannes, S. M., & Kintsch, W. (1987). Knowledge organization and text organization. *Cognition and Instruction, 4*, 91–115.

Mazzoni, G., & Cornoldi, C. (1993). Strategies in study-time allocation: Why is study time sometimes not effective? *Journal of Experimental Psychology: General, 122*, 47–60.

McDaniel, M. A., Einstein, G. O., Dunay, P. K., & Cobb, R. E. (1986). Encoding difficulty and memory: Towards a unifying theory. *Journal of Memory and Language*, 25, 645–656.

McDaniel, M. A., & Fisher, R. P. (1991). Test and test feedback as learning sources. *Contemporary Educational Psychology, 16*, 192–201.

McDaniel, M. A., & Masson, M. E. J. (1985). Altering memory representation through retrieval. *Journal of Experimental Psychology: Learning, Memory, and Cognition, 11*, 371–385.

McNamara, D. S., Kintsch, E., Songer, N. B., & Kinstch W. (1996). Are good texts always better? Text coherence, background knowledge, and levels of understanding in learning from text. *Cognition and Instruction, 14*, 1–43.

Metcalfe, J. (2002). Is study time allocated selectively to a region of proximal learning? *Journal of Experimental Psychology: General, 131*, 349–363.

Miles, J., & Stine-Morrow, E. (2004). Adult age differences in self-regulated learning from reading sentences. *Psychology and Aging, 19*, 626–636.

Muramoto, T. (1996). Test recall and text recognition with and without a title. *Japanese Psychological Research*, 38, 240–244.

Neisser, U. (1976). *Cognition and reality*. San Francisco: Freeman.

Nelson, T. O., & Dunlosky, J. (1991). When people's judgments of learning (JOLs) are extremely accurate at predicting subsequent recall: The "delayed-JOL effect." *Psychological Science, 2*, 267–270.

Nelson, T. O., & Leonesio, R. J. (1988). Allocation of self-paced study time and the "labo-in-vain effect." *Journal of Experimental Psychology: Learning, Memory, and Cognition, 14*, 676–686.

Nelson, T. O., Leonesio, R., Shimamura, A., Landwehr, R., & Narens, L. (1982). Overlearning and the feeling of knowing. *Journal of Experimental Psychology: Learning, Memory, and Cognition, 8*, 279–288.

Nelson, T. O., & Narens, L. (1990). Metamemory: A theoretical framework and new findings. In G. Bower (Ed.), *The psychology of learning and motivation: Advances in research and theory* (Vol. 26, pp. 125–173). San Diego, CA: Academic Press.

Nelson, T. O., & Narens, L. (1994). Why investigate metacognition? In J. Metcalfe and A. P. Shimamura (Eds.), *Metacognition: Knowing about knowing* (pp. 1–25). Cambridge, MA: MIT Press.

Nelson, T. O., Narens, L., & Dunlosky, J. (2004). A revised methodology for research on metamemory: Pre-judgment recall and monitoring (PRAM). *Psychological Methods, 9,* 53–69.

Roediger, H. L., III, & Karpicke, J. D. (2005). Test-enhanced learning: Taking memory tests improves long-term retention. *Psychological Science, 17,* 249–255.

Shaddock, A., & Carroll, M. (1997). Influences on metamemory judgements. *Australian Journal of Psychology, 49,* 21–27.

Simon, D. A., & Bjork, R. A. (2001). Metacognition in motor learning. *Journal of Experimental Psychology: Learning, Memory, and Cognition, 27,* 907–912.

Thiede, K. W. (1996). The relative importance of anticipated test format and anticipated test difficulty on performance. *Quarterly Journal of Experimental Psychology: Human Experimental Psychology, 49A,* 901–918.

Thiede, K., Anderson, M., & Therriault, D. (2003). Accuracy of metacognitive monitoring affects learning of texts. *Journal of Educational Psychology, 95,* 66–73.

Thiede, K. W., & Dunlosky, J. (1999). Toward a general model of self-regulated study: An analysis of selection of items for study and self-paced study time. *Journal of Experimental Psychology: Learning, Memory, and Cognition, 25,* 1024–1037.

Thorndyke, P. W. (1977). Cognitive structures in comprehension and memory of narrative discourse. *Cognitive Psychology, 9,* 77–110.

Weaver, C. A., III, & Bryant, D. S. (1995). Monitoring of comprehension: The role of text difficulty in metamemory for narrative and expository text. *Memory & Cognition, 23,* 12–22.

Wheeler, M. A., & Roediger, H. L., III (1992). Disparate effects of repeated testing: Reconciling Ballard's (1913) and Bartlett's (1932) results. *Psychological Science, 3,* 240–245.

Wiley, J., Griffin, T., & Thiede, K. W. (2005). Putting the comprehension in metacomprehension. *Journal of General Psychology, 132,* 408–428.

Metacognition in Education:
A Focus on Calibration

Douglas J. Hacker, Linda Bol, and Matt C. Keener

Introduction

"Why investigate metacognition?" Thomas Nelson and Louis Narens asked this question in the title to a chapter they authored in 1994. Their question was not asked in a disparaging way but was intended to encourage reflection on the reasons for the lack of "cumulative" progress in research on learning and memory over the last half century. Nelson and Narens speculated that this lack of cumulative progress was due, in part, to three shortcomings: (1) lack of a target for research, (2) overemphasis on a nonreflective-organism approach, and (3) short-circuiting via experimental control (i.e., researchers' attempts to control variations in participants' self-directed cognitive processing). Of these three shortcomings, the first was the inspiration for the present chapter.

Nelson and Narens (1994) explained that a target for research "should be defined in terms of some to-be-explained behavior of a specific category of organism in a specific kind of environmental situation" (p. 3). In their own work, they addressed this "lack of a target for research" by specifically identifying the to-be-explained behavior as mnemonic behavior, the specific category of organism as college students, and the environmental situation as studying for and taking an examination. They went on to argue that targets for research in the area of learning and memory typically have been restricted to the laboratory, and that although there is a continued need for laboratory work, there is also a need for researchers to go outside the laboratory into more ecologically valid environmental situations. A quotation from the Nelson and Narens chapter, provided by Parducci and Sarris (1984), aptly encapsulates this view:

> The desire for ecological validity ... cannot be separated from the concern to make psychology more practical. ... Scientists continue to study psychological problems without apparent concern for practical applications. ... There do seem to be strong forces pushing even traditional areas of psychological research in practical directions. (pp. 10–11)

We have resonated strongly with Nelson and Narens's arguments, and in this chapter, we follow their guidelines in identifying a target for research: Calibration is the to-be-explained behavior; students — elementary to graduate — constitute the specific category of organism; and the classroom is the environmental situation.

Our plan for this chapter is first to expand on Nelson and Narens's (1994) argument to go outside the laboratory into more naturalistic environmental situations to study learning and memory. The environment in which metacognition is examined can have an impact on the results of studies and therefore can have an impact on our notions of the general character of metacognition. Second, we present a brief overview of Nelson and Narens's (1990) model of metacognition for the purpose of describing the metacognitive monitoring and control processes that potentially interact in educational contexts. Last, as mentioned, we narrow our focus on meta-cognition in education to calibration, how calibration is measured, and calibration of students in classroom contexts.

Laboratories versus Classrooms

A common practice of researchers who conduct laboratory studies in learning and memory is to generalize their results to educational contexts. Discussion sections often provide suggested educational implications, some of which may be readily and productively applied to educational contexts, others that are not likely practical, and still others that are intended only as a call for future research. We are not advocating that learning and memory researchers should stop this practice. Providing educa-tional implications should be a major concern for psychologists wishing to make their work more applicable to "naturalistic contexts" and can be quite helpful to research-ers and practitioners interested in improving learning environments.

However, generalizing findings from studies that have used content and proce-dures that have little resemblance to actual classroom practices is risky and in some cases may be unwarranted (Lundeberg & Fox, 1991; McCormick, 2003; Winne, 2004). In a laboratory context, the goal is to control materials, procedures, participants, and experimental conditions, and the greater extent to which control can be achieved the more certain researchers can be that causes for thought or behavior have been identified. In the area of metacognition, this experimental rigor has been applied to a limited range of learning, most often including feeling of knowing (FOK), ease of learning (EOL), judgments of learning (JOLs), confidence in retrieval, allocation of study time, or comprehension of short narrative or expository texts (Nelson & Narens, 1994).

In naturalistic contexts, especially classroom contexts, such controls are difficult to manage. Conditions for learning are massively complex in comparison to labora-tories. Information can be encoded in multiple ways, including but not limited to lec-ture, reading, participation in group discussions, question and answer, and in some cases by physically manipulating materials (Maki & McGuire, 2002). Moreover, in general, students are likely more motivated to perform well on a classroom test that is going to contribute to their overall grade for a course than on a test that has little long-term consequence for them. And, the interval between learning and testing in a classroom context can be considerably longer than in a laboratory context, in which it is often the case that barely an hour passes between learning and testing. In sum, differences between laboratory and classroom contexts entail not only the type of learning but also the depth, breadth, and motivation for learning, all of which can have an impact on one's ability to monitor and control learning.

Space does not permit an extensive analysis of the issues surrounding generalizability between laboratory and classroom contexts or between different classroom contexts. However, allow us to provide an illustration that may shed additional light on some of the issues.

Lundeberg and Fox (1991) conducted a meta-analysis of laboratory and classroom studies investigating a form of metacognition called the *test expectancy effect*. The test expectancy effect was first reported by Meyer (1934), who found that students who were expecting to receive an essay test performed better on both an essay test and a multiple-choice test than students who were expecting to receive a multiple-choice test. Since then, the recommended study skill strategy has been to prepare for an essay test regardless of the actual type of test a person is to receive. Lundeberg and Fox's (1991) results showed that the test expectancy effect was true, but only for studies that were conducted in laboratory contexts. In studies conducted in classroom contexts, the exact opposite result was found. As a result of their meta-analysis, Lundeberg and Fox recommended that, "In the classroom, the simplest advice, akin to the encoding specificity view, would be: Study for the type of test you expect to receive" (p. 97).

In addition to the practical advice that can be garnered from this study (Lundeberg & Fox, 1991), the results point directly to our argument that generalizing findings from laboratory studies of metacognition to classroom contexts can at times be risky. Before such generalization can occur, there needs to be a better understanding of the factors that contribute to metacognitive judgments concerning the selection and use of study strategies and the conditions under which those judgments are made. If the conditions in a laboratory context approximate conditions in classrooms, generalizing from one to the other would not be controversial. However, if conditions differ, and they likely do, factors that are known to affect metacognitive judgments in classroom contexts (e.g., depth and breadth of knowledge, input from colearners, motivation, or the social comparisons that learners make in a social setting) will need to be introduced and controlled in the laboratory. Until these factors are more thoroughly investigated, one should be cautious about generalizing from the laboratory to the classroom.

Metacognitive Monitoring and Control

Nelson and Narens (1990) proposed a theoretical framework for metacognition that has served well as a description of the components and processes that comprise this concept. Their framework is based on three principles: (1) Mental processes are split into an object-level (i.e., cognition) and a meta-level (i.e., metacognition); (2) the meta-level contains a dynamic model of the object-level, which is the source of metacognitive knowledge or understanding of the object-level; and (3) there are two processes corresponding to the flow of information from the object-level to the meta-level (i.e., monitoring) and from the meta-level to the object-level (i.e., control). Metacognition can be viewed as monitoring and control of a lower level of thought by a higher level of thought (Broadbent, 1977). Through monitoring, people obtain information at the metacognitive level about the status of knowledge or strategies at a cognitive level;

through control, people can use their metacognitive knowledge or understanding at the metacognitive level to regulate thought at the cognitive level (Hacker, 1998, 2004).

To illustrate the dynamic interplay between monitoring and control, consider calibration. In brief, *calibration* is a measure of the degree to which a person's judged ratings of performance correspond to his or her actual performance (Keren, 1991; Lin & Zabrucky, 1998; Winne, 2004; Yates, 1990). Although there are several significant contributors to calibration accuracy, the underlying psychological process reflected in calibration entails a person's monitoring of what he or she knows about a specified topic or skill and judging the extent of that knowledge in comparison to some criterion task, such as an examination. For instance, while studying for an hour or two for an upcoming chemistry test on chemical nomenclature, students may continuously monitor what they know and judge that more studying is necessary to get a decent grade. They can exert further control over their studying for several more hours, at which time they will again monitor what they know and judge that a grade of about 90% correct is possible and acceptable. That judgment of 90% is then compared to their actual performance, which for illustrative purposes turns out to be 95% correct. Calibration in this case is the difference between the judged 90% and the actual 95% correct, which indicates not only that the students were fairly accurate in monitoring their knowledge but also that they were slightly underconfident.

This example illustrates how people, as agents of their own thoughts and behaviors, can monitor their knowledge or skills, establish their own goals for learning, develop plans to achieve their goals, control the deployment of those plans, monitor the progress of their plans, further control the plans if necessary, and judge when they have been achieved. In other words, people can be self-regulators of their behaviors (Zimmerman, 2000). Thus, this example also highlights the importance of calibration in educational contexts. As a further illustration, consider how inaccurate calibration during reading could sway students to ineffectively regulate their learning of text (Lin & Zabrucky, 1998). On the one hand, strong overconfidence during reading could fail to trigger appropriate control processes necessary for students to attain greater comprehension of the text. On the other hand, strong underconfidence could cause students to misallocate precious study time to continue reading in the hopes of further comprehending the text when in fact their comprehension may be more than sufficient for the task.

In summary, Nelson and Narens's (1990) theoretical framework of metacognition provides important insights into the dynamic interplay that exists between monitoring and control processes as people attempt to influence their learning and memory. Although this theoretical framework is based almost entirely on laboratory research, the classroom context provides fertile ground for the application of theory to practice. At a minimum, to become self-regulated learners, students at the metacognitive level need to accurately monitor their ongoing cognitive states and processes, and the information obtained from such monitoring must be used to exert control to regulate those cognitive states and processes. The importance of accurate monitoring and control in relation to calibration has been succinctly summarized by Winne (2004): "Learning will be inversely proportional to the degree of calibration bias and proportional to calibration accuracy" (p. 476).

A Focus on Calibration

At this point, we would like to focus our attention more squarely on calibration, which is a type of metacognition that has been investigated perhaps more extensively in educational contexts than other types of metacognition. In the sections that follow, we give a fuller description of calibration, describe the various ways in which it is measured, more fully discuss the importance of calibration to learning and memory in educational contexts, and describe patterns of findings in classroom contexts. We end with a discussion of directions for future research.

What Is Calibration?

Calibration is the degree to which a person's perception of performance corresponds with his or her actual performance (Keren, 1991; Lichtenstein, Fischhoff, & Phillips, 1982; Nietfeld, Cao, & Osborne, 2006). In other words, learners make judgments about what knowledge or skill they have learned, and those judgments are compared to an objectively determined measure of that knowledge or skill (Winne, 2004; for other measures of judgment accuracy, please see Benjamin & Diaz, this volume). As in the example given in the section on metacognitive monitoring and control, a student can monitor his or her learning before testing and make a prediction that 90% of the to-be-tested material has been mastered. In addition, the student's subjective judgment concerning which material has been mastered can occur after testing. Monitoring judgments that follow performance are commonly called *postdictions* (Lin & Zabrucky, 1998).

Nelson and Narens (1994) drew a distinction between prospective monitoring judgments and retrospective monitoring judgments that clarifies the distinction between prediction judgments and postdiction judgments. Figure 1 (adapted from Nelson & Narens, 1994) shows three stages of learning (i.e., acquisition, retention, and retrieval), the various monitoring judgments that a person can make (e.g., judgments of learning, feeling of knowing), and the control processes that are informed by monitoring (e.g., allocation of study time, termination of study). We have added to this figure where we believe prediction and postdiction judgments fit within the stages of learning. A *prediction judgment* is a monitoring judgment that comes after acquisition and retention but prior to retrieval; a *postdiction judgment* follows retrieval. Therefore, predictions can be thought of as prospective monitoring judgments (i.e., a person monitors his or her knowledge or skill before retrieval of the knowledge or skill). In some respects, a prediction judgment is a type of self-efficacy judgment (Hertzog, Dixon, & Hultsch, 1990) in that the magnitude of the judgment reflects a person's belief in his or her mastery of some learning or memory task. A postdiction judgment can be thought of as a retrospective monitoring judgment (i.e., a person monitors his or her knowledge or skill after retrieval). Both judgments can be used to inform control processes (Nelson & Narens, 1990, 1994). Optimistic predictions may lead people directly into retrieval, believing they have mastered the material or skill; pessimistic predictions may convince people they need to return to acquisition and retention. Postdictions, which overlap to some degree with "confidence in retrieved

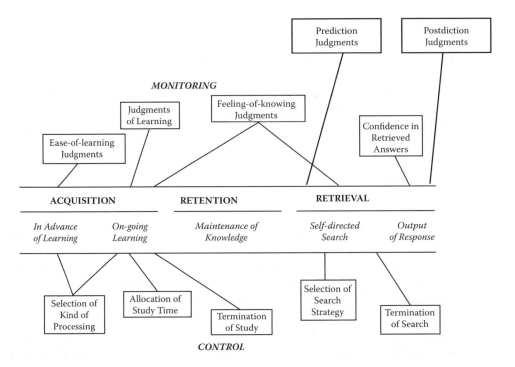

Figure 1 Nelson and Narens's framework showing memory stages, examples of monitoring and control components, and the locations where prediction and postdiction judgments occur. (Adapted from Nelson & Narens, 1994.)

answers," provide learners with more accurate feedback on their monitoring proficiency (Maki, 1998; McCormick, 2003; Pressley & Ghatala, 1990). Based on this feedback, learners may employ different control processes during their next acquisition and retention task.

An important distinction must be made between calibration, which is referred to as absolute accuracy, and resolution or discrimination, which are referred to as relative accuracy. The two types of accuracy are often confused, although they represent two very different aspects of metacognitive monitoring and are measured in very different ways (Nelson, 1996). In a study by Maki, Shields, Wheeler, and Zacchilli (2005), in which absolute and relative accuracy were compared, no significant correlation was found between the two, suggesting that the two types of accuracy tap different metacognitive processes.

Absolute accuracy (also known as calibration) refers to the degree of correspondence between a person's judged level of performance and his or her actual performance. Calibration judgments provide important estimates of overall memory retrieval; however, they do not provide good discrimination between what a person may or may not know. *Relative accuracy* does this by providing a measure of the degree to which a person's judgments can predict the likelihood of correct performance of one item relative to another (Nelson, 1984, 1996) or whether a target event will or will not occur (Yates, 1990). In other words, relative accuracy provides a measure of whether a person can discriminate between what is known or not known, whereas absolute accuracy indicates whether a person can estimate actual overall test performance (Nelson, 1996; Nietfeld, Cao, & Osborne, 2005; Nietfeld, Enders, & Schraw, 2006).

In educational contexts, measures of absolute accuracy tend to show better reliability than measures of relative accuracy and are more likely to show stable individual differences (Maki et al., 2005). Nevertheless, both measures can be quite useful. Calibration provides important estimates of overall recall levels, and relative accuracy provides important estimates of which items are correct or incorrect. Maki and colleagues argued that if students are overconfident in their predicted performance, they may prematurely end studying, thinking that they have mastered the to-be-tested material. Moreover, those same students may not know which specific topics within the to-be-tested material need further study. Thus, inability to predict overall test performance and to discriminate among known and unknown topics can have dire consequences for achievement on tests.

How Calibration Is Measured

Although there is one commonly used measure of relative accuracy, that is, γ (Maki et al., 2005; Nelson, 1984, 1996; Wright, 1996), there is a variety of methods used to measure calibration. These methods can be grouped roughly into two categories: difference scores and calibration curves. Difference scores all involve taking the difference between judged performance and actual performance; however, there are at least four questions that should be considered: (1) What kind of judgment is being made? (2) What level of performance is being judged? (3) When is the judgment being made? (4) How is the difference between judged and actual performance calculated? First, judgments can be made on a percentage of likelihood scale or confidence scale (i.e., 0%, no likelihood or confidence in knowing; 20% chance or confidence in knowing up to 100% chance or confidence in knowing). Often, participants are restricted to six probabilities (0, 20, 40, 60, 80, 100) but in other cases are given a choice to select any value along a continuous line, with 0% at one end and 100% at the other (Schraw, Potenza, & Nebelsick-Gullet, 1993). Judgments also can entail asking participants to state how many items they expect to get correct of the total number of items (e.g., Of the 35 items, how many do you expect to get correct?). Second, judgments can be directed at a local level (e.g., the mean of the judgments made on individual items on a test) or at a global level (i.e., all the items as a whole) on a test (Schraw, 1994). Third, as discussed, judgments can be made before or after performance, that is, predictions or postdictions, respectively (Pressley & Ghatala, 1989; Pressley, Levin, Ghatala, & Ahmad, 1987; Pressley, Snyder, Levin, Murray, & Ghatala, 1987; see also Lin & Zabrucky, 1998, for predictions and postdictions made in calibration of comprehension studies).

Finally, the difference between judged and actual performance can be calculated in several ways. Perhaps the most straightforward measure of calibration concerns global-level judgments in which the absolute value of the difference between judged and actual performance is calculated (e.g., Hacker, Bol, Horgan, & Rakow, 2000; Pressley & Ghatala, 1989; Pressley, Levin, et al., 1987; Pressley, Snyder, et al., 1987). For instance, students will be asked to predict or postdict their performance by making a judgment on how many items on a test they expect to get correct or got correct, respectively. Once their actual performance is assessed, their actual scores are subtracted from their predicted and postdicted judgments, and the absolute value of that difference is taken. Values closer to zero indicate greater accuracy. If the absolute value is not taken, the resultant differences produce a bias score. That is, negative values indicate underconfident judgments, and positive values indicate overconfident judgments. A student who predicts a score of 80 but actually scores a 70 would be overconfident and positively biased.

Measures of calibration involving local-level judgments are a bit more complicated but still relatively straightforward (see Keren, 1991, or Yates, 1990, for a detailed description of these measures). For each item, participants are asked to predict or postdict their performance. These predictions or postdictions are usually given as a confidence judgment expressed as a probability statement in answering the item correctly (e.g., 75% confident that I will get the answer correct). Performance is assessed with a 0 assigned to incorrect items and a 1 to correct items. Calibration is calculated by taking the absolute value of the difference between the confidence judgment (expressed as a proportion) and performance. The differences calculated for the individual items are then summed, and this sum is divided by the total number of items. People are said to be well calibrated if, in the long run, their assigned probabilities to the items are equal to their performance on the items (Lichtenstein et al., 1982). Thus, the closer to zero the mean difference score is, the better calibrated a person is. A bias score also can be calculated at the item level by calculating the mean probability judgment and subtracting from it the mean performance score. Negative values indicate overall underconfidence and positive values overconfidence. Yates (1990) also suggested squaring the differences between probabilities assigned to each item and actual scores, producing a probability score (also known as a quadratic score or the Brier score). The mean probability score then can be used to assess calibration accuracy (see Yates, 1990, for a discussion of standards of accuracy).

The other method for measuring calibration is the calibration curve or graph (Keren, 1991; Yates, 1990). Actual performance is plotted on the y axis, and predicted or postdicted performance is plotted on the x axis. The 45° line represents perfect calibration in which predictions or postdictions are exactly equal to actual performance. Points below perfect accuracy indicate overconfidence, and points above indicate underconfidence. Calibration graphs provide easily interpretable representations of the ways in which accuracy varies across performance levels rather than a single measure of the relation between predictions or postdictions and actual performance (Weingardt, Leonesio, & Loftus, 1994). Moreover, calibration graphs demonstrate the ways in which overconfidence and underconfidence in judgments vary with performance.

Figure 2 is a calibration graph that reflects calibration of test performance in a classroom context (Hacker et al., 2000). In this case, the values on the y axis represent students' actual percentage correct on the first of three tests, and the values on the x axis represent students' predicted and postdicted scores on the test expressed as percentages. The five groups are approximate groupings representing students' overall academic performance across the semester-length course, with Group 1 earning As, Group 2 earning Bs, Group 3 earning Cs, Group 4 earning Ds, and Group 5 earning

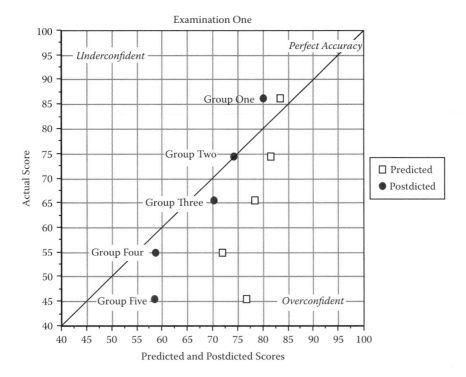

Figure 2 A calibration graph plotting predicted and postdicted scores against actual scores. The calibration accuracy of each performance group can be compared against perfect calibration, represented by the diagonal line. (Adapted from Hacker et al., 2000.)

Fs. Predicted scores are represented by the hollow squares, and postdicted scores are represented by the filled circles.

As can be seen in this figure, as a general rule, predictions tend to exceed postdictions, and postdictions tend to be more accurate than predictions, although in this example the highest-performing group is an exception. Greater accuracy of postdictions over predictions is a common finding in calibration research, and Pressley and Ghatala (1990) referred to this phenomenon as the *testing effect*. What is striking about the results displayed in the figure is that higher-achieving students tended to be underconfident in their predictions and postdictions, whereas lower-achieving students tended to be overconfident, with their predictions grossly overconfident.

In sum, all measures of calibration provide a quantitative assessment of the degree of discrepancy between perceived performance and actual performance. The discrepancy can be calculated at the item level and averaged over multiple items, or the discrepancy can be calculated at global levels in which students are asked to make a single judgment over multiple items. The closer to zero the discrepancies become, the better calibrated a person is said to be, with perfect calibration attained when the discrepancies are zero. A person is overconfident if the calculated discrepancies are positive values and underconfident if they are negative. In educational contexts, the general finding observed has been that underconfidence is associated with higher performance and overconfidence with lower performance.

Why Is Calibration Important in Educational Contexts?

In many professions, the inability to make accurate, realistic predictions can have dire consequences (Allwood & Granhag, 1999; Dunning, Heath, & Suls, 2004). Such dire consequences are exemplified by a physician who is unrealistically confident in her diagnoses, a lawyer who may be unduly optimistic when predicting the verdicts of his court cases, or an airline pilot who overestimates her ability to handle challenging weather conditions. In classrooms, although the consequences of overconfidence or underconfidence may not be life threatening, they may certainly affect students' academic achievement and motivation. Students who are strongly underconfident may fail to disengage from studying for a test and misallocate precious study time because they assume that they have not mastered the material (Maki et al., 2005). Strong overconfidence while employing a specific learning strategy can provide a false sense of the strategy's effectiveness (Hacker, 1998). And, relatedly, students could intentionally inflate their overconfidence during test preparation as a self-handicapping strategy that provides a ready excuse when performance is poor (Winne, 2004). For example, "I studied really hard for the test, so the teacher must have given an unreasonably difficult test."

In an era of high-stakes accountability, the ability to perform well on tests has become increasingly important (Bol & Nunnery, 2004). Student performance on high-stakes tests has an impact on educational placements, grade promotion, academic major, college admissions, graduation, and entry into various professions. Therefore, students' ability to judge how well they have studied for an exam and how well they are likely to perform on the exam, as well as how well they can monitor performance during the exam, are essential skills contributing to their performance. Inaccurate calibration judgments have been linked to poor performance on various types of exams (e.g., Barnett & Hixon, 1997; Bol & Hacker, 2001; Bol, Hacker, O'Shea, & Allen, 2005; Hacker et al., 2000; Kruger & Dunning, 1999; Nietfeld et al., 2005). Thus, there is good evidence suggesting that if students are unable to produce accurate calibration judgments, they may not take the remedial steps necessary to promote their achievement or carefully evaluate their responses during or after the exam.

Overconfidence in judging one's knowledge, skill, comprehension, or test preparedness is a robust phenomenon observed across many subject areas (e.g., Allwood & Granhag, 1999; Bol & Hacker, 2001; Bol et al., 2005; Dunning et al., 2004; Flannelly, 2001; Glenberg, Wilkinson, & Epstein, 1982; Grimes, 2002; Hacker et al., 2000; McCormick, 2003; Nelson, 1999). To further complicate matters, Winne and Jamieson-Noel (2002) have shown that students also can be biased with respect to their self-reporting of study techniques. They found that students appeared overconfident in their self-reports of whether their studying was guided by objectives and a planned method of studying. Thus, drawbacks associated with overconfident predictions may be compounded by overconfident self-appraisals regarding the efficacy of any particular study strategy employed.

Overconfidence may influence attention or preparation more selectively. Students may not allocate their study efforts to those topics for which they are least prepared. Many studies have shown that students tend to be more overconfident when the material or test items are difficult and underconfident when the material or test items are easy, a phenomenon dubbed the *hard–easy* effect (Flannelly, 2001; Juslin, Winman, & Olsson, 2000; Nietfeld et al., 2005; Winne, 2004; Winne & Jamieson-Noel, 2002). Therefore, students may allocate the least amount of time to difficult material that is, ironically, most in need of additional study effort due to their unrealistic confidence judgments. In testing situations, students may not critically reconsider their responses because they are unjustifiably confident in their knowledge (Flannelly, 2001). Because students need to feel a degree of uncertainty in their responses before they will begin to reconsider the question and answer, this overconfidence could easily override feelings of uncertainty, and incorrect answers are left unchallenged (Gaskins, Dunn, Forte, Wood, & Riley, 1996).

Overconfidence in calibration judgments also may have an impact on student satisfaction with academic courses and choice of academic majors. In his study of undergraduates enrolled in a macroeconomics course, Grimes (2002) found that overconfidence was linked to unmet student expectations and dissatisfaction. He concluded that, for some students, "Unmet performance expectations lead to dissatisfaction with the course, the instructor, and perhaps, the economics discipline in general" (p. 8). Although Grimes did not collect student satisfaction data, the argument makes intuitive sense and rings true for instructors who teach difficult or technical subjects. Whether overconfidence and violations of expectations affect course evaluations and other indices of student satisfaction is a question that awaits further empirical study.

Underconfidence also may adversely affect student monitoring and control of comprehension and studying. Not recognizing what one does or does not understand is a failure of metacomprehension (Maki et al., 2005). That is, students may not monitor and allocate their reading or study efforts in the most efficient ways. Because students tend to be less confident on easy materials or items (Juslin et al., 2000; Lin & Zabrucky, 1998; Maki et al., 2005), they may inappropriately devote more time than necessary to their study of material they have already mastered. In testing situations, attention and effort may be inefficiently distributed across questions and responses.

Patterns of Findings in Classroom Contexts

In this section, we describe patterns of findings from studies conducted in naturalistic classroom settings. As mentioned, findings obtained in laboratory settings often provide critical insights into psychological phenomena; however, generalizing those findings to different contexts, especially classroom contexts, can sometimes be risky. Establishing strong ecological validity by generalizing laboratory findings to naturalistic classroom contexts is a different area of research and one that most often falls to educational psychologists. We have attempted to collect as much of this research on calibration in classrooms as possible, but the list may not be exhaustive and should be considered representative of this line of research. Table 1 provides an overview of these studies in terms of their characteristics and major findings. These studies are discussed in the next section.

TABLE 1   Characteristics and Major Findings of Calibration Studies Conducted in Classroom Contexts

Study	Subjects and Context	Research Design	Treatment/Factors	Measures	Major Findings
Barnett & Hixon (1997)	62 elementary school students in Grades 2, 4, and 6 in spelling, math, and social studies	Descriptive, comparative	Grade level; subject area	Absolute, global prediction and postdiction accuracy on class assessments; scores on standardized test	Predictions more accurate in spelling and social studies than in math; no consistent grade-level differences; strong correlations between calibration accuracy and achievement
Bol & Hacker (2001)	59 graduate students enrolled in two sections of an introductory research methods in education course	Quasi-experiment	Practice test versus traditional review for midterm and final exams; achievement level; item format	Absolute, global prediction and postdiction accuracy on course exams; achievement on course exams	Students receiving practice tests less accurate on predictions and scored lower on multiple-choice items; high achievers better calibrated; predictive accuracy did not differ by item format for high achievers, but low achievers more accurate in their predictions of scores on essay versus multiple-choice items
Bol et al. (2005)	356 undergraduates enrolled in several sections of social and cultural foundations in education course	True experiment	Calibration practice on five online quizzes versus no quiz practice; achievement level	Absolute, global prediction and postdiction accuracy on quizzes and final exam; achievement on quizzes and final exam; explanatory style scores	No effect of the practice treatment on calibration or achievement; high achievers better calibrated; low achievers less accurate, overconfident; explanatory style accounted for a large portion of the variance in the dependent measures
Flannelly (2001)	66 senior year undergraduate nursing students enrolled in a psychiatric mental health course	True experiment	Practice test and feedback on confidence ratings versus no practice test or feedback; achievement; item difficulty (hard or easy)	Judgment bias (calculated by subtracting mean performance from mean confidence) on hard and easy exam items; scores on individual items	Students who received practice test with feedback exhibited less overconfidence on hard items and less underconfidence on easy items; lower achievers overconfident but high achievers underconfident on hard items; low achievers more confident on wrong answers and less confident on right answers

	Sample	Design	Variables	Measures	Findings
Garavalia & Gredler (2002)	69 senior year undergraduates enrolled in two sections of a health science course	Quasi-experiment	Goals instruction versus comparison (case study); calibration accuracy (high versus low)	Self-efficacy for self-regulated learning; goal analysis; prior achievement; final course grade	Accurate predictors who had goal-setting intervention obtained higher grades than inaccurate predictors in comparison condition; inverse relationship between expected grades with actual grades and grade point average
Grimes (2001)	253 undergraduates enrolled in a principles of macroeconomics course	Descriptive, comparative	Gender; age; race; grade point average; previous exposure to content; absence; study practices	Absolute, global predictive accuracy; relative global predictive accuracy (better or worse compared to first exam); exam scores	Large degree of overconfidence on both absolute and relative predictive measures; older students less likely to overpredict performance; inverse relationship between overconfidence and grade point average; previous exposure to content resulted in greater overpredictions
Hacker et al. (2000)	99 undergraduates enrolled in two sections of an introductory educational psychology course	Preexperiment, comparative	Self-assessment instruction and practice tests; achievement level	Absolute global, predictive and postdictive accuracy; hours spent studying	Strong relationship between performance and predictive, postdictive accuracy; overconfidence among lowest-scoring groups, gains in calibration accuracy among high achievers; students relied on prior calibration judgments rather then prior performance; study time unrelated to prior performance
Hacker et al. (2007)	137 undergraduates enrolled in one of four sections of an introductory educational psychology course	Quasi-experiment	Extrinsic incentives, reflection, both incentives and reflections, or neither; achievement level	Absolute global predictions, postdictions; predictive, postdictive accuracy; exam sores; explanatory style scores	Both extrinsic incentive conditions led to greater improved accuracy among low achievers; high achievers more accurate calibrators; for lower achievers, the explanatory style constructs predicted both predictions and postdictions

TABLE 1 Characteristics and Major Findings of Calibration Studies Conducted in Classroom Contexts (Continued)

Study	Subjects and Context	Research Design	Treatment/Factors	Measures	Major Findings
Nietfeld et al. (2005)	27 undergraduates enrolled in an educational psychology survey course	Preexperiment, comparative	Feedback; item difficulty; grade point average	Global and local monitoring accuracy (mean difference between confidence and performance); bias scores (signed mean differences); exam scores	Monitoring remained stable over the semester; global monitoring more accurate than local monitoring; high-achieving students more accurate in monitoring their performance; students better calibrated and underconfident on easy items but overconfident on difficult items
Nietfeld et al. (2006)	84 undergraduate students enrolled in two sections of an educational psychology survey course	Quasi-experiment	Weekly monitoring exercises and feedback versus feedback only; gender	Local monitoring accuracy (mean difference between confidence and performance); bias scores (signed mean differences); exam and course project scores; self-efficacy	Monitoring exercises and feedback improved monitoring accuracy and performance on exams and course project; students who improved their calibration also improved their exam scores; improved calibration associated with modest increased self-efficacy
Shaughnessy (1979)	47 undergraduate students enrolled in an introductory psychology course	Descriptive	Achievement levels (quartiles)	Local confidence levels (midpoint between mean on correct versus incorrect items; confidence-judgment accuracy (ratio of local confidence over pooled variance)	Some confidence judgment accuracy even among lowest achievers; higher achievers had higher confidence-judgment accuracy scores; low-achieving students overconfident but high-achieving students tended to be underconfident

Sinkavich (1995)	67 undergraduate students enrolled in two sections of an educational psychology course	Preexperiment, comparative	Extra credit for replacing incorrect with correct items on final; feedback and comparison of exam scores with classmates	Confidence ratings; exam scores	A relationship between confidence ratings and exam performance; good students had higher correlations between confidence ratings and exam performance; both good and poor students improved their scores on tests by using the replacement items

Achievement Level and Bias   As described, calibration accuracy has been linked to student achievement: At the global level of calibration, lower-achieving students tend to show low accuracy and overconfidence on exams, and higher-achieving students tend to show high accuracy but underconfidence (see Figure 2). This pattern has been observed among students enrolled in education, psychology, nursing, health sciences, and economics at both the graduate and undergraduate levels. The overconfidence among lower-achieving students in particular has been termed the *unskilled but unaware* effect (Kruger & Dunning, 1999).

Our own studies exemplify both of these effects. In both Hacker et al. (2000) and Bol and Hacker (2001), we observed this same pattern for undergraduates enrolled in an introductory educational psychology course and graduate students enrolled in a research methods course. A somewhat unexpected result in the latter study was a significant interaction between the independent variables of achievement level and item type. The calibration accuracy of higher-achieving students was similar on both multiple-choice and essay items, but the lower-achieving students were significantly less accurate on their predictions of multiple-choice items across both the midterm and final exams. These interactions did not emerge for postdiction accuracy. In Bol et al. (2005), we further replicated the findings with respect to the impact of achievement on calibration accuracy and direction of bias. This study was conducted with students enrolled in undergraduate educational foundations courses. Again, higher-achieving students were more accurate but somewhat underconfident in their predictions and postdictions than were lower-achieving students, who were largely overconfident.

Other researchers have confirmed the link between calibration accuracy and achievement. Grimes (2002) found that lower-scoring economics students were less accurate and more overconfident than their better-performing peers. Similarly, Shaughnessy (1979) found a strong positive relationship between calibration accuracy and performance on a series of four classroom exams among psychology undergraduate students. He posited that poorly performing students, when judging overall performance on each exam, demonstrated "an inability to distinguish adequately between known and unknown information" (p. 510). These findings were mirrored by Sinkavich (1995), who reported stronger correlations between confidence ratings and exam performance among higher-achieving compared to lower-achieving students enrolled in an undergraduate educational psychology course. Garavalia and Gredler (2002) discovered an inverse relationship between students' expected grades in an undergraduate health science course with their actual grades and grade point average (GPA). Furthermore, students were divided into groups of accurate or inaccurate calibrators based on their accuracy in predicting their final grades. More accurately calibrated students who received a goal-setting intervention received higher actual grades than did students who were less accurately calibrated in the control condition. This last result supports the link between calibration accuracy and achievement.

The link between achievement level and accuracy is well established, but the relationship seems to be complicated by item difficulty. Nietfeld et al. (2005) studied undergraduate students enrolled in an educational psychology course and employed calibration measures at both global (i.e., confidence ratings on overall performance after taking the test) and local (i.e., confidence ratings for each item) levels. Student performance, as measured by GPA and test scores, was a strong predictor of local accuracy and monitoring. Not unexpectedly, higher-performing students were more accurate than lower-performing students. In terms of item difficulty, students showed more accurate calibration on easy compared to difficult items. Similar to other studies that have shown the hard–easy effect (Flannelly, 2001; Juslin et al., 2000; Nietfeld et al., 2005; Winne, 2004; Winne & Jamieson-Noel, 2002), students displayed under-confidence on easy items but overconfidence on difficult items.

Of particular note is that only local measures of calibration were linked to student achievement levels. Nietfeld and colleagues' (2005) global measure of calibration, which was similar to the postdiction measure used in our own studies (Bol & Hacker, 2001; Bol et al., 2005; Hacker et al., 2000), did not show a relationship with achievement. Therefore, their results seemingly contradicted what we had found. Our results showed a significant interaction between achievement level and item type, such that the calibration accuracy of higher-achieving students did not differ between multiple-choice and essay items, but lower-achieving students were significantly less accurate on their predictions of multiple-choice items. However, this contradiction might be explained by item difficulty. The multiple-choice items we had used (Bol & Hacker, 2001) were more difficult than essay items. Therefore, lower-achieving students, presumably with less knowledge of the tested content, should display less accuracy with difficult items. Flannelly (2001) also discovered calibration bias that varied as a function of item difficulty. In her study using undergraduate nursing students, she relied only on local confidence ratings for each test item on content related to psychiatric mental health nursing. Students' bias scores were similar on easy items regardless of achievement level but differed on difficult items.

We identified only one classroom study that did not rely on college students in their calibration research. During individual interviews, Barnett and Hixon (1997) assessed whether second, fourth, and sixth graders could predict and postdict their classroom performance in spelling, math, and social studies. Overall, the students' global-level prediction accuracy was significantly correlated with achievement: High scores on the classroom tests were correlated with greater prediction accuracy. Evidence did not support uniform patterns of findings across grade levels and subject areas. This was most likely due to the fact that the difficulty of classroom tests varied across grade levels and subject areas. For the youngest students, who faced less-difficult tests than the oldest students, accuracy was quite good; however, for the oldest students tests were more difficult, and their accuracy suffered. Similar to the argument that we have proposed in this chapter, Barnett and Hixon suggested that when the self-assessment capabilities of students is being investigated, the context in which it occurs must be considered.

Improving Calibration Accuracy   Whether calibration accuracy can be improved is a question that has not been definitively answered. Some studies have shown that improvements are difficult to obtain or are not durable (e.g., Bol & Hacker, 2001; Bol et al., 2005; Koriat, 1997; Nietfeld et al., 2005; Nietfeld & Schraw, 2002), whereas other studies have shown that various types of intervention can lead to improvements (e.g., Glenberg, Sanocki, Epstein, & Morris, 1987; Hacker et al., 2000; Nietfeld, Cao et al., 2006; Schraw et al., 1993; Yates, 1990). Three studies that were conducted in classroom contexts (Bol & Hacker, 2001; Bol et al., 2005; Nietfeld et al., 2005) demonstrated that student calibration tends to be stable despite feedback and practice.

Bol and Hacker (2001) investigated the effectiveness of using practice tests versus traditional review to improve calibration accuracy on midterm and final exams. The findings indicated that students who reviewed the content via practice tests were less accurate than students who experienced traditional review. Furthermore, calibration accuracy did not improve across exams. One explanation for the lack of improvement may be that the study included only two trials or measures, the final and midterm exam.

To address this limitation, Bol et al. (2005) investigated the impact of calibration practice on five quizzes that preceded students' predictions and postdictions on the final exam in an undergraduate educational foundations course. Feedback on quiz scores was provided immediately to students after taking each of the online quizzes. Similar to our earlier findings, calibration accuracy on the final exam was similar for students assigned to the practice condition when compared to students who were not asked to predict and postdict their performance on the quizzes. Therefore, the practice intervention did not seem to be effective in improving calibration accuracy. Nietfeld et al. (2005) also reported that students' calibration accuracy did not improve across four course exams even though students had an opportunity to review their exam results as well as their item-level confidence ratings. The authors posited that self-directed feedback, without explicit training in monitoring, was insufficient to improve accuracy.

In contrast to studies that suggest resistance to improving calibration accuracy, other experimental interventions have been successful. In some instances, the difference in results between classroom-based studies showing no change in calibration accuracy and those showing at least modest improvement may be attributable to the power or strength of the intervention.

Nietfeld, Cao et al. (2006) investigated the impact of an explicit monitoring intervention on calibration accuracy, self-efficacy, and performance. Recall that in their previous study (Nietfeld, Cao et al., 2005) they failed to establish the effectiveness of repeated feedback for improving calibration accuracy and suggested that explicit training in monitoring may be necessary. Therefore, in Nietfeld et al. (2006), two sections of an undergraduate educational psychology course were randomly assigned to the monitoring and comparison groups. The monitoring intervention consisted of exercises that asked students to assess their learning for the current class session as well as their study preparation, respond to and provide confidence ratings on review items, and reflect on the accuracy of their confidence ratings. In addition to weekly feedback, the students were given feedback and interpretation on their calibration accuracy the week following the three course exams. Calibration accuracy and performance both improved, supporting the authors' prediction that a more powerful explicit monitoring intervention is necessary to realize positive changes in accuracy.

Hacker, Bol, and Bahbahani (2007) not only studied the impact of reflection and feedback on calibration accuracy, but also the provision of extra credit points if students' predicted and postdicted scores minimally deviated from their actual scores. In their factorial design, four sections of an undergraduate educational psychology course were randomly assigned to one of four conditions: incentives and feedback, reflection and feedback, a combined treatment condition (reflection, incentives, and feedback), or a comparison condition. The reflection treatment consisted of providing students with feedback on their calibration accuracy and a questionnaire asking them to reflect on explanations for their performance, on any discrepancies between their performance and calibration judgments, and on strategies they might use to improve their calibration accuracy. We found that our intervention was successful in increasing postdiction accuracy on the last two exams for lower-achieving students in the two groups that received incentives; however, lower-achieving students in the reflection-only condition were less accurate in their postdictions. There were no significant differences on measures of predictive accuracy.

Even though our (Hacker et al., 2007) reflection and feedback condition was similar to that reported by Nietfeld, Cao et al. (2006), we found contradictory results. However, different calibration measures were used in the two studies. Nietfeld et al. relied on confidence judgments at both global and local levels (item by item), whereas our measures of calibration were global-level predictions and postdictions of actual test scores, not confidence judgments. Although performance, predictions/postdictions, and confidence judgments can be conceptualized as self-efficacy judgments, predictions/postdictions of performance entail other aspects of memory in addition to self-efficacy, such as appraisal of the memory task to be completed and translating one's ability to perform the task into a specific estimate of performance (Hertzog et al., 1990). These differences between confidence judgments and performance judgments could account for differences between the two studies, and it is up to future research to discern these differences.

Finally, findings in the Hacker et al. (2000) study illustrated the effectiveness of a complex treatment consisting of feedback, practice tests, and course instruction that included the benefits of accurate self-assessment for goal setting, time management, and academic performance. The results revealed that prediction and postdiction accuracy improved, but only for higher-achieving students. Flannelly (2001) also compared the calibration accuracy of students who prepared for the exam by taking practice tests combined with review of the content with those who prepared via review only. Practice tests were effective in decreasing overconfidence on difficult items and underconfidence on easy items. The common element shared by these two studies that may have contributed to improved calibration was making students familiar with the type of test and test content. Thus, creating this familiarity may be a necessary condition for calibration accuracy (for a counterexample, see Bol & Hacker, 2001).

Overall, findings on the effectiveness of various interventions applied in classroom settings have yielded mixed results. It appears that feedback and practice alone are insufficient for improving calibration accuracy. With one exception (Flannelly, 2001), practice tests alone do not seem to improve calibration accuracy. Reflection and instruction on self-assessment and monitoring were clearly effective in improving calibration judgments in the Nietfeld, Cao et al. study (2006) but were found to be effective only for higher-achieving students in the Hacker et al. (2000) study. Finally, external rewards or incentives were effective in increasing the accuracy of calibration judgments only among lower-achieving students (Hacker et al., 2007).

Explanatory Style   The stability of calibration accuracy demonstrated in many of the classroom studies reviewed is vexing. One would expect that students who are repeatedly provided with evidence about the inaccuracy of their calibration would modify their judgments. This does not seem to be the case. Several studies have shown that the stability of students' predictions and postdictions across multiple exams is often significantly higher than the stability of their performance (e.g., Hacker et al., 2000, 2007; Schraw et al., 1993). Thus, rather than basing their calibration judgments on actual performance, past or present, which would likely be two of the best predictors of future performance, people appear to base their calibration judgments on stable persistent beliefs about their performance (Nisbett & Ross, 1980; Schraw et al., 1993). Stable beliefs about performance are encompassed under theories of explanatory or attributional style. The tendency for people to attribute failures to external causes and successes to internal causes is known as *hedonic bias* (Weiner, 1986) or *protection of self-worth* (Covington, 2004). For students, this means that they are more likely to attribute failure on an exam to external factors such as the trickiness of the items or inadequate instructor direction. Conversely, students' success on an exam is more likely to be attributed to internal causes such as the student's own ability and effort. Researchers have established links between explanatory style and metacognitive knowledge (Kurtz, Schneider, Carr, Borkowski, & Turner, 1988), which may at least partially account for the persistent stability of calibration judgments.

To investigate the potential influence of attributions on calibration, we analyzed the results obtained from an explanatory-style questionnaire in our most recent studies (Bol et al., 2005; Hacker et al., 2007). Using regression analyses, we examined the unique contribution of patterns in explanatory style to prediction and postdiction accuracy on a final exam. For the outcome of prediction accuracy, we found that the more students attributed their poor calibration accuracy to task-centered sources (external causes), the more overconfident they were in their predictions of performance. Moreover, the more students attributed their poor calibration accuracy to their own testing abilities (internal causes), the more underconfident they were in their predictions. For postdictions, only responses to the items related to task-centered (external) sources emerged as significant. The pattern observed, however, was opposite from prediction accuracy: The more students attributed their poor calibration accuracy to task-centered causes, the more underconfident they were in their postdictions (Bol et al., 2005).

The findings related to predictive accuracy seem intuitively clear because one would expect overconfidence to be associated with external explanations and lower achievement levels (e.g., "I expected to do well on the test, but the teacher wrote a terrible exam"). The findings for postdiction accuracy are more difficult to interpret. We do know that students' postdictions tend to be more realistic or accurate because they have completed the exam (i.e., the "testing" effect), and they are better able to judge how they performed. One interpretation is that after completing the exam, students have a better notion of just how many items on the exam were unknown or guessed at, which, if substantial, could lead to underconfident judgments based on a perceived difficult exam.

Social Influences   Social variables influence metacognition as well as explanatory style. The influence of explanatory style in classroom contexts may be more potent due to social pressures. For example, some lower-achieving students may demonstrate a self-serving attributional style and overestimate their performance to protect their perceptions of self-worth and image of themselves as good students in comparison with their classmates.

There have been a number of studies investigating the influences of social variables on metacognition generally. For example, in a series of four laboratory studies, Karabenick (1996) reported that the presence of colearners' questions elicited responses reflecting cognitive dissatisfaction and feelings of confusion. Fewer studies have focused on how social variables influence calibration. Caravalho, Moisses, and Yuzawa (2001) manipulated social cues in a laboratory setting by presenting participants with information about comparative student performance from a fictitious study. Social cues had more impact on students with low versus high metacognitive ability. In a second study, they found that social cues influenced confidence judgments for only low self-regulators. The results from both studies led the authors to conclude that students with low metacognitive skills may be particularly susceptible to social influences.

We identified only two studies that investigated social influences on calibration in a classroom context. Puncochar and Fox (2004) examined undergraduate students' accuracy and confidence while cooperatively completing quizzes in small groups during class. They showed groups to be more accurate than individuals who worked alone, and that groups were more confident in their right answers. However, group confidence for wrong answers continued to increase across quizzes. The authors coined this finding as the "two heads are worse than one" effect. The effect did not diminish as a result of feedback, directions, class readings, or lectures on metamemory and confidence. "Group work appears to produce the undesirable byproduct of being highly confident when wrong" (p. 590).

The second study to investigate social influences on student calibration in the classroom was conducted by Sinkavich (1995). Although the stated purpose was not to investigate social influences, the study is discussed here because the procedure clearly involved social comparisons among students on calibration accuracy. After two of the three course exams, students from two course sections were given individualized, detailed feedback on their performance and confidence ratings. In addition, they were provided with summary statistics for the class and instructed to compare their examination feedback to their neighbors to evaluate their relative accuracy. Correlations between confidence ratings and total scores increased only for one of the two course sections and only from the second to the third exam. In the other course section, a marked decrease in prediction accuracy from the second to the third exam was observed. The author speculated that the third exam, which was a final comprehensive exam and longer than the other two, was more difficult than the earlier exams. Other findings confirmed the now-familiar pattern of higher-achieving students exhibiting significantly greater calibration accuracy than their lower-achieving classmates. Sinkavich concluded that higher-achieving students were better predictors of what they do or do not know on a test, indicating better calibration accuracy. However, there was mixed support for the effectiveness of social comparisons for improving calibration judgments.

Conclusions

We introduced this chapter by adopting Nelson and Narens's (1994) guidelines for identifying our "target for research." We focused on calibration as the to-be-explained behavior, students — elementary to graduate — as the specific category of organism, and the classroom as the environmental situation. The laboratory work that has been conducted on calibration has provided many important insights into this metacognitive monitoring process, and we acknowledge that there is a continued need for such research. However, we also acknowledge that there is a need to go outside of the laboratory into more ecologically valid environmental situations. We focused our attention on classroom applications of calibration.

There are some findings that appear to transcend context. For example, the testing effect appears to be salient in laboratory as well as classroom contexts: Calibration judgments made after testing tend to be more accurate than calibration judgments made prior to testing. This seems intuitively clear in that the participants or students have much more information about the type of test, the testing items, and their performance after the test and should be able to make more accurate judgments. Also, the hard–easy effect is apparent in both contexts: In general, participants or students demonstrate overconfidence on difficult items but underconfidence on easy items.

However, in classroom settings, the hard–easy effect is compromised by achievement level. Higher-achieving students tend to be underconfident on difficult items, whereas lower-achieving students tend to be overconfident (i.e., the unskilled but unaware effect). Similar patterns of findings have been found in laboratory studies investigating age-related differences in calibration: Older adults as compared to younger adults tend to be overconfident in their judgments concerning subsequent recall of low-association items (e.g., Connor, Dunlosky, & Hertzog, 1997). There are obvious differences between these classroom and laboratory studies, which may make generalizations among them difficult, but there may be similar issues at stake. Perhaps variations in confidence are due to methods of calibration measurement, anchoring, or scaling effects, or perhaps underconfidence of higher-achieving students and overconfidence of lower-achieving students are the result of personal strategies used to maintain engagement in the task or to save face, respectively. Nelson and Narens (1994) argued that in laboratories, researchers attempt to control variations in participants' self-directed cognitive processing (i.e., short-circuiting via experimental control). In the classroom, however, the self-directed cognitive processing of students may provide us with much better understanding of how metacognitive monitoring is adaptively used.

Classroom investigations of calibration have shown that improving calibration accuracy is not easily accomplished. Simply providing students with practice tests and feedback on calibration accuracy is not enough to significantly improve their accuracy. Nietfeld et al. (2005) posited that explicit training in monitoring with self-directed feedback may be necessary for improved accuracy. And, in Nietfeld,

Cao et al. (2006), this was shown to be the case. This finding resonates well with the reading strategy research, which has shown the necessity for explicit training not only for monitoring strategies but also for control strategies to increase reading comprehension (Hacker, 2004). Other classroom results showed that improvements in calibration accuracy could be accomplished through the use of external rewards or incentives, but these appeared to be effective for only lower-achieving students. In addition, working in small groups may increase calibration accuracy yet produce the undesirable by-product of increasing overconfidence in wrong answers (i.e., the two heads are worse than one effect).

Identifying factors that contribute to calibration judgments remains a fertile area for investigation. When making local-level judgments (i.e., at the item level), students may be directly accessing their memories in search for information pertinent to the questions being asked. If memories are retrievable, high levels of confidence will be given, and more often than not, high but not perfect accuracy will result — after all, memory is fallible (for a critique of this interpretation, see Koriat, 1997).

When making global-level judgments (i.e., at the test level), the contributing factors likely become much more complex. Before a test is given, students may directly access their memories, develop an inventory of the knowledge they possess, and make a prediction about their performance on a test of that knowledge. However, several of the studies we reviewed would suggest a more complicated picture. Explanatory style (i.e., the causes to which people attribute their successes and failures) accounts for a significant amount of the variance in calibration judgments, with different patterns of explanatory style observed for higher- versus lower-achieving students. As noted, calibration judgments tend to be relatively stable across tasks and time. Such stability could be explained, in part, by stable personality traits, such as explanatory style. Moreover, social factors have been found to influence calibration accuracy (Caravalho et al., 2001; Karabenick, 1996; Puncochar & Fox, 2004; Sinkavich, 1995). In classroom contexts, in which social influences are highly salient, finding connections between calibration accuracy and social forces would not be unexpected.

Directions for Future Research

An obvious direction for future research is to heed Nelson and Narens's (1994) advice to venture from the laboratory into the more naturalistic setting of the classroom. Given that many researchers employ convenience samples, it is not surprising that researchers tend to use their own classes. With one exception, the studies reviewed here were conducted with college students, usually enrolled in educational psychology courses. More research on student calibration across grade levels, courses, and tasks is clearly warranted. Longitudinal or cross-sectional designs will help us better understand developmental changes in calibration within classroom contexts. We further endorse Nelson and Narens's position that laboratory studies are certainly beneficial when concerns about internal validity are paramount, but we also need to investigate the generalizability of these findings to the messy world of real-life classrooms using authentic tasks.

As mentioned, student behavior in classrooms is influenced by social variables. Metacognition and calibration more specifically are no exceptions. Given the scant research examining the impact of social variables on calibration accuracy, replication studies across tasks, group compositions, and types of feedback are needed. For instance, social comparison data in the form of calibration and performance could vary as well as the achievement level of students within groups. Lower-achieving students may benefit from social comparisons with students who demonstrate more accuracy in their calibration judgments. Such findings would be relevant to both students and teachers.

Explanatory style and other motivational variables are linked to social influences and may illuminate why calibration judgments seem to be resistant to improvement in the absence of more powerful interventions. Studies have demonstrated that feedback and practice alone are insufficient in improving calibration accuracy. This may be particularly problematic in the case of lower-achieving students, who are largely overconfident. In classroom situations, lower-achieving students may be more motivated to preserve their sense of self-worth and use ego-protecting strategies, such as persevering in overconfident, unrealistic predictions and relying on external attributions to explain their performance. Attributional retraining to promote more realistic metacognitive judgments, which in turn should improve monitoring ability during test preparation, represents one avenue for future study.

A final direction for future research is to augment quantitative data collection strategies with qualitative strategies in mixed-method designs. Nearly all of the classroom studies we reviewed employed quantitative designs. In our most recent study, we asked students to respond to open-ended questions to explain any discrepancies between their predictions and their actual scores. We have attempted to align these responses with findings obtained from our close-ended questionnaire assessing explanatory style related to calibration accuracy (Hacker et al., 2007). In their study of student calibration within elementary school classrooms, Barnett and Hixon (1997) relied on their analysis of classroom tests, student interviews, and classroom observations to detect patterns that may have been influenced by pedagogy, test preparation, and student expectations across teachers, subject areas, and grade levels. Qualitative data, rich with contextual information, may direct us toward more successful interventions to improve calibration accuracy in classroom settings and ultimately improve academic achievement.

References

Allwood, C. M., & Granhag, P. A. (1999). Feelings of confidence and the realism of confidence judgments in everyday life. In P. Juslin & H. Montgomery (Eds.), *Judgment and decision making: Neo-Brunswikian and process-tracing approaches* (pp. 123–146). Mahwah, NJ: Erlbaum.

Barnett, J. E., & Hixon, J. E. (1997). Effects of grade level and subject on student test score predictions. *The Journal of Educational Research, 90*, 170–174.

Bol, L., & Hacker, D. J. (2001). A comparison of the effects of practice tests and traditional review on performance and calibration. *The Journal of Experimental Education, 69*, 133–151.

Bol, L., Hacker, D. J., O'Shea, P., & Allen, D. (2005). The influence of overt practice, achievement level, and explanatory style on calibration accuracy and performance. *The Journal of Experimental Education, 73*, 269–290.

Bol, L., & Nunnery, J. A. (2004). The impact of high-stakes testing on restructuring efforts in schools serving at risk students. In G. Taylor (Ed.), *In pursuit of equity and excellence: The educational testing and assessment of diverse learners* (pp. 101–117). Lewiston, NY: Mellon Press.

Broadbent, D. E. (1977). Levels, hierarchies, and the locus of control. *Quarterly Journal of Experimental Psychology, 29*, 181–201.

Caravalho, F., Moisses, K., & Yuzawa, M. (2001). The effects of social cues on the confidence judgments mediated by knowledge and self-regulation of cognition. *The Journal of Experimental Education, 69*, 325–343.

Connor, L. T., Dunlosky, J., & Hertzog, C. (1997). Age-related differences in absolute but not relative metamemory accuracy. *Psychology and Aging, 12*, 50–71.

Covington, M. V. (2004). Self-worth theory goes to college: Or do our motivation theories motivate? In D. M. McInerney & S. Van Etten (Eds.), *Big theories revisited: Research on sociocultural influences on motivation and learning* (Vol. 4, pp. 91–114). Greenwich, CT: Information Age.

Dunning, D., Heath, C., & Suls, J. M. (2004). Flawed self-assessment: Implications for health, education, and the workplace. *Psychological Science in the Public Interest, 5*, 69–106.

Flannelly, L. T. (2001). Using feedback to reduce students' judgment bias on test questions. *Journal of Nursing Education, 40*, 10–16.

Garavalia, L. S., & Gredler, M. E. (2002). An exploratory study of academic goal setting, achievement calibration and self-regulated learning. *Journal of Instructional Psychology, 29*, 221–230.

Gaskins, S., Dunn, L., Forte, F., & Riley, P. (1996). Student perceptions of changing answers on multiple choice questions. *Journal of Nursing Education, 35*, 88–90.

Glenberg, A. M., Sanocki, T., Epstein, W., & Morris, C. (1987). Enhancing calibration of comprehension. *Journal of Experimental Psychology: General, 116*, 119–136.

Glenberg, A. M., Wilkinson, A. C., & Epstein, W. (1982). The illusion of knowing: Failure in the self-assessment of comprehension. *Memory & Cognition, 10*, 597–602.

Grimes, P. W. (2002). The overconfident principles of economics students: An examination of a metacognitive skill. *The Journal of Economic Education, 33*, 15–30.

Hacker, D. J. (1998). Metacognition: Definitions and empirical foundations. In D. J. Hacker, J. Dunlosky, & A. C. Graesser (Eds.), *Metacognition in educational theory and practice* (pp. 1–23). Mahwah, NJ: Erlbaum.

Hacker, D. J. (2004). Self-regulated comprehension during normal reading. In R. B. Ruddell & N. Unrau (Eds.), *Theoretical models and processes of reading* (5th ed., pp. 775–779). Newark, DE: International Reading Association.

Hacker, D. J., Bol, L., & Bahbahani, K. (2007). *Explaining calibration accuracy in classroom contexts: The effects of incentives, reflection, and explanatory style.* Manuscript under review.

Hacker, D. J., Bol, L., Horgan, D., & Rakow, E. A. (2000). Test prediction and performance in a classroom context. *Journal of Educational Psychology, 92*, 160–170.

Hertzog, C., Dixon, R. A., & Hultsch, D. F. (1990). Relationships between metamemory, memory predictions, and memory task performance in adults. *Psychology and Aging, 5*, 215–227.

Juslin, P., Winman, A., & Olsson, H. (2000). Naïve empiricism and dogmatisim in confidence research: A critical examination of the hard-easy effect. *Psychological Review, 107*, 384–396.

Karabenick, S. A. (1996). Social influences on metacognition: Effects of colearner questioning on comprehension monitoring. *Journal of Educational Psychology, 88*, 689–703.

Keren, G. (1991). Calibration and probability judgments: Conceptual and methodological issues. *Acta Psychologica, 77*, 217–273.

Koriat, A. (1997). Monitoring one's own knowledge during study: A cue-utilization approach to judgments of learning. *Journal of Experimental Psychology: General, 126*, 297–316.

Kruger, J., & Dunning, D. (1999). Unskilled and unaware of it: How difficulties in recognizing one's incompetence lead to inflated self-assessments. *Journal of Personality and Social Psychology, 77*, 1121–1134.

Kurtz, B. E., Schneider, W., Carr, M., Borkowski, J. G., & Turner, L. A. (1988). Sources of memory and metamemory development: Societal, parental, and educational influences. In M. Gruneberg, P. Morris, & R. Sykes (Eds.), *Practical aspects of memory* (Vol. 2, pp. 537–542). New York: Wiley.

Lichtenstein, S., Fischhoff, B., & Phillips, L. D. (1982). Calibration of probabilities: The state of the art to 1980. In D. Kahneman, P. Slovic, & A. Tversky (Eds.), *Judgment under uncertainty: Heuristics and biases* (pp. 306–334). Hillsdale, NJ: Erlbaum.

Lin, L., & Zabrucky, K. M. (1998). Calibration of comprehension: Research and implications for education and instruction. *Contemporary Educational Psychology, 23*, 345–391.

Lundeberg, M. A., & Fox, P. W. (1991). Do laboratory findings on text expectancy generalize to classroom outcomes? *Review of Educational Research, 61*, 94–106.

Maki, R. H. (1998). Test predictions over text material. In D. J. Hacker, J. Dunlosky, & A. C. Graesser (Eds.), *Metacognition in educational theory and practice* (pp. 117–144). Mahwah, NJ: Erlbaum.

Maki, R. H., & McGuire, M. J. (2002). Metacognition for text: Findings and implications for education. In T. J. Perfect & B. L. Schwartz (Eds.), *Applied metacognition* (pp. 39–67). New York: Cambridge University Press.

Maki, R. H., Shields, M., Wheeler, A. E., & Zacchilli, T. L. (2005). Individual differences in absolute and relative metacomprehension accuracy. *Journal of Educational Psychology, 97*, 723–731.

McCormick, C. B. (2003). Metacognition and learning. In W. M. Reynolds & G. E. Miller (Eds.), *Handbook of psychology: Vol. 7, educational psychology* (pp. 79–102). New York: Wiley.

Meyer, G. (1934). An experimental study of old and new types of examination: The effects of examination set on memory. *Journal of Educational Psychology, 25*, 641–661.

Nelson, T. O. (1984). A comparison of current measures of the accuracy of feeling-of-knowing predictions. *Psychological Bulletin, 95*, 109–133.

Nelson, T. O. (1996). Gamma is a measure of the accuracy of predicting performance on one item relative to another item, not of the absolute performance on an individual item. *Applied Cognitive Psychology, 10*, 257–260.

Nelson, T. O. (1999). Cognition versus metacognition. *American Psychologist, 51*, 102–116.

Nelson, T. O., & Narens, L. (1990). A theoretical framework and new findings. *The Psychology of Learning and Motivation, 26*, 125–141.

Nelson, T. O., & Narens, L. (1994). Why investigate metacognition? In J. Metcalfe & A. P. Shimamura (Eds.), *Metacognition: Knowing about knowing* (pp. 1–25). Cambridge, MA: MIT Press.

Nietfeld, J. L., Cao, L., & Osborne, J. W. (2005). Metacognitive monitoring accuracy and student performance in the postsecondary classroom. *The Journal of Experimental Education, 74*, 7–28.

Nietfeld, J. L., Cao, L., & Osborne, J. W. (2006). The effect of distributed monitoring exercises and feedback on performance, monitoring accuracy, and self-efficacy. *Metacognition and Learning, 1*, 159–179.

Nietfeld, J. L., Enders, C. K., & Schraw, G. (2006). A Monte Carlo comparison of measures of relative and absolute monitoring accuracy. *Educational and Psychological Measurement, 66*, 258–271.

Nietfeld, J. L., & Schraw, G. (2002). The effect of knowledge and strategy training on monitoring accuracy. *The Journal of Educational Research, 95*, 131–142.

Nisbett, R., & Ross, L. (1980). *Human inference: Strategies and shortcomings of social judgment*. Englewood Cliffs, NJ: Prentice-Hall.

Parducci, A., & Sarris, V. (1984). *Perspectives in psychological experimentations: Toward the year 2000*. Hillsdale, NJ: Erlbaum.

Pressley, M., & Ghatala, E. S. (1989). Metacognitive benefits of taking a test for children and young adolescents, *Journal of Experimental Child Psychology, 47*, 430–450.

Pressley, M., & Ghatala, E. S. (1990). Self-regulated learning: Monitoring learning from text. *Educational Psychologist, 25*, 19–33.

Pressley, M., Levin, J. R., Ghatala, E. S., & Ahmad, M. (1987). Test monitoring in young grade school children. *Journal of Experimental Child Psychology, 43*, 96–111.

Pressley, M., Snyder, B. L., Levin, J. R., Murray, H. G., & Ghatala, E. S. (1987). Perceived readiness for examination performance (PREP) produced by initial reading of text and text containing adjunct questions. *Reading Research Quarterly, 22*, 219–236.

Puncochar, J. M., & Fox, P. W. (2004). Confidence in individual and group decision making: When "two heads are worse than one." *Journal of Educational Psychology, 96*, 582–591.

Schraw, G. (1994). The effect of metacognitive knowledge on local and global monitoring. *Contemporary Educational Psychology, 19*, 143–154.

Schraw, G., Potenza, M. T., & Nebelsick-Gullet, L. (1993). Constraints on the calibration of performance. *Contemporary Educational Psychology, 18*, 455–463.

Shaughnessy, J. J. (1979). Confidence-judgment accuracy as a predictor of test performance. *Journal of Research in Personality, 13*, 505–514.

Sinkavich, F. J. (1995). Performance and metamemory: Do students know what they don't know? *Journal of Instructional Psychology, 22*, 77–87.

Weiner, B. (1986). Interpersonal and intrapersonal theories of motivation from an attributional perspective. *Educational Psychology Review, 12*, 1–14.

Weingardt, K. R., Leonesio, R. J., & Loftus, E. F. (1994). Viewing eyewitness research from a metacognitive perspective. In J. Metcalfe & A. P. Shimamura (Eds.), *Metacognition: Knowing and knowing* (pp. 157–184). Cambridge, MA: MIT Press.

Winne, P. H. (2004). Students' calibration of knowledge and learning processes: Implications for designing powerful software learning environments. *International Journal of Educational Research, 41*, 466–488.

Winne, P. H., & Jamieson-Noel, D. L. (2002). Exploring students' calibration of self-reports about study tactics and achievement. *Contemporary Educational Psychology, 27*, 551–572.

Wright, D. B. (1996). Measuring feeling of knowing: Comment on Schraw (1995). *Applied Cognitive Psychology, 10*, 261–268.

Yates, J. F. (1990). *Judgment and decision making*. Englewood Cliffs, NJ: Prentice Hall.

Zimmerman, B. J. (2000). Attaining self-regulation: A social cognitive perspective. In M. Boekaerts, P. R. Pintrich, & M. Zinder (Eds.), *Handbook of self-regulation* (pp. 13–39). San Diego, CA: Academic Press.

Author Index

A

Aarts, H., 122, *132*
ABC Research Group, 216, *241*
Adam, S., 255, *261*
Adams, C. M., 362, *371*
Adams, J. K., 221, *241*
Ahmad, M., 396, 397, *408*, 435, *455*
Aldridge, V. J., 375, *389*
Alexander, K. W., 322, *328*
Alexander, M., 365, 366, *371*, 380, 382, 383, *389*
Alexander, M. P., 374, *389*
Allain, P., 365, *370*, 380, 381, *388*
Allen, D., 438, 440, 444, 445, 446, 448, *453*
Allwood, C. M., 177, *189*, 438, *452*
Anderson, D., 74, *93*
Anderson, J. R., 216, *239*, 269, *281*
Anderson, M., 419, *427*
Anderson, M. C., 269, *281*
Anderson, M. C. M., 158, *171*, 342, *351*
Anderson, R. E., 211, *239*
Andrews, S., 421, 422, *425*
Angstadt, P., 215, 216, *243*, 266, *283*
Ansay, C., 43, *44*, 61, *66*, 118, *132*
Aristotle, 47, *65*
Armstrong, D., 29, *43*
Armstrong, E., 384, *389*
Arndt, J., 214, 215, *241*
Ashby, W. R., 50, 51, *65*, *66*
Atkinson, R. C., 12, 23, *26*, 139, *153*, 215, *239*, 265, 266, *281*, 334, 337, 339, 340, *348*
Aurobindo, S., 47, *65*
Awh, E., 378, 379, *385*
Ayers, M. S., 215, 216, *243*, 266, *283*

B

Bacon, E., 357, 361, 362, 363, 364, 366, 367, 368, *369*, *371*, 373
Baddeley, A., 250, *259*
Baddeley, A. D., 177, *190*, 346, *348*, 405, *405*
Badre, D., 377, 384, *385*, *386*
Bahbahani, K., 441, 446, 447, 448, 452, *453*
Bahrick, H. P., 139, *152*, 158, *169*
Bain, J. D., 266, 269, *282*
Baird, J. A., 374, *386*

Baker, J. M. C., 16, 17, *27*, 59, 65, *66*, 356, 357, *369*, 420, *425*
Baldo, J. V., 378, 381, *385*
Balota, D. A., 59, *66*, 317, *331*
Baltes, P. B., 79, *93*
Banks, W. P., 78, *91*, 212, 215, *239*
Bar, S. K., 55, 56, 65, *67*, 111, *113*, 117, 121, *133*, 167, *169*, 219, *242*, 394, *407*
Barcelo, F., 380, *385*
Barch, D. M., 377, *385*
Barlow, M. R., 130, *132*
Barnett, J. E., 438, 440, 445, 452, *452*
Batchelder, E., 234, *240*
Batchelder, W. H., 211, 212, 216, 223, 224, 225, 229, 230, 231, 234, 239, *240*, *242*, *243*, *244*
Battig, W. F., 272, *281*
Baumeister, R. F., 319, 323, *330*
Bawa, S., 219, *240*
Bayen, U. J., 212, 221, 223, 224, 225, *240*
Bechara, A., 384, *385*
Begg, I., 74, *91*, 137, *152*, 346, *348*
Begg, J. M., 61, 65, *65*
Bell, H. M., 334, 335, *348*
Belli, R. F., 122, *135*
Benjamin, A. S., 49, 59, 61, 64, *65*, 74, 75, 79, 83, 85, 86, 89, 90, *91*, *92*, 119, *132*, 137, *152*, 164, 167, *168*, 214, 216, 219, 220, 221, *240*, 273, *281*, 346, *348*, 394, *405*, 414, *424*
Benton, A. L., 381, *385*
Berie, J. L., 362, *369*
Bering, J. M., 401, *405*
Bernstein, D., 159, *170*
Bernstein, D. M., 320, *328*
Berntsen, D., 159, *168*
Berrigan, M., 361, 363, 364, *369*
Berry, D. C., 251, *259*
Bharucha, J., 411, *424*
Bianco, C., 159, 163, *168*
Binder, N., 251, *263*
Bink, M. L., 289, 295, *305*, *306*, 311
Bird, R., 346, *348*
Bird, R. D., 74, *92*
Birdsall, T. G., 76, 78, 90, *93*, *94*
Bisanz, G. L., 396, *405*
Bjork, E. L., 342, *348*

D

E

Subject Index